Two week loan
Benthyciad pythefnos

Please return on or before the due date to avoid overdue charges
A wnewch chi ddychwelyd ar neu cyn y dyddiad a nodir ar eich llyfr os gwelwch yn dda, er mwyn osgoi taliadau

EUROPEAN SECURITY LAW

European Security Law

Edited by

MARTIN TRYBUS

Senior Lecturer in Law at the University of Sheffield

and

NIGEL D WHITE

*Professor of International Law at the University of Sheffield
and Director of the Centre for Law in its International Context*

OXFORD
UNIVERSITY PRESS

OXFORD
UNIVERSITY PRESS

Great Clarendon Street, Oxford OX2 6DP

Oxford University Press is a department of the University of Oxford.
It furthers the University's objective of excellence in research, scholarship,
and education by publishing worldwide in

Oxford New York

Auckland Cape Town Dar es Salaam Hong Kong Karachi
Kuala Lumpur Madrid Melbourne Mexico City Nairobi
New Delhi Shanghai Taipei Toronto

With offices in

Argentina Austria Brazil Chile Czech Republic France Greece
Guatemala Hungary Italy Japan Poland Portugal Singapore
South Korea Switzerland Thailand Turkey Ukraine Vietnam

Oxford is a registered trade mark of Oxford University Press
in the UK and in certain other countries

Published in the United States
by Oxford University Press Inc., New York

Preface

In September 2006 troops from European countries were sent to Lebanon as a key component in the international effort to produce peace after a brutal war between Israel and Hizbollah forces. This is the latest evidence of a growing European military confidence, which in turn is a reflection of a developing competence in security matters. The creation of the European Union (EU) and its Common Foreign and Security Policy by the Maastricht Treaty of 1992 heralded this development, though the idea of a common defence can be traced to the beginnings of European integration. This book provides an analysis of the EU's evolving legal framework and powers on such matters, but it also recognizes that such a framework sits (maybe uneasily) within the wider body of international law. Moreover, it needs to be coherent with other fields of EU law and policy. The EU's security and defence policy also brings it up against other organizations such as the Organization for Security and Cooperation in Europe (OSCE), but more especially the North Atlantic Treaty Organisation (NATO). EU relations with NATO have, in particular, caused some concern and are still evolving as both organizations seek to play a wider security role in the post-Cold War, and now post-9/11, era. With security now dominating political agendas at the domestic, regional, and international levels, it is no surprise that the EU's concern for security has grown apace, and, following the Union's respect for the rule of law, has been shaped legally as well as politically. This book evaluates the progress of the Union in this regard in its international context and in its wider context of European integration generally. The analysis is in the main a legal one, but is placed squarely within wider historical and political perspectives.

This book emerged out of a project funded by the Centre for Conflict and Security Law based in the School of Law at Sheffield University and linked to the Faculty of Law at the University of Utrecht. With the exception of three chapters, earlier versions of all contributions were presented and discussed at a workshop held at Nottingham University in April 2005. Thanks go to Professor Sue Arrowsmith, Dr Olympia Bekou, Dr Robert Cryer, Matthew Happold, Professor Tamara Hervey, Professor Jeffrey Kenner, and Dr Eric Myjer who chaired, discussed, and contributed greatly to the various sessions at this workshop. Thanks also go to Marco Odello for his help organizing the workshop and to Jeremy Wickins of the University of Sheffield for his preparation of the manuscript.

Martin Trybus
Nigel D White

Centre for Law in its International Context
University of Sheffield, UK
October 2006

Contents

List of Abbreviations

ACV	Armoured Combat Vehicle
AFSOUTH	Allied Forces Southern Europe
AMIS	African Union Mission in Sudan
AMM	Aceh Monitoring Mission
APF	African Peace Facility
APSA	Architecture for Peace and Security in Africa
ASEAN	Association of Southeast Asian Nations
AU	African Union
BiH	Bosnia and Herzegovina
C3I	Communications, Command, Control and Intelligence
CASA	*Construcciones Aeronáuticas*
CBRN	Chemical, Biological, Radiological, or Nuclear
CCP	Common Commercial Policy
CEUMC	Chairman of the European Union Military Committee
CFC	Ceasefire Commission in the Darfur area of Sudan
CFE	Conventional Armed Forces in Europe
CFI	Court of First Instance
CFSP	Common Foreign and Security Policy
CiO	Chairman in Office
CIS	Commonwealth of Independent States
CJTF	Combined Joint Task Forces
COMESA	Common Market for Eastern and Southern Africa
COPPS	European Union Coordinating Office for Palestinian Police Support
COPS	European Union Political and Security Committee
COREPER	European Union Committee of Permanent Representatives
CPCO	Centre de Planification et de Conduite des Opérations
CPD	Coherent Policy Document
CRT	Civilian Response Team
CSBMs	Confidence and Security Building Measures
CSCE	Conference for Security and Cooperation in Europe
CSDP	Common Security and Defence Policy
CSO	Committee of Senior Officers
DASA	Defence Analytical Services Agency
DCI	Defence Capabilities Initiative
DDI	Developing Defence Industries
DRC	Democratic Republic of Congo
D-SACEUR	Deputy Supreme Commander Allied Forces Europe
EAA	European Armaments Agency
EAC	East African Community
EADC	European Aerospace and Defence Company
EADS	European Aeronautic Defence and Space Company
EC	European Community

ECAP	European Capabilities Action Plan
ECHR	European Convention on Human Rights
ECJ	European Court of Justice
ECMM/EUMM	European Community/European Union Monitoring Mission
ECOMICI	Economic Community of West African States Mission in Ivory Coast
ECOWAS	Economic Community of West African States
ECSC	European Coal and Steel Community
ECtHR	European Court of Human Rights
EDA	European Defence Agency
EDC	European Defence Community
EDEM	European Defence Equipment Market
EDF	European Defence Force
EDF	European Development Fund
EDTIB	European Defence Technological and Industrial Base
EEC	European Economic Community
EMU	European Monetary Union
EPC	European Political Cooperation
ERRF	European Rapid Reaction Force
ESDI	European Security and Defence Identity
ESDP	European Security and Defence Policy
ESS	European Security Strategy
EU	European Union
EU BAM Rafah	European Union Border Assistance Mission at Rafah Crossing Point in the Palestinian Territories
EUCE	European Union Command Element
EUF	European Union-led Forces
EUFOR	European Union Force in Bosnia and Herzegovina
EUJUST	European Rule of Law Mission
EUJUST LEX	European Rule of Law Mission for Iraq
EUMC	European Union Military Committee
EUMS	European Union Military Staff
EUPAT	European Union Police Advisory Team in Former Yugoslavian Republic of Macedonia
EUPM	European Union Police Mission
EUPOL	European Union Police Mission
EUPOL COPPS	European Union Police Mission in the Palestinian Territories
EUPT	European Union Planning Team
EURATOM	European Atomic Energy Community
EUROCORPS	Force for Europe and the Atlantic Alliance
EUROFOR	French /Italian/Portuguese/Spanish European Force
EUROMARFOR	European Maritime Force
EUSEC	European Union Security Sector Reform Mission
EUSOFA	Status of Forces Agreement concerning forces seconded to the European Union
EUSR	European Union Special Representative
FYROM	Former Yugoslavian Republic of Macedonia
GAM	Free Aceh Movement

HCNM	High Commissioner on National Minorities
HQ	Headquarters
HRC	United Nations Human Rights Committee
ICCPR	International Covenant on Civil and Political Rights
ICJ	International Court of Justice
IEMF	International Emergency Multinational Force
IEPG	Independent European Programme Group
IFOR	Implementation Force
IGAD	Intergovernmental Authority on Development
IGC	Intergovernmental Conference
IHL	International Humanitarian Law
IIA	Ituri Interim Administration
ILC	International Law Commission
IMP	Initial Monitoring Presence
INTERFET	International Force for East Timor
IPTF	United Nations International Police Task Force
IPU	Integrated Police Unit
KFOR	Kosovo Enforcement Force
KLA	Kosovo Liberation Army
LoI	Letter of Intent
MERCOSUR	*Mercado Commun Del Sur*
MONUC	United Nations Mission in the Democratic Republic of Congo
MoU	Memorandum of Understanding
NAC	North Atlantic Council
NATO	North Atlantic Treaty Organisation
OAS	Organization of American States
OAU	Organisation for African Unity
OCCAR	Organisation for Joint Armaments Co-operation
ODIHR	Office for Democratic Institutions and Human Rights
OHQ	Operation Headquarters
OMIK	Organisation for Security and Co-operation in Europe Mission in Kosovo
OSCE	Organization for Security and Co-operation in Europe
PJCC	Police and Judicial Cooperation in Criminal Matters
POLARM	Ad Hoc European Union Working Party on a European Armaments Policy
PSC	Political and Security Committee
PSI	Proliferation Security Initiative
QMV	Qualified Majority Vote/Voting
RRF	Rapid Reaction Force
SACEUR	Supreme Allied Commander Europe
SADC	Southern African Development Community
SC	Security Council
SEA	Single European Act
SFOR	United Nations Stabilization Force in Bosnia and Herzegovina
SG/HR	Secretary General/High Representative
SHAPE	Supreme Headquarters Allied Powers Europe

SOFA	Status of Forces Agreement
SOMA	Status of Mission Agreement
TECE	Treaty Establishing a Constitution for Europe
TEU	Treaty on European Union
UMFA	Union Minister for Foreign Affairs
UN	United Nations
UNMIK	United Nations Interim Administration Mission in Kosovo
UNPROFOR	United Nations Protection Force
UNSC	United Nations Security Council
UNTAET	United Nations Transitional Administration in East Timor
US/USA	United States of America
USSR	Union of Soviet Socialist Republics
WEAG	Western European Armaments Group
WEAO	Western European Armaments Organization
WEU	Western European Union
WMD	Weapons of Mass Destruction
WTO	World Trade Organisation
WU	Western Union

List of Contributors

Ademola Abass is Reader in Law at the University of Reading, United Kingdom. Educated at the Universities of Lagos, Nottingham, and Cambridge, he previously taught collective security law at the University of Nottingham, under the auspices of Nigel White, and at the University of the West of England, Bristol. His research interests include collective security law, regional organizations, peace and security, and international criminal law. He was African Union Expert on regional mechanisms and European Union Expert on capacity building for African regional organizations. He is the author of *Regional Organisations and the Development of Collective Security: Beyond chapter VIII of the UN Charter* (Hart Publishing, 2004), several refereed articles in *International and Comparative Law Quarterly*, *Netherlands International Law Review*, *Texas International Law Journal*, and *International Criminal Law Review* amongst others. He has also contributed chapters to books including Malcolm Evans (ed) *International Law* (OUP, 2003, 2006). He is a regular guest lecturer at the European Masters in Human Rights and Democracy, University of Seville, Spain and is a member of the Academic Council on the United Nations Systems (ACUNS), the International Law Association, and is a Fellow of the Cambridge Commonwealth Society.

Aris Georgopoulos read law at the Capodistrian University of Athens, in Greece and the Catholic University of Leuven, in Belgium. He read for a PhD at the Law School of the University of Nottingham after having received a doctoral scholarship from the same academic institution. His PhD thesis on European Defence Procurement Integration was awarded a special distinction by the European Group of Public Law in 2004. His main research interests lie within the area of European law and international trade law and policy. While at Nottingham he taught EU law and worked also as a researcher with the Public Procurement Research Group (PPRG). He joined the School of Law of the University of Dundee in December 2004 and the School of Law of the University of Nottingham in September 2006. He has published a number of articles and book chapters on aspects of European Community Law and European Security and Defence Policy and has presented at various conferences in Europe, North and Latin America. Dr Georgopoulos is a member of the editorial board of the Public Procurement Law Review. He has acted as expert advisor to national authorities on the review of their domestic public procurement legislation as well as with the OECD (training and advising public procurement officials and judges of sixth enlargement countries.) He is a member of the Athens Bar Association registered at the Athens Court of Appeal.

Panos Koutrakos is Professor of European Law at the University of Bristol, United Kingdom. He is a graduate of the Universities of Athens, London, and Birmingham and has been a stagiaire at the European Commission in Brussels. He has taught at the University of Durham and the University of Birmingham. He has been Jean Monnet Research Fellow at the University of Michigan Law School and Visiting Professor at the University of Iowa College of Law. He is the Book Reviews Editor of *European Law Review* and a contributor to *Smits and Herzog on the Law of the European Union*, writing about the

Common Foreign and Security Policy. He has contributed to training programmes for judges from central and eastern Europe. He is the author of *EU International Relations Law* (Hart Publishing, 2006) and *Trade, Foreign Policy and Defence in EU Constitutional Law* (Hart Publishing, 2001). In addition to EU external trade and political relations, his research interests cover the law of the single market, in particular the free movement of goods and services.

Heike Krieger is Professor of Public Law and Public International Law at the Free University of Berlin, Germany. Until recently she was Associate Professor of Public Law, Public International Law, European Law and Comparative Public Law at the University of Göttingen, Germany. She studied law at the Universities of Göttingen and Bonn in Germany and at the National University of Singapore. In 2003 she was Visiting Lecturer at the School of Law, University of Nottingham and in the academic year 2005/2006 she taught Constitutional Law as Visiting Professor at the Faculty of Law, University of Munich, Germany. She has published a number of articles and book chapters on human rights law, EU law, and German constitutional law. She is author of *Das Effektivitätsprinzip im Völkerrecht (The Principle of Effectiveness in Public International Law)* 2000, co-author with Georg Nolte of *Europäische Wehrrechtssysteme (European Military Law Systems)* 2002, and editor of the document volumes *East Timor and the International Community* 1997 and *The Kosovo Conflict and International Law* 2001. In 2004 she completed a book on *Streitkräfte im demokratischen Verfassungsstaat (Armed Forces in Democracies)* for which she received the *Helmuth-James-von-Moltke-Preis 2005* of the *Deutsche Gesellschaft für Wehrrecht und Humanitäres Völkerrecht e.V.*

Frederik Naert is a legal advisor in the Directorate General Legal Support and Mediation of the Belgian Ministry of Defence in Brussels and regularly deals with ESDP in practice. He was also assigned to the Belgian ISAF Detachment for four months in early 2006, including a deployment to Kabul in March 2006. He is a voluntary researcher at the Institute for International Law, KU Leuven, where he is preparing a PhD on international law aspects of the European Security and Defence Policy. He studied law at the Catholic University of Leuven, Belgium and the University of Melbourne, Australia. He was a research and teaching assistant at the University of Leuven's Institute for International Law from 1998 until 2004. He has published on European security organizations, especially the EU, peace operations, international humanitarian and human rights law, terrorism, European and international criminal law, and international immunities, and is co-editor of *Legal Instruments in the Fight Against International Terrorism. A Transatlantic Dialogue* (Martinus Nijhoff, 2004). He lectures regularly at the Royal Defence College (Brussels), has spoken at national and international conferences and is a member of the editorial board of the Flemish Yearbook of International Humanitarian Law, is assistant to the editor of the *International Encyclopaedia of Laws: Intergovernmental Organisations* and the Director of the Documentation Centre of the International Society for Military Law and the Law of War, as well as being editor of a 'current developments' section in the latter's *Newsletter* and a member of the Scientific Board of its Belgian branch.

Marco Odello is Lecturer in Law at the University of Wales, Aberystwyth, United Kingdom. He studied at the Universities of Genoa, Rome, Nottingham, Madrid, and Sheffield. He worked with UNICEF-Italy and the Institute for University Co-operation in Rome. He has been a Researcher at the European Public Law Center (Athens) and at the Centre for Conflict and Security Law, University of Nottingham. He has taught international law, international organizations, comparative law, and human rights in Peru and Mexico. He was invited professor at the Central University of Venezuela (Caracas) and at the University of Maracaibo (Venezuela). He lectures regularly at the Summer University of Human Rights (Geneva) and at the International Institute of Humanitarian Law. Between 2000 and 2003 he was involved as an expert consultant by the University of Bologna in the EU Tempus Project 'Towards a European Model Judge' for which he developed a module on International Human Rights and Humanitarian Law. He is a member of the International Institute of Humanitarian Law, and is Assistant Editor of the *Journal of Conflict and Security Law*. He has published numerous articles and is co-author of *La Convenzione Internazionale sui Diritti del Minore e l'Ordinamento Italiano*, Naples, ESI, 1994, co-editor of Mazzarelli and Odello (eds), *L'insegnamento dei Diritti Umani*, Rome, EDIUN, 1999, and co-author of *Problemas actuales del derecho público en Mexico*, México DF, Porrúa, 2004.

Mirko Sossai is research fellow at the LUISS University in Rome, Italy. He studied International Relations and Law at the University of Padua and at the University of Siena, where he completed a PhD thesis on State Responsibility for Terrorist Acts (2005). In spring 2003 he undertook a period of research at the Max-Planck Institute for Comparative Public Law and International Law in Heidelberg, Germany. In Padua, he collaborated with the Interdepartmental Centre on Human Rights (2004–2005). His publications include papers on international terrorism, including an article on the application of measures under SC Res 1373 to the conflict in Colombia. More recently, he wrote on the domestic enforcement of ICJ Judgments. He is currently a member of the Research Unit coordinated by Prof Natalino Ronzitti (LUISS, Rome) on the topic 'Access to justice and compensation for violations of the law of war'.

Fabien Terpan is Maître de conférences in public law at the University of Grenoble, France. He studied public law and political science in Strasbourg (Institut des hautes études européennes) and Grenoble (Institut d'études politiques et faculté de droit). He wrote a PhD Thesis on the 'Common Foreign and Security Policy of the European Union' and has published several articles and four books, two of them related to European security law (*La politique étrangère et de sécurité commune de l'UE*, Bruylant, 2003, and *La politique européenne de sécurité et de défense*, Presses de l'Institut d'études politiques de Toulouse, 2004). He started his academic career at the University of Toulouse where he taught European Union law, international relations and international politics. As a member of the Morris Janowitz Center on 'armed forces and security' (Toulouse) he has been responsible for several research programmes on European security. Fabien Terpan has editorial responsibilities in the French review *Défense nationale et sécurité collective*, where he tries to improve knowledge of CFSP and ESDP. He also participates in the activities of TEPSA (Trans-European Policy Studies Association, Brussels). Apart from CFSP/ESDP, he has research interests in other EU policies such as immigration and asylum, regional policy, culture cooperation, and the fight against terrorism. Since September 2006, Fabien Terpan has been Maître de conférences at the Institute of Political Studies in Grenoble, where he helps to coordinate a Master's degree programme in European Union studies.

Martin Trybus is Senior Lecturer in Law at the University of Sheffield, United Kingdom. He studied law at the Free University of Berlin, Germany and the University of Wales,

Aberystwyth before starting his academic career at the University of Nottingham, United Kingdom where he taught EU law and public procurement law. In 2002 he collaborated with Nigel White to develop a postgraduate course in EU Defence Law. Over the past few years, Martin Trybus has published a number of articles and book chapters on the application of the EC Treaty to aspects of the security and defence policies of the EU Member States. More recently he wrote on the European Defence Agency and the security aspects of the EU Constitutional Treaty. He is the author of *European Union Law and Defence Integration* (Hart Publishing, 2005) and *European Defence Procurement Law* (Kluwer, 1999). In the context of his other main research interest, public procurement law, he has published widely, including the edited collection *Public Procurement: The Continuing Revolution* (Kluwer, 2002) with Sue Arrowsmith. He has recently completed a secondment as Senior Adviser to the Organisation for Cooperation and Development (OECD) in Paris, where he coordinated three major studies on public procurement financed by the European Commission.

Nicholas Tsagourias is Lecturer in law at the University of Bristol, United Kingdom. He studied law in Greece, at the Aristotelian University of Thessaloniki and also holds degrees from the University of Bristol (LLM) and the University of Nottingham (PhD). Nicholas Tsagourias has written extensively on international law, including on the use of force, collective security, peacekeeping, and the theory of law. He wrote the book *Jurisprudence of International Law: The Humanitarian Dimension* (Manchester University Press, 2000). He is member of the editorial board of the *Journal of Conflict and Security Law*.

Ramses A Wessel is Professor of the Law of the European Union and other International Organizations and Co-Director of the Centre for European Studies at the University of Twente, the Netherlands. He is Director of the European Studies programme and Senior Research Fellow of the University's Institute for Governance Studies. Ramses Wessel is a senior member of the Netherlands Institute of Government and associate member of the research school Ius Commune. His additional functions include: Editor-in-Chief and founder of the *International Organizations Law Review* and Editor-in-Chief of the Dutch journal and yearbook on peace and security, *Vrede en Veiligheid*. Ramses Wessel graduated at the University of Groningen in International Law and International Relations and was subsequently an assistant professor there and at the Department of the Law of International Organizations at Utrecht University. He is the author of *The European Union's Foreign and Security Policy: A Legal Institutional Perspective* (Kluwer Law International, 1999) and of a number of other publications in the field of European security law. His general research interests lie in the field of international and European institutional law, with a focus on international organizations, peace and security, and European foreign, security, and defence policy.

Nigel D White is Professor of International Law at the University of Sheffield and Director of the Centre for Law in its International Context. He was formerly Professor of International Organizations in the School of Law at the University of Nottingham. He is the author of numerous articles and books including *Keeping the Peace: The United Nations and the Maintenance of International Peace and Security* (Manchester University Press, 1997), *The Law of International Organisations* (Manchester University Press, 2005), and *The UN System: Toward International Justice* (Lynne Rienner, 2002) and editor of *Collective Security Law* (Ashgate, 2004). He is also co-editor of the *Journal of Conflict and Security Law*, published by Oxford University Press.

Table of Cases

ICTY cases

UK cases

German cases

INTRODUCTION

1

An Introduction to European Security Law

Martin Trybus, Nigel D White, and authors

The European security landscape has been rapidly changing recently. In 1991, in Maastricht, the Member States of the European Communities created the Common Foreign and Security Policy (CFSP) as an intergovernmental second pillar of the Treaty on European Union (TEU). Moreover, since 1998 they have been developing the security aspect of this policy into a European Security and Defence Policy (ESDP). This policy now even includes a plan for a European Rapid Reaction Force of 60,000–100,000 troops with army, air force, and navy components. The necessary institutional structures to back up this independent military capability of the European Union (EU) have started to operate. These developments are the most significant innovations towards European security integration since the failure of the European Defence Community (EDC) in the 1950s. Since then the security of the old continent had been dependent largely on the US-dominated North Atlantic Treaty Organisation (NATO), complemented by her largely dormant European sister the Western European Union (WEU).

After two devastating World Wars, the prohibition of the use of force limited the legality of war to the right to self-defence or military action taken under United Nations (UN) authority. Consequently the ministers and departments of war gradually became ministers and departments of defence. Theoretically the sole tasks of the armed forces were to organize the defence of their country, especially against the threat of the other military bloc during the Cold War. However, during the same period new tasks for the armed forces developed. Mainly within the framework of the United Nations, the armed forces of many countries were deployed to keep peace between warring parties, to enforce peace, or more generally for humanitarian tasks. Today missions can take the modern soldier to the other end of the world where he or she is not necessarily expected to fight but to prevent bloodshed. The armed forces serve a broader notion of international or regional security that goes beyond the classical defence of the state. After the end of the Cold War the military threat posed by NATO and the Warsaw Pact vanished. As the extensive defence effort of the past was no longer necessary the armed forces of many countries had to find new reasons for their expensive existence in a time of tight budgets. These security activities, from humanitarian action to peacemaking, seem to have developed into the new raison d'être for the military. Moreover, more recently the fight against terrorism was added to these tasks. Just as the focus shifted from 'war' to 'defence' after World War II, the emphasis has been shifting from 'defence' to 'security'. Moreover, the word 'security' can be understood as a wider term that also includes the classical function of 'defence'. Indeed, the concept of 'security' can take on a specifically regional character that may be created by the EU but also influenced by other European regional actors such as NATO or the Organization for Security and Co-operation in Europe (OSCE), as well as by international institutions. This book considers the political and legal development of European security as understood in its external aspects—security from threats and attacks—rather than what could be called internal security or police matters.

The evolution of the EU into a security actor poses numerous legal problems. Unlike the failed EDC Treaty of 1952, the ESDP is part of the intergovernmental CFSP. The regulation in a separate pillar causes problems with the Community pillar when a policy or measure requires instruments from both pillars, for example in relation to sanctions. This leads to the more general problem of the coherence of the CFSP with the elements of external relations already conducted in the Community framework. The 2004 EU Constitutional Treaty, if it ever comes into force, aims to overcome the multi-pillar structure of the EU. It builds on the peacekeeping *acquis* of the current second pillar, which has already led to several missions. It also includes a mutual defence clause, which raises questions of neutrality concerning some of the Member States. Moreover, the emergence of a new defence and security actor raises questions of compatibility with NATO and other elements of the European and transatlantic security structure, most notably the collective security system of the UN, as well as basic principles of international law governing the use of both forcible and non-forcible measures. The necessity to establish a European defence equipment market through the introduction of a European Defence Agency (EDA) is a third element of the defence dimension of the EU envisaged by the Constitutional Treaty. This edited collection addresses the legal dimension of European security in three parts. Part I deals with the origins and future of European security integration before Part II covers the elements of the current European security policy, followed by a final Part III on the consistency of the European security framework.

Before Parts II and III of this collection look at European security law in its actual and present context, Part I discusses past and future visions of European security and defence integration. Co-editor Martin Trybus covers the origins and future of European defence integration in two chapters. This aims to facilitate the understanding of the discussion of the present system in the following parts and explores alternative models to the current approach at the same time. Both chapters have in common that they deal with major European treaty projects which did not become reality. In Chapter 2, 'The Vision of the European Defence Community and a Common Defence for the European Union', he investigates the relevance of the dawn of European integration for the present and the future. In the early 1950s the six founding Member States of the European Coal and Steel Community (ECSC) envisaged a supranational EDC in charge of a European defence policy which would even have included a European army. This most ambitious project of European security integration to date failed. The objective of this chapter is to provide an overview of the Community envisaged in the EDC Treaty. The method to achieve an understanding of the scale of security and defence integration planned in the 1950s is to compare the EDC Treaty with defence-related provisions in later European treaties and legislation, most notably those on the CFSP, ESDP, and the Common Security and Defence Policy (CSDP) under the 2004 EU Constitutional Treaty. After a brief introduction to the history of the EDC Treaty, the chapter will discuss the supranational nature of the EDC as reflected in its institutional law, its defensive character, its principle of non-discrimination between Member States, and the connection to NATO. Within the limits set by a book chapter and considering the different historical and strategic contexts, the reader will be able to compare the comprehensive legal framework with the current efforts discussed in other chapters of this collection.

In Chapter 3 Trybus discusses another ambitious and ill-fated project of European security integration, this time set in an uncertain future rather than in the past. 'On the Common Security and Defence Policy of the EU Constitutional Treaty' deals with the innovations regarding security and defence envisaged under the EU Constitutional Treaty mentioned above. The three main policy fields of the CSDP, namely, armaments policy, crisis management, and collective defence, will be addressed. These policy fields will be discussed at length in their current context in Part II of the collection. The analysis in Chapter 3 takes different versions of the Constitutional Treaty into account: from the draft presented by the Convention in July 2003 to the final version published in December 2004. It will be argued that the future of the CSDP does not depend on the entering into force of the Constitutional Treaty. The CSDP armaments policy has been detached from the Constitutional Treaty and implemented through a Joint Action. It is already developing on the basis of the current framework, as will be discussed in Chapter 9. Moreover, the CSDP crisis management policy and the EU's military institutions do not differ substantially from those of the ESDP presently conducted under the Treaty of Nice. They can be developed on the basis of the current framework, which is discussed extensively in Chapters 4 to 6. Finally, the collective defence commitment, and the office of the Union Minister for Foreign Affairs envisaged in the Constitutional Treaty, could also be introduced on the basis of Article 17(1) of the Treaty on European Union. The collective defence commitment is discussed in Chapter 8.

Following the discussion of past and future visions of European security and defence integration, Part II covers the various elements of European security policy, mainly in its current context of the Treaty of Nice. Part II has six chapters. Three chapters cover legal problems of the EU crisis management policy, and one chapter each is dedicated to mutual defence, anti-terrorism policy, and armaments policy.

Peacekeeping has been one of the most important EU activities under the second pillar of the current Treaty of Nice. Therefore three chapters cover the evolving EU crisis management policy. In Chapter 4, 'ESDP in Practice: Increasingly Varied and Ambitious EU Security and Defence Operations', Frederik Naert analyses the main legal aspects of the first eleven of the thirteen ESDP operations launched since 2003, ie, the military operations CONCORDIA (Former Yugoslavian Republic of Macedonia, FYROM), ARTEMIS (Democratic Republic of Congo, DRC) and ALTHEA (Bosnia and Herzegovina), the police operations EUPM (Bosnia and Herzegovina), PROXIMA (FYROM) and EUPOL KINSHASA (DRC), the rule of law mission EUJUST THEMIS (Georgia), the integrated rule of law mission EUJUST LEX for Iraq, the security sector reform mission EUSEC DRC (DRC), the civil-military EU Support to AMIS II (African Union Mission in Darfur, Sudan) and the EU monitoring mission in Aceh (AMM). After an analysis of each operation, focusing on common elements and peculiar aspects, Naert draws some general conclusions regarding the scope of ESDP operations, international mandate, legal status and applicable law, third State participation and some institutional issues.

In Chapter 5, 'EU Peacekeeping Operations: Legal and Theoretical Issues', Nicholas Tsagourias explores the theoretical, political, and legal aspects of EU peacekeeping. The first of the issues examined is the institutional mechanisms and legal framework for peacekeeping contained in the EU constitutive treaties as well as the rationale behind EU peacekeeping. It will be argued in this regard that peacekeeping is a manifestation of the EU's 'civilian' identity. The second of the issues which will be examined is the relationship between the EU, the UN, and NATO in peacekeeping. Notwithstanding the close cooperation and the structured dialogue between these organizations, it is submitted that legally or politically the EU can act more independently. The third of the issues which will be examined, and which has received minimum attention, concerns the application of international humanitarian law and human rights law to peacekeeping operations, as well as the international responsibility of the EU. It will be argued that the operations are those of the EU and that the latter has de facto personality. However, because of ambiguities with regards to the international personality of the EU, the above issues will be considered from a number of different perspectives.

In Chapter 6, 'Extraterritorial Collective Security: The European Union and Operation ARTEMIS', Ademola Abass discusses Operation ARTEMIS, undertaken by the EU in the Democratic Republic of Congo in 2003 at the request of the UN. He examines the various legal issues that arise from the operation, which not only became the first time the EU has conducted an enforcement action properly so-called, but also the first time it had done so outside Europe. In particular, the chapter considers why the Security Council authorized the operation under Chapter VII and not Chapter VIII of the UN Charter, especially being, it is argued, the first time the Security Council had utilized a regional organization in the proper understanding of the Chapter VIII framework. The chapter studies the non-involvement of the African Union (AU) in an operation concerning one of its Member States, and elucidates the wider implications of the operation for the inter-institutional relationship between the EU and the AU.

In Chapter 7 Mirko Sossai explores 'The Anti-Terrorism Dimension of ESDP'. The progressive development of an ESDP coincided with the urgency, perceived also at the EU level, to combat the global threat to peace and security constituted by trans-national terrorist networks. Since the 2002 Seville meeting, the European Council has gradually identified the main characters of the ESDP contribution against terrorism. In this regard, two essential steps are represented by the approval of the Declaration on combating terrorism, soon after the terrorist attacks in Madrid of 11 March 2004, and the adoption of the Conceptual Framework on the ESDP dimension of the fight against terrorism. This chapter seeks to evaluate the changes terrorism has made to the nature of ESDP against the background of the nego-tiation on the Constitutional Treaty and therefore the possible role of the EU as a regional organization under Chapter VIII of the UN Charter. It is important to understand how the military option can complement the EU's counter-terrorism action in the crucial areas of judicial and police cooperation, civil protection and assistance to third countries.

In Chapter 8 Heike Krieger covers mutual defence in a European context by ask-ing 'Common European Defence: Competition or Compatibility with NATO?'. Since the end of the cold war new security structures have emerged within Europe. The end of the bi-polar security system has enlarged the number of actors with overlapping competences. While NATO broadened its range of permissible activ-ities through the new Strategic Concept of 1999, efforts within the EU aim at closer co-operation on mutual defence including an automatic action commit-ment. After examining legal limitations for overlapping treaty obligations of NATO and EU Member States the chapter will argue that the EU should not pursue the idea of creating a traditional defence alliance. Rather, because of the changing understanding of defence and security, an alliance based on a clause comparable to the solidarity clause in the envisaged EU Constitutional Treaty could be a more appropriate approach in the future.

In Chapter 9, 'European Armaments Policy: A *Conditio Sine Qua Non* of the European Security and Defence Policy', Aris Georgopoulos describes the land-scape of the European armaments market. The existence of a vibrant and com-petitive European defence and industrial base is widely considered as a necessary condition for an effective and credible ESDP. With this as its starting point the chapter focuses on examination of the emerging institutional framework of a European armaments policy in the light of the recent developments in the field, namely, the establishment of the European Defence Agency and the initiatives of the European Commission. There are various reasons which make this examin-ation necessary. First, the institutional arrangement of European armaments cooperation has immediate consequences for the effectiveness of efforts to create a healthy and competitive European defence technological and industrial base.

As argued in the chapter, the limited effectiveness witnessed so far is to a large extent attributable to what appears to be an environment of unnecessary institutional balkanization of European armaments cooperation. The chapter further submits that the subordination of European armaments cooperation under the EU did not eradicate duplication completely because there are other fora of armaments cooperation outside the EU. More importantly, the initiatives within the Union do not appear to be complementary but inherently antagonistic. Finally, the chapter argues that the new institutional framework, although much more streamlined than in the recent past, develops like a creature with two heads. Until there is a clear allocation of roles the aim of sustaining a vibrant and competitive European defence industrial and technological base would be simply a chimaera with immediate negative repercussions on the credibility of the ESDP as a whole.

After the discussion of the scope of the ESDP and its legal problems in Part II, Part III discusses the coherence of European security law, in five chapters. The discussion refers both to the internal coherence of the security policy of the EU and to its external coherence with policies outside the Union.

Two chapters deal with the internal coherence of the security policies of the Union. In Chapter 10 Ramses A Wessel addresses 'Differentiation in EU Foreign, Security and Defence Policy: Between Coherence and Flexibility'. While the relatively new security and defence policy may contribute to positioning the Union as a cohesive force in international relations, the current legal regime explicitly allows for differentiation in this area. The purpose of this contribution is to analyse the variations in foreign, security, and defence policy as well as the consequences of a possible fragmentation on the positioning of the Union as a united global force. Is it possible for Member States not to participate in the security and defence integration or does the single legal order of the Union prevent this variation? A second question concerns the different possibilities for closer (or 'enhanced') cooperation. While the Treaty on the one hand allows for groups of Member States to work closer together in the area of CFSP, on the other hand the possibilities for an enhanced cooperation in ESDP are less evident. And, finally, the question is to what extent the new European Constitution discussed in Chapter 3 further consolidates the somewhat fragmented legal regime on differentiation in the area of foreign, security, and defence policy.

In Chapter 11 Panos Koutrakos examines 'Security and Defence Policy within the Context of EU External Relations: Issues of Coherence, Consistency, and Effectiveness'. ESDP is devised and carried out in the context of EU external relations. This chapter sheds some light on the various linkages between the conduct of an efficient ESDP and the law and practice of EU external relations and the various ways in which the Union institutions and the Member States seek to ensure the consistency and coherence of EU international actions. It identifies normative, political, and practical mechanisms and examines their interactions in the context of an evolving Union.

The last three chapters of Part III deal with the coherence of the security policy of the EU with other international security frameworks. In Chapter 12 Fabien Terpan explores 'EU-NATO Relations: Interoperability as a Strategic Consideration and a Legal Requirement'. In both NATO and the EU there is a legal basis for the development of a European role in defence and security. Arrangements have been made to fully cooperate in these matters. However, EU-NATO relations face three major challenges: subsidiarity, interoperability, and a more balanced partnership between European members and the United States. Neither the treaties nor the political declarations have given a precise view of the way these challenges are supposed to be faced. A permanent Treaty should help to better shape the future of EU-NATO relations. Before that, however, some political clarifications have to be provided, especially on the idea of European autonomy.

In Chapter 13 Marco Odello examines the relationship between 'The Organization for Security and Co-operation in Europe and European Security Law'. The OSCE defines security and cooperation as one of its main purposes. Security is a wide concept that does not always have well-defined limits. It can expand and include both military and non-military elements. The OSCE was the largest organization in the widened European region well before the end of the Cold War. For this reason, it is not possible to speculate on the idea of European security law without dealing with the pan-European organization par excellence. The content of the concept of security adopted by OSCE documents will be related to other organizations to provide a general framework of the developments concerning the definition(s) of this concept. The chapter focuses on legal aspects of institutional action in the area of security law. Its central idea is to evaluate whether the legal and institutional structure of the organization may undermine its role as the leading European organization in the area of security. It also considers the possible positive aspects of the peculiar legal framework of the OSCE.

In Chapter 14 Nigel White discusses 'The EU as a Regional Security Actor within the International Legal Order'. The UN Charter envisaged the universal organization it constituted working on security matters alongside regional security actors. More widely, the Charter formed part of the post-1945 international legal order, contributing in varying degrees to the principles and rules governing the use of military force, the imposition of non-forcible measures, and the protection of human rights and self-determination. In the period 1956–1992 the impact of these international rules and institutions on the predecessors of the EU was limited. With the EU's entrance as a serious security actor on the international stage in 1992, with the adoption of the Maastricht Treaty, it became more pressing to evaluate the position, powers, and limitations of the EU in the international legal order. The questions to be considered within this chapter concern the rights and duties of the EU and the UN in international law in the related areas of peace and security, human rights, and democracy, as well as the legal relationship between the two bodies. This will then provide a clearer framework within which better cooperation can be achieved. The process of positioning the organizations within the international legal order should result in enhancing the legitimacy and arguably the effectiveness of the two organizations, whether they act singly or together. It is important to identify the underlying principles governing the organizations and their activities. It will be argued that there are fundamental (legal) principles underlying the function of collective security in the international community that have to be recognized and reinforced if we are to have organizational activity that is not just simply discretionary or arbitrary.

In the final Chapter on 'Conclusions on the Current State of European Security Law' Nigel White and Martin Trybus draw conclusions on the scope and coherence of European security law.

PART I

ORIGINS AND FUTURE OF EUROPEAN SECURITY INTEGRATION

2

The Vision of the European Defence Community and a Common Defence for the European Union

*Martin Trybus**

1. Introduction

In August 1954 the French parliament effectively refused to ratify the European Defence Community (EDC) Treaty. The most ambitious project of European security and defence integration to date failed. The EDC Treaty between the six Member States (Belgium, France, Germany, Italy, Luxembourg, and the Netherlands) had envisaged nothing less than the creation of a supranational organization to supervise integrated European Defence Forces. However, the end of the EDC project did not mean the end of the European security and defence integration process. Later in 1954 the Western European Union (WEU), an intergovernmental organization, was established, this time with the inclusion of the United Kingdom. However, it took another 38 years before European leaders created the intergovernmental Common Foreign and Security Policy (CFSP) as part of the Treaty on European Union (TEU), thus putting European security and defence integration back on the agenda. It took even longer, 45 years, before an equally intergovernmental European Security and Defence Policy (ESDP) started to develop as a part of the CFSP.

The EDC Treaty has not been receiving much academic attention recently.[1] Most publications and conference contributions come from political scientists. The main textbooks on European law briefly mention the failure of the project in their introductory chapters on the history of European integration. Even more

* Senior Lecturer in Law, University of Sheffield, United Kingdom. Thanks to Tamara Hervey (Nottingham) for useful comments when discussing a previous version of this chapter on a workshop in Nottingham in April 2005. I am also grateful to Aris Georgopoulos (Nottingham), Heike Krieger (Berlin), and Steve Peers (Essex) for their observations during the workshop. Any mistakes, however, remain my own. All website addresses cited were active on 17 October 2006, unless otherwise specified.
[1] E Fursdon, *The European Defence Community: A History* (Macmillan: London, 1980) remains the most comprehensive analysis of the EDC to date.

specialized works on European security and defence law do not dedicate more than a paragraph to the subject. However, it is submitted that study of the EDC Treaty is timely and worthwhile, since Maastricht Article 17(1) TEU stipulates that the CFSP 'might lead to a common defence'. This 'common defence' is vague, uncertain, and set in the future. Article I-41(2) of the envisaged European Union (EU) Constitutional Treaty replaces the word 'might' with the more certain 'will', although the introduction of a common defence would still be subject to an uncertain decision of the European Council. A common defence would go beyond the current CFSP and ESDP or the Common Security and Defence Policy (CSDP) envisaged in the EU Constitutional Treaty. The failed EDC also consisted of many elements that would have gone further than these EU policies. It represents a project of the past regulating many aspects of a vague and uncertain common defence which is set in the future of European security and defence integration. Hence the EDC Treaty gives an idea of what a 'common defence' might actually entail.

The objective of this chapter is to provide an overview of the Community envisaged in the EDC Treaty. The method to achieve an understanding of the scale of security and defence integration planned in the 1950s is to compare the EDC Treaty with defence-related provisions in later European treaties and legislation, most notably those on the CFSP, the ESDP, and the CSDP. With regards to the EDC, this comparison is necessarily limited to a textual analysis, as the Community to be established by the EDC Treaty remained a vision and never became a reality. Hence it is unclear whether it would have actually worked in practice. This reservation applies equally to the CSDP, discussed in Chapter 3, since the EU Constitutional Treaty might never enter into force either. After a brief introduction to the history of the EDC Treaty, this chapter will discuss the supranational nature of the EDC as reflected in its institutional law, its defensive character, its principle of non-discrimination between Member States, and the connection to the North Atlantic Treaty Organisation (NATO). Within the limits set by a book chapter, and considering the different historical and strategic contexts, the reader will be able to compare the comprehensive legal framework prepared by an army of lawyers, policy-makers, soldiers, and diplomats with the current efforts discussed in other chapters of this collection.

2. A Short History of the European Defence Community Treaty

European integration is a reaction to World War II. The war had resulted in more than 40 million dead Europeans, a largely destroyed infrastructure in many countries, and a political landscape dominated by the Soviet threat.[2] This experience

---

[2] Winston Churchill summarized the situation in his famous speech on 19 September 1946 in Zurich as follows: 'What is the plight to which Europe has been reduced? [...] Over wide areas a vast

taught European leaders a lesson: a new approach to European relations had to be developed to overcome the traditional antagonisms which had led to so much hardship and destruction. The fundamental Schuman Declaration of 1950 put this connection between European integration and the prevention of another war in no uncertain terms.[3] While, so far, post-war relations had followed the traditional intergovernmental approach,[4] Schuman proposed—and in 1952 achieved—a supranational European Coal and Steel Community (ECSC) with the power to take binding decisions on the Member States: Belgium, France, Germany, Italy, Luxembourg, and the Netherlands.

The next step for integration directly concerned the sensitive defence area: the establishment of a more supranational EDC with the participation of the six ECSC Member States. The EDC envisaged nothing less than the merger of the armed forces of the Member States into European Defence Forces (EDF), including newly-created German divisions. These forces were to be organized and supervised by a supranational EDC administration answerable to a European Assembly. During the New York and Washington conferences in September 1950 the French Prime Minister René Pléven made an unofficial proposal for an EDC. The war in Korea had started three months before this proposal. Communist North Korea had invaded South Korea with the help of the Communist People's Republic of China. A UN military force under the leadership of the USA intervened. A first armed conflict between Communist states and the West had started and made the organization of the defence of Europe, with the inclusion of a substantial German contribution, an urgent matter. All six governments signed the EDC Treaty resulting from the Pléven Proposal in May 1952. The German, Dutch, Belgian, and Luxembourg legislatures had also ratified the Treaty by the summer of 1954. It was sent for ratification in the French parliament and Italian ratification was anticipated soon afterwards.[5] The EDC project consisted of the

shivering mass of tormented, hungry, care-worn and bewildered human beings gape at the ruins of their cities and homes and scan the dark horizons for the approach of some peril, tyranny or horror'. Some 40 million were dead and in 1946 100 million were living near starvation levels. In Germany 3 million out of 5.5 million houses were destroyed, Frankfurt was destroyed by 45 per cent, Cologne 66 per cent, Düsseldorf 93 per cent. All Rhine bridges, 75 per cent of all other bridges, and most of the railway track were destroyed. Belgium and Poland lost 60 per cent of their locomotives and rolling stock. In France, Belgium, the Netherlands, Greece, Poland, and Yugoslavia industrial production was only 20 per cent of pre-war figures. Coal output in Europe was 42 per cent of what it was before the war. A massive inflation forced a rapid devaluation in France, Italy, and Germany. Finally, living in defiance of authority and without the law had led to moral disintegration in the formerly occupied countries. See A Nutting, *Europe Will not Wait: A Warning and a Way Out* (Hollis & Carter: London, 1960), 1–3.

   [3] Schuman Declaration of 9 May 1950, *Bulletin of the European Communities* 13 (1980) 14, 15; available at: <http://europa.eu/abc/symbols/9-may/decl_en.htm>: 'A united Europe was not achieved and we had war'.

   [4] The Brussels Treaty on Western Union 1948 (19 UNTS 51), the Council of Europe (87 UNTS 103; ETS 1), and the (NATO) Washington Treaty (34 UNTS 243) all represent intergovernmental frameworks.

   [5] For the chronology of EDC, see D Lerner and R Aron, *France Defeats EDC* (New York: Frederick A Praeger, 1957), XV–XVI.

Treaty itself[6] with a preamble and 132 articles,[7] a number of protocols,[8] and other instruments.[9]

The next parts of this chapter will discuss the central characteristics of the EDC, which are its supranational nature reflected in the institutional law of the EDC Treaty, its exclusively defensive orientation, and its interdependence with NATO. The regulation of these issues in the EC Treaty will be compared to regulation in the EU under the current Treaty of Nice and the envisaged EU Constitutional Treaty.

3. The Supranational Nature of the European Defence Community

In intergovernmental organizations the participating states take the decisions. Most international organizations, including the UN and NATO, are intergovernmental in character. By contrast, a supranational organization has independent

---

[6] *La Traité Instituant la Communauté Européene de Défense—La Documentation Française* was originally published by the *Ministère des Affaires Etrangères* in Paris (undated, 1952?). There are two English translations. One was presented to the United Kingdom Parliament in April 1954 as *The European Defence Community Treaty Paris, May 27, 1952 (together with related documents)*, Cmd 9127 (London: HMSO, 1954). This excluded translation of the protocols on jurisdiction, military penal code, finance, conditions of pay of the military and civil personnel and their pension rights, and the status of the European Defence Forces and that of the commercial and fiscal regime of the EDC (see below). The Office of the United States Special Representative in Europe published a separate and slightly different unofficial translation of the EDC Treaty on 26 January 1953 based on the United States Senate publication 94118 (82nd Congress 2nd session), on the NATO version published on 12 July 1952, and on a translation of one of the agreements by the Allied High Commission's Secretariat.

[7] Part I: Fundamental Principles, Chapter I: The European Defence Community (Articles 1–8), Chapter II: European Defence Forces (Articles 9–18); Part II: The Institutions of the Community, Chapter I: The Board of Commissioners (Articles 19–32), Chapter II: The Assembly (Articles 33–38), Chapter III: The Council (Articles 39–50), Chapter IV: The Court (Articles 51–67); Part III: Military Provisions, Chapter I: Organization and Administration of the European Defence Forces (Articles 68–79), Chapter II: Status of the European Defence Forces (Articles 80–82); Part IV: Financial Provisions (Articles 83–100); Part V: Economic Provisions (Articles 101–111); Part VI: General Provisions (Articles 112–132).

[8] The Military Protocol, the Jurisdictional Protocol, the Protocol relating to Military Penal Law, the Financial Protocol, the Protocol on the Conditions of the Remuneration of Military and Civilian Personnel within the Community and on their Pension Rights, the Protocol regarding the Grand Duchy of Luxembourg, the Protocol regarding the Relations between the EDC and NATO, the Protocol on Guarantees given by Member States of the EDC to Parties to the North Atlantic Treaty, the Protocol relating to the Status of the European Defence Forces and the Commercial and Fiscal Administration of the EDC, the Protocols of Signature, and the Protocol on the Interim Committee.

[9] The Common Declaration of the Defence Ministers on the Duration of the Treaty, the Agreement envisaged in Article 107 (Paragraph 4b), the Exchange of Letters between the Government of the Federal Republic of Germany and the Governments of the Co-signatory States to the EDC Treaty concerning Article 107 of the Treaty, the Treaty between the United Kingdom and the member States of the EDC, the Protocol to the Atlantic Treaty on guarantees given by the Parties to the North

institutions that have the power to take decisions which are binding on the participating states. This can include an independent court with the authority to issue
binding judgments. Moreover, the institutions representing the participating
states can take at least some decisions by qualified and even simple majority,
thereby opening the possibility of a state being out-voted. Following the example
of the ECSC Treaty, the EDC Treaty envisaged a supranational organization.
It should be pointed out, however, that the intergovernmental/supranational
dichotomy is problematic. The European Community, for example, is generally
seen as a supranational organization, but it consists of both intergovernmental
and supranational elements. The Council, for example, is an intergovernmental
institution where the Member States take decisions. However, many decisions
may be taken by qualified majority voting, thereby opening up the possibility
of a Member State being bound by a decision it voted against. Moreover, many
decisions on legislation are also subject to a vote of the supranational European
Parliament and judicial review of the supranational European Court of Justice.
While the dichotomy is problematic, the EDC Treaty nevertheless envisaged a
more supranational organization based on the model of the ECSC. Article 1 EDC
Treaty expressly established the supranational character of the Community, comprising common institutions, common armed forces, and a common budget.[10]
This supranational character manifested itself mainly in the competencies and
independence of the executive organ and the court in comparison to the role of
the main intergovernmental institution.

3.1. The Board of Commissioners

Articles 19 to 32 EDC Treaty regulated the composition and powers of the Board
of Commissioners, the executive institution of the Community. The nine
Commissioners had to be nationals of a Member State, were appointed by agreement between the national governments, and would normally serve for six years.
One third of the members would be replaced every two years and not more than
two were to come from one Member State.[11] The Board was the most important
element of the more supranational character of the EDC, since they were to be

Atlantic Treaty to the Members of the EDC, the Tripartite Declaration by the Foreign Ministers of
the United States, France and the United Kingdom, and the Exchange of Letters between the
Government of the Federal Republic of Germany and the Governments of France, the United States
and the United Kingdom (one concerning the control of atomic energy and the other concerning
civilian aircraft).

[10] Article 1 EDC Treaty: 'The High Contracting Parties, by the present Treaty, set up among
themselves a European Defence Community, supra-national in character, comprising common
institutions, common Armed Forces, and a common budget'. The EDC proposal has been even
called 'supranational *par exellence*': see P Koutrakos, *Trade, Foreign Policy and Defence in EU
Constitutional Law: The Legal Regulation of Sanctions, Exports of Dual Use Goods and Armaments*
(Oxford: Hart, 2001) 9.
[11] Article 21 EDC Treaty.

independent from the governments of the Member States and empowered to take binding decisions. An 'important direction on their independence'[12] was stated in Article 20 EDC Treaty:

In the accomplishment of their duties, the members of the Board of Commissioners shall neither ask for or receive instructions from any government. They shall refrain from any action inconsistent with the supranational character of their duties.[13]

The Board would have a quorum of five and decisions were to be taken by a majority of those present.[14] The governments of the Member States, after consulting the Board, would appoint a Chairman of the Board of Commissioners from among its members by mutual agreement for four years.[15]

The Board of Commissioners was to have executive and supervisory powers.[16] According to Article 27 EDC Treaty, in the exercise of its powers it was to take Decisions, make Recommendations, and express Opinions. Decisions were to be binding in all their aspects. Recommendations were to be binding in respect of the purposes which they laid down, but were to leave to whom they were addressed the choice of the means of achieving that purpose. Opinions were to have no binding force. According to Article 30 EDC Treaty the Board was to have at its disposal the civil and military personnel necessary to enable it to carry out all the tasks devolving on it under the Treaty. The military and civilian personnel in the services they were to form for this purpose were to be subordinate to the Board on the same footing and on the same basis. Article 31 EDC Treaty dealt with its powers in respect of EDF ranks and appointments.[17] Thus the Board of Commissioners would have been the EDC ministry of defence. Moreover, it would have had the power to pass secondary legislation in the form of binding Decisions and Recommendations. The latter follows the example of the powers of the High Authority of the ECSC, which was the only model at the time.

The independent Board of Commissioners was to be the institutional manifestation of the supranational character of the EDC. It was the crucial supranational institutional element, in contrast to the intergovernmental element represented by the Council. The Board was to be the only institution the EDC was not to 'borrow' from the ECSC. Hence it was the only wholly separate EDC institution safeguarding the interests of only that Community. This emphasized the supranational character of the Community. However, there was an important intergovernmental element in the fact that the members of the Board were to be appointed by agreement of the governments of the Member States.

The far-reaching independence and powers of the Board of Commissioners were one of the reasons for the French opposition to the EDC Treaty. In Chapter II

---

[12] Fursdon, above, note 1, at 155.   [13] Article 20 EDC Treaty.
[14] Article 24(1) EDC Treaty.   [15] Article 25 EDC Treaty.   [16] Article 19 EDC Treaty.
[17] Article 31 EDC treaty.

of its *Projet de Protocole d'Application du Traité instituant la Communauté Européenne de Défense*[18] of 19 August 1954 the French Government proposed to limit the task of the Board of Commissioners to the management, administration, and equipment of the EDF. It was to have no political prerogatives and be subordinate to the Council. Moreover, for eight years after the Treaty came into force a Member State could have suspended any decision of the Board of Commissioners which it considered as affecting its vital interests. Equally, for the same period, the latter's right of appeal would have been suspended. This would have eroded the supranational character of the EDC enshrined mainly in the provisions on the Board of Commissioners. As Fursdon wrote, 'the once-powerful Board of Commissioners would have been downgraded to a Board of Technical Management only'.[19] It would have been harder for the Board to come to decisions, and executive implementation of these decisions would have been very difficult. Thus the French proposals would have 'removed the whole supranational concept'.[20]

In the context of the Community pillar of the current Treaty of Nice, the European Commission, which is the executive organ and civil service of the EU, has no general powers comparable to that of the Board of Commissioners under Article 30 EDC Treaty. Most general decisions are taken by the intergovernmental Council who are also the co-legislator with the European Parliament. The European Commission itself has only very limited legislative powers[21] and an almost exclusive right of initiating legislation. In the context of the ESDP, which is part of the second pillar of the current Treaty of Nice, the Commission does not even have the powers of the initiator of legislation which it has under the first pillar. As outlined in the next section, the organizational structures involved in the ESDP are all under the supervision of the Council, and the Commission is largely excluded from this policy. This would not even change under the envisaged EU Constitutional Treaty discussed in Chapter 3.[22] The Western Union (WU),[23] NATO, or the WEU did or do not have an institution with powers comparable to those of the EDC Board of Commissioners either. Moreover, at the time of writing there is no plan to create an equally powerful supranational institution in the area of defence and security. Hence the Board of Commissioners remains the most powerful institution ever envisaged for an international defence and security

[18] *Projet de Protocole d'Application du Traité instituant la Communauté Européenne de Défense*, later published by the Belgian Government: *Textes et Documents*, Brussels, Ministère des Affaires Etrangères et du Commerce Extérieur, 24 August 1954.   [19] Fursdon, above, note 1, 284.
[20] Nutting, above, note 2, 67.
[21] Under Articles 39(3)(d) and 86(3) EC and when legislation is delegated from the Council to the Commission (which means that the Council can also take these powers back), see P P Craig and G de Búrca, *EU Law*, 3rd edn (Oxford: OUP, 2002) 140.
[22] See also M Trybus, *European Union Law and Defence Integration* (Oxford: Hart Publishing, 2005) 381–2.
[23] An organization established by the Brussels Treaty (see above), preceding the WEU.

organization. Its supranational character was to be the essential component of the supranational character of the EDC.

3.2. The Council

The significance of the position of the independent Board of Commissioners for the supranational character of the EDC becomes clear when compared to the position of the intergovernmental institution. The Council of the EDC, which was to be the Council of the ECSC, was to be composed of representatives from each Member State government, each becoming chairman by turn of alphabetical order. Hence the Council was the intergovernmental element in the institutional structure of the EDC. They were to meet as often as necessary, but at least every three months, and could be called into session on the initiative of the Chairman or a member of the Council or the Board of Commissioners. In order to function at any time, a deputy could represent a Council Member and also each Member State had to have a permanent representative nominated.

In broad terms, the task of the Council was to harmonize the activities of the Board of Commissioners with the policies of the governments of the Member States.[24] Its main function was similar to that of the Council in the context of the ECSC or the later European Economic Community, and EU: the Council was to be a legislator. It was to issue Directives to guide the activities of the Board of Commissioners, to give approvals, which the Board of Commissioners had to obtain before taking Decisions or making Recommendations, and to take Decisions. However, in contrast to the role of the Council in the EC and the EU, the EDC Treaty also envisaged a strong legislative role for the Board of Commissioners, both as a legislator and as an initiator of legislation. This followed the example of the High Authority in the ECSC. Broadly speaking, the fundamental decisions were to be taken by the Council but generally the Board of Commissioners was to take the decisions. For example, Article 31(1) EDC Treaty provides that ranks higher than those of Commander of a basic unit of homogeneous nationality were to be conferred by Decision of the Board of Commissioners, on approval by the Council acting unanimously.[25] Article 31(2) EDC Treaty provides that the respective Member State was to make decisions on ranks in homogeneous units. According to Article 31(3)(b) EDC Treaty decisions concerning 'all other military appointments', in other words of lower ranks in heterogeneous units, were to be taken by the Board of Commissioners. This example illustrates the point made above that the Council was to take only the more political decisions. The less political and more administrative the decision, the less the involvement of the Council.

Article 43 EDC Treaty dealt with the voting procedure to be followed in implementing the different types of decisions called for in the Treaty. There were three

---

[24] Article 39(1) EDC Treaty.

[25] A similar procedure applies to other high appointments under Article 31(3)(a) EDC Treaty.

variations: a simple majority, a specified or qualified majority, and unanimity. A simple majority meant an absolute majority of representatives or, in the event of a tie, a majority of representatives of the Member States which together made available to the Community at least two thirds of the contribution of Member States. The term 'contribution', as used in the simple or specified majority voting procedure, was taken as meaning the percentage of financial contribution actually paid during the previous financial year and the percentage of manpower composing the EDF on the first day of the current half year. The voting procedure was thus in certain circumstances subject to a 'weighting' dependent on the size of a nation's contributory defence effort towards the EDC. Obviously, it would be some time before such contributions were formed into the echelons of the EDF and so an agreed scale was required to enable the Council to function over this interim period. Article 43 *bis* EDC Treaty gave this on a forfeiture basis as Germany, France, and Italy three each, Belgium and Netherlands two each, and Luxembourg one. A specified or qualified majority was to be achieved either by the proportion of votes so specified, provided that such a majority included the votes of the Member States which together made available to the Community two thirds of the contribution of Member States, or by the vote of five Member States. According to Article 39(4) EDC Treaty the decisions and approval of the Council were to be decided by simple majority unless the EDC Treaty provided otherwise. However, as the Treaty required qualified majorities or unanimity for most conceivable decisions, decision-making by simple majority would have been of little importance in practice.

A qualified two-thirds majority was required with regards to matters of a lesser, managerial, or administrative nature with regards to general principles, the EDF, or finance and budget.[26] In broad terms the unanimous vote of the Council was required on important matters affecting the EDC generally, modifications to

---

[26] A two-thirds majority Council decision was required for: general matters in Article 46 subparagraph 1 EDC Treaty on inviting the Board of Commissioners to take any measure within its competence; Article 114 (1) subparagraph 2 EDC Treaty on laying down directives governing the transfer of information from the Member States to the Board of Commissioners considered necessary for the exercise of the latter's duties; Article 123 (2) subparagraph 1 EDC Treaty regarding provisional measures taken in the context of this article; Article 126 subparagraph 1 EDC on convening a conference for the amendment of EDC Treaty; for matters regarding the European Defence Forces in Articles 13 subparagraph 1, 14 subparagraph 1, 77 (2) subparagraph 1, 78 *bis* (4.2) EDC Treaty; and for finance and budget in Article 85 subparagraph 2 EDC Treaty on the nomination of the members of the Board of Auditors and its Chairman, Article 87(2)(b) EDC Treaty on the allocation of expenditure, Article 89 subparagraph 4 EDC Treaty on the choice of a common accounting currency for the budget, Article 90(1) EDC Treaty regarding transfers of credits between the chapters of responsibility of the Board of Commissioners, Article 102(2) EDC Treaty on general instructions regarding common programmes for the armament, equipment, supply, and infrastructure of the EDF, Article 103(2) EDC Treaty on the Council approval of the seven-year programmes of the Board of Commissioners regarding common armaments programmes, Article 104(4) and (5) subparagraph 3 EDC Treaty on the Council approval of regulations regarding public procurement and contract management of common armaments programmes submitted by the Board of Commissioners, and Article 107(2) subparagraph 2 EDC Treaty regarding amendments to the list of armaments in Annex I to Article 107 EDC Treaty.

any arrangements relating to the EDF and their associated common equipment programmes, on financial arrangements, and on the common budget.[27] A unanimous decision was achieved if the votes in its favour included those of all Member States represented on the Council. Abstentions could not prevent the adoption of such a decision.

There are two remarks to be made about these voting procedures. First, the allocation of votes took the different contributions of the Member States into account. However, as the provisional allocation of votes indicates, this did not take the real differences in contribution into account but balanced them with the fact that every Member State had to have a vote. Second, the distribution between simple majority voting, qualified majority voting, and unanimous vote indicates a fine balance between the intergovernmental and the supranational. The intergovernmental institution Council were to take decisions on the more important matters on an intergovernmental basis: unanimity means that there is no possibility of being out-voted, there is a national *veto*. All Member States are equal: one government, one vote. Decisions on less important matters are taken on a more supranational basis: simple and qualified majority means that there is a possibility of being out-voted, there is no national *veto*, and the number of votes takes the 'size' of the Member States into account.

Lastly, the Council alone was responsible for decisions regarding any joint sessions with the NATO Council or in regard to an EDC-NATO Protocol. The joint sessions were essentially sessions of the EDC Council extended by the representatives of the USA, Canada, Portugal, Denmark, Norway, and the United Kingdom. Any decision taken unanimously during such joint meetings of the two Councils was to be automatically binding on the EDC institutions.[28] The joint sessions of the Councils were to be one of the links between NATO and EDC as two interdependent elements of the European security and defence architecture. The EDC was to be the first and only 'floor' based on the 'basement' of NATO, in turn based on the 'foundations' of the UN. The EDC link to NATO is discussed further below.

---

[27] Unanimous Council decision was required for: general matters in Articles 119 EDC Treaty regarding the linguistic system of the institutions of the Community, Article 123 (1) EDC Treaty for decisions taken in the context of cases of grave and urgent necessity, Article 124 subparagraphs 1 and 2 EDC Treaty for the approval of Board decisions to be taken in cases not provided in the Treaty, Article 125 subparagraph 1 EDC Treaty regarding adjustments of the rules relating to the exercise by the Board of Commissioners of the powers granted to it due to unforeseen difficulties, Article 129 EDC Treaty regarding accession to the EDC; matters concerning the European Defence Forces in Articles 15(2) EDC Treaty regarding the organization of the EDF, Article 39(2) EDC Treaty regarding the directives guiding the activities of the Board, Article 44 EDC Treaty regarding modifications to the text defining the status of the personnel and the texts governing the general organization, recruitment, strength, and officering of the forces, and modifications to the plan constituting the EDF, Article 48 EDC Treaty regarding relations between NATO and the EDC, Articles 68(2), 69(2), 77(1), and 78 *bis* (1.1) EDC Treaty on specific rules relating to the organization and administration of the EDF; and for finance and budget in Articles 84, 85 subparagraph 2, 87(2), 95(1), 99 subparagraph 3, EDC Treaty and the economic provisions in Articles 104(7), 105 subparagraph 2, and 107(4)(d) EDC Treaty.   [28] Article 47 (2) EDC Treaty.

According to Article 46 EDC Treaty, acting on a two-thirds majority, the Council could invite the Board of Commissioners to take any measure within its competence. The Board did not have to comply with this invitation. If they did not comply then the Council or any Member State could call the Assembly into session with a view to obtaining a motion of censure and hence the Board's resignation. This scenario would have involved a serious confrontation between the institutions and Member States amounting to a 'constitutional crisis'. Such a crisis would have undermined the coherence of the EDC and the security of Western Europe and therefore it is unlikely it would ever have happened. As the Council would have had to overcome such a high hurdle to overcome their resistance to comply with their invitation, Article 46 EDC Treaty did not represent a significant limitation on the Board of Commissioners' right to initiative.

In contrast to the EDC, the institutional structure of the current ESDP is that it is exclusively part of the Council. The High Representative for the Common Foreign and Security Policy, the Political and Security Committee,[29] the European Union Military Committee,[30] the European Union Military Staff,[31] and the Committee for Civilian Aspects of Crisis Management, and even the new European Defence Agency discussed in Chapter 3 and by Georgopoulos in Chapter 9, are all Council bodies. The ESDP peacekeeping dimension (discussed by Naert in Chapter 4 and by Tsagourias in Chapter 5) and the European armaments policy are policies conducted exclusively by the intergovernmental Council deciding by unanimity. This 'Council-driven' and 'Council-controlled' security and defence policy would also continue with the new office of the Union Minister for Foreign Affairs envisaged under the EU Constitutional Treaty.[32] The almost unlimited control of the Council acting by unanimity is the main characteristic of the intergovernmental security and defence policy of the EU.

3.3. The Court

Articles 51 to 57 EDC Treaty regulated the Court of the EDC, which was to be the ECSC Court of Justice.[33] It was to ensure respect for the law in the interpretation and application of the EDC Treaty and its regulations[34] and to have jurisdiction to hear appeals by Member States, the Council, or the Assembly against Decisions or Recommendations of the Board of Commissioners.[35] Similarly, it was to be competent to give judgment on appeals brought against the proceedings of the Council brought by a Member State, by the Board of Commissioners, or by the Assembly.[36] Appeals could be made on grounds of lack of legal competence, violation of procedure, violation of the Treaty or any legal rules concerning its

---

[29] Article 25 TEU.
[30] Annex VI to the Presidency Report, Annexes IV to VI on the EUMC, M Rutten (ed) *From St-Malo to Nice, European Defence: Core Documents*, Chaillot Paper 47 (Paris: Institute of Security Studies of the European Union, 2001) 193–6.   [31] Ibid, 196–9.
[32] See Trybus, above, note 22, 360–80.   [33] Article 52 EDC Treaty.
[34] Article 51 EDC Treaty.   [35] Article 54 EDC Treaty.   [36] Article 57 EDC Treaty.

application, or misuse of powers, as outlined in Articles 54(1) and 57(1) EDC Treaty. The Court could set aside the Recommendations or Decisions of the Board and at the request of a Member State, or the Board of Commissioners, set aside the proceedings of the Assembly. However, according to Article 58(1) sub-paragraph 2 EDC Treaty such an appeal could only be based on grounds of lack of legal competence or violation of requisite formalities. Action had to be brought within one month from the notification or publication of the act in question,[37] for reasons of legal certainty. The EDC Treaty did not provide for individual action, in other words appeals of natural or legal persons. Under the ECSC Treaty this was possible within certain limits. However, Article 62 EDC Treaty provided for a procedure whereby only the Court was competent to rule on the validity of decisions taken by the Council or the Board of Commissioners. Thus the Court had the function of a constitutional court in the framework of the EDC.

The Court was independent from the influence of the governments of the Member States. Even the International Court of Justice is independent. However, in the ECSC, the EDC, and later the EC, the Court exercises its jurisdiction over the Member States without their specific consent to individual cases. Thus the jurisdiction of the Court is also an element of the supranational character of the EDC.

The strong position of a court of law in a defence organization was and is unprecedented. Neither the WU of 1948, NATO, nor later the WEU provided for judicial review. The jurisdiction of the European Court of Justice is excluded from the ESDP and the CFSP of the EU according to Article 46 TEU, although as explained by Koutrakos in Chapter 11 the Court has decided on the limitations of the Community pillar. Moreover, even under the envisaged EU Constitutional Treaty the security and defence policy remains excluded from the jurisdiction of the Court. The nonchalance with which the Member States provided for judicial review in the EDC Treaty can partly be explained by the fact that in the early 1950s they could not be aware of the pivotal role of the Court of Justice, a role that only became apparent with the Luxembourg jurisprudence of the 1960s. Had the Member States known about *Van Gend*[38] and *Costa v ENEL*[39] at the time it can be assumed that judicial review would have been a more controversial issue. Another reason might be the desire of the Member States as the creators of the EDC Treaty to introduce some form of control of the powerful Board of Commissioners. Finally, in a Community largely replacing the defence efforts of the Member States rather than forming a military alliance of still independent national forces, administrative and legislative actions have to be subjected to the same checks and balances as those of the Member States. This is necessary to meet

---

[37] Articles 54(2) and 57 subparagraph 2 EDC Treaty.
[38] Case C-32/84 *Van Gend en Loos NV Algemene Transporten Expeditie Onderneming* v *Nederlandse Administratie der Belastingen* [1963] ECR 1.
[39] Case C-6/64 *Costa* v *Ente Nazionale per l'Energia Elettrica (ENEL)* [1964] ECR 585, [1964] CMLR 425.

the minimum requirements of democracy, legitimacy, and accountability. In other words, when the state is replaced in a particular field, the replacing entity should be subjected to the same level of judicial control as previously the state.

3.4. The Assembly

Article 33 to 38 EDC Treaty dealt with the Assembly, which was the Assembly of the ECSC increased by three delegates each for Germany, France, and Italy. The members were to be elected on the same terms as the other delegates by the national parliaments, not directly by the peoples of the Community. Hence the Assembly was one of the institutions the EDC 'borrowed' from the ECSC.[40] It was to meet annually and members of the Council and the Board of Commissioners could attend and address it. The latter had to report to the Assembly, who would discuss the report, make suggestions and comment thereon. The Assembly could pass a censure motion forcing the entire Board of Commissioners to resign. It is submitted that for various reasons, that go beyond the aim of this chapter, the EDC would have suffered from a democratic deficit. Suffice it to say that the similar provisions of assemblies and the European Parliament in other European treaties caused criticism of the democratic structure.[41] The EDC would not have had a directly elected institution, this at least indirectly-elected institution would have had only a consultative function, it could not elect the Board of Commissioners, and a Council made up of representatives of Member State governments and an executive Board of Commissions would have passed legislation.

While the European Parliament has been a directly-elected institution since 1979, its role under the CFSP and ESDP is reduced to the bare minimum.[42] It suffers from a democratic deficit.[43] Article 21 TEU allocates a very rudimentary and vague right of consultation to the successor of the ECSC and the EEC Assembly. This would not change under Articles I-41(8) and III-304(1) and (2) of the EU Constitutional Treaty,[44] a fact criticized by the European Parliament itself.[45] However, while the weakness of the European Parliament in the context

---

[40] R A Wessel, *The European Union's Foreign and Security Policy: A Legal and Institutional Perspective* (The Hague/London/Boston: Kluwer Law International, 2000) 2.

[41] See J Weiler, U Haltern, and F Meyer, 'European Democracy and its Critique' in J Hayward (ed), *The Crisis of Representation in Europe* (Frank Cass, 1995) 32–3; J Weiler, 'European Models: Polity, People and System' in P Craig and C Harlow, *Lawmaking in the European Union* (The Hague/London/Boston: Kluwer Law International, 1998), chapter 7; P Craig, 'The Nature of the Community: Integration, Democracy and Legitimacy' in Craig and de Búrca, *The Evolution of EU Law* (Oxford: Oxford University Press, 1999) 1; G de Búrca, 'The Quest for Legitimacy in the European Union' (1996) 59 MLR 349; Craig and de Búrca, *EU Law*, above, note 21, 167.

[42] Trybus, above, note 22, 76–8.   [43] Wessel, above, note 38, 213.

[44] Trybus, above, note 22, 382–5.

[45] 'European Parliament Resolution on the Annual Report from the Council to the European Parliament on the Main Aspects and Basic Choices of CFSP, including Financial Implications for the General Budget of the EU, Strasbourg, 23 October 2003' in A Missiroli, *From Copenhagen to Brussels: European defence: core documents*, Volume IV, Chaillot Paper No 67 (Paris: Institute of Security Studies of the European Union, December 2003) 229.

of security and defence policy is only one aspect of the weakness of the all more supranational institutions in this policy field, it is also a regular feature of the security and defence polices of many Member States that the role of the legislature is reduced and that of the executive enhanced. A comprehensive discussion of this issue, however, would go beyond the aims of this chapter.

3.5. The European Defence Forces

The EDC Treaty was to establish a permanent European army. Articles 9 to 18 EDC Treaty laid down the principles for the constitution and organization of the EDF. Units from the Member States were to be made available to the Community 'with a view of their fusion'. No Member State could recruit or maintain national armed forces other than those for which the EDC Treaty had made special provision.[46] Such circumstances were to apply only where the Member State would have assumed defence responsibilities for non-European territories or for the fulfilment of international missions in Berlin, Austria, or under United Nations' auspices. On completion of such missions, the troops were either to be disbanded or made available to the Community. Such forces could, with the agreement of the Supreme Commander NATO, be rotated with those assigned to the EDF. Troops intended for the personal protection of the Head of State could remain national. Navies, in addition to the general provision regarding territories outside Europe, could be used nationally to protect communications with and between overseas territories and for the fulfilment of NATO tasks accepted prior to entry into force of the EDC Treaty. The total size of national armed forces for non-European tasks was not to be so large as to prejudice contributions to the EDF. Article 11 EDC Treaty allowed Member States to recruit and maintain police and gendarmerie forces but stated that these should in size and nature not 'exceed the requirements of their mission'. Hence the EDF was to largely replace the armed forces of the Member States.

Articles 12, 13, and 14 EDC Treaty laid down the conditions under which a Member State might, with the authority of the Board of Commissioners, temporarily withdraw part of its EDC force contribution to meet national requirements. The situations envisaged were those of disorder or threatened disorder in the Member State's own territory, in the event of a major crisis affecting a non-European territory for which it has assumed responsibility, or to fulfil an international mission entrusted to it outside the EDC area. Whereas in the first case the requirement was for the Board of Commissioners merely to notify the Council, in the latter two cases the formal approval of the Council by a two-thirds majority and the agreement of the Supreme Commander NATO were necessary.

Neither NATO nor the WEU have integrated the armed forces of their Member States to the extent envisaged in the EDC Treaty. There are many units

---

[46] Article 9 subparagraph 2 EDC Treaty.

which are integrated to various different degrees, eg, the Eurocorps, the Dutch-German Corps, and the Dutch and Belgian navies. However, these are bilateral or multilateral arrangements which normally only affect parts of the armed forces of the participating countries. The project of an autonomous European military capacity, first put forward by the French and United Kingdom governments at the 1998 Saint-Malo Summit,[47] adopted as an EU policy at the Cologne European Council in 1999,[48] and later developed to a plan for a European Rapid Reaction Force (ERRF) of the EU of 60,000 soldiers and their respective equipment in the Helsinki Headline Goal,[49] is the most ambitious project in this area since the EDF. This new force is to serve as an instrument of the ESDP; in other words, it is to be a security force in the context of the Petersberg tasks discussed in Chapters 4 and 5, not an instrument of a common defence. Most Member States would only assign a small part of their armed forces to this project. However, not even the ERRF project compares to the comprehensive approach of the EDF which would have largely replaced the national armed forces of the Member States with a European army.

3.6. The supranational heritage of the European Defence Community

There are arguments for a more supranational European defence organization. The preamble of the EDC Treaty calls this 'speed and efficiency'[50] to attain the objectives of the Community. A supranational organization with its independent institutions which can take binding decisions, if necessary against the will of individual Member States, can achieve cohesion between the combined military efforts of its Member States. It is this cohesion which represents the added value of such an organization. Instead of six small or medium-size military efforts there is one combined organization and army. An international or supranational organization taking over the responsibility for defence and national security from her Member States in response to a considerable military threat needs the power to

---

[47] Franco-British Summit, 'Joint Declaration on European Defence: Saint-Malo', 3–4 December 1998 <http://www.weu.int/eng/info/d981204a.htm>. See also Rutten, *From St-Malo to Nice*, above, note 30, 8. See on the Declaration: A Deighton, 'The Military Security Pool: Towards a New Security Regime for Europe?' (2000) 35 *The International Spectator* 41–54; J Howorth, 'Britain, France and the European Defence Initiative' (2000) 42 *Survival* 33–55.

[48] Declaration of the European Council on Strengthening the Common European Policy on Security and Defence, European Council Meeting in Cologne, 3–4 June 1999, at point 1 paragraph 2, as cited by Rutten, above, note 30, 42–3.

[49] European Council, Presidency Conclusions: European Council Meeting in Helsinki, 10–11 December 1999 <http://europa.eu.int/council/off.concl>.

[50] Paragraph 3 of the preamble of the EDC Treaty reads: '... considering the fullest possible integration to the extent compatible with military necessities, of the human and material elements of their Defence Forces assembled within a supra-national European organization to be the best means for the attainment of this aim with the necessary speed and efficiency'.

make binding decisions. Otherwise, Member States can undermine the cohesion of the organization to further their individual national agendas. For example, they can refuse to follow individual decisions, withdraw troops or other means from the Community without approval, or leave the Community altogether, in the worst case during a crisis. Examples of such a scenario are the withdrawal of France and Greece from the military structure of NATO, in 1966 and 1981 respectively. Undermining the cohesion of the smallest military unit means compromising effectiveness: the unit cannot do its job.[51] Compromising effectiveness means compromising security. Similarly, it could be argued that undermining the cohesion of an organization or Community in charge of defence means undermining efficiency, thereby undermining national or Community security. Supranationality as a prerequisite for cohesion is therefore also a prerequisite for deterrence. Only a cohesive Community deters potential enemies. The deterrent effect of a Community of medium and small states as compared to the deterrent effect of an individual Member State is only enhanced through the cohesion of the Community. An incoherent or even divided Community will not be taken as a serious deterrent. For the EDC project, due to the Soviet threat, deterrence was the main objective. It is submitted that in a military Community which does not include a military superpower that can easily compensate for the lack of cooperation of any of the other participating states, the cohesion of the medium and small countries that make up such a Community is of even greater importance. NATO is the most successful military international organization. However, the membership of the USA makes it essentially an organization made up of a superpower plus a number of considerably smaller allies, essentially under the protection of the superpower. The dominance of the USA ensures cohesion and makes it less important at the same time. As will be explained below, certain provisions of the EDC Treaty connected the Community to NATO, thereby also aiming to use the impact of the involvement of the superpower USA to further the cohesion of the European security architecture. However, the EDC, as a strong European component of a transatlantic alliance and as the framework for a German contribution perceived to be crucial to ensure a sufficient defence effort, could not afford to remain intergovernmental. An intergovernmental Community would have required the establishment of sovereign German armed forces. The other conceivable alternative, a European defence for Germany and a national defence for everybody else, would have been discriminatory and hence unacceptable for Germany. Hence supranationality was essential for the EDC project.

This general approach followed the example of the ECSC. Supranationality, also featuring prominently in the preamble to the Treaty,[52] was the most

---

[51] See M Trybus, 'Sisters in Arms: European Community Law and Sex Equality in the Armed Forces' (2004) 9 Eur L J 631–58 on this issue of cohesion.

[52] See paragraph 3 of the preamble, above, note 48.

controversial aspect of the EDC and ultimately the reason for the failure of the project.[53] At a conference in Brussels in August 1954, a few weeks before the French Parliament rejected ratification, the French Government under Prime Minister Pierre Mendès-France put forward proposals that essentially undermined the supranational character of the EDC.[54]

Even now, a supranational common defence organization goes too far for many European states. This is not surprising, as establishing such an organization would be equal to a considerable transfer of sovereignty over defence issues from the participating nations to the organization. As defence and national security are at the heart of sovereignty, it is not easily acceptable for States to forfeit something they perceive to be such an essential part of their independence. Consequently, the WEU, the European defence alliance within NATO founded after the failure of the EDC in 1954, was an intergovernmental organization without any significant supranational features. However, it was also irrelevant for most of its existence. Moreover, the EEC Treaty, the next major integration project after the failed EDC, included defence exemptions to clarify that defence matters were largely outside the application of the Treaty.[55] As pointed out by Georgopoulos in Chapter 9 below, any attempts of the Commission to regulate even the economic aspects of defence were repeatedly rebuked. In 1991, in Maastricht, the CFSP was established as an intergovernmental second pillar of the TEU, separate from the supranational first pillar of the EC. This was controversial: during the Dutch Presidency of the EC in 1991 the Hague Government had unsuccessfully proposed to integrate the CFSP into the more supranational EC legal order.[56] Finally, although the Constitutional Treaty of 2004 aims to overcome the three-pillar structure of the TEU, it leaves the intergovernmental character of the CFSP and what is envisaged as the CSDP intact. As far as the supranational character of the failed EDC is concerned, the heritage of that Community appears to be that defence and security integration on a supranational basis is not feasible.

It is submitted that even in a strategic environment characterized by a shift from defence to security, the supranationality of defence and security à la EDC would represent an added value. Deterrence and effectiveness through coherence

---

[53] Fursdon, above, note 1, chapter 7: 'Prelude to failure', at 227–65 and chapter 8: 'La ronde est complète', 266–99.

[54] *Projet de Protocole d'Application du Traité instituant la Communauté Européenne de Défense*, later published by the Belgian Government: *Textes et Documents, Brussels, Ministère des Affaires Etrangères et du Commerce Extérieur*, 24 August 1954. See in particular Chapter I Point 2 and Chapter II Point 6.

[55] See M Trybus, 'The EC Treaty as an instrument of defence integration: judicial scrutiny of defence and security exemptions' (2002) 39 CML Rev 1347–72 on these provisions.

[56] See: 'First Dutch Draft Treaty Proposal from the Dutch Presidency, 30 September 1991', in, F S Laursen and S Vanhoonacker, *The Intergovernmental Conference on Political Union: Institutional Reforms, New Policies and International Identity of the European Community* (Maastricht: European Institute of Public Administration, 1992) 407–12.

are also important with respect to security policy. A supranational ESDP would have been taken more seriously by its partners and opponents in the conflicts on the Balkans.

4. Defence and Security

The sole purpose of the EDC was the defence of Western Europe against the Soviet threat. The Community was not to have a 'peacekeeping mission'. In contrast, the current ESDP and the future CSDP put a strong emphasis on security, whereas defence is of rather minor importance.

4.1. The defensive character of the European Defence Community

Article 2(1) EDC Treaty provided that the objectives of the Community were exclusively defensive. On a literal interpretation this means that the EDC would not have participated in UN missions in the context of chapters VI and VII of the UN Charter, for example the war in Korea. Security policy, in other words humanitarian, peacekeeping, and peacemaking missions were to be conducted in the context of the UN, not the EDC. As outlined in the previous section of this chapter, the Member States of the EDC would have had the right, in their capacity as Member States of the UN, to withdraw troops from the EDF to participate in UN missions. This was stipulated in Article 14 EDC Treaty: while on an international mission, 'the contingents thus detached [from the EDF] shall cease to be responsible to the Community until they are once again made available to it on being no longer needed to meet the crisis'. Article 14(2), in conjunction with Article 13(2), EDC Treaty authorized the Board of Commissioners and the Council to settle the economic and financial implications of such a temporary withdrawal. Hence the EDC did not establish a European security policy separate from that of the UN. The European security law of the EDC was 'negative': Articles 10(2), 13(2), and 14 EDC Treaty provide that the Member States shall temporarily detach contingents from the EDF to participate in such missions and to re-integrate or disband them once these missions have been completed. This is a reflection of the political situation and the different international positions of the Member States: France had a permanent seat in the Security Council, Italy and the Benelux countries were 'regular members', and Germany was not even a Member State of the UN until the 1970s. Therefore the responsibilities of the European Member States vis-à-vis the UN would have been substantially different. Moreover, the EDC was founded as an instrument of defence against the Soviet Union. Security policy in the context of the UN could only be conducted with the agreement of the Soviet Union, which as a permanent member of the Security Council had a right of veto. It would have been diplomatically difficult to directly contribute EDF contingents to UN missions. Thus the EDC was limited to a common defence.

The WEU initially inherited the exclusively defensive character of the EDC. However, from the early 1990s the WEU developed a security policy with the so-called 'Petersberg Tasks'. During the same period the EU started developing the security aspect of its CFSP. Security policy under the ESDP will be covered extensively in chapters 4 and 5 below. Suffice it here to point out that in contrast to the exclusively defensive character of the EDC, the current EU, the WEU, and the Organization for Security and Cooperation in Europe (OSCE) discussed by Odello in Chapter 13 below, all put an emphasis on security rather than defence. Nevertheless, as mentioned above, Article 17(1) of the current Treaty of Nice also raises the issue of defence by stipulating that the CFSP might lead to a common defence. This reference to a common defence goes beyond the content of the forms of European Political Cooperation (EPC) before Maastricht and has been called an 'important difference'[57] or 'the major innovation'[58] of the CFSP. 'Common defence policy' and 'common defence' necessarily require aspects which add to the security aspects of foreign policy that had been a part of EPC before 1991. Possible additional aspects which amount to a defence policy would involve the co-ordination of national defence capabilities or even the creation of European capabilities. Defence capabilities could include, inter alia, troops, military intelligence, logistic support, and military training. However, the issue of capabilities is not mentioned in the Maastricht and Amsterdam versions of the TEU. The wording of Article 17(1) TEU shows that because of the sensibility of the subject a careful approach was chosen, which started or continued a process of defence integration without really committing the Member States to any tangible steps in the immediate future. The use of words such as 'might' and 'eventual' in the Maastricht version of the provision reveals that the advocates of defence integration had to reach a compromise with its opponents.[59] The word 'might' was still there after Amsterdam, whereas the more determined 'progressive' replaced the Maastricht 'eventual'. The compromise thesis is supported by the fact that according to Article 23(2) subparagraph 3 last sentence TEU issues having defence implications were expressly excluded from qualified majority voting and therefore subject to the requirement of unanimity. As pointed out above,

---

[57] T Marauhn, *Building a European Security and Defence Identity*, Bochumer Schriften zur Friedenssicherung und zum Humaniären Völkerrrecht 30 (Bochum: Universitätsverlag Dr N Brockmeyer, 1996) 94; M R Eaton, 'Common Foreign and Security Policy' in D O'Keefe and P Twomey, *Legal Issues of the Maastricht Treaty* (London: Wiley Chancery Law, 1994) 215 at 219–20 calls it a 'a main difference' and at 216 a 'significant change'.

[58] F Fink-Hooijer, 'The Common Foreign and Security Policy of the European Union', (1994) 3 Eur J of Intl L 173 at 194.

[59] N Neuwahl, 'A Partner with a Troubled Personality: EU Treaty-Making in Matters of CFSP' (1998) 3 *Eur Foreign Affairs Rev* 177, at 232: 'No great steps forward can therefore be expected to be taken in the near future'; Eaton, above, note 57, 218: 'The compromise is that it is there but a long way off'.

a common defence is vague, uncertain, and set in the future. However, the reference in Article 17 TEU was a beginning that might well allow the new Union to assert a European security and defence identity on the international stage. Hence this first reference confirmed in Amsterdam can be seen as the beginning of a dynamic process. After 37 years, defence was put back on the European agenda.

As outlined above, Article I-41(2) of the 2004 EU Constitutional Treaty adopts the approach of Article 17(1) TEU with regards to a common defence and only develops the security aspect of the CFSP by adding the concept of an autonomous military capacity. The military capacity is designed as an instrument of security policy rather than defence policy. It is submitted that a common defence will remain vague, uncertain, and set in the future for the foreseeable future. The fact that defence remained national is a crucial part of the heritage of the failure of the EDC in 1954. This is partly due to the same reasons that contributed to this failure: a common defence requires the transfer of a core part of any Member State's sovereignty and the main middle powers of Europe, the United Kingdom[60] and France, were not (yet) prepared to consent to this transfer. Other factors are no longer comparable to those of the 1950s. It is no longer necessary or possible to prevent an independent German military capability. Moreover, the Soviet threat has disappeared. Hence defence is simply less important than it used to be until the 1980s. Security is now the main field of military cooperation in Europe. Moreover, keeping sovereignty over defence might also provide a feeling of compensation for the transfer or loss of sovereignty over other matters, which had not yet occurred in 1954.

4.2. The European Defence Community and collective defence

The EDC was also a defence alliance beyond the common defence through the EDF. Article 2(3) and (4) EDC Treaty provided:

3. Any armed attack against any of the Member States in Europe or against the European defence forces shall be considered an armed attack on all Member States.
4. The Member States and the European Defence Forces shall afford to the State or force so attacked all the military and other aid in their power.

---

[60] The United Kingdom did not want to be a Member State of the EDC. However, its government signed a 'Memorandum regarding United Kingdom Association with the European Defence Community, an Agreement regarding Co-operation between the United Kingdom and the European Defence Community, a Statement of Common Policy on Military Association between the Forces of the United Kingdom and the European Defence Community' (1952) Cmd 9126, and a Declaration in which it committed itself to the continuous stationing of troops on the European continent, most notably in Germany. Moreover, the government declared that it would consider a military attack on any of the Member States of the EDC an attack on the United Kingdom. Thus the United Kingdom aligned herself closely to the EDC, even partly integrating her armed forces with the EDF and making a defence guarantee. However, the United Kingdom did not join the above national structures of the Community as a full Member State.

This 'all-important "automatic action" commitment'[61] made the EDC a military alliance comparable to the WU,[62] NATO,[63] or later the WEU.[64] However, comparison with the similar Article 5 Washington (NATO) Treaty reveals that the commitment in Article 2 EDC Treaty went much further, as it did not subject the action to be taken by the other Member States to reservations. Action was to be automatic, which could be considered yet another expression of the more supranational character of the EDC. Not only the Member States but also the supranational EDF are obliged to take unlimited military and other action to the aid of the attacked Member State. The Member States were to transfer sovereignty and therefore responsibility for defence to the supranational EDC. They therefore had to be sure that in the case of an attack, against which, due to the lack of armed forces of their own, they would not take individual military action regarding their self-defence, the Community would commit all its power to their defence. Therefore, the supranational EDC, merging the armed forces of its Member States into supranational armed forces, had to assume the responsibility for the military security of the Member States. The automatic action commitment, in other words an action commitment without reservations, was therefore the necessary compensation for the transfer of sovereignty. Moreover, the military apparatus now committed to their defence would have been considerably more substantial than in the case of individual self-defence. Therefore the national

---

[61] Fursdon, above, note 1, at 153.   [62] See above.

[63] Article 5 Northern Atlantic Treaty. It reads:

The Parties agree that an armed attack against one or more of them in Europe or North America shall be considered an attack against them all and consequently they agree that, if such an armed attack occurs, each of them, in exercise of the right of individual or collective self-defence recognised by Article 51 of the Charter of the United Nations, will assist the Party or Parties so attacked by taking forthwith, individually and in concert with the other Parties, such action as it deems necessary, including the use of armed force, to restore and maintain the security of the North Atlantic area. Any such armed attack and all measures taken as a result thereof shall immediately be reported to the Security Council. Such measures shall be terminated when the Security Council has taken the measures necessary to restore and maintain international peace and security.

See: <http://www.nato.int/docu/basictxt/treaty.htm>. Article 51 of the UN Charter reads:

Nothing in the present Charter shall impair the inherent right of individual or collective self-defence if an armed attack occurs against a Member of the United Nations, until the Security Council has taken measures necessary to maintain international peace and security. Measures taken by Members in the exercise of this right of self-defence shall be immediately reported to the Security Council and shall not in any way affect the authority and responsibility of the Security Council under the present Charter to take at any time such action as it deems necessary in order to maintain or restore international peace and security.

See: <http://www.nato.int/docu/basictxt/bt-un51.htm>.

[64] Article V WEU (Brussels) Treaty. Article V reads:

If any of the High Contracting Parties should be the object of an armed attack in Europe, the other High Contracting Parties will, in accordance with the provisions of Article 51 of the Charter of the United Nations, afford the Party so attacked all the military and other aid and assistance in their power.

See: <http://www.weu.int/Treaty.htm>.

security of the Member States was, at least in theory, enhanced. The influence of the individual Member States on their defence was to be more limited than before because action was ultimately determined by the institutions of the EDC. However, it can be assumed that the more supranational character and the automatic action commitment would have made the EDC a mighty military power posing a considerable deterrent. It is likely that the enhanced military and political power, combined with the protection of the USA through NATO, addressed below, would have deterred the Soviet Union from an invasion of Western Europe.

The segment 'in Europe' clarified that the overseas territories of the Member States, such as the Dutch Antilles, the Belgian Congo, or the French departments in Algeria, were excluded from this protection. This segment represented the only limitation of the automatic action commitment. Therefore the respective Member States had to ensure the defence of these territories on a national basis.[65] In other words, as they did not transfer the sovereignty and responsibility for these territories to the EDC, they would be allowed to keep national armed forces and to withdraw parts of their troops from the EDF[66] in case the security of one of these territories so required.

The fact that, alongside the EDF, the other Member States also have to help an attacked Member State refers to non-military aid, eg, civil supplies, money, and civil defence, and possibly national armed units permanently or temporarily outside the EDF.

With the exception of the special case of Germany, all prospective Member States of the EDC were also Member States of NATO. This allowed them, after the failure of the EDC, in 1954 to transfer the automatic action commitment of the EDC Treaty to the Modified Brussels Treaty, the founding document of the intergovernmental WEU. Hence with the automatic action commitment the WEU carries the heritage of the EDC, although strictly speaking the commitment is not the heritage of the EDC but of the older Brussels Treaty establishing the WU. It was the foundation of the EU and the gradual transfer of the functions of the WEU to the CFSP that brought the commitment on to the agenda of the EU. Nevertheless, it was not included in Maastricht, Amsterdam, or Nice. As discussed in Chapter 3 below, the neutral status of some of the Member States led

---

[65] The WEU Treaty, ibid, contains a similar limitation to Europe. The NATO Treaty, above, note 51, has different approach in Article 6, which reads:

For the purpose of Article 5, an armed attack on one or more of the Parties is deemed to include an armed attack: on the territory of any of the Parties in Europe or North America, on the Algerian Departments of France, on the territory of or on the Islands under the jurisdiction of any of the Parties in the North Atlantic area north of the Tropic of Cancer; on the forces, vessels, or aircraft of any of the Parties, when in or over these territories or any other area in Europe in which occupation forces of any of the Parties were stationed on the date when the Treaty entered into force or the Mediterranean Sea or the North Atlantic area north of the Tropic of Cancer.

[66] Subject to an approval procedure: see below.

to problems and modifications with regards to the EU Constitutional Treaty. Article I-40(7)[67] of the June 2004 version of the Constitutional Treaty contains an automatic action commitment comparable to that of the EDC and Modified Brussels Treaties. However, Article I-41(6) of the October 2004 version of the Constitutional Treaty signed by the Member States in Rome modifies the traditional mutual defence clause considerably. It reads:

If a Member State is the victim of an armed aggression on its territory, the other Member States shall have towards it an obligation of aid and assistance by all the means in their power, in accordance with Article 51 [UN] Charter. This shall not prejudice the specific character of the security and defence policy of certain Member States. Commitments and cooperation in this area shall be consistent with commitments under [NATO], which, for those States which are members of it, remains the foundation of their collective defence and the forum for its implementation.

On a literal interpretation Article I-40 (7) subparagraph 1 sentence 1 of the October 2004 version of the Constitutional Treaty does not exclude the neutral Member States. Under sentence 2 the non-aligned Member States are under no obligation to aid and assist the other Member States in case of an armed aggression, despite being entitled to such aid and assistance. In other words, a Member State such as Sweden, for example, is entitled to aid and assistance in case of an armed aggression, without being obliged to give it. Hence the October 2004 version of the Constitutional Treaty legalizes 'free riding' in collective defence. Prima facie this appears unfair and excessively favourable to the interests of the neutral Member States. However, due to the fact that an armed aggression against any of the Member States seems very unlikely, the collective defence commitment is mainly political and diplomatic rather than military and strategic. Therefore this arrangement has clear advantages since it accommodates the reservations of the neutral Member States while at the same time including them in collective defence.[68] Moreover, since this arrangement addresses a serious concern of the neutral Member States, it is to be welcomed.

The mutual defence clause of the EDC Treaty was transferred to the WEU. Since the functions of the WEU are in the process of being transferred to the EU the clause needs to be transferred as well before the WEU can be dissolved. The mutual defence clause of the Constitutional Treaty will become a part of the heritage of the EDC in the EU, as part of the Constitutional Treaty, or in case of a failure, another Treaty amendment.[69]

[67] Article I-40 (7) of the June 2004 version reads (with emphasis added):

Under this cooperation, if one of the Member States participating in such cooperation is the victim of armed aggression on its territory, the other participating States shall give it aid and assistance *by all the means in their power*, military or other, in accordance with Article 51 of the United Nations Charter.

[68] The notion of 'mutual defence' is not entirely accurate here, since the arrangement is one-sided and the notion of 'mutual' requires some form of 'give and take'.

[69] See on this in detail: M Trybus, 'With or without the EU Constitutional Treaty: towards a Common Security and Defence Policy?' (2006) 31 ELR 145, at 162–5.

5. The Principle of Non-discrimination between Member States

Article 6 EDC Treaty provided that there should be no discrimination between Member States.[70] This requirement was important to Germany. As outlined above, a major motivation for the EDC project was to integrate the necessary German contribution to the defence of Western Europe into a European framework; independent German armed forces were to be avoided. This was also the German position.[71] The new Community was to be a safeguard against another war between the Member States, and a defence against the Soviet threat. However, many politicians in France, Italy, and the Benelux countries were only prepared to give up their national armed forces as a lesser evil than a new '*Wehrmacht*'. The German Government, however, also saw its contribution to the EDC as an instrument to gain full or partial sovereignty and wanted to avoid the status of a second-class Member State.[72] The Bonn Convention,[73] which was to give the Federal Republic of Germany its sovereignty, was negotiated at the same time as the EDC, was linked to the EDC, and could not come into effect separately.[74] The fact that one of the basic motivations of the EDC was to avoid national German armed forces, however, in itself already represented discrimination against Germany, which due to its recent history was not seen as a state like the others.[75] Moreover, since the Federal Republic was not a Member State of the UN and had no overseas territories, there was little potential for the use by Germany of the provisions on withdrawing troops from the EDF described under the section on the EDF above. In contrast to the French EDF troops, for example, the German contingents would have always stayed integrated in the European army. To this day the greater part of the German armed forces is under direct NATO command rather than that of the German defence minister. Nevertheless, the young Federal Republic of Germany signed and ratified the EDC Treaty because this was a step towards becoming a state like the others. The inherent discrimination was a lesser evil than the disarmed status quo.

In its *Projet de Protocole d'Application du Traité instituant la Communauté Européenne de Défense*[76] of 19 August 1954, mentioned above, the French Government asked for changes in the military provisions of the EDC Treaty. Integration of forces would only apply to German forces, and to forces of the other Member States stationed in Germany. This meant, as Nutting pointed out,

---

[70] Article 6 EDC Treaty reads: 'The present Treaty shall in no way discriminate against its Member States'.   [71] Nutting, above, note 2, 36.

[72] See Fursdon, above, note 1, 96, 107–8, 116, 122, 153; Nutting, ibid, 38.

[73] See on the Bonn and Paris Conventions: W A Kewenig, 'Bonn and Paris Agreements (1952 and 1954)' in R Bernardt (ed), *Encyclopedia of International Law* (Amsterdam/New York/Oxford: North Holland, 1982), Volume III, 56.   [74] Nutting, above, note 1, 42 and 69.

[75] I would like to thank Heike Krieger for bringing this point to my attention.

[76] Above, note 18.

that the French Government 'was asking for a European army for the Germans and a French army for the French'.[77] It is submitted that this could not have been reconciled with Article 6 EDC Treaty as it discriminated against Germany. Moreover, it shows that such a provision was necessary, as non-discrimination cannot be taken for granted.

A similar provision to Article 6 EDC Treaty is implied in all European treaties, including the EC Treaty, and can be called a basic rule of European integration. In the context of the EDC it emphasized that the different sizes of the Member States in relation to territory, population, and military would not lead to discriminatory treatment in relation to the other Member States and the EDC. Apart from the special case of Germany, which had no sovereignty over defence to transfer,[78] the non-discrimination rule is an important assurance for a Member State transferring sovereignty to a more supranational Community, which requires trust in the other Member States. This does not mean that different financial and military contributions would not be taken into account, for example in relation to defence procurement. Moreover, it is generally doubtful that there is no discrimination between Member States in practice. A large Member State will often throw its weight around to promote a national or Community agenda. An example is the hefty reaction of the Member States of the EU against the inclusion of the right wing Freedom Party in the Federal Government of the small Member State Austria in 1999. The inclusion of the right wing National Alliance in the Government of the large Member State Italy did not cause comparable reactions. However, these might also be isolated examples. Nevertheless, in practice a large Member State such as France will exercise more influence in a Community like the EDC, than a small Member State such as Luxembourg, especially in the context of intergovernmental institutions such as the Council.

6. The Close Connection of the European Defence Community to NATO

The Treaty envisaged an EDC that was to be closely connected to NATO. This close connection and interdependence had four elements: a general rule of close cooperation, specific rules on close cooperation, the status of the Supreme Commander NATO as an organ of the Community, and a mutual defence clause with NATO. This firm connection to NATO would be a more controversial issue today, as explained by Krieger in Chapter 8 and Terpan in Chapter 12 below.

---

[77] Nutting, above, note 2, 67.

[78] The Federal Republic of Germany had only the prospect of sovereignty to transfer. However, this prospect materialized with the establishment of the *Bundeswehr* (German armed forces) after the failure of the EDC Treaty in 1955 and the full sovereignty of the reunited Germany in 1990.

6.1. General rule of close cooperation

First, the EDC Treaty contained a general rule of close cooperation with NATO. The preamble stipulated that the new organization aimed at 'ensuring the defence of Western Europe against any aggression in close collaboration with organizations having the same purpose'. This referred mainly to NATO as the main international organization dedicated to the defence of Western Europe, but also to the WU. More specifically, Article 5 EDC Treaty provided in Part I on 'fundamental principles' that 'The Community shall work in close cooperation with the Northern Atlantic Treaty Organization'. It is submitted that this rule was of subsidiary character and could be relied on whenever none of the more specific rules on close cooperation discussed below applied.

As will be discussed in more detail by Krieger in Chapter 8 and Terpan in Chapter 12 below, both the TEU in its current form of the Treaty of Nice and the envisaged EU Constitutional Treaty contain comparable rules on NATO compatibility. Article 17(1) paragraph 2 TEU provides:

[The Union] shall respect the obligations of certain Member States, which see their common defence realised in the Northern Atlantic Treaty Organization (NATO), under the Northern Atlantic Treaty and be compatible with the common security and defence policy established within that framework.

This provision is interpreted as giving priority for established NATO policy in the event of a conflict:[79] the CFSP has to be consistent with NATO policy. The special provisions on Denmark and the non-aligned Member States in the TEU and the EU Constitutional Treaty were not required at the time of the EDC because all prospective Member States, with the special exception of Germany, were members of NATO. The rules on NATO compatibility in all these treaties are a reflection of the fact that NATO was and is the dominant defence and security organization in Europe. The Member States, both NATO members and non-aligned States, do not wish to establish a competitor to NATO with regards to defence.

However, there is a clear difference between the close cooperation with NATO in the EDC Treaty and NATO compatibility in the TEU and the EU Constitutional Treaty. EDC and NATO were to be in the same business of the defence of Western Europe. The EDC was an integral part of NATO just like the armed forces of the United Kingdom or Norway. In the EU of Nice and the Constitutional Treaty a common defence is set in an uncertain future whereas the EDC would already have represented a common defence. The issue of conflict between norms of the NATO and EDC Treaties did not even occur to the fathers of the EDC. In contrast, NATO and the EU have been competing to a certain

---

[79] Wessel, above, note 38, 137; L Münch, 'Die gemeinsame Außen-und Sicherheitspolitik (GASP): ein Schaf im Wolfspelz?' (1997) *Zeitschrift des Öffentlichen Rechts* 389, 404.

extent on the same field of security since the end of the Cold War. Since the early 1990s the EU has been developing a security policy, while NATO has been searching for new areas of activity.

6.2. Specific rules on general cooperation

Secondly, the EDC Treaty contained many specific rules on close cooperation. Articles 10(2) and (4), 13, 14, 18, 48, 68(2) and (3), 69(2) and (3), 70(3), 78 bis(1), 87 bis(4), 94, 102, 120(3), 123(1), 127, 128 EDC Treaty and Article 26 of the Military Protocol, Protocol No 3 Regarding the Relations Between the European Defence Community and the North Atlantic Treaty Organisation provided such specific rules on closer cooperation. For example, according to Articles 101 to 111 EDC Treaty the Board of Commissioners was to prepare and execute common programmes for the armament, equipment, supply, and infrastructure of the EDF. It was to simplify and standardize armaments, equipment, supplies, and infrastructure 'as much and as rapidly as possible', also with regards to compatibility with NATO requirements.[80]

The TEU and the EU Constitutional Treaty do not contain such an extensive set of specific rules on NATO cooperation. This is partly due to the fact that the EU does not provide such a comprehensive defence policy as was envisaged in the EDC Treaty. However, the current regime of closer cooperation with NATO is not limited to the treaties. Most importantly, the 'Berlin-Plus Agreement' between NATO and the EU discussed by Terpan in Chapter 12 below allows the EU access to the military assets of NATO. The EU does not have the military assets to conduct an extensive defence and security policy. Consequently, it could be said that the connection of the EU to NATO is closer than that of the EDC to NATO would have been, since the CFSP, the ESDP, and the CSDP are, or would be, dependent on NATO assets.

6.3. The role of the Supreme Commander NATO

Thirdly, the EDC Treaty envisaged the Supreme Commander NATO as an organ of the Community. Hence NATO and the EDC were to have a common institution. For example, the Supreme Commander NATO was authorized to ensure that the EDF were organized, equipped, trained, and prepared for duty in a 'satisfactory manner'. As soon as national contributions were ready they were to be placed at the disposal of the Supreme Commander who, in turn, would give the Community his requirements regarding the articulation and deployment of such forces. Part III of the Treaty and the Military Protocol contained the military provisions. Articles 68, 69, and 70 EDC Treaty covered the basic structure of the army, air force, and navy elements of the EDF. The army corps would be

---

[80] Article 102(1)(c) EDC Treaty.

composed of basic units of different nationalities, other than in exceptional circumstances resulting from tactical or organizational situations proposed by the Supreme Commander NATO, determined by the Board of Commissioners, and approved by the Council. European naval forces would consist of what was required for protection of the home waters of the Member States' European territories. Contingents were to form groups of the same nationality for single tactical tasks but have European status; they could be incorporated in part or whole, as an integrated force into NATO commands. The deployment of the EDF in the framework of the Supreme Commander NATO's recommendations was also to be the Board's responsibility, as was the administration of its personnel and equipment.

6.4. The European Defence Community-NATO mutual defence clause

Fourthly, Article 1 of Protocol No 4 to the EDC Treaty on Guarantees given by the Member States of the European Defence Community to the Parties to the North Atlantic Treaty provided:

An armed attack—

(i) on the territory of any of the Parties to the Northern Atlantic Treaty in the area described in Article 6 (i) of the said Treaty, or
(ii) on the forces, vessels or aircraft of any of the Parties to the North Atlantic Treaty when in the area described in Article 6 (ii) of the said Treaty,

shall be considered an armed attack on the members of the European Defence Community and the European Defence Forces.

In the event of such an armed attack, the members of the European Defence Community, in respect of themselves and the European Defence Forces, shall have the same obligations towards the Parties to the North Atlantic Treaty as those Parties undertake towards the members of the European Defence Community and the European Defence Forces, in virtue of the Protocol between the Parties to the North Atlantic Treaty referred to in Article 2 below.

Article 2 of the same Protocol provided:

The present Protocol shall enter into force at the same time as the Protocol signed by the Parties to the North Atlantic Treaty granting reciprocal guarantees to the members of the European Defence Community and the European Defence Forces.

The Protocol envisaged a mutual defence clause between the EDC and NATO. The EDC would have had a status comparable to that of a member of NATO. There is no mutual defence clause in the TEU. Article 5 of the Modified Brussels (WEU) Treaty contains the 'European' mutual defence clause and all WEU members are also NATO members. As outlined in Chapter 3 below, the EU Constitutional Treaty is the first 'mainstream' European treaty to contain a mutual defence clause

(Article I-41(7)). This led to controversy between the NATO Member States and the non-aligned Member States. The clause had to be changed several times and now provides a flexible framework. For the NATO Member States the arrangement is comparable to that of the EDC Treaty and its Protocol No 4. For non-aligned Member States there is no obligation to help the other Member States in the case of an attack.

7. Conclusions

The Treaties of Maastricht, Amsterdam, and Nice stipulate that the progressive framing of a common defence policy *might* lead to a common defence. According to the envisaged EU Constitutional Treaty it *will* lead to such a policy. Hence, since 1991 the more or less certain final destination of European security and defence integration has been a common defence of the Union. This raises the question as to what a common defence would entail: a collective defence commitment, supranational military structures, or even a European army? The failed EDC Treaty had envisaged many elements that go well beyond the current state of European security and defence integration with its evolving Petersberg tasks, incremental military institutions, intergovernmental decision-making, and plans for an ERRF. An unconditional mutual defence commitment, supranational institutions, and fully integrated and permanent EDF are only the most notable elements. Hence the EDC Treaty provides the most detailed and comprehensive description to date of what a common defence may entail.

Many of the political, economic, and strategic factors that influenced the European integration process after World War II still prevail today. For example, many still see European integration as a welcome cage for the German tiger. The United Kingdom is still opposed to defence integration on a more supranational basis and France is still concerned about its sovereignty. This led to a central feature of the evolution of European defence integration that dominated the early years and still prevails today: the question as to whether European defence should be organized on a more supranational or a more intergovernmental basis. The supranational model, first introduced by the ECSC and later developed in the EEC and Euratom, disappeared from the European defence integration agenda with the failure of the EDC. The intergovernmental model, introduced to the process with the Dunkirk and Brussels Treaties, prevailed with the Modified Brussels Treaty and the CFSP, the ESDP, and the envisaged CSDP. However, the supranational model did not establish a common defence. Europe continued to have largely national armed forces using largely different equipment within largely independent organizational structures. The only cohesion was achieved through the leadership of the USA in NATO and the fear of Soviet aggression. The United Kingdom, Denmark, the neutral Member States, and many of the central and eastern European countries that joined the Union might still have strong reservations about a more supranational common defence. However, there are also Member States such as Germany, Belgium, Luxembourg, Hungary, Greece, ultimately France and Italy, and possibly the Netherlands and Spain, who are working towards an ever-closer union of their defence efforts.

The EDC project remains the only precedent for a more supranational European defence organization. Civil servants, military officers, and politicians prepared it over many years. The representatives of six different countries reached agreement over the precise contents of such a Community, which included issues such as institutional structure, military organization, procurement, and finance. The provisions of the EDC are therefore a benchmark for the current state of European defence and security integration, and a source of inspiration for future defence integration projects leading to a common defence.

3

On the Common Security and Defence Policy of the EU Constitutional Treaty

Martin Trybus *

1. Introduction

The future of the EU Constitutional Treaty[1] is uncertain after the Dutch and French rejected the symbolic document in referenda held in 2005. In response, the June 2005 Brussels European Council suggested a 'pause for reflection'. Whilst the reasons for the 'nee' and the 'non' are complicated and go beyond the aim of this chapter, it is submitted that they were not directed against its subject matter, the Common Security and Defence Policy (CSDP) envisaged in the new text.[2]

* Senior Lecturer in Law, University of Sheffield, United Kingdom. This chapter is based on a presentation, 'The Constitutional Treaty and EU Defence Policy', to the Utrecht International and European Study Association Symposium *The Role of the EU in International Conflicts*, University of Utrecht, the Netherlands, November 2005, published as 'On the Future of the Common Security and Defence Policy envisaged in the EU Constitutional Treaty' (2005) 23 MERCURIOS: Utrecht J of Eur and Intl L 46–60. All website addresses cited were active on 17 October 2006, unless otherwise specified.

[1] Treaty establishing a Constitution for Europe, Conference of the Representatives of the Governments of the Member States, Brussels, 13 October 2004 (Orfr) CIG 87/1/04 REV 1. This version included a number of considerable changes in comparison to the Draft Treaty prepared by the Convention and agreed at the Summit in June 2004. The version published on 16 December 2004 [2004] OJ L-310/1 contained only minor changes to the October 2004 version. The discussion in this chapter will refer to the December 2004 version unless otherwise indicated. The Constitutional Treaty consists of the Treaty itself, divided into four parts, preceded by a preamble, and a number of Protocols and Declarations. Part I covers, in 60 articles (I-1 to I-60) divided into nine titles, the objectives, principles, competencies, legal instruments, finances, membership, and institutions of the Union. Part II consists of the Charter of Fundamental Rights of the Union, consisting of a separate preamble and 54 articles (II-61 to II-114) divided into seven titles. Part III consists of 322 articles (III-115 to III-436) divided into seven titles containing the detailed provisions on the *acquis communautaire* and the *acquis* of the second and the third pillars. Finally, Part IV contains twelve general and final articles (IV-437 to IV-448). A reference to the relevant part needs to be included when indicating individual articles of the Constitutional Treaty, for example Article I-40 or III-210 Constitutional Treaty. Parts I and III regulate the Community polices and the CFSP and CSDP.

[2] According to Eurobarometer, Wave 57, which questioned 15,987 individuals in face-to-face interviews between 29 March and 1 May 2002, a common defence and security policy among the EU Member States is supported by 71 per cent of individuals questioned in the EU of the 15: 49 per cent

This policy is to replace the European Security and Defence Policy (ESDP) under the current framework of the Treaty of Nice. Most Member States of the EU will continue the integration of their security and defence efforts, through the new document, the current regime, or alternative frameworks inside or outside the Union. This chapter will argue that the innovations of the CSDP do not necessarily require the entering into force of the Constitutional Treaty.

The EU security and defence policy started as the 'junior partner' of a European foreign policy with the Common Foreign and Security Policy (CFSP) of the 1991 Treaty of Maastricht. It was further developed in the Treaties of Amsterdam and Nice, and has been implemented most notably through the increasingly ambitious military missions since 2003 discussed in the chapters by Naert and Tsagourias.[3] The EU does not have armed forces, a ministry of defence, a military administration, a comprehensive security and defence policy, European defence industries, a procurement programme, or a collective defence commitment. However, important developments regarding a European Rapid Reaction Force (ERRF), EU military institutions, an ESDP including a European Security Strategy, intra-Community mergers in the defence industries, a European Capabilities and Armaments Policy, and the assimilation of the WEU show that the Union has been working hard to fill the void. The Constitutional Treaty addresses most of these issues. For example, it develops the tasks of the EU security institutions and introduces the office of the Union Minister for Foreign Affairs who is also a 'Union Minister for Security and Defence' in all but name. A new European Defence Agency is to conduct a common armaments policy and European procurement programmes. Moreover, for the first time a collective defence commitment appears in a fundamental document of the EU. Nevertheless, this chapter argues that most of the aspects of the CSDP can be developed without the entry into force of the Constitutional Treaty. This is due to the fact that certain innovations do not require a Treaty base, can be launched through the current framework of the Treaty of Nice, or can be introduced through the next Treaty revision, which might not necessarily require referenda. The analysis will start with a brief discussion of the fundamental context of the envisaged CSDP. It will focus on the three main aspects of the new policy, namely, crisis management, armaments policy, and collective defence, excluding the institutional aspects, such as the CSDP role of the Union Minister for Foreign Affairs.

---

in the UK, 50 per cent in Ireland, 53 per cent in Sweden, 54 per cent in Finland, 61 per cent in Austria, 65 per cent in Denmark, 67 per cent in Portugal, 71 per cent in France, 72 per cent in Greece, 75 per cent in Belgium, 76 per cent in Spain, 79 per cent in both Germany and the Netherlands, 82 per cent in Italy and 87 per cent in Luxembourg. Support was particularly strong in France with 71 per cent and the Netherlands with 79 per cent. Opposition was strongest in the neutral Member States and the United Kingdom with Austria 20 per cent, United Kingdom and Republic of Ireland both 29 per cent, Denmark 30 per cent, Finland 37 per cent, and Sweden 38 per cent. Source: J-Y Haine, *From Laeken to Copenhagen, European Defence: Core Documents*, Chaillot Paper No 57 (Paris: Institute of Security Studies of the European Union, February 2003) 55.

[3] See Chapters 4 and 5, below, respectively.

2. The CSDP, the CFSP, and the Constitutional Treaty

Since Maastricht, the Treaty on European Union (TEU) regulates the CFSP and later the ESDP in a second pillar separate from the (first) Community pillar. In contrast to the EC and its sui generis legal nature, characterized by supremacy and direct effect, the CFSP and ESDP are governed by international law. The dominance of the intergovernmental Council, which in the context of the ESDP always takes decisions by unanimity, the exclusion of judicial and parliamentary scrutiny, and the insignificant role of the Commission, set the second pillar apart. The Dutch Presidency had suggested the use of the Community method in 1991, but most Member States resisted its use for the CFSP in Maastricht, Amsterdam, and Nice. Governments are afraid to lose control over what they perceive as one of their core functions. However, there are also concerns whether an enlarged Union of 25, 27, or more will be able to make an efficient and coherent foreign, security, and defence policy by unanimity and whether the exclusion of Court, Parliament, and Commission are justified.

Under the Constitutional Treaty the EU will have legal personality and will replace the Community.[4] The new Treaty envisages the abolition of the three-pillar structure of the TEU by establishing a single legal framework of the Union. However, the characteristics of the current second pillar,[5] namely Council dominance, unanimity, the exclusion of judicial review, the lack of parliamentary scrutiny, and Commission insignificance, prevail in the context of the new CSDP. Therefore, it is submitted, the second pillar continues to exist almost untouched, somehow hidden in the 'post-pillar' structure of the Constitutional Treaty.[6]

With regards to a 'common defence', the new Treaty keeps the status quo of the Treaty of Nice intact by adopting the approach of Article 17(1) TEU.[7] According to Article I-41(2), the Constitutional Treaty does not introduce a common defence. The provision reads:

The [CSDP] shall include the progressive framing of a common Union defence policy. This will lead to a common defence, when the European Council, acting unanimously, so decides ...

---

[4] Article IV-438(1) Constitutional Treaty (October 2004 version: see below) 'Succession and legal continuity' reads: 'The European Union established by this Treaty shall be the successor to the European Union established by the Treaty on European Union and to the European Community'. Article IV-437(1) Constitutional Treaty reads: 'Repeal of earlier Treaties. This Treaty establishing a Constitution for Europe shall repeal the Treaty establishing the European Community, the Treaty on European Union and, [...] the acts and treaties which have supplemented or amended them [...]'.

[5] According to Article I-41(1) Constitutional Treaty the 'common security and defence policy shall be an integral part of the [CFSP]'.

[6] For more detail see, 'The old players and a new minister: the institutional structure of the Common Security and Defence Policy under the Constitutional Treaty' in M Trybus, *European Union Law and Defence Integration* (Oxford: Hart Publishing, 2005) 354–94.

[7] Article 17 (1) TEU reads: 'The common foreign and security policy shall include all questions relating to the security of the Union, including the progressive framing of a common defence policy, [...] which might lead to a common defence, should the European Council so decide'.

Hence a common defence remains uncertain and set in the future. Moreover, it is not clear what it would entail. However, Article I-41(2) is useful for the definition of the scope of the CSDP since it clearly spells out that it does *not* amount to the establishment of a common defence. Consequently, a common defence would go beyond the CSDP. Moreover, the provision indicates that the EU would add to the then *acquis* of the CSDP under the Constitutional Treaty, which is to be understood as a further step towards a common defence.

3. Crisis Management

After having explained the fundamentals of the CSDP, the three main elements of the new policy will be discussed. The first aspect builds on the current ESDP. Crisis management is addressed in Articles I-41(1) and III-309(1) and covers the 'Petersberg Tasks' initially developed in the context of the WEU during the 1990s. According to Article I-41(1) these are: 'peacekeeping, conflict prevention and strengthening international security in accordance with the United Nations Charter'. More detail is added by Article III-309(1).[8] Article III-310(1) provides:

Within the framework of the European decisions adopted in accordance with Article III-309, the Council may entrust the implementation of a task to a group of Member States which are willing and have the necessary capability for such a task. Those Member States, in association with the Union Minister for Foreign Affairs, shall agree among themselves on the management of the task.

This suggests that crisis management can be subject to a degree of flexibility. First, the Council will decide unanimously on a mission,[9] without flexibility. However,

---

[8] Article III-309 Constitutional Treaty reads:

The tasks referred to in Article I-41 (1), in the course of which the Union may use civilian and military means, shall include joint disarmament operations, humanitarian and rescue tasks, military advice and assistance tasks, conflict prevention and peace-keeping tasks, tasks of combat forces in crisis management, including peacemaking and post-conflict stabilisation. All these tasks may contribute to the fight against terrorism, including by supporting third countries in combating terrorism in their territories.

See A Missiroli, 'The European Union: Just a Regional Peacekeeper?' (2003) 8 *Eur Foreign Affairs Rev* 493 (hereinafter 'Regional Peacekeeper'), at 495. Missiroli considers this to be a considerable broadening of the Petersberg Tasks. It covers both missions undertaken under Chapter VI of the UN Charter (blue helmet operations, eg, Cyprus) and humanitarian peace-enforcement missions undertaken under Chapter VII of the UN Charter (possibly involving the use of force, eg, Somalia or Bosnia); see A Missiroli, *CFSP, Flexibility and Defence*, Chaillot Paper No 38 (Paris: Institute of Security Studies of the Western European Union, 2000) 14.

[9] Article III-309(2) sentence 1 Constitutional Treaty reads: 'The Council shall adopt European decisions relating to the tasks referred to in paragraph 1 [the 'Petersberg Tasks'], defining the objectives and the scope and the general conditions for their implementation'. Unanimity is always required in the context of military action. Article III-297(1) sentence 1 reads: 'When the international situation requires operational action by the Union, the Council shall adopt the necessary European decisions'. Article I-40(6) sentence 1 reads: 'European decisions relating to the common

this adoption stage will be followed by an ad hoc decision of each individual Member State on whether to contribute to the implementation of the Decision. This arrangement represents an element of informal flexibility, as possibly only some of the 24 or 26 Member States,[10] which would have adopted the Decision, would contribute to its implementation. This principle of voluntarism is the normal practice in the context of crisis management missions conducted by international organizations such as the United Nations.[11] In the context of the WEU the Member States have shown a clear preference for 'one-off ad hoc operational coalitions rather than more structured [formal] multilateral frameworks'.[12] This ad hoc flexibility is an appropriate practice as Member States differ enormously with regards to their financial and military means. It is already available under the Treaty of Nice and has been practised during the first crisis management operations of the EU in 2003.[13] However, flexible arrangements such as these will lead to problems when there are no Member States willing to contribute and there is a clear need for action. The alternative is a more permanent 'rapid reaction force' with long-term contributions of the Member States raised for a multitude of future missions to be decided on at a later stage. This would provide the Union with an autonomous military capacity and ensure the implementation of the relevant Council Decisions. Value would be added by the increased coherence of the component national contributions through more permanent common service in such a force.

An autonomous military capacity was proposed at the French-British Summit in Saint-Malo in 1998,[14] adopted by the Cologne European Council in 1999, and developed into a plan for an ERRF of 60,000 in the Helsinki Headline Goal.[15]

---

foreign and security policy shall be adopted by the European Council and the Council unanimously, except in cases referred to in Part III'. The possibility of moving to qualified majority voting in Article III-300(2) and (3) is blocked by paragraph 4 of that provision, which provides: 'Paragraphs 2 and 3 shall not apply to decisions having defence implications'.

[10] Denmark does not participate in the CFSP with regards to measures having defence implications under the TEU. Denmark would continue this practice under the Constitutional Treaty.

[11] See Articles 43 and 44 of the UN Charter. Contributions are voluntary. Nevertheless, the experience of the UN also shows that the practice has disadvantages. These concern the uncertainty of contributions, funding, and the coherence of a corps made up of many different national contingents.

[12] Missiroli, *CFSP, flexibility and defence*, above, note 8, vii.

[13] See the lists of contributions to these missions ('EUPM' in Bosnia and Herzegovina and 'Concordia' in FYR Macedonia) in Missiroli, 'Regional Peacekeeper', above, note 8, at 497 and 499. Notable are the contributions of countries outside the EU, Canada in particular. 1,800 mainly French soldiers conducted the 'ARTEMIS' mission in the DR Congo.

[14] '[In order for the EU] to be in a position to play its full role on the international stage the Union must have the capacity for *autonomous* action, backed up by credible military forces, the means to decide to use them and a readiness to do so, in order to respond to international crises' [emphasis added]. Franco-British Summit, 'Joint Declaration on European Defence: Saint-Malo', 3–4 December 1998, <http://www.weu.int/eng/info/d981204a.htm>. See also M Rutten (ed), *From St-Malo to Nice, European Defence: Core Documents*, Chaillot Paper No 47 (Paris: Institute of Security Studies of the European Union, 2001) 8.

[15] European Council, Presidency Conclusions: European Council Meeting in Helsinki, 10–11 December 1999 <http://europa.eu.int/council/off.concl>.

It is an example of cooperation developed in practice under the Treaty of Nice and not even expressly mentioned there. This shows that cooperation in crisis management policy is not Treaty-dependent and, therefore, that the entry into force of the Constitutional Treaty is not a condition for the further development of this policy field. Article I-41(1) mentions the autonomous military capacity: '[The CFSP] shall provide the Union with an operational capacity drawing on assets civil and military', but not the more tangible Helsinki Headline Goal and the plan for the ERRF. The provision establishes an independent EU military capacity as an objective of the EU. However, the EU may use this independent military capacity only on missions outside the Union for peacekeeping, conflict prevention, and strengthening international security in accordance with the principles of the UN Charter. Hence the military capacity is only an instrument of crisis management, not a defence force.

A military capacity is also mentioned in Article 1 of Protocol 23 on Permanent Structured Cooperation established by Article I-41(6) and Article III-312 of the Constitution (hereinafter 'Protocol 23'):

The permanent structured cooperation referred to in Article I-41(6) of the Constitution shall be open to any Member State which undertakes, from the date of entry into force of the [Constitutional Treaty], to: . . .

(b) have the capacity to supply by 2007 at the latest, either at national level or as a component of multinational force groups, targeted combat units for the missions planned, structured at a tactical level as a battle group, with support elements including transport and logistics, capable of carrying out the tasks referred to in Article III-309, within a period of 5 to 30 days, in particular in response to requests from the [UN], and which can be sustained for an initial period of 30 days and be extended up to at least 120 days.

This addresses another variation of flexibility in crisis management, the concept of 'permanent structured cooperation', newly provided in Article I-41 (6):

Those Member States whose military capabilities fulfil higher criteria and which have made more binding commitments to one another in this area with a view to the most demanding missions shall establish structured cooperation within the Union framework. Such cooperation shall be governed by the provisions of Article III-312. It shall not affect the provisions of Article III-309.

According to Article III-312(1) and (2):

1. Those Member States which wish to participate in the permanent structured cooperation referred to in Article I-41(6), which fulfil the criteria and have made the commitments on military capabilities set out in [Protocol 23] shall notify their intention to the Council and to the Union Minister for Foreign Affairs.
2. Within three months following the notification referred to in paragraph 1 the Council shall adopt a European decision establishing permanent structured cooperation and determining the list of participating Member States. The Council shall act by a qualified majority after consulting the Union Minister for Foreign Affairs.

Permanent structured cooperation is designed for the crisis management and armaments aspects of the CSDP, not for the aspect of collective defence discussed below. This is confirmed by the fact that Protocol 23 only deals with crisis management and armaments policy. The reasons for this exclusion of collective defence are connected to the special nature of, and controversy over, this aspect of the CSDP. This will be discussed below. In comparison to the Treaty of Nice, under which enhanced cooperation is not available for matters having military or defence implications, the possibility of using permanent structured cooperation with regards to the crisis management and armaments policies is a major innovation of the Constitutional Treaty.

Whilst the June 2004 version of the Constitutional Treaty used the term 'structured cooperation', the December 2004 version uses the term 'permanent structured cooperation'. The notion of 'permanent' emphasizes the difference from the 'one-off ad hoc' flexibility regarding the implementation of Article III-309 Decisions outlined above. It might be interpreted as an argument supporting the thesis outlined below that permanent structured cooperation envisages some form of permanent 'ERRF'.

The concept of 'permanent structured cooperation' in Articles I-41(6) and III-312 needs to be differentiated from the 'general'[16] concept of 'enhanced cooperation' in Articles I-44 and III-416–23. The major difference relates to the participation of Member States at a later stage. In a case of enhanced cooperation the Commission decides on 'accession' to the respective policy field according to Article III-418(1).[17] This excludes cases in the context of the CFSP where the Council, acting on a proposal from the Union Minister for Foreign Affairs,[18] takes this decision according to Article III-420 (2).[19] Enhanced cooperation is open to

[16] This term was suggested by R A Wessel, in a paper on 'Differentiation in EU Security Law' (hereinafter 'Differentiation') presented to the Workshop on European Security Law at the University of Nottingham School of Law in April 2005. See also Chapter 10 below.

[17] III-Article 418 (1) reads:

When enhanced cooperation is being established, it shall be open to all Member States, subject to compliance with any conditions of participation laid down by the European authorising decision. It shall also be open to them at any other time, subject to compliance with the acts already adopted within that framework, in addition to any such conditions. The Commission and the Member States participating in enhanced cooperation shall ensure that they promote participation by as many Member States as possible.

[18] This office is to be introduced by the Constitutional Treaty.

[19] Article III-420 (2) reads:

Any Member State which wishes to participate in enhanced cooperation in progress in the framework of the common foreign and security policy shall notify its intention to the Council, the Union Minister for Foreign Affairs and the Commission. The Council of Ministers shall confirm the participation of the Member State concerned, after consulting the Union Minister for Foreign Affairs and, after noting, where necessary, that any conditions of participation have been fulfilled. The Council, on a proposal from the Union Minister for Foreign Affairs, may also adopt any transitional measures deemed necessary with regard to the application of the acts already adopted within the framework of enhanced cooperation. However, if the Council considers that any conditions of participation have not been fulfilled, it shall indicate the arrangements to be adopted to fulfil those conditions and shall

as many Member States as possible and, provided they comply with the conditions of participation laid down by the authorizing decision according to Article III-418(1), they may join at any time. Member States that wish to participate in enhanced cooperation have a right to do so. Moreover, EU institutions representing all Member States take the relevant Decisions. In contrast, Article III-312(3) provides that if a Member State wishes to participate in a policy field subject to permanent structured cooperation at a later stage, '[o]nly the members of the Council representing the participating Member States shall take part in the vote'. Moreover, according to Article III-312(1) permanent structured cooperation is designed only for those Member States 'which fulfil higher military capability criteria'. Only those who *can* go ahead *may* go ahead. Permanent structured cooperation is therefore not as open to Member States wishing to join at a later stage as enhanced cooperation is. Member States are not entitled to participate. Moreover, a 'Council within the Council' representing only the Member States already participating in permanent structured cooperation will decide on the accession of newcomers. This arrangement is designed as an 'incentive' for Member States to participate from the beginning, a design that has already been successful in the context of armaments, as will be explained below.

It is highly likely that the regulations on permanent structured cooperation are mainly designed to accommodate the ERRF envisaged in the Helsinki Headline Goal. The ERRF would overcome the ad hoc nature of the implementation stage of crisis management missions and represent a binding commitment of the participating Member States. For example, after a Decision to deploy troops on a peacekeeping mission there would be certainty regarding the contribution of troops to implement it. The Council could deploy the ERRF, a force made up of Member State contributions on the basis of long-term or medium-term commitments. In other words, the forces for the implementation of a Decision would be ready before the Decision was taken. The crisis management policy of the EU could rely on a standing force. Such a force would eliminate the element of informal flexibility and therefore uncertainty formed by the ad hoc character of the forces implementing Decisions under the regime of the Treaty of Nice. However, as the ERRF would be formed on the basis of permanent structured cooperation, in other words on the basis of voluntary commitments, another element of differentiation would be introduced instead. Therefore, a more permanent ERRF would take an element of uncertainty out of the European crisis management policy without eliminating the advantages of flexibility, and would still follow the tradition of voluntarism used in international crisis management missions.

Do these arrangements on permanent military cooperation amount to the creation of a 'European army'? The Helsinki Headline Goal, which provided a detailed description of the envisaged autonomous military capacity of the EU,

---

set a deadline for re-examining the request for participation. For the purposes of this paragraph, the Council shall act unanimously and in accordance with Article I-44(3).

contained a sentence that it did not 'imply the creation of a European army'. However, the legal significance of the passage in the Helsinki Headline Goal is questionable and neither the Constitutional Treaty nor its Protocol 23 contains a comparable sentence. The passage has political rather than legal importance, since a European army was considered too controversial. Moreover, whether the achievement of the Helsinki Headline Goal, through the Constitutional Treaty, the Treaty of Nice, or otherwise would imply the creation of a European army depends on its definition. If the completely integrated European Defence Forces envisaged in the failed 1950s European Defence Community Treaty discussed in the previous chapter[20] are the benchmark for a 'European army', then neither the current arrangements under the Treaty of Nice nor those laid out under the Constitutional Treaty go far enough. However, if merely a certain size, coherence, and permanence are required, then the future ERRF of the Helsinki Headline Goal may be considered a European army in all but name. Similarly, EUFOR, an already existing peacekeeping force of 7,000 composed mainly of European contingents under a common command at least until 2008, and discussed in the next chapter by Naert, comes very close to more liberal definitions of a European army.[21]

If the Constitutional Treaty does not enter into force, crisis management has to continue on the basis of the current framework of the Treaty of Nice until the next Treaty revision. First, an ERRF could not be established on the basis of permanent structured cooperation. Because of the military and defence exception in Article 27b TEU[22] it could not be established on the basis of enhanced cooperation either. It can be conducted only by all Member States acting in unison within the EU or by a number of Member States outside the Union. Whether such a force would find the support of all the Member States is uncertain but not unlikely. The force is still not operational in 2005, although it was to be established by 2003.[23] Whether the establishment of such a force outside the EU is compatible with the obligations under the Treaty of Nice is not clear. However, it would clearly undermine the CFSP and ESDP or CSDP when such visible aspects of security

---

[20] As outlined in Chapter 2, the European Defence Community Treaty had provided for national contingents being made available to the Community in view of their fusion. The individual divisions were to be composed of soldiers of the same nationality but there was to be a single command structure, a single armaments policy, a single 'ministry of defence' with an independent Board of Commissioners, and soldiers wearing the same uniform.

[21] Although the notion of a 'European army' would probably require that force to have a more general mandate than that of Operation 'ALTHEA' in Bosnia-Herzegovina.

[22] Article 27b sentence 2 TEU reads: '[enhanced cooperation] *shall not relate to matters having military or defence implications*' (emphasis added).

[23] According to the Presidency Conclusions at the European Council meeting in Thessaloniki, 19–20 June 2003, 'The EU now has operational capability across the full range of the Petersberg Tasks, limited and constrained by recognised shortfalls, which can be attained by the further development of the EU's military capabilities': A Missiroli, *From Copenhagen to Brussels: European Defence: Core Documents*, Chaillot Paper No 67 (Paris: Institute of Security Studies of the European Union, December 2003) at point 56, p 144. See also General Affairs and External Relations Council, Brussels, 19–20 June 2003. This appears to fall short of the ERRF envisaged in the Helsinki Headline Goal.

and defence policy were conducted outside the Union. This is the main reason why Belgium, France, Germany, and Luxembourg never realized their April 2003 plans for a military alliance outside the EU.[24] Assuming the continuation of the status quo on the basis of the Treaty of Nice, the forces necessary for the implementation of crisis management Decisions would have to be formed on an ad hoc basis, with the implication of uncertainty as described above. Alternatively, all Member States have to agree on the ERRF, thereby making flexibility unnecessary. This would be difficult but not impossible.

Since 2003 the EU has conducted the first missions within the current framework of the Treaty of Nice.[25] However, so far these missions have been small and at the 'low end' of security, involving police work or military missions in areas that were relatively safe for the troops involved. They were also very limited in terms of time. The EU missions continued the tradition of WEU crisis management, which was equally limited. The EUFOR mission in Bosnia-Herzegovina is larger in size but still 'low end' and 'second-hand' since hostilities have ceased and EUFOR is taking over from a NATO mission.[26]

Without an autonomous ERRF, the EU will not be able to react quickly and with a sizeable force to a humanitarian crisis or a substantial security challenge.[27] Without that ability it will not develop into 'a power to be reckoned with' in international affairs, but will remain a civilian power, occasionally conducting limited crisis management operations. There is a danger that the Union has raised expectations it cannot fulfil. The current crisis management policy of the EU is discussed at length in later chapters by Naert and Tsagourias, and the chapter by Wessel provides a more comprehensive analysis of the issue of flexibility or differentiation in the context of EU security and defence law.

4. The European Capabilities and Armaments Policy

The second aspect of the CSDP is the 'European Capabilities and Armaments Policy' conducted through the European Defence Agency (EDA) outlined in Articles I-41(3) subparagraph 2 and III-311.[28] The creation of this Agency

---

[24] 'Gang of Four', *Financial Times*, 28 April 2003; 'European leaders unveil plan for central military HQ', *Financial Times*, 30 April 2003.

[25] For brief descriptions of these missions see Missiroli, 'Regional Peacekeeper', above, note 8, at 498–500.

[26] 'Changing of the guard: the EU seeks to show the US it is serious about defence', *Financial Times*, 2 December 2004.

[27] Missiroli, *CFSP, Flexibility and Defence*, above, note 8, at 14, argues that there is agreement amongst all EU Member States regarding peacekeeping in the sense of Chapter VI of the UN Charter but not (yet) with regards to peacemaking involving the use of force in the sense of Chapter VII. However, it is likely to become increasingly difficult to exclude the necessity to use force in a peacekeeping mission.

[28] See on this new agency in detail: M Trybus, 'The New European Defence Agency: A Contribution to a Common European Security and Defence Policy and a Challenge to the Community *acquis*?' (2006) 43 CML Rev 667–703.

addresses the need for a common approach to the planning, production, and procurement of weapons, ammunitions, and other war material. This includes issues such as the research and development of new armaments, the preservation of the European defence industrial base, and the European armaments market;[29] areas remarkably close to subject matters currently regulated by Community law.[30] The EDA became operational independent of the Constitutional Treaty[31] since it was already established in 2004 by a Joint Action[32] of the Council on the basis of Article 14 of the Treaty of Nice. All Member States with the exception of Denmark[33] participate in the Agency, which was set up in Brussels.[34] Thus the European Capabilities and Armaments Policy aspect of the CSDP is independent from the Constitutional Treaty. The wording of the EDA Joint Action closely follows that of the relevant provisions of the Constitutional Treaty, which is the subject matter of this article.

Article III-311(2), which provides that '[t]he Agency shall be open to all Member States wishing to be part of it' suggests the basic institutional structure of the EDA be construed as a flexible framework.[35] However, with the exception

---

[29] According to Article III-311(1) Constitutional Treaty the EDA will be required to:

a) contribute to identifying the Member States' military capability objectives and evaluating observance of the capability commitments given by the Member States;

b) promote harmonisation of operational needs and adoption of effective, compatible procurement methods;

c) propose multilateral projects to fulfil the objectives in terms of military capabilities, ensure coordination of the programmes implemented by the Member States and management of specific cooperation programmes;

d) support defence technology research, and coordinate and plan joint research activities and the study of technical solutions meeting future operational needs;

e) contribute to identifying and, if necessary, implementing any useful measure for strengthening the industrial and technological base of the defence sector and for improving the effectiveness of military expenditure.

[30] The defence procurement agencies of the Member States have to procure civil and dual-use supplies (goods), works (construction), and services on the basis of the EC Treaty and above certain thresholds on the basis of the EC Public Procurement Directives. The EC Treaty also covers the procurement of armaments, as do (possibly) the Directives, but the Member State can invoke security exemptions in the Treaty and Directives, subject to review by the European Court of Justice. On EC law and defence procurement see: M Trybus, 'Procurement for the Armed Forces: Balancing Security and the Internal Market' (2002) 27 ELRev 692–713.

[31] A Georgopoulos, 'The New European Defence Agency: Major Development or a Fig Leaf?' (2005) 14 Public Proc L Rev 103 puts it as follows: 'its establishment was dissociated with the adoption of the European Constitutional Treaty'.

[32] Council Joint Action 2004/551/CFSP of 12 July 2004 on the establishment of the European Defence Agency [2004] OJ L-245/17. Article 1(1) of the Joint Action reads: 'An Agency in the field of defence capabilities development, research, acquisition and armaments (the European Defence Agency), hereinafter referred to as "the Agency", is hereby established'. For a critical account of the EDA Joint Action see Georgopoulos, ibid.

[33] See Section 21 of the Preamble to the EDA Joint Action.

[34] 'Making forces work together', *Financial Times*, 2 December 2004. The EDA currently has a staff of around 80.

[35] This interpretation is supported by Article 1(a) of Protocol 23 to the Constitutional Treaty, which envisages the EDA to be subject to permanent structured cooperation together with the crisis management policy discussed above. This is also confirmed by Article 1(3) and (4) EDA Joint Action

of Denmark, all Member States are participating in this basic institutional structure in practice. Therefore, the possibility to withdraw from EDA under the
Constitutional Treaty makes it a flexible framework in theory only. Moreover,
Article III-311(2) determines 'the level of effective participation in the Agency's
activities. Specific groups shall be set up within the Agency bringing together
Member States engaged in joint projects'. This indicates flexibility regarding participation in individual programmes and projects conducted within the basic
institutional framework of the EDA.[36] Following the tradition of European
collaborative projects, eg, the British-German-Belgian-Spanish 'Eurofighter'/'and
if Typhoon', the groups of Member States cooperating in an individual project are
formed on an ad hoc basis.[37]

Organizational structures outside the EU, such as the Western European
Armaments Group and Organization in the context of the WEU[38] and the
British-French-German-Italian Organisation for Joint Armaments Co-operation
(OCCAR),[39] are currently promoting European cooperation in armaments policy. The arrangements of the Constitutional Treaty and the EDA Joint Action are
welcomed since Member States wishing to establish a more coherent defence procurement regime can now do so inside rather than outside the Union. The import
of the external *acquis* of the Western European Armaments Organisation (WEAO)

which differentiates between Member States who wish to participate immediately on the one hand
and those who wish to participate after its adoption or withdraw from it. Article 1(3) EDA Joint
Action reads:

The Agency shall be open to participation by all Member States bound by this Joint Action [not
Denmark, see ibid]. Member States who wish to participate immediately in the Agency shall notify
their intention to do so to the Council and inform the [Secretary General/High Representative for
the CFSP] at the time of the adoption of this Joint Action.

Paragraph (4) reads:

Any Member State wishing to participate in the Agency after the adoption of this Joint Action or
wishing to withdraw from the Agency shall notify its intention to the Council and inform the
SG/HR. Any necessary technical and financial arrangements for such participation or withdrawal
shall be determined by the Steering Board.

[36] This is also expressed in the definition of 'contributing Member States' as Member States of the
EU contributing to a particular project or programmes in Article 3 EDA Joint Action.

[37] This finding is confirmed by, inter alia, the Preamble and Chapter IV of the EDC Joint Action
on 'ad hoc projects or programmes and associated budgets'. Section 17 of the Preamble to the EDA
Joint Action reads: 'The Agency, while being open to participation by all Member States, should
also provide for the possibility of specific groups of Member States establishing ad hoc projects or
programmes.'

[38] Austria, Belgium, the Czech Republic, Denmark, Finland, France, Germany, Greece, Hungary,
Italy, Luxembourg, the Netherlands, Norway, Poland, Portugal, Spain, Sweden, Turkey, and the
United Kingdom are full members of the WEAG, which forms the background for the WEAO.
See: <http://www.weu.int/weao/site/frameset.htm>.

[39] See: Convention on the Establishment of the Organisation for Joint Armaments Co-operation
OCCAR, reproduced in B Schmitt, *European Armaments Cooperation: Core Documents*, Chaillot
Paper No 59 (Paris: Institute for Security Studies of the European Union, April 2003) 45–59. OCCAR
is based in Bonn and manages several programmes: the Franco-German 'Tiger' attack helicopter, the
Franco-Italian Future Surface-to-Air Missile Family, the Belgian-British-French-German-Spanish-
Turkish A400M transport aircraft. The latter involves non-OCCAR members.

and OCCAR into the EU[40] can overcome the fragmentation of a European armaments policy and avoid duplication. The new Agency and the European armaments policy are discussed in detail in Chapter 9, by Georgopoulos, below.

5. Collective Defence

The third aspect of the CSDP is a major innovation of the Constitutional Treaty. Collective defence has never been on the agenda of the EC or EU before. It has been the domain of NATO and the WEU since the failure of the European Defence Community in 1954 discussed in the previous chapter. The final version of the Constitutional Treaty provides in Article I-41(7):

If a Member State is the victim of an armed aggression on its territory, the other Member States shall have towards it an obligation of aid and assistance by all the means in their power, in accordance with Article 51 [UN] Charter. This shall not prejudice the specific character of the security and defence policy of certain Member States.

Commitments and cooperation in this area shall be consistent with commitments under [NATO], which, for those States which are members of it, remains the foundation of their collective defence and the forum for its implementation.

This provision represents a mutual defence clause comparable to Article 5 of the WEU's 1954 Modified Brussels Treaty[41] and to Article 5 of NATO's 1949 Washington Treaty.[42] It would make the EU a military alliance comparable to the

---

[40] Missiroli, *CFSP, Flexibility and Defence*, above, note 8, 37; P de Vestel, 'The Future of Armament Cooperation in NATO and the WEU' in Kjell E Eliassen (ed), *Foreign and Security Policy in the European Union* (London: Sage, 1998) 197–215.

[41] Article 5 of the Modified Brussels Treaty (Protocol (with Exchange of Letters) Modifying and completing the Brussels Treaty, signed 23 October 1954, 211 UNTS 342) reads:

If any of the High Contracting Parties should be the object of an armed attack in Europe, the other High Contracting Parties will, in accordance with the provisions of Article 51 of the Charter of the United Nations, afford the Party so attacked all the military and other aid and assistance in their power.

[42] Article 5 Washington Treaty, 34 UNTS 243, reads:

The Parties agree that an armed attack against one or more of them in Europe or North America shall be considered an attack against them all and consequently they agree that, if such an armed attack occurs, each of them, in exercise of the right of individual or collective self-defence recognised by Article 51 of the Charter of the United Nations, will assist the Party or Parties so attacked by taking forthwith, individually and in concert with the other Parties, such action as it deems necessary, including the use of armed force, to restore and maintain the security of the North Atlantic area. Any such armed attack and all measures taken as a result thereof shall immediately be reported to the Security Council. Such measures shall be terminated when the Security Council has taken the measures necessary to restore and maintain international peace and security.

J S Ignarski, entry on 'NATO', in R Bernardt, *Encyclopedia of Public International Law* (Amsterdam: North Holland, 1983) at 269, considers this a qualified provision which 'compares unfavourably with the equivalent Article V of the Modified Brussels Treaty'. Article 5 was invoked only once. The USA invoked it after the attacks on New York and Washington on 11 September 2001.

WEU by uniting the remaining *acquis* of the latter with the *acquis* of the earlier. After the transfer of the crisis management policy and the activities of the WEAG/WEAO outlined above the mutual defence clause is the only substantial remaining part, and also the 'original core function',[43] of the WEU.[44] Thus the introduction of a mutual defence clause in the Constitutional Treaty completes a transfer process of the functions of the WEU to the EU.[45]

The mutual defence clause in the Draft Constitutional Treaty envisaged by the Convention in 2003 and agreed by the European Council in June 2004[46] differs from that eventually signed in October 2004 and published in December of the same year. These differences are a reflection of considerable disagreements over the transformation of the EU into a military alliance. First, the concept of 'closer cooperation' contained in the Draft and the June 2004 version was removed from the provision. This would have introduced a specific category of formal flexibility where most but not all Member States would have participated in EU collective defence. The non-aligned Member States—Austria, Finland, Ireland, and Sweden—demanded the removal of flexibility from the clause. This was to prevent a 'vanguard' of Member States such as France, Belgium, and Germany from using the 'label of the EU' in collective defence without really representing the EU as a whole.[47] Second, the notion 'military or other' was deleted after the

---

[43] Wessel, 'Differentiation', above, note 16.

[44] On another important function, that of parliamentary scrutiny through the WEU Assembly, see: Trybus, *European Union Law and Defence Integration*, above, note 6, at 106–8. Other activities of the WEU include disarmament and non-proliferation of weapons. For a detailed analysis see: R A Wessel, 'The EU as Black Widow: Devouring the WEU to Give Birth to a European Security and Defence Policy' in V Kronenberger (ed), *The European Union and the International Legal Order—Discord or Harmony?* (The Hague: TMC Asser Press, 2001) 405.

[45] The WEU itself uses the term 'transition'; see the Marseille Declaration, WEU Ministerial Council, Marseille, 13 November 2000, Paragraph 5: 'They [the ministers] also agreed to suspend application of the routine consultation mechanisms in force between the WEU and the EU, without prejudice to the cooperation required within the framework of the transition process'. During the same meeting it was decided that the dialogue and cooperation, which the WEU at 28 and 21 had developed with the associate members, associate partners and observers, would cease. See at Paragraph 4: '[. . .] these responsibilities would be taken up within the existing framework of political dialogue between the EU and the countries concerned'. Rutten, *From Saint Malo to Nice*, above, note 14, 147, at 148.

[46] Article I-41(7) of the Convention in the June 2004 version reads:

Until such time as the European Council has acted in accordance with paragraph 2 of this Article, closer cooperation shall be established, in the Union framework, as regards mutual defence. Under this cooperation, if one of the Member States participating in such cooperation is the victim of armed aggression on its territory, the other participating States shall give it aid and assistance by all the means in their power, military or other, in accordance with Article 51 of the United Nations Charter.

Article I-40 (2) of the Draft Treaty presented by the Convention read:

The common security and defence policy shall include the progressive framing of a common Union defence policy. This will lead to a common defence, when the European Council, acting unanimously, so decides. It shall in that case recommend to the Member States the adoption of such a decision in accordance with their respective constitutional requirements.

[47] See in particular the letter, dated 4 December 2003, written by the Finnish Foreign Secretary Erkki Tuomioja and his colleagues Brian Cowen from Ireland, Benita Ferrero-Waldner from Austria,

notion of 'all the means in their power', which could be interpreted as excluding military means. However, it is submitted that this notion is sufficiently wide to include military means. Furthermore, the provision deals with the response to an armed aggression. Third, the reference to close cooperation with NATO was omitted, but the new subparagraph 2 introduces an even clearer requirement of consistency with NATO. Moreover, it could be interpreted as reducing the mutual defence commitment of subparagraph 1 to a commitment subsidiary to NATO corresponding to the general arrangements between the two organizations. Taken together the deletion of 'military or other', of the reference to NATO, and of Article III-214,[48] could be interpreted as a 'demilitarization' of the clause, transforming the mutual defence commitment into a mere solidarity clause. However, even the final version of the Constitutional Treaty includes a separate solidarity clause in Article I-43, covering terrorist threats as well as natural or man-made disasters. This provision and Article I-41 (7) must have separate fields of application.

Fourth, the new sentence '[t]his shall not prejudice the specific character of the security and defence policy of certain Member States' accommodates the reservations of the neutral Member States with regards to the old Article I-40(7). The thus extended provision no longer obliges the neutral Member States to aid and assistance of the other Member States in case of an armed aggression. On the other hand, the provision does not exclude the non-aligned Member States from being entitled to such aid and assistance. In other words, the new Article I-41 codifies 'free riding' in collective defence. While this appears unreasonably favourable to the interests of the neutral Member States, it should be kept in mind that an armed aggression against any of the Member States is very unlikely. The collective defence commitment has mainly a political and diplomatic rather than a military and strategic nature. Moreover, the military capacities of the non-aligned Member States do not make a difference. Therefore the arrangement has advantages since it accommodates the reservations of the neutral Member States without excluding them from collective defence,[49] and allows the transfer of the WEU collective defence *acquis* to the EU. Common defence is discussed in detail in Chapter 8 by Krieger, which, like Chapter 12 by Terpan, also looks at the relationship of the EU with NATO.

and Leaila Freivalds from Sweden, in Missiroli, *From Copenhagen to Brussels*, above, note 23, 437 (hereinafter 'Letter of 4 December 2003'), the article by Toumioja, 'Europe needs to act as a whole on defence', *Financial Times*, 28 October 2003, and the article he published together with his colleague Laila Freivalds from Sweden, in *Dagens Nyhetter* (Sweden), 11 November 2003 (a translation into English was provided by Sweden's Permanent Representation to the EU in Missiroli, ibid, 430). See also: 'Four EC States Fight to Guard Neutrality', *The Guardian*, 9 December 2003; 'Selbst entscheiden wie wir helfen', *Kurier* (Austria), 11 December 2003; 'Tuomioja welcomes Italian compromise on security guarantees' *Helsingin Sanomat* (Finland), 10 December 2003.

[48] Which included references to the EU Political and Security Committee, the EU Military Committee, NATO and the UN Security Council.

[49] The notion of 'mutual defence' is not accurate here, since the arrangement is one-sided, and the notion of 'mutual' requires some form of 'give and take'.

6. Conclusions

The CSDP envisaged in the Constitutional Treaty builds on the security and defence *acquis* of the ESDP developed in the context of the current framework of the Treaty of Nice. Many aspects, such as its intergovernmental nature, security institutions, and the uncertain future 'common defence', remain untouched. However, it also introduces considerable innovations in the core areas of security and defence policy, namely, crisis management, armaments policy, and collective defence. The degree to which these innovations depend on the entry into force of the Constitutional Treaty, however, varies considerably.

With regards to crisis management the new concept of 'permanent structured cooperation' could facilitate the establishment of a more permanent military capacity of the EU to overcome the current ad hoc character of the implementation stage of this policy. Moreover, the new text provides a Treaty base for an autonomous military capacity. However, it is doubtful whether a Treaty base and permanent structured cooperation are needed to develop the crisis management policy of the Union. Missions from 'Concordia' to 'ALTHEA' are possible under the current framework and even an ERRF could be established under the Treaty of Nice. This policy aspect is not controversial and will develop independently from the entry into force of the Constitutional Treaty.

The creation of the EDA ahead of the entry into force of the Constitutional Treaty teaches two important lessons. First, certain elements of the CSDP can be detached from the Constitution and introduced on the basis of the current framework of the Treaty of Nice, eg, through a Joint Action. Second, policy fields designed as flexible frameworks might still lead to (almost) all Member States participating. This avoids the disadvantages of flexibility, namely fragmentation. The possibility of withdrawing from a certain policy at a later stage appears to encourage participation.

Collective defence is not as independent from the Constitutional Treaty as the crisis management and armaments policies are. Without the Constitutional Treaty entering into force the EU will not develop into a military alliance. However, Member States aiming at a defence alliance and possibly a common defence, such as Belgium, France, Greece, Hungary, Luxembourg, Spain, and Germany, will not necessarily wait for the next Treaty revision. Therefore a military alliance of EU Member States outside the EU becomes a possibility. Alternatively, the WEU will continue to exist in its current form. Both scenarios would undermine the coherence and consistency of the CFSP and vice versa. However, in the strategic situation of Europe today, collective defence is simply not as important as it was during the Cold War. Therefore, the crisis management and armaments policies, which do not depend on the entry into force of the Constitutional Treaty, are the crucial elements of the CSDP. Ultimately, the success or failure of the Giscard text will make little difference to the development of an EU security and defence policy.

PART II

ELEMENTS OF EUROPEAN SECURITY POLICY

4

ESDP in Practice: Increasingly Varied and Ambitious EU Security and Defence Operations

*Frederik Naert**

1. Introduction

The EU has been developing a (Common) European Security and Defence Policy (ESDP) since the Cologne and Helsinki European Council decisions of June and December 1999.[1] Since then the EU has gradually put into place the building blocks of the ESDP,[2] enabling it to declare the ESDP operational and to launch its first ESDP operation in 2003.[3] At the time of writing,[4] the

---

* Legal advisor, Directorate General Legal Support and Mediation, Belgian Ministry of Defence. The views expressed in this contribution are solely those of the author and do not necessarily reflect the views of the Belgian Government, its Ministry of Defence, or its General Directorate Legal Support and Mediation. All website addresses cited were active on 17 October 2006, unless otherwise specified.

[1] European Council conclusions since 1993 are available at <http://ue.eu.int/cms3_fo/showPage .asp?id=432&lang=en&mode=g>.

[2] See, in addition to other chapters in this volume: N Gnesotto (ed), *EU Security and Defence Policy. The First Five Years (1999–2004)* (Paris: EU ISS, 2004) available at <http://www.iss-eu.org>; A Dumoulin, R Mathieu, and G Sarlet, *La Politique Européenne de Sécurité et de Défense. De l'opéra-toire à l'identitaire* (Brussels: Bruylant, 2003), and S Duke, *The EU and Crisis Management. Development and Prospects*, (Maastricht: EIPA, 2002). For key documents, see Chaillot papers Nos 47, 51, 57, 67, and 75, available at <http://www.iss-eu.org>. See also <http://ue.eu.int/ cms3_fo/showPage.asp?id=261&lang=en&mode=g>. For the impact of the Treaty Establishing a Constitution for Europe (EU Constitution) (Rome, 29 October 2004, [2004] OJ C-310, not yet entered into force), see F Naert, 'European Security and Defence in the EU Constitutional Treaty', (2005) 10 J of Conflict & Security L 187–207 (prior version available at <http://www.mil.be/rdc/ viewdoc.asp?LAN=nl&FILE=doc&ID=143>).

[3] According to para 56 of the 19–20 June European Council conclusions, 'The EU now has operational capability across the full range of Petersberg tasks, limited and constrained by recognized shortfalls, which can be alleviated by the further development of the EU's military capabilities'. In the European Council conclusions of 14–15 December 2001 (para 6), ESDP had already been declared operational for some missions. See also N Tsagourias, Chapter 5 of this volume.

[4] The research for this chapter was concluded on 25 September 2005. However, key developments up to 28 January 2006 have been included wherever possible. In respect of the proposed

ever-increasing number of past and present ESDP operations stands at four-
teen: the military operations CONCORDIA in the Former Yugoslav Republic
of Macedonia (FYROM), ARTEMIS in the Democratic Republic of the Congo
(DRC) and ALTHEA in Bosnia and Herzegovina (BiH); police operations EUPM
(European Union Police Mission) in BiH, PROXIMA in FYROM, EUPOL
KINSHASA (European Union Police Mission in Kinshasa, DRC), and EUPOL
COPPS (EU Police Mission in the Palestinian Territories); the rule of law
mission EUJUST THEMIS in Georgia, the integrated rule of law mission
EUJUST LEX for Iraq; the security sector reform mission EUSEC DRC (EU
Security Sector Reform Mission in the DRC); the mixed civilian-military EU
Support to AMIS II (African Union Mission in the Darfur region of Sudan);
the EU AMM (Aceh Monitoring Mission); EUPAT (EU Police Advisory
Team) in FYROM; and EU BAM Rafah (EU Border Assistance Mission at Rafah
Crossing Point in the Palestinian Territories).[5] The most recent operation,
EUFOR DR Congo in the DRC to temporarily reinforce the UN's mission there,
was decided upon too late to be discussed in this chapter and is not included in
this number (see especially Council Joint Action 2006/319/CFSP of 27 April
2006 on the European Union military operation in support of the United Nations
Organization Mission in the Democratic Republic of the Congo (MONUC)
during the election process ([2006] OJ L-116/98), and UN Security Council
Resolution 1671 of 25 April 2006). Furthermore, the EU is planning a possible
future EU crisis management operation in Kosovo (see Council Joint Action
2006/304/CFSP of 10 April 2006 on the establishment of an EU Planning Team
(EUPT Kosovo) regarding a possible EU crisis management operation in the field
of rule of law and possible other areas in Kosovo ([2006] OJ L-112/19)). This list
excludes European Community/EU missions launched before 1999 which would
probably qualify as crisis management operations today, in particular the EU's
administration of the city of Mostar (BiH)[6] and the EC/EU Monitoring Mission
(ECMM/EUMM) in the former Yugoslavia.[7] It also excludes the EU Border

EU Constitution, the text is written in the conditional tense to reflect its uncertain future after the
referenda rejecting it.

    [5] See generally <http://ue.eu.int/cms3_fo/showPage.asp?id=268&lang=en&mode=g>; COSAC
Secretariat, *Fourth Bi-Annual Report*, October 2005 <http://www.cosac.eu/en/documents/biannual>; G
Lindstrom, 'On the Ground: ESDP Operations', in N Gnesotto (ed), above, n 2, 111–30; D Lynch and
A Missiroli, 'ESDP Operations', EU Institute for Security Studies <http://www.iss-eu.org/esdp/
09-dvl-am.pdf> and UK FCO, 'ESDP Operations' <http://www.fco.gov.uk/servlet/Front?pagename
=OpenMarket/Xcelerate/ShowPage&c=Page&cid=1077042145284>.

    [6] See F Pagani, '*L'administration de Mostar par l'Union européenne*', 42 *Annuaire français de droit
international* (1996) 234–54; J Wouters and F Naert, 'How Effective is the European Security
Architecture? Lessons from Bosnia and Kosovo', (2001) 50 ICLQ 555 and Special Report No 2/96
[1996] OJ C-287/1.

    [7] The ECMM was established by a Memorandum of Understanding signed on 13 July 1991 and
was renamed EUMM by Council Joint Action 2000/811/CFSP of 22 December 2000 ([2000] OJ

Assistance Mission to Moldova and Ukraine, which does not appear to be an ESDP operation.[8]

The purpose of this chapter is to examine the main legal aspects of these operations and to draw some conclusions from and make some remarks on this. In the first section all these operations (with the exception of EUPAT,[9] COPPS,[10] and EU BAM Rafah[11] which were launched to late to be fully covered by this study), will be addressed in chronological order, starting with a general overview[12] and followed by an analysis of their international mandate, the legal status of the force/mission, and the applicable law and the participation of third States in the operation. The focus will be on common elements on the one hand and on peculiar aspects on the other. In the second section, some general conclusions will be drawn and remarks made regarding the scope of ESDP operations, the international mandate, the legal status and applicable law, third State participation and

L-328/53), most recently amended and extended by Council Joint Action 2005/807/CFSP of 21 November 2005 ([2005] OJ L-303/61). On the ECMM, see J Wouters and F Naert, above, previous note, 547–50, 558, and 560. The status of this mission is governed by, inter alia, agreements with FYROM ([2001] OJ L-241/2), Albania ([2003] OJ L-93/50) and the Federal Republic of Yugoslavia ([2001] OJ L-125/2). On the EUMM generally, see <http://www.eusrbih.org/euinbih/?cid=23,1,1>.

[8] For instance, it does not seem to be based on a Joint Action, is funded by the European Commission, and was announced by the External Relations Commissioner and the SG/HR. See on this mission generally <http://www.eubam.org> and <http://ue.eu.int/cms3_fo/showPage.asp?id=986&lang=en&mode=g>.

[9] Established by Council Joint Action 2005/826/CFSP of 24 November ([2005] OJ L-307/61). See generally <http://ue.eu.int/cms3_fo/showPage.asp?id=994&lang=en&mode=g> and <http://www.eu-pat.org> (latter site active on 28 January 2006, but no longer). This is a follow-on mission after Concordia and Proxima (see below), which aims to further support the development of an efficient and professional police service based on European standards of policing for a six-month period, after which EC support initiatives for FYROM are planned. Art 11(1) of the EUPAT Joint Action provides for efforts to extend the Proxima Status of Mission Agreement (SOMA) (see below, n 138) to EUPAT.

[10] COPPS stands for the EU Coordinating Office for Palestinian Police Support and was initially not a formal ESDP mission: see EU Doc S308/05, 26 September 2005 <http://ue.eu.int/uedocs/cms_Data/docs/pressdata/fr/discours/86356.pdf>. It was initially based on an exchange of letters signed on 20 April 2005 (see EU Doc S163/05, <http://ue.eu.int/ueDocs/cms_Data/docs/pressData/en/declarations/84603.pdf>). It currently aims to contribute to the establishment of sustainable and effective policing arrangements under Palestinian ownership in accordance with best international standards. See generally Council Joint Action 2005/797/CFSP of 14 November 2005 ([2005] OJ L-300/65) and <http://ue.eu.int/cms3_fo/shwPage.asp?id=974&lang=en&mode=g>.

[11] Established by Council Joint Action 2005/889/CFSP of 12 December 2005 ([2005] OJ L-327/28). The aim of EU BAM Rafah is to provide a third party presence at the Rafah Crossing Point in order to contribute, in cooperation with the Community's institution-building efforts, to the opening of the Rafah Crossing Point and to build up confidence between the Government of Israel and the Palestinian Authority. See generally <http://ue.eu.int/cms3_fo/showPage.asp?id=979&lang=en&mode=g>.

[12] While this will usually include the number of forces/personnel and the contributing states, the author has not always been able to collect this information and no breakdown is provided for each

some institutional issues. While the budget for each operation will be specified to give an idea of the operation's costs, financing issues will otherwise only be dealt with marginally.[13]

However, all this is preceded by an introduction to the legal framework of ESDP operations. First, the international mandate will usually be based on a UN Security Council mandate, peace agreement, and/or host state consent. Second, the EU will normally conclude a status of Mission/Forces Agreement (SOMA/SOFA) with the host state which will regulate the status and activities of an operation in the host state. Third, there will be an EU Council Joint Action[14] establishing the operation and in some cases separate Council Decisions launching the operation and/or appointing the Head of Mission or Operation and Force Commanders. Fourth, there may be various decisions of the Political and Security Committee (PSC), which exercises political control and strategic direction of EU crisis management operations,[15] eg, a decision setting up a Committee of Contributors. Fifth, there are often EU agreements with third states participating in an operation. Sixth, for military operations there will be an Operation Plan and rules of engagement[16] (not in the public domain). Furthermore, there may be additional agreements between participating states, which are often not in the public domain either.

contributing state. For this information the reader is referred to the publications listed in n 5 and in the general note accompanying the title of each operation. It may be noted that the Conference of Committees for European and Community Affairs of the European Parliaments (COSAC) has welcomed the Council's decision to publish information on which Member States participate in which ESDP operations: see [2005] OJ C-322/1, para 1.

[13] See on this: Article 28 TEU (see below, n 76); Art III-313 proposed EU Constitution, above, n 2; Council Decision 2004/197/CFSP of 23 February 2004 ([2004] OJ L-63/68), as amended by Council Decision 2004/925/EC of 22 December 2004 ([2004] OJ L-395/68) and Council Decision 2005/68/CFSP of 24 January 2005 ([2005] OJ L-27/59); D Scannel, 'Financing ESDP Military Operations', 9 *Eur Foreign Affairs Rev* (2004) 529–49 and A Missiroli, *€uros for ESDP: Financing EU Operations*, Occasional Paper No 45 (Paris: EU ISS, June 2003) and 'Ploughshares into Swords? Euros for European Defence', (2003) 8 *Eur Foreign Affairs Rev* 5–33. See also N Tsagourias, Chapter 5 of this volume.

[14] Joint Actions are based on Art 14 TEU (below, n 76). See also N Tsagourias, Chapter 5 of this volume.

[15] Art 25 TEU (below, n 76), which reads in relevant part:

[...] a Political and Security Committee shall monitor the international situation in the areas covered by the common foreign and security policy and contribute to the definition of policies by delivering opinions to the Council at the request of the Council or on its own initiative. It shall also monitor the implementation of agreed policie [...]. Within the scope of this title, this Committee shall exercise, under the responsibility of the Council, political control and strategic direction of crisis management operations. The Council may authorise the Committee, for the purpose and for the duration of a crisis management operation, as determined by the Council, to take the relevant decisions concerning the political control and strategic direction of the operation, without prejudice to Article 47.

See also N Tsagourias, Chapter 5 of this volume.

[16] The Operation Plan contains the specifics of the operation and is often lengthy, in part due to many annexes, which normally also address legal issues and the use of force. The rules of engagement may be described in short as instructions concerning the use of force.

2. An Overview of ESDP Operations

2.1. European Union Police Mission (EUPM) in Bosnia and Herzegovina (BiH)[17]

The EU has been involved in BiH for quite some time.[18] Especially after the end of NATO's military operation over Kosovo in 1999, the EU adopted a broader and more ambitious regional approach to South-Eastern Europe, including the Stability Pact for South-Eastern Europe and the Stabilization and Association Process, with the aim of eventually integrating the countries of this area into the EU.[19]

Subsequently, on 1 January 2003, the EU launched its first ESDP operation, the EU Police Mission in Bosnia and Herzegovina (EUPM), which succeeded the UN's International Police Task Force (IPTF). In December 2004 the EU also took over the military stabilization force from NATO through operation ALTHEA (discussed below in 2.6). The EUPM was planned well in advance: the EUPM Joint Action was adopted on 11 March 2002 and a planning team had been established already.[20] The Head of Mission would lead the planning team and was appointed on that day too.[21] This also made possible the timely conclusion and entry into force of a Status of Mission Agreement (SOMA).[22]

The EUPM is part of the broader EU rule of law follow-up in BiH.[23] This is reflected in the chain of command, where the EU Special Representative (EUSR) for Bosnia and Herzegovina acts as an intermediary between the High Representative for the Common Foreign and Security Policy and Secretary-General of the Council of the EU (SG/HR) on the one hand and the Head of Mission on the other.[24]

The objective of the mission is 'to establish sustainable policing arrangements under BiH ownership in accordance with best European and international practice, and thereby raising current BiH police standards' through monitoring, mentoring and inspecting; the mission does not include executive powers or the deployment of an armed component.[25]

[17] See generally A Nowak, *L'Union en action: la mission de police en Bosnie* Occasional Paper No 42 (Paris: EU ISS, January 2003); <http://www.eupm.org> and <http://ue.eu.int/cms3_fo/showPage .asp?id=585&lang=en&mode=g>.
[18] See J Wouters and F Naert, above, n 6, 553 and 555. The EU's involvement included the ECMM (discussed above), humanitarian aid, political and diplomatic involvement, monitoring of sanctions, substantial financial support, and leading the reconstruction efforts (together with the World Bank).
[19] See ibid, 566–8, and <http://ec.europa.eu/enlargement/enlargement_process/accession_process/ how_does_a_country_join_the_eu/sap/index_en.htm>.
[20] Council Joint Action 2002/210/CFSP of 11 March 2002 [2002] OJ L-70/1.
[21] Council Decision 2002/212/CFSP of 11 March 2002 [2002] OJ L-70/8.
[22] [2002] OJ L-293/2, concluded in accordance with Art 11(1) EUPM Joint Action, above, n 20.
[23] Art 7 EUPM Joint Action, above, n 20.   [24] Ibid, Arts 6–7.
[25] Ibid, annexed mission statement and Art 1 EUPM SOMA, above, n 22. Its revised mission statement for 2006–7 is 'through mentoring, monitoring and inspecting, to establish in BiH a

The mission was intended to run from 2003 till 2005,[26] but was extended (with a revised mandate) for another two years in late 2005.[27] For its initial duration, it had an estimated total budget of €129.7 million, including €75.7 million from the Community budget.[28] The amount funded by the Community budget was reduced by approximately €2.5 million for 2004 and 2005,[29] presumably reflecting the amount paid by third States participating in the mission (as explained below).[30]

The mission was initially led by Commissioner Sven Frederiksen,[31] who was succeeded by Assistant Commissioner Kevin Carty[32] and Mr Vincenzo Coppola.[33] It numbers about 500 police officers from 33 countries (detailed below) with headquarters in Sarajevo and 24 monitoring units co-located within police units throughout BiH.[34] The PSC exercises political control and strategic direction of the operation.[35]

2.1.1. Mandate

The Council of the EU expressed its readiness to take over the UN's IPTF on 18 February 2002, an offer that was accepted by the Peace Implementation Council Steering Board (which supervises the implementation of the General Framework Agreement for Peace in Bosnia and Herzegovina, the Dayton Peace Agreement)[36] ten days later and welcomed by the UN Security Council on 5 March 2002 in Resolution 1396.[37] On 4 March 2002 the Bosnian authorities invited the EU to undertake this mission. The EUPM is therefore based on the consent of the authorities of Bosnia and Herzegovina. This is reflected in the wording of UN Security Council Resolution 1396, which welcomes rather than authorizes the EUPM.

---

sustainable, professional and multiethnic police service operating in accordance with best European and international standards' (Art 1(1) Joint Action 2005/824/CFSP, below n 27).

[26] Art 1(3) EUPM SOMA, above, n 22.

[27] Council Joint Action 2005/824/CFSP of 24 November 2005 [2005] OJ L-307/55, Arts 1 and 15.

[28] Art 9 EUPM Joint Action, above, n 20; Council Joint Action 2003/141/CFSP of 27 February 2003 ([2003] OJ L-53/63) and Council Decision 2002/968/CFSP of 10 December 2002 ([2002] OJ L-335/1).

[29] Council Decision 2003/856/CFSP of 8 December 2003 ([2003] OJ L-323/13) and Council Decision 2004/837/CFSP of 6 December 2004 ([2004] OJ L-360/32).

[30] See <http://europa.eu.int/comm/external_relations/cfsp/fin/actions/eupm03.htm> (active on 28 January 2006, but no longer).   [31] Council Decision 2002/212/CFSP, above, n 21.

[32] Council Decision 2004/188/CFSP of 23 February 2004 ([2004] OJ L-58/27), extended by Council Decision 2005/81/CFSP of 31 January 2005 ([2005] OJ L-29/48).

[33] PSC Decision EUPM/1/2005 of 25 November 2005, [2005] OJ L-335/58.

[34] Art 3 EUPM Joint Action, above, n 20 and Art 1(2) EUPM SOMA, above, n 22.

[35] Art 7 EUPM Joint Action, above, n 20.

[36] Paris, 14 December 1995, (1996) 35 ILM 75.

[37] EUPM Joint Action, above, n 20, preamble. All UN Security Council Resolutions are available at <http://www.un.org/documents/scres.htm>.

2.1.2. Legal status and applicable law

The EUPM SOMA was concluded on time[38] and entered into force before the start of the mission. The key provision on the status of the mission is Article 4, which grants the EUPM a status equivalent to that of a diplomatic mission, makes all its offices and means of transport inviolable, and gives EUPM personnel all privileges and immunities equivalent to those of the personnel of embassies (differentiating between EUPM personnel, administrative and technical staff, and locally hired auxiliary personnel), adding that the EU Member States and other Sending Parties shall have priority of jurisdiction. It may be noted that it is common for states and international organizations to seek privileges and immunities for personnel participating in operations/missions (and even exercises) abroad. Some reflections on this point are included in the final remarks below. Remarkably, there is no provision at all on applicable law.[39]

In line with the nature of the mission (as discussed above, this does not include executive functions), Article 5(1) EUPM SOMA states that 'Members of the EUPM shall not carry arms'. It is for BiH to take 'all necessary measures for the protection, safety and security of the EUPM and its members' (Article 6(1) EUPM SOMA). Furthermore, according to Article 6(2) EUPM SOMA 'Members of the EUPM shall not undertake any action or activity incompatible with the impartial nature of their duties'.

2.1.3. Participation of third States

All fifteen 'old'[40] EU Member States (including Denmark[41]) participate in the EUPM, as well as the ten 'new' Member States, the candidate Member States Bulgaria, Romania, and Turkey, the NATO Member States Iceland, Norway, and Canada, and also Russia, Switzerland, and Ukraine.[42]

The participation of third States that are Members of the Organization for Security and Co-operation in Europe (OSCE) was permitted by Article 8 EUPM Joint Action, which also provided for the conclusion of detailed agreements to be concluded with those states.[43]

---

[38] Above, n 22.

[39] Applicable law refers to the law applicable to the personnel of an operation. This law is complex and normally includes international law, the law of the state(s) sending the personnel, and local (meaning host state) law. status of Forces Agreements (SOFAs)/SOMAs usually stipulate respect for local law (see the discussion below on the SOFAs/SOMAs for other missions and especially n 303 and accompanying text).   [40] Ie, the EU Member States before the 2004 accession wave.

[41] The participation of Denmark is not evident given its special position in respect of the ESDP, which is discussed below, n 62 and accompanying text.

[42] See <http://www.eupm.org/FactSheet.asp?lang=eng>.

[43] Most of the agreements have been published in [2003] OJ L-239. For the agreement with Poland, see [2003] OJ L-64/38 and for that with Russia, see [2003] OJ L-197/38. The author has not been able to find an agreement with Canada. For more details on the agreements, see the OJ and the Council's agreements database: <http://ue.eu.int/cms3_fo/showPage.asp?id=252&lang=en&mode=g>.

On the basis of a selective survey, these agreements share the following elements: the participating state associates itself to the Joint Action establishing the EUPM and commits itself to seconding a specified number of personnel to this mission. It bears the costs thereof and it pays a share in the common costs. Its personnel are covered by the EUPM SOMA. EU decision-making autonomy is safeguarded but all participating states have the same rights and obligations in terms of day-to-day management of the operation as participating EU Member States,[44] and the EU will consult with participating states when ending the mission. The agreements also contain a clause on classified information[45] and on claims linked to the secondment of personnel to the EUPM.

2.2. CONCORDIA (FYROM)[46]

CONCORDIA was the EU's second ESDP operation and its first military one. The EU had already played a role in FYROM at the time of the crisis in Kosovo,[47] and following its regional approach to South-Eastern Europe (mentioned above in 2.1) and when tensions increased in early 2001 the EU and NATO undertook coordinated efforts to avoid an escalation,[48] resulting in the 13 August 2001 Ohrid Framework Agreement.[49]

The EU was involved in the implementation and supervision of this agreement, but the military presence was initially led by NATO, which conducted operations Essential Harvest, Amber Fox, and Allied Harmony in FYROM.[50] However, on 31 March 2003 the EU took over NATO's peacekeeping mission.[51] The Operation Plan and rules of engagement were adopted on 18 March 2003.[52] CONCORDIA was to last six months[53] but was extended until 15 December 2003.[54] It was then followed by EUPOL PROXIMA (discussed below in 2.4).

The aim of the operation was to contribute to stability and security in FYROM and to further the implementation of the Ohrid Agreement.[55]

---

[44] It is apparently assumed that all contributions are significant in the sense of Art 8 EUPM Joint Action, above, n 20.

[45] The sharing of classified information with non-Member States requires regulation and can be problematic (compare the position of Malta and Cyprus in EU-led operations with recourse to NATO assets, discussed below in n 187).

[46] See generally G Lindstrom, above, n 5, 116–8; <http://www.delmkd.cec.eu.int/en/Concordia/main.htm> and <http://ue.eu.int/cms3_fo/showPage.asp?id=594&lang=en&mode=g>.

[47] J Wouters and F Naert, above, n 6, 559–60.

[48] J Wouters and F Naert, *'Europese defensie in de NAVO en de Europese Unie: eenheid en complementariteit'* (2002) 31 *Vrede en Veiligheid*, 215 and 223 (n 71).

[49] Text at <http://faq.macedonia.org/politics/framework_agreement.pdf>.

[50] See <http://www.nato.int/fyrom/home.htm>.

[51] Art 1 Council Decision 2003/202/CFSP of 18 March 2003 [2003] OJ L-76/43. See also Council Joint Action 2003/92/CFSP of 27 January 2003 [2003] OJ L-34/26.

[52] 18 March 2003 Council conclusions.

[53] Art 3 Council Decision 2003/202/CFSP, above, n 51.

[54] Council Decision 2003/563/CFSP of 29 July 2003 [2003] OJ L-190/20.

[55] Joint Action 2003/92/CFSP, above, n 51, 1st consideration preamble.

CONCORDIA was an operation with recourse to NATO assets and only became possible once EU-NATO arrangements had been agreed upon, a difficult process only successfully concluded in March 2003.[56] A specific EU-NATO exchange of letters was concluded for CONCORDIA on 17 March 2003.[57] The EU operational headquarters were located at (NATO's) Supreme Headquarters of Allied Powers in Europe (SHAPE) and the Operation Commander was the Deputy Supreme Allied Commander for Europe (D-SACEUR).[58] The responsibilities at Force Headquarters level were first exercised by France as 'framework nation' and as of 1 October 2003 by EUROFOR (the French-Spanish-Italian-Portuguese European Force established to conduct peace support operations).[59]

The PSC, under the responsibility of the Council, exercised the political control and strategic direction of the operation, and was authorized to take 'the relevant decisions', including the powers to amend the Operation Plan, the chain of command, and the rules of engagement, whereas the powers of decision with respect to the objectives and termination of the operation remained vested in the Council.[60]

Some 400 military personnel from 27 countries were engaged in this operation,[61] ie, all EU Member States except Denmark, which does not participate in the elaboration and the implementation of decisions and actions of the Union which have defence implications, does not participate in their adoption, and is not obliged to contribute to the financing of operational expenditure arising from such measures,[62] and except Ireland, which, under Irish law, can only take part in missions with a UN mandate,[63] and 14 third States (detailed below).

[56] The 'Berlin Plus package' on these relations was agreed on 17 March 2003 (<http://www.nato.int/issues/nato-eu/chronology.html>) and mainly consists of the 16 December 2002 NATO-EU 'Berlin Plus' agreement, the December 2002 EU-NATO Declaration on ESDP (<http://www.nato.int/docu/pr/2002/p02-142e.htm>), and the EU-NATO Security Agreement of 14 March 2003 ([2003] OJ L-80/36, entered into force 14 March 2003). On NATO-EU relations, see Heike Krieger, Chapter 8 of this volume; J-Y Haine, 'ESDP and NATO', in N Gnesotto (ed), above, n 2, 131–43; <http://ue.eu.int/cms3_fo/showPage.asp?id=282&lang=en&mode=g> and <http://www.nato.int/issues/nato-eu/index.html>. See also M Reichard, 'Some Legal Issues Concerning the EU-NATO Berlin Plus Agreement' (2004) 73 Nordic J of Intl L 37–67.

[57] Council Decision 2003/202/CFSP, above, n 51, 4th consideration preamble. This agreement was extended with CONCORDIA's extension, see Council Decision 2003/563/CFSP, above, n 54, 6th consideration preamble.

[58] EU Doc 6158/03, 7 February 2003 and Art 2 Joint Action 2003/92/CFSP, above, n 51. Unless indicated otherwise, numbered EU documents are available at <http://register.consilium.eu.int>.

[59] EU Doc 11881/03, 29 July 2003; Art 2 Council Decision 2003/563/CFSP, above, n 54 and <http://www.eurofor.it/Mission_CONCORDIA_03%20INDEX.htm>.

[60] Art 4(1) Joint Action 2003/92/CFSP, above, n 51.

[61] See <http://ue.eu.int/cms3_fo/showPage.asp?id=594&lang=en&mode=g>.

[62] See Art 6 Protocol on the Position of Denmark, annexed to the TEU (below, n 76) since the Treaty of Amsterdam (2 October 1997 [1997] OJ C-340/1, entered into force 1 May 1999]). This is recalled in the 8th consideration of the preamble of Council Decision 2003/202/CFSP, above, n 51. This position would remain the same under the proposed EU Constitution (above, n 2), see Art 5 of the Protocol on the Position of Denmark.

[63] Eg, Parliamentary debates, 24 November 2004 (<http://debates.oireachtas.ie/DDebate.aspx?F=JUS20041124.xml&Ex=All&Page=2>). Even a positive UN attitude and host state consent did not suffice.

The budget for the common costs amounted to €6.2 million[64] and was managed through a specific financial mechanism. The other costs were funded by the participating states on a 'costs lie where they fall' basis.[65]

2.2.1. Mandate

CONCORDIA was undertaken following a request by the FYROM President.[66] In addition, UN Security Council Resolution 1371 of 26 September 2001 welcomed the presence of international observers (Article 4) and strongly supported 'the establishment of a multinational security presence in [FYROM] at the request of its Government to contribute towards the security of the observers' (Article 5). So here too the main legal basis was the consent of the Government and the UN Security Council merely endorsed the operation rather than authorized it. The significance of the latter point will be addressed below in the concluding remarks.

2.2.2. Legal status and applicable law

Article 12 of Joint Action 2003/92/CFSP[67] provided for a Status of Forces Agreement (SOFA). On this basis, the CONCORDIA SOFA was concluded on 21 March 2003[68] and entered into force on 31 March 2003,[69] ie, the day the operation started. This agreement also covered personnel and assets of a third State participating in CONCORDIA.[70]

Pursuant to article 2 of this SOFA, the European Union-led forces (EUF) were to respect FYROM laws and regulations, and Article 9 added an obligation to respect international conventions and FYROM laws regarding the protection of the environment and cultural heritage, albeit 'subject to the requirements of the operation'. Furthermore, Article 2 obliged mission staff to refrain from any activity incompatible with the impartial and international nature of the operation. Pursuant to Article 5, EUF premises, accommodation, archives, and documents were inviolable, its premises and accommodation and assets therein, and their means of transport were immune from search, execution, etc, and EUF correspondence was granted a status equivalent to that of diplomatic correspondence. Article 6 granted EUF personnel treatment, including immunities and privileges, equivalent to that of diplomatic agents. Article 7(2) permitted EUF personnel to carry arms and ammunition 'on condition that they [were] authorized to do so by their orders'. In respect of claims for death, injury, damage, or loss, Article 13 distinguished between two categories of claims. Claims arising out of activities in connection with civil disturbances, protection of the EUF, or which were

---

[64] <http://ue.eu.int/cms3_fo/showPage.asp?id=594&lang=en&mode=g>.   Initially,   only €4.7 million had been allocated: see Art 9(3) Joint Action 2003/92/CFSP, above, n 51.

[65] Art 9 and 11th consideration preamble Joint Action 2003/92/CFSP, above, n 51.

[66] 18 March 2003 Council conclusions. The CONCORDIA extension was also based on such a request: see EU Doc 11881/03, 29 July 2003.   [67] Above, n 51.

[68] [2003] OJ L-82/46.   [69] See the Council's agreements database, above, n 43.

[70] Art 1(3)(c) and (g) CONCORDIA SOFA.

incidental to operational necessities were not to be the subject of any reimbursement by states participating in the operation or by the EU financing mechanism. All other claims were to be dealt with by a Joint Claims Commission composed of representatives of the EUF and FYROM authorities. Settlement of the latter claims was to occur after previous consent of the state concerned or the mechanism.

Finally, Article 16 provided that a number of separate implementing agreements were to be concluded on, inter alia, the status of local staff and contractors, procedures for addressing and settling claims, and the exchange of information.

2.2.3. *Participation of third States*

The CONCORDIA Joint Action provided for the participation of third States, in particular non-EU European NATO Members, candidate EU Member States, and other 'potential partners'.[71]

This participation was without prejudice to EU decision-making autonomy, and third States making 'significant military contributions' were to have the same rights and obligations in the day-to-day management of the operation as participating EU Member states.[72] The PSC was authorized to take the relevant decisions on acceptance of the proposed contributions, upon the recommendation of the Operation Commander and the EU Military Committee (EUMC).[73]

On 18 March 2003 the Council welcomed the participation of 14 third States.[74] These states were the (then) candidate Member States Bulgaria, the Czech Republic, Estonia, Hungary, Latvia, Lithuania, Poland, Romania, Slovakia, Slovenia, and Turkey and the NATO Member States Iceland and Norway. Canada initially participated but later withdrew.[75]

Detailed arrangements regarding third State participation were to be the subject of an agreement under Article 24 of the Treaty on European Union (TEU[76]), although the SG/HR, 'assisting the Presidency', was authorized to negotiate such arrangements on the Presidency's behalf.[77] Agreements were concluded with 12 third States.[78]

---

[71] Joint Action 2003/92/CFSP, above, n 51, Art 8.   [72] Ibid, Art 8(1) and (4).

[73] Ibid, Art 8(2).   [74] Council conclusions of 18 March 2003.

[75] Canada was initially listed (see <http://ue.eu.int/uedocs/cmsUpload/Fourteen% 20non-EU% 20countries.pdf>) but no longer afterwards (see <http://www.eurofor.it/Mission _CONCORDIA_03%20INDEX.htm>). According to G Lindstrom, above, n 5, 125, Canada withdrew over financing arrangements. Also, the author has not found an EU-Canada participation agreement for CONCORDIA.

[76] Maastricht, 7 February 1992 ([1992] OJ C-224/1), entered into force 1 November 1993, as subsequently amended. In this chapter, unless indicated otherwise, references are made to the consolidated version as in force at the time of writing and published in [2002] OJ C-325/5.

[77] Joint Action 2003/92/CFSP, above, n 51, Art 8(3).

[78] Czech Republic ([2003] OJ L-229/39), Estonia ([2003] OJ L-216/61), Latvia ([2003] OJ L-313/79), Lithuania ([2003] OJ L-234/19), Poland ([2003] OJ L-285/44), Romania ([2004] OJ L-120/62), Slovak Republic ([2004] OJ L-12/54), and Turkey ([2003] OJ L-234/23). The agreements with Hungary (18 June 2003), Iceland (3 July 2003), Norway (17 June 2003), and Slovenia

On the basis of a selective survey, these agreements share the following elements: the participating state associates itself to the Joint Action establishing the operation and commits itself to seconding personnel to this mission (in most cases to be determined at a Force Generation Conference). It bears the costs thereof, except common costs, and pays a specified share of the common costs. Participating state personnel are covered by the CONCORDIA SOFA and the participating third State exercises jurisdiction over its personnel. All forces and personnel remain under the full command of their national authorities, who transfer operational control to the EU operation commander. EU decision-making autonomy is safeguarded, but all participating states have the same rights and obligations in day-to-day management of the operation as participating EU Member States.[79] The agreements also contain a clause on classified information and on claims for damage to the local population caused by personnel seconded by a third State to the operation.

Furthermore, a Committee of Contributors for this operation was set up by the PSC,[80] which had been authorized to do so by the Council.[81]

2.3. ARTEMIS (DRC)[82]

ARTEMIS was an operation in an area where the EU was already involved: the EU had taken initiatives at the continental level,[83] at the (sub)regional level of the Great Lakes region,[84] and specifically regarding the DRC,[85] which has long suffered from internal armed conflicts with foreign intervention. Obviously, operation ARTEMIS signified a greater EU involvement on the field. Moreover, the EU later also launched a police operation in Kinshasa, a security sector reform mission in the DRC (discussed below in 2.7 and 2.8) and a second military operation there, namely EUFOR DR Congo.

(31 July 2003) do not seem to have been published in the OJ. The author has not found any agreement with Bulgaria or Canada.

[79] It again was apparently assumed that all contributions were significant in the sense of Art 8(4) Joint Action 2003/92/CFSP, above, n 51.

[80] PSC Decision FYROM/1/2003 of 18 February 2003 [2003] OJ C-62/1.

[81] Joint Action 2003/92/CFSP, above, n 51, Art 8(5).

[82] See generally <http://ue.eu.int/cms3_fo/showPage.asp?id=605&lang=en&mode=g>; UN Peacekeeping Best Practices Unit (PBPU), *Operation Artemis: The Lessons of the Interim Emergency Multinational Force*, October 2004, available at <http://pbpu.unlb.org>; C Mace, 'Operation Artemis: Mission improbable?', *Eur Security Rev* No 18, July 2003, available at <http://www.isis-europe.org>; and <http://www.defense.gouv.fr/sites/ema/enjeux_defense/operations_exterieures/documentation/republique_democratique_du_congo/>.

[83] Eg, Council Common Position 2004/85/CFSP of 26 January 2004 [2004] OJ L-21/25. See also <http://ue.eu.int/showPage.asp?id=400&lang=en&mode=g>.

[84] Eg, the EU Special Representative for this region, see: <http://ue.eu.int/showPage.asp?id=263&lang=en&mode=g>.

[85] See generally: <http://europa.eu.int/comm/development/body/country/country_home_en.cfm?cid=cd&lng=en&status=old>.

In May 2003 intense fighting erupted in and around Bunia in the DRC's Ituri region, leading to many deaths and refugees. As the United Nations Organization Mission in the DRC (MONUC) was unable to deal with the situation, the UN Secretary-General called for 'the rapid deployment to Bunia of a highly trained and well-equipped multinational force, under the lead of a Member State, to provide security at the airport as well as to other vital installations in the town and to protect the civilian population'.[86] Subsequently, France indicated its readiness to deploy a force to Bunia and on 30 May 2003, in Resolution 1484, the Security Council authorized the deployment, until 1 September 2003, by which date MONUC was to be sufficiently reinforced, of an International Emergency Multinational Force (IEMF) in Bunia 'to contribute to the stabilization of the security conditions and the improvement of the humanitarian situation in Bunia, to ensure the protection of the airport, the internally displaced persons in the camps in Bunia and, if the situation requires it, to contribute to the safety of the civilian population, [UN] personnel and the humanitarian presence in the town'.

France successfully appealed to the EU Member States to make this an EU operation. The preparations took place very quickly[87] and the decision to undertake the operation was adopted on 5 June.[88] The Operation Plan and rules of engagement were adopted on 12 June and on that same day the operation was formally launched,[89] although French forces were already on the ground on 6 June.[90]

ARTEMIS was an autonomous EU operation, without recourse to NATO assets. This required the designation of a 'Framework Nation' since the EU itself has no proper headquarters (yet).[91] France was the 'Framework Nation' and contributed the multinationalized Headquarters, the Operation and Force Commanders (Generals Bruno Neveu and Jean-Paul Thonier), and the majority of the troops.[92] The operational Headquarters, which became operational on 16 June 2003,[93] were located in Paris and the Force Headquarters in Entebbe, Uganda, with an outpost in Bunia. ARTEMIS's full strength was 1,800 troops and these were all deployed by early July.[94] The mission ended on 1 September 2003

---

[86] S/2003/574, 15 May 2003, available at <http://www.un.org/documents/xchgesc.htm>.

[87] The Council asked the SG/HR for a feasibility study on 19 May 2003.

[88] Council Joint Action 2003/423/CFSP of 5 June 2003 [2003] OJ L-143/50.

[89] Council Decision 2003/432/CFSP of 12 June 2003 [2003] OJ L-147/42. By 13 June, 400 troops were in Bunia, see: <http://www.reliefweb.int/rw/rwb.nsf/AllDocsByUNID/af53b8f764b3e760c1256d470029cff1>.   [90] UNPBPU, above, n 82, 19.

[91] ARTEMIS Joint Action, above, n 88, 5th consideration preamble. The extent of proper EU planning facilities or headquarters is a controversial issue. A compromise was adopted in late 2003 to have a small planning cell at the EU Military Staff and an EU planning cell at SHAPE; see J-Y Haine, above, n 56, 140–1.   [92] ARTEMIS Joint Action, above, n 88, Arts 2–5.

[93] French Defence Ministry press release, 16 June 2003, available at <http://www.defense.gouv.fr/sites/ema/enjeux_defense/operations_exterieures/documentation/republique_democratique_du_congo>.

[94] Council factsheet on ARTEMIS, July 2003 and H L Stimson Center, 'Review of European Union Field Operations', March 2004 <http://www.stimson.org/fopo/pdf/Factsheet_EUFieldOperations.pdf>, 4. The total number of personnel involved may have run up to 2,200:

with a handover to MONUC and the last ARTEMIS troops left Bunia on 7 September. The political control and strategic direction of the operation was exercised by the PSC under the responsibility of the Council and the PSC was authorized to take 'the relevant decisions', including the powers to amend the Operation Plan, the chain of command, and the rules of engagement, but excluding the powers of decision with respect to the objectives and termination of the operation, which remained vested in the Council.[95]

Six EU Member States participated both in the headquarters and with forces (Belgium, France, Germany, Greece, Sweden, and the UK) and another six participated in the headquarters only (Austria, Ireland, Italy, the Netherlands, Portugal, and Spain).[96] Obviously, Denmark did not participate in this military operation (as explained above),[97] and neither did Luxemburg or Finland.[98] The then candidate Member States Cyprus and Hungary participated in the headquarters and Canada, South Africa, and Brazil participated too (as explained below).

The Council set up an arrangement for the common costs, estimated at €7 million, and the remaining costs were borne by the participating states on a 'costs lie where they fall' basis.[99] In contrast to earlier operations, third participating states did not contribute to the common costs.[100]

2.3.1. Mandate

Operation ARTEMIS was based on UN Security Council Resolution 1484 of 30 May 2003, adopted under Chapter VII[101] of the UN Charter[102] and authorizing the participating states to 'take all necessary measures to fulfil [the Force's] mandate' (Article 4). However, in the preamble of this Resolution, the Security Council took note of the support of the DRC, Rwanda, Uganda, and the Ituri parties for the deployment of the force.

Hence the operation contains both elements of peacekeeping, with consent of the parties and Chapter VII peace enforcement. ARTEMIS was conducted in a dangerous environment, witness the subsequent heavy MONUC

---

see J Howorth, 'The Capacities at Europe's Disposal' in Royal Defence College and Royal Institute for International Relations (eds), *Able and Willing...* (Brussels: Belgian Ministry of Defence, 2004) 25, <http://www.mil.be/rdc/viewdoc.asp?LAN=nl&FILE=doc&ID=131>.

[95] ARTEMIS Joint Action, above, n 88, Art 7.   [96] G Lindstrom, above, n 5, 120.

[97] ARTEMIS Joint Action, above, n 88, 13th consideration preamble.

[98] The author is not aware of the reasons for this non-participation, nor of those that led some Member States to only participate in the headquarters. However, the speed with which the operation was set up in combination with the recourse to ad hoc internationalized French headquarters might have been among these reasons.   [99] ARTEMIS Joint Action, above, n 88, Art 11.

[100] C Mace, above, n 82, 2.

[101] This Chapter allows the Security Council to determine the existence of any threat to the peace, breach of the peace, or act of aggression and to make recommendations or decide upon measures to be taken to maintain or restore international peace and security, including sanctions and the use of force.   [102] Charter of the United Nations, San Francisco, 26 June 1945.

fighting with various militias, but was not confronted with major hostile actions against it.[103]

UN support for ARTEMIS was renewed in Security Council Resolutions 1493 (28 July 2003) and 1505 (26 August 2003). The latter Resolution authorized ARTEMIS to provide assistance to MONUC in and around Bunia if MONUC requested such assistance during the period of ARTEMIS's disengagement, until 15 September 2003 at the latest.

2.3.2. *Legal status and applicable law*

Article 13 of the ARTEMIS Joint Action[104] provided that, 'If required, the status of the EU-led forces in the [DRC] shall be the subject of an agreement with the Government of the [DRC] . . . on the basis of Article 24 [TEU]'. However, a SOFA was only concluded with Uganda, or rather, the SOFA between France and Uganda was extended to the EU,[105] and none was concluded with the DRC.

2.3.3. *Participation of third States*

Article 10 of the ARTEMIS Joint Action[106] provided for the participation of third States, without prejudice to the EU's decision-making autonomy. It authorized the PSC to 'take appropriate action with regard to participation arrangements', to take, upon the recommendation of the Operation Commander and the EUMC, the relevant decisions on acceptance of proposed contributions, and to set up a Committee of Contributors, in case the third States provided significant military contributions.

Pursuant to this authority, the PSC accepted contributions from Hungary, Canada, Brazil, and South Africa on 1 July[107] and established a Committee of Contributors on 11 July.[108] On 31 July it accepted the Cypriot participation.[109] Cyprus and Hungary only participated in the headquarters, whereas Canada and South Africa sent troops, and Brazil did both.[110] The participation of Canada, South Africa, and Brazil was limited to 5 July.[111]

The short time limits may explain why no participation agreements seem to have been concluded (the ARTEMIS Joint Action did not provide for

---

[103] However, on 14 June a patrol was attacked by rebel militias and returned fire ('*Une patrouille d'Artemis prise à partie*', 14 June 2003, available at the French ARTEMIS web page, above, n 82) and on 16 June EU forces under attack returned fire and killed two attackers (C Mace, above, n 82, 3, n 3).   [104] Above, n 88.

[105] See EU Documents 12225/03 (4 September 2003) and 10773/03 (26 June 2003, partially in the public domain) and the text of and information on the French-Ugandan SOFA of 18 June 2003 (2227 *UNTS* 267 and *J Officiel de la République Française* 29 August 2003) on <http://www.doc. diplomatie.fr/pacte>.   [106] Above, n 88.

[107] PSC Decision DRC/1/2003 of 1 July 2003 [2003] OJ L-170/19.

[108] PSC Decision DRC 2/2003 of 11 July 2003 [2003] OJ L-184/13.

[109] PSC Decision DRC/3/2003 of 31 July 2003 [2003] OJ L-206/32.

[110] Council factsheet on ARTEMIS, July 2003.   [111] G Lindstrom, above, n 5, 120.

agreements under article 24 TEU[112]), except with Cyprus,[113] even though the Council did adopt a model participation agreement specifically for this operation.[114] Alternatively, the agreements exist but are not in the public domain. Either way, only the agreement with Cyprus can be discussed. This agreement more or less follows the agreements on CONCORDIA (discussed above), with the exception of the lack of contribution to the common costs.[115]

2.4. PROXIMA (FYROM)[116]

The EU Police Mission PROXIMA in FYROM was launched on 15 December 2003 at the same time that the EU's military operation CONCORDIA there ended.[117] It was initially established for twelve months,[118] but was extended by another year.[119] After its termination, on 14 December 2005, it was followed by the EU Police Advisory Team (EUPAT).[120]

PROXIMA had the competences to monitor, mentor, and advise the local police, in order to support, inter alia, the consolidation of law and order, including the fight against organized crime, the implementation of the comprehensive reform of the Ministry of the Interior, including the police, the creation of a border police, support of the local police in building confidence within the population, and enhanced police cooperation with neighbouring states.[121] Although executive functions were excluded, PROXIMA was authorized to have an armed protection unit, unlike the EUPM.[122]

The strength of the mission was up to around 200 police officers and civilians,[123] coming from the fifteen 'old' Member States, nine 'new' Member States

---

[112] This provision reads:

1. When it is necessary to conclude an agreement with one or more States or international organisations in implementation of this title, the Council may authorise the Presidency, assisted by the Commission as appropriate, to open negotiations to that effect. Such agreements shall be concluded by the Council on a recommendation from the Presidency. 2. The Council shall act unanimously when the agreement covers an issue for which unanimity is required for the adoption of internal decisions. 3. When the agreement is envisaged in order to implement a joint action or common position, the Council shall act by a qualified majority in accordance with Article 23(2). [. . .] 5. No agreement shall be binding on a Member State whose representative in the Council states that it has to comply with the requirements of its own constitutional procedure; the other members of the Council may agree that the agreement shall nevertheless apply provisionally. 6. Agreements concluded under the conditions set out by this Art shall be binding on the institutions of the Union.

[113] [2003] OJ L-253/23.   [114] EU Doc 11468/03, 16 July 2003.

[115] The agreement is also less extensive, but this is logical as it only concerns participation in a headquarters.

[116] See generally <http://ue.eu.int/cms3_fo/showPage.asp?id=584&lang=en&mode=g>.

[117] Council Joint Action 2003/681/CFSP of 29 September 2003 [2003] OJ L-249/66. On the EU's involvement in FYROM and CONCORDIA, see above, 2.2.   [118] Ibid, Art 14.

[119] Council Joint Action 2004/789/CFSP of 22 November 2004 [2004] OJ L-348/40.

[120] Briefly mentioned above in n 9.

[121] Joint Actions 2003/681/CFSP and 2004/789/CFSP, above, nn 117 and 119, Art 3.

[122] Arts 9(3) and 8(3)–(7) PROXIMA SOMA, below n 138.

[123] See <http://ue.eu.int/cms3_fo/showPage.asp?id=584&lang=en&mode=g>. This number was not maintained throughout the operation.

and Turkey, Norway, Switzerland, and Ukraine (as explained below) and 140 local staff.[124] The operation was initially led by Commissioner Bart D'Hooge,[125] who was succeeded by Mr Jürgen Paul Scholz.[126] PROXIMA had, in principle, a head-quarters in Skopje, one central co-location unit at the Ministry of Interior level, and other units co-located within FYROM at appropriate levels.[127] The PSC exer-cised, under the responsibility of the Council, the political control and strategic direction of the mission, and was authorized to take the relevant decisions.[128] The PSC could therefore amend the Operation Plan, the chain of command, and the rules of engagement, but the powers of decision with respect to the objectives and termination of the operation remained vested in the Council.[129] The Joint Action extending the mission added that the EUSR for FYROM 'shall provide local political guidance to the Police Head of Mission [and] shall ensure coordination with other EU actors as well as relations with host party authorities and media'.[130] The EUSR also acted as the communication channel between the SG/HR and the Head of Mission.[131]

The mission costs initially foreseen were up to €15.006 million out of the Community budget,[132] while costs related to the police officers seconded by participating states were to be borne by them, except per diems.[133] In January 2004, up to €6.555 million for per diems of €100 per person for 2004 out of the Community budget were added,[134] and the Joint Action extending the mission fixed the financial reference amount covering the expenditure related to the extended mission at €15.95 million.[135]

2.4.1. Mandate

PROXIMA, like CONCORDIA, was undertaken following a request by FYROM[136] and was, at least partly, covered under the EU's role welcomed in UN Security Council Resolution 1371 of 26 September 2001 (as noted above in 2.2).

---

[124] See <http://www.eupol-proxima.org> (last visited 25 September 2005). Ireland was not represented anymore in the later stages of the operation.
[125] Council Decision 2003/682/CFSP of 29 September 2003 [2003] OJ L-249/70.
[126] PSC Decision PROXIMA/2/2004 of 30 November 2004 [2004] OJ L-367/29.
[127] Joint Actions 2003/681/CFSP and 2004/789/CFSP, above, nn 117 and 119, Art 4.
[128] Ibid, Art 8.
[129] Joint Action 2003/681/CFSP, above, n 117, Art 8. Under Joint Action 2004/789/CFSP, above, n 119, the power to appoint the Head of Mission was added (and was exercised by the PSC, see above, n 126) but rules of engagement were dropped. However, since the listing does not appear to have been exhaustive and the latter power was not explicitly reserved for the Council, this may not have made a difference.   [130] Joint Action 2004/789/CFSP, above, n 119, Art 8(2).
[131] Joint Actions 2003/681/CFSP and 2004/789/CFSP, above, nn 117 and 119, Art 7.
[132] Joint Action 2003/681/CFSP, above, n 117, Art 10.
[133] Joint Actions 2003/681/CFSP and 2004/789/CFSP, above, nn 117 and 119, Art 6(2).
[134] Council Joint Action 2004/87/CFSP of 26 January 2004 [2004] OJ L-21/31.
[135] Joint Action 2004/789/CFSP, above, n 119, Art 10.
[136] Joint Action 2003/681/CFSP, above, n 117, 6th consideration preamble. The extension of the operation was also based on such a request: see Joint Action 2004/789/CFSP, above, n 119, 8th consideration preamble.

Consequently, the main legal basis for the operation was the consent of the FYROM Government.

2.4.2. Legal status and applicable law

Article 13 of the PROXIMA Joint Action provided for the conclusion of a SOMA in accordance with Article 24 TEU, although the SG/HR was authorized to negotiate such arrangements on the Presidency's behalf.[137] The SOMA was concluded only four days before the start of the mission.[138]

Pursuant to Article 2 of this SOMA, the mission forces, headquarters, and assets (EUPOL PROXIMA) were to respect the laws and regulations of FYROM, including those regarding the protection of the environment and cultural heritage, and mission staff were to refrain from any activity incompatible with the impartial and international nature of their duties or inconsistent with the SOMA.

The privileges and immunities of EUPOL PROXIMA, and EUPOL PROXIMA personnel, were governed by Articles 5 and 6 respectively. EUPOL PROXIMA was granted the status equivalent to that of a diplomatic mission, with corresponding inviolability and immunity from the criminal, civil, and administrative jurisdiction of FYROM, in accordance with the Vienna Convention on Diplomatic Relations.[139] EUPOL PROXIMA personnel were granted all privileges and immunities of diplomatic agents, and the mission's administrative and technical staff enjoyed a status equivalent to that of administrative and technical staff from Sending States employed in diplomatic missions. However, for the first time in an EU SOMA/SOFA, it was stipulated that the SG/HR 'shall, with the explicit consent of the competent authority of the Sending State, waive the immunity enjoyed by EUPOL Proxima personnel where such immunity would impede the course of justice and it can be waived without prejudice to the interests of the EU'. Local personnel employed by EUPOL PROXIMA who were nationals of, or permanently resident in, the Host Party enjoyed the status enjoyed by locally employed staff in diplomatic missions in FYROM (Article 7).

While FYROM was responsible for the security of EUPOL PROXIMA personnel, EUPOL PROXIMA did have the right to establish, within the Mission, an armed protection element of around thirty police officers to ensure the protection and possible rescue of EUPOL PROXIMA and local personnel, as well as EUMM or OSCE personnel, and this element had the right to use all means necessary, including weapons (see also Article 9(3)), to perform its tasks in accordance with rules determined by the EU, though it did not have an executive policing role (Article 8).

---

[137] Above, n 117, Art 13(1).

[138] [2004] OJ L-16/66. Pursuant to its Art 18(1), this agreement shall enter into force upon written notification of the Parties that the internal requirements have been complied with. However, the EU Council's agreements database (above, n 43) does not mention a FYROM notification.

[139] Vienna, 18 April 1961, 500 *UNTS* 95.

In respect of claims for death, injury, damage, or loss, Article 14 distinguished between two categories of claims. Participating states or the EU were not obliged to reimburse claims arising out of activities in connection with civil disturbances, protection of the EU mission (personnel), or which were incidental to operational necessities. Any other claim of a civil law character, to which the Mission or any member thereof was a party and over which the courts of the Host Party did not have jurisdiction because of the SOMA, was to be submitted to the Head of Mission, and was to be dealt with by separate arrangements establishing procedures for settling claims, after previous consent of the state concerned.

It may be added that a State or Community institution having seconded a staff member was responsible for answering any claims linked to the secondment, from or concerning the staff member, and was also responsible for bringing any action against the secondee.[140]

2.4.3. Participation of third States

Article 9 of the PROXIMA Joint Action[141] provided for the participation of third States, distinguishing between the acceding states which were invited and other states which could be invited, without prejudice to EU decision-making autonomy. It authorized the PSC to take, upon the recommendation of the Head of Mission and the Committee for Civilian Aspects of Crisis Management,[142] the relevant decisions on acceptance of proposed contributions and to take 'appropriate action with regard to participation arrangements'. Furthermore, third participating States were to bear the cost of sending the police officers and/or civilian staff seconded by them and were to contribute to the running costs of PROXIMA 'as appropriate'. Moreover, third participating States had the same rights and obligations in day-today management of the operation as participating EU Member States. Article 9(4) did not require a 'significant' contribution, as was demanded in the previous operations but ignored in practice (as noted above), thus reflecting existing practice.

Detailed arrangements regarding third State participation were to be the subject of an agreement under Article 24 TEU. On 10 February 2004 the PSC accepted the participation of Turkey, Norway, Switzerland, and Ukraine[143] and agreements with these countries were concluded.[144] These agreements are very similar to the ones for the EUPM, although the number of staff to be seconded was not specified and for the common costs only a voluntary contribution was

---

140 Joint Actions 2003/681/CFSP and 2004/789/CFSP, above, nn 117 and 119, Art 13(2).

141 Above, n 117 and Joint Action 2004/789/CFSP, above, n 119, Art 9.

142 Established by Council Decision 2000/354/CFSP of 22 May 2000 [2000] OJ L-127/1.

143 PSC Decision PROXIMA/1/2004 of 10 February 2004 [2004] OJ L-60/54.

144 All published in [2004] OJ L-354 (respectively at 90, 86, 78, and 82). The EU Council's agreements database (above, n 43) suggests that the agreement with Turkey has not yet entered into force and the same is true for that with Ukraine, although the latter was provisionally applied from 8 July 2004.

requested. All personnel remained under the full command of their national authorities, who transferred operational control to the Head of Mission. The clause on claims included a mutual waiver for most claims between participating states, which was not the case in participation agreements for earlier operations.

In addition, nine acceding Member States participated (all but Malta).[145] There seem to have been no agreements with the acceding states so presumably this was not deemed necessary in light of their imminent accession.

2.5. EUJUST THEMIS (Georgia)[146]

After two military and two police operations, the EU launched its first rule of law mission, EUJUST THEMIS in Georgia, in June 2004.[147] The mission could be seen as a conflict prevention effort: according to the preamble of the THEMIS Joint Action, 'The security situation in Georgia is stable but may deteriorate with potentially serious repercussions on regional and international security and the strengthening of democracy and the rule of law. A commitment of EU political effort and resources will help to embed stability in the region'.[148] In any event, this operation clearly intensified the EU's role in this country.[149]

On 16 July the Council approved the Operational Plan for EUJUST THEMIS and launched the mission, which lasted twelve months and was successfully concluded on 14 July 2005.[150] Ms Sylvie Pantz was the Head of Mission of THEMIS,[151] which had a Head Office in Tbilisi and experts co-located at several key positions with the Georgian authorities.[152] Mission experts were seconded by EU Member States or institutions; international and local staff were recruited on a contractual basis, as required,[153] and would number about ten, plus some local staff.[154] As in other missions, the PSC exercised, under the responsibility of the Council, the political control and strategic direction of the mission, and was authorized to take the relevant decisions, including the powers to appoint a Head of Mission and to amend the Operation Plan and the chain of command but excluding the powers of decision with respect to the objectives and termination of

---

[145] See <http://www.eupol-proxima.org> (last visited 25 September 2005).

[146] See generally <http://ue.eu.int/cms3_fo/showPage.asp?id=701&lang=EN>.

[147] Council Joint Action 2004/523/CFSP of 28 June 2004 [2004] OJ L-228/21.

[148] Ibid, 3rd consideration preamble.

[149] On EU relations with Georgia, see <http://europa.eu.int/comm/external_relations/georgia/intro/index.htm> and the EU factsheet of 26 October 2004 at <http://ue.eu.int/uedocs/cmsUpload/Factsheet%20THEMIS%20041026.pdf>, 4–5.

[150] EU factsheet, above, and EU Doc THE/03 (update 3), 22 July 2005, <http://ue.eu.int/uedocs/cmsUpload/050722_Themis_UPDATE_3_final_briefing.pdf>. The mission was followed by an enhanced mandate of the EUSR for the South Caucasus; see Council conclusions of 18 July 2005 EU Doc 10813/05 (Presse 177) and <http://europa.eu.int/comm/external_relations/cfsp/fin/pja_eusr.htm>.

[151] PSC Decision THEMIS/1/2004 of 30 June 2004 [2004] OJ L-239/35.

[152] THEMIS Joint Action, above, n 147, Art 3.   [153] Ibid, Art 6(2)–(3).

[154] See <http://ue.eu.int/cms3_fo/showPage.asp?id=701&lang=en&mode=g>.

the operation.[155] In this mission too, an EUSR functioned at the level between the SG/HR and the Head of Mission.[156] There was no participation of third States, because of the limited size of the mission.[157]

The mission of THEMIS was, in coordination with and complementary to EC and other donors' programmes, to assist in 'the development of a horizontal governmental strategy guiding the reform process for all relevant stakeholders within the criminal justice sector'. It was also to 'help develop an overall policy and improve top-level planning and performance capabilities in the areas identified as requiring urgent assistance'.[158]

The financial reference amount intended to cover the expenditure related to the mission was initially set at €2.05 million.[159] It was later raised to €2,307,873.[160] Member States—apparently in contrast to institutions—bore the costs related to the mission experts seconded by it, except per diem allowances.[161]

2.5.1. Mandate

THEMIS was undertaken at the request of the Georgian authorities,[162] which formed the legal basis for this mission.

2.5.2. Legal status and applicable law

Pursuant to Article 7 of the THEMIS Joint Action,[163] a SOMA was concluded on 3 December 2004, ie, more than four months after the start of the mission.[164] It is not clear whether this SOMA entered into force.[165]

Article 2 of the SOMA demanded that the mission and mission personnel respect the laws and regulations of Georgia, and obliged mission staff to refrain from any activity incompatible with the impartial and international nature of their duties or inconsistent with the SOMA. Moreover, under the THEMIS Joint Action, 'both during and after the mission, the mission experts shall exercise the greatest discretion with regard to all facts and information relating to the mission'.[166]

The privileges and immunities of THEMIS and THEMIS personnel were governed by, respectively, Articles 5 and 6 THEMIS SOMA and seem identical to those of EUPOL PROXIMA.[167] THEMIS personnel are granted all privileges and immunities of diplomatic agents and the clause on waiver of immunity[168] is, mutatis mutandis, identical to that in the PROXIMA SOMA.[169] Apparently,

---

155 THEMIS Joint Action, above, n 147, Art 9.   156 Above, n 147, Art 8.
157 Ibid, 6th consideration preamble.   158 Ibid, Art 2.   159 Ibid, Art 10.
160 Council Joint Action 2004/638/CFSP of 13 September 2004 [2004] OJ L-291/17.
161 THEMIS Joint Action, above, n 147, Art 6(2).   162 Ibid, 4th consideration preamble.
163 Ibid.   164 [2004] OJ L-389/42.
165 The Council's agreements database (above, n 43) does not give a date of entry into force nor does it mention a provisional application.   166 THEMIS Joint Action, above, n 147, Art 4(3).
167 See the PROXIMA SOMA, above, n 138, discussed above, in 2.4.
168 Art 6(2) THEMIS SOMA.
169 Compare with Art 6(3) PROXIMA SOMA (above, n 138).

there was some discussion over the extent of staff immunities, since delegations noted in the Council that the provisions of the draft Agreement were without prejudice to provisions that might be agreed for future missions and that, in particular, 'the extent of the privileges and immunities foreseen for staff of the Mission [did] not constitute a precedent'.[170] Since the only difference with PROXIMA is the broader immunity of administrative and technical staff,[171] this is probably what was being referred to.

In respect of claims for death, injury, damage, or loss, Article 13 distinguishes between two categories of claims, similarly to the PROXIMA SOMA. It may be added that a state or Community institution having seconded a staff member shall be responsible for answering any claims linked to the secondment, from or concerning the staff member, and shall be responsible for bringing any action against the secondee.[172]

Finally, on 10 July, the Government of Georgia adopted a decree on cooperation between EUJUST THEMIS and all the major stakeholders in Georgia.[173]

2.6. ALTHEA (BiH)[174]

In taking over the military presence in BiH from the NATO-led Stabilization Force (SFOR)[175] on 2 December 2004 by operation ALTHEA, the EU was undertaking its biggest and most challenging mission so far and further enhancing its role in BiH, where the EU was already very active and already ran the EUPM (as explained above in 2.1).

ALTHEA had been prepared for quite some time and the Council had already adopted a Joint Action on this operation in July 2004, appointing the Operation Commander, D-SACEUR,[176] and the EU Force Commander (General A David Leakey), and designating the EU Operational Headquarters as being located at SHAPE.[177] The Head of the EU Command Element at Naples, General Ciro Cocozza, was appointed in October 2004,[178] and the Operation Plan was adopted that same month.[179] The decision on the launching of ALTHEA was taken on 27 November 2004 and the operation commenced

---

[170] EU Doc 10651/04, 18 June 2004, para 3.

[171] Compare Art 6 THEMIS SOMA with Art 6 PROXIMA SOMA (above, n 138).

[172] THEMIS Joint Action, above, n 147, Art 7(2).

[173] EU factsheet on THEMIS, above, n 149.

[174] See generally <http://ue.eu.int/cms3_fo/showPage.asp?id=745&lang=en&mode=g> and <http://www.euforbih.org>.

[175] On SFOR, see <http://www.nato.int/issues/sfor/index.html>.

[176] Consequently, following appointment of a new D-SACEUR, the Operation Commander was also replaced: see PSC Decision BiH/2/2004 of 24 September 2004 [2004] OJ L-324/22.

[177] Council Joint Action 2004/570/CFSP of 12 July 2004, [2004] OJ L-252/10, especially Arts 2–4. General Gian Marco Chiarini was later appointed the new Force Commander as of 5 December 2005; see PSC Decision BiH/6/2005 of 14 June 2005 [2005] OJ L-173/14.

[178] PSC Decision BiH/4/2004 of 19 October 2004 [2004] OJ L-357/38.

[179] Council conclusions of 11 October 2004.

on 2 December 2004.[180] No date was fixed for the end of this operation.[181] ALTHEA is a mission with recourse to NATO assets and is governed by the EU-NATO arrangements mentioned above (2.2), but the entire chain of command of the EU Force remains under the political control and strategic direction of the EU, after consultation with NATO, and NATO is only informed by the PSC and by the Chairman of the EUMC (CEUMC).[182] Initially, 7,000 troops have been deployed[183] from more than 30 countries.[184] The Force headquarters are established in Sarajevo.[185] Twenty-two Member States participate in ALTHEA (all but Denmark,[186] Cyprus, and Malta[187]), as do 11 third States (see details below).[188] The force will include an Integrated Police Unit (IPU) style capability with executive powers.[189]

ALTHEA's mission is two-fold: first, to provide deterrence and continued compliance with Annexes 1A and 2 of the Dayton Agreement, and, second, to contribute to a safe and secure environment in BiH.[190]

As in previous operations, the PSC, under the responsibility of the Council, exercises the political control and strategic direction of the EU military operation and is authorized to take the relevant decisions, which include amending the Operation Plan, the chain of command, and the rules of engagement and decisions on the appointment of the EU Operation and Force Commander, while the powers of decision with respect to the objectives and termination of the EU military operation remain vested in the Council.[191] The EUMC monitors the proper execution of the operation, conducted under the responsibility of the EU Operation Commander, with the Chairman of the EUMC acting as point of contact for the Operation Commander.[192] A six-monthly review is envisaged.[193]

A number of measures have been adopted to ensure coherence of ALTHEA with other EU actions in BiH, with a key role for the EUSR.[194]

As to financing, the common costs are administered by Athena, ie, the financing mechanism set up to administer common costs of ESDP operations,[195] and the financial reference amount for the common costs is set at €71.7 million.[196]

---

[180] Council Decision 2004/803/CFSP of 25 November 2004 [2004] OJ L-353/21.

[181] The operation shall end on a date to be decided by the Council: see ALTHEA Joint Action, above, n 177, Art 17(2). See also Council Decision 2004/803/CFSP, above, previous note, Art 3.

[182] ALTHEA Joint Action, above, n 177, Arts 1(3) and 13(1).

[183] See the Council factsheet of 29 November 2004 at <http://ue.eu.int/uedocs/cmsUpload/041129%20Althea%20update%203.pdf>.   [184] EU Doc S0337/04, 2 December 2004.

[185] See the Council factsheet on ALTHEA, above, n 183.

[186] ALTHEA Joint Action, above, n 177, 19th consideration preamble.

[187] Cyprus and Malta do not have a security agreement with NATO and cannot participate in EU operations with recourse to NATO assets, such as ALTHEA.

[188] See <http://www.euforbih.org/organisation/organisation.htm>.

[189] See the Council factsheet on ALTHEA, above, n 183. An Integrated Police Unit is a multinational force composed mainly of police forces, but includes military components (see <http://www.euforbih.org/forum/special/html/t241a.htm>).

[190] ALTHEA Joint Action, above, n 177, Art 1(1).   [191] Ibid, Art 6.   [192] Ibid, Art 8.

[193] Ibid, Art 16.   [194] Ibid, Art 7.   [195] See the Council Decisions cited above, n 13.

[196] ALTHEA Joint Action, above, n 177, Art 12.

2.6.1. Mandate

The EU's intention to take over from SFOR was welcomed in UN Security Council Resolution 1551 of 9 July 2004 (para 10). However, the legal situation is somewhat complicated since SFOR, although mandated by the UN Security Council, also worked on the basis of the Dayton Agreements, which specifically envisaged a NATO-led force.[197] This was solved by the Security Council, which, in para 10 of its Resolution 1575 of 22 November 2004, authorized:

> ... the Member States acting through or in cooperation with the EU to establish for an initial planned period of 12 months a multinational stabilization force (EUFOR) as a legal successor to SFOR under unified command and control, which will fulfil its missions in relation to the implementation of Annex 1-A and Annex 2 of the Peace Agreement in cooperation with the NATO HQ presence in accordance with the arrangements agreed between NATO and the EU as communicated to the Security Council in their letters of 19 November 2004, which recognize that the EUFOR will have the main peace stabilization role under the military aspects of the Peace Agreement.

However, the Security Council did acknowledge the support of the Bosnian authorities for this solution and their confirmation that both the EU force and the remaining NATO presence are the legal successors to SFOR (para 7). Consequently, the combination of the Dayton Agreement and Resolution 1575 constitutes the legal basis for ALTHEA.

The Resolution also authorizes the new NATO presence (para 11). Furthermore, it states that references in the Dayton Agreement and relevant Resolutions to IFOR (Implementation Force, SFOR's predecessor) and/or SFOR, NATO and the North Atlantic Council (NAC, NATO's main political decision-making body) shall henceforth be read as applying, as appropriate, to the NATO presence, EUFOR, the EU and the PSC, and the Council of the EU (para 12; see also below), and accords both missions the necessary powers under the Dayton Agreements and the relevant Security Council Resolutions (paras 14–16). It also expresses the intention to consider the terms of further authorization as necessary in the light of developments in the implementation of the Dayton Agreement and the situation in BiH (para 13).

2.6.2. Legal status and applicable law

Regarding the SOFA, a similar problem arose as with the mandate because the SFOR SOFA was included in the Dayton Agreement and only applied to a NATO-led force.[198] Here too, the two Security Council Resolutions already

---

[197] See above, n 36, Annex 1-A, Art 1. Whilst Art 1(a) seems sufficiently general to cover an EU force ('Member States or regional organizations and arrangements'), the remainder of Art 1 frequently refers to NATO.   [198] Ibid, Appendix B to Annex 1A, especially para 1.

cited provided a solution. First, pursuant to para 20 of Resolution 1551, the status of forces agreements currently contained in the Dayton Agreement applied provisionally in respect to the (then) proposed EU mission and its forces, including from the point of their build-up in BiH, in anticipation of the concurrence of the parties to those agreements to that effect. Secondly, according to *para* 12 of Resolution 1575 all references to NATO and/or the NATO operation in the Dayton Agreement, 'in particular in Annex 1-A and its appendices'—which include the SFOR SOFA—shall henceforth be read as applying, as appropriate, to NATO and/or the NATO presence and to the EU and/or EU mission. The SFOR SOFA is thereby made applicable to ALTHEA.

It may suffice to mention the key elements of the SOFA, replacing 'NATO' by 'EU'. The SOFA makes applicable, mutatis mutandis, the provisions of the Convention on the Privileges and Immunities of the United Nations[199] to the EU, and those provisions concerning experts on mission to EU personnel involved in the operation, except as otherwise provided for in the SOFA (para 2). As experts on mission, EU personnel are immune from personal arrest or detention (para 8) and EU military personnel are subject to the exclusive jurisdiction of their national elements in respect of any offences committed by them in BiH (para 7). All mission personnel must respect the laws of BiH 'insofar as it is compatible with the entrusted tasks/mandate' and shall refrain from activities not compatible with the nature of the operation (para 3). EU personnel may possess and carry arms if authorized to do so by their orders (para 4). Local personnel hired also enjoy some privileges and immunities (para 16). The SOFA also applies to the civilian and military personnel, property, and assets of national elements/units of EU States, acting in connection with the operation or the relief for the civilian population (para 19), and BiH shall accord non-EU States and their personnel participating in the operation the same privileges and immunities as those accorded under this agreement to EU States and personnel (para 21). Claims for damage or injury to government personnel or property, or to private personnel or the property of BiH, shall be submitted through Bosnian governmental authorities to the designated NATO Representatives (para 15). Finally, supplemental arrangements may be concluded (para 20).

2.6.3. *Participation of third States*

The non-EU European NATO Members and Canada are allowed to participate if they so wish and candidate Member States, potential partners, and other third States may also be invited to participate in the operation, obviously without prejudice to the decision-making autonomy of the EU.[200] Third States making

---

[199] 13 February 1946, 1 *UNTS* 15.   [200] ALTHEA Joint Action, above, n 177, Art 11(1).

'significant military contributions' have the same rights and obligations in day-to-day management of the operation as participating EU Member States.[201] The PSC is authorized to take the relevant decisions on acceptance of proposed contributions, upon the recommendation of the Operation Commander and the EUMC, and to set up a Committee of Contributors.[202] As in previous missions, detailed arrangements regarding third State participation are to be the subject of an agreement under Article 24 TEU, but where the EU and a third State have concluded an agreement establishing a framework for the participation of this state in the EU operations, such an agreement shall apply.[203] This presumably applies to Bulgaria,[204] Romania,[205] and Norway.[206]

On 21 September 2004 the PSC accepted contributions from Argentina, Bulgaria, Canada, Chile, Morocco, New Zealand, Norway, Romania, Switzerland, and Turkey[207] and on 3 November 2004 also from Albania.[208] A Committee of Contributors was set up on 29 September 2004.[209] So far, agreements have been concluded with Switzerland,[210] Morocco,[211] Albania,[212] New Zealand,[213] Chile,[214] and Argentina,[215] apparently on the basis of a mission-specific model participation agreement.[216] At first sight, these agreements do not differ substantially from participation agreements in previous missions, but they require no contribution to the common costs from the participating state, and they provide for the transfer of operational and tactical command and/or control to the EU Operation Commander, who is entitled to delegate his authority.

2.7. EUPOL KINSHASA[217]

The EU Police Mission to Kinshasa (DRC) has its antecedents in the DRC peace and transition agreement of 17 December 2002, and especially the Memorandum

---

[201] ALTHEA Joint Action, above, n 177, Art 11(1).
[202] Ibid, Art 11(2) and (5).   [203] Ibid, Art 11(3).
[204] [2005] OJ L-46/50, provisionally applied as from 24 January 2005.
[205] [2005] OJ L-67/14, entered into force 1 December 2004.
[206] [2005] OJ L-67/8, entered into force 1 January 2005.
[207] PSC Decision BiH/1/2004 of 21 September 2004 [2004] OJ L-324/20.
[208] PSC Decision BiH/5/2004 of 3 November 2004 [2004] OJ L-357/39.
[209] PSC Decision BiH/3/2004 of 29 September 2004 [2004] OJ L-325/64.
[210] [2005] OJ L-20/42, entered into force 1 February 2005, provisionally applied from 22 December 2004.
[211] [2005] OJ L-34/47, not yet entered into force but provisionally applied from 1 February 2005.
[212] [2005] OJ L-65/35, entered into force 1 August 2005, provisionally applied from 7 March 2005.
[213] [2005] OJ L-127/28, not yet entered into force, provisionally applied from 4 May 2005.
[214] 25 July 2005, [2005] OJ L-202/40, not yet entered into force.
[215] [2005] OJ L-156/22, entered into force 9 June 2005.
[216] EU Doc 12382/04, 14 September 2004, listed but not published in the Council's register.
[217] See generally <http://ue.eu.int/cms3_fo/showPage.asp?id=788&lang=en&mode=g>.

on Security and the Army of 29 June 2003, which provided for the establishment of an Integrated Police Unit (IPU).[218] Following a DRC Government request for EU assistance in October 2003, the PSC agreed in December 2003 that the EU should support the establishment of the IPU.[219] EUPOL KINSHASA is the third EU initiative in support of the IPU, following a Commission initiative under the European Development Fund and an earlier Council Joint Action assisting the establishment of the IPU by contributions with funds and/or in kind to provide the government of the DRC with the law enforcement equipment, arms, and ammunition necessary for the establishment of the IPU.[220]

The mission was prepared by a Planning Team[221] and was launched on 30 April 2005.[222] It was only intended to be active until the end of 2005[223] but was extended for a further year.[224] It has about thirty staff[225] under the command of the Head of Mission (Police Commissioner Adilio Custodio)[226] and should cost no more than €4.37 million.[227] The mission's objective is to 'monitor, mentor, and advise the setting up and the initial running of the IPU in order to ensure that the IPU acts following the training received in the Academy Centre and according to international best practices in this field' and shall be focused on the IPU chain of command.[228] As usual, the PSC exercises political control and strategic direction of the mission.[229]

As noted above, this EU operation is based on the consent of the DRC Government. Article 13 of the EUPOL KINSHASA Joint Action[230] provided for the conclusion of a SOMA. A SOMA was concluded but only on 1 September

---

[218] On the role of the IPU, see H Boshoff, *Summary Overview of the Security Sector Reform Process in the DRC. ISS Situation Report*, 6 January 2005 <http://www.iss.co.za/af/current/2005/050110DRC.pdf>, 11–13.

[219] See the preamble of Council Joint Action 2004/847/CFSP of 9 December 2004 [2004] OJ L-367/30. The EU's involvement in the DRC is discussed above, in 2.3.

[220] Council Joint Action 2004/494/CFSP of 17 May 2004 [2004] OJ L-182/41.

[221] Joint Action 2004/847/CFSP, above, n 219, Art 1.

[222] See EU Doc S173/05 of that date: <http://ue.eu.int/uedocs/cmsUpload/050430_Visite_Afrique.en.pdf>.

[223] See Art 14 Joint Action 2004/847/CFSP, above, n 219 (expires 31 December 2005).

[224] See Council Joint Action 2005/847/CFSP of 21 November 2005, [2005] OJ L-305/44, 3rd consideration preamble *juncto* Art 1(6).

[225] On 31 August 2005, only six Member States had staff contracted or seconded to the mission: Belgium, France, Italy, the Netherlands, Portugal, and Sweden; see COSAC Secretariat, above, n 5, 15.

[226] See EU Documents 15855/04 (Presse 349), 9 December 2004 (<http://ue.eu.int/ueDocs/cms_Data/docs/pressData/en/misc/83090.pdf>) and RDC/00 (initial), 23 May 2005 (<http://ue.eu.int/uedocs/cmsUpload/Background-23.5.05.en.pdf>). This appointment was extended by PSC Decision EUPOL KINSHASA/2/2005 of 22 November 2005 [2005] OJ L-335/57.

[227] Joint Action 2004/847/CFSP, above, n 219, Art 10.

[228] Ibid, Art 3. This was slightly broadened by Art 1(2) Council Joint Action 2005/847/CFSP, above, n 223 to include 'further advice on other issues complementary to the effective conduct of policing in DRC, and shall enhance liaison with EUSEC RD CONGO in the field of security sector reform'. [229] Joint Action 2004/847/CFSP, above, n 219, Arts 7 and 8.

[230] Ibid.

2005. It, inter alia, grants the mission and its staff protection equivalent to that of diplomatic missions and staff, including the possibility of waiver, demands respect for local law, allows the carrying of side-arms for self-defence, and contains a claims provision.[231] The participation of third States is provided for in article 9 EUPOL KINSHASA Joint Action,[232] but it does not appear as if any third State does in fact participate.

2.8. EUSEC DRC[233]

The EU's involvement in the DRC, discussed above (2.3 and 2.7), was further extended by the launching of yet another new type of mission, namely a security sector reform mission (EUSEC DRC), in response to a DRC Government request in April 2005.[234] This operation was launched on 8 June 2005, is to cover a period of twelve months but was subsequently extended until 30 June 2007,[235] is led by General Pierre Joana, comprises eight experts seconded by the Member States and by the EU institutions, and has an estimated cost of €1.6 million.[236] The mission aims:

... to provide advice and assistance for security sector reform in the [DRC] with the aim of contributing to a successful integration of the army in the DRC [...], while taking care to promote policies compatible with human rights and international humanitarian law, democratic standards and the principles of good governance, transparency and respect for the rule of law.[237]

As usual, the PSC exercises political control and strategic direction of the mission.[238] The mission is formally a civilian one, but is in reality rather a mixed civilian-military operation.

---

[231] [2005] OJ L-256/58, entered into force 1 September 2005.   [232] Above, n 219.

[233] See generally <http://ue.eu.int/cms3_fo/showPage.asp?id=909&lang=en>.

[234] Council Joint Action 2005/355/CFSP of 2 May 2005, [2005] OJ L-112/20, especially 8th consideration preamble, later amended by Council Joint Action 2005/868/CFSP of 1 December 2005 [2005] OJ L-318/29.

[235] Council Joint Action 2005/355/CFSP, above, previous note, Art 15. For its extension with a somewhat amended structure and additional expenditure of €4.75 million, see Council Joint Action of 25 April 2006 amending and extending Joint Action 2005/355/CFSP on the European Union mission to provide advice and assistance for security sector reform in the Democratic Republic of the Congo (DRC) (2006/303/CFSP) [2006] OJ L-112/18, as corrected by the Corrigendum to Council Joint Action 2005/355/CFSP of 2 May 2005 on the European Union mission to provide advice and assistance for security sector reform in the Democratic Republic of the Congo (DRC) (OJ L-112, 3 May 2005) [2006] OJ L-169/60.

[236] See EU Doc RDC/00 (initial), above, n 226. The size of the mission dictates that only some Member States will participate in it.

[237] EUSEC Joint Action (above, n 234), Art 1. See also ibid, Art 2.

[238] Ibid, Arts 7 and 8.

As noted above, the mission is based on the consent of the DRC Government. The SOMA for this mission should be the same as that for EUPOL KINSHASA,[239] and there was initially no participation of third States in EUSEC DRC.[240]

2.9. EUJUST LEX[241]

As part of the EU's support for post-Saddam Iraq,[242] the EU decided late in 2004 to set up an expert team to consider an integrated rule of law mission[243] and early in 2005 indeed decided to establish such a mission.[244] The aim of EUJUST LEX is to address the urgent needs in the Iraqi criminal justice system through providing training for some 770 senior and high potential officials, primarily from the police, judiciary, and prison service[245] in senior management, and in skills and procedures in criminal investigation, in full respect for the rule of law and human rights, in order to improve the capacity, coordination, and collaboration of the different components of the Iraqi criminal justice system.[246]

EUJUST LEX comprises a planning phase which was to begin no later than 9 March 2005 and an operational phase beginning no later than 1 July 2005 and lasting one year.[247] A particular feature of this operation is that it takes place mostly outside Iraq: the training activities take place in the EU (with a coordinating office in Brussels employing 16 staff) or in the region, and there is only a liaison office in Baghdad (5 staff), although, depending on developments in Iraq, the Council shall examine the possibility of training within Iraq and, if necessary, shall amend the Joint Action accordingly.[248] Mr Stephen White was appointed Head of Mission[249] and the financial reference amount from the EU budget is €10 million, with Member States contributing training courses and trainers

[239] Ibid, 11th consideration preamble: 'The status of the mission will be subject to consultation with the DRC government with a view to ensuring that the [SOMA] relating to EUPOL Kinshasa is applicable to the mission and its staff'.

[240] However, Art 1(3) of Council Joint Action 2005/868/CFSP (above, n 234) inserted an amendment allowing for the participation of third States in the chain of payments project set up by this Joint Action.

[241] See generally <http://ue.eu.int/cms3_fo/showPage.asp?id=823&lang=en>.

[242] For the EU's role in Iraq, see generally 'EU support for Iraq', factsheet, June 2005, <http://ue.eu.int/uedocs/cmsUpload/Factsheet-Iraq-June2005.pdf>. As EU Member States were divided on the legality and opportunity of the 2003 war against Iraq, the EU played hardly any role before and during this war. Even in the aftermath, its role has remained limited.

[243] Council Joint Action 2004/909/CFSP of 26 November 2004 [2004] OJ L-381/84.

[244] Council Joint Action 2005/190/CFSP of 7 March 2005 [2005] OJ L-62/37.

[245] See the fact sheet above, n 242.   [246] EUJUST LEX Joint Action, above, n 244, Art 2.

[247] Ibid, Arts 1 and 14. The Council welcomed the first training sessions in its 18 July 2005 conclusions.

[248] EUJUST LEX Joint Action, above, n 244, Arts 2 and 3. At the time of writing, no such amendment had been adopted.

[249] PSC Decision EUJUST LEX/1/2005 of 8 March 2005 [2005] OJ L-72/29.

as well as some additional financial support.[250] The PSC exercises the political control and strategic direction of the mission.[251]

The mission was undertaken with the consent of the Iraqi Government.[252] As to the SOMA, the situation is not very clear. Article 7(1) of the EUJUST LEX Joint Action states that '[w]here required, the status of EUJUST LEX staff, including where appropriate the privileges, immunities and further guarantees necessary for the completion and smooth functioning of EUJUST LEX shall be agreed in accordance with...Article 24 [TEU]'.[253] However, to the author's knowledge, at the time of writing no such agreements have been concluded. Given that the training will take place in different countries, both EU Member States and third States, and that it may be necessary to also regulate the status of Iraqi trainees and not just the trainers, any SOMAs concluded are likely to contain peculiar features. Furthermore, the EUJUST LEX Joint Action devotes considerable attention to the security of the mission and its staff, eg, 'Member States shall endeavour to provide EUJUST LEX, in particular the Liaison Office, secure accommodation, body armour and close protection within Iraq'.[254] Participation of third States is not provided for, although training in the region will obviously require the cooperation of some third States.

2.10. EU Support AMIS II[255]

The EU support for the peace process in Sudan[256] has so far culminated in a mission in support of the AU mission to Sudan (AMIS II),[257] at the request of the AU,[258] which has taken the lead in attempting to bring security to the population of the Darfur region in Sudan, where international crimes against the population have been committed in recent years.[259] One of the peculiar elements of this mission is its mixed civil-military nature: it consists of a civilian (police) and a military component, with different tasks and financing arrangements.[260] The PSC exercises political control and strategic direction and is advised by both the Committee for Civilian Aspects of Crisis Management and the EUMC (assisted

---

[250] EUJUST LEX Joint Action, above, n 244, Art 11, and the factsheet above, n 242.

[251] EUJUST LEX Joint Action, above, n 244, Arts 8(2) and 9.

[252] See ibid, 2nd and 5th considerations preamble and EU Doc S211/05, 9 June 2005 <http://ue.eu.int/ueDocs/cms_Data/docs/pressData/en/declarations/85157.pdf>.

[253] Above, n 244.   [254] Ibid, Art 10, especially Art 10(8).

[255] See generally <http://ue.eu.int/cms3_fo/showPage.asp?id=956&lang=en>.

[256] For other EU actions, see the preamble of the Joint Action below, next note. See also Council Joint Action 2005/556/CFSP of 18 July 2005 [2005] OJ L-188/43.

[257] Council Joint Action 2005/557/CFSP of 18 July 2005 [2005] OJ L-188/46.

[258] Ibid, 11th consideration preamble.

[259] The Darfur situation has been referred to the International Criminal Court by the UN Security Council; see <http://www.iccpi.int/cases/current_situations/Darfur_Sudan.html>.

[260] Ibid, respectively Sections II and III. See also Council Decision 2005/806/CFSP of 21 November 2005 [2005] OJ L-303/60.

by the EU Military Staff (EUMS)), in the field of their respective competences.[261] The EUSR for Sudan, Mr Pekka Haavisto, is assisted by a police advisor,[262] who is the Head of the police team, and by a military advisor,[263] who shall 'help to ensure coherence of the military component of the EU supporting action'.[264] The duration of the mission is not yet determined.[265] The support is varied and includes assistance in the field of training, planning, and transport.[266] The mission reportedly comprises 30 military personnel and up to 50 police officers (but currently only 25).[267]

2.10.1. Mandate

As already mentioned, the mandate is based on an AU request for assistance to the AU mission, which in turn is based on a UN Security Council mandate adopted on the basis of a ceasefire/peace agreement and a Sudanese request.[268] Moreover, EU support to AMIS I was welcomed by the UN Security Council in its Resolution 1556 of 30 July 2004 (para 3).

2.10.2. Legal status and applicable law

Pursuant to Article 12 of the AMIS II Joint Action,[269] the SG/HR was to secure legally binding assurances from the African States on the territory of which EU supporting action personnel are or will be deployed that their status is governed by the Status of Mission Agreement (SOMA) on the Establishment and Management of the Ceasefire Commission in the Darfur area of Sudan (CFC),[270] and by the General Convention on the Privileges and Immunities of the Organization for African Unity.[271] These assurances appear to have been obtained, as the fifteenth consideration of the preamble of this Joint Action states that:

The exchange of letters between the SG/HR and the President of the [AU] Commission confirming the arrangements for the EU supporting action to AMIS II also confirms that

---

[261] AMIS Joint Action, above, n 257, Art 4.

[262] Mr Douglas Brand, appointed by PSC Decision DARFUR/2/2005 of 29 July 2005 [2005] OJ L-241/58.

[263] Mr Philippe Mendez, appointed by PSC Decision DARFUR/1/2005 of 29 July 2005 [2005] OJ L-241/57.   [264] AMIS Joint Action, above, n 257, respectively Arts 7 and 10.

[265] Ibid, Art 16(2).

[266] Ibid, respectively Arts 6 and 9 and EU Doc. AMIS II/01, July 2005 <http://ue.eu.int/uedocs/cmsUpload/AMIS_II_July.pdf>.

[267] COSAC Secretariat, above, n 5, 11.

[268] See Resolutions 1547 (11 June 2004), 1556 (30 July 2004), 1564 (18 September 2004, especially para 3), 1574 (19 November 2004), and 1590 (24 March 2005).   [269] Above, n 257.

[270] Concluded between the AU and the Government of Sudan on 4 June 2004 and available at <http://www.africa-union.org/DARFUR/Agreements/soma.pdf>.

[271] Accra, 25 October 1965, available at <http://www.africa-union.org/Official_documents/Treaties_%20Conventions_%20Protocols/offTreaties_Conventions_&_Protocols.htm>. It would seem that this convention is applicable to the AU.

all EU personnel already deployed or to be deployed in Sudan and other African States in the context of the EU supporting action are covered, as far as their status is concerned, by the agreement between the AU and Sudan on the status of the AU mission.

As with ALTHEA and ARTEMIS, this is a SOMA construction of a particular nature. Moreover, in addition to privileges and immunities, the AU SOMA contains some peculiar elements, such as respect for international humanitarian law (the significance thereof is discussed below).[272]

2.10.3. Participation of third States

The AMIS II Joint Action does not mention the participation of third States but does refer to the need for coordination with the UN and NATO, in addition to the AU.[273]

2.11. EU AMM[274]

The EU, together with countries from the Association of Southeast Asian Nations (ASEAN), and Norway and Switzerland, has deployed a monitoring mission in Aceh (Indonesia) to monitor the implementation of various aspects of the peace agreement set out in the Memorandum of Understanding (MoU) between the Government of Indonesia and the Free Aceh Movement of 15 August 2005,[275] which will, it is hoped, bring an end to a lengthy conflict in this Indonesian province.[276]

The AMM, led by Mr Pieter Feith,[277] became operational on 15 September 2005, the date on which the decommissioning of the Free Aceh Movement (GAM) armaments and the relocation of non-organic military and policy forces began,[278] although an initial monitoring presence (IMP) of 80 staff was already deployed on 15 August 2005.[279] The mission is estimated to cost €15 million, including €9 million out of the EU budget, and was scheduled to end in March 2006 but was repeatedly extended, most recently until 15 December 2006.[280]

---

[272] Above, n 270, Title IV, paras 8–9.

[273] Above, n 257, Art 3. On NATO's assistance to AMIS, see <http://www.nato.int/issues/darfur/index.html>.

[274] See generally <http://www.aceh-mm.org> and <http://ue.eu.int/cms3_fo/showPage.asp?id=957&lang=en>.

[275] Text at <http://ue.eu.int/uedocs/cmsUpload/MoU_Aceh.pdf>.

[276] Council Joint Action 2005/643/CFSP of 9 September 2005 [2005] OJ L-234/13.

[277] Ibid, Art 5(1).

[278] In the MoU (above, n 275), 'organic' police/military forces seems to refer to officially recognized and constituted police/military forces.

[279] EU Doc ACH/02, 15 September 2005, <http://ue.eu.int/uedocs/cmsUpload/AcehCouncil%20FactsheetREV2bis.pdf>.

[280] Ibid and Arts 12(1) and 16 AMM Joint Action, above, n 276. For the extensions, see Council Joint Action of 27 February 2006 amending and extending Joint Action 2005/643/CFSP on the European Union Monitoring Mission in Aceh (Indonesia) (Aceh Monitoring Mission—AMM) (2006/202/CFSP) [2006] OJ L-71/57; Council Joint Action of 7 June 2006 amending and extending

In order to monitor the implementation of the commitments under the MoU, the AMM's tasks include, inter alia, monitoring the GAM demobilization and decommissioning, the re-location of non-organic military forces and non-organic police troops, the reintegration of active GAM members, and the process of legislation change, as well as monitoring the human rights situation and providing assistance in this field in the context of the other tasks, ruling on disputed amnesty cases, and investigating and ruling on complaints and alleged violations of the MoU.[281]

The mission consists of 226 international unarmed personnel (130 from EU Member States, Norway, and Switzerland, and 96 from the participating ASEAN countries), spread over the Headquarters in Banda Aceh, 11 geographically distributed District Offices conducting monitoring tasks and 4 Decommissioning Teams.[282] The PSC exercises political control of, and provides strategic direction to, the mission.[283] The mission is formally a civilian one, but is in reality rather a mixed civilian-military operation.

2.11.1. *Mandate, legal status, and applicable law*

The mission is based on the MoU[284] and therefore on the consent of the Indonesian Government[285] and GAM. Both the MoU and the AMM Joint Action[286] provided for the conclusion of a SOMA, which was signed on 14 September and 3 October 2005 and provisionally applied from 15 September 2005.[287] It is not clear under what status the IMP operated.

2.11.2. *Participation of third States*

Pursuant to Article 10 of the AMM Joint Action,[288] acceding states were to be invited and third States could be invited to participate in the AMM, and all third States making contributions (whether significant or not) to the AMM have the same rights and obligations in terms of day-to-day management of the mission as participating EU Member States. Only Norway and Switzerland participate.[289] In addition, this operation is conducted under EU leadership but jointly with the

---

Joint Action 2005/643/CFSP on the European Union Monitoring Mission in Aceh (Indonesia) (Aceh Monitoring Mission—AMM) (2006/407/CFSP) [2006] OJ L-158/20 and Council Joint Action of 7 September 2006 amending and extending Joint Action 2005/643/CFSP on the European Union Monitoring Mission in Aceh (Indonesia) (Aceh Monitoring Mission—AMM) (2006/607/CFSP) [2006] OJ L-246/16.

[281] AMM Joint Action, above, n 276, Art 2.

[282] Ibid, Art 4 and EU Doc ACH/02, above, n 279.

[283] AMM Joint Action, above, n 276, Arts 8 and 9.   [284] Above, n 275, title V.

[285] See also AMM Joint Action, above, n 276, 3rd consideration preamble.

[286] Respectively in para 5(3) and Art 7.

[287] Text in [2005] OJ L-288/60. The Agreement entered into force on 3 October 2005. The agreement was repeatedly extended along with the mandate (see above).

[288] AMM Joint Action, above, n 276.

[289] EU Doc ACH/02, above, n 279. For the agreement with Switzerland, see [2005] OJ L-349/31.

ASEAN Member States Brunei, Malaysia, the Philippines, Singapore, and Thailand. Agreements with the ASEAN participating states have been or will be adopted in the form of exchanges of letters.[290] There is one deputy Head of Mission from an ASEAN country.[291] Finally, the PSC set up a Committee of Contributors in November 2005.[292]

3. Some General Remarks and Conclusions

First, the survey above clearly shows that the ESDP works and is developing rapidly. Moreover, in this process, the EU is gradually developing doctrines and model documents/agreements, some of which are relevant to legal issues. In this respect, it is commendable that many EU documents relating to ESDP operations are in the public domain. Nevertheless, some interesting documents are not in the public domain and some issues therefore cannot be addressed in as much detail as they deserve.

3.1. The scope of ESDP operations

First, the operations the EU undertook in the first three years after the launch of its first operation illustrate quite well the broad variety of possible ESDP tasks and the advantage this choice of instruments offers. Some of the more recent operations in particular, such as the EUJUST THEMIS (which, moreover, may be regarded as a conflict prevention mission), EUSEC DRC, EUJUST LEX, the AMM, the AMIS II Supporting Mission, EUPAT, and the Border Assistance Mission EU BAM Rafah, reflect the flexibility of these instruments. Moreover, in most cases both military and civilian operations have been or are being conducted in the same country, although the relationship in time varies: in BiH the EUPM is now accompanied by ALTHEA; in the DRC, ARTEMIS was, after a time gap, followed by EUPOL KINSHASA, EUSEC DRC, and EUFOR DR Congo; and in FYROM CONCORDIA was immediately succeeded by PROXIMA, which was in turn followed by EUPAT. In fact, the AMIS II Supporting mission was a mixed mission from the start, albeit with two quite distinct elements. This development of a more integrated approach, based on a broad security concept,[293] is a positive development but brings with it new challenges, eg, given the institutional

---

[290] The Council's register lists documents in this respect, but they are not published in the register.
[291] EU Doc ACH/02, above, n 279.
[292] PSC Decision ACEH/1/2005, 15 November 2005, [2005] OJ L-317/16.
[293] See for the EU, *A Secure Europe in a Better World. European Security Strategy*, adopted by the 12 December 2003 European Council <http://ue.eu.int/cms3_fo/showPage.asp?id=266&lang=en&mode=g> and, for further references, J Wouters and F Naert, 'The EU and Conflict Prevention: a Brief Historic Overview' in V Kronenberger and J Wouters (eds), *The European Union and Conflict Prevention. Legal and Policy Aspects* (The Hague: TMC Asser Press, 2004) 37–8. See also N Tsagourias, Chapter 5 of this volume.

differences between military and civilian missions. Moreover, the different status of EU BAM Rafah, which is an ESDP operation, and the EU Border Assistance Mission to Moldova and Ukraine, which is not,[294] raises the question when an operation must be regarded as an ESDP operation. It would appear that the security of the operation personnel and in the operation zone is important in this respect.[295] Finally, it may be mentioned that the EU is developing 'civilian response teams' (CRTs), which are civilian crisis management rapid reaction capabilities of flexible size and composition, consisting of Member State experts with, in principle, Council Secretariat participation, and drawn from an EU-wide pre-selected pool of experts,[296] able to quickly launch civilian ESDP missions.

Secondly, the geographical reach of the ESDP is clearly expanding: after starting with the Balkans, the EU now also conducts operations in Africa and Asia, including the Middle East. While it is sometimes questioned whether regional organizations should act outside their own region, it is submitted that there is no a priori obstacle to such actions as long as they are based on an appropriate international mandate (as discussed above and below). Furthermore, the AMIS Support Mission and AMM illustrate the EU's readiness to support other regional organizations and to cooperate with them.

Thirdly, in parallel, as regards the military operations, there is the increasing size and difficulty of the missions: while CONCORDIA was very limited; ARTEMIS was already bigger and fairly challenging given its autonomous nature, the distance involved, the quick deployment and the dangerous environment; and ALTHEA is also a major challenge in light of the size of the mission and the possibly considerable duration, although it relies on NATO assets. Admittedly, it remains to be seen whether the EU could deal with a high-intensity conflict and/or a significantly larger military operation. While this is essentially a military issue,[297] from an institutional perspective the main question would seem to be whether the EU has a sufficient headquarters and command structure at its disposal for such an eventuality. This might be a problem if it would not have recourse to NATO assets in such a case and if none of the Member States with major military capabilities would be willing to assume the role of framework nation either. However, it is questionable whether in that case there would be sufficient political will to launch an ESDP operation at all.

Fourthly, ARTEMIS shows that the ESDP missions are not limited to peace-keeping in the traditional consensual sense, but may include peace enforcement, since ARTEMIS, while conducted with the consent of the parties involved, acted

---

[294] See above, nn 11 and 8.

[295] See the 13th consideration of the preamble of the EU BAM Rafah Joint Action, above, n 11.

[296] See EU Doc 10462/05, 23 June 2005. See also N Tsagourias, Chapter 5 of this volume.

[297] See Royal Defence College and Royal Institute for International Relations (eds), above, n 94 and see also N Tsagourias, Chapter 5 of this volume. It is submitted that the usual comparison with the US is not the most relevant one and that a comparison with potential hostile forces in potential ESDP operation zones would be more relevant.

under a Chapter VII mandate,[298] had an enforcement mission, albeit a limited one, and was called in precisely because the UN peacekeeping force in place was unable to cope with the situation. It is submitted that this is and has always been the case and that the 'tasks of combat forces in crisis management, including peacemaking' mentioned in Article 17(2) TEU[299] include peace enforcement.[300] This would arguably be clearer under the proposed EU Constitution, of which Article I-41(1) lists, next to peacekeeping, missions for 'strengthening international security' and in which Article III-309(1) sums up 'tasks of combat forces in crisis management, including peacemaking and post-conflict stabilization' in addition to peacekeeping tasks. Moreover, in the preamble of the Protocol on permanent structured cooperation established by Article I-41(6) and Article III-312 of the Constitution, it would be recognized that the EU may be called upon by the UN to assist in implementation of missions undertaken under Chapter VII of the UN Charter.[301]

3.2. International mandate

All ESDP missions so far have had a clear basis in international law. In all cases this was the invitation or consent of the host state government and other parties involved, sometimes in the form of a peace agreement and often reinforced by Security Council support or endorsement and, in the case of ARTEMIS and ALTHEA, by Security Council authorization.

That the Security Council merely endorsed some of the operations, notably consensual ones, indicates that no Security Council authorization is required for such operations, at least when they have the support of all the parties concerned in the theatre of operation. It is submitted that this is both correct and desirable and that Security Council authorization is only required for enforcement operations.[302]

---

[298] The scope of this Chapter is discussed above, in n 101.

[299] Art 17 reads:

1. The common foreign and security policy shall include all questions relating to the security of the Union, including the progressive framing of a common defence policy, which might lead to a common defence, should the European Council so decide. It shall in that case recommend to the Member States the adoption of such a decision in accordance with their respective constitutional requirements. [...] 2. Questions referred to in this Article shall include humanitarian and rescue tasks, peacekeeping tasks and tasks of combat forces in crisis management, including peacemaking [...].

[300] See J Wouters and F Naert, above, n 48, 211 and n 41 and the author's book review of S Duke's *The EU and Crisis Management* in (2002) 9 Maastricht J Eur & Comparative L 311. But see F Pagani, 'A New Gear in the CFSP Machinery: Integration of the Petersberg Tasks in the Treaty on European Union' (1998) 9 Eur J of Intl L 741–2 and UK House of Commons, Select Committee on Defence, *Eighth Report*, 11 May 2000 (<http://www.parliament.the-stationery-office.co.uk/pa/cm199900/cmselect/cmdfence/264/26402.htm>), paras 41–2. But see N Tsagourias, Chapter 5 of this volume.   [301] See also M Trybus, Chapters 2 and 3 of this volume.

[302] See also N Tsagourias, Chapter 5 of this volume.

3.3. Legal status and applicable law

In the SOFAs and SOMAs there has been some evolution but there are also a number of common elements.

First, in the first (EUPM) SOMA, it was striking that there was no reference to an obligation to respect local law, a clause which is common in SOFAs.[303] Fortunately, this obligation was introduced in later SOMA/SOFAs, and in two instances specific mention was additionally made of respect for local laws regarding environmental protection and the protection of cultural heritage, albeit in the case of CONCORDIA 'subject to the requirements of the operation'. It is remarkable that respect for international humanitarian law is never mentioned, except in the case of the AMIS Supporting Mission via the AU SOMA. Admittedly, (almost) all ESDP operations so far did not include active participation in hostilities, which is required for international humanitarian law to become applicable. However, this was not obvious for ARTEMIS. Moreover, this threshold is not required for human rights, which are also not mentioned in the SOFA/SOMAs, to apply, although their extraterritorial application, and their relation to international humanitarian law, is controversial.[304] Obviously, the mere absence of a clause pertaining to either body of law does not mean that this body of law would or will not be respected, and it is submitted that Article 6 TEU requires such respect.[305]

Secondly, the frequent granting of privileges and immunities equivalent to that of a diplomatic mission and diplomatic personnel is also unusual,[306] although perhaps less so for the smaller civilian missions such as THEMIS. It is particularly unusual for a military operation like CONCORDIA, where it is normally rather

---

[303] See, eg, para 6 UN Model SOFA, UN Doc A/45/594, 9 October 1990, and para 3 SFOR SOFA, above, n 198 (where this is, however, qualified somewhat).

[304] See on this, eg, International Court of Justice, Advisory Opinion of 9 July 2004 on the *Legal Consequences of the Construction of a Wall in the Occupied Palestinian Territory* (available at <http://www.icj-cij.org>), paras 108–11; Human Rights Committee, General Comment 31 (21 April 2004, CCPR/C/74/CRP4/Rev 6, available at <http://www.ohchr.org/english/bodies/hrc/comments.htm>), paras 10–11; F Coomans and T Kamminga (eds), *Extraterritorial Application of Human Rights Treaties* (Antwerp: Intersentia, 2004), and the case-law discussed in J Wouters and F Naert, 'Shockwaves through International Law after 11 September: Finding the Right Responses to the Challenges of International Terrorism', in C Fijnaut, J Wouters and F Naert (eds), *Legal Instruments in the Fight Against International Terrorism. A Transatlantic Dialogue* (Leiden/Boston, Mass: Martinus Nijhoff, 2004) 514–25 (available at <http://www.law.kuleuven.ac.be/iir/eng/research/publications/NaertWoutersIL.pdf>). See also N Tsagourias, Chapter 5 of this volume.

[305] See F Naert, *'De binding van NAVO- en EU-strijdkrachten aan mensenrechten bij operaties tegen terrorisme'* 30(7) Nederlands Juristen Comité voor de Mensenrechten-Bulletin (2005) 909–19. See also N Tsagourias, Chapter 5 of this volume; however, Tsagourias' view that if peacekeepers become engaged in an armed conflict, it would always be an international one, may be questioned, in particular where the 'opponent' does not represent a state.

[306] It is more common to reserve the diplomatic status for the top officials of a mission and accord other mission members lesser immunities: see, eg, paras 24–8 UN Model SOFA, above, n 303, and paras 2 and 8 SFOR SOFA, above, n 198.

stipulated that the forces shall be under the exclusive criminal jurisdiction of their Sending State.[307] The inclusion of a clause providing for a waiver of immunity in the more recent SOMA/SOFAs is a welcome development. However, it would be very exceptional for such a waiver to be granted. To the author's knowledge, this has not yet happened and states are very reluctant to grant a waiver. Obviously, to the extent that they take the necessary remedial or judicial actions themselves, this need not be a problem.[308] Moreover, in many cases the reluctance to hand over personnel to local jurisdictions is understandable, given that such jurisdictions do not always exist and rarely function in accordance with international human rights standards in conflict zones in which operations usually take place. Taking into consideration that staff of international organizations generally enjoy wide immunities in a host state, and that personnel of an operation will usually be called upon to take more intrusive actions than such staff, such immunities do not seem excessive.

Thirdly, for claims, the SOMA/SOFAs distinguish between two categories of claims: claims arising out of activities in connection with the operation are not subject to any reimbursement by participating states or the EU, whereas all other claims, if they are not within the jurisdiction of the local courts, are dealt with by specific mechanisms. The issue of claims is complex and deserves further discussion, but is addressed here only briefly. In any event, in at least one NATO-led operation, compensation is sometimes awarded even where a SOFA does not require it. Hence one has to look beyond the texts and take into account practice in this field. However, the author has not been able to verify whether such a practice has also occurred in EU-led operations. Finally, while in light of human rights considerations[309] a complete exclusion of some categories of claims would seem to be problematic, a mission-specific SOFA/SOMA is normally only applicable in the host state and may not preclude claims in the states participating in an operation, although this course of action may be very difficult for host state residents to pursue.

Fourthly, the mechanisms used to make applicable SOFA/SOMAs of related missions and of other international organizations or countries constitute an interesting and practical approach to the status issue.

---

[307] Eg, paras 27 and 47(b) UN Model SOFA, above, n 303 and para 7 SFOR SOFA, above, n 198. Compare N Tsagourias, Chapter 5 of this volume.

[308] Admittedly, the immunities of international organizations are being increasingly challenged from a human rights perspective. However, the jurisprudence suggests there is no problem where an adequate alternative remedy is available (see especially European Court of Human Rights, *Beer and Regan* v *Germany* and *Waite en Kennedy* v *Germany*, both 18 February 1999, and *McElhinney* v *Ireland*, *Fogarty* v *United Kingdom* and *Al-Adsani* v *United Kingdom*, all three 21 November 2001 and all five available at <http://www.echr.coe.int>). Court proceedings in the Sending State of the personnel concerned could be such a remedy, although in civil suits for damages this venue may be very difficult for host state residents.   [309] See previous note.

Finally, it should be noted that there exist model SOFAs and SOMAs for police,[310] civilian, and military ESDP missions, but only the former is in the public domain.[311]

3.4. Third State participation

The larger and more traditional types of EU operations so far have been reinforced by third States' participations, while most of the smaller and newer ones have not. Many of these participations came from candidate Member States (including Turkey), most of which have now acceded to the EU. However, the non-EU NATO Member States Iceland, Canada, and Norway have also been active participants, as has Switzerland and, to a lesser extent, Ukraine. Russia and Albania each participated in one mission, as did the non-European countries Brazil, South Africa, Argentina, Chile, Morocco, New Zealand, Brunei, Malaysia, the Philippines, Singapore, and Thailand.

This openness to third States provides an added value and may be enhanced by their full participation in the day-to-day running of the operation, including for small contributors,[312] and the tendency in the more recent participation agreements to not demand a contribution to the common costs. Obviously, the latter somewhat increases the share of the common costs for the participating EU Member States. However, if this helps to attract contributions from third States, which in any event pay the non-common costs for their forces/personnel, it is probably more advantageous in the end. The inclusion of mutual waivers of claims reflects the position between Member States under the EU Claims Agreement concluded between the Member States on 28 April 2004.[313]

The participation agreements with third States do not differ very much, except where they reflect specificities proper to an operation. In fact, in addition to mission-specific model participation agreements,[314] there now exist general (draft) model participation agreements for military and civilian ESDP missions, but they are not in the public domain.[315] Moreover, several third States have now concluded framework agreements on participation in ESDP operations, thereby avoiding the need to conclude a specific agreement for every operation.[316]

[310] EU Doc 14612/4/02 REV 4, 29 April 2003.
[311] See the references in EU Doc 10607/05 (27 June 2005, partially in the public domain) and EU Doc 8886/05 (18 May 2005, not in the public domain).
[312] Ie, by not reserving this participation for those who provide 'significant' contributions.
[313] [2004] OJ C-116/1, especially Arts 3–4 (not yet entered into force).
[314] See above, nn 114 (ARTEMIS) and 216 (ALTHEA).
[315] The most recent versions listed in the Council's register appear to be, respectively, EU Documents 12047/04 (3 September 2004) and 12050/04 (3 September 2004), not in the public domain.
[316] Bulgaria (above, n 204), Iceland (21 February 2005 [2005] OJ L-67/2), Norway (above, n 206), Romania (above, n 205), Ukraine (13 June 2005 [2005] OJ L-182/29, not yet entered into force), and Canada (24 November 2005 [2005] OJ L-315/21).

3.5. Some institutional issues

First, practice so far has clarified to some extent what is meant by political control and strategic direction and what powers may be exercised by the PSC. The PSC is usually granted the authority to amend the Operation Plan, the chain of command, sometimes including the appointment of the Head of Mission, and the rules of engagement, to accept third States' contributions, and to set up a Committee of Contributors, while the powers of decision concerning the objectives and termination of the operation remain vested in the Council. The role of the PSC would essentially remain the same under the proposed EU Constitution.[317]

Secondly, practice shows that not all Member States participate in every mission and that, even when this is the case, contributions may differ greatly. Although this does not seem to have caused any problems and may reflect what Member States have always envisaged, one may question whether this non-participation, except for Denmark,[318] 'the specific character of the security and defence policy of certain Member States'[319] and states that make use of the 'constructive abstention' mechanism,[320] is justified for *military operations* under the letter of the TEU, given that it is not specifically authorized in the TEU and that Article 27B TEU only permits enhanced cooperation[321] in the Common Foreign and Security Policy for the implementation of a Joint Action or Common Position and excludes such cooperation for matters having military or defence implications.[322] Incidentally, it may be noted that Denmark's participation in police operations indicates that civilian and police operations are not considered to have military or defence implications. Be that as it may, under the proposed EU Constitution, entrusting a mission to a group of Member States would clearly be possible.[323] Moreover, the 'battle group' concept already endorsed by the EU, which envisages the quick availability of national or multinational force packages, including headquarters, for specified time periods,[324] implies the acceptance of participation of a limited number of Member States, at least on the ground.

---

[317] Above, n 2, Art III-307(2).

[318] The special position of Denmark has been mentioned above: see n 61 and accompanying text.

[319] This reservation, included in Art 17(1), second subpara EU Treaty, may cover the Irish position (see above, n 62 and accompanying text).

[320] Under Art 23(1), second subpara, EU Treaty, a member of the Council who abstains may qualify its abstention by making a formal declaration, in which case it shall not be obliged to apply the decision, but shall accept that the decision commits the Union.

[321] Ie, cooperation between some Member States within the framework of the EU and making use of EU institutions.

[322] See on these elements of differentiation N Tsagourias, Chapter 5 and R A Wessel, Chapter 10, both of this volume.

[323] Above, n 2, Arts I-41(5), III-310(1), and III-310. Note also the permanent structured cooperation envisaged in the Protocol (No 23) on permanent structured cooperation established by Arts I-41(6) and III-312 of the Constitution.

[324] On the 'battle group' concept, see <http://ue.eu.int/uedocs/cmsUpload/Battlegroups.pdf> and N Tsagourias, Chapter 5 of this volume.

Thirdly, it is submitted that the elaborate treaty practice in the field of ESDP operations, namely the SOFA/SOMAs and participation agreements, clearly illustrates that treaties are concluded *by and on behalf of the EU* and that the EU consequently possesses international legal personality.[325] In any event, this issue would also be settled by the EU Constitution, should it enter into force.[326] Moreover, the said practice contains some particular features such as the frequent entry into force of agreements on the date of signature or, where this is not the case, provisional application from this date. However, in a number of cases it would appear that agreements never entered into force, although apparently this has not posed any problems so far.

3.6. Cooperation with other international organizations

Most EU operations take place in countries where the EU and other international actors are already involved. In the case of ARTEMIS, the cooperation with the UN has definitely contributed to enhanced EU-UN relations.[327]

CONCORDIA and ALTHEA illustrate that EU operations with recourse to NATO assets function quite well. On the other hand, one may wonder whether the parallel EU and NATO support for AMIS II is not an unnecessary duplication.

Finally, the AMIS Supporting Mission and the AMM may be good starting points for developing closer cooperation with the AU and ASEAN respectively.

---

[325] It has long been controversial whether the EU has international legal personality (in contrast with the EC, for which this is generally accepted), and whether agreements concluded under Art 24 TEU are concluded on behalf of the EU or of the Member States. See also N Tsagourias, Chapter 5 of this volume.

[326] Above, n 2, Arts I-7 (although this provision speaks of legal personality generally, it is not disputed that this includes international legal personality) and IV-438(1).

[327] See J Wouters and F Naert, 'Linking Global and Regional Organizations: the Case of the United Nations and the European Union', April 2004 <http://www.law.kuleuven.ac.be/iir/nl/opinies/FNJWeuun.pdf>, 4–5. See also N Tsagourias, Chapter 5 of this volume.

5

EU Peacekeeping Operations: Legal and Theoretical Issues

*Nicholas Tsagourias**

1. Introduction

Peacekeeping has become one of the headline goals of the European Union's security and defence policy and a manifestation of its participation in the international arena. In this chapter we will study the place and role of peacekeeping within the EU legal and political order, examine the available legal, institutional, and operational resources, consider the application of international humanitarian and human rights law to EU peacekeeping forces, and examine the international responsibility of the Union. In a more theoretical context, we shall consider the Union's evolving security and defence identity, and reflect on the Union's future direction in this area.

2. Historical Overview: The Development of European Security and Defence Policy

The history of the project to integrate European foreign, security and defence policy is relevant to an understanding of its present condition.[1] Since the early days of European integration, the process of formulating and operating a common foreign, security, and defence policy has been characterized by the interlacing of common interests with national interests of Member States.[2]

* Lecturer in law, University of Bristol, United Kingdom. I would like to thank Dr Frederik Naert, University of Leuven, and Aurel Sari, PhD Candidate, UCL for their comments and suggestions. The usual disclaimer applies. All website addresses cited were active on 17 October 2006, unless otherwise specified.
    [1] S Duke, *The Elusive Quest for European Security: From EDC to CFSP* (Basingstoke: Macmillan Press, 2000) 12–81.
    [2] C Hill, 'EU Foreign Policy since 11 September 2001', (2004) 42 *J Common Market Studies* 143, at 160.

In the 1950s the ambitious plan for a European Defence Community (EDC),[3] with a common European Army and a European Political Community, was rejected by the French Parliament because it compromised French interests in developing national military and nuclear capabilities. A decade later, the Fouchet Plan (1961–2) provided for a 'Treaty on the Union of States' leading to a unified foreign policy and coordination of defence policies. This plan too was rejected. Although dressed in idealistic language, with a European theme, it was deemed to serve the particular interests of its author-state. The other EEC Member States were not convinced; instead, they saw NATO as the most effective defence organization, that also interlocked the USA in Europe.

The predecessor to a Common Foreign and Security Policy (CFSP) was the European Political Cooperation[4] (EPC) which, however, excluded defence or security issues. EPC fostered European political unity and solidarity through harmonization of policies, common positions on international events, and concerted diplomacy. The political and economic aspects of security were added later in the Solemn Declaration of Stuttgart, whereas the Single European Act (1987) institutionalized the EPC practices, amongst others, through the EPC Secretariat.[5] The Treaty on European Union (TEU) introduced CFSP and the progressive framing of a common defence policy under the second pillar.[6] This pillar is intergovernmental, meaning that the role of the institutions in decision-making is rather weak. However, the introduction of a foreign, security, and defence policy betrays acceptance of the fact that challenges facing Europe or the world at large require concerted and coordinated action and that the Union's participation in this policy area will complement its overall economic and political achievements. The CFSP objectives, as stated in the TEU, include: the strengthening and safeguarding of the common values, fundamental interests, and security of the Union; preserving international peace and security; and promoting the values of democracy, the rule of law, and respect of human rights and fundamental freedoms.[7] They are formulated in broad terms and reflect values and ideological precepts which are internal to the Union. Because they are prescriptive,[8] their realization requires a combination of policies, initiatives, resources, and instruments, and this is the particular trait of the CFSP, as we shall see later.

---

[3] E Fursdon, *The European Defence Community: A History* (London: Macmillan, 1980). See also M Trybus, Chapter 1 of this volume.

[4] S Nuttall, *European Political Co-operation* (Oxford: Clarendon Press, 1992); P Ifestos, *European Political Cooperation* (Aldershot: Avebury, 1987).

[5] R Dehousse, J H H Weiler, 'EPC and the Single Act: From Soft Law to Hard Law?' in M Holland (ed), *The Failure of European Political Cooperation. Essays on Theory and Practice* (London: Macmillan, 1991) 128.

[6] E Regelsberger, W Wessels, 'The CFSP Institutions and Procedures: A Third Way for the Second Pillar', (1996) 1 *Eur Foreign Affairs Rev* 29, at 42; M E Smith, 'The Legalization of EU Foreign Policy' (2001) 39 *J Common Market Studies* 79.   [7] Art 11 TEU.

[8] M Koskenniemi, 'International Law Aspects of the Common Foreign and Security Policy' in M Koskenniemi, *International Law Aspects of the European Union* (The Hague/Boston/London: Martinus Nijhoff, 1998) 27, at 28.

The security and defence policy (ESDP) was developed in response to various exogenous and endogenous events. On the one hand, the end of the Cold War brought radical changes to the international political environment with the emergence of new types of security threats, whereas, on the other, the Union pursued an active policy of projecting itself as a geopolitical actor. What energized the Union was the Yugoslav wars that brought into light its complacency, the lack of security capabilities, or strategy, and its negligible input and leverage in international affairs, even in its immediate neighbourhood. Thus, the Union decided to strengthen its security and defence capabilities in order to address such flaws.

The ESDP gathered momentum when the European Council in Helsinki (1999) decided on a number of headline goals evolving around the Petersberg tasks, ie, humanitarian and rescue tasks, peacekeeping, and tasks of combat forces in crisis management, including peacemaking.[9] The Headline Goal of crisis management provided for the creation of a Rapid Reaction Force comprising 50,000–60,000 troops to perform the Petersberg tasks, to be deployable within 60 days and capable of being sustained for at least a year. It was completed in May 2003, when the Capability Conference declared that 'the EU now has operational capability across the full range of Petersberg tasks, limited and constrained by recognised shortfalls'.[10] The Constitutional Treaty added to the existing tasks 'joint disarmament operations, humanitarian and rescue tasks, military advice and assistance tasks, conflict prevention and peace-keeping tasks, tasks of combat forces in crisis management, including peace-making and post-conflict stabilisation'.[11]

Civilian crisis management, as the other Headline Goal, includes police, civilian administration, civil protection, and strengthening the rule of law. For this reason, provisions were made for the creation of a Police Unit of 5,000 police officers capable of being deployed within 30 days, as well as for a pool of judges, prosecutors, prison officers, election monitors, humanitarian assistance teams, or other experts. The Civilian Capabilities Commitment Conference confirmed that 'Member States' voluntary commitments are now 5,761 officers in the area of police, 631 for rule of law, 562 for civilian administration and 4,988 for civil protection. With these commitments, Member States have well exceeded the concrete targets set by the European Council'.[12]

The civilian and military crisis management projections of the Union are now spelled out in the Headline Goal 2010. The military projections focus on interoperability, deployability and the sustainability of deployed troops, and the ability to 'deploy force packages . . . either as stand alone force or as part of a larger

---

[9] Art 17 TEU. Petersberg Declaration, Western European Union Council of Ministers, Bonn, 19 June 1992. The Petersberg tasks were inserted in the TEU with the Treaty of Amsterdam.

[10] Declaration of EU Military Capabilities, Capability Conference, Brussels, 19 May 2003.

[11] Art III-309.

[12] Civilian Capabilities Commitment Conference: Ministerial Declaration, Brussels, 22 November 2004.

operation enabling follow-on phases . . . based on the EU battlegroups concept'.[13] The battlegroup concept is based on 'combined arms, battalion sized force and reinforced with Combat Support and Combat Service Support elements . . . could be formed by a Framework Nation or by a multinational coalition of Member States'. The aim is to have, by 2007, the capacity to 'undertake two concurrent single Battlegroup-size rapid response operations, including the ability to launch both such operations nearly simultaneously'.[14] The action plan for civilian crisis management focuses on: multifunctional civilian crisis management resources; complementarity and coherence between all Union instruments; improvements in operationability, training, and recruitment; and more efficient cooperation with the UN and the OSCE.[15]

The Union also streamlined its security and defence policy by adopting the European Security Strategy (2003). The ESS provides strategic focus for the EU, whose geographic borders are loose and whose enemies are diffuse. It identifies a number of key threats such as terrorism, proliferation of weapons of mass destruction, regional conflicts, state failure, and organized crime and identifies a combination of political, economic, and social responses with recourse to military ones only as a last resort.[16] The types of threats and responses that this document identifies are a recognition of the fact that current threats are multifarious and their sources are obscure, denationalized, and de-territorialized. Finally, the Constitutional Treaty not only spells out the principles that guide the Union's action on the international scene,[17] but also includes a solidarity clause in cases of terrorist attacks and natural or man-made disasters,[18] as well as a mutual defence provision.[19]

Before discussing the Union's security identity, we should say that the EU is an atypical security actor. It is institutionally multi-layered and, policy-wise, multi-faceted. Furthermore, the Union does not embody the reflexive security identity of nation states, which is often ethno-culturally determined. In the absence of personified threats, but facing security challenges, the Union has formulated more elaborate instruments to attain security through political, economic, social, or cultural interaction building upon a network of values, rules, and behaviours. As a consequence, the Union's security and defence policy may appear rather eccentric or atavistic in a world intellectually dominated by hard security. At other times it may appear clumsy because it is not only about Union policies but also about

[13] General Affairs and External Relations Council Conclusions, Brussels, 17 May 2004, approved by the European Council, 17–18 June 2004.

[14] Military Capability Commitment Conference, Declaration on European Military Capabilities, Brussels, 22 November 2004.

[15] Action Plan for Civilian Aspects of ESDP, European Council, 17–18 June 2004.

[16] European Security Strategy, Brussels, 12 December 2003, 2–8 <www.consilium.europa.eu./uedocs/cmsUpload/78367.pdf>.   [17] Art I-3(4); Art III-292 (2).

[18] Art II-42.

[19] Art I-41 (7); M Krajewski, 'Foreign Policy and the European Constitution', (2003) 22 Ybk Eur L 435; F Naert, 'European Security and Defence in the EU Constitutional Treaty' (2005) 10 J Conflict and Security L 187.

the foreign and defence policies of the Member States. Having said that, its contribution to international security is very distinct. As the ESS says, 'an active and capable European Union would make an impact on a global scale. In doing so, it would contribute to an effective multilateral system leading to a fairer, safer and more united world'.

3. Peacekeeping and European Security and Defence Identity

The Union's identity in security and defence is the system of principles, values, meanings, and instruments that embody internal trajectories and understandings which become referential points and orientation sources for external action.[20] Indeed, the Constitutional Treaty spells out the values that have inspired the Union's creation, development and enlargement, namely the values of 'democracy, the rule of law, the universality and indivisibility of human rights and fundamental freedoms, respect for human dignity, equality and solidarity and respect for the principles of the United Nations Charter and international law'.[21] These values also become the Union's objectives in external relations and are attained through a combination of 'civilian' methods including economic, political, and judicial assistance, cooperation, and 'know how'. For instance, the ESS recognizes that the causes of terrorism are not exclusively military and that neither should the responses be exclusively military.[22] It then goes on to mention preventive action, but couched in a web of multilateral and multidimensional responses. These include intelligence, police, and judicial assistance or political, economic, social assistance, and initiatives. Military instruments are to be used only as a means of last resort. Thus, prevention does not convey the same meaning as it does in the US National Security Strategy (2002).[23] Rather, it implies political, economic, and social prevention of the causes of terrorism. Related to this is the Union's policy of extending security by fostering well-governed countries through commitment to democratic reform, human rights, the rule of law, and market economics. The policy of enlargement is a prime example[24] and, as the ESS says, the 'European countries are committed to dealing peacefully with disputes and to co-operating through common institutions'.

---

[20] B Tonra, 'Constructing the Common Foreign and Security Policy: The Utility of a Cognitive Approach' (2003) 41 *J Common Market Studies* 731; M Williams, 'Identity and the Politics of Security' (1998) 4 *Eur J Intl Relations* 204.

[21] Compare Art III-292(1) and (2). Art 11 TEU. Also see Art 2 EC Treaty and Art 6 TEU.

[22] European Security Strategy, n 16, above, 3, 7. See also Common Position on Terrorism 2001/930/CFSP [2001] OJ L-344/90.   [23] <www.whitehouse.gov>.

[24] See, for example, the criteria as set by the Copenhagen Council:

... the associated countries ... that so desire shall become members of the European Union. Accession will take place as soon as an associated country is able to assume the obligations of membership by satisfying the economic and political conditions required. Membership requires that the candidate country has achieved stability of institutions guaranteeing democracy, the rule of law,

It is in this context that we should consider peacekeeping as an expression of the Union's civilian identity. Although the concept of peacekeeping has changed meaning,[25] it remains a civilian instrument for attaining humanitarian and peace-maintaining objectives that uses military symbols.[26] Peacekeeping is a hybrid instrument that requires quantitatively and qualitatively different capabilities, resources, and strategies from those required by hard security[27]. For the Union, peacekeeping as a civilian security instrument is embedded in its ideological, structural, and historical experiences as described above. It also befits the Union as an atypical actor that lacks the concrete attributes of the state and, consequently, the territorially defined, historically solidified, and interest specific character of national foreign and security policies.

4. An Overview of EU Peacekeeping Operations

The Union's peacekeeping policy has been gradualist but expansive.[28] Instead of pre-empting events, as happens in other areas, peacekeeping operations were emplaced only when resources became available in 2003. The diversity of the operations also shows that the Union has been testing its potential in terms of resources, difficulties, geographic reach, or cooperation with other security actors.

The first Union operation was the EU Police Mission (EUPM) in Bosnia and Herzegovina (BiH).[29] It was launched on 1 January 2003 and runs until 31 December 2006. This operation took over from the UN International Police Task Force (IPTF), put in place to oversee the implementation of the Dayton

human rights and respect for and protection of minorities, the existence of a functioning market economy as well as the capacity to cope with competitive pressure and market forces within the Union. Membership presupposes the candidate's ability to take on the obligations of membership including adherence to the aims of political, economic and monetary union.

Presidency Conclusions: Copenhagen European Council (1993). European Commission, 'Agenda 2000', Bull EU, Suppls 5–15/97 (1997). J Gow, 'Security and democracy: the EU and Central and Eastern Europe', in K Henderson (ed), *Back to Europe: Central and Eastern Europe and the European Union* (London: UCL Press, 1999) 23.

[25] *An Agenda for Peace: Preventive Diplomacy, Peacemaking and Peace-keeping*, A/47/277—S/24111 (1992), para 20; *Supplement to An Agenda For Peace*, A/50/60—S/1995/1(1995), paras 33–6; *Report of the Panel on United Nations Peace Operations*, paras 9–83; *The Blue Helmets: A Review of United Nations Peacekeeping*, 2nd edn (New York: UN Department of Public Information, 1990) 5–8; E Suy, 'Peace-keeping Operations' in R-J Dupuy (ed), *A Handbook on International Organizations*, 2nd edn (The Hague/London/Boston: Martinus Nijhoff, 1998) 539ff.

[26] *Supplement to An Agenda for Peace*, paras 34–5.

[27] It is interesting to note in this regard that the ESDP does not mention peace restoration. The latter is a robust concept that requires peace enforcement against a designated enemy and would have required a fundamental shift in paradigm.

[28] G Lindstrom, 'On the Ground: ESDP operations' in N Gnesotto (ed), *EU Security and Defence Policy: The First Five Years (1999–2004)* (Paris: Institute for Security Studies, 2004) 111ff, available at <www.iss-eu.org>.

[29] Council Joint Action 2002/210/CFSP [2002] OJ L-70/1; Council Joint Action 2005/825/CFSP [2005] OJ L-307/59. K M Osland, 'The EU Police Mission in Bosnia and Herzegovina' 11 *Intl Peacekeeping* (2004) 544.

Peace Accord of 1995.[30] EUPM was created following an invitation by the BiH government. It was welcomed, but not authorized, by the Security Council (SC) in Resolution 1396 (2002) following the acceptance of the EU offer by the Peace Implementation Council Steering Board.[31] It consists of 530 police officers, the majority of whom are from EU Member States, whereas a small number are from third States such as Russia, Iceland, Romania, Bulgaria, Canada, Turkey, Norway, Switzerland, and Ukraine. EUPM's mandate is to 'establish sustainable policing arrangements under BiH ownership in accordance with best European and International practice, thereby raising current BiH police standards'.[32] The operational objectives are to 'monitor, mentor and inspect'[33] in cooperation and consultation with the UN or other organizations and in conjunction with the whole cadre of EU activities in the country. This mission will be followed by a refocused EUPM mission for an additional period of two years.[34]

The second peacekeeping operation was Operation *Concordia* in FYROM, which was also the first EU military operation.[35] The operation was launched in March 2003, following an invitation by the government of FYROM, and took over NATO's operation 'Allied Harmony'. The Security Council (SC) did not create the operation, but in Resolution 1371 (2001) it expressed its support for the establishment of a multinational security presence in FYROM. Its mandate was to 'contribute to a stable, secure environment, to allow the Macedonian Government to implement the Ohrid Framework Agreement'.[36] The negotiation of the agreement was facilitated by the EU and US special representatives; the agreement provided for non-discrimination and the equitable representation of the Albanian minority in public life, the development of decentralized government, the use of the Albanian language, and the recognition of the unitary character of the state.[37] Its implementation was supported politically and financially by the EU whilst NATO launched operation *Essential Harvest* to disarm Kosovo Liberation Army (KLA) fighters. Operation *Concordia* benefited from NATO's assets, following the 'Berlin Plus' agreement between the EU and NATO on the sharing of assets, whereas France was designated the 'framework nation'. The mission consisted of 357 personnel from EU Member States (with the exception of Ireland and Denmark) and from third countries such as Canada, Bulgaria, Turkey, Iceland, Romania, and Norway. The force patrolled FYROM's borders with Albania, Kosovo, and Serbia where ethnic Albanian populations live. The operation was concluded on 15 December 2003 and was followed by a light police

[30] 'General Framework Agreement for Peace in Bosnia and Herzegovina with Annexes, 1995' in (1996) 35 ILM 89.
[31] Communiqué by the PIC Steering Board, 28 February 2002, available at <www.ohr.int/pic/default.asp?content_id=7009>.
[32] Council Joint Action 2002/210/CFSP [2002] OJ L-70/5 (Annex).   [33] Ibid.
[34] Council Joint Action 2005/824/CFSP [2005] OJ L-307/55.
[35] C Mace, 'Operation Concordia: Developing a 'European' Approach to Crisis Management?' (2004) 11 *Intl Peacekeeping* 474.   [36] Council Joint Action 2003/92/CFSP [2003] OJ L-34/26.
[37] <www.president.gov.mk>.

mission, EUPOL, for a period of one year.[38] The mandate of operation *Proxima*, was to assist in raising police standards and it did not act under the Berlin Plus framework. On 11 October 2004 the Council decided to extend the mission for another 12 months, following an invitation by FYROM's government.[39]

The fourth operation is Operation ARTEMIS, launched in Bunia in the Democratic Republic of Congo (DRC) from 12 June until 1 September 2003.[40] It followed the escalation of ethnic violence that hindered the provision of humanitarian assistance, created refugees and displaced persons, and threatened to derail the peace process. It was established after the SC, acting under Chapter VII, determined in Resolution 1484 (2003) that the situation in the Ituri region and in Bunia constituted a threat to the peace process and to the peace and security in the Great Lakes region and authorized 'the deployment of an Interim Emergency Multinational Force [IEMF] in Bunia in close coordination with MONUC' until 1 September 2003. The SC also authorized the Member States participating in the IEMF to take all necessary measures to fulfil its mandate. Following this, operation ARTEMIS was launched; its mandate was the 'stabilisation of the security conditions and the improvement of the humanitarian situation in Bunia, to ensure the protection of the airport, the internally displaced persons in the camps in Bunia and, if the situation requires it, to contribute to the safety of the civilian population, United Nations personnel and the humanitarian presence in the town'.[41] It was the first peacekeeping operation launched outside Europe and France was again appointed the 'framework nation'. The other main contributors were Sweden, Belgium, Britain, Germany, Greece, Brazil, Canada, and South Africa; Denmark, following the Protocol annexed to the TEU, did not participate. The operation comprised 1,800 personnel and engaged in military operations to demilitarize Bunia. It was succeeded by a robust UN force.

On 16 July 2004 EUJUST THEMIS was launched in Georgia. It ran until July 2005.[42] This was an EU Rule of Law Mission whose mandate was to assist the reform of Georgia's criminal justice sector by supporting and providing guidance to local authorities. The operation consisted of experts in the field and was part of the civilian aspect of ESDP. It was launched following an invitation of the Georgian Government. Membership was limited to EU Member States.

On 12 July 2004 the EU decided to launch operation EUFOR ALTHEA in BiH,[43] following NATO's decision to terminate its own operation. This has been welcomed by the SC in Resolution 1551 (2004).[44] The Union eventually

---

[38] Council Joint Action 2003/681/CFSP [2003] OJ L-249/66.
[39] Conclusions, General Affairs and External Relations Council, 11 October 2004.
[40] Council Joint Action 2003/432/CFSP [2003] OJ L-147/42.
[41] SC Res 1484 (2003) Council Joint Action 2003/423/CFSP [2003] OJ L-143/50; S Ulriksen, C Gourlay, C Mace, 'Operation *Artemis:* The Shape of Things to Come?' (2004) 11 *Intl Peacekeeping* 508.   [42] Council Joint Action 2004/523/CFSP [2004] OJ L-228/21.
[43] Council Joint Action 2004/570/CFSP [2004] OJ L-252/10.   [44] SC Res 1551 (2004).

launched Operation ALTHEA on 2 December 2004.[45] The mission's mandate is to ensure compliance with the Peace Agreement, and to contribute to a safe and secure environment in BiH. The mission is using NATO's capabilities and DSACEUR (Deputy Supreme Commander Allied Forces Europe) has been appointed operation commander. It comprises 7,000 troops from 22 Member States and from 11 third States such as Albania, Argentina, Norway, Canada, and Turkey. The SC, in Resolution 1575 (2004) and acting under Chapter VII, welcomes the EU's intention to launch this operation and:

> authorizes the Member States acting through or in cooperation with the EU to establish for an initial period of 12 months a multinational stabilization force (EUFOR) as a legal successor to SFOR under unified command and control, which will fulfil its missions in relation to the implementation of Annex 1-A and Annex 2 of the Peace Agreement in cooperation with the NATO HQ presence in accordance with the arrangements agreed between NATO and the EU . . . [46]

The operation is part of a comprehensive policy towards BiH that may eventually lead to its accession to the EU.

In April 2005 the EU launched EUPOL KINSHASA, a police mission in Kinshasa, DRC.[47] The mission's mandate is to 'monitor, mentor and advise the setting up and the initial running of the IPU (Integrated Police Unit) in order to ensure that the IPU acts . . . according to international best practices'.[48] It comprises 30 staff. It was only intended to be active until the end of 2005 but was extended for a further year. In June 2005, the EU launched operation EUSEC DR Congo,[49] with the aim of integrating the Congolese army and of promoting human rights, democratic standards, good governance, and humanitarian law. This was an advisory and assistance mission lasting twelve months.

In February 2005 the EU decided to launch EUJUST LEX, the European Union Integrated Rule of Law Mission for Iraq.[50] The mission became operational on 1 July 2005. Its mandate is to train in the EU or in the region high- and mid-level officials in senior management and criminal investigation. If the situation in Iraq permits, training will take place in Iraq.[51] This mission was initially for 12 months but, due to progress, the Council extended the mission for another 18 months.

The Union also decided to support the AU mission AMIS II in Darfur, Sudan. For this reason, in July 2005 it established the AMIS EU Supporting Action to support to the military and police component of AMIS II.[52]

---

[45] Conclusions, General Affairs and External Relations Council, 25 November 2004.
[46] SC Res 1575 (2004).   [47] Council Joint Action 2004/847/CFSP [2004] OJ L-367/30.
[48] Ibid.   [49] Council Joint Action 2005/355/CFSP [2005] OJ L-112/20.
[50] Council Joint Action 2005/190/CFSP [2005] OJ L-62/37.   [51] Ibid.
[52] Council Joint Action 2005/557/CFSP [2005] OJ L-188/46.

5. Actors and Policy Instruments in Security and Defence Policy: The Case of Peacekeeping

The Union's political structure in security and defence privileges intergovernmentalism.[53] The European Council is the principal organ that 'identifies the strategic interests and objectives of the Union'.[54] The Council of Ministers is entrusted with decision-making powers to implement the objectives set out by the European Council.[55] The role of the Commission is generally circumscribed. It is 'fully associated to the work' of the CFSP[56] but its powers of initiative are limited.[57] The European Parliament's role in the second pillar is very weak and the Constitutional Treaty proposes limited consultation.[58] The European Court of Justics (ECJ) lacks jurisdiction, perhaps for reasons of expediency and efficiency.[59] According to the Constitutional Treaty, the ECJ would have jurisdiction over the legality of restrictive measures against legal or physical persons,[60] and would also adjudicate on the division of the Union's competences.[61] Another important organ is that of the High Representative, who is also Secretary General (SG-HR) of the Council. The role of the SG-HR is to assist in the formulation and implementation of policies and offer coordination, coherence, and visibility. If the Constitutional Treaty is ratified this post will be replaced by the Union Minister for Foreign Affairs (UMFA), who will also be Vice President of the Commission.[62] The role of UMFA is to contribute 'towards the preparation of a CFSP and [. . .] ensure implementation of the European decisions adopted by the European Council and the Council'.[63] The UMFA will have double allegiances and responsibilities: to the Commission for the Union's external relations and to the Council for the Union's foreign, security, and defence policy.[64]

An organ that plays a prominent role in ESDP is the Political and Security Committee (PSC).[65] It consists of permanent staff, representatives of Member

---

[53] This does not imply that the Second Pillar is more akin to international law cooperation as per E Denza, *The Intergovernmental Pillars of the European Union* (Oxford: Oxford University Press, 2002) 19. See C W A Timmermans, 'The Constitutionalisation of the European Union', (2002) 21 Ybk Eur L 1.
[54] Arts 13 and 4 TEU; Art III-293.   [55] Arts 13(3) 14, 15, 17 TEU.   [56] Art 27 TEU.
[57] Art 22(1) TEU. According to the Constitutional Treaty, the power of initiative belongs to Member States, the Union Minister of Foreign Affairs acting alone, or the Commission. Arts I-40(6) and III-299(1).   [58] Art 21 TEU, Art III-304.
[59] Art III-376. According to Art 47 TEU legal competence under the first pillar prevails over those of the second and third pillars. See Case C-170/96 *Commission v Council* [1998] ECR I-2763; P Eeckhout, *External Relations of the European Union: Legal and Constitutional Foundations* (Oxford: Oxford University Press, 2004) 147–52. We should also say that the weak input of parliaments or courts is not a particularly EU phenomenon but is common in many national systems. L Henkin, *Foreign Affairs and the United States Constitution* (Oxford: Clarendon Press, 1996) 146.
[60] Art III-376. Case T-306/01 R, *Yusuf v Council and Commission*, Order of the President of the Court of First Instance (7 May 2002); Case T-47/03 R, *Jose Maria Sison v Council of the European Union*, Order of the President of the Court of First Instance (15 May 2003).   [61] Art III-308.
[62] Art I-27.   [63] Art III-296.   [64] Arts I-27 and I-28.
[65] Council Decision 2001/78/CFSP [2001] OJ L-27/1.

States at ambassadorial level, and representatives of the Commission and the Council. According to Article 25 TEU, its role is to define policies, monitor the international situation, and advise the Council, and also to ensure political control and strategic direction over military operations. Its place within the institutional structure of the Union means that the PSC promotes Union rather than national interests. Other institutions involved in ESDP include the European Union Military Committee (EUMC),[66] which is composed of the Member States' Chiefs of Defence and whose role is to 'provide the PSC with military advice and recommendations on all military matters'. The European Union Military Staff (EUMS)[67] is composed of seconded military personnel from the Member States, and its role is to 'perform early warning, situation assessment and strategic planning for Petersberg tasks including identification of European national and multinational forces', and to implement policies and decisions as directed by the EUMC. Finally, there is the Committee on Civilian Aspects of Crisis Management and the Situation Centre, which analyses options for the EUMC and the PSC.

The decision-making process in foreign policy, security, and defence is a balancing act between institutional efficiency and protection of national interests. Where Member States share common interests the European Council can adopt common strategies unanimously.[68] Their implementation, however, can be the object of QMV. Joint Actions address specific situations where operational action may be required and they lay down their objectives, scope, and means.[69] They are adopted unanimously or by QMV when a common strategy exists. Common positions[70] define the Union's approach thematically or geographically, and are adopted unanimously or by QMV when a common strategy exists. In cases where QMV applies and a Member State invokes vital reasons of national policy, the European Council can adopt a decision only by unanimity.[71] The Constitutional Treaty proposes a single legislative instrument, the European Decision,[72] and decisions that have defence or military implications are exempted from QMV because they refer to areas where Member States traditionally enjoy exclusive competence.[73]

Concerning the legal effect of these instruments, Joint Actions 'commit Member States in the positions they adopt and in the conduct of their activity'.[74] From this—read in conjunction with Article 14(3), (6), and (7) TEU, according to which national measures should not impair the objectives or the effectiveness of Joint Actions—one may reasonably conclude that Member States are under an obligation to conform with the object of the Joint Action. Such obligation does not, however, have any internal legislative effect.[75] The legal effect of common positions varies according to their object,[76] and provided that they identify a

---

[66] Council Decision 2001/79/CFSP [2001] OJ L-27/4.
[67] Council Decision 2001/80CFSP [2001] OJ L-27/7.   [68] Art 13 TEU.
[69] Art 14 TEU.   [70] Art 15 TEU.   [71] Art 23 (2) TEU; Art III-300(2).
[72] Arts I-40(3) and III-294(3).   [73] Art 23(2) TEU; Art I-41 and Art III-300(4).
[74] Art 14(3) TEU.   [75] Denza, n 55, above, 145.   [76] Eeckhout, n 60, above, 403–5.

specific course of action, they may introduce a legislative obligation since Member States 'shall ensure that their national policies conform to the common position'.[77] Common strategies are Framework Decisions. They are not binding[78] as such but acquire legal effect through the common positions or Joint Actions that implement them. With the introduction of a single instrument, that of the European Decision, decisions on foreign, security, and defence policy will enjoy primacy as they do in other areas of Union competence[79] and Member States 'shall comply' with them.[80]

Two important instruments in the implementation of ESDP are the mechanisms of enhanced cooperation and constructive abstention. The former allows a group of Member States to go ahead with the implementation of a common position or Joint Action not relating to matters having military or defence implications,[81] whilst the latter allows Member States to exempt themselves from a common position or Joint Action.[82] Such decisions 'commit the Union', whereas the constructive abstainer undertakes to 'refrain from any action likely to conflict with or impede Union action'. In addition, Member States are exhorted to support the relevant policies 'actively and unreservedly in a spirit of loyalty and mutual solidarity'.[83] Whether this commitment is legal or simply political,[84] and whether it can be enforced, is difficult to fathom, although the language is peremptory rather than instructive; the underlying aim is to project the Union with a single voice.[85] According to the Constitutional Treaty, implementation of the security and defence tasks may be carried out by a group of Member States 'which are willing and have the necessary capability'.[86] These States should regularly inform the Council, either voluntarily or at the request of another Member State, or when the mandate requires amendment, or the task entails major consequences. The Constitutional Treaty also establishes the mechanism of permanent structured cooperation that will include Member States with advanced or similar capabilities and commitments and where the decisions are taken by unanimity among the participants.[87] Partial cooperation, in its different forms, and constructive abstention introduce flexibility in policy formation and policy implementation, efficient allocation of resources, and, by default, reveal a degree of solidarity and trust between Member States.[88] On the other hand, their frequent use may fragment the Union's identity[89] and impede the solidification of the

---

[77] Art 15 TEU.   [78] Cf Denza, n 54, above, 140.
[79] Art I-6.   [80] Art I-16(2).   [81] Art 27(a), (b), (c) TEU.
[82] Art 23(1) TEU and Arts 1–41(2) and III-300(1).   [83] Art III-294.
[84] D Curtin and I Dekker, 'The Constitutional Structure of the European Union: Some Reflections on Vertical Unity-in-Diversity' in P Beaumont, C Lyons, N Walker (eds), *Convergence and Divergence in European Public Law* (Oxford: Hart Publishing, 2002) 59, at 69–71.
[85] See also Art I-16(2), according to which Member States 'shall comply' with the Union's action in CFSP.   [86] Arts I-41 (5) and III-310.
[87] Arts I-41 (6) and III-312. See also Protocol on permanent structured cooperation established by Arts I-41(6) and III-312 of the Constitution.
[88] There is a protective mechanism with regards to enhanced cooperation in Art 27(c) TEU.
[89] S Peers, 'Common Foreign and Security Policy 1999–2000' (2001) Ybk Eur L 531, at 550–2.

Union's security *acquis*. The most extreme situation would be for a Joint Action adopted whilst certain state(s) constructively abstain, to be implemented by a group of cooperating states. Such action would formally maintain its Union character but its internal and/or external legitimacy and authority might be affected. Fragmentation cannot be averted by the caveat of prior agreement and authorization[90] because decisions are formulated in general terms and are open to construction. It is too presumptuous to believe that agreement on a course of action necessarily means agreement on the means of implementation. In effect, the enhanced cooperation group appropriates for itself strategic independence because the follow-up monitoring procedure is weak. This becomes even more problematic in cases where the group requests changes to the mission. In such cases 'the Council shall adopt the necessary European decisions'. The language used is affirmative, as if the Council will immediately give its assent, although it seems that the Council should act unanimously.[91] In brief, the institutionalization of cooperation in its different forms may eventually undermine the Union's purpose of 'asserting its identity' on the international scene, and jeopardize the loyalty and solidarity of its Members since the risk of polarization and division is greater in security and defence matters, as the recent Iraq war has shown. Moreover, ESDP is still embryonic and the Union has not as yet solidified its identity but instead it seeks to reinforce its identity through its actions. It can become an effective policy instrument only when deeper cohesiveness, trust, and solidarity are forged among the Member States and the Union maintains full political and strategic control over the operations at all levels.

   As far as the decision-making process in peacekeeping operations is concerned, they are established by the Council (General Affairs Council), whereas political and strategic control is exercised by the PSC. Coordination with third States is achieved through the Committee of Contributors.[92] The chain of command is to some extent similar to the command structure in UN operations.[93] The European Union Special Representative (EUSR) reports to the Council and EU Commanders should coordinate closely with the EUSR. The EU Operation Commander and EU Force Commander are responsible for the running of the operation and are appointed by the Council of the EU but the PSC may be authorized by the Council to take further decisions on the appointment of the EU Operation or Force Commander.[94] The headquarters can be national and/or multinational, depending on the composition of the force. Where NATO resources are used, operational control is exercised by DSACEUR, who is appointed EU Operation Commander and reports to the EUMC under the 'double hatting' system. In such cases, the Operational HQ is located within

---

[90] Art 27 TEU.   [91] Art I-41 (4).

[92] Council Joint Action 2003/423/CFSP [2003] OJ L-143/52.

[93] The SC is responsible for 'overall political direction', the S-G for 'executive direction', and command in the field is entrusted to the chief of mission by the S-G. See *Supplement to an Agenda for Peace* (1995), para 38.   [94] Council Joint Action 2004/570/CFSP [2004] OJ L-252/10, para 6.

SHAPE (Supreme Headquarters Allied Powers Europe). Finally, the EU Framework Nation Concept means that a particular State leads the operation and provides the operational HQ.

Operations are financed from the EC budget, except those having defence or military implications or when the Council unanimously decides otherwise.[95] For example, operational costs for ARTEMIS were charged to the Member States because of its military character,[96] whereas for the EUPM, start-up costs and operational expenditure fell within the Community budget and annual travel costs 'lie where they fall'.[97] If a State opts out, it is not obliged to contribute financially.[98] A new mechanism, called *Athena*, was established to administer the financing of the common costs of EU operations having military or defence implications.[99] *Athena* will act on behalf of the EU Member States, except Denmark or, depending on the operation, on behalf of the Union or third States contributing to the operation.[100] For this reason it provides for standing or ad hoc arrangements with third States. The Annexes contain a list of common costs to be borne by *Athena*. These include costs, whenever they are incurred, such as operational common costs relative to the preparatory and active phase of the operation, with the exception of costs for transport, barracks, and lodgings unless the Council decides otherwise. Following this, the common costs of EUFOR will be borne by *Athena* with the exception of those for barracks, lodgings, and transportation. This scheme may contribute to coherent and long-term financial planning, better coordination with third countries and auditing, although still a division into 'military' or 'civilian' is not always possible.[101]

6. The Application of Humanitarian and Human Rights Law to EU Peacekeeping Operations and the Union's International Responsibility

6.1. The EU and humanitarian law

International humanitarian law (IHL) consists mainly of the Hague and Geneva law and applies to any factual situation of armed conflict, ie, to situations where hostile armed exchanges become intense and sustained, as opposed to sporadic or

---

[95] Art 28 TEU.   [96] Council Joint Action 2003/423/CFSP [2003] OJ L-143/50.
[97] Council Joint Action 2002/210/CFSP [2002] OJ L-70/3.
[98] For example, Denmark did not contribute financially to Operation ARTEMIS on the basis of the Protocol annexed to the TEU exempting her from decisions having defence implications. Council Joint Action 2003/423/CFSP [2003] OJ L-143/50.
[99] Council Decision 2004/197/CFSP [2004] OJ L-63/68.   [100] Ibid, Arts 1 and 2.
[101] A Missiroli, 'Euros for ESDP: Financing EU Operations' Occasional Papers No 45 (Paris: ISS, June 2003) <www.iss-eu.org>.

random.[102] This means that, with respect to peacekeeping, IHL applies whenever the peacekeepers are involved in hostile armed exchanges.

In order to determine whether IHL applies to the Union's peacekeeping operations, we need first to establish whether the Union has international legal personality. International personality enables states or other entities such as international organizations to assume rights and obligations[103] and can be either a *de jure* or a *de facto* attribute. The constituent treaties confer legal personality on the EC[104] but there is no such provision with regard to the EU and although the Treaty on the Constitution for Europe confers international legal personality on the EU[105] its status is at the moment uncertain. Be that as it may, the Union may instead have *de facto* personality if it satisfies certain conditions, for example, if it has distinct aims and objectives and distinct organs that act independently of the founding states.[106] The Union satisfies the above conditions and thus it is submitted here that it has *de facto* legal personality.[107] A manifestation of its distinct legal personality is the agreements on the participation of third States in EU-led operations, or agreements on the status of EU-led forces that were signed by the Council on the basis of Article 24 and on behalf of the EU without the participation of the Member States.[108] Having said that, third parties may

---

[102] Common Art 2, Geneva Conventions 1949; Art 1(1) AP II; *Tadic* (IT-94-1) Appeals Chamber, 2 October 1995, para 70; UK Ministry of Defence, *The Manual of the Law of Armed Conflict* (Oxford: Oxford University Press, 2004) paras 14.3–8, pp 376–7.

[103] I Brownlie, *Principles of Public International Law*, 6th edn (Oxford: Oxford University Press, 2003) 57.

[104] Art 281 EC; Case C-22/70 *Commission* v *Council* [1971] ECR 263, at 274, paras 13–16.

[105] Art I-7.

[106] *Reparations for Injuries Suffered in the Service of the United Nations*, Advisory Opinion, ICJ Rep (1949) 174, at 178–9. Brownlie, n 103, above, 648–9; P Sands, P Klein, *Bowett's Law of International Institutions*, 4th edn (London: Sweet & Maxwell, 2001) 470–532. H G Schermers and N M Blokker, *International Institutional Law: Unity within Diversity*, 3rd edn (The Hague/London/Boston: Martinus Nijhoff, 1995), paras 1562–70, pp 976–81. For objective personality see N White, *The Law of International Organisations* (Manchester: Manchester University Press, 1996) 27–56 and G Gaja, *First Report on Responsibility of International Organisations of 26 March 2003* UN DocA/CN4/532, para 18. On 'presumptive' personality see J Klabbers, *An Introduction to International Institutional Law* (Cambridge: Cambridge University Press, 2002) 52–9.

[107] Eeckhout, n 59, above, 154–60; C Tomuschat, 'The International Responsibility of the European Union' in E Cannizzaro (ed), *The European Union as an Actor in International Relations* (The Hague/London/Boston: Kluwer, 2001) 177, at 183; R A Wessel, 'The Inside Looking Out: Consistency and Delimitation in EU External Relations' (2000) 37 CMLRev 1135, at 1138–45; Editorial Comment 'The European Union: A New International Actor' (2001) 38 CMLRev 825. Contrary, J W de Zwaan, 'Legal Personality of the European Communities and the European Union' (1999) 30 Netherlands Ybk Intl L 75; Denza, n 54, above, 173–8.

[108] For example, see 'Agreement between the European Union and the Republic of Estonia on the participation of the Republic of Estonia in the European Union-led forces (EUF) in the Former Yugoslav Republic of Macedonia', Council Decision 2003/624/CFSP [2003] OJ L-216/60 or 'Agreement between the European Union and the Republic of Cyprus on the participation of the Republic of Cyprus in the European Union-led forces (EUF) in the Democratic Republic of Congo', Council Decision 2003/693/CFSP [2003] OJ L-253/22; 'Agreement between the European Union and the Former Yugoslav Republic of Macedonia on the status of the European Union-led forces in the Former Yugoslav Republic of Macedonia', Council Decision 2003/222/CFSP [2003] OJ L-82/45; 'Agreement between the European Union and Bosnia and Herzegovina (BiH) on the activities of the European Union Police Mission (EUPM) in BiH' [2002] OJ L-293/2.

challenge its standing, although not those that have recognized its personality, for example those that entered into legal relations with the Union. The requirement of unanimity in ESDP may be a ground for such challenge, but in this case one needs to consider: whether unanimity is the only available method; whether the decision is the sum of individual and separate decisions; and, finally, whether the decision binds all the members regardless of their vote.[109] From our preceding discussion, it appears that the Union's decisions on peacekeeping are institutional, but this does not detract from the fact that the Union's *de facto* personality can be challenged.

Having established that the Union has legal personality, the question that immediately follows is whether the EU is bound by IHL. This issue was also raised in the context of UN peacekeeping and thus we shall use the same reasoning, where applicable. Although the Union is not party to IHL treaties, the bulk of humanitarian law provisions have customary status and as such bind the Union because, according to a well-established principle of international law, international organizations are bound by customary international law.[110] Looked at from another perspective, adherence to IHL can also be seen as part of the Union's human rights and rule of law policies.[111] Indeed, the Union has emphasized the 'primary importance it attaches to the four Geneva Conventions as the basic treaties of international humanitarian law'[112] and on many occasions the Union has contributed to the dissemination of IHL through declarations or by drawing attention to violations thereof.[113] Furthermore, the Union issued guidelines to promote compliance with IHL which apply to all those taking action within the framework of the Union.[114]

As far as accession to IHL treaties is concerned, it should be looked at from a Union perspective but also from the perspective of IHL treaties. Article 24 TEU endows the Union with the necessary competence but the accession should also

---

[109] A Geslin, '*Réflexions sur la répartition de la résponsabilité entre l'organisation internationale et ses états membres*' 109 RGDIP (2005) 539, at 566; Opinion of A-G Darmon in Case C-241/87 *Maclane Watson and Company Ltd* v *Council and Commission* [1998] ECR I-1797, paras 134–6.

[110] *Reparations Case*, n 106, above, 180; *Interpretation of the Agreement of 25 March 1951 between the WHO and Egypt* ICJ Rep (1980) 72, at 90; Schermers and Blokker, n 106, above, paras 1575–81, pp 982–90; K Lanaerts and E De Smijter, 'The European Union as an Actor under International Law' (1999/2000) 19 Ybk Eur L 95, at 122–6; A Peters, 'The Position of International Law within the European Community Legal Order' (1998) German Ybk Intl L 9.   [111] Art III-193.

[112] Declaration by the Presidency on behalf of the European Union on the Occasion of the 50th Anniversary of the four Geneva Conventions (12 August 1999), available at <http://presidency.finland.fi>.

[113] Common Position 95/379/CFSP [1995] OJ L-227/3; Common Position on Rwanda 2000/558/CFSP [2000] OJ L-236/1; Common Position on Rwanda 2001/799/CFSP [2001] OJ L-303/1; Council Common Position 2001/443/CFSP [2001] OJ L-155/19. See also declarations in relation to Israel, Iraq, and Sudan: EFP Bull, Doc No 00/089. T Ferraro, '*Le droit international humanitaire dans la politique étrangère et de sécurité commune de l'Union européene*' 84 IRRC (2002) 435; R Desgagné, 'European Union Practice in the Field of International Humanitarian Law: An Overview' in V Kronenberger (ed), *The European Union and the International Legal Order* (The Hague: TMC Asser Press, 2001) 455.

[114] European Union Guidelines on promoting compliance with international humanitarian law (IHL), 2005/C 327/04 [2005] OJ C-327/4.

satisfy the rules and mechanisms provided for in the referent treaties. The current position is that IHL treaties are open only to states,[115] thus, non-state entities cannot accede thereto. One may say that this argument is rather unconvincing in view of the evolving competence of international organizations and of their activities in areas covered by IHL. This being so, it is submitted that the Union should at least declare that it will abide by the principles and rules of IHL or promulgate a detailed list of humanitarian law rules and principles that will apply to its own peacekeeping operations.[116]

6.2. EU peacekeeping and human rights

The scope of humanitarian and human rights law application has been the subject of intense debate.[117] One line of reasoning advocates complete separation because humanitarian and human rights law have a different locus, purpose, and content whereas another advocates their concurrent application. It is submitted here that the application of humanitarian and human rights law is concurrent and complementary, creating a multilevel system of protection. To put it differently, human rights apply concurrently but also complementarily with humanitarian law and fill in the gaps of the latter, whereas in cases where rights such as the right to life are regulated by both branches of law, IHL as lex specialis takes precedence. As the ICJ said in the *Wall Advisory Opinion*, there may be rights that are exclusive matters of international humanitarian or human rights law, yet others that may be matters of both branches.[118] In relation to peacekeeping, human rights apply to non-coercive operations whereas in coercive operations human rights and humanitarian law apply concurrently and complementarily.

This being said, one needs to identify the Union's human rights obligations. The EU is not party to the ECHR[119] or to any other human rights treaty and the EU

---

[115] See common Arts 1 and 2 Geneva Conventions. C Greenwood, 'International Humanitarian Law and United Nations Peace Operations' (1998) 1 Ybk Intl Humanitarian L 3, at 16.

[116] Common Art 1, Geneva Conventions. By analogy, see 'Secretary-General's Bulletin: Observance by United Nations Forces of International Humanitarian Law' para 4 UN Doc ST/SBG/199/13.

[117] R Provost, *Human Rights and Humanitarian Law* (Cambridge: Cambridge University Press, 2002).

[118] *Legal Consequences of the Construction of a Wall in the Occupied Palestinian Territory, Advisory Opinion of 9 July 2004*, para 106; *Legality of the Threat or Use of Nuclear Weapons, Advisory Opinion of 8 July 1996*, para 25, both at <http://www.icj-cij.org>. Human Rights Committee, General Comment 31, 'Nature of the General Legal Obligation Imposed on States Parties to the Covenant', UN Doc CCPR/C/21/Rev1/Add13 (2004); General Comment No 29 (50), States of Emergency (Art 4), 24 July 2001, UN Doc CCPR/C/21/Rev1/Add11. The HRC has also rejected the Israeli argument that the ICCPR does not apply to the occupied territories because humanitarian law applies thereto: Concluding Observations of the Human Rights Committee; Israel, 21 August 2003, UN Doc CCPR/CO/78/ISR, para 11.

[119] Opinion 2/94 *Accession by the Communities to the Convention for the Protection of Human Rights and Fundamental Freedoms* [1996] ECR I-1759; Art I-9(2) Constitutional Treaty.

Charter of Fundamental Rights is not legally binding, nor will its inclusion in the Constitutional Treaty change this state of affairs as long as the Constitutional Treaty's status remains uncertain. However, human rights are part of the European *acquis* as general principles of law inspired by the constitutional traditions of Member States and the European Convention on Human Rights (ECHR).[120] Being part of the Union *acquis*, human rights, and indeed customary and non-derogable rights, bind the institutions and the Member States when they implement or derogate from Union law.[121] The question then is whether they apply extraterritorially, since peacekeeping operations usually take place outside the Union's territory. According to international jurisprudence, effective control is the source of extra-territorial jurisdiction. The ECHR organs applied this reasoning to cases arising out of the Turkish invasion of Northern Cyprus. As the ECtHR said, Turkey's jurisdiction extends to 'all persons under their [Turkish armed forces] actual authority and responsibility, whether that authority is exercised within their own territory or abroad'.[122] Such control need not necessarily be tantamount to occupation, as the aforementioned *Cyprus* v *Turkey* case or the HRC report on Israel[123] may imply. If that were the case, it would be difficult to apply this construction to peacekeeping, since belligerent occupation is inimical thereto. What is actually required is military or civilian control over an area which can even be temporary or exercised via a subordinate local administration.[124] As the ECtHR said in the *Banković* case, 'the State through the effective control of the relevant territory and its inhabitants abroad as a consequence of military occupation or through the consent, invitation or acquiescence of the Government of the territory, exercises all or some of the public powers normally to be exercised by that Government'.[125] We also submit

---

[120] Art 6 (2) TEU; Art I-9(3) Constitutional Treaty; Case-11/70 *Internationale Handelsgesellschaft* [1970] ECR 1125.   [121] Art II-111 Constitutional Treaty.

[122] *Cyprus* v *Turkey* (Appl Nos 6780/74 and 6950/75). ECommHR 26 May 1975, 2 DR (1975) 125, at 136; *Loizidou* v *Turkey* (Preliminary Objections) ECtHR 23 March 1995 <www.echr.coe.int/ECHR/EN/header/Case-law/HUDOC/HUDOC + database> paras 61–4.

[123] Concluding Observations of the Human Rights Committee: Israel, 5 August 2003, UN Doc CCPR/CO/78/ISR (2003), para 11.

[124] *Loizidou* (1995), para 62; *Ilaşcu and Others* v *Moldova and the Russian Federation* (Appl No 48787/99) ECtHR, 8 July 2004, paras 314, 316; *Issa and Others* v *Turkey* (Appl No 31821/96) ECtHR, 16 November 2004, paras 68–74; *Öcalan* v *Turkey* (Appl No 46221/99) ECtHR, 12 March 2003, para 93. <www.echr.coe.int/ECHR/EN/header/Case-law/HUDOC/HUDOC + database>. With regards to ICCPR, see Human Rights Committee, General Comment 31, 'Nature of the General Legal Obligation Imposed on States Parties to the Covenant', UN Doc CCPR/C/21/Rev1/Add13 (2004). According to the Comment the Covenant applies in respect of anyone within the power or effective control of the state 'even if not situated within the territory of the State Party'. This principle also applies 'to those within the power of effective control of the forces of a State Party acting outside its territory, regardless of the circumstances in which such power or effective control was obtained, such as forces constituting a national contingent of a State party assigned to an international peacekeeping or peace enforcement operation'. Ibid, para 10. F Coomans and M T Kamminga (eds), *Extraterritorial Application of Human Rights Treaties* (Antwerp and Oxford: Intersentia, 2004).

[125] *Banković and Others* v *Belgium and 16 Other Contracting States* (Appl No 52207/99) ECtHR, 12 December 2001, para 71 <www.echr.coe.int/ECHR/EN/header/Case-law/HUDOC/HUDOC

that effective control is not confined to the geographical reach of the referent human rights instrument as the ECtHR indicated in the *Banković* case.[126] Instead, it should be seen as a condition that applies anywhere in the world. In sum, the extraterritorial application of human rights with regard to peacekeeping complements the current system of extraterritorial application based on the effects that external acts have within the Union.[127] Where factual gaps exist in the exercised control, these must be assessed in relation to the operation's mandate. For example, if the operation's mandate is to exercise full jurisdiction over a territory, as in the case of extraterritorial administration, jurisdiction is presumed to be exercised over the whole territory. Even if the exercise of jurisdiction is limited because of factual gaps, the referent authority is not released from its international responsibility but should seek to fulfil its human rights responsibilities through other means.[128] Finally, we should note that the situation that gives rise to peacekeeping cannot possibly justify derogations from human rights, even in cases of robust operations. Peacekeeping is not about the life of the nation[129] and even if the language of the Constitutional Treaty on derogations is vague, it can hardly justify derogations from human rights with regards to peacekeeping.[130]

Concerning the human rights that apply to peacekeeping, this depends on its mandate. If the peacekeeping operation exercises total control over a territory, then the whole cadre of human rights should apply,[131] otherwise only those rights connected with the particular exercise of jurisdiction. This being said, when the operation is subject to a SC resolution, the latter can trump human rights.[132] Recently, the Court of First Instance (CFI) exercised incidental review of SC resolutions on the basis of *jus cogens*.[133] If the European Union Courts continue to assert their competence to review SC Resolutions, the risk of contradictory decisions cannot be underestimated, which will put states in the invidious position of having to choose between their Union and UN obligations.

+database>. See also the HRC's views with regards to BiH in UN Doc CCPR/C/79/Add14, paras 4–5 and with regards to Croatia in UN Doc CCPR/C/79/Add15, para 6. A different approach was taken in *R (on the application of Al-Skeini) v Secretary of State for Defence* [2004] EWHC 2911 where control was limited to prisons.

[126] As to the interpretation of what is the ECHR's legal space, see *Banković*, paras 79–80. *Cyprus v Turkey* (Appl No 25781/94) ECtHR, 10 May 2001, para 78.

[127] Case-36/74, *Walgrave v Union Cycliste Internationale* [1974] ECR 1405.

[128] *Ilaşcu*, paras 333–5.

[129] Art 15 ECHR; *Ireland v UK* (1978) 2 EHRR 25; D J Harris, M O'Boyle, C Warbrick, *Law of the European Convention on Human Rights* (London: Butterworths, 1995) 489–507.

[130] Art II-112 Constitutional Treaty.

[131] *Cyprus v Turkey* (Appl No 25781/94), ECtHR, 10 May 2001 para 77.

[132] Art 103 UN Charter.

[133] Case T-306/01 *Ahmed Ali Yusuf and Al Barakaat International Foundation v Council and Commission* Judgment of 21 September 2005, paras 260–82. Also Case T-315/01, *Yassin Abdullah Kadi v Council and Commission* Judgment of 21 September 2005.

6.3. The international responsibility of the EU and peacekeeping

International responsibility is closely related to that of international personality. On the basis of what has been said above about the Union's legal personality, we shall consider this issue from a number of different perspectives and also borrow heavily from the law on state responsibility, since the law on the responsibility of international organizations is not codified.

International responsibility arises when an international obligation is violated and the wrongful act is attributed to the holder of said obligation. With respect to peacekeeping, the Union is under the customary law obligation to respect and ensure respect of humanitarian law.[134] This obligation is fulfilled by monitoring and supervising the seconded troops, issuing instructions to enforce respect of IHL and, when needed, taking action to suppress violations of humanitarian law or ensure that such action is taken.[135] Troop-contributing states have similar obligations and this formula of overlapping obligations ensures respect of humanitarian law. Concerning human rights, the Union should respect its own human rights law as well as customary human rights. Moreover, Member States are not released from their own human rights obligations[136] and they should also comply with the Union's human rights *acquis* when they implement Union policies. Whereas the former obligations give rise to Member States' international responsibility, the latter give rise to internal responsibility.

What we need to examine next is the criteria according to which a wrongful conduct can be attributed to the Union. Effective command and control[137] is the

---

[134] Common Art 1, 1949 Geneva Conventions; Art 1 (1) Additional Protocol I; *Case Concerning Military and Paramilitary Activities in and against Nicaragua*, ICJ Rep (1986) 14 at 114, para 220; *Nuclear Weapons Advisory Opinion*, n 118, above, ICJ Rep (1996) 257, para 79. J-M Henckaerts and L Doswald-Beck, *Customary International Humanitarian Law, Vol 1: Rules* (Cambridge: Cambridge University Press, 2004) 495–550.

[135] *Nicaragua Case*, n 134, above, paras 220 and 254–6, pp 114 and 129–30.

[136] *Matthews v UK* (Appl No 24833/94) 28 EHRR 361, at para 32.

[137] In relation to the UN, see 'United Nations General Assembly: Report of the Secretary-General Administrative and Budgetary Aspects of the Financing of the United Nations Peacekeeping Operations' (20 September 1996) UN Doc A/51/389, in 37 ILM 700 (1998) adopted by GA Res 257 (1998) A/RES/52/247. According to the report:

The international responsibility of the United Nations for combat-related activities of United Nations forces is premised on the assumption that the operation in question is under the exclusive command and control of the United Nations (para 17). In joint operations, international responsibility for the conduct of the troops lies where operational command and control is vested according to the arrangements establishing the modalities of cooperation between the State or States providing the troops and the United Nations. In the absence of formal arrangements between the United Nations and the State or States providing troops, responsibility would be determined in each and every case according to the degree of effective control exercised by either party in the conduct of the operation. (para 18). The principle that in coordinated operations liability for combat-related damage in violation of international humanitarian law is vested in the entity in effective command and control of the operation or the specific action reflects a well-established principle of international responsibility (para 19).

main criterion, which means that the EU will be responsible if it exercises effective command and control over the operation or the force is an organ of the Union. As we said earlier, peacekeeping operations are established by the Council, which is a Union institution and the decision binds the Union as such. Secondly, the PSC exercises political control and strategic direction and can change the mandate or even abolish the whole operation.[138] Even if its membership is not exclusively *communautaire*, the PSC is attached to the Council and represents the Union. Thirdly, the EU Operation and Force Commander is appointed by the Council or the PSC if authorized by the Council. From the above it transpires that the peacekeeping force is in fact a Union organ and is controlled by the Union. In this case, and provided that the Union has legal personality, if a breach occurs that is attributable to the Union the latter incurs international responsibility. It may be said on the other hand that the peacekeeping force constitutes a pool of independent contingents coordinated under the second pillar. According to this line of argument, the peacekeeping force is not an organ of the Union but states act in concert, using the decision-making facilities available in the second pillar. In this case, it is the Member States that incur responsibility. Such responsibility should be joint, although this does not preclude the existence of an internal mechanism to apportion responsibility and probably recover damages.

One may also say that in any case the Union and the Member States should have concurrent or at least subsidiary responsibility because of their close links and cooperation in peacekeeping. After all, it is the Member States' troops that act, albeit on EU instructions.[139] The upshot of this position is that individual states will not be able to hide behind the institution and the Union will not be able to hide behind its members.

Be that as it may, the simple truth is that only states can be brought before courts because no court can exercise jurisdiction over the Union. Even if according to Article 6 (2) TEU it is the Union that should respect human rights and human rights apply to Union institutions and Member States alike the ECJ does not have jurisdiction over CFSP[140] unless jurisdiction is established by attributing such responsibility to the EC on the assumption that the EC and the EU form a single legal entity.[141] The ICJ does not have jurisdiction either, since only states

---

Nicaragua Case, n 134, above, para 115; Case No IT-94-1-A, *The Prosecutor* v *Dusko Tadić* (Appeals Chamber), Judgment of 15 July 1999, paras 131–7. M Perez-Gonzalez, 'Les organisations internationales et le droit de la résponsabilité' 92 *RGDIP* (1988) 63, at 81–5; M Hirsch, *The Responsibility of International Organisations towards Third Parties: Some Basic Principles* (The Hague/London/Boston: Martinus Nijhoff, 1995) 64–5; *Second Report on Responsibility of Inter-National Organisations*, A/CN4/541, para 40. See also Arts 4, 5, 8 of Draft Articles on State Responsibility (2001).

[138] For example, see Art 6 of Operation ALTHEA. Council Joint Action 2004/570/CFSP [2004] OJ L-252/10.

[139] With regards to states see *Nicaragua Case*, n 134, above, paras 115, 116, 255–6. Also Responsibility of States for Internationally Wrongful Acts (2001), Art 6 UN Doc A/56/10.

[140] Art 46 TEU.

[141] D M Curtin, I F Dekker, 'The EU as a 'Layered' International Organization: Institutional Unity in Disguise' in P Craig, G de Burca, *The Evolution of EU Law* (Oxford: Oxford University

can be parties thereto. With regard to violations of human rights, again the EU is immune, due to lack of forum. The EU is not party to the ECHR or to any other human rights treaties and although it is bound by customary human rights, it does not have locus standi before international human rights courts. From the above it transpires that no internal judicial remedies exist, whereas internationally it is only the Member States that can be held responsible.[142]

6.4. Privileges, immunities, and third-party liability

Civilian peacekeeping operations, such as EUF, EUJUST, or EUPM, enjoy the status of diplomatic missions. This means that the Vienna Convention on Diplomatic Relations (1961) applies and not the Protocol on the Privileges and Immunities of the European Communities.[143] Accordingly, the peacekeeping staff enjoys complete immunity from criminal, and certain immunities from civil, jurisdiction. Immunities are functional[144] and as the Agreement with BiH states, they are granted during the mission and thereafter 'with respect to official acts previously performed in the exercise of their mission'.[145] The immunities of technical staff are concurrent with their duties.[146] With regards to military operations, customarily the contributing states exercise criminal jurisdiction over their troops and the troops enjoy immunity from the civil jurisdiction of the host state only for official acts.

Issues of immunity and of privileges are dealt with in SOFAs signed between the sending state or organization and the host state. For EUFOR it is the status of forces agreement contained in the Framework Agreement and applied to NATO's SFOR operation that will apply.[147] According to this agreement, immunity

Press, 1999) 83; P Eeckhout, *External Relations of the European Union: Legal and Constitutional Foundations* (Oxford: Oxford University Press, 2004) 152–4.

[142] *Matthews* v *UK*, n 136, above; *Beer and Regan* v *Germany* [2001] 22 EHRR 3.

[143] 'Agreement between the European Union and Bosnia and Herzegovina (BiH) on the activities of the European Union Police Mission (EUPM) in BiH' [2002] OJ L-293/2, Art 4; Council Joint Action 2004/523/CFSP of 28 June 20004 on the European Union Rule of Law Mission in Georgia, EUJUST THEMIS, Art 7; Council Decision 2003/693/CFSP [2003] OJ L-253/22; 'Agreement between the European Union and the Former Yugoslav Republic of Macedonia on the status of the European Union-led forces in the Former Yugoslav Republic of Macedonia', Council Decision 2003/222/CFSP [2003] OJ L-82/45, Art 6.

[144] This is a customary norm: see Schermers and Blokker, n 106, above, para 324, pp 235–6.

[145] 'Agreement between the European Union and Bosnia and Herzegovina (BiH) on the activities of the European Union Police Mission (EUPM) in BiH' [2002] OJ L-293/2.

[146] Arts 31 and 37 Vienna Convention on Diplomatic Relations (1961).

[147] Council Joint Action 2004/570/CFSP [2004] OJ L-252/10, para 8. Appendix B to Annex 1-A 'Agreement between the Republic of Bosnia and Herzegovina and the North Atlantic Treaty Organisation (NATO) Concerning the Status of NATO and its Personnel' (1996) 35 ILM 102. The agreement provides for the application of the 1946 Convention on the Privileges and Immunities of the United Nations concerning experts in mission (para 2); the exclusive jurisdiction of the national state in respect of criminal and disciplinary offences (para 7); claims for damages or injury to government or private persons or property to be submitted by BiH governmental authorities to NATO representatives (para 15); accords the same privileges and immunities to non-NATO states (para 21).

covers both civilian and military personnel and is total in respect of criminal and disciplinary offences. When the EU peacekeeping force is a component of another operation, it may conclude a separate SOFA or apply an existing SOFA. For example, EU Support AMIS II is governed by the AU SOFA and the general Convention on the Privileges and Immunities of the OAU.

According to the SOFA concerning forces seconded to the EU[148] (EUSOFA), the military or civilian staff seconded to the EU institutions shall enjoy immunity from legal process for acts or words performed in the exercise of their official functions and this immunity continues even after the end of secondment. The immunity is granted in the interests of the EU and can be waived either by the sending state or by the EU institutions.[149] For military and civilian staff at HQ or forces, the sending state can exercise criminal and disciplinary jurisdiction but, concerning civilian staff, only if their status is subject to the law governing the armed forces. The sending state can also exercise jurisdiction with respect to offences to its security if not punishable by the law of the receiving state.[150] The receiving state can exercise jurisdiction over all other offences and also over offences relating to its security that are not punishable by the law of the sending state. In a way, this SOFA establishes the primacy of the sending state in all juris-dictional matters and contains rules to solve issues of concurrent jurisdiction.[151] Furthermore, it does not affect the obligations of Member States towards the ICC.[152] The EUSOFA is an international law agreement because it needs to be approved according to the constitutional procedures of each Member State and then deposited with the SG of the Council of the European Union.[153] The EUSOFA follows closely the NATOSOFA and thus it introduces a degree of consistency when the same forces are used by both organizations.

The Convention on the Safety of United Nations and Associated Personnel[154] may apply to EU peacekeepers to the extent that they are considered 'associated per-sonnel'. The Convention obligates states to criminalize certain acts and to either prosecute or extradite persons responsible for committing such acts.[155] It applies to conventional operations and does not apply to enforcement actions under Chapter VII of the UN Charter where peacekeepers are engaged as combatants.[156] In order to fall within the meaning of 'associated personnel', and therefore within the protec-tion of the Convention, peacekeepers must carry out activities 'in support of the ful-filment of the mandate of a United Nations operation' and must be assigned with the 'agreement of the competent organ of the United Nations'.[157] Although EU

---

[148] Document 2003/C 321/02, 'Agreement between the Member States of the European Union concerning the status of military and civilian staff seconded to the institutions of the European Union, of the headquarters and forces which may be made available to the European Union in the context of the preparation and execution of the tasks referred to in Art 17(2) of the Treaty on European Union, including exercises, and of the military and civilian staff of the Member States put at the disposal of the European Union to act in this context' (EU SOFA).   [149] Art 8.
[150] Art 17.   [151] Art 17(6).   [152] Para 4.   [153] Art 19(1) and (4).
[154] UN Doc A/RES/49/59 (1995).   [155] Arts 9, 10, 15 of Convention.
[156] Arts 1 and 2(2) of Convention.   [157] Art 1 of Convention.

operations may support the 'mandate' of a UN operation, there may be problems with regards to more independent operations, as for example in 'bridging' operations where there is no UN operation yet on the ground.

Concerning the relations of Member States with the ICC, all EU Member States are parties to the ICC and the latter can exercise jurisdiction on the basis of the principle of complementarity.[158] The Union has often expressed its firm support towards the ICC and the Council has issued guidelines on the surrender agreements signed by the USA and ICC state parties.[159] According to the guidelines, existing agreements that reserve the Court's jurisdiction should be accepted but new agreements only if they contain temporal limitations and guarantees against impunity and concern persons who are not nationals of any ICC state party. Otherwise, they will be inconsistent with the ICC Statute.[160]

With regards to third-party liability arising from the peacekeeping operation, according to the status of staff provisions in Operations THEMIS, EUPOL KINSHASA, and EUJUST LEX, the seconding Member State or EU institution is 'responsible for answering any claims linked to the secondment, from or concerning the staff member' and the Member State or the EU institution 'shall be responsible for bringing any action against the secondee'. It is not clear what the phrase 'responsible for answering' means but if it means liability in tort it invokes rules of administrative liability[161] and possibly the non-contractual liability of the Union.[162] With regards to the latter, the problem of locus standi reappears. The Courts do not have jurisdiction with regards to the EU and, therefore, any action for damages on the basis of Article 288(2) TEC will be dismissed for lack of competence[163] unless non-contractual liability is established on the presumption that the Community and the Union are in fact one legal and political entity with common institutions. If the above is correct, liability is established on the basis of the secondee's attachment to a particular institution regardless of the classification of the operation as an EU operation. Again, this construction is not safe because even if this hurdle is overcome, there remains the hurdle of locus standi with regards to claimants. Because of these problems, it would have been more practical to establish review boards attached to the mission, as is the case in UN operations.[164]

---

[158] Art 17 ICC Statute.   [159] Art 98 ICC Statute.

[160] Conclusions of the Council of the European Union on the ICC, Brussels, 30 September 2002; Council Common Position 2003/444/CFSP [2003] OJ L-150/67, Art 5.

[161] Art 288 (4). Staff Regulations and Conditions of Employment of other Servants, Reg 259/68 [1968] OJ L56/1. In relation to UN responsibility see United Nations General Assembly: Report of the Secretary-General Administrative and Budgetary Aspects of the Financing of the United Nations Peacekeeping Operations (20 September 1996) UN Doc A/51/389, para 22.

[162] Art 288 (2). H G Schermer and C R A Swaak, 'Official Acts of Community Servants and Art 215 (4)' in T Heukels, A McDonnell, *Action for Damages in Community Law* (The Hague/London/Boston: Kluwer, 1997) 167.   [163] Art 46 TEU.

[164] See United Nations General Assembly: Report of the Secretary-General Administrative and Budgetary Aspects of the Financing of the United Nations Peacekeeping Operations (20 September 1996) UN Doc A/51/389, according to which 'such liability would be entailed if the damage was caused in violation of international humanitarian rules and could not be justified on grounds of "military necessity"' (para 16).

7. Inter-organizational Relations in Peacekeeping: EU-UN-NATO

The EU has cooperated with other actors in peacekeeping operations and, therefore, it is necessary to examine the political and legal conditions of such cooperation.[165] The most important actor in peace and security is the UN. Its security competence is global and primary but the UN Charter acknowledges in Chapter VIII the role that regional security agencies or organizations can play. However, the Charter does not contain any definition of what is 'regional'. Still, any definition based on geographic, cultural, linguistic, or political factors will be inconclusive. For this reason, we submit that the classification of an actor as regional should be approached constructively and should embrace subsystems or subgroups of states that are security providers. To put it differently, for Chapter VIII purposes it is the limited membership and the security mandate that place an actor under the 'regional' rubric.[166] It seems that the Union satisfies the above conditions and consequently it can be classed as a security agent for Chapter VIII purposes. However, in the absence of a formal designation, the question remains as to who decides whether a particular agency is regional. In the past, the UN has implied that the European Community and its Members resemble a regional organization,[167] but in recent resolutions such as those on Congo or BiH, the SC did not invoke Chapter VIII or indicate in any manner whatsoever that it considers the EU a regional agency. In the absence of any formal declaration, this issue can only be solved in concreto by using functional criteria. For example, were the Union to invoke collective self-defence following the provisions on mutual defence contained in the TECE, this would place the Union outside Chapter VIII and within the scope of Article 51 UN Charter on self-defence. For all other security matters the EU will be classed as a regional agent.

The question as to whether regional organizations can establish peacekeeping operations is an internal matter of the organization. The UN Charter neither prohibits nor permits regional organizations to establish peacekeeping operations.[168] Consequently, the Union's competence in peacekeeping can only derive from its constitutive treaties. Where the UN and regional organizations interact though is

---

[165] A Novosseloff, 'EU-UN Partnership in Crisis Management and Prospects' International Peace Academy, June 2004 <www.ipacademy.org>; T Tardy, 'Limits and Opportunities of UN-EU Relations in Peace Operations: Implications for DPKO' September 2003 <http://pbpu.unlb.org>.

[166] Art 53 UN Charter does not contain any geographic limitation as to the scope of regional action and this is true of Art 52 as well. What the latter implies is that regional organizations can deal with matters pertaining to international peace and security to the extent that they relate to a particular region.   [167] SC Res 713 (1991); SC Res 727 (1992).

[168] For the legal basis of UN peacekeeping see *Certain Expenses of the United Nations (Art 17, Paragraph 2, of the Charter)* Advisory Opinion, ICJ Rep (1962) 151, at 177; B Simma (ed), *The Charter of the United Nations* (Oxford: Oxford University Press, 2002) 684–6. With regards to regional systems, see Simma, ibid, 807–970.

with regards to the use of force where regional agencies or organizations are subordinate to the UN Security Council.[169] Thus, one needs to make a distinction between coercive operations that, according to Article 53 UN Charter, require SC authorization and non-coercive ones that may be emplaced without authorization provided that the interested parties have consented thereto.[170] To give an example, Operation ARTEMIS in Congo or ALTHEA in BiH were authorized by the SC because of their coercive character,[171] whereas Operation CONCORDIA was launched without authorization in response to an invitation by the government of FYROM. Moreover, no SC authorization is needed for coercive operations if the host State or the parties concerned have given their consent.[172] In sum, no SC authorization is needed for non-coercive operations or coercive but consensual peacekeeping operations.

As far as the geographical scope of the peacekeeping operation is concerned, it is true that certain regional organizations limit their geographical reach.[173] Any such attempt on the part of the EU would, however, be completely unwarranted. It is not only difficult to demarcate Europe's borders geographically but borders are porous and the impact of any crisis in moral, political, economic, or social terms is often beyond its specific locality. As the ESS rightly says, 'global communication increases awareness in Europe of regional conflicts and humanitarian tragedies in the world'. Moreover, the Union's objectives are not 'time or place' specific but global in their reach, and their aim is to project the Union as a global player. Thus the geographic projection of the Union's peacekeeping missions is global. Having said that, what may pose limits are the available resources, the strength of political will, and the reception of the Union's forces by third States.

Related to the above is the question as to whether the Union can emplace a peacekeeping operation within its Member States. Although membership implies internalization of the Union's values, principles, and methods, there is no guarantee that problems will never appear. Since the Union's primary concern is to preserve its values internally and externally, the Union has not just responsibility but also a duty to respond to such a crisis. This view is also supported from the principle that underlines Article 52(2) and (3) UN Charter, according to which regional organizations have primary responsibility in the pacific settlement of

---

[169] See Art 52 and 53 UN Charter.

[170] Consent was the basis of the first UN operation (UNEF) in 1956; see UN Doc A/3302 (6 November 1956) and GA Res 1001 UN Doc A/RES/1001 (ES-I). See N Tsagourias, 'Consent, Impartiality/Neutrality and the Use of Force in Self-defence: Their Constitutional Role in Peacekeeping' (2006) (forthcoming) J Conflict and Security Law.

[171] We should say in this regard that the SC Resolution mentions Chapter VII and not Chapter VIII. This is probably due to the fact that it is both states and organizations that participated in the operation. Therefore, a general authorization under Chapter VII was more convenient. Having said that, the SC has often avoided indicating under which Chapter authorization was given, an event that has raised questions about the character of the action.

[172] The ICJ made a similar distinction in the *Certain Expenses* Advisory Opinion, n 169, above, 170.

[173] Arts 3(f) and 4(e) Constitutive Act of the African Union (2000); Arts 3 and 4 Treaty of ECOWAS. See also A Abass, Chapter 6 of this volume.

regional disputes. Although this is a theoretical possibility, in practical terms any operation with military or defence implications needs the consent of all states, including the one(s) concerned. Consequently, whether this is a realistic option depends on the density of integration and the degree of trust. Second, in order for this to happen, the ESDP needs to change orientation. Currently it is placed within the CFSP of the Union and it is outward instead of inward looking.

Another area where the EU and the UN interact is in the management and interoperability of mixed operations. The Joint Declaration on EU-UN Cooperation in Crisis Management[174] established a framework of cooperation between the two organizations. The declaration recognizes the primary respon-sibility of the UNSC for the maintenance of peace and security and 'reasserts its [Union's] commitment to contribute to the objectives of the United Nations in crisis management'. In order to coordinate civilian and military crisis manage-ment, a joint consultative mechanism—a Steering Committee—was established to examine 'mutual co-ordination and compatibility' in planning, training, com-munication, and best practices. This led to the 'EU-UN Co-operation in Military Crisis Management Operations: Elements of Implementation of the EU-UN Joint Declaration' adopted in 2004.[175] This document identifies 'modalities under which the EU could provide military capabilities in support of the UN'. The two options identified are: (1) the provision of national military capabilities in the framework of a UN operation and (2) an EU operation in answer to a request from the UN. Concerning the first option, it states that the decision whether to participate in a UN operation is national but that the EU can play the role of a 'clearing house process', in particular with regard to 'enabling capabil-ities', that is, 'expensive capabilities requiring a very high level of expertise'. Concerning the second option, the document states that the operation will be 'under the political control and strategic direction of the EU'. Such operations will either be 'stand alone' or follow the 'modular approach', that is, take responsibility for a specific component of the UN operation. Concerning operations calling for a rapid response, it identifies operations of the 'bridging model', that is, oper-ations being emplaced rapidly and with agreed duration until a UN force arrives, and operations of the 'stand by model', that is, a reserved EU force in support of a UN mission. The above moves coincide with the Declaration following the Franco-British Summit of 24 November 2003 that proposed 'rapid reaction capabilities to enhance its [Union's] ability to support the UN in short-term crisis management situations'. According to the Declaration the Union should be able to deploy within 15 days battle-group sized forces, each around 1,500 troops, offered by a single nation or through a multinational or framework nation force package, with appropriate transport and sustainability, and operating under

[174] Joint Declaration on EU-UN Cooperation in Crisis Management (24 September 2003) <www.europa-eu-un.org>.
[175] Presidency Conclusion Thessaloniki European Council, 17–18 June 2004.

a Chapter VII mandate either at the request of the UN or until UN or other regional forces arrive.[176]

This type of EU involvement raises complex issues of authority and decision-making, but it also makes apparent the need and the possible benefits of closer cooperation between the EU and the UN. To this we should add the cooperation on civilian crisis management which includes exchange of information; the Union acting as a 'clearing house'; or the Union contributing to a UN operation, either as a component of such operation or independently of the UN operation.[177]

Although the structural dialogue and working partnership between the EU and the UN is progressing and the ESS unequivocally states that 'strengthening the United Nations, equipping it to fulfil its responsibilities and to act effectively is a European priority', there is no legal or political undertaking that the EU will defer to the UN organs. On the contrary, one may trace an independent and assertive streak in EU relations with the UN. This can be contrasted with the WEU Petersberg Declaration, according to which 'decisions to use military units...will be taken...in accordance with the provisions of the UN Charter'.[178] Such language was not inserted in the EU Treaties. One may also add other more cogent political and legal reasons for such an attitude. EU operations are those that are controlled politically and strategically by the Union institutions. Subordination to the UN will weaken such control but also undermine the Union's aim of visibility in security and defence. Secondly, when NATO resources are used, the EU will be even more cautious in submitting to UN control, considering the fact that NATO has resisted such control. Thus, the subcontracting model appears to be the only viable option because it offers flexibility and independence.

We should also add at this juncture that the prospect of a coercive operation without SC authorization cannot be ruled out.[179] Even if one treats the EU as a regional organization, the relation between the UN and regional systems is not linear and post-1945 practice reveals a tendency towards a more decentralized and horizontal security system where the UN and its SC do not enjoy exclusive decision-making power. This is mainly due to the fact that the SC and regional actors approach the meaning and source of security threats differently, and also due to the SC's failure to be more inclusive in its deliberations and decisions. Moreover, the SC is not the linchpin of legitimacy and efficiency.[180] It is thus our view that the EU may undertake coercive peacekeeping operations with or without SC authorization. The legitimacy of such autonomous operations can be traced back

---

[176] *Strengthening European Cooperation in Security and Defence*, Declaration, Franco-British Summit, London, 24 November 2003.

[177] 'EU-UN cooperation on civilian crisis management', Presidency Report, Council Document 16062/04, 13 December 2004.

[178] Petersberg Declaration, Western European Union Council of Ministers, Bonn, 19 June 1992.

[179] The existence of SC authorization for operation ALTHEA in BiH or ARTEMIS in Congo does not contradict the above statement, because these were components of a wider UN operation.

[180] N Tsagourias, 'The Shifting Laws on the Use of Force and the Trivialization of the UN Collective Security System: The Need to Reconstitute it' (2003) 34 Netherlands Ybk Intl L 55.

to the procedural and substantive conditions contained in the EU constitutive treaties. As we have already said, the constitutive documents contain a list of substantive values that constitute the benchmarks for external action, being at the same time internal benchmarks of legitimacy. This can be contrasted to the nominal value input in SC deliberations or decisions. Secondly, the EU ascribes to the UN principles that have acquired constitutional validity by being inserted in its constitutive treaties. Thus EU operations are not inconsistent with UN principles and purposes.

This being said, we do not propose a total decoupling between the EU and the UN in peacekeeping. What we suggest is a decentralized security system where actors are identified because of their capabilities and efficiency, and where effective communication between actors is established. The structural dialogue to rationalize and streamline planning, resourcing, and management will contribute towards this end and we believe that the involvement of both the UN and the EU will also enhance the legitimacy and efficiency of any operation. On the other hand, if such coordination and cooperation is not possible, it is our view that the Union should be able to proceed independently.

Relations between the EU and NATO are much thicker than a mere sharing of capabilities.[181] According to the Berlin Plus agreements, where NATO as a whole is not involved, the EU can have 'assured access' to NATO's planning capabilities. From this it follows that access to other capabilities or assets is not assured; however, such assets have been identified and the EU may be allowed to use them. Berlin Plus also solved the thorny, if somewhat artificial, problem of participation of non-EU NATO members in the decision-making process and in the conduct of operations. When NATO resources are used, these states are invited to participate in the planning and operational process and if operations are conducted in their near proximity they will be consulted. We should say however at this juncture that Berlin Plus is a package of agreements between the EU and NATO whose content is secret and what is in the public domain is the 'NATO-EU Declaration on ESPD'[182] and the letters exchanged between the SG/HR and SG NATO,[183] which are not binding as such. Recently, certain EU States have proposed independent planning capabilities. Instead, it was decided to establish an EU cell at SHAPE for Berlin Plus operations, whereas for autonomous operations the national headquarters will be in charge. It was also acknowledged that there may be circumstances where a 'joint civil/military response is required and where no national headquarters is identified'. In such cases '[a] civilian/military cell in the EUMS would have responsibility for generating the capacity to plan and run the operation'.[184]

[181] J-Y Haine, 'ESDP and NATO' in N Gnesotto (ed), *EU Security and Defence Policy: The First Five Years (1999–2004)* (Paris: Institute for Security Studies, 2004) 131 <www.iss-eu.org>. See also F Terpan, Chapter 12 of this volume.
[182] 'EU-NATO Declaration on ESDP' 42 ILM 242 (2003).
[183] EU-NATO: The Framework for Permanent Relations and Berlin Plus (17 March 2003).
[184] 'European Defence: NATO/EU Consultation, Planning and Operations', Presidency Conclusions, Brussels European Council, 12 December 2003.

In brief, future relations between the EU and NATO will be informed by the direction the two organizations take. NATO needs to revisit its strategic dogma and position, particularly in view of the US preference for unilateral actions and haphazard 'coalitions of the willing' where established organizations such as NATO are dispensable. On the other hand, the EU will continue to invest in security and will continue to project its identity. Consequently, the extent to which their relationship will become antagonistic or cordial depends on whether there are overlaps or duplication in objectives, operational areas, and resources. It is our opinion that, although the EU and NATO share certain common objectives, they have a distinct security culture, posture, potential, and resources. They should therefore continue to develop their distinct personalities without trying to undermine each other, but instead establish distinct channels of communication and asset distribution as needed.

8. Conclusion

Peacekeeping combined with the other—political, economic, social—instruments used by the Union in its external relations is an instrument of soft security that eventually attains hard security. The Union should continue to develop its professional expertise in this area whilst at the same time establishing mechanisms to facilitate security and defence cooperation with other organizations. At this point we should express a note of caution as to whether the Union should develop hard security policy and dogma. The EU represents a polity of multilevel governance with multiple clusters of legitimacy. People who primarily identify themselves with the state unit because of the deeper sense of sharing and solidarity that exists at the national level,[185] and the tangible sense of security that it offers, may be reluctant to transfer their loyalties to the EU. At the Union level no amalgamated security and defence policy exists because it is practically impossible for the Union to absorb each and every security interest. The 'civilian' character of the ESDP is also supported by a number of other factors. In the first instance, soft security and civilian identity is exactly how the Union has understood and experienced security since its creation. The aim behind integration is to attain peace and security through political, economic, and social interaction and communication, and through de-securitization of threats. The Union's policies, particularly towards CEEC or the Balkans, show how this security paradigm is projected to the outside world. Indeed, the European Security Strategy's motto of 'a secure Europe in a better world' implies affirmative structural action. Secondly, the adoption of full military capabilities for hard security will inexorably transform the way the Union is perceived internally and externally. It may jeopardize the

---

[185] W Bloom, *Personal Identity, National Identity and International Relations* (Cambridge: Cambridge University Press, 1990) 79.

internal consensus if states start antagonising each other. A military mentality may also affect or compromise other areas of EU action such as humanitarian aid and assistance or reintroduce intergovernmentalism in current federal areas. There is also the possibility that third States may change the way they view the EU.[186] How other states see the Union is a combination of history, internal politics, and culture as well as conduct in external relations. The Union has not been involved in wars, does not have enemies as such, and employs civilian tools in its external relations. Thus its identity is less polarizing or threatening. Moreover, the 'Europeanization' of peacekeeping operations, particularly in Africa, will help to overcome local sensitivities because forces, even if coming from former colonial states, will benefit from the legitimacy that the parent institution enjoys. Thirdly, full military capabilities may lead to internal differentiation and fragmentation. Member States have different military traditions, dogmas, and capabilities; whilst some among them are neutral, others, such as France and the UK, have a long tradition of military activism. Thus it will not come as a surprise if some sort of a directorate is established.[187] If this happens, smaller states will feel sidelined or blackmailed to agree on the proposed action. As we said above, the ESDP is an arena where Member States' foreign, security, and defence policies interact and it manifests itself as univocal policy only when there is overlapping agreement. The divisions during the Iraqi saga are proof of what may happen when sensitive issues are at stake. On the other hand, the consensus on the post-conflict reconstruction of Iraq reveals the depth of agreement on the civilian aspects of crisis management.[188] Fourthly, duplication of tasks should be avoided. The UN, NATO, or the OSCE, for instance, use different methods, military or political, in order to attain peace and security. Since the present threats are complex and require comprehensive and multi-sourced responses, there is a need for better coordination of strategies, instruments, and implementation methods. A better distribution of labour and allocation of competence among the existing institutions, which can then use their expertise and experience in their relevant fields, is needed.[189] Finally, the obsession with military capabilities derives from a mono-optical view of the world where credibility and success are measured by military victories. The credentials of military power to solve problems are sometimes overestimated, not only due to the complexity of the issue at hand, but also because there is often

[186] M Ortega, 'Conclusion: Regional Building in Europe and across the World' in M Ortega (ed), *Global Views on the European Union* Chaillot Paper 72 <www.iss-eu.org>.

[187] B Crowe, 'A Common European Foreign Policy after Iraq?' (2003) 79 *Intl Affairs* 533, at 545–6.

[188] 'The European Council reaffirms that the stability of Iraq is a shared interest and reiterates the Union's commitment to supporting the political as well as the economic reconstruction of the country . . . ' *Presidency Conclusions, Brussels European Council* 12 December 2003.

[189] M Jopp, '*The Strategic Implications of European Integration*, Adelphi Paper no 290, (London: Brassey's, 1994) 67. For the relations between the EU and the AU see Council meeting—External Relations, Brussels 17 November 2003; Council Common Position 2004/85/CFSP [2004] OJ L-21/25; 'The European Union and peacekeeping in Africa', Document C/1880 Assembly of WEU <www.assembly-weu.org/en/documents/sessions_ordinaires/rpt/2004/1880.html>.

a lack of projection or willingness to use military power.[190] As the Iraqi case has proven, winning the peace is just as important as, or more important than, winning the war. Nor should the Union compete with the USA or aspire to become its counterweight. These options are not only self-indulgent but also unrealistic because neither the USA nor the Union present a fundamentally different order of values and rules. As a conclusion, we submit that the Union's capabilities and resources should be directed towards a wide concept of peace-keeping that includes the political, social, and civil aspects in addition to the security ones. In this way, the Union will project itself as an actor in international affairs being informed and guided by values that are genuine expressions of its internal identity and experience because, contrary to projected images, peace-keeping is not apolitical but indeed a manifestation of the political values and wishes of its authors.[191] In order to succeed in this task, the Union needs to develop a comprehensive and transparent peacekeeping strategy.

---

[190] 'There is dangerous over-confidence in military force in some quarters, which recent history does not support': K Booth, 'Military Intervention: Duty and Prudence' in L Freedman (ed), *Military Intervention in European Conflicts* (Oxford: Blackwell, 1994) 56, at 67.

[191] A James, 'The Dual Nature of Peacekeeping', in D Bourantonis and M Evriviades (eds), *A United Nations for the Twenty-First Century: Peace, Security and Development* (The Hague, London, Boston: Kluwer Law International, 1996) 171, at 172.

6

Extraterritorial Collective Security: The European Union and Operation ARTEMIS

*Ademola Abass**

1. Introduction

On 12 June 2003 the European Union launched its first military operation outside Europe and the first to be undertaken without recourse to NATO assets under the Berlin-Plus framework.[1] The mission, codenamed Operation ARTEMIS, was mandated by the UN Security Council to stabilize Bunia in the Ituri region of the Democratic Republic of Congo (DRC).[2] The military component of Operation ARTEMIS—the Interim Emergency Multinational Force (IEMF)— was deployed to the DRC in June 2003 and was authorized by the Security Council, under Chapter VII of the UN Charter, to use force to implement its mandate.[3] Although France served as the 'framework nation'[4] for this operation and worked under the auspices of the EU, Operation ARTEMIS benefited from the participation of several non-EU states, thus making it one of the most widely-subscribed regional actions in history.

There is no doubt that the complex nature of international relations has increased the cooperation between international organizations, such as the UN and the EU on the one hand, and between international organizations and states, such as between the EU and African states, on the other.[5] Vertical interaction

---

* Reader in Law, University of Reading, UK. All website addresses cited were active on 17 October 2006, unless otherwise specified.

[1] For a comprehensive analysis, see: M Reichard, 'Some Legal Issues Concerning the EU-NATO Berlin Plus Agreement' (2004) 73 Nordic J of Intl L 37; R Rummel 'From Weakness to power with the ESDP?' (2002) 7 *Eur Foreign Affairs Rev* 467; Å Missiroli, 'Euros for ESDP—Financing EU Operations' *Occasional Paper* 45 (Paris: Institute for Security Studies, June 2003); C Heusgen, 'Implementing the European Security Strategy' in S Biscop (ed), *Audit of European Strategy* Egmont Paper (No 3) (Brussels: Royal Institute for International Relations, 2004).

[2] UN Res 1484 (2003), 30 May 2003.   [3] Operative paragraph 1.

[4] This follows from the EU's adoption, on 24 July 2002, of the concept of 'framework nation' as the basis for the conduct of autonomous EU-led operations. These are operations that do not make use of NATO assets.

[5] On the various aspects of the powers and functions of international organizations, see generally G J Magone, *A Short History of International Organization* (New York: McGraw-Hill, 1954);

(international organizations-to-states) is as important to today's world order as horizontal relationships (states-to-states), especially in the field of peace and security.[6] Yet, while it is common for states and international organizations to cooperate in order to achieve specific goals, the use of military force by international organizations on the territory of non-Member States is a rarity in state relations.

This chapter therefore examines the 2003 armed intervention, by the European Union, in the conflict in the DRC. The author discusses the various legal questions that arise from the EU's extension of its collective security regime beyond Europe, especially in respect of a conflict that did not, at least directly, concern any of its Member States. Considering also that Operation ARTEMIS forms part of a much broader commitment by the EU to assist African states and organizations to deal with the various problems besieging their continent, this chapter ponders the wider implications of the cooperation between the EU and AU and attempts to understand how this might develop in the future.[7]

Given that Operation ARTEMIS was authorized by the UN Security Council, acting under Chapter VII rather than Chapter VIII of the UN Charter, the author discusses the increasing interaction between the Chapters VII and VIII frameworks in the context of the delegation of collective security powers to regional organizations.[8]

2. An Overview of the Issues

From 12 June to 15 September 2003 the European Union deployed the IEMF in the conflict in the Bunia region of the DRC.[9] The mission was launched in response to the request, made by the UN Secretary-General, Kofi Annan, to the President of the Security Council, for 'the rapid deployment to Bunia of a highly trained and well-equipped multinational force, under the lead of a Member State,

F Amerasinghe, *Principles of Institutional Law of International Organisations*, 2nd edn (Cambridge: Cambridge University Press, 2005); D Sarooshi, *International Organizations and the Exercise of their Sovereign Powers* (Oxford: Oxford University Press, 2005).

  6 Outside the United Nations Systems the EU is probably leading the development of a vertical relationship between international organizations and individual states and this effort is more pronounced in the EU's relationship with Africa. See 'EU Support for Peace and Security in Africa', European Union Factsheet, available at <http://ue.eu.int/uedocs/cmsUpload/Africa.pdf>.

  7 For comprehensive coverage of the EU operation in Africa, see Fernanda Faria, 'Crisis Management in Sub-Saharan Africa. The Role of the European Union', EU-ISS Occasional Paper No 51, April 2004, available at <http://aei.pitt.edu/1615/01/occ51.pdf>.

  8 See D Sarooshi, *The United Nations and the Development of Collective Security. The Delegation by the UN of its Chapter VII Powers* (Oxford: Oxford University Press, 1999).

  9 The force was commanded by the French General Jean-Paul Thonier. Peacekeeping Best Practices Unit, *Operation Artemis: The Lessons of the Interim Emergency Multinational Force* (United Nations Peacekeeping, 2004), available at <http://pbpu.unlb.org/pbpu/view/viewdocument.aspx?id=2&docid=572>, at 18.

to provide security at the airport as well as to other vital installations in the town and to protect the civilian populations'.[10]

Although Operation ARTEMIS was the EU's second peace-support operation—following the path-breaking Operation Concordia in Macedonia[11]—the operation represented several significant developments. Apart from being the first time an international organization intervened in a conflict affecting a non-member State and outside its territory,[12] the EU launched a self-contained military operation, even if small, without the usual recourse to the assets and capabilities of NATO under the so-called Berlin Plus formula. Operation ARTEMIS thus affords the EU an opportunity to assess the readiness and endurability of the European Security and Defence Policy (ESDP), which continues to attract considerable criticism.[13]

Despite the catalogue of 'firsts', Operation ARTEMIS raises a plethora of legal questions. As concerns constitutionality, question marks arise as to the competence of the EU to undertake collective security operations outside its region. Furthermore, whereas the EU should operate on a regional basis under the constitutional framework of Chapter VIII of the UN Charter,[14] Operation ARTEMIS was mandated by the UN Security Council under Chapter VII and not Chapter VIII. The provisions of the latter Chapter govern the delegation of collective security powers by the Security Council to regional organizations, especially when such delegated powers involve the use of force by the beneficiaries.[15]

Consequently, situating the legal basis of Operation ARTEMIS outside the perimeters of Chapter VIII potentially revamps the doctrinal debate about the limits of the powers of the Security Council to 'utilize' regional organizations for the maintenance of peace and security, as well as the nature of 'situations' such delegated powers could be directed at.[16] Various shades of debate exist in legal discourse to the effect that the Security Council can only use regional organizations to perform operations within their own regions and only for matters contained in the constituent instruments of such organizations.[17] If this rather narrow interpretation of Chapter VIII is correct, then question marks are raised about the validity of Operation ARTEMIS.

[10] UN Res 2003/574, 28 May 2003. See C Mace, 'Operation Artemis: Mission Improbable?' (2003) 18 *Eur Security Rev*.

[11] J Wouters and F Naert, 'How Effective is the European Security Architecture? Lessons from Bosnia and Kosovo', (2001) 50 *ICLQ*, 555; G Lindstrom, 'On the Ground: ESDP Operations' in N Gnesotto (ed), *EU Security and Defence Policy. The First Five Years* (1999–2004) (Paris: EU Institute for Security Studies, 2004), also available at <http://www.iss-eu.org>.

[12] G Grevi, D Lynch and A Missiroli, *ESDP Operations* (Paris: Institute for Security Studies, 2005), available at <http://www.iss-eu.org/esdp/09-dvl-am.pdf>.

[13] Rummel, n 1, above; F Fink-Hooijer, 'The Common Foreign and Security Policy of the European Union' (1994) 3 Eur J of Intl L 173.   [14] See below.

[15] See Sarooshi, n 8, above; A Abass, *Regional Organisations and the Development of Collective Security: Beyond Chapter VIII of the UN Charter* (Oxford: Hart Publishing, 2004).

[16] B Simma, *The Charter of the United Nations: A Commentary*, 2nd edn, (Oxford: Oxford University Press, 2002).   [17] Ibid, 859–90, for a more recent examination of the arguments.

The previous occasions when the Security Council could be said to have, for lack of a better term, 'utilized' regional organizations are too shrouded in legal ambiguities to serve great precedential value. The first were the two instances in which the Council retroactively 'legitimized' unilateral regional actions, which, in any case, were actions conducted *within* the concerned organization's region and against two of its Member States.[18] Although some writers view these episodes as the Council effectively *utilizing* the concerned regional organization within the purview of Chapter VIII, serious doubts have been raised against such interpretations.[19]

Another situation was when the Security Council, through Resolution 1244, coordinated its post-conflict efforts in Kosovo with NATO (under KFOR), despite the fact that NATO had previously conducted an enforcement action against Yugoslav forces in Kosovo without Security Council authorization.[20] However, the legal permutations of this case clearly preclude any conclusion that the Council's subsequent rapport with NATO unequivocally amounted to a utilization of NATO in the spirit of Chapter VIII.[21] Perhaps the closest it could be said that the Security Council really came to utilizing a regional organization was through Resolution 787 concerning Yugoslavia.[22] Even then, that resolution had addressed states 'acting nationally or through regional agencies or organizations'. The only organization that responded to this resolution, NATO, did not claim to do so under Chapter VIII.[23]

Although this was the first time that the EU was, as a collective body, directly involved in 'peacekeeping' efforts in Africa, Operation ARTEMIS forms part of a much wider EU effort in Africa. In May 2004 the EU established the African Peace Facility (APF),[24] at the request of the African Union Commission,[25] as a basket fund totalling some €250 million, to assist the AU to implement its objectives. The APF was to be resourced from the 9th European Development Fund

[18] On the Security Council's dealing with Liberia and Sierra Leone crises, see A C Ofodile, 'The Legality of ECOWAS Intervention in Liberia' (1994–5) 32 Columbia J of Transnational L 381; A Abass, 'The Implementation of ECOWAS New Protocol and Security Council Resolution 1270 in Sierra Leone: New Development in Regional Intervention' (2002) 10 Miami Intl and Comparative L Rev 177.   [19] See Abass, n 15, above, particularly Chapter 5.

[20] See N Krisch, 'Unilateral Enforcement of the Collective Will: Kosovo, Iraq, and the Security Council' (1999) 3 Max Planck Ybk of United Nations L 59; J Lobel and M Ratner, 'Bypassing the Security Council: Ambiguous Authorizations to Use Force, Ceasefires and the Iraqi Inspection Regime' (1999) 93 AJIL 124.

[21] See N D White, 'The Legality of Bombing in the Name of Humanity' (2000) 5 (1) J of Conflict and Security L 27.   [22] UN Doc S/RES/787, 16 November 1992.

[23] See E Beckett, *The North Atlantic Treaty, the Brussels Treaty and the Charter of the United Nations* (London: Stevens & Sons, 1950); Hans Kelsen, 'Is the North Atlantic Treaty a Regional Arrangement?' (1950) AJIL 162.

[24] R Keane, 'The EU's African Peace Facility Uncovered: Better Late than Never?' (2004) 24 *Eur Security Rev*, available at <http://www.isis-europe.org/ftp/Download/ESR%2024%20-%20APF.pdf>.

[25] See 'Introductory Note to the Report of the Interim Chairperson of the Commission of the African Union, Assembly of the African Union, Second Ordinary Session' 4–12 July 2003, Maputo, Mozambique. It is stated in this report that, 'At its Extraordinary Session held in Sun City/Sandton,

(EDF) and would cover objectives including peace support operations and the establishment and sustenance of an African Standby Force,[26] as well as the pursuit of a Capacity Building programme of the AU Commission at large. However, it must be emphasized that the APF was not directly mandated to support the institutional reform of the AU, although, as one commentator has argued, 'the success of the APF and the EU's ability to engage with the AU will depend on the future development and cohesion of the Peace and Security Council',[27] by far the most powerful organ of the AU.

Before embarking on a full analysis of Operation ARTEMIS, it is pertinent to stress that while it is desirable to first consider whether the EU is a regional organization within Chapter VIII of the UN Charter, the discussion below avoids this inquiry for two reasons. First, the adoption of the resolution enabling Operation ARTEMIS under Chapter VII renders such an exercise rather superfluous. Secondly, the question whether the EU is a regional organization in international law has been sufficiently addressed elsewhere in this book.[28] Consequently, the present writer takes the view that the EU is a regional organization within Chapter VIII of the UN Charter.

3. The Contextual Background to Operation ARTEMIS

The crisis in the DRC is one of the most enduring conflicts in the world, as it is also one that continues to frustrate the UN and African organizations in their peacekeeping efforts.[29] The conflict, originating in the attainment of Congo's political independence from Belgium in 1960, rapidly became entwined with the political evolution of that country, as reflected in its nomenclatural transformations. From Congo to Zaire, and then to the incumbent Democratic Republic of Congo, the conflict in the DRC remains a constant reminder of both the consequences of the Cold War on satellite states in the Third World and the lacklustre commitment of the United Nations to effect collective security in the continent.

The origins of the crisis in the DRC can be traced back to at least the early 1960s, when secession attempts by the Katangese region of the country were

Council was informed about the initial consultation between the African Union and European Union Commissions intended to get the EU to provide strategic and more concrete support for peace efforts of the African Union, including peace support operations', at 49.

[26] See M Joannidis, ' "Africanisation" of Peacekeeping in Africa', available at <http://www .diplomatie.gouv.fr/en/IMG/pdf/3.pdf>. At the time of writing, the AU has deployed up to 8,000 troops of the African Standby Force to Darfur, Sudan.

[27] Keane, n 24, above, at 2.   [28] See N White, Chapter 14 of this volume.

[29] For an excellent account for the Congo crisis, see W Durch (ed) *The Evolution of UN Peacekeeping: Case Studies and Comparative Analysis* (New York: St Martin's Press, 1993); M Doyle (ed) *Peacemaking and Peacekeeping for the New Century* (Oxford: Rowman and Littlefield Publishers, 1996).

repressed with the help of the UN.[30] More recently those internecine conflicts have resurfaced amongst the many tribes of the DRC, including those in the Ituri region of the DRC, spreading quickly to the region's capital, Bunia.[31] Escalating in the late 1990s, the conflict between the two major rival tribes of Ituri, the Lendu and the Hema minority, has claimed at least some 50,000 lives with nearly half a million people internally displaced. Ituri, as with the rest of the country equating roughly to the size of Western Europe, was the responsibility of the UN Mission in Congo, the MONUC.

However, the spread of the conflict to the regional capital city of Bunia resulted in heavy loss of life. The situation was worsened by the intervention of two neighbouring countries, Uganda and Rwanda, an intervention brought to an end only after the long-awaited Ituri Interim Administration (IIA) was installed in April 2003.

In early May 2003 Ugandan forces withdrew from Ituri at the instance of the Security Council.[32] Up until then, Uganda had constituted itself as the de facto authority in the Ituri District.[33] Uganda's disruptive withdrawal left a security vacuum that MONUC was unable to fill despite reinforcement by nearly 700 Uruguayan troops.[34] The ensuing crisis, which forced many to flee their homes and seek refuge in MONUC sector 2 Headquarters and the airport, forced the withdrawal of the UN peacekeepers from the area, and prompted the UN Secretary-General, Kofi Annan, to ask the EU for a stabilization force.[35]

In response to the Secretary-General's request, the EU adopted a Joint Action on 5 June 2003,[36] which established the first EU interventionist mission outside Europe. Composed of 1,850 troops from France ('the framework nation'),[37] Canada, Belgium, and Uganda,[38] Operation ARTEMIS arrived in the DRC on 6 June, a day after the Security Council ratified the operation. However, it was not until 12 June that the Security Council formally launched the operation, four days before the EU mission opened fire on rebels who had fired on its troops. The operation remained in the DRC until 1 September 2003 when, following the enlargement of MONUC by the Security Council on 28 July 2003, and its authorization to 'use all necessary means'[39] to fulfil its mandate, the IEMF transferred its entire missions to MONUC.

---

[30] N D White, *Keeping the Peace*, 2nd edn (Manchester: Manchester University Press, 1997); F T Liu, 'Peacekeeping and Humanitarian Assistance' in L Gordenker and T Weiss (eds), *Soldiers, Peacekeepers and Disasters* (Basingstoke: Macmillan, 1991).

[31] For an account of the crisis, see Faria, n 7, above.

[32] *Operation Artemis: The Lessons of the Interim Emergency Multinational Force*, n 9, above.

[33] Ibid.   [34] Ibid.   [35] See below.

[36] 2003/423/CFSP, 5 June 2003, in OJ L-253/23.

[37] See Grevi, Lynch and Missiroli, *ESDP Operations*, n 12, above.

[38] See below for analysis of the participation of these non-EU (third) States.

[39] S/RES/1484 (2003), 30 May 2003.

4. Operation ARTEMIS and Collective Security Law

A determination of the legality of Operation ARTEMIS under international law or, more specifically, under collective security law at both regional (EU) and international (UN) levels requires an analysis of the interplay between Chapters VII and VIII of the UN Charter, and an appreciation of the various EU legal regimes governing the operation.

4.1. The EU legal regime and Operation ARTEMIS

Under the EU legal system, the overall responsibility for Operation ARTEMIS rested with the Political and Security Committee (PSC), which, in accordance with Article 25 of the EU Treaty, exercises strategic and political control of all EU operations. The PSC has powers not only to take 'relevant decisions' that fundamentally affect the operation, but it also exercises authority over the command and control of the operation. The main limit to the PSC's powers is that it cannot, on its own, authorize the alteration or termination of a mission.

Article 13 of the Joint Action on ARTEMIS provides the constitutional basis for the operation. This article states that 'if required, the status of the EU-led forces in the Democratic Republic of Congo shall be the subject of an agreement with the Government of the [DRC] to be concluded on the basis of Article 24 [EU Treaty]'.[40] France also required that Rwanda and Uganda, whose forces were very active in the region, give written consent to the deployment.[41] The EU Military Committee (EUMC) was responsible for implementing the operation while coordination with the UN was ensured through the interaction between the High Representative and the EU Special Representative from the Great Lakes region, acting in close coordination with the EU Presidency.[42]

From an analytical standpoint, it is much easier to explain the various EU legal regimes and institutional mechanisms—the EU Treaty, the PSC, and the Joint Action—than to reconcile the various legal rules that are potentially applicable to the operation under the UN system, as later analysis will show. That does not mean, however, that the EU system is necessarily coherent. As has been observed elsewhere in this book,[43] it seems curious that Article 13 had based the question whether the EU should conclude a Status of Forces Agreement (SOFA) with the DRC on the latter's request to do so.

In practice, the EU, and, for that matter, any state or international organization that wishes to intervene in a conflict occurring in another state, would normally conclude a SOFA or Status of Mission Agreement (SOMA) with the host State

---

[40] Council Joint Action 2003/432/CFSP, 5 June 2003, OJ L-143, 11 June 2003.
[41] See 'Lessons', n 11, above, 12.   [42] See Mace, n 10, above, 2.
[43] See F Naert, Chapter 4 of this volume.

prior to the deployment of its troops. In accordance with Article 12 of the Joint Action on Concordia,[44] the EU concluded, on 21 March 2003,[45] such an agreement with the Former Yugoslav Republic of Macedonia (FYROM) in relation to Operation Concordia, an EU mission that took over from NATO.[46] A consistent approach by the EU would have been for its Joint Action on ARTEMIS to have explicitly specified, or decisively exempted, the conclusion of a SOFA with the DRC.

However, as fuller analysis will later show, there is a significant difference between Operation Concordia and Operation ARTEMIS in terms of their legal character, and it is this difference that underlines why Concordia expressly included a SOFA with the host State (FYROM) and ARTEMIS did not. Whereas Operation Concordia was essentially a peacekeeping operation, ARTEMIS was, in all its legal ramifications, an enforcement action. While it was mandatory for FYROM to consent or accede to Operation Concordia (hence the need to have a status of force agreement with that state), as a prerequisite for deployment of foreign troops on its soil, such consent is not applicable to a non-consensual enforcement operation such as Operation ARTEMIS.

Therefore, when the EU referred to a possible requirement of a SOFA in its Joint Action, it was superfluous: the EU was not legally bound to obtain such consent as a precondition for deploying its troops in the DRC. Nor, indeed, was France under any obligation to obtain consent from other parties to the conflict—Uganda and Rwanda—prior to deploying the IEMF. The requirement of host State consent is an essential feature that distinguishes a peacekeeping operation, such as Operation Concordia, from an enforcement action like Operation ARTEMIS.

4.2. Operation ARTEMIS and the UN Charter: the conflict within

Technically speaking, there should be no problem with conducting a legal analysis of Operation ARTEMIS under the UN Charter rules. After all, the operation could pass off as a simple case of the Security Council calling to service one of the numerous regional organizations that the UN Charter empowers it to utilize under Chapter VIII, as and when it desires. In such a legal analysis, the exercise of the Security Council's powers, in the manner the Security Council related to the EU in this case, would primarily, and almost exclusively, focus on the construction of Article 39 of the UN Charter. This article entitles the Security Council to make any recommendations with regards to any situations it has decided threaten or actually breach international peace and security. However, complications arise where the Security Council, in the exercise of this power in a given situation, conflates different legal regimes, such as the UN Charter and the constitution of the concerned

---

[44] 2003/92/CFSP.   [45] OJ L-82, 29 March 2003, 45–6.
[46] Art 1 Council Decision 2003//202/CFSP, 27 January 2003, restated in OJ L-34, 11 February 2003 at 26. For a fuller account of Operation Concordia, see F Naert, Chapter 4 of this volume.

regional organization, in a manner both alien to the Security Council's practice and unsupported by the concerned organization's constitutional order.

Had the Security Council merely authorized a coalition of 'able and willing' states to use 'all necessary means' to stabilize Bunia, as it often does when acting under Chapter VII,[47] legal analysis would have invariably turned on, and in all likelihood been confined to, whether 'all necessary means', in this context, includes the use of force, an interpretation that most commentators seem to favour today.[48] The other possible area that would have merited attention would be to investigate whether the authorization to use all necessary means came *before*, *after*, or *simultaneously* with the beneficiary state's exercising the right of self-defence (Article 51). An exercise of a right of self-defence under Article 51 of the UN Charter does not require authorization by the Security Council, as shown clearly by the US-led military action to expel Iraqi troops from Kuwait in 1990.

Unfortunately, Operation ARTEMIS did not benefit from such an accumulation of legal certainties as described above. There had been no attack on any EU Member States by the DRC—which could have activated Article 51 and justified the EU's action against elements within that country under Article 51. Nor could it be justifiably asserted that the humanitarian situation in Bunia, at the relevant period, was of the magnitude that could warrant the invocation of the controversial doctrine of humanitarian intervention as NATO had done four years earlier in Kosovo.[49] Although there was undeniably a desperate humanitarian situation in most parts of the DRC, Resolution 1484, for whatever reasons, did not invoke humanitarian reasons as a basis for the intervention by the EU. The Security Council had simply acted under Chapter VII of the UN Charter.

By determining in Resolution 1484 that the situation in the Ituri region and Bunia threatened international peace and security, the Security Council undoubtedly avoided the limitations contained in Article 2(7) of the UN Charter which forbid the UN to interfere in matters that are essentially within the domestic jurisdiction of its Member States. And once the Security Council removed this restraint, it was free to authorize the multinational stabilization force to 'take all necessary means to fulfil its mandate'.[50]

---

[47] See L Sohn, 'The Authority of the United Nations to Establish and maintain a Permanent United Nations force' (1958) AJIL 229; N White and Ö Ülgen, 'The Security Council and the Decentralised Military Option: Constitutionality and Function' (1997) XLIV Netherlands Intl L Rev 378.

[48] See N Blokker, 'Is Authorization Authorized? Powers and Practice of the UN Security Council to Authorize the Use of Force by "Coalitions of Able and Willing"' (2000) Eur J of Intl L 541; M Koskenniemi, 'The Place of Law in Collective Security' (1999) 17 Michigan J of Intl L 455; T Gill, 'Legal and Some Political Limitations of the Security Council to Exercise Its Enforcement Powers under Chapter VII of the Charter' (1995) 25 Netherlands Intl Ybk of Intl L 33.

[49] See A Cassesse, '*Ex Injuria ius Oritur*. Are We Moving Towards Legitimation of Forcible Humanitarian Countermeasures in the World Community?' (1999) 10(1) Eur J of Intl L 23; B Simma, 'NATO, the UN and the Use of Force: Legal Aspects' (1999) 10(1) Eur J of Intl L 1; N White, 'The Legality of Bombing in the Name of Humanity' (2000) 5(1) J of Conflict and Security L 27.

[50] S/RES/1484 (2003), 30 May 2003.

However, in choosing not a group of random states but a regional organization to implement its mandate, the resolution opened up more doctrinal controversy on Chapter VIII. The power so delegated to Operation ARTEMIS was to execute an *enforcement* action, an interpretation that is justified by the reference to 'all necessary measures' in contradistinction to a classical peacekeeping operation. Doubtless the Security Council has the authority to do this, but the question is whether it also has the authority to endow an organization foreign to the region of a conflict, and none of whose members is affected by it, with the power to intervene in the conflict?

It might be argued that by authorizing the EU to act outside Europe, the Security Council acted ultra vires its constitutional powers and that the EU, in accepting, also went beyond what was legally permissible under its treaty. While the former rationale is worthy of examination—if, at least, to ensure that the Security Council had not acted illegitimately on this occasion—it is rather pointless to engage in studying whether or not the EU, by acting outside its region, acted ultra vires its constitution, for two reasons. First, the decision to go to the DRC was not taken by the EU but by the Security Council acting under Chapter VII.[51] The relevant question therefore should be whether the Security Council can legally authorize a regional organization to act under Chapter VII and, if it does, whether a regional organization is under an obligation (under Article 25 of the UN Charter) to implement the decision of the Security Council. Put differently, is the EU, as a regional organization, bound by the obligation in Article 25 to implement the Security Council decision to intervene in Bunia since that article addresses states not organizations?

This query is fundamentally different from that concerning the Security Council's competence to authorize a regional organization to act outside its region. The present inquiry is important to our analysis because it cannot simply be assumed that the Security Council is always free to imply powers not expressly conferred on it in the Charter, particularly when there are specific provisions in the Charter—in this case Chapter VIII—that cater for the situation.

There is nothing in the UN Charter that explicitly grants the Security Council the liberty to authorize regional actions alternately under Chapters VIII and VII, as though both chapters were appropriate or equally apply to regional actions. Chapter VIII is the substantive framework governing how the Security Council could delegate powers to regional organizations. As far as the formal scheme of the Charter on regional actions is concerned, therefore, the question whether the Security Council could authorize regional organizations under Chapter VII is a valid one.

If we overlook the apparent inconsistency of the Security Council in authorizing Operation ARTEMIS under Chapter VII instead of Chapter VIII, it is doubtful whether states escape obligations they individually incur under the UN Charter by the mere fact of becoming members of international organizations (for the purpose

---

[51] But see below for analysis of the path taken by the Security Council to authorize the EU.

of Article 25), or simply because the Security Council decides to delegate its powers to them under a different Charter framework. Article 39 of the UN Charter states that the Security Council shall make 'recommendations, *or* decide what measures shall be taken' in order to deal with a situation in respect of which it has determined that a threat to, or breach of, peace has occurred.[52] That provision does not only cover the kind of measures the Security Council could prescribe, but it also governs the range of recommendations that it might decide. There is no sensible reason why such recommendations could not include the Security Council delegating its powers to regional organizations under Chapter VII.

Although in accordance with the above analysis the Security Council is able to authorize regional organizations to take enforcement actions under Chapter VII, it is important to note that it adopted a different approach with regards to Operation ARTEMIS. The Security Council had specifically called on France—as an independent member state of the UN—not the EU, as a regional organization to intervene in Bunia, although France had, in turn, proposed that the mission become an EU operation.[53] The Security Council adopted a similar method in 1999 when it called on Australia to lead other nations to restore peace and security in East Timor, following Indonesia's disruptive exit from that country in the aftermath of East Timor's referendum favouring autonomy from Indonesia.[54] Although the resultant mission, the International Force for East Timor (INTERFET) was led by Australia and was not, strictly speaking, a UN operation, it was nevertheless approved by the Security Council acting under Chapter VII.[55] The main difference between Operation ARTEMIS and INTERFET is that, whereas both operations were authorized under Chapter VII, INTERFET, unlike ARTEMIS, did not take place under the auspices of any regional organization.

The second reason why it is not important to investigate whether by acting in the DRC the EU acted ultra vires its constitution is that it is not unusual for the EU to intervene in foreign countries. Whilst the Helsinki and the Ferreira frameworks concerning the powers and functions of the European Rapid

---

[52] See H Vetschera, 'International Law and International Security: The Case of Force Control' 24 German Ybk of Intl L 144; I Osterdahl, *Threat to the Peace: The Interpretation by the Security Council of Article 39 of the UN Charter* (Uppsala: Iustus Forlag, 1998); Y Dinstein, *War, Aggression and Self-Defence*, 3rd edn (Cambridge: Cambridge University Press, 2001) 247 et seq.

[53] See F Grignon, 'The Artemis Operation in the DRC. Lessons Learned for the Future of EU Peacekeeping in Africa' IGC, in a paper presented at the IEEI International Conference on 'The Challenges of Europe-Africa Relations: An Agenda of Priorities' Lisbon, 23–24 October 2003, cited by Faria, n 7, above, at 41.

[54] S/RES/1269 (1999) 15 September 1999; S/RES/1272(1999) 25 October 1999; S/RES/1319 (2000) 20 September 2000. See A Cobb, 'East Timor and Australia's Security Role: Issues and Scenarios', available at <http://wopared.parl.net/library/pubs/CIB/1999–2000/2000cib03.htm#3>.

[55] INTERFET was not a UN mission in the sense of its being adopted by the UN. Its main mandate was to maintain peace and security in East Timor and protect the UN Transitional Administration in East Timor (UNTAET) from the rampaging Indonesian and local Timorese militiamen who resorted to violence in protest at the result of the referendum favouring autonomy for the East Timorese from Indonesia. See B Gill and J Reilly, 'Sovereignty, Intervention and Peacekeeping: The View from Beijing', available at <http://www.csis.org/media/csis/press/00fallgill_reilly.pdf>.

Reaction Force speak of the EU being able to deploy where NATO cannot—a phrase which could mean EU undertaking collective security *within* its Member States, unlike NATO—it has been said that the EU cannot intervene militarily in Member States' conflicts.[56] Whether this represents a correct reading of the legal authority of the EU collective security mechanism remains to be seen, and given the acute sensitivity of NATO to EU's projected involvement in collective security in Europe, this issue seems destined for much greater political attention.

The issue remains though as to whether the Security Council acted intra vires the UN Charter in authorizing Operation ARTEMIS to act in the DRC. As stated above, this is a separate and distinct issue from whether the Security Council is competent to authorize regional organizations under Chapter VII.

It might be argued that the Security Council cannot authorize an organization to act outside its region and on issues not contained in the organization's constituent instrument.[57] This view is based on the argument that when Article 52(1) of the UN Charter talks about situations 'appropriate to regional agencies', it is referring to the particular region of the concerned organization.[58] This argument is also supported by the contention that the word 'situation' is used in that article to preclude situations of armed hostilities.[59]

It is tempting to, yet again, engage in discussion about the Security Council's powers under Chapter VIII, but it is not the intention here to deal extensively with these issues as this has been done more fully elsewhere.[60] Moreover, it is now beside the point whether the Security Council *can* utilize a regional organization outside its own region as it did so in the instant case. The question is whether, in so doing, the Security Council acted under the appropriate constitutional framework of the UN Charter. What is certain is that it appears both presumptuous and unconvincing to limit the Security Council's ability to delegate its powers only to organizations acting within their regions. Nothing in the history of the negotiation of the UN Charter or its texts supports this interpretation.[61] One recognizes, however, that this summation does not explain why, despite authorizing the EU collectively, the Security Council failed to refer to Chapter VIII. After all, its action in Bosnia-Herzegovina indicated its preference for *simultaneously* acting under Chapter VII and Chapter VIII whenever it wishes to make use of states acting per se and those acting under the auspices of regional organizations. The involvement of non-EU members in Operation ARTEMIS would suggest that the operation was conducted under Chapter VII and Chapter VIII.

[56] Comment by the Norwegian Representative to the AU/G8 Summit, held on 26 October 2005, Addis Ababa, Ethiopia, attended by this writer.

[57] On the general point on whether regional organizations can act outside their regions, see Simma, n 16, above.

[58] See J-P Cot and A Pellet (eds) *La Charte des Nations Unies: Commentaire: article par article*, 2nd edn (Paris : Economica) 810; Simma, 'Commentary', n 16, above, 691.

[59] See Simma, 'Commentary', n 16, above, 807; De Wet, 'The Relationship between the Security Council and Regional Organizations during Enforcement Action under Chapter VIII of the United Nations Charter' (2002) 71 Nordic J of Intl L 1.   [60] See Abass, n 6, above.

[61] See UNCIO Document, vol 12, 708.

From the records of the Security Council's meeting leading to the adoption of Resolution 1484, there is virtually no indication as to why the Security Council ignored Chapter VIII. It is common knowledge that the Security Council is inconsistent when it comes to applying Charter provisions. Certainly, it would have been constitutionally correct for the Security Council to have invoked Chapter VIII. Yet no provisions of the UN Charter make such a reference indispensable, and considering that the Security Council had not directly approached the EU to lead the mission, such a specific reference to Chapter VIII is therefore not necessary.

Also, it is not implausible to argue that had it acted under Chapter VIII specifically, the Security Council would have made itself vulnerable to criticism by African regional organizations, if not others, as to why it did not call on any of them to implement Resolution 1484 in Bunia. And such reactions, had they come particularly from African states, would have been difficult to dispel. True, there may be a shortage of material capacity on the part of African organizations to undertake the enormous challenge in the DRC, but the Security Council would have had a difficult time convincing these organizations, and perhaps the rest of the world, that there was a shortage of human resources in Africa to implement its mandate in Bunia. At the peak of the crisis, the Economic Community of West African States (ECOWAS) had deployed almost 17,000 troops to Sierra Leone.[62] When this is compared to the less than 2,000 forces that eventually made up Operation ARTEMIS, or the initial 5,000 or so in the UN's own Mission in Congo (MONUC), any arguments by the Security Council that African organizations lack human capacity for peace support operations would have flown in the face of the evidence. Whatever accounts for the Council's choice of authority in mandating Operation ARTEMIS, it does not prejudice or weaken the mission's constitutional basis in the UN Charter. The Security Council had acted under the authority of Chapter VII and, as far as legality is concerned, its action is unassailable. The interesting question then is what is the constitutional character of Operation ARTEMIS under the UN Charter?

4.2.1. *Operation ARTEMIS as an enforcement action under Chapter VII*

As noted above, the Security Council acted under Chapter VII, not Chapter VIII, in authorizing Operation ARTEMIS. Through Resolution 1484, the Security Council authorized the deployment of the IEMF in Bunia to:

[c]ontribute to the stabilization of the security conditions and the improvement of the humanitarian situation in Bunia, to ensure the protection of the airport, the internally displaced persons in the camps in Bunia and, if the situation requires it, to contribute to the safety of the civilian population, [UN] personnel and the humanitarian presence in the town.

---

[62] See K Nowrot and E Schabaker, 'The Use of Force to Restore Democracy: International Legal Implications of ECOWAS Intervention in Sierra Leone' (1998) 14(2) American U J of Intl L Rev 321.

The resolution empowered Operation ARTEMIS to 'take all necessary measures to fulfil its mandate'.[63] Legal analysis of similar provisions in Security Council practice, for example in Resolution 678,[64] leads to an interpretation of this paragraph as authorizing Operation ARTEMIS to use force to implement the mandate in the Resolution. But care must be taken not to confuse the legal authority for the use of force in Resolution 1484, as an enforcement action, with the kind of force that peacekeepers are traditionally entitled to use even when undertaking a consensual peacekeeping operation.[65] The assumption that the troops of Operation ARTEMIS had already 'proved themselves willing [to use force] if necessary',[66] as an indication that the operation was willing to take enforcement action prior to the authorization of force by the Security Council under Chapter VII, is erroneous. The return of fire with fire, as the troops of Operation ARTEMIS did on 16 June, was a legitimate use of force in self-defence of peacekeepers under the permissible rules of peacekeeping operations, which do not require any Security Council authorization.[67] Such uses of force are distinguishable from the use of force for enforcement purposes, which Resolution 1484 authorized Operation ARTEMIS to take.

The use of force by peacekeepers in self-defence is a lawful action that can only be taken *after* peacekeepers have been fired on by rebels or combatants (or where their lives are otherwise preponderantly imperilled) but not *before* any of these conditions have occurred. Conversely, the use of force in the lawful pursuit of enforcement action is not based on a reciprocal doctrine of returning fire with fire, and indeed peace enforcers can resort to such uses of force proactively or offensively.[68]

Another significant difference between the two uses of force is that where the use of force by peacekeepers in self-defence must be confined to the removal of (or, in compelling cases, the prevention of) dangers or threats to peacekeepers, enforcement actions can be used to determine the outcome of conflict situations and to achieve ends that do not directly relate to the forces.

As stated above, whilst the adoption of the resolution enabling Operation ARTEMIS under Chapter VII possibly explains the non-reference to the 'host' country, the DRC, it has wider implications for that country. Adopting Resolution 1484 under Chapter VII means that Operation ARTEMIS forces could actually

---

[63] Operative para 4.

[64] See J Quigley, 'The United States and United Nations in the Persian Gulf: New World or Disorder' (1992) 25 Cornell Intl L J 1; B Weston, 'Security Council Resolution 678 and the Persian Gulf Decision Making: Precarious Legitimacy' (1991) AJIL 516.

[65] See R Higgins, *United Nations Peacekeeping, 1946–1967: Documents and Commentary, Vol 3 Africa* (Oxford: Oxford University Press, 1980); G Abi-Saab, *The United Nations Operation in Congo, 1960–1964* (Oxford: Oxford University Press, 1978).   [66] See Mace, n 10, above, 1.

[67] See generally Higgins, n 65, above; Abi-Saab, n 65, above; White, n 30, above.

[68] See the *Repertory of Practice of United Nations*, II, 443, available at <http://www.un.org/law/repertory/>.

take action, not only against the rebel forces or warring factions in the DRC, but also against the forces of the legitimate government of the country, especially where the latter act in a way that hinders IEMF in the execution of its mandate.[69]

The instances are rare, however, where a UN mandated force would act against the interests of the legitimate government, especially where such an operation is there for the purpose of restoring peace and security to the country and supporting the rule of law. But rarity does not equate impossibility, although the common practice is for such operations to seek the support of host State governments. The UN Security Council showed acute awareness of the value of such cooperation when it took note, in the preamble to Resolution 1484,[70] of the support for Operation ARTEMIS by the DRC President, parties to the conflict, and even interested outsiders such as Rwanda and Uganda.

4.3. Operation ARTEMIS and the obligation to report under the UN Charter

Authorizing Operation ARTEMIS under Chapter VII reveals a lacuna in the application of the Charter rules to regional organizations mandated by the Security Council. Article 54 of the UN Charter obliges regional organizations to keep the Security Council informed, at all times, of measures they take or contemplate taking towards resolving conflicts.[71] But nothing in this provision limits that obligation to when regional organizations act in respect of conflicts occurring in their own regions. Additionally, it is certain that, given the desire of the Security Council to use this provision as leverage on regional enforcement actions in particular, the rule applies also to actions taken by regional organizations outside their own regions.

Problems arise where a regional organization is authorized under Chapter VII and not Chapter VIII, as with Operation ARTEMIS. Does this exempt the EU from the obligation to report, thereby implying that it is entirely free to decide on or contemplate any measure to implement the Council resolution? If the rationale of Article 54 is confined to Chapter VIII, then there can be no doubt that the chain of reporting is broken once the Security Council authorizes a regional organization under Chapter VII. However, such an interpretation flies in the face of common sense, and also is inconsistent with the *travaux préparatoires* of Chapter VIII as a whole. The entire framework of Chapter VIII itself was origi-

---

[69] An example is Liberia under Samuel Doe's regime where ECOWAS stated clearly that it required no authorization from any of the parties to the conflict in order to implement its mandate. See K O Kufor, 'The Legality of the Intervention in the Liberia Civil War by the Economic Community of West African States' (1993) (5) African J of Intl L and Comparative L 525.

[70] Preamble para 7.

[71] 'The Security Council shall at all times be kept informed of activities undertaken or in contemplation under regional arrangement or by regional agencies for the maintenance of international peace and security.'

nally intended to form part of Chapter VII's legal continuum;[72] it is a matter of convenience that Article 54, as with the rest of Chapter VIII, finds itself disconnected from Chapter VII.[73]

There is an acknowledged interrelationship between certain provisions of Chapters VII and VIII.[74] For instance, Article 51 in Chapter VII governing self-defence was inserted in the UN Charter in order to protect regional organizations, which, of course, falls under Chapter VIII. The Inter-American System was particularly concerned that if all powers to authorize the use of force in all situations were left to the Security Council as originally intended, then states' survival would be endangered when faced with attacks.[75] The fear then was that a member of the permanent Security Council would use its veto to prevent the Council from acting decisively in the face of serious threat to life and limb in the concerned UN Member State.[76] Some of the regional organizations that predated the UN Charter thus insisted on their names being specifically inserted in the Charter to guarantee their security.[77] But instead of obliging this request, a compromise was reached whereby Article 51 would be incorporated in the Charter as an interim measure to enable states to defend themselves until the Security Council took measures prescribed under that provision.[78] Although the text of Article 51 would eventually address 'states' as the beneficiaries of this protection, it is incontrovertible that Article 51 owes its existence to the foresight of regional organizations, and, as such, its provisions apply *mutatis mutandi* to such organizations as they do to states. Evidently, Article 51 is contained in Chapter VII of the Charter, whereas its original principal beneficiaries (regional organizations) reside in Chapter VIII.

The conclusion to be drawn from the above brief exploration of Chapters VII and VIII is that there is need to accommodate some level of interaction between the provisions of the two chapters when applying them to specific situations. Hence, in light of the purpose and objectives of Chapter VIII, as an instrument of delegation by the Security Council, and given that certain elements of Chapter VII apply to Chapter VIII actors, the adoption of Operation ARTEMIS resolution

---

[72] See Doc 576III/4/9, May 25 1945, UNCIO vl 12, particularly the statement of the Colombian Foreign Minister Lleras-Camargo, serving then as the Chairman of the Committee III/4 responsible for regional arrangements, at 680.   [73] Ibid, 680–681.

[74] See E V Rostow, ' "Until What"? Enforcement or Collective Self-Defence?' (1991) 85 AJIL 452.

[75] See C Fenwick, 'The Inter-American Regional System: Fifty Years of Progress' (1956) 50 AJIL 18; J Frowein and R Wolfrum, 'Security Council Control over Regional Action' (1997) 1 Max Planck Ybk of United Nations L 129.

[76] See L Goodrich, 'Regionalism and the United Nations' (1949) Columbian J of Intl Affairs 10; E Padilla, 'The American System and the World Organization' (1945) 24 *Foreign Affairs* (October) 104.

[77] See Docs 576 III/4/9, 25 May 1945, *United Nations Conference on International Organization* Vol 12, 684; Simma, 'Commentary', n 16, above, 687.

[78] See R Russell, *A History of the United Nations Charter: The Role of the United States 1940–1945* (Washington, DC: The Brookings Institution, 1958) 688 et seq; J Sutterlin, *The United Nations and the Maintenance of International Peace and Security: A Challenge to be Met* (Connecticut: Praeger, 1995) 93.

under Chapter VII does not free the EU from its obligations under Article 54. On the contrary, the utilization of a regional organization outside its own region actually raises the stake of that obligation much higher than when regional organizations act within their own regions. Consequently, there was a stricter requirement on the EU to comply with Article 54 of the UN Charter when implementing Resolution 1484.[79]

5. Operation ARTEMIS and the Third States

An examination of Operation ARTEMIS would be incomplete without considering the participation of third States in the operation. 'Third States' as used in this chapter refers to those states, which are not EU Member States (although some of them are European states), whose contributions to the operation are not only significant to the success of the operation, but whose 'identity' makes Operation ARTEMIS one of the most unique operations undertaken by a regional organization. These states are: Cyprus and Hungary, (both European but non-EU Member States), South Africa and Uganda (African states), and, finally, Brazil and Canada (South and North American states respectively). Clearly, in terms of geographical spread, few regional actions, if any, benefited from wider participation than Operation ARTEMIS. Also, the involvement of these individual countries in an operation undertaken by a regional organization adds a new dynamic to the way the Security Council conceives of its powers vis-à-vis regional organizations.[80]

Article 10 of the Joint Action provides the legal basis for the participation of third States in Operation ARTEMIS. This article empowers the PSC to 'take appropriate action with regard to participation arrangement'. Accordingly, the PSC approved third States' participation on 1 July 2003, according special recognition to Canada in the process.[81] It is the responsibility of the Operation Commander and the EUMC to access proposals for contributions from interested states and take decisions on this. Such a proposal was accepted from Cyprus, which decided to join the operation after the deployment.

The degrees of participation by third States differ. Brazil and Canada[82] (alongside Germany, Greece, and the UK) contributed to troops and strategic airlifting,

---

[79] At the political level, the EU did not accept a subordination of its PSC to the Security Council although it (the EU) did report to the Security Council measures taken towards implementing the mandate in UN Res 1484. See S Biscop and E Drieskens, 'Effective Multilateralism and Collective Security: Empowering the UN', Working Paper 16, available at <http://aei.pitt.edu/3075/01/IIEBWP016-DRIESKENS-BISCOP.pdf> 14.   [80] See below for analysis.
[81] For a detailed analysis of Canada's participation in EU missions, see J Fraterman, *Canada–EU Cooperation in Military Crisis-Management: Principles, Modalities and Practice, European Foreign Policy Unit Working Paper*, 2006/1 available at <http://www.lse.edu/Depts/intrel/pdfs/EFPU%20Working%20Paper%202006%201.pdf>.
[82] See N Neuwahl, 'Editorial: The Atlantic Alliance: For better or for Wars . . . ' (2003) 8 *Eur Foreign Affairs Rev* 427.

while South Africa supplied troops and helicopters.[83] Uganda provided the mission with a logistics and communication base at Entebbe, even though operational planning was conducted from the French *Centre de Planification et de Conduite des Opérations* (CPCO) at Creil, to 'which were seconded officers from thirteen other countries, thus demonstrating the potential for multinationalisation of a national HQ'.[84] Cyprus and Hungary participated in mission headquarters administration only, probably because Cyprus did not join the mission until after the deployment of troops.[85] Brazil was the only third State that rendered both services.

However, contrary to precedents laid down in Operation Concordia in Macedonia,[86] certain third State participants in Operation ARTEMIS were exempted from financial obligations under the agreement. On 10 June the EU informed Canada of its readiness to waive all costs incurred by Canada in the operation.[87] There are two possible explanations for this exemption. First, it seems that the reluctance of Canada to 'commit a force contingent without first receiving assurances that it would not be forced to foot a disproportionate amount of the associated common costs',[88] as was the case with Concordia, compelled the EU to so decide. Secondly, Operation ARTEMIS was not, strictly speaking, an EU operation, as it was mandated by the Security Council. Conversely, it can be argued that since Canada did not legally require the approval of the EU to participate in the operation, it equally was under no obligation to contribute to the EU's operation costs.[89]

Constitutionally, it is correct to hold that there is no legal obligation for Canada to obtain the EU's approval as a condition for participating in Operation ARTEMIS, especially since the UN called on individual members, not the EU as an organization, to lead the operation.[90] But that leaves unsolved the question of who then pays for Canada? It is doubtful whether the EU would be under an obligation to settle costs incurred by Canada in these circumstances. However, given that Canada's participation was expressly welcomed and politically approved by the EU, this brings Canada within the EU fold for the purpose of cost administration. It does seem likely that, as a kind gesture, the EU decided to waive the costs incurred by Canada. In any case, the total costs of the Operation were about

---

[83] J Howorth, 'Spending Patterns and Defence Budgets', available at <http://www.mil.be/rdc/viewdoc.asp?LAN=nl&FILE=doc&ID=131>.   [84] Ibid.

[85] Cyprus only participated in the Headquarters administration.

[86] D Corin, 'EU facing Battle over Costs of Peacekeeping in Bosnia', *Eur Voice*, 23 September 2004.

[87] Cited by Fraterman, n 81, above, 16. As one commentator opined, the decision to exempt third States from financial obligations was motivated by the withdrawal from Operation Concordia of one of the third States which participated in that operation. The said state objected to the financial contribution assessed to it under Operation Concordia, and being also a third State participant in ARTEMIS, it lobbied for a complete exemption of third States from common costs. However, it is premature to assume that this exemption constitutes a precedent for future operations. See Mace, n 10, above, 2.   [88] Fraterman, n 81, above, 17.

[89] Ibid, 16.   [90] See above.

€7 million, and 'it seems unlikely that Brussels would have risked quibbling over a small amount'.[91]

An important question with regards to third States' participation in Operation ARTEMIS, and the EU, concerns the responsibility for command and control vis-à-vis the UN. As stated, the third States that took part in Operation ARTEMIS are non-EU members and to that extent do not fall under Chapter VIII. This means that these states cannot be subject to any degree of control by the Security Council under Chapter VIII or by the EU itself under its legal regime, not being signatories to such. It seems arguable, however, that since the operation was authorized under Chapter VII, then the Security Council would be able to exercise direct control over the activities of those states, although nothing prevents the states from acting in tandem with the EU states.

Models for the Security Council directly controlling states, which act alongside regional organizations in the same operation, exist in the Security Council's handling of the Cote d'Ivoire crisis.[92] Here, the Security Council dealt with ECOMICI (the ECOWAS Mission in Ivory Coast) and France (operating individually) separately.[93] Usually, the mandating resolution, or subsequent resolutions detail the responsibilities of such states. But the parallels of the UN mission in North Korea (1950–3) and the Gulf crises (1990) do not provide worthy examples.[94] Although these operations did not involve regional organizations as such, the UN had nevertheless entrusted responsibility to the USA with the expectation that the USA would report its activities to the Security Council. In both cases, not only did the USA not comply with its reporting obligations under the enabling resolutions, but it also took the unusual step of informing the media of its actions before the UN knew about them.[95] Fortunately, Operation ARTEMIS was relatively short (three months altogether) and benefited from better coordination between the EU and the UN than those aforementioned operations. It might have helped that whereas it was states (particularly the USA) that initiated the operation in North Korea and the Gulf before the involvement of the Security Council, Operation ARTEMIS was deployed under the authority of the Security Council.

---

[91] Fraterman, n 81, above, 16.

[92] S/RES/1514 (2003) 13 November 2003. For analysis of the Third Party Formula in ECOMICI, see Abduolaye Fall, 'ECOWAS Mission in Cote d'Ivoire: Partnership for Peace', available at <http://www.inwent.org/ef-texte/military/fall.htm>.

[93] L Grebie and P Addo, 'Challenges of Peace Implementation in the Cote d'Ivoire', Report on an Expert Workshop by KAIPTC and ZIF, available at <http://www.iss.org.za/pubs/Monographs/No105/3ECOWAS.htm>.

[94] See statement by Pérez de Cuéllar reported in West Africa 3581 (1–7 July 1991), 1076; D A Leurdijk, 'Before and After Dayton: The UN and NATO in the Former Yugoslavia' in T G Weiss (ed), *Beyond Subcontracting: Task-Sharing with Regional Arrangements and Service-Providing NGOs* (Basingstoke: Macmillan, 1998) 49; Quigley, n 64, above.

[95] US Policy in the Persian Gulf: Hearing before the Senate Committee on Foreign Relations 101st Cong, 2d Sess 107 (pt 1) (1990). See T Lie, *In the Cause of Peace* (New York: Macmillan, 1954); M Halberstam, 'The Right of Self-Defense Once the Security Council Takes Action' 17 Michigan J of Intl L 229.

6. The Implications of Operation ARTEMIS for the ESDP and EU/AU Cooperation

Notably, the EU did not involve the AU or any other African organization in Operation ARTEMIS. In fact, there are no records of any formal discussion between the EU and the AU on the operation. The crucial question therefore is: what are the implications of Operation ARTEMIS for the future of the ESDP and EU/AU cooperation, especially in the field of peace and security?

The impact of Operation ARTEMIS on the ESDP is extensive. The operation demonstrated that the EU is capable of undertaking decisive military operations in one of the world's largest countries without the help of home-grown troops and local organizations.[96] Hence those who are cynical about the integrity of the ESDP now have, to some extent, reasons to be optimistic. Although limited in scope and duration, Operation ARTEMIS also confirmed that the EU is able to function independently of NATO, a realization that did not appear to have gone down well with certain NATO states, particularly the USA, which insisted that the EU should desist from taking such autonomous actions as Operation ARTEMIS.[97] It is curious though that the USA was antagonistic to Operation ARTEMIS, given that neither the USA nor NATO manifested any particular interest in intervening in the DRC crisis.[98] Be that as it may, Operation ARTEMIS could be regarded as a clear signpost, a 'watch-this-space' gesture by the EU to NATO that in the maintenance of international peace and security, be it in Europe, the Balkans or Africa, the EU welcomes NATO as a credible partner, but to no greater extent than it (the EU) is prepared to go it alone if it considers that such solo performances are consonant with the interests of its Member States and augur well for the direction of its security and defence policy.

It might be too early to claim that Operation ARTEMIS confirmed the EU's capacity to act alone at all times,[99] in the light of the limited scope of the operation, compared to those usually confronted by such collective security actors as NATO and ECOWAS. Nevertheless, Operation ARTEMIS has emboldened the EU and given its authorities the necessary platform to advance the course of the ESDP with the required expediency and determination. Although the EU had already operationalized its Rapid Reaction Force (RRF) before deploying ARTEMIS[100], it established in 2004 an agency devoted to defence capabilities, research, and acquisition of armaments.[101]

Operation ARTEMIS also affects the EU/UN relationship. As stated earlier, the EU did not subordinate its PSC to the UN Security Council during

---

[96] On the capacity of the EU for crisis management, see H-C Hagman, 'European Crisis Management and Defence: The Search for Capabilities' *Adelphi Paper* 353.
[97] See Faria, n 7, above, 47.   [98] Ibid, 47 et seq.   [99] Ibid, 47.
[100] The RRF was operationalized in May 2003, notwithstanding that only 20,000 out of its projected 60,000 forces were ready. See Faria, n 7, above, 48.
[101] General Affairs Council Conclusions, 17 November 2003; see also Faria, n 7, above, 48.

Operation ARTEMIS. Yet the operation 'highlighted the need . . . to detail the relations between the UNSC and the EU when acting on behalf of the former'.[102] Increased participation by the EU in military operations in Europe and Africa will inevitably increase the frequency with which the EU and UN will have to coordinate their activities.[103] Since most such joint operations will probably happen in Africa, and given that the AU currently lacks the required capacity for effective collective security operations, the EU's contributions to police and military missions will go a long way in filling the 'glaring gap between the demand and the supply of capable peacekeeping forces that the international community can mobilize'.[104]

The non-inclusion of AU forces in Operation ARTEMIS speaks to a different impact of the ESDP on EU/AU cooperation. As a matter of practice, the EU, unlike the AU, does not operate on the basis of European sub-regional organizations, nor does it, as yet, have such a holistic framework of continental architecture for peace and security as the AU is currently developing. In the Architecture for Peace and Security in Africa (APSA), the AU will function in collaboration with sub-regional organizations. Hence, the troops of the African Standby Force to be deployed to conflict situations from time to time will be composed of troops from sub-regional brigades. It is possible therefore that, with no formal scheme of collaboration between the EU and European sub-regional groupings, the EU did not feel any particular need to act in conjunction with either the AU, which, in any case, was barely two years old when ARTEMIS was deployed.[105]

It is even possible that involving African sub-regional organizations that are immediately concerned with the crisis—the Southern African Development Community (SADC), the Intergovernmental Authority on Development (IGAD), and the Common Market for Eastern and Southern Africa (COMESA)—would be counter-productive. There is a deep involvement of members of some of these organizations in the crisis in the DRC. In addition, the intense diplomatic battle between especially IGAD, COMESA, and the East African Community (EAC) for the control of the Eastern Brigade (EastBrig) that would compose the African Standby Force in any resultant operation in the DRC makes the involvement of those organizations in Operation ARTEMIS highly unattractive. Although this brigade had not been formed at the time Operation ARTEMIS was deployed, the present disagreement would certainly have emerged in one

---

[102] Biscop and Drieskens, n 79, above, 14, quoting T Tardy, *L'Union Européenne et L'ONU dans la Gestion de crise: Opportunités et Limites d'une relation Déséquilibrée*, Recherches et Documents No 32 (Paris: Fondation pour la recherché Stratégique, 2004).

[103] On EU/UN cooperation, see K Lenaerts and De Smijter, 'The United Nations and the European Union: Living Apart Together' in K Wellens and E Suy (eds), *International Law: Theory and Practice. Essays in Honour of Eric Suy* (The Hague: Martinus Nijhoff, 1998) 439.

[104] M O'Hallon and P W Singer, 'The Humanitarian Transformation: Expanding Global Intervention Capacity' (2004) 46(1) *Survival* 77.

[105] As confirmed by this writer, there was no record of any discussion between the EU and the AU on this mission.

form or another had any attempt been made to involve any of these three organizations. It does not help either that there is cross-pollination and proliferation of memberships amongst these three organizations, especially COMESA and SADC. All these make it extremely difficult to achieve consensus or take collective decisions with expediency.

Yet not involving African organizations in Operation ARTEMIS, while militarily expedient, is fraught with certain sociological risks. The concept of ownership is a strong factor in the process of conflict mediation, either in peacekeeping or post-conflict operations such as peacebuilding. This is all the more so in the DRC case where African organizations have been actively engaged in the crisis for decades. It may be that the urgency of the Bunia situation made any coordination with African organizations infeasible at the time. But perpetuating the culture of exclusive European military operations in African conflicts can easily be (mis)-read as an acute manifestation of insensitivity, or that the EU is merely interested in convincing NATO that it could do it alone, rather than helping develop local initiatives and actors in Africa.

The fact, however, that the EU established, in May 2004, the African Peace Facility, totalling €250 million, devoted to supporting African peace operations indicates that encouraging the development of local initiatives and African capacities, rather than direct military interventions, is the future direction of the EU security and defence policy in Africa. To be sure, the EU may yet directly intervene in future African conflicts, but such actions will probably be exceptional and taken in consultation with African organizations.

All told, the deployment of European troops on African soil ends (at least for now) decades of fence-sitting, thereby removing the suspicion amongst African states that Western powers are not genuinely interested in assisting Africans to find concrete solutions to their many crises. The often-generous financial and material contributions Europe has always made available to African states have been perceived as an easy way out for European powers eager to keep their forces within their borders and not send them to the killing fields of Africa.

7. Conclusion

Operation ARTEMIS opened a remarkable chapter in the implementation of collective security by regional organizations, not only because it was the first time the EU had undertaken a direct enforcement operation in Africa, but more because it was the first time the Security Council had unequivocally utilized a regional organization outside its region. The resolve by the international community to stabilize Bunia using not the instrumentality of African organizations but an apparently neutral foreign body might tempt one to conclude that interventions by organizations not familiar with parties to conflicts stand a much better chance of success than the involvement of neighbours.

Yet care must be taken not to exaggerate the future value of Operation ARTEMIS. The operation had a rather limited and, to a large extent, a much simpler mission to accomplish: it would go into the DRC, stabilize Bunia, and get out within three months. It was not saddled with understanding the genesis of the conflict in the DRC as a prerequisite to achieving an abiding truce. It did not have to show particular awareness of the cultural or social dynamics of contending parties, as most peacekeeping operations do with much longer and more delicate mandates. Nor did Operation ARTEMIS troops need to show particular friendliness to any side or waste time on winning the battle for hearts and minds before the real battle in the field. The main mandate for Operation ARTEMIS was to use force to stabilize the region. With such a mandate, troops are placed in a far more secure terrain to operate than when they attempt to create buffer zones across enemy lines.

Of course, some might argue that since Operation ARTEMIS achieved success without seeking knowledge of the local dynamics of the conflict as a condition for intervention, this undermined the usefulness of such a method of conflict resolution. Such a conclusion is not only incorrect, but also does not take into account the context of operations such as ARTEMIS. True, Operation ARTEMIS was swift and surgical and achieved its result as far as its main mandate is concerned. Yet there can hardly be any doubt that such a victory would itself be pyrrhic if not located within a broader context of post-conflict reconstruction.

Thus, to measure the true achievement of Operation ARTEMIS, we need to situate its mandate—stabilization of the Ituri region—within the overall quest to establish peace and security in the DRC. Short EU military operations are not the long-term solution to African problems.[106] The mission of Operation ARTEMIS was one of the very many efforts geared towards accomplishing this broader aim. Other efforts, such as peacekeeping and post-conflict reconstruction, whether these take place long before or after Operation ARTEMIS, will determine the place of Operation ARTEMIS in the conflict in the DRC. Operation ARTEMIS was swift and compact, the sustenance of its success would be a function for MONUC, and its gains can only be consolidated by further efforts. It is in those implicit collaborative efforts that the achievement of Operation ARTEMIS can be truly realized.

---

[106] Faria, n 7, above, 53.

7

The Anti-Terrorism Dimension of ESDP

*Mirko Sossai**

1. Introduction

The response at the EU level to the threat posed by global terrorist networks has increasingly shown its cross-pillar dimension: all policies are involved.[1] The Action Plan on combating terrorism, adopted for the first time on 21 September 2001 and regularly revised, now identifies well over 100 initiatives, listed under the four strands of the EU Counter-Terrorism Strategy endorsed by the European Council in December 2005: prevent, protect, pursue, and respond.[2] Among the priority areas of action, mention should be made of: addressing radicalization and recruitment, information-sharing, combating terrorism financing, mainstreaming counterterrorism in the EU's external relations, and improving civil protection and the protection of critical infrastructure.

It is necessary to situate in that context the issue of the ESDP contribution to the fight against terrorism. By way of introduction, a general point should be made: one of the theoretically challenging aspects of this topic is represented by the process of interdependence between, on one side, the urgency to use all the means available to react against such a threat to internal and international security and, on the other side, the contemporary rapid development of a European security and defence policy. In the meanwhile, the international legal framework has been exposed to interpretative pressure, especially with regard to the discipline of the use of force and the right of self-defence.

---

* Research fellow, LUISS University, Rome, Italy. All website addresses cited were active on 17 October 2006, unless otherwise specified.

[1] See, eg, S Peers, 'EU Responses to Terrorism', (2003) 52 ICLQ 227 et seq; N Vennemann, 'Country Report on the European Union', in C Walter et al (eds), *Terrorism as a Challenge for National and International Law: Security versus Liberty?* (Berlin: Springer, 2004), 217 et seq; A Reinisch, 'The Action of the European Union to Combat International Terrorism' in A Bianchi (ed), *Enforcing International Law Norms Against Terrorism* (Oxford: Hart, 2004) 119–62.

[2] For the Action Plan, see the last updated version Doc 11882/06, *EU Action Plan on Combating Terrorism*, available at <http://register.consilium.europa.eu/pdf/en/06/st11/st11882-re01.en06.pdf>; for the strategy, see Doc 14469/05, *The EU Counter-Terrorism Strategy*, available at <http://register.consilium.europa.eu/pdf/en/05/st14/st14469-re04.en05.pdf>.

This chapter therefore identifies two, albeit connected, levels of analysis: the fight against terrorism in the framework of the Common Foreign and Security Policy (CFSP) and the possible role of the European Union as a regional organization under international law.[3] The following issues need to be investigated: first, the changes terrorism has made to the nature of ESDP against the background of the negotiations on the Treaty establishing a Constitution for Europe;[4] secondly, the consistency of the EU military contribution to the fight against terrorism with general international law and the collective security system.

2. The Contribution of ESDP in the Fight against Terrorism: from Seville to Madrid

When the EU reacted to the terrorist attacks of 11 September 2001 in the USA, the European Council recognized that its contribution to the international fight against terrorism would be enhanced by its budding security and defence policy.[5] However, it took until the 2002 Seville Summit almost a year later to explicitly state that the second pillar would be an anti-terrorist tool as part of the Union's comprehensive approach to the global problem. The Seville Declaration prioritized the Union's external instruments, such as providing anti-terrorism-related assistance to third countries, intelligence cooperation and in general promoting solidarity and international joint efforts, also in the framework of multilateral organizations such as the UN.[6] As for the possible future actions in the field of the ESDP, the European Council stated that the development of the defence policy 'must take fuller account of the capabilities that may be required, in accordance with the Petersberg tasks and the provisions of the Treaty to combat terrorism'.[7]

The recognition of the link between the Union's military capabilities and the goal of fighting terrorism gradually gained acceptance, as evidenced in the

---

[3] See N White, Chapter 14 of this volume.   [4] OJ C-310, 16 December 2004.

[5] *Extraordinary European Council Meeting: Conclusions and Plan of Action*, 21 September 2001: 'It is by developing the Common Foreign and Security Policy (CFSP) and by making the European Security and Defence Policy (ESDP) operational at the earliest opportunity that the Union will be most effective'. Available at <http://eceuropa.eu/justice_home/news/terrorism/documents/concl_council_21sep_en.pdf>.

[6] *Presidency Conclusions—Seville 21 and 22 June 2002* (13463/02), Annex V: *Declaration by the European Council on the Contribution of the CFSP, including the ESDP, to the Fight against Terrorism*, available at <http://ue.eu.int/ueDocs/cms_Data/docs/pressData/en/ec/72638.pdf>. Paras 3 and 4 read as follows:

The Common Foreign and Security Policy, including the European Security and Defence Policy, can play an important role in countering this threat to our security and in promoting peace and stability. Closer cooperation among the Member States is being put into practice to take account of the international situation created by the terrorist attacks of 11 September. The European Council welcomes the progress achieved since September 11 on incorporating the fight against terrorism into all the aspects of the Union's external relations policy.

[7] Ibid, para 6.

European Security Strategy adopted by the European Council on 12 December 2003.[8] Terrorism is recognized as one of the key threats faced by Europe in the twenty-first century, besides the proliferation of weapons of mass destruction, regional conflicts, state failure, and organized crime. The document prepared by Javier Solana, the EU's High Representative for the CFSP, observing the inherent relationship of all the elements, emphasizes that 'the most frightening scenario is one in which terrorist groups acquire weapons of mass destruction'. 'A more capable Europe'—as one of the paragraphs suggests—requires that the EU 'should think in terms of a wider spectrum of missions'. This is already a creative application of the second pillar, in comparison not only with its origins at Maastricht in the early 'nineties but also with the definition of the Petersberg missions included in Article 17(2) TEU after Amsterdam:[9] the reference in the text to 'joint disarmament operations, support for third countries in combating terrorism and security sector reform' mirrored the new provisions included in the Treaty establishing a Constitution for Europe, then signed in Rome on 29 October 2004. However, how the 'Petersberg tasks' might be used in the fight against terrorism was still open to doubt.

The Madrid terrorist attacks of 11 March 2004 sounded a shocking wake-up call for the European public in general. They laid open an internal vulnerability to such attacks which had hitherto not been addressed by the EU or its Member States in a systematic way. The Declaration on Combating Terrorism approved by the European Council on 25 March 2004 was followed by vigorous activity in various fields.[10] For the first time, the European Council emphasized the role which the ESDP could play to improve security within the EU borders. A Solidarity Clause was included in the Declaration,[11] which essentially

---

[8] *A Secure Europe in a Better World: European Security Strategy*, 12 December 2003, available at <http://ue.eu.int/uedocs/cmsUpload/78367.pdf>.

[9] Article 17(2) of the TEU reads as follows: 'Questions referred to in this Article shall include humanitarian and rescue tasks, peacekeeping tasks and tasks of combat forces in crisis management, including peacemaking'. The consolidated version of the Treaty on European Union is published in OJ C-325, 24 December 2002.

[10] The urgency to react against the threat, perceived as imminent, posed by global terrorist networks, made it necessary to enhance the 2001 Plan of Action to Combat Terrorism. Updated strategic objectives were agreed in the Declaration on combating terrorism: (1) deepen the international consensus and enhance international efforts to combat terrorism; (2) reduce the access of terrorists to financial and other economic resources; (3) maximize capacity within EU bodies and Member States to detect, investigate, and prosecute terrorists and prevent terrorist attacks; (4) protect the security of international transport and ensure effective systems of border control; (5) enhance the capability of Member States to deal with the consequences of a terrorist attack; (6) address the factors which contribute to support for, and recruitment into, terrorism; (7) target actions under EU external relations towards priority third countries where counter-terrorist capacity or commitment to combating terrorism needs to be enhanced.

[11] The Declaration on Solidarity against Terrorism (available at <http://www.consilium .europa.eu/uedocs/cmsUpload/79635.pdf>) reads as follows:

We, the Heads of State or Government of the Member States of the European Union, and of the States acceding to the Union on 1 May, have declared our firm intention as follows:

In the spirit of the solidarity clause laid down in Article 42 of the draft Treaty establishing a Constitution for Europe, the Member States and the acceding States shall accordingly act jointly in

constituted a restatement, albeit with some significant changes, of Article I-42 (Article I-43 in the final text) of the draft Constitutional Treaty.[12] Apart from the discussion over its legal nature, the adoption of the Declaration on solidarity against terrorism imparted new vigour to the debate on collective self-defence in the terrorism context and on the specific character of the mutual solidarity against a terrorist attack compared to the mutual assistance clause in Article I-41(7).[13] Another important issue became how to use military capabilities to protect the civilian population against terrorist attacks within the Union.

Since the terrorist attacks in Madrid, the EU counterterrorism initiatives were focused mainly on the internal aspects. Meanwhile, a comprehensive strategy to identify the main elements of the ESDP contribution to the fight against terrorism was in the making. In June 2004 the European Council[14] requested the Political and Security Committee to elaborate a Conceptual Framework. The document was adopted by the Council on 22 November 2004 and then endorsed by the European Council in December 2004. The Framework identifies the main areas of action in which the civilian and the military capabilities can play a role: prevention, protection, response/consequence management, and support to third countries in the fight against terrorism.[15]

This chapter will present the EU's anti-terrorism measures as a cross-cutting issue in principle, which, however, has an increasingly visible ESDP dimension. In particular it will emphasize how the use of ESDP overcomes the distinction between external and internal security. It remains to be seen to what extent EU military capabilities might complement and enhance the diplomatic and financial dimensions of the fight against terrorism.

---

a spirit of solidarity if one of them is the victim of a terrorist attack. They shall mobilise all the instruments at their disposal, including military resources to:
– prevent the terrorist threat in the territory of one of them;
– protect democratic institutions and the civilian population from any terrorist attack;
– assist a Member State or an acceding State in its territory at the request of its political authorities in the event of a terrorist attack.
It shall be for each Member State or acceding State to the Union to choose the most appropriate means to comply with this solidarity commitment towards the affected State.

[12] See section 6 of this chapter, below.

[13] Art I-41:

If a Member State is the victim of armed aggression on its territory, the other Member States shall have towards it an obligation of aid and assistance by all the means in their power, in accordance with Article 51 of the United Nations Charter. This shall not prejudice the specific character of the security and defence policy of certain Member States.

Commitments and cooperation in this area shall be consistent with commitments under the North Atlantic Treaty Organisation, which, for those States which are members of it, remains the foundation of their collective defence and the forum for its implementation.

[14] Doc 10679/2/04 REV 2 *Presidency Conclusions of the Brussels European Council* (17 and 18 June 2004) available at <http://ue.eu.int/ueDocs/newsWord/en/ec/81742.doc>.

[15] Doc 14797/04, *Conceptual Framework on the European Security and Defence Policy Dimension of the Fight against Terrorism*, 18 November 2004, available at <http://register.consilium.eu.int/pdf/en/04/st14/st14797.en04.pdf>.

3. Terrorism as a Key Threat in the European Security Strategy

Terrorism is identified by the European Security Strategy (ESS) as a new threat relatively intangible in comparison with the traditional aggression of a state against another state, since it is less visible and less predictable.[16] Even though terrorist activities had already affected societies in several European countries throughout the second part of the twentieth century, the events of 11 September 2001 in New York and Washington drew attention to the emergence of a new generation of terrorism aimed above all at maximizing human casualties (*hyperterrorisme*, catastrophic terrorism).[17]

The ESS addresses precisely these peculiar aspects of the global fundamentalist networks: international terrorists are less dependent on state sponsorship and they form transnational affiliations having financial and strategic autonomy. Acting through small cells, they are 'willing to use unlimited violence to cause massive casualties'. The strategy recognizes that Europe represents at the same time 'a target and a base for such terrorism'. In this context, the uncontrolled spread of Weapons of Mass Destruction (WMD), their means of delivery and related material by non-state actors for terrorist purposes, is perceived as the worst danger.

Several references to the use of military capabilities in the fight against terrorism are made in the document. A crucial aspect underlined by the Strategy is the need to reconsider the notion of self-defence, which is no longer based on the threat of invasion. Rather, 'the first line of defence will often be abroad'. However, it is hard to infer from these few words the intention to take up a definitive position on the highly-debated issue of the use of force against a terrorist attack under Article 51 of the UN Charter. The sibylline reference to the concept of defence could perhaps be better understood against the background of the principles subsequently affirmed in the document. Attention is given to threat prevention and to the readiness to act before a potential threat occurs. The ESS states furthermore that 'preventive engagement can avoid more serious problems in the future', while the previous version delivered in June 2003 referred to 'pre-emptive engagement'. The different wording could be interpreted as a deliberate move to avoid any possible reference to the doctrine of pre-emption introduced in the National Security Strategy of

---

[16] See further UN Doc A/59/565, *A More Secure World: Our Shared Responsibility: Report of the High-level Panel on Threats, Challenges and Change*, 2 December 2004, 38 et seq, para 107 et seq, available at <http://www.eisil.org/index.php?sid=882305233&id=1834&t=link_details&cat=511>.

[17] See W Laqueur, 'Postmodern Terrorism: New Rules for an Old Game', *Foreign Affairs*, September/October 1996; W Laqueur, *The New Terrorism. Fanaticism and Arms of Mass Destruction* (Oxford: Oxford University Press, 1999); F Heisbourg, *Hyperterrorisme: la nouvelle guerre* (Paris: Odile Jacob, 2001); J Burke, *Al Qaeda, Casting a Shadow of Terror* (London: Penguin, 2004).

the United States.[18] The final version of the ESS would thus confirm the pre-eminence of the non-military option in the context of prevention.[19] However, it does not exclude the use of military means while countering terrorism: 'Dealing with terrorism may require a mixture of intelligence, police, judicial, military and other means'.[20] In this respect, the ESS suggests, in conformity with the redefinition of Petersberg tasks introduced in the Treaty on the European Constitution,[21] an expansion of the scope of crisis management operations: 'we should think a wider spectrum of missions. This might include joint disarma-ment operations, support for third countries in combating terrorism and security sector reform'.

Finally, the European Security Strategy affirms the EU commitment to multi-lateralism: it recognizes the primary responsibility of the UN Security Council for the maintenance of international peace and security and intends to contribute, whenever possible, to UN action in cases of crisis management.

The improvement of 'co-ordination with international organisations on man-aging the response to terrorist attacks and other disasters' is also set out as a key priority by the EU Counter-Terrorism Strategy.[22] It is significant that the docu-ment, which represents the most recent step in the definition of the EU strategic commitment in the fight against terrorism, was adopted by the European Council in line with the ESS.[23]

A comparative analysis of the American and the European approaches on secur-ity issues offers a valuable perspective on the process of re-definition of the notion.[24] In the present changed global context, the traditional concept of *state security* risk is considered to be counter-productive, being unable to tackle the new interrelated threats of the twenty-first century. A recent report, presented by the Study Group on Europe's Security Capabilities, proposes a 'Human Security Doctrine'.[25] Based on the theoretical elaboration of the Commission on Human Security,[26] the report suggests a security approach which 'should contribute to the protection of every individual human being and not focus only on the defence of the Union's borders'.[27]

---

[18] *The National Security Strategy of the United States of America*, 20 September 2002, available at <http://www.whitehouse.gov/nsc/nss.pdf>.
[19] See S Duke, 'The European Security Strategy in a Comparative Framework: Does it Make for Secure Alliances in a Better World?' (2004) 9 *Eur Foreign Affairs Rev* 459, at 473.
[20] ESS, n 8, above, 7.
[21] See Art I-309 of the Constitutional Treaty, section 5 of this chapter, below.
[22] *EU Counter-Terrorism Strategy*, n 3, above, 16.   [23] Ibid, 7.
[24] See, eg, V Petrovsky, F Kratochwil, E Lanc, 'Security: New Threats and New Strategies: Theme II' in (2003) 16 Leiden JIL 873.
[25] See *A Human Security Doctrine for Europe*, The Barcelona Report of the Study Group on Europe's Security Capabilities, 15 September 2004, available at <http://www.lse.ac.uk/Depts/global/Publications/HumanSecurityDoctrine.pdf>.
[26] See *Final Report of the Commission on Human Security*, 1 May 2003, available at <http://www.humansecurity-chs.org/finalreport/index.html>.
[27] *A Human Security Doctrine for Europe*, n 25, above, 9.

4. The Conceptual Framework of the ESDP Dimension of the Fight against Terrorism

The contribution of ESDP to the fight against terrorism has recently been made clearer in the Conceptual Framework prepared by the Political and Security Committee and endorsed by the Brussels European Council on 3 December 2004. The Framework clearly draws inspiration from the ESS and the Declaration on combating terrorism, both in the definition of the fundamental principles[28] which should apply to the use of civilian and military capabilities in the field of counterterrorism and in the identification of the four main areas of action.

The six principles reaffirm the crucial aspects of solidarity and collective action, as stated in the Declaration on combating terrorism and in the ESS: 'concerted European action is indispensable'. Common threat assessment is needed to develop effective policies. The urgency to mobilize all the instruments at the disposal of the EU and of the Member States, including military resources, is then affirmed in the spirit of the solidarity clause: the ESDP provides a meaningful, though complementary, contribution to the overall approach to the fight against terrorism. In this regard, the wide spectrum of measures requires effective cross-pillar coordination, which the EU Counter-terrorism Coordinator is called upon to ensure. Emphasis is laid on the fundamental principle of the voluntary nature of States' contribution, in accordance with the decisions taken at the Helsinki and Feira European Councils.[29] Finally, strengthening international cooperation, in particular with international organizations, remains a priority of the EU efforts in accordance with the commitment to an effective multilateralism affirmed in the ESS.

The focus on prevention, protection, consequence management, and support to third countries reflects the range of priority issues identified by the Declaration and then included in the Revised Plan of Action to combat Terrorism endorsed by the European Council on 17 and 18 June 2004.[30]

It is noteworthy that the document considers not only the scope of crisis management operations outside the Union under Article 17(2) TEU but also the contribution which EU Member States' military resources could offer with regard

---

[28] The following six basic principles apply: (1) solidarity between EU Member States; (2) voluntary nature of Member States' contributions; (3) clear understanding of the terrorist threat and full use of available threat analysis; (4) cross pillar coordination in support of the EU common aim in the fight against terrorism; (5) cooperation with relevant partners; (6) complementary nature of the ESDP contribution, in full respect of Member States' responsibilities in the fight against terrorism and with due regard to appropriateness and effectiveness considerations.

[29] See also Art I-40(3) of the Constitutional Treaty.

[30] The implementation of strategic objective 3 (to maximize capacity within EU bodies and Member States to detect, investigate, and prosecute terrorists and prevent attacks) and objective 5 (to enhance the capability of the EU and of Member States to deal with the consequences of a terrorist attack) requires a specific contribution of the ESDP.

to preventing and limiting the consequences of terrorist attacks within EU borders, as indicated in the Solidarity Clause.

Therefore, in the next two paragraphs the analysis will focus first on the process of expansion of crisis management operations to include the fight against terrorism and on the on-going elaboration of an EU Solidarity programme on assistance between Member States in the prevention, and against the consequences of, terrorist threats and attacks.

5. Petersberg Missions and the Fight against Terrorism

The process of reformulation of the Petersberg tasks in the Treaty establishing a Constitution for Europe led to the adoption of Article I-41(1), which provides that the Union may use civil and political assets 'on missions outside the Union for peace-keeping, conflict prevention and strengthening international security in accordance with the principles of the United Nations Charter'. Article III-309 includes a further definition of the tasks, in which explicit reference is made to the fight against terrorism: they shall include joint disarmament operations, humanitarian and rescue missions, military advice and assistance programmes, conflict prevention and peacekeeping operations and, in addition, 'tasks of combat forces in crisis management, including peace-making and post-conflict stabilisation. All these tasks may contribute to the fight against terrorism, including by supporting third countries in combating terrorism in their territories'.[31]

As is well known, this formulation is broader and more detailed than that included in Article 17(2) TEU. Whether Article III-309 introduces a wider competence of the Union in this field is still far from clear, since the list included in Article 17 does not seem to be exhaustive.[32] In any case, the Conceptual Framework, coming before the entry into force of the Treaty on a Constitution for Europe, has already interpreted the task of EU crisis-management mission in the spirit of Article III-309.[33] This is even more evident in the *potential* scenarios considered by the Conceptual Framework in which missions by EU military forces could operate under Title V of the TEU.

5.1. Prevention

As for the contribution to the prevention of terrorism, the Conceptual Framework interestingly refers to 'maritime and airspace control-type operations'.[34] The kind of operation envisaged here aims at preventing terrorist-related activities

---

[31] See M Ortega, 'Beyond Petersberg: Missions for the EU Military Forces', in N Gnesotto (ed), *EU Security and Defence Policy. The First Five Years (1999–2004)* (Paris: EU-ISS, 2004) 73.

[32] For a discussion of the tasks included in Art 17, see F Pagani, 'A New Gear in the CFSP Machinery: Integration of Petersberg Tasks in the Treaty of the European Union' (1998) 9 EJIL 741.

[33] *Conceptual Framework*, n 15, above, para 4.   [34] Ibid, para 13.

and especially illicit trafficking of nuclear, chemical, and biological weapons and related material by both state and non-state actors. In a similar context, NATO launched Operation *Active Endeavour* on 6 October 2001, following the invocation of Article V of the North Atlantic Treaty: extended in March 2004 after the Madrid terrorist attacks to the whole of the Mediterranean, the mission has the mandate to monitor shipping and to provide escorts to non-military shipping through the Straits of Gibraltar.[35] NATO claims that it has, inter alia, reduced the cost of maritime insurance in the Mediterranean by 20 per cent.[36]

Furthermore, since the attacks of 11 September 2001, the prevention of the illicit trafficking of WMD has gained increasing relevance, as demonstrated by the recent adoption of Security Council Resolution 1540 (2004):[37] several initiatives have been launched in the framework of the political cooperation among G8 members[38] and through the Proliferation Security Initiative (PSI).[39] Announced by President Bush on 31 May 2003, the initiative, which involves fifteen countries and has received widespread support, is aimed at strengthening the necessary capabilities to detect and interdict vessels and aircraft suspected to be trafficking WMD. A Statement of Interdiction Principles was agreed at a PSI plenary meeting in Paris on 4 September 2003.[40] The General Affairs and External Relations Council adopted a statement of support for the initiative on 17 May 2004.[41]

At the moment it is far from clear whether the EU might take over the NATO operation in the Mediterranean in the near future. The 'Berlin Plus' Agreement of 16 December 2002[42] would allow the EU to enhance its operational capabilities,

---

[35] NATO Press Release 2004 (40), 17 March 2004. In an exchange of letters with Russia (9 December 2004) and Ukraine (21 April 2005), NATO defined the modalities of the support of these two countries to the Operation Active Endeavour, which continues to be carried out under Article V of the North Atlantic Treaty.

[36] G Robertson, speech at the BMVG-FAZ Forum, Berlin, 24 June 2003, available at <http://www.bmvg.de/sicherheit/print/030624_bmvg_faz_rede_robertson.php>.

[37] UN Doc S/RES/1540 (2004), 28 April 2004.

[38] *The G8 Global Partnership Against the Spread of Weapons and Materials of Mass Destruction*, available at <http://www.g8.gc.ca/2002Kananaskis/kananaskis/globpart-en.asp>; *G8 Action Plan on Non Proliferation*, available at <http://www.sipri.org/contents/expcon/seaisl2004_nonprolif.html>.

[39] M Byers, 'Policing the High Seas: The Proliferation Security Initiative' (2004) 98 AJIL 526; D H Joyner, 'The Proliferation Security Initiative: Nonproliferation, Counterproliferation, and International Law' (2005) 30 Yale J Intl L 507; J I Garvey, 'The International Institutional Imperative for Countering the Spread of Weapons of Mass Destruction: Assessing the Proliferation Security Initiative' (2005) 10 J Conflict and Security L 125.

[40] See *Proliferation Security Initiative: Statement of Interdiction Principles*, 4 September 2003, available at <http://www.proliferationsecurity.info/principles.html>.

[41] *2582nd Council Meeting, General Affairs and External Relations—GENERAL AFFAIRS, Brussels, 17 May 2004*, available at <ue.eu.int/ueDocs/newsWord/en/gena/80498.doc>:

The European Union and its Member States commit themselves to contribute to the PSI and will take the necessary steps in support of interdiction efforts to the extent their national and Community legal authorities permit and consistent with their obligations under international law and frameworks.

[42] 42 ILM 2003, 42. See M Reichard, 'Some Legal Issues Concerning the EU-NATO Berlin Plus Agreement' (2004) 73 Nordic J Intl L 37.

having recourse to NATO military assets. It should be remembered, however, that *Active Endeavour* is based on Article 5 of the North Atlantic Treaty and it is one of the measures adopted in reaction to an armed attack and not a crisis management operation.

A maritime-type control operation finally raises the issue of the respect of relevant international legal obligations and in particular the question of the applicable provisions of the Convention on the Law of the Sea:[43] for instance, the right of visit in the high seas is limited to the cases provided for in Article 110 of the Convention, 'except where acts of interference derive from powers conferred by treaty'. At the moment, customary international law does not allow high seas interdiction of vessels flagged by non-consenting States, which are suspected of transporting WMD.

5.2. Protection

In the field of protection, the Conceptual Framework identifies the scenario in which EU military forces committed in a crisis management operation under Title V of the EU treaty could be victims of a terrorist attack. The document recognizes the necessity to 'minimise the vulnerabilities of EU personnel, material, assets and, as appropriate, possible key civilian targets, including critical infrastructure' in the area of the crisis management operation.

The updated version of the 'EU Plan of Action on combating terrorism', adopted on 19 November 2004,[44] contains a brief description of the on-going initiatives taken by the Political and Security Committee to implement this aspect of the Conceptual Framework: its preliminary recommendations were expected to be presented to the Council in June 2005.

5.3. Response/consequence management

The scenario here envisaged is slightly different from the previous one, since it refers to the management of consequences after a terrorist act has occurred in an area in which an EU mission under Article 17 of the EU Treaty is already on the ground. The Conceptual Framework affirms that 'in full compliance with the objective of the mission, the EU-led force should be ready to "fill the gap" with military and civilian capabilities while waiting for an expected international civil protection support at high readiness'.

In this context, action 3.7.7 of the revised Action Plan on combating terrorism is aimed at developing a visible and effective rapid response protection capability, which 'would allow an *immediate reaction in the affected area in the immediate*

---

[43] UN Convention on the Law of the Sea, opened for signature 10 December 1982, 1833 United Nations Treaty Series 397.
[44] Doc 14330/04, *EU Plan of Action on Combating Terrorism—Update*, action 3.7.4.

aftermath of a possible terrorist attack, in most cases in support of local authorities and pending the arrival of further expected aid from the international community'.[45] The elaboration of the concept was expected by June 2005: the protection component of the EU-led crisis management operation seems to have a clear humanitarian task, to support third countries in the event of a terrorist attack, providing help to the civilian population. The term 'immediate reaction', although ambiguous, should not be interpreted as permitting a use of force in response to the attack, as confirmed by the explicit limitation provided by the reference to the primary 'objective of the mission'.

5.4. Third countries

Assistance to third countries is one of the crucial recommendations included in Security Council Resolutions 1373 (2001) and 1377 (2001).[46] The ESS had already underlined the need to help third countries respond more effectively against terrorist activities.[47] Counterterrorism technical assistance is becoming a fundamental aspect of EU relations with countries lacking the capacity to implement the mandatory measures provided for, in particular, by Resolution 1373 (2001): lastly, the Hague Programme on freedom, security, and justice, adopted by the EU on 5 November 2004, urges the Council and the Commission to set up a network of national experts for technical assistance and to increase the funding for counter-terrorism related capacity building projects in third countries.[48]

In contrast, the Conceptual Framework does not explain in detail the nature of the ESDP missions in support of third countries for the fight against terrorism in their territory: at first the document recalls the European Security Strategy, when it suggests the development of 'a wider spectrum of missions'. Action point (g) mentions 'the development of appropriate cooperation programmes to promote trust and transparency, the support in planning activities related to the fight against terrorism including consequences management or support in training and exercise'.[49] This kind of activity—reorganization of the armed forces, exchange of good practices, and police training measures—is definitively covered by the list included in Article III-309 of the Treaty on a Constitution for Europe, since it also includes 'military advice and assistance tasks'.[50]

---

[45] *Conceptual Framework*, n 15, above, para 19.i.

[46] UN Doc S/RES/1373 (2001), 28 September 2001; S/RES/1377 (2001), 17 November 2001. See C A Ward, 'Building Capacity to Combat International Terrorism: The Role of the United Nations Security Council' (2003) 8 J Conflict and Security L 289.

[47] Cf Doc SEC (2004) 332, *Commission Staff Working Paper, European Security Strategy: Fight against Terrorism*, 19 March 2004.

[48] Doc 14292/04, Annex I, *The Hague Programme: Strengthening Freedom, Security, Justice in the European Union*, para 2,2 available at <http://ec.europa.eu/justice_home/doc_centre/doc/hague_programme_en.pdf>.   [49] *Conceptual Framework*, n 15, above, para 19.g.

[50] On the development of the ESDP civilian dimension, see Doc 15863/04, *Civilian Headline Goal 2008*, 7 December 2004, available at <http://register.consilium.europa.eu/pdf/en/04/st15/st15863.en04.pdf>. Incidentally, this task definition is very similar to OSCE activity in its first

Whether the support for a third country might entail military operations on the ground to combat terrorist groups is still open to discussion: this activity seems to go beyond the competences of EU military forces under Article 17 of the TEU. In addition, the Conceptual Framework mentions 'the wider issue of the protection of EU citizens in third countries [. . .] especially in the case of EU citizens taken hostage by terrorist groups'. A twenty-year-long doctrinal debate has not solved the question of the lawfulness of the use of force to protect citizens endangered in the territory of a third State, in the absence of its explicit consent.[51] Since a broadening of the scope of self-defence under Article 51 of the UN Charter has been rejected by the International Court of Justice and part of the doctrine,[52] some authors investigated the existence of a customary rule in statu nascendi permitting intervention for protecting nationals abroad.[53]

6. Solidarity against Terrorism

6.1. The content of the Declaration on Solidarity against terrorism

Adopted under the direct impression of the terrorist attacks in Madrid, the Declaration on Solidarity against terrorism states that all Member States shall act jointly in a spirit of solidarity if one of them is the victim of a terrorist attack, mobilizing all the instruments at their disposal, including military resources. It does not constitute a simple political restatement of the Solidarity Clause included in Article I-43 of the Treaty on the Constitution for Europe. Two main differences should be pointed out. First, in the Declaration on Solidarity there is no mention of the Union ('Member States and the acceding States'), whereas Article I-43 refers to the 'Union and its Member States'. Secondly, a final paragraph is added in the Declaration which leaves the Member States free to 'choose the most appropriate means to comply with this solidarity commitment towards the affected State'. These changes appeared to be aimed at reaffirming the sovereignty of the Member States, which 'prevailed over acknowledging any

(political-military) dimension in the same field, particularly with OSCE partner States. Cf OSCE Bucharest Plan of Action for Combating Terrorism (Ninth Meeting of the Ministerial Council, 3 and 4 December 2001) and OSCE Strategy to Address Threats to Security and Stability in the Twenty-First Century (Eleventh Meeting of the Ministerial Council, 1 and 2 December 2003). On the security issues within the OSCE, see the chapter by M Odello, Chapter 13 of this volume.

[51] On this issue, see, eg, N Ronzitti, *Rescuing Nationals Abroad through Military Coercion and Intervention on Grounds of Humanity* (Dordrecht, Boston, Lancaster: Martinus Nijhoff, 1985); T Franck, *Recourse to Force* (Cambridge: Cambridge University Press, 2002); Y Dinstein, *War, Aggression and Self-Defence*, 3rd edn (Cambridge: Cambridge University Press, 2001); A Randelzhofer, 'Article 51', in B Simma (ed), *The Charter of the United Nations: A Commentary* (Oxford: Oxford University Press, 2002) 788.   [52] See section 6 of this chapter, below.

[53] Cf A Randelzhofer, 'Article 2 (4)', in B Simma (ed), *The Charter of the United Nations*, n 51, above, 112, at 133.

Union competence';[54] yet the European Council asked the Commission and the Council to assess Member States' capabilities and to propose the necessary measures.[55]

The recourse to the *travaux préparatoires* of Article I-43 helps, in any case, to shed light on the content of the Declaration. The introduction of a Solidarity clause in the Treaty on the Constitution for Europe was intended to provide a different instrument, in addition to the mutual defence clause included in Article I-41(7), to respond multilaterally to the asymmetric threat represented by the terrorist activities of non-state actors. The suggestions submitted by several members of Working Group VIII demonstrate the variety of approaches on the solidarity clause: whilst some of them argued for the inclusion of an explicit mutual defence clause against terrorism, others supported the deletion of the proposal because of its uselessness.[56] The final report of the Working Group in December 2002 affirmed that: 'Such a clause would not be a clause on collective defence entailing an obligation to provide military assistance, but would apply to threats from non-State entities'.[57] Although the reference to military assistance in the report of the Working Group sounds ambiguous—indeed Article I-43 does not exclude the use of military resources—the peculiar nature of the Solidarity clause is corroborated by two specific elements. The obligation to provide assistance to the state victim of a terrorist attack is restricted to its territory and it is subjected to the express request of its political authorities. A risk of unilateral abuse of the Solidarity clause results from the provision on prevention. In this scenario, the assisting state does not need the previous consent of a state to intervene, even with military force, in its territory: this conduct would definitely amount to a violation of Article 2(4) of the UN Charter and of the correspondent obligation under general international law.

Therefore, further analysis should be devoted to the separation—so clear, at least theoretically—between mutual defence and solidarity. As one author has recently noted, 'the dividing line between mutual defence against an armed aggression, included in Article I-41 and mutual solidarity against a terrorist attack may prove very thin indeed'.[58] There might be an overlap in their scope of application to the extent that a terrorist act might be seen to amount to an armed attack under Article 51 of the UN Charter. After emergence of the US doctrine of

---

[54] See M Reichard, 'The Madrid Terrorist Attacks: A Midwife for EU Mutual Defence?' (2004) 7 *Zeitschrift für Europarechtliche Studien* 313.

[55] Doc 10679/2/04 REV 2, *Presidency Conclusions of the Brussels European Council* (17 and 18 June 2004), n 14, above, para 19.

[56] Proposed Amendments to the text of the Articles of the Treaty Establishing a Constitution for Europe, Part One of the Constitution.

[57] The European Convention, Final Report of the Working Group VIII—Defence, 16 December 2002, para 58.

[58] A Missiroli, 'Mind the Steps: The Constitutional Treaty and Beyond', in N Gnesotto (ed), *EU Security and Defence Policy. The First Five Years (1999–2004)* (Paris: EU ISS, 2004) 149; see also F Naert, 'European Security and Defence in the EU Constitutional Treaty' (2005) 10 J Conflict and Security L 187.

pre-emption, legal debate has focused on the constitutive elements of the notion of armed attack and on its progressive expansion. Some scholars criticized the necessity to attribute an armed attack to a state[59] while others argued for reconsideration of the element of gravity as a defining parameter: in the event of a terrorist act committed by private groups, a military response would not be precluded.

The International Court of Justice in the recent advisory opinion on the 'Legal Consequences of the Construction of a Wall in the Occupied Palestinian Territory', refused to recognize such an evolution in the right of self-defence. Having rejected the argument submitted by Israel, according to which 'the fence is a measure wholly consistent with the right of States to self-defence enshrined in Article 51 of the Charter', the Court strongly stated that 'Article 51 of the Charter thus recognizes the existence of an inherent right of self-defence in the case of armed attack by one State against another State'.[60]

Moreover, the Declaration on Solidarity needs to be interpreted, as for its defence implications, in accordance with Article 11 of the TEU, which affirms the objective to safeguard the common values, fundamental interests, independence, and integrity of the Union in conformity with the principles of the United Nations Charter.[61]

6.2. The problem of the legal nature of the Declaration

The content of the Solidarity clause does not find correspondence in any provision of the TEU. In addition, as acknowledged by the Seville European Council in June 2002, 'the Treaty on the European Union does not impose any binding mutual defence commitments'.[62]

The activation of the Solidarity clause resulted from the urgency perceived by the Member States to elaborate measures in the spirit of Article I-43, before the

---

[59] C Greenwood, 'International Law and the War Against Terrorism' (2002) 78 *Intl Affairs* 301, at p 308; S Murphy, 'Terrorism and the Concept of Armed Attack in Article 51 of the Charter' (2002) 43 Harvard Intl L J 42; C Stahn, ' "Nicaragua is Dead, Long Live Nicaragua"—The Right to Self-defence Under Article 51 UN Charter and International Terrorism', in C Walter et al (eds), *Terrorism as a Challenge for National and International Law: Security versus Liberty?* (Berlin: Springer-Verlag, 2004) 827; contra, G Gaja, 'In What Sense Was There an Armed Attack?' available at <http://www.ejil.org/forum_WTC/ny-gaja.html>.

[60] Para 139 of the Advisory Opinion, 9 July 2004, available at <http://www.icj -cij.org/icjwww/idocket/imwp/imwpframe.htm>. For different perspectives on the position of the Court concerning self-defence, see R Wedgwood, 'The ICJ Advisory Opinion on the Israeli Security Fence and the Limits of Self-Defense' (2005) 99 AJIL 52; S Murphy, 'Self-Defense and the Israeli Wall Advisory Opinion: An Ipse Dixit from the ICJ?' (2005) 99 AJIL 62; I Scobbie, 'Words My Mother Never Taught Me—"In Defense of the International Court" ' (2005) 99 AJIL 76. However, cf separate opinions by Judge Kooijmans and by Judge Simma in the case concerning 'Armed Activities on the Territory of the Congo' (Democratic Republic of the Congo v Uganda), 19 December 2005.   [61] Article 11 of the TEU.

[62] *Annex IV to the Presidency Conclusions of the Sevilla European Council* (21–22 June 2002), para 4, available at <http://www.ecre.org/seville/sevconc.pdf >.

entry into force of the Treaty on the Constitution for Europe: yet any attempt, in light of the law of treaties as codified in the 1969 Vienna Convention, to argue for the legally binding nature of the Declaration must be dismissed.[63] It is excluded that the Member States considered the Declaration a decision under Article 17 of the TEU on the creation of the defence clause. Moreover, the Declaration did not constitute a provisional application of draft Article 42 in accordance with Article 25 of the 1969 Vienna Convention. They did not intend to conclude a new treaty outside the TEU either.[64]

Nevertheless, an interesting approach would be—from a different perspective—to consider the Declaration as 'subsequent practice in the application of the treaty which establishes the agreement of the parties regarding its interpretation'.[65] However, such an interpretation is far from convincing: the wording of the TEU does not admit a mutual defence or solidarity clause.

Thus there is no doubt that the Declaration is a political instrument, as confirmed by the European Council in the Declaration on combating terrorism: 'the political commitment of the Member States and of the acceding States, taken as for now, to act jointly against terrorist acts, in the spirit of the Solidarity Clause contained in Article 42 of the draft Constitution for Europe'.

6.3. Initiatives for the implementation of the Declaration at the EU level

The European Council, in its Conclusions on the fight against terrorism on 17–18 June 2004, invited the Council and the Commission to 'assess the capabilities of Member States both in preventing and coping with the consequences of any type of terrorist attack, to identify best practices and to purpose the necessary measures. Existing cooperation on civil protection should be enhanced, *reflecting the will of Member States to act in solidarity in the case of terrorist attack in any Member States or in the case of attack against EU citizens abroad'*.[66]

On 22 October 2004 the Commission submitted to the Council four Communications on the issue of the 'prevention, preparedness and response to terrorist attacks'.[67] On 2 December 2004 the Justice and Home Affairs Council also adopted conclusions on prevention, preparedness, and response to terrorist

---

[63] 1155 United Nations Treaty Series 331.

[64] Cf M Reichard, 'The Madrid Terrorist Attacks', n 54, above, 327.

[65] Article 31, para 3(b) of the Vienna Convention on the Law of Treaties.

[66] *Presidency Conclusions of the Brussels European Council* (17 and 18 June 2004), n 14, above (emphasis added).

[67] See Commission communications on: Prevention, preparedness and response to terrorist attacks (COM(2004) 698 final); Critical Infrastructure Protection in the fight against terrorism (COM(2004) 702 final); Preparedness and consequence management in the fight against terrorism (COM(2004) 701 final); Prevention of and fight against terrorist financing through measures to improve the exchange of information, to strengthen transparency and enhance the traceability of financial transactions (COM(2004) 700 final).

attacks[68] and an EU Solidarity Programme on the consequences of terrorist threats and attacks.[69]

The latter document, which obviously remains a political instrument, constitutes a revised version of the 2002 Programme to improve cooperation in the European Union for preventing and limiting the consequences of chemical, biological, radiological, or nuclear (CBRN) terrorist threats.[70] The issue of how military assets and capabilities could be used to protect civilian populations against the consequences of terrorist attacks, including CBRN ones, had already emerged in the course of 2003.[71] On 17 May 2004 the General Affairs and External Relations Council endorsed a report submitted by the Political and Security Committee on 'modalities, procedures and criteria for making available to the Community Civil Protection Mechanism the content of military assets and capabilities relevant to the protection of civilian populations against the effects of terrorist attacks, including CBRN'. In the Solidarity Programme Member States are invited to expand and deepen the content of the database.

7. Conclusions

In the aftermath of the Madrid terrorist attack, the external dimension of the fight against terrorism is emerging as a crucial element of the EU strategy. The recent document prepared by Mr Javier Solana, entitled 'Integrating the Fight against Terrorism into EU External Relations Policy',[72] includes a range of proposals to enhance the external action. It focuses on cooperation with the UN, in particular with regard to the fight against the financing of terrorism and the provision of technical assistance, and on the adoption of counterterrorism clauses in the agreements with third countries.

In the global effort to combat international terrorism, an EU which is more active in the enhancement of the peaceful responses 'will be one which carries greater political weight'.[73] The complementary nature of the ESDP contribution has been recently emphasized by Mr Javier Solana as follows:

I firmly believe that the military option alone cannot offer a solution [. . .] [J]udicial, police cooperation, intelligence sharing, should be the center of gravity of our action. This does not mean that we are not working on how European Security and Defence Policy can offer a meaningful contribution. Quite the contrary, work is ongoing in the field, e.g. of consequence management. But, I repeat, ESDP is not at the core of our efforts.[74]

---

[68] Doc 15232/04.   [69] Doc 15480/04.   [70] Doc 14627/02.
[71] *Annex I of the Presidency Conclusions of the Thessaloniki European Council* (19–20 June 2003) para 4, available at <http://www.ecre.org/eu_developments/debates/grconcl.pdf>.
[72] Doc 150082/04, *Integrating the Fight against Terrorism into EU External Relations Policy*
[73] ESS, n 8, above.
[74] *Terrorism in Europe: How does the Union of 25 Respond to this Phenomenon?*, Remarks by *Javier Solana*, Berlin, 7 October 2004.

The present contribution, however, demonstrates the increasing relevance in the debate about the military option in the fight against terrorism. Both the Declaration on Solidarity of 25 March 2004 and the Conceptual Framework on the ESDP dimension of the fight against terrorism recently endorsed by the European Council demonstrate the tendency to interpret the current binding provisions of the TEU in the light of the new discipline provided by the Treaty on the Constitution for Europe. Furthermore, the analysis of the relationship between ESDP and the fight against terrorism is not just a theoretical one: Operation ALTHEA in Bosnia and Herzegovina[75] already has a clear counter-terrorism mandate.[76] A first report on the implementation of the Conceptual Framework was endorsed by the Council on 23 May 2005: it focuses on the extension of the database on military assets and capabilities relevant to the protection of civilian population against terrorist attack and more generally on the interoperability between military and civilian assets.

The potential scenarios for military missions outside the Union envisaged by the Conceptual Framework open up the discussion on the issue of the relationship of this kind of action with the UN collective security system and their respect of general international law. Once the EU is recognized as a regional organization under Chapter VIII of the UN Charter, it must respect the provisions contained therein. In particular, the Report of the High Level Panel on Threats, Challenges and Change significantly confirms the reading of Article 53, which is shared by the majority of international law scholars,[77] according to which enforcement actions by regional organizations involving the use of armed force have to be authorized by the UN Security Council.[78]

[75] See F Naert, Chapter 4 of this volume, and N Tsagourias, Chapter 5 of this volume.

[76] Doc 12576/04, *Concept for the European Union Military Operation in Bosnia and Herzegovina—Operation ALTHEA*, 29 September 2004.

[77] Cf, eg, U Villani, 'Les rapports entre l'ONU et les organisations régionales dans le domaine du maintien de la paix' (2001) 290 *Recueil des cours* 225 and, most recently, 'La politica europea in materia di sicurezza e di difesa e i suoi rapporti con le Nazioni Unite' (2004) 59 *La Comunità internazionale* 63.

[78] UN Doc A/59/565, *A More Secure World*, 71: 'Authorization from the Security Council should in all cases be sought for regional peace operations'.

8

Common European Defence: Competition or Compatibility with NATO?

*Heike Krieger**

1. Introduction

Since the end of the Cold War new security structures have emerged within Europe. The end of the bi-polar security system has enlarged the number of actors with overlapping competences. While NATO broadened its range of permissible activities through the new Strategic Concept of 1999, efforts within the EU aim at closer cooperation on mutual defence, including an automatic action commitment. After examining legal limitations for overlapping treaty obligations of NATO and EU Member States, this chapter will argue that the EU should not pursue the idea of creating a traditional defence alliance. Because of the changing understanding of defence and security an alliance based on a clause comparable to the Solidarity clause in the Draft Constitutional Treaty could be a more appropriate approach in the future.

2. Why Common European Defence?

Since the late 1990s the idea of common European defence has been back on the political agenda. There are several internal as well as external reasons which speak in favour of a common European defence project. From the point of view of the internal development of the EU the creation of common defence structures enhances the process of European integration. At present the future direction of European integration is increasingly unclear. Common European defence structures, including a European army, would be a major goal for any truly political union.[1] A security aspect has always been part of the European integration

* Professor of Public Law and Public International Law at the Free University of Berlin, Germany. All website addresses cited were active on 17 October 2006, unless otherwise specified.
[1] J Solana, *'Die Gemeinsame Europäische Sicherheits- und Verteidigungspolitik—Das Integrationsprojekt der nächsten Dekade'*, *Integration* 2000, 1–6; see for the German debate: W Schäuble, *'Die*

process. It was one of the original motives behind the process of European integration, most clearly in the attempt to establish a supranational European Defence Community in 1952.[2] Even the process of economic integration always included some security interests, because the European Steel and Coal Community was directed against possible threats from Germany.[3] The end of the Cold War, however, changed the perception of security interests. Common security is no longer an internal concept but an external one.[4]

In this respect common European defence seems more and more inevitable because a single Member State is no longer capable of providing for its military security on its own, in terms of resources and policy options. Public demands for cutbacks in national defence spending and the rising costs of standing armies, professional training, and armaments research and development make EU Member States recognize the need to share their capabilities. Pooling of resources is a major argument for any European army.[5] Moreover, the new security agenda which is no longer based on considerations of the balance of power, prompts the emergence of new security actors. In the case of the EU there are three main reasons for its increasing importance in security matters. (1) Europe is presently developing common interests in external security affairs. (2) Its external security interests seem to differ from those of the USA. (3) These differences lead to different interpretations of pertinent legal concepts.

(1) In the past, observers claimed that any meaningful common external policy on security matters would be illusionary because of a lack of common security interests. Developments after 11 September 2001 have changed this perception. The European Security Strategy initiated by Mr Javier Solana provides an analysis of security threats which is shared by Member States.[6] The European Institute for Security Studies has proposed a substantive White Paper on European Defence.[7] The fact that new security threats, such as international terrorism, have blurred

---

europäische Integration voranbringen', *Frankfurter Allgemeine Zeitung,* 25 January 2005, 9; see, however, J Holst, 'Ambiguity and Promise' in B von Plate (ed), *Europa auf dem Weg zur kollektiven Sicherheit?* (Baden-Baden: Nomos Verlag, 1994), 13, at 27 who characterizes common defence as a consequence of integration not as vehicle for its promotion.

[2] For an analysis of the European Defence Union see M Kleine, *Die militärische Komponente der Europäischen Sicherheits- und Verteidigungspolitik* (Baden-Baden: Nomos Verlag, 2005) 40–56; T Marauhn, *Building a European Security and Defence Identity: The Evolving Relationship between the Western European Union and the European Union* (Bochum: Universitätsverlag N Brockmeyer, 1996); M Trybus, Chapter 2 of this volume.

[3] J Varwick, *'Die ESVP-Eine folgerichtige Weiterentwicklung der Gemeinsamen Außen- und Sicherheitspolitik (GASP)?'* in W Hoyer and G Kaldrack (eds), *Europäische Sicherheits- und Verteidigungspolitik* (Baden-Baden: Nomos, 2002) 96 at 99 et seq.   [4] Ibid, at 101 et seq.

[5] See H Borchert, 'Rollenspezialisierung und Zusammenlegung von Ressourcen' in J Varwick (ed), *Die Beziehungen zwischen NATO und EU: Partnerschaft, Konkurrenz, Rivalität?* (Opladen: Barbara Budrich Verlag, 2005) 155 et seq; P Fitschen, '*"Rollenspezialisierung" und "Pooling"—Zauberformeln für ESVP und NATO?'* in J Varwick (ed), op cit, 139 et seq.

[6] J Solana, 'A Secure Europe in a Better World; European Security Strategy', document adopted at the European Council, Brussels, 12 December 2003, available at <http://www.iss-eu.org/solana/solanae.pdf>.

[7] EU Institute for Security Studies, *European Defence—A Proposal for a White Paper* (Paris: 2004).

the lines between internal and external security may have had a catalytic effect in this respect. Before 2001 Member States had already identified common threats for their internal security and had acted not only within the third but also within the first pillar of the EU. Europol, Eurojust, and the Schengen System are striking examples of the willingness to coordinate and harmonize action in relation to internal security threats. Since international terrorism is a threat to internal as well as to external security and requires internal as well as external responses it became easier for Member States to agree on external security policy goals. Thus, according to Article 11(1) and Article 2 TEU it is an objective of the EU to safeguard 'the integrity of the Union in conformity with the principles of the United Nations Charter, strengthening the security of the Union in all ways and preserving peace and strengthening international security, in accordance with . . . the objectives of the Paris Charter, including those on external borders'. The phrase 'external borders' is particularly striking and suggests that the territorial integrity of the Union is an objective of the CFSP.[8]

(2) At the same time there is an increasing recognition of, and emphasis on, the different security interests of Europe and the USA. The redefinition of US defence policy after the Cold War accelerated ESDP. Nowadays the main security threats are not built up in Europe but originate from other parts of the world. Therefore, the USA predominantly addresses challenges outside Europe. This development has strengthened the European intention to guarantee its own security in order to compensate for the diminishing US security interest in Europe.[9] Moreover, military observers have noted that the EU-US capability gap is constantly increasing. With or without ESDP it will be very difficult for European forces to remain interoperable with US forces in the full range of military missions. The US is likely to play a decreasing military role within NATO, reserving its military power for high-intensity high-technology operations. Developments in military technology might well prompt complementary roles of EU and NATO in defence matters. In such circumstances the prospect of military autonomy ceases to be a simple political aspiration and becomes, more and more, a functional necessity. The development of an independent ESDP is a first step towards enabling the EU to pursue its own security concerns.

(3) Simultaneously, norms of collective responsibility weaken. Although NATO has been the only international organization whose members continuously subscribe to collective self-defence, the political heterogeneity of its Member States is now NATO's main characteristic. European states disagree with the global agenda

---

[8] S Graf von Kielmansegg, *Die Verteidigungspolitik der Europäischen Union* (Stuttgart: Boorberg, 2005) 133; see, however, P d'Argent, *'Le traité d'Amsterdam et les aspects militaire de la PESC'* in Y Lejeune (ed), *Le traité d'Amsterdam. Espoir et déceptions* (Brussels: Bruylant, 1998) 383, at 387; see, on the objectives of the CSDP in the Draft Constitution, M Trybus, *European Union Law and Defence Integration* (Oxford: Oxford University Press, 2005) 296.
[9] S Larabee, 'ESDP and NATO: Assuring Complementarity' *The International Spectator* 1/2004, 51, at 53.

which is set by Washington.[10] The USA concentrates on its actions against terrorism worldwide. While the EU acknowledges the threats of international terrorism and the proliferation of weapons of mass destruction, it is increasingly critical towards the American agenda. Even where the EU agrees with the objectives, it often disapproves of the means to achieve them. The EU favours multilateralism, especially through the UN, while the USA advocates coalitions of the willing.[11]

Thus the legal dispute which affects in particular the concept of self-defence in Article 51 of the UN Charter endangers an alliance such as NATO, which is based on collective self-defence. In the past NATO worked smoothly because Member States shared the basic understanding of the applicable legal principles. Now there is a divide over these principles.[12] At present the USA and many European states follow differing interpretations of international public law regarding the use of force.[13] The US doctrine of pre-emptive self-defence is rejected by most EU Member States. Although the first version of the European Security Strategy by Mr Javier Solana included a statement that 'pre-emptive engagement can avoid more serious problems in the future' the sentence was changed in the final version of the paper.[14] The divergence over the interpretation of 'imminent danger' and thus the legitimate conditions for the use of force persists.[15] Moreover, the dispute is constantly expanding and stretches into the realm of humanitarian and human rights law and its applicability in the fight against terrorism. It increasingly concerns the fundamental values of the EU which the EU cannot renounce, especially in regard to human rights protection.[16] The resulting fragmentation of the transatlantic security order can be observed in terms of real or perceived interests and the interpretation of applicable norms. In consequence, it seems to become politically easier to act collectively in defence and security matters within the EU than within NATO.

3. Defence in a Multilevel System

With the end of the Cold War European security policy is no longer exclusively state-centred and bi-polar in its focus on NATO. Instead, security is provided

---

[10] See V Mauer, 'Von der Hegemonie zum kooperativen Gleichgewicht' in J Varwick (ed), *Die Beziehungen zwischen NATO und EU: Partnerschaft, Konkurrenz, Rivalität?* (Opladen: Barbara Budrich Verlag, 2005) 257 et seq.   [11] ISS, *White Paper*, n 7, above, at 35.

[12] Ibid, 33.

[13] For an analysis of the US concept of pre-emptive self-defence see M Bothe, 'Terrorism and the Legality of Pre-Emptive Force' (2003) 14 Eur J Intl L 227 et seq.

[14] Solana, n 6, above; Larabee, n 9, above, at 56 et seq.   [15] N 12, above.

[16] See the diverging positions of the EU and the Council of Europe on CIA flights and secret prisons in Europe as well as the dispute about the interpretation of what constitutes torture and degrading treatment; for instance: Craig Whitlock, 'Europeans Probe Secret CIA Flights, Questions Surround Possible Illegal Transfer of Terrorism Suspects' *Washington Post Foreign Service*, 17 November 2005, A 22.

by different networks with a multiplicity of actors and organizations.[17] Such a multilevel security system is characterized by a number of international organizations which are competent to deal with security and defence. Moreover, since in no case has sovereignty been transferred to one of the organizations, Member States themselves remain the primary actors. They do not only define the organizations' competences from the inside but also from the outside as members of other international organizations. Thus, to a large extent the relationship between the different security actors is not a question of law and applicable conflict norms but will be solved on the political level.

However, the debate over the indivisibility of security structures still continues. It is partly informed by a traditional understanding of a security architecture where security relations between diverse groups of actors have been conceived in terms of competing alliances.[18] This traditional approach is the basis of Article 8 of the NATO Treaty which prohibits participation in an alliance which is directed against NATO. However, this understanding does not properly address the question of effective coordination and distribution of authority between different security actors when security and defence are no longer clear-cut matters within the exclusive competence of one military alliance but are embedded in a multilevel system.

3.1. NATO as a forum for competition?

Achieving complementarity in a multilevel system is a problem for many EU policies. In the case of economic policies, for instance, there are divergent players whose actions must be coordinated: the Member State, the EU, and the WTO. Because of the extent of competence that the EU already possesses, complementarity is achieved through EU representation in the WTO. Member States' interests are more or less realized through the EU, which utilizes the WTO as a platform for political competition with the USA.[19]

However, the model does not work for multilevel security. First, integration in defence matters is not as advanced as integration in economics. Member States have only started to develop common interests, but in contrast to economic policies they are not yet willing to transfer any sovereignty in defence matters. Final decisions in defence rest with the nation states. Moreover, the WTO and NATO are differently

---

[17] See NATO's Rome Declaration of 8 November 1991, No 3: 'The challenges we will face in this new Europe cannot be comprehensively addressed by one institution alone, but only in a framework of interlocking institutions tying together the countries of Europe and North America', available at <http//www.nato.int/docu/basictxt/b911108b.htm>.

[18] E Krahmann, 'The Emergence of Security Governance in Post-Cold War Europe', Working Paper 36/01, University of Sussex, 2001, 7.

[19] See on conceptions for the relationship between the EU, the WTO, and Member States: A v Bogdandy and T Makatsch, ' "Kollision, Koexistenz oder Kooperation"?—Zum Verhältnis on WTO-Recht und europäischem Außenwirtschafsrecht in neueren Entscheidungen', Europäische Zeitschrift für Wirtschafsrecht 2000, 261 et seq.

structured. Whereas the WTO through its organs can impose binding decisions on its Member States, NATO is based to a larger extent on consensus, which in turn requires Member States' willingness for compromise instead of competition.

Above all, the EU as a security actor is not as potent as the EU as an economic actor. Thus, it is more difficult to enforce security interests. Although the very idea of a European Defence Identity implies that there are specific European security concerns which a European Defence Union could express in opposition to the USA, there are clear factual limits to any European aspirations. Compatibility is a political necessity. Most EU Member States do not possess sufficient military capabilities to guarantee their own defence in case of a territorial attack. Probably only the British and the French armed forces are capable of deploying troops abroad on their own.[20] An effective military defence without US participation and thus without NATO is not possible for the time being. Moreover, most of the basic European forces will remain virtually unchanged whether deployed by NATO or by the EU. Since there will only be one set of forces and one set of equipment in Europe, much of each will be double-hatted, for instance the Eurocorps is already available for deployment under either EU or NATO command.[21]

3.2. Preventing overlapping competences

Taking into account the comparable weakness of the EU as a security actor, one way to realize the required complementarity in a multilevel security system is to prevent overlapping competences or commitments.

3.2.1. *Common defence and common defence policy*

When the EU started a Common Foreign and Security Policy the Single European Act focused on the political aspects of security (Article 30(VI)a SEA). Military security remained a prerogative of the Member States and was realized through NATO.[22] However, from Maastricht to the Nice Treaty EU Member States developed a Common Security and Defence Policy which includes military aspects of security. Thus Articles 11(1) and 17(1) TEU refer to an understanding of security which covers political, economic, and military aspects. Article 17(1) TEU also introduces the concepts of defence policy and defence into the Treaty.[23]

---

[20] J Lindley-French and F Algieri, *A European Defence Strategy* (Gütersloh: Bertelsmann Foundation, 2004) 32 et seq; see, however, S Biscop, 'Able and Willing?', (2004) 9 *Eur Foreign Affairs Rev* 509, at 514 et seq.   [21] Kleine, n 2, above, 217 et seq.

[22] See M Warnken, *Der Handlungsrahmen der Europäischen Union im Bereich der Sicherheits- und Verteidigungspolitik* (Baden-Baden: Nomos, 2002) 35.

[23] Art 17:

1. The common foreign and security policy shall include all questions relating to the security of the Union, including the progressive framing of a common defence policy, which might lead to a common defence, should the European Council so decide. It shall in that case recommend to the Member States the adoption of such a decision in accordance with their respective constitutional requirements . . . 2. Questions referred to in this Article shall include humanitarian and rescue tasks, peacekeeping tasks and tasks of combat forces in crisis management, including peacemaking.

According to the wording and history of the article, defence policy has been a subject matter of the EU Treaty since the Amsterdam Treaty[24] while common defence is still a future perspective.

3.2.1.1. The meaning of 'defence' in the TEU

In its traditional understanding, defence means military defence against external aggression which is directed against a state's territory. Taking into account that the TEU even mentions the external borders of the EU in Article 11(1) subparagraph (3) the classical understanding of defence as territorial defence against an armed attack is clearly covered by the concept of defence in the EU Treaty. However, the concept of defence in the EU Treaty is broader.[25] ESDP was introduced into the Maastricht Treaty as a response to European experiences in the Yugoslav conflict in order to enable the EU to address the military aspects of security and to conduct military operations for crisis management. Thus, crisis management operations are not covered by the concept of 'security' in the Treaty but are based on the provisions on defence. According to Article 17(2) TEU, the wording of which refers to Article 17(1) TEU, defence includes humanitarian and rescue tasks, peacekeeping tasks, and tasks of combat forces in crisis management, including peacemaking. The missions are those defined in the so-called Petersberg tasks of the WEU.[26] However, the understanding of Petersberg tasks has subsequently been expanded. At the 1999 Cologne Council the declaration stated that these tasks included 'the full range of conflict prevention and crisis management tasks'.[27] The Laeken Council, which proclaimed the ESDP operational, emphasized that the further development of means and capabilities would permit the Union 'progressively to take on more demanding operations'.[28] In reaction to the events of 11 September 2001, the extraordinary European Council of 21 September stressed that it would fight terrorism in all its forms, and that 'the fight against terrorism will be a priority objective of the EU'.[29] The European Council in Seville in June 2002 decided to boost the Union's involvement in the fight against terrorism through a coordinated interdisciplinary approach 'embracing all Union policies, including by developing the CFSP and by making the ESDP operational'. It was recalled that the 'the CSFP, including the ESDP, can play an important role in countering this threat to our

---

[24] Kleine, n 2, above, 77.

[25] S Duke, 'CESDP: Nice's Overtrumped Success?' (2001) 6 *Eur Foreign Affairs Rev* 155, at 157.

[26] Western European Union, Council of Ministers, Bonn, 19 June 1992, Petersberg Declaration; *Bulletin der Bundesregierung No 68*, 23 June 1992, 649–53; see M Fleuß, *Die operationelle Rolle der WEU in den neunziger Jahren* (Frankfurt am Main: Lang, 1996); M Kleine, n 2, above, 92–4.

[27] Cologne European Council, Presidency Conclusions, Cologne 3 and 4 June 1999, printed in M Rutten (ed), *From St Malo to Nice, European Defence: Core Documents, Vol I*, Chaillot Paper 47 (Paris: Institute of Security Studies of the European Union, 2001) 41 et seq; see D Thym, *'Die Begründung einer europäischen Verteidigungspolitik'*, *Deutsches Verwaltungsblatt* 2000, 676.

[28] European Council, Laeken, 14–15 December 2001, Report of the Presidency, printed in M Rutten (ed), *From Nice to Laeken, European Defence: Core Documents, Vol II*, ,Paris 2002, 196 et seq.

[29] Extraordinary European Council, 21 September 2001, Conclusions and Action Plan, printed in Rutten, n 28, above, *Vol II*, 158 et seq.

security'.[30] The EU Draft Treaty establishing a Constitution for Europe draws an even more detailed picture of the Petersberg tasks. According to the Draft Treaty, EU missions shall include joint disarmament operations, military advice and assistance tasks, and post-conflict stabilization (Article III-309(1)). Since the Council expanded the interpretation of Petersberg missions, defence now includes nearly every aspect of military security.[31]

3.2.1.2. The differentiation between common defence and common defence policy

This leaves the question open as to how to differentiate between common defence and common defence policy. It is particularly difficult to clarify what *common* defence means because 'common defence' is not informed by a clear political concept. On a political level Member States chose to act in constructive ambiguity so that a political compromise could be achieved in Maastricht.[32] Thus, the literature provides numerous different interpretations of 'common defence' which include the establishment of integrated military structures,[33] the inclusion of an automatic action commitment,[34] or the deployment of cooperating troops.[35]

An analysis of the Treaty provisions suggests that the general difference lies in different options to act. Certain options of a supranational or binding character as well as those actions that would fundamentally change the nature of the TEU are not part of a common defence policy. First, neutral Member States were clearly opposed to any automatic action clause during negotiations in Maastricht and Amsterdam. States, such as the UK, which do not want to endanger the transatlantic relationship likewise wanted to keep the competences of NATO and the EU apart. Thus, Member States' intentions speak in favour of a delineation of competences that does not conflict with NATO competences in relation to collective self-defence. Secondly, according to Article 17(1) TEU common defence is not yet a EU competence but a future option which would need ratification by Member States. Thus, the clause aims to protect Member States' sovereignty. States are not yet willing to give up sovereignty in relation to military defence. All those measures that are particularly critical for Member States' sovereignty and would require restrictions on, or a transfer of, sovereignty are excluded from the concept of defence policy but would require an amendment of the Treaty according to

---

[30] European Council, Seville, 21–22 June 2002, Presidency Conclusions, Annex V; printed in J-Y Haine (ed), *From Laeken to Copenhagen, European Defence: Core Documents, Vol III*, Chaillot Paper No 57 (Paris: Institute of Security Studies of the European Union, February 2003) 272.

[31] ISS, *White Paper*, n 7, above, at 47.   [32] Von Kielmansegg, n 8, above, 119.

[33] H Krück in J Schwarze (ed), *EU-Kommentar* (Baden-Baden: Nomos, 2000) Art 11–28 no 36.

[34] R Wessels, 'The State of Affairs in EU Security and Defence Policy' (2003) 8 J of Conflict and Security Law 265, at 286 et seq.

[35] H-J Cremer in Christian Calliess and Matthias Ruffert (eds), *Kommentar des Vertrages über die Europäische Union und des Vertrages zur Gründung der Europäischen Gemeinschaft*, 2nd edn (Neuwied: Hermann Luchterhand Verlag, 2002) Art 17 no 7; R Geiger, *EUV, EGV: Vertrag über die Europäische Union und Vertrag zur Gründung der Europäischen Gemeinschaft*, 3rd edn (Munich: CH Beck, 2000), Art 17 no 3.

either Article 17 or Article 48 TEU. Common defence therefore means that the military defence of a Member State against external aggression on its territorial integrity would be an EU competence.[36] The establishment of legal obligations to use national forces or to take specific measures concerning structures and capabilities of national forces belongs to the realm of common defence. The same is true for an automatic action commitment.[37]

Another yardstick is the question whether any decision would fundamentally change the nature of the EU. The establishment of integrated forces and command structures of the EU, or the creation of a supranational defence structure comparable to the European Defence Union, is therefore not part of a common defence policy. For this reason the EU does not possess military forces or headquarters but has to rely on its Member States and NATO. Consequently, common defence policy can be defined as a common policy to react to immediate military threats through actions which do not require a transfer of sovereignty or which do not change the nature of the EU fundamentally.[38] Thus, it includes coordinated military crisis operations on a voluntary basis. Since the voluntary nature is decisive to delineate the difference between common defence and common defence policy it is submitted that operations for territorial defence would be part of a common defence policy as long as they were conducted voluntarily and no integrated military structures were established. Only an automatic action commitment or the establishment of integrated military structures would lead to an overlap of treaty commitments because only in such a case would the EU compete with NATO for the military resources of its Member States or direct its Member States' behaviour in case of territorial defence.[39] Thus, under the present arrangements of the TEU, there are no overlapping or conflicting treaty commitments in the realm of collective self-defence.

3.2.1.3. NATO's 1999 Strategic Concept

However, the exclusion of collective self-defence could not prevent overlaps in the application of the EU Treaty and the NATO Treaty. NATO itself broadened its range of permissible activities through the new 1999 Strategic Concept.[40] Throughout the 1990s NATO had adapted to the profound changes of the international order. In the Concept, the parties express their will to explicitly expand

---

[36] J Frowein, 'Auf dem Weg zu einer gemeinsamen Sicherheits- und Verteidigungspolitik' in C Tomuschat (ed), *Rechtsprobleme einer europäischen Sicherheits- und Verteidigungspolitik* (Heidelberg: Muller, 1997) 11 et seq; Warnken, n 22, above, 146.   [37] Von Kielmansegg, n 8, above, 129.

[38] J Frowein, n 36, above, 11; M Warnken, n 22, above, 142; for arguments why military crisis management is not covered by the general provisions on security policy according to the TEU see von Kielmansegg, n 8, above, 123 et seq.

[39] H-J Cremer in Calliess and Ruffert (eds), n 35, above, Art 17 no 1; von Kielmansegg, n 8, above, 130 et seq.

[40] 'The Alliance's Strategic Concept, Approved by the Heads of State and Government participating in the meeting of the North Atlantic Council in Washington DC on 23rd and 24th April 1999', printed in Rutten, n 27, above, *Vol I*, 24 et seq.

NATO's aims by crisis response operations, which go beyond Article 5 of the NATO Treaty.[41] If a conflict has developed into a crisis that has become so critical that preventive action no longer seems promising, the Council can become active, in cooperation with the competent international organizations. For this, it can make use of a series of instruments of action. These instruments include non-Article 5 crisis response operations, which are of a military nature. Thus a non-Article 5 crisis response operation is an operation which does not have an attack of the territory of a party to the treaty as a prerequisite.[42] The operation is to be carried out in accordance with the international law that is applicable in the respective case.

The new 1999 Strategic Concept leaves the Alliance's function of collective defence unaffected. The aim and the purpose of NATO continue to be the defence against, or deterrence of, any aggression by a third State.[43] The re-organization of military capabilities to act is to explicitly remain oriented towards this function of NATO.[44] The possibility of so-called crisis response operations, however, constitutes an important expansion of NATO's tasks, which has not been implied in the Treaty.[45] Although the Strategic Concept has considerably expanded the realm of application of the NATO Treaty this has not yet been regarded as an objective amendment of the NATO Treaty.[46]

3.2.2. Towards mutual defence?

The realm of application of the ESDP and the NATO Treaty does not only overlap in relation to crisis response operations. The EU Constitutional Treaty obligations may also overlap in relation to collective self-defence.

The progressive development of the ESDP did not stop with the crisis management operations. Especially, France and Germany foster the idea of a European Security and Defence Union, which was first proposed at the Brussels summit of 29 April 2003.[47] Although the proposal could not be brought into the EU Draft Constitution, some Member States, in particular Germany, continue to

---

[41] Strategic Concept Part III, Nos 31–32.

[42] Strategic Concept Part III, Nos 29 and 31–32, and Part IV, Nos 41 and 53, letter c; also cf Part I, No 10, Part II, No 24.   [43] Strategic Concept, Part I, No 10.

[44] Strategic Concept, Part III, No 28, Part IV, Nos 41 et seq.

[45] H McCoubrey and J Morris, 'International Law, International Relations and the Development of European Collective Security' (1999) 4 J of Armed Conflict L 195, at 208 et seq; G Nolte, 'Die "neuen Aufgaben" von NATO und WEU: Völker- und verfassungsrechtliche Fragen' in: (1994) 54 *Zeitschrift für ausländisches öffentliches Recht und Völkerrecht* 95–123.

[46] For instance: NATO Strategic Concept Case, Judgment of the German Constitutional Court of 22 November 2001, Decisions of the German Constitutional Court (BVerfGE) vol 104, 151 et seq; see A Paulus, '*Quo vadis* Democratic Control? The Afghanistan Decision of the Bundestag and the Decision of the Federal Constitutional Court on the NATO Strategic Concept Case', 3 German L J No 1, available at <http://www.germanlawjournal.com>.

[47] *Gemeinsame Erklärung Deutschlands, Frankreichs, Luxemburgs und Belgiens zur Europäischen Sicherheits- und Verteidigungspolitik*, Brüssel, 29 April 2003; available at <http://www.auswaertiges-amt.de/www/de/ausgabe_archiv?archiv_id=4385>.

explore options and limits for a Defence Union and the establishment of a European Army.[48]

3.2.2.1. The first version of the EU Constitutional Treaty

The first version of the Constitutional Treaty provided for closer cooperation on mutual defence. It included an automatic action commitment which relied on Article V of the WEU Treaty: 'Under the close cooperation, if one of the Member States participating in such cooperation is the victim of an armed aggression on its territory, the other participating States shall give it aid and assistance by all means in their power, military and other, in accordance with Article 51 of the UN Charter'.

According to the wording, this clause can be read as an unconditional and binding automatic commitment to assistance. If all EU members that are also members of the WEU had subscribed to the closer cooperation clause on mutual defence, the Article V commitment of the WEU Treaty could have been considered as derogated. This would have meant the end of a long process to integrate the WEU fully into the EU. Some EU Member States, headed by France and Germany, had suggested merging the EU and WEU in 1997. As a result, the WEU's automatic action clause would have been integrated into the EU. However, this plan was vigorously rejected by the British government.[49] The dispute continued within the Convention's Working Group on Defence.[50]

Nonetheless, the Working Group did not only suggest introducing a solidarity clause into the Constitutional Treaty, together with procedures for the case of a terrorist attack. It also included an opt-in provision which would have authorized those Member States who wished to integrate the mutual assistance clause of the WEU Treaty to subscribe to such a clause within the framework of the Union.[51] In parallel, the Brussels summit proposed to include in the Constitutional Treaty 'a general clause on solidarity and common security, binding all Member States in the European Union, and allowing for a response to risks of any sort that threaten the Union'.[52] Both options, automatic commitment and the Solidarity clause, were included in the Convention's draft text of 18 July 2003. The new formulation in Article I-40(2) supported the idea of the European Security and Defence

[48] See for instance, W Schäuble, *'Die europäische Integration voranbringen', Frankfurter Allgemeine Zeitung*, 25 January 2005, 9; U Diedrichs, M Jopp, S Sandawi, *'Möglichkeiten und Grenzen militärischer Integration im Rahmen der ESVP', Integration* 3/04, 223 et seq. The article is based on a study on 'Options and Limits for Military Integration within ESDP' commissioned by the German Ministry of Defence.

[49] J Howorth, 'The European Draft Constitutional Treaty and the Future of the European Defence Initiative: A Question of Flexibility', (2004) 9 *Eur Foreign Affairs Rev* 483 at 492.

[50] Secretariat of the Working Group in Defence, 'Summary of the meeting held on 29 October 2002', CONV 399/02 (12 November 2003).

[51] Final Report of the Working Group VIII-Defence, no 57 and 63; Howorth, n 49, above, at 493.

[52] *Gemeinsame Erklärung Deutschlands, Frankreichs, Luxemburgs und Belgiens zur Europäischen Sicherheits- und Verteidigungspolitik, Brüssel*, 29 April 2003; available at <http://www.auswaertiges-amt.de/www/de/ausgabe_archiv?archiv_id=4385>.

Union: 'The common security and defence policy shall include the progressive framing of a common Union defence policy. This will lead to a common defence, when the European Council, acting unanimously, so decides'.

This wording was considerably stronger than the wording in Article 17 TEU. It justified Article I-40(7), according to which those Member States which want to go further would be allowed to anticipate the European Council's decision on common defence, at least in terms of the mutual assistance clause.[53] Despite this shift the compatibility clause in relation to NATO was comparatively weak. It stated that in the execution of closer cooperation on mutual defence, the participating Member States shall work in close cooperation with NATO (Part I, Article 40(7)). In addition, the article shall not affect the rights and obligations resulting from the North Atlantic Treaty (Part III, Article 214(4)).

3.2.2.2. The compromise achieved

However, for several reasons this approach could not be realized in its entirety. First, the proposal was objectionable for neutrals, who were afraid of involvement despite the opt-in mechanism, and to Atlanticists, who feared the consequences for NATO. The three controversial issues concerned the voluntary nature of participation, the formula on the relation to NATO, and the idea of anticipating the EU's decision on common defence.[54] The clause on mutual defence was criticized as political symbolism since it seemed pointless to pretend that European defence can be militarily efficient without major American contributions.[55] Moreover, for Eastern Europeans territorial defence is still a valid issue and the value of defence guarantees not trivial. Their support for a development of the ESDP which openly competes with, or seeks to supplant, NATO is unlikely. Finally, in the EU it can be argued that the relevance of defence guarantees is reduced. Because of the war-excluding effects of the Union itself the purpose of defence guarantees within an alliance to ban intra-allied attacks and reduce competition is more or less meaningless.[56]

In response to the criticism a new text was proposed under the Italian presidency. The text was an acceptable compromise for all parties concerned. Above all, the first sentence of Article 40-I(7), which anticipated the decision of the EU on mutual defence, was cancelled as well as any formula concerning 'mutual defence' and the detailed arrangements under Article III-241. Moreover, the requirement to 'give' aid and assistance to a Member State under attack 'by all means in their power, military and other' was rephrased as an obligation of aid and assistance.[57] The explicit reference to military assistance was cut out in the

---

[53] Art 40-I(7) 'Until such time as the European Council has acted in accordance with paragraph 2 of this Article, closer cooperation shall be established, in the Union framework, as regards mutual defence . . .' [54] Howorth, n 49, above, at 495

[55] A Bailes, 'The Institutional Reform of ESDP and Post-Prague NATO', *The International Spectator* 3/2003, 31, at 34. [56] Ibid, note 12.

[57] Howorth, n 49, above, at 495.

interests of the neutral Member States.[58] Thus, the clause is less explicit than the WEU or the NATO clause. On the other hand, the wording does not give room for Member States' discretion. In this respect the clause is stricter than Article V of the NATO Treaty. Thus, it still qualifies as an automatic action commitment.

The clause on mutual defence in Article I-40(7) would still have meant a qualitative difference in the concept of the ESDP and thus the face of the EU. With the clause the EU would no longer have been an economic or political union but also a defence alliance. Thus not only peacekeeping missions such as ARTEMIS and Concordia,[59] but also military combat operations, such as Enduring Freedom, could have been led under the aegis of the EU. Within the limits of Article 51 UN Charter the EU would have been enabled to lead military missions without the authorization of the UN Security Council, unlike military operations based on the Petersberg tasks which require, in principle, an authorization under the UN Charter or the consent of the state concerned. The different kinds of missions involve a different profile and they are based on a completely different kind of foreign policy rhetoric. Above all, the clause implied a qualitative shift in the relation to NATO. The ESDP would have been directed to territorial defence. However, the clause does not transform the EU into an organization of collective self-defence. It provides no competence to build up integrated military structures but establishes a horizontal duty between the Member States to give assistance.[60] Thus, as long as the EU does not possess integrated military structures the possibility of EU missions based on territorial self-defence is, in the end, not a practical reality.

By way of a formal amendment of the Treaty Member States intended to establish a structure which belongs to the realm of common defence.[61] Thus, with the introduction of an obligation to military assistance in the case of an armed attack the question arises whether there are any further aspects of common defence which are still a future option. On the one hand, the Draft Constitution still includes the clause on common defence. Since the Declarations of Helsinki[62] and Laeken[63] stated that 'the development of military capabilities does not imply the creation of a European army' it is, on the other hand, unclear what is left for the Council to decide on. As described above it is submitted that the concept of 'common defence' includes more than the introduction of an automatic action

---

[58] 'If a Member State is the victim of armed aggression on its territory, the other Member States shall have towards it an obligation of aid and assistance by all means in their power, in accordance with Art 51 of the United Nations Charter . . .'. See, for the effects of the clause on neutral EU Member States, F Naert, 'European Security and Defence in the EU Constitutional Treaty' (2005) 10 J of Conflict and Security L 187, at 193 et seq.   [59] See Chapter 4 of this volume.

[60] Von Kielmansegg, n 8, above, 234.

[61] Von Kielmansegg, n 8, above, 212 et seq; see, however, Howorth, n 49, above, at 495.

[62] Helsinki European Council, Presidency Conclusions, Helsinki 10 and 11 December 1999, printed in Rutten, n 27, above, *Vol I*, 82.

[63] European Council, Laeken, 14–15 December 2001, Report of the Presidency, printed in Rutten, n 28, above, *Vol II*, 196 et seq.

commitment. The difference in terminology between 'mutual' and 'common' defence in the first version of the Draft Treaty supports this idea. Thus, the establishment of legal obligations to use national forces or to take specific measures concerning structures and capabilities of national forces would be left for the Council to decide. In order to clarify the limits of the concept of 'common defence' it is helpful to look for the purpose of the clause. The clause establishes a simplified procedure for making defence a competence of the EU.[64] It deviates from the general procedure for amendments of the Treaty. Taking into account that the general amendment clause would still apply to amendments of Article 40-I of the Constitutional Treaty itself[65] it is submitted that the simplified procedure will mean fundamental changes to the general amendment procedure.[66] Moreover, Article 40-I(1) subparagraph 4 and (3) subparagraph 1 underline that ESDP operations will be conducted with recourse to Member States' capabilities. Thus, a decision on the introduction of a European army would require a formal amendment of Article 40-I itself.[67] The requirement of a formal Treaty amendment is justified because a decision on a European army would change the nature of the EU itself, as well as alter its relation to NATO fundamentally. This would include the establishment of a supranational defence union comparable to the plans for the European Defence Union as well as the establishment of integrated military structures close to those of NATO.

3.3. Regulation of overlapping commitments: applicable conflict norms

Since the extension of EU and NATO competences at present and probably in the future will lead to an overlap of competences, regulations are required. Overlapping commitments and competences are regulated by conflict norms. The norms which are contained in the NATO Treaty and the WEU Treaty do not severely restrict European aspirations to realize a common defence project which co-exists or even competes with NATO. In contrast, the TEU and ESDP declarations clearly establish NATO's primacy in collective self-defence as well as crisis management operations.

3.3.1. *Obligations arising from the NATO and WEU Treaties: room for co-existence and competition*

The US Foreign Secretary Ms Madeleine Albright identified the so-called three 'D's as standards for judging any autonomous action regarding defence within Europe. Any initiative must avoid duplication of existing efforts, must avoid

---

[64] H-J Cremer in Calliess and Ruffert (eds), n 35, above, Art 17 no 1; M Warnken, n 22, above, 146 et seq.   [65] Art 17(5) TEU includes a reference to Art 48 TEU in this respect.
[66] Von Kielmansegg, n 8, above, 117.   [67] Ibid, 146.

decoupling European defence from NATO, and must avoid discrimination against non-EU members, such as Turkey.[68] In the course of the discussion NATO Secretary Lord Robertson summarized these objections and turned the debate into a set of positive formulations: improvement of European defence capabilities, inclusiveness and transparency for all allies, and indivisibility of transatlantic security. The US government endorsed the three 'I's' and translated the third one to 'indivisibility of security structures'.[69] However, while these standards might form indispensable political parameters for future cooperation between EU and NATO they are not set by any legal obligations arsing from the present European Security architecture.[70]

3.3.1.1. Duplication of military structures

Under the Washington or WEU Treaties EU Member States are free to create their own military structures even if certain structures were duplicated. A legal barrier might be found in Article IV(2) of the WEU Treaty. The WEU Treaty includes applicable legal standards because all Member States of the WEU are Member States of the EU. Moreover, Article 17(2) Amsterdam Treaty enabled the WEU to provide the EU with access to its operational capabilities, thus integrating important parts of the WEU into the EU.

In Article IV(2) the WEU Treaty recognizes NATO's primacy in military matters: 'Recognising the undesirability of duplicating the military staffs of NATO, the Council and its Agency will rely on the appropriate military authorities of NATO for information and advice on military matters'.

If this provision could be read as prohibiting any overlap with the activities of NATO organs, it might serve as a legal barrier against any autonomous EU military institutions. However, according to the wording this provision only contains a political command. It is a mere factual finding that the organization does not possess any military planning bodies and is therefore unable to organize any common military operation.[71] The provision does not set up any legal barrier.[72] Even if Article IV(2) WEU Treaty is conceived as a legal obligation it does not bind EU Member States. All WEU Member States are members of the EU. These Member States could derogate from Article IV(2) WEU Treaty through their explicit or implicit subsequent behaviour according to Article 31(3) of the Vienna Convention on the Law of Treaties or restrict the applicability of the earlier treaty according to Article 30(3) of the Vienna Convention.

---

[68] M Albright, 'The Right Balance will Secure NATO's Future' *Financial Times* 7 December 1998.
[69] M Albright and W Cohen, 'Get ESDI Right: Europe Should Beef up its Military Capabilities' *Wall Street J Europe* 24 March 2000, 70.
[70] See also H Krieger, *'Äußere Sicherheit durch europäische Streitkräfte'* in R Scholz (ed), *Europa der Bürger?* (Cologne: Hanns-Martin-Schleyer-Stiftung, 2002) 156–63.
[71] T Stein, *'Die Verträge über den deutschen Verteidigungsbeitrag'* in *Deutschlandvertrag, westliches Bündnis und Wiedervereinigung* (Berlin, Duncker & Humblot, 1985) 77 at 87.
[72] See, however, Kleine, n 2, above, 185 et seq.

3.3.1.2. Decoupling European defence from NATO

Moreover, Article 8 of the NATO Treaty might set a standard for any attempt to decouple European defence from NATO:

Each Party declares that none of the international engagements now in force between it and any other of the Parties or any third State is in conflict with the provisions of this Treaty, and undertakes not to enter into any international engagement in conflict with this Treaty.

The article requires the conformity of a Member State's international obligations with the NATO Treaty but it does not prohibit that EU Member States design their common security and defence policy as an alliance as long as the obligations undertaken by EU Member States do not directly oppose NATO. Article 8 was directed against pacts of mutual assistance into which France and the UK had entered with the USSR and which were still in existence at the time of concluding the NATO Treaty.[73] The pacts of 10 December 1944 and 26 May 1942 obliged France, the UK, and the USSR not to enter into alliances which were directed against one of them. When plans for an Atlantic alliance became public the USSR stated that the accession of France or the UK to NATO would infringe their duties under the respective pacts of mutual assistance.[74] Thus it can be concluded that an international obligation only infringes the NATO Treaty if it is directed against the Alliance. This would be the case if a party were to collaborate in military affairs with an adversary of the Alliance or if cooperation were directed against a Member of the Alliance.

There is a second barrier in Article 8 of the NATO Treaty: a common defence policy must not be framed in a manner that EU Member States would no longer have the capacities to meet obligations which arise from NATO decisions. Besides, Article 3 NATO Treaty requires Member States to maintain and develop their individual and collective capacity to resist armed attack. However, the single fact that EU Member States deal with the issue of defence in different treaties in a different manner does not infringe the NATO Treaty. NATO Member States are entitled to conduct all missions through the EU which a single Member State could take on its own without infringing the NATO Treaty. Even the establishment of integrated military structures would not contravene the NATO Treaty as long as these structures do not factually exclude participation in NATO.[75]

An autonomous automatic action clause as envisaged in the First Draft of the EU Constitutional Treaty does not constitute a conflicting commitment either. First, the automatic action commitment clause does not include a competence to build up integrated military structures. Thus, the enforcement of military assistance will remain NATO's task.[76] Secondly, the WEU Treaty has always included

---

[73] K Ipsen, *Rechtsgrundlagen und Institutionalisierung der Atlantisch-Westeuropäischen Verteidigung* (Hamburg: Heitman, 1967) 23 et seq.
[74] Memorandum of the USSR of 31 March 1949, Europa-Archiv 1949, 2120.
[75] See, however, von Kielmansegg, n 8, above, 317.   [76] Ibid, 358.

an automatic action commitment[77] which is tighter than Article 5 of the NATO Treaty,[78] and both treaty obligations co-existed for fifty years. Nonetheless, in the past it has been argued that the strict automatic action commitment of Article V of the WEU Treaty would not be in conformity with the NATO Treaty. It would infringe Articles 5 and 8 because Article 5 of the NATO Treaty includes a more flexible commitment which would be unjustifiably limited by the stricter obligation which arises from Article V of the WEU Treaty.[79] However, this assumption does not seem justified either in the case of the WEU or in the case of the EU. The NATO Treaty can neither be considered as a subsequent treaty in terms of Article 59 of the Vienna Convention on the Law of Treaties nor is there any clue in the WEU Treaty that Member States wanted to suspend their obligations for the duration of the NATO Treaty. Likewise, the relation between the EU Treaty and the NATO Treaty would not fall under Article 59 Vienna Convention.

Moreover, commitment to an automatic action clause would not contradict NATO obligations. As a consequence of an inclusion of an autonomous action clause comparable to the WEU clause EU Member States would be limited in the discretion which they exercise in the consultations of the NATO Council. At least one could argue that they would be excluded from rejecting any military support or from claiming neutrality. If NATO did not decide on any military assistance EU Member States would remain obliged to provide assistance to the Member State under attack.[80] This interpretation is in line with the concept of NATO's primacy. In addition, an automatic action commitment does not mean that Member States must automatically use all military means available. A flexible approach which is part of the NATO Strategy would not be in contrast with an automatic action commitment. The commitment just excludes the possibility of remaining neutral.[81] Other obligations which are included in the NATO Treaty are also broadly framed and give room for Member States' discretion. Article 4 of the Treaty, for instance, is in line with this interpretation. The article contains a duty to consult together whenever, in the opinion of any of them, the territorial

---

[77] Art V WEU Treaty:

If any of the High Contracting Parties should be the object of an armed attack in Europe, the other High Contracting Parties will, in accordance with the provisions of Article 51 of the Charter of the United Nations, afford the Party so attacked all the military and other aid and assistance in their power.

[78] Art 5 NATO Treaty:

The Parties agree that an armed attack against one or more of them in Europe or North America shall be considered an attack against them all and consequently they agree that, if such an armed attack occurs, each of them, in exercise of the right of individual or collective self-defence recognised by Article 51 of the Charter of the United Nations, will assist the Party or Parties so attacked by taking forthwith, individually and in concert with the other Parties, such action as it deems necessary, including the use of armed force, to restore and maintain the security of the North Atlantic area.

[79] K Ipsen, 'Die rechtliche Institutionalisierung der Verteidigung im atlantisch-westeuropäischen Raum' (1972) 21 *Jahrbuch des Öffentlichen Rechts* 1, at 29.   [80] Stein, n 71, above, at 88.
[81] In relation to the WEU see on this point the statement of the Dutch government, Kamerstuken 1947–8, 774, No 3 p 3.

integrity, political independence, or security of any of the parties is threatened. But it does not oblige the parties to come to certain conclusions on the provision of military support.[82]

It has been argued that Article 5 of the Washington Treaty limits aspirations for a supranational Defence Union. Although certain limitations on Member States' discretion under Article 5 NATO Treaty are permissible it has been proposed that the treaty would be infringed if no exercise of discretion is possible at all. Thus, the clause would imply a prohibition against transferring the sovereign rights over a Member State's armed forces to a supranational organization in a legally binding way without any possibility of withdrawing the forces and bringing them back under national command.[83] In such a case, a Member State would no longer be able to make the sovereign decision to deploy armed forces under Article 5 of the NATO Treaty. On the other hand, France withdrew from NATO's military structures between 1966 and 1993. This has never been considered as an infringement of the NATO Treaty.[84] To that extent, NATO practice supports the argument that Article 5 does not limit efforts for a European Defence Union. In addition, the NATO Treaty does not contain any duty to assign or earmark armed forces for NATO or to place armed forces under NATO command, even in the case of an Article 5 situation. Such an act of assignment is a sovereign decision of a Member State which can always be revoked or limited.[85] Already by the time of the Kosovo campaign, more than 90 per cent of the US force structure was not earmarked for assignments to NATO.[86] Thus it is conceivable that the exercise of discretion under the NATO Treaty does not strictly require Member States to consider the assignment or deployment of armed forces. In any event, the question would probably not arise in practice because in the case of the establishment of a supranational defence union its position within or towards NATO would be a major issue to be resolved on the political plane.

3.3.1.3. Discrimination against non-EU NATO Members

In 2002 the issue of discrimination against non-EU States was particularly problematic. The Greek-Turkish dispute about cooperation with NATO was a threat to the EU-led mission in Macedonia.[87] Mutual defence within the EU would make this problem even more severe. Ireland, Sweden, Finland, Austria but also Cyprus and Malta are not NATO Member States. Iceland, Norway, and Turkey, on the other hand, are NATO members but will not be EU members within the near future. The credibility of the EU's commitment to defence could have been tested if EU countries that are neither neutral nor members of NATO, such as Cyprus or Malta, had subscribed to mutual defence.[88]

From a legal point of view the NATO Treaty does not generally forbid different treatment between NATO members. Even though NATO Member States are not

---

[82] Von Kielmansegg, n 8, above, 230. [83] Ibid, 357.
[84] Stein, n 71, above, 88 et seq. [85] Ipsen, n 73, above, 158 et seq.
[86] ISS, *White Paper*, n 7, above, at 45. [87] See F Naert in Chapter 4 of this volume.
[88] See Naert, n 58, above, at 195 on the issue of mutual defence and neutral EU Member States.

allowed to act against each other, Article 8 of the Treaty does not forbid acting without another Member State. The USA, for instance, has conducted its military operations since 11 September 2001 without relying on NATO, although NATO invoked Article 5 for the first time in its history. European contributions are provided on an exclusively bilateral basis. The unilateral actions of the USA have never been seen as a legal discrimination against other NATO Member States. There is no reason to qualify autonomous actions of other Member States within the EU in a different manner.

Finally, the NATO Treaty as a treaty of alliance includes a general duty to consult and inform Member States, if some of the partners take autonomous measures within the treaty's realm of application. For the Petersberg tasks these requirements are met by EU-NATO security arrangements on effective consultation and cooperation which were concluded in 2003.[89] They enable the EU to use NATO planning capacities while imposing duties to consult and inform on the EU.[90]

3.3.2. *Obligations arising from EU Law: NATO's primacy*

Whilst the already existing treaties on defence set practically no legal obligations on Member States, EU law imposes some stricter limits which shall guarantee NATO's primacy.

3.3.2.1. The clause on respect and compatibility in Article 17(1) TEU

Article 17(1) subparagraph 2 TEU states that the policy of the Union shall respect the obligations of certain Member States which see their common defence realized in NATO under the North Atlantic Treaty and shall be compatible with the common security and defence policy established within that framework.[91] The first part of Article 17(1) subparagraph 2 asks for respect for the obligations arising from the NATO Treaty. Since the obligations which arise from the NATO Treaty are broadly framed with a wide discretion for Member States[92] it is submitted that no further legal limitations arise from the first part of Article 17(1) subparagraph 2 TEU.

The second part, however, calls for compatibility with the NATO Treaty not in terms of obligations but in terms of actual policy. On the one hand, this clause could just be a political statement which emphasizes that the ESDP is not a surrogate for NATO.[93] On the other hand, it is the centrepiece of the compromise

---

[89] See 'Agreement between the European Union and the North Atlantic Treaty Organisation on the Security of Information', OJ L-080, 27 March 2003 P 0036–0038. The agreement is part of the Berlin Plus package.   [90] See Chapter 4 of this volume.

[91] The Draft Constitution Art I-4l(7) reads: 'Commitments and cooperation in this area shall be consistent with commitments under NATO, which, for those States which are members of it, remains the foundation of their collective defence and the forum for its implementation'; Final Version of Draft Constitutional Treaty, 6 August 2004; see M Trybus, n 8, above, 350–2.

[92] See Chapter 4 of this volume.

[93] Kaufmann-Bühler in E Grabitz and M Hilf, *Das Recht der Europäischen Union* (München: C H Beck Verlag, 1999), Art 17 no 22; see also H-J Cremer in Calliess and Ruffert (eds), n 35, above,

which was reached between Member States in Maastricht when defence was introduced into the Treaty. It is therefore submitted that the clause limits European defence policy to a policy which is compatible with NATO. Thus, according to the treaty, earlier NATO decisions take precedence over EU decisions. The EU has to make sure unilaterally that its decisions do not counteract or jeopardize NATO decisions.[94] Thus, the clause addresses the problem that the EU's various involvements with an international crisis will complicate the issue as to how NATO's primacy can be regained or asserted after the EU was already exercising most of its responsibilities. During a conflict the EU will probably already be involved in attempts to solve the crisis diplomatically. ESDP mechanisms will probably already operate before NATO responds to the conflict at all. The clause expresses the attempt to build the EU into the European security architecture without destroying present structures.[95] However, this cannot mean that the EU would be restricted to enacting NATO decisions. With the ESDP the EU established itself as a security actor in its own right and so the requirement of compatibility must be read restrictively. Thus the clause does not include a duty to support but only a prohibition to counteract. Likewise, it does not establish the principle 'NATO first' so that NATO would have a right to be consulted first or to take decisions first. Nor is there a general primacy of NATO to use Member States' military resources.[96] Here, EU obligations do not exceed obligations arising from the NATO Treaty.

To sum up, the clause aims at preventing conflicting decisions in operative terms. It is conceivable that NATO and the EU act in parallel in a crisis situation. Under such circumstances the EU is prohibited from counteracting concrete decisions of NATO. Accordingly, the EU would not be allowed to have recourse to Member States' armed forces which are assigned to a concrete crisis management operation under NATO command. The EU would not be allowed to make a decision that would require Member States to withdraw their armed forces from a NATO operation without the alliance's consent.[97] However, taking into account the overlapping membership of both organizations as well as the requirement to decide unanimously such conflicts are hardly conceivable.[98]

3.3.2.2. NATO's right to first refusal in ESDP declarations
The EU Helsinki summit tried to address the overlapping realm of application by ensuring NATO's primacy. The European Council underlined its determination to launch and conduct EU-led military operations in response to international crises only where NATO as a whole is not engaged.[99] The Council assured that the

---

Art 17 no 5; J Frowein, *'Auf dem Weg zu einer gemeinsamen Sicherheits- und Verteidigungspolitik'* in Tomuschat (ed), n 36, above, 15.

[94] Von Kielmansegg, n 8, above, 232.   [95] Wessels, n 34, above, at 278.
[96] Von Kielmansegg, n 8, above, 232.   [97] Ibid, 356.
[98] Wessels, n 34, above, at 278.
[99] Helsinki European Council, Presidency Conclusions, Helsinki 10 and 11 December 1999, printed in Rutten, n 27, above, *Vol I*, 82.

'process will avoid unnecessary duplication and does not imply the creation of a European Army'.

The phrase 'where NATO as a whole is not engaged' is often read as NATO's right of first refusal.[100] Accordingly, EU crisis operations would only be permissible when NATO refused to take responsibility.[101] The clause aims at the compatibility of the ESDP with NATO. The alliance shall not be endangered by some of its Member States which prefer to conduct crisis management operations by excluding other NATO members. This is emphasized by the formula 'NATO as a whole'. On the other hand, the EU stresses, in principle, its equality as a security actor in ESDP documents. Consequently, in line with the primary obligations of the TEU, the clause stresses the primacy of NATO missions and contains a prohibition against circumventing NATO. EU Member States shall only use the ESDP as a framework for military operations when NATO agrees or is not willing to act in a manner which is, in principle, consistent with European policy goals or is simply not interested in a mission.[102] Thus ESDP documents show that the ESDP is complementary to NATO and not conceived as a forum for competition. However, these documents do not bind Member States legally insofar as they could still extend the EU's military competence in the EU Treaty.[103]

4. Conclusion: from Defence to Solidarity

However, the present compromise might as such not be an adequate distribution of legal powers and political responsibility for future developments. The reason for this is grounded in the changing understanding of security and defence.

4.1. The changing concept of security and defence

Security is no longer reduced to the absence of war. Since the end of the Cold War European governments are increasingly free to address less fundamental security threats than those which challenge their state borders. At present a broad notion of security prevails which includes internal conflict, transnational crime, and terrorism. Beyond the military aspect security is also applied to the protection of societies and individuals within states. Correspondingly, threats are also perceived in broader terms. Thus societies and individuals face a multitude of dangers ranging from the inadequacies of political and social structures to environmental

---

[100] C V Buttlar, 'The EU's New Relations with NATO Shuttling between Reliance and Autonomy', 6 *Zeitschrift für europarechtliche Studien* (2003) 399, at 426; M Quinlan, *European Defence Cooperation. Asset or Threat to NATO?* (Washington, DC: Woodrow Wilson Center Press, 2001) 36 et seq.
[101] See A Bagett, 'The Development of the European Union Common Defence and its Implications for the United States and NATO' (2000) 5 Georgia J of Intl and Comparative L 377, at 391.
[102] Von Kielmansegg, n 8, above, 238.   [103] Ibid, 238 et seq.

degradation.[104] The expansion of the concept of security into non-military issues has therefore led to a reconsideration of the political structures through which security can be achieved. It has made an international organization such as the EU with broad competence in almost every aspect of governance an appropriate actor for security.

Likewise, the concept of defence starts to be expanded. While defence used to describe the territorial defence of a state and its boundaries against external military aggression through another state the concept at present starts to broaden into two directions: on the one hand, the territorial aspect of defence loses its importance. On the other hand, defence is no longer an exclusive response to actions of state actors. In this respect the German Defence Policy Guidelines released in May 2003 by the Ministry of Defence[105] are illustrative. They recognize that traditional territorial defence no longer responds to present security policy requirements. On the one hand, it is acknowledged that international crisis management in times of non-state attacks and weapons of mass destruction serves defence interests. Because international terrorism is a global threat, it must be countered by a comprehensive approach, ranging from political and diplomatic initiatives to military operations. As argued above, this understanding of defence is already part of the TEU. On the other hand, it is emphasized that the lines between internal and external security have become blurred. Armed forces may therefore increasingly be deployed within the state in order to perform functions comparable to the police. Thus, the German Defence Policy Guidelines state that in future defence will comprise more internal missions directed against non-state actors.[106] The guidelines show that the classic differentiation between security missions, such as the Petersberg tasks, collective self-defence, and police actions starts to blur. The circumstances of possible terrorist attacks do not easily fit the traditional form of defence guarantees nor the traditional military responses prepared for giving effect to them.[107]

4.2. Solidarity as a future option

Future relations between the ESDP and NATO should take these developments into account. The EU should not focus too much on the traditional concept of a

---

[104] O Waever, 'European Security Identities', 34 *J Common Market Studies* (1996) 103 at 104 et seq.

[105] '*Verteidigungspolitische Richtlinien für den Geschäftsbereich des Bundesministers der Verteidigung vom 21.05.2003*', No 80, available at <http://www.bmvg.de/pic/sicherheit/vpr_broschuere.pdf>.

[106] On the legal implications of attacks by private actors on the right of self-defence see: T Ruys and S Verhoeven, 'Attacks by Private Actors and the Right of Self-defence' (2005) 10 J of Conflict and Security L 289–320; M Krajewski, 'Selbstverteidigung gegen bewaffnete Angriffe nicht-staatlicher Organisationen—Der 11 September und seine Folgen' (2002) 40 *Archiv des Völkerrechts* 187 et seq; E Myers and N White, 'The Twin Towers Attack: An Unlimited Right to Self-Defence?' (2002) 7 J of Conflict and Security L 5 et seq; C Stahn, 'International Law at the Crossroads: The Impact of September 11' (2002) 62 *Zeitschrift für ausländischer öffentliches Recht und Völkerrecht* 214 et seq.

[107] Bailes, n 55, above, at 34 et seq.

Defence Union. The Solidarity clause which is included in the EU Draft Treaty provides a more appropriate answer to present security threats. In terms of solidarity with European Member States, Article 15 states that 'the Member States shall actively and unreservedly support the Union's common foreign and security policy in a spirit of loyalty and mutual solidarity'. The Solidarity clause (Article I-43) is more explicit. It requires the Union to mobilize all instruments available to prevent the terrorist threat in the territory of the Member States, and to protect democratic institutions and the civilian population from any terrorist attack:

> The Union and its Member States shall act jointly in a spirit of Solidarity if a Member State is victim of terrorist attacks or natural or man-made disaster. The Union shall mobilise all the instruments at its disposal, including the military resources made available by the Member States to prevent the terrorist threat in the territory of the Member States . . .

Since the European Council Declaration of 25 March 2004, the Solidarity clause in the event of terrorist attacks has already been applied on a political basis. Following the 11 March 2004 terrorist attacks in Madrid, the European Council declaration on combating terrorism confirmed 'the political commitment . . . to act jointly against terrorist acts, in the spirit of the Solidarity Clause contained in Article 42 of the draft Constitution for Europe'.[108] The Solidarity clause cannot be considered as a conflicting obligation since it does not create any obligation to provide military assistance on the part of the Member States. But what is more important is that the clause permits the use of military or civil EU capabilities within the EU's territory. They are not restricted to territorial self-defence but include police measures. Thus the clause offers the necessary variety of means for appropriate actions when external and internal security are no longer clear-cut concepts.

Thus the clause covers certain aspects of homeland defence in case of terrorist attack. Consequently, the proposal for a White Paper on Defence which was made by a Study Group of the European Institute for Security Studies suggests that the EU should consider developing a homeland defence capability, bringing together the collective assets of the Council and the Commission, including a military component with a European equivalent of the recently created US Northern Command.[109] The development of such a military component, however, would probably imply the creation of integrated military structures and would therefore require an amendment of the TEU.[110]

What is more important is that for parts of the new security scenario the concept of solidarity is more appropriate because, unlike defence, it has not yet been defined in political let alone in legal terms. Thus it could be designed to fit a multilevel security system. An EU state under a terrorist attack, for example,

---

[108] European Council, 'Declaration on Combating Terrorism', Brussels, 25 March 2004; printed in EUISS (ed), *European Security and Defence: Core Documents Volume 5*, Chaillot Paper 75 (Paris: Institute of Security Studies of the European Union, 2005) 31.
[109] ISS, *White Paper*, n 7, above, at 98.   [110] See above, sections 3.2.1.2 and 3.2.2.2.

would need Member States' support in the form of medical emergency support and energy supplies. Cooperation would be required to track down suspects and extradite them. Likewise, military assistance would not be needed to resist a territorial military invasion in the form of high-technology operations but might have to cope with outbreaks of disease, energy shortages, or sabotage of key infrastructures. From an institutional point of view the concept fits into the EU because it would involve actions by the European Commission as well as in the intergovernmental sphere. Reflecting the multi-dimensional nature of EU solidarity could deal with actions in all dimensions of human and functional security except for military territorial defence and high-technology operations.[111] Many of the existing political conflicts over the relationship between NATO and the EU could be avoided and the danger of competition between the EU and NATO would be reduced.

[111] Bailes, n 55, above, at 36 et seq.

9

The European Armaments Policy: A *conditio sine qua non* for the European Security and Defence Policy?

Aris Georgopoulos *

1. Introduction

The establishment of the European Security and Defence Policy (ESDP) demonstrates that the EU is prepared to move into more sensitive areas previously considered beyond its reach. By doing so the EU aims to consolidate[1] its role as a global political actor. Nevertheless, as stated by the European Commission[2] and seconded by the High Representative of the Common Foreign and Security Policy (CFSP)[3] and others,[4] the credibility and, therefore, the success of the ESDP depends heavily on its capabilities, and, in particular, on the existence of a competitive and rationalized European Defence Technological and Industrial Base (EDTIB).[5]

---

* Lecturer in Law, University of Nottingham, United Kingdom. All website addresses cited were active on 17 October 2006, unless otherwise specified.

[1] The notion of *consolidation* implies that the EU is already a significant global player as a result of its economic might. It further refers to the support of the EU's current soft power with hard power capabilities (projection of power in the archetypal military sense). It should be mentioned at this point that the author's view is that a precondition for this consolidation is primarily the consistency in the field of CFSP and the ESDP, as for example in the case of the Common Commercial Policy.

[2] COM (2003) 113 final, *European Defence—Industrial and Market Issues—Towards an EU Equipment Policy*, Brussels, 2003, 8 and 11. For an analysis of COM (2003) see Aris Georgopoulos, 'Industrial and Market Issues in European Defence: The Commission Communication of 2003 on Harmonisation and Liberalisation of Defence Markets' (2003) 12 Public Procurement L Rev NA 82 et seq.

[3] J Solana, 'Europe Should Pool Its Defence Resources', *Financial Times*, 23 May 2005.

[4] For example, this view was also advocated by Lord Robertson of Port Ellen (former Secretary General of NATO), in 'The Future of Transatlantic Relations', Annual Lecture of the Institute for Transatlantic, European and American Studies (ITEAS), 7 November 2005, University of Dundee.

[5] It should be noted that the idea of a strong European Defence Technological and Industrial Base does not negate in principle the possibility of cooperation in armaments with countries which are not Member States of the European Union.

This requirement is also highlighted in Article 17 TEU[6] which stipulates that '[T]he progressive framing of a common defence policy will be supported, . . . *by cooperation in the field of armaments*' [emphasis added], and also Article 2 of Protocol 23 of the Treaty establishing a Constitution for Europe (the Constitutional Treaty), discussed by Trybus in Chapter 3. The latter provides that the participation in European or joint armaments projects is one of the main criteria for partaking in the permanent structured cooperation,[7] the new flexibility mechanism in the field of ESDP envisaged by the Constitutional Treaty, discussed by Wessel in Chapter 10.[8] Both provisions underline without any doubt the importance of European armaments cooperation and its direct link with the effectiveness of the ESDP.

Thus it becomes clear that the furtherance of European armaments cooperation as a means to enhance the competitiveness of the EDITB is seen as a necessary condition for enabling the ESDP to carry out its missions effectively. At the political level this need was recognized during the Greek EU Presidency of 2003 and the debate for 'more Europe' in armaments gained a renewed impetus. As a result two major parallel initiatives—one by the Council of the EU and one by the European Commission—were launched with the aim of shaping the future of European armaments cooperation/integration.

In the meantime fora outside the EU, such as the Organisation for Joint Armaments Co-operation (OCCAR)—and until very recently the Western European Armaments Group[9] (WEAG)—continue to operate albeit in a modest manner.

The present chapter focuses on the examination of the emerging institutional framework of a European armaments policy as the latter manifests itself from the recent developments in the field. This examination is necessary for a number of reasons.

First, the institutional layout of European armaments cooperation has immediate consequences for the effectiveness of efforts to create a healthy and competitive EDTIB and therefore ultimately affects the effectiveness and credibility of the ESDP. As argued further below the limited effectiveness witnessed so far in European armaments cooperation is to a large extent attributable to what appears to be an environment of unnecessary and wasteful institutional balkanization.

---

[6] Art 17 sentence 4 TEU.

[7] The permanent structured cooperation foreseen in Arts I-41(6) and III-312 of the Constitutional Treaty is a new flexibility mechanism which allows those Member States who fulfil higher military capability criteria and are willing to do so to commit themselves more in the area of the ESDP. See also M Trybus, Chapter 3 of this volume.

[8] It is believed that flexibility mechanisms such as the permanent structured cooperation will still be relevant even if the Constitutional Treaty is not eventually ratified.

[9] The Western European Armaments Group stopped being operational in May 2005. Most of its workings have been, or soon will be, transferred to the European Defence Agency (see further below).

Secondly, the institutional arrangement of the European armaments policy determines the direction into which the latter will eventually develop. It is submitted that there are various alternative scenarios which could serve as blueprint for European armaments cooperation. These scenarios determine the intensity of integration in this area. For example, the European armaments policy may take the form of a fully competitive integrated market, part of the wider internal market under the supervision of a supranational body like the European Commission (this could be termed the 'pure supranational' scenario). Alternatively, it could progress as an area of intergovernmental cooperation among Member States under the loose supervision of an intergovernmental body, for example the European Defence Agency (this could be termed the 'pure inter-governmental' scenario).[10] Of course, other hybrid scenarios are also conceivable.[11] The issue of which institutions eventually emerge as the key actors in the area will be an influential factor on the intensity of integration.

Finally, the examination of the institutional framework of European arma-ments cooperation provides an illuminating example of the lack of consistency that occasionally accompanies EU initiatives in the area of the ESDP.[12] As argued in this chapter, the recent subordination of European armaments cooperation under the EU did not eradicate duplication since even the initiatives that take place therein seem, beneath a thin layer of prima facie complementarity, poten-tially antagonistic.

This chapter begins with a brief presentation of the political/security, eco-nomic, and industrial background of the European defence market, with the purpose of assisting the better understanding of the particularities of this area. It continues by examining European armaments cooperation so far undertaken in fora outside the EU, with the aim of providing the context which to a large extent explains the current developments within the EU. Then it explores the ongoing initiatives of the EU and evaluates their possible impact. Finally, the chapter concludes that although the new initiatives constitute welcome developments they have not managed so far to tackle completely the issue of institutional duplication—instead they simply replicated it within the framework of the EU. The chapter argues that only when the institutional side of European armaments cooperation is arranged properly, with a clear allocation of roles, will it be possible to attain the objectives of a competitive EDITB and as a result the credibility of the ESDP. In this effort the sustained political will of the Member States is consid-ered to be an indispensable condition.

---

[10] On more supranational and more intergovernmental approaches to European security and defence integration see also Trybus in Chapter 3 of this volume.

[11] For instance, a certain segment of the armaments market may be subject to intergovernmental cooperation while others may fall under supranational instruments.

[12] On the issue of consistency of the ESDP in the context of EU external relations see Koutrakos in Chapter 11 of this volume.

2. The Background

2.1. Political and security

The European political and security environment is a mosaic of multiple actors with partially overlapping competencies and membership. The EU, NATO (discussed by Krieger in Chapter 8 and Terpan in Chapter 12), the WEU, and the OSCE (discussed by Odello in Chapter 13), and individual countries all have their share in the formation of the European political and security agenda. Nevertheless, in spite of this 'institutional congestion', which admittedly adds to the complexity of the European security edifice, there is one clear underlying factor. When it comes down to security and defence, national sovereignty remains the jewel in the crown in any relevant forum or effort. This is the reason why, thus far, cooperation in the field of security and defence has been carried out in an intergovernmental rather than a supranational manner.[13]

This observation is important because it also explains why initiatives in the field of the European defence market, presented further below, have not gone beyond the level of intergovernmental cooperation. As Walker and Gummett rightly point out, defence market issues, despite straddling both the economic and defence spheres, were thought to belong more to the domain of European defence cooperation than to the economic one.[14]

The assiduity on national sovereignty in defence and security matters is emphatically illustrated in the course of European integration. Initially, despite the fact that the rationale behind the creation of the European Communities was political par excellence—the avoidance of a new war in Europe—the issues of security and defence were left en bloc outside the new European edifice. As discussed extensively by Trybus in Chapter 2, René Pléven's plan for the creation of a European Defence Community (EDC) with a standing European army, which led to the signing of the EDC Treaty,[15] was put to an inglorious end by the French National Assembly in 1954. Likewise, the project for a European Political Community which would supplement the EDC with the establishment of

---

[13] The terms *intergovernmental* and *supranational* are used in this context as legal rather than political terms. Thus by the term *intergovernmental* is meant a legal process which leads to binding decisions only upon consenting parties/governments—according to the classic paradigm of public international law. In contrast by the term *supranational* is meant a legal process which, in the specific fields where governments have knowingly relinquished their sovereign competences, may lead to binding decisions even upon non-consenting parties—governments. (It should be clarified that the process which has been described above as supranational *from a legal point of view* may still demonstrate a lot of intergovernmental traits *from a political point of view*, such as the so-called intergovernmental bargaining).

[14] W Walker and P Gummett, *Nationalism, Internationalism and the European Defence Market*, Chaillot Paper No 9 (Paris: Institute of Security Studies of Western European Union, 1993) 4.

[15] The EDC Treaty was signed by Belgium, Netherlands, Luxembourg, France, Germany, and Italy on 27 May 1952.

federal-like political institutions was also abandoned. Both initiatives were distinctively 'supranational'. As a result, efforts for political integration including defence were relinquished or remained in a 'semi-dormant' condition. This was expressed by the inclusion of Article 223 (now 296 EC) in the Treaty of the European Economic Community, which allows Member States to adopt measures *they* consider necessary in the production or trade of arms, munitions, and warlike material. Subsequent efforts for cooperation in foreign and security policy have been purely intergovernmental.

First, the European Political Cooperation (EPC), which began in Luxembourg in 1970 with the approval of the 'Davignon Report' by the Foreign Ministers of the six founding Member States, aimed at the coordination of their foreign policies. Initially EPC did not include any issues related to defence. It was not until the Solemn Declaration of Stuttgart in 1983 that the political and economic (though not the military) aspects of security became part of the EPC's scope. This cooperation was carried out until 1986 in the margins of European communities and it was based on informal consultations, reports, and agreements. However, even after its formal embrace by the Single European Act,[16] EPC remained a forum of intergovernmental cooperation.[17]

Later the end of the Cold War and the transformation of the global security landscape led to a revival of the idea of a European common foreign policy— something more than the cooperation of the EPC framework. Hence the Common Foreign and Security Policy (CFSP) was established by the Treaty of Maastricht as the second pillar of the European Union edifice, with the purpose of asserting the Union's identity in the international scene.[18] Later the creation of the position of High Representative of the CFSP by the Treaty of Amsterdam[19] aimed first to better coordinate the CFSP agenda and secondly to associate the concept of the CFSP with a 'recognizable personality' of high political calibre.

Subsequent developments, such as the introduction of 'constructive abstention' with the Treaty of Amsterdam and 'enhanced cooperation' with the Treaty of Nice, did not change the intergovernmental character of the CFSP but rather aimed at improving the efficiency of the decision-making process, envisaged within a purely intergovernmental environment. The hard nucleus of intergovernmentalism, enjoining that a decision or norm cannot bind a country if the latter refuses to accept it, has not changed. The CFSP was not underpinned by significant defence structures and capacities, a remnant of the Communities' civil tradition and a direct consequence of NATO's position as the centrepiece of Europe's defence. The mismatch between aspirations and means was more than apparent.

[16] Art 1, Art 3(2), and Art 30 or Title III of the Single European Act.

[17] On EPC see P Koutrakos, *Trade Foreign Policy and Defence in EU Constitutional Law: The Legal Regulation of Sanctions, Export of Dual Use Goods and Armaments* (Oxford: Hart Publishing, 2001) at 9 et seq.

[18] Art 2 (former Art B) TEU. See in detail R A Wessel, *The European Union's Foreign and Security Policy: A Legal and Institutional Perspective* (The Hague: Kluwer, 1999).

[19] Art 26 (former Art J 16) TEU.

The British initiative which led to the Franco-British Summit in St-Malo in December 1998 constituted the beginning of a European Security and Defence Policy (ESDP). In the Joint declaration the two countries agreed that the '... Union must have the capacity for autonomous action, backed up by credible military forces, the means to decide to use them and a readiness to do so, in order to respond to international crises'.[20] Nevertheless the breakthrough came in the aftermath of the intervention in Kosovo, where the embarrassing reality of the EU's impotence to deal with a medium-scale security hazard in its neighbourhood led to drastic developments culminating in the Helsinki Summit in 1999. The Presidency Conclusions of the Helsinki European Council established the 'head-line goal', namely the capacity for the EU to deploy within sixty days and sustain for at least one year up to sixty thousand troops, by the year 2003.[21]

The creation of military structures within the EU, even with the initial modest assignment of Petersberg tasks[22]—namely rescue tasks, peacekeeping tasks, and tasks of combat forces in crisis management, including peacemaking,[23] discussed by Naert in Chapter 4 and Tsagourias in Chapter 5—admittedly signalled a significant shift in the European integration agenda. Defence was not a 'taboo' issue any more for the European venture. Nevertheless, despite its significance this shift did not amount to a radical change which could challenge the supremacy of national sovereignty over defence matters. The vision for an EDC as conceived in Pléven's plan constitutes a distant possibility. In the foreseeable future it seems that national governments, ministries of defence, and national armies will still play the predominant role in defence.

2.2. Economic

The defence budgets of the EU Member States[24] have suffered a long period of lean years since the beginning of 1990s. The end of the Cold War, with the disappearance of the Soviet threat and the belief that the likelihood of a new security risk for Europe was rather slim in the foreseeable future, opened the way for the

[20] Text of Joint Declaration on European Defence, UK-French Summit 3–4 December 1998, para 2, House of Commons Select Committee on Defence. See also M Trybus, *European Union Law and Defence Integration* (Oxford: Hart Publishing, 2005) at 92–120.

[21] Helsinki European Council of 10 and 11 December 1999, Presidency Conclusions para 28, available at <http://europa.eu.int/council/off/conclu/dec99/dec99_en.htm#security>. This development was accompanied by the establishment of the Political and Security Committee which, in a nutshell, prepares the Union's response to international crises falling within the scope of the CFSP (see Council Decision 2001/78/CFSP of 22 January 2001 setting up the Political and Security Committee of the European Union [2001]OJ L-27/1). The Committee is assisted in carrying out its duties by the Military Committee (see Council Decision 2001/79/CFSP of 22 January 2001 setting up the Military Committee of the European Union [2001] OJ L-27/4) and the Military Staff (see Council Decision 2001/80/CFSP of 22 January 2001 on the establishment of the Military Staff of the European Union [2001] OJ L-27/7).

[22] The Petersberg tasks were first stipulated in June 1992 at the Ministerial Council of the Western European Union (WEU) held at the Hotel Petersberg near Bonn.   [23] Art 17(2) TEU.

[24] With the exception of Greece.

re-allocation of public resources in less war-like directions.[25] It is estimated that between 1989 and 1994 there was a 12 per cent reduction in defence expenditure by the European NATO countries.[26] The aggregate defence budgets of EU Member States fell from US$181 billion in 1985 to US$171 billion in 1993[27] and further to US$140billion in 1999.[28] Likewise, defence equipment expenditure declined from US$38 billion in 1983 to US$28 billion in 1999.[29] As a result, the workforce in European defence-related industries fell from approximately 1.6 million in 1984 to 1 million in the mid-1990s, a decrease of 37 per cent.[30] Currently the workforce in the European defence industry is estimated at approximately 800,000.[31] A further consequence was that within this environment of stagnation European governments resorted to introversion and protectionism of their troubled defence industries. The trend of decreasing defence budgets continued until 2001. There was a small increase in defence expenditure in 2002. France and the UK announced some substantial increases in 2003, whereas Germany decided to freeze its defence expenses until 2006.

Nevertheless, these increases do not match the US performance. The American defence budget in 2003 increased by 14 per cent to an astonishing $369 billion[32] (this figure does not include the additional $80 billion appropriated for the war in Iraq)[33] and it is expected to increase further until 2007. It is important to note that currently the aggregate defence expenditure of all EU Member States is less than half of the US defence expenditure. What is more, due to fragmented defence markets, duplications in defence spending and R&D expenditure, the modest European resources are spent unwisely.

Thus the gap between the USA and the EU is not only a matter of quantity but also of quality. It has been estimated that a Europe with fragmented defence markets would have to spend 10 to 15 per cent more than the USA in order to achieve comparable results.[34]

---

[25] Apart from the peace dividend explanation it has also been suggested that the aforementioned period coincided with the convergence criteria foreseen by the Maastricht Treaty—apart from the UK—especially the 3% upper limit on public deficits. See Mark Guyot and Radu Vranceanu, 'European Defence: The Cost of Partial Integration' (2001) 12 *Defence & Peace Economics* 158.

[26] P de Vestel, 'Defence Markets and Industries in Europe: Time for Political Decisions', Chaillot Paper No 21 (Paris: Institute of Security Studies of Western European Union, 1995).

[27] COM (96) 10 final, *The Challenges Facing the European Defence-related Industry*, Brussels, 1996, Annex.

[28] C Langton (ed), *The Military Balance 2001–2002* (Oxford: Oxford University Press, 2001), 35.   [29] Ibid.

[30] COM (96) 10 final.

[31] E Liinkanen, 'The Role of EU and European Commission Initiatives to Promote a Competitive European Defence Technological and Industrial Base', Forum Europe 5th European Defence Industries Conference, Brussels, 23 May 2000.

[32] M Evans, 'Rise in US Arms Budget Leaves Europe Far Behind', *The Times*, 12 February 2002.

[33] Stockholm International Peace Research Institute, Recent trends in military expenditure, available at <http://www.sipri.org/contents/milap/milex/mex_database1.html>.

[34] R Seidelmann, 'Costs, Risks and Benefits of a Global Military Capability for the European Union', (1997) 8 *Defence & Peace Economics* 129.

2.3. Industrial

The European defence industrial environment is quite complex. To begin with, until relatively recently defence companies had a distinct affiliation with a particular Member State and as a result they were more national than European. The fragmentation of the European defence market from the demand point of view into many small national markets in combination with domestic security and industrial and political considerations had a mirror image on the supply side.

The most common method of transnational collaboration between Europe's defence firms was the establishment of strategic partnerships and joint ventures. These forms of collaboration had beneficial synergy effects but were by definition unable to lead to substantial industrial restructuring because the various partners remained separate operating companies. In addition, there are different degrees of defence industrial capabilities in the various Member States. Eighty per cent of Europe's defence industrial capacity is concentrated between the so-called 'Big Four', namely France, Germany, Italy, and the UK.[35] Furthermore, the divergence relates not only to the different industrial capabilities among the various Member States but has also a very important structural dimension. For example, the defence industry in Germany and the UK has been largely privatized whereas in France and Greece state control over the defence industry has been much stronger. Often state ownership of the defence industry is connected with the allocation of civil servant status to their workers, an element which may hinder restructuring.

The European defence industrial background has changed significantly over the last five years. Until 1997 European defence consolidation took the form of acquisition of smaller firms by larger ones within the borders of domestic markets. The idea was to create national champions, which would consolidate domestic defence markets and ensure favourable conditions—due to their size—in case of cooperation with enterprises from other countries. Until 1999 the creation of a Pan-European major defence firm, the so called European Aerospace and Defence Company (EADC), was seen as the response to the American defence industry consolidation that took place in the first half of the 1990s with the creation of American giants such as Boeing, Lockheed Martin, and Raytheon. The subsequent creation of the European Aeronautic Defence and Space Company (EADS) in 2000 signalled a significant change in the European defence industrial landscape. The company emerged from the merger of DASA, the French Aérospatiale Matra, and Construcciones Aeronáuticas (CASA) of Spain. EADS is active in the field of aerospace and defence and has a strong presence in the civil market through the Airbus consortium.[36]

---

[35] Walker and Gummett distinguish European countries into five groups according to their defence industrial capacities. The first group consists of France and the UK because of their largely autonomous defence industrial capabilities. The second group comprises Germany, Italy, and possibly Spain. The third group consists of Belgium, Norway, Denmark, and Switzerland whereas the fourth comprises Greece, Portugal, and Turkey. Sweden is considered as *sui generis* because, despite its small size, it has a considerable defence industrial capability. Walker and Gummett, n 14, above.

[36] BAe Systems is the other partner of Airbus.

The establishment of EADS constituted the first major cross-border merger in the European defence industrial environment, but it is only a beginning. Although the field of aerospace and electronics reached a high level of rationalization with EADS, BAe Systems, and Thales (formerly Thomson-CSF) as the main players, other fields such as shipbuilding and land systems remain fragmented. The reasons for higher consolidation in aerospace could be explained by the fact that companies in the field have had a strong civil presence with previous experience of successful cross-border partnerships—for example Airbus—and were more exposed to the free market culture.

3. The European Defence Procurement Edifice

There have been various initiatives so far dealing with European armaments cooperation. Most of these initiatives, however, took place outside the framework of the EU.

3.1. The Western European Armaments Group (WEAG) and Western European Armaments Organization (WEAO)

As already mentioned, the WEAG ceased being operational at the end of May 2005. Nevertheless, it still needs to be discussed here because its achievements and most significantly its failures explain the shape of the current institutional layout of European armaments cooperation.

The WEAG constituted the oldest forum of European cooperation in the field of armaments. It was established in 1992 under the ambit of the WEU, although its origins can be traced back to 1976 when the defence ministers of the European NATO nations[37] established the Independent European Programme Group (IEPG), a forum of armaments cooperation with the aim of promoting cooperation between participating countries and enhancing their defence industries. In 1992 the functions of the IEPG were transferred to the WEAG. The latter lacked legal personality and functioned more as a forum of political consultation. WEAG objectives were: the more efficient use of resources, the opening-up of national defence markets to cross-border competition, the strengthening of the European defence industrial base, and the promotion of cooperation in research and development.

The WEAG was organized in three panels. Panel I aimed at promoting cooperative equipment programmes which met the military requirements of WEAG members. Panel II dealt with defence research and technology. Panel III dealt with aspects of common defence economics policy and armaments cooperation

---

[37] Apart from Iceland.

procedures. The main project of this panel was the drafting of the Coherent Policy Document (CPD), a non-enforceable agreement, adopted in 1990 by defence ministers, which set the principles for the creation of a European Defence Equipment Market (EDEM). EDEM was intended to open up domestic markets in the areas of development, procurement, and maintenance of war-like material for contracts of a value exceeding €1 million. The main features of EDEM were the application of the *juste retour* principle together with the support of countries with Developing Defence Industries (DDI), the requirement of publication of future contracts, and the non-enforceable character of the CPD framework.[38]

Juste retour can be described as the equitable industrial return that states require for their national enterprises, either from the state's financial participation in a cooperative project or for providing market access to foreign firms. The principle is very important for countries with small or medium-sized defence industries because it secures the involvement of their domestic firms in the defence procurement market.

The requirement of publication of future defence contracts was aimed at the dissemination of information to other, non-domestic, European firms of contractual opportunities in the various Member States. In contrast to the public procurement regime of the EU, the publication of future defence contract opportunities was not carried out centrally. Instead, there was a decentralized system whereby each Member State was supposed to publish its future defence contracts, either in a separate contracts bulletin or in the official state gazette. Contracts bulletins were to be available from the focal point designated for each member. The non-enforceable character of EDEM rules has been considered as the primary reason for the framework's limited practical impact.[39]

The main characteristic of WEAG was its wide membership. At the time of its closure it comprised nineteen members.[40] This broad participation was WEAG's strongest advantage and at the same time its main weakness.

First of all, it was an advantage because it enabled WEAG to claim to be the most inclusive forum for European defence industrial cooperation. Nevertheless, this inclusiveness in combination with the fact that all members irrespective of size had equal rights and responsibilities had an adverse effect on the flexibility of WEAG. The agendas of big country producers and countries with medium- and small-sized defence industries have not always coincided, to say the least. For example, big country producers (France, Germany, Italy, and the UK) argued

---

[38] For an analysis of the EDEM framework see M Trybus, *European Defence Procurement Law: International and National Procurement Systems as Models for a Liberalised Defence Procurement Market in Europe* (The Hague, London, Boston: Kluwer Law International, 1999) 31–44.

[39] Trybus, ibid.

[40] Austria, Belgium, Czech Republic, Denmark, Finland, France, Germany, Greece, Hungary, Italy, Luxembourg, Netherlands, Norway, Poland, Portugal, Spain, Sweden, Turkey, and the UK.

that the juste retour in collaborative projects, in particular if calculated on the basis of each collaborative programme separately, might render collaboration cumbersome, costly, and limit its effect on the rationalization of the European defence industrial base.

On the other hand, smaller countries were more sceptical about this approach. According to them, juste retour was a significant tool which could promote their defence industrial bases and as a consequence increase competition across Europe at a later stage. They were also unconvinced about the true motives of larger countries. It seemed to them quite hypocritical to blame the fragmentation of European defence market on juste retour, which benefits smaller countries, when all big country producers protected—in some cases outspokenly—their defence industries. Thus the rhetoric for the abolition of juste retour as a means to achieve economies of scale was seen by small members as a pretext on the part of big country producers in order to extend the dominance of their defence firms. This sort of disagreement prevented radical solutions from being adopted, thus leading to the enfeeblement of WEAG's credibility as the preferred forum for European defence market integration.

In an effort to address the European defence market's fragmentation, in 1993 WEAG set up an ad hoc Study Group whose task was to assess the politico-economic environment and opine on the possibilities for the creation of a European Armaments Agency (EAA). Because of the unripe politico-economic circumstances the ad hoc group avoided recommending the immediate creation of an EAA. Instead, in 1996 defence ministers proceeded to the creation of the Western European Armaments Organization (WEAO). The WEAO was a subsidiary body of the WEU and shared its legal personality. This meant that the WEAO[41] was able to conclude contracts on behalf of its members.

A second attempt at the creation of an EAA took place in 1999 when the defence ministers decided at their Erfurt meeting to develop a plan with a timetable, known as 'Masterplan'. Despite the endorsement of Masterplan's proposals by defence ministers,[42] it is clear that by the end of 2002 the idea of creating an EAA within the WEAG had lost its momentum.[43] It is believed that an additional factor in the limited impact of the WEAG, EDEM, and WEAO was their timing. Their establishment coincided with the lean years of the European defence industrial market, when the natural reaction of national governments was to adopt 'introverted' defence industrial policies.

[41] The WEAO's activities were limited to the field of research and technology despite the fact that according to Art 6 of its Charter its activities could expand in other areas such as defence procurement and management of assets and facilities.

[42] WEAG Rome Declaration, 16 May 2002, para 4.

[43] B Schmitt, *The European Union and Armaments: Getting a Bigger Bang for the Euro*, Chaillot Paper No 63 (Paris: European Union Institute for Security Studies, 2003) 22; Assembly of the Western European Union, 'First Part of the Forty-eighth Annual Report of the Council to the Assembly on the Initiatives of the Council', Document/A1807, 12 November 2002, 3.

3.2. The Organisation for Joint Armaments Co-operation (OCCAR)

The Organisation for Joint Armaments Co-operation (OCCAR)[44] was formed on 12 November 1996[45] by France, Germany, Italy, and the UK.[46] The OCCAR Convention was signed by the defence ministers at the Farnborough Air Show on 9 September 1998. OCCAR attained legal personality on 28 January 2001.

Thus far OCCAR has been developed into a management agency of defence collaborative projects, although it has the potential for covering a much wider range of activities. The main aim of OCCAR is to enhance efficiency in the management of defence-related collaborative projects. Currently it manages six collaborative programmes.[47]

OCCAR is based on five principles, namely: cost-effectiveness of collaborative programmes, harmonization of requirements, competitiveness of defence industrial base, renunciation of juste retour, and openness to participation of other European Member States in the organization. The participation of other European countries is conditional upon their involvement in collaborative programmes and acceptance of OCCAR's principles, rules, and procedures. Its legal status, namely the capacity to conclude and manage contracts and to institute proceedings[48] on behalf of its members, initially rendered OCCAR one of the main contenders for becoming a fully-fledged European Armaments Agency.[49]

The establishment of OCCAR has been considered as the response of the big European country producers to the inability of the WEAG/WEAO to agree on the establishment of a European Armaments Agency.[50] Initially it was hailed by commentators[51] and industry[52] alike as a fresh breeze in the somewhat inauspicious field of European defence market integration.[53] It was believed that the

---

[44] The acronym derives from the French *Organisme Conjoint de Cooperation en Matière d'Armement.*

[45] The origins of OCCAR can be traced to the earlier decision taken by the Franco-German Defence and Security Council in 1994 and the subsequent official announcement of the initiative at the Franco-German meeting of Baden-Baden in 1995. See J Mawdsley, *The Gap Between Rhetoric and Reality: Weapons Acquisitions and ESDP* BICC Paper 26 (Bonn: Bonn International Center for Conversion, 2002) 14.   [46] Belgium joined OCCAR in 2003 and Spain in 2005.

[47] ROLAND (a short-range optical/radar guided surface-to-air missile), FSAF (surface-to-air anti-missile system family), BOXER (armoured utility vehicle), TIGER helicopter, COBRA (counter-battery radar) and last but not least the A400M (medium/long transport aircraft formerly known as Future Large Aircraft or FLA).

[48] Art 39(a), (b), (c) of the Convention on the Establishment of the Organisation for Joint Armaments Co-operation.

[49] B Schmitt, n 43, above; K Hayward, *Towards a European Weapons Procurement Process: The Shaping of Common European Requirements for New Arms Programmes*, Chaillot Paper No 27 (Paris: Institute of Security Studies of Western European Union 1997) 21.

[50] Assembly of Western European Union, Document A/1840, *The Development of Armaments Policy in Europe—Reply to the Annual Report of the Council*, 3 December 2003, para 37; K Hayward, ibid.   [51] Mawdsley, n 45, above.

[52] De Briganti, 'Poll Discounts Small Nations in European Industry Effort' *Defense News*, 6 November 1995, 24.

[53] J Mawdsley and G Quille, *Equipping the Rapid Reaction Force: Options for and Constraints on a European Defence Equipment Strategy*, BICC Paper 33 (Bonn: International Center for Conversion, 2003) 30–1.

Big Four were paving the way for European defence market liberalization.[54] However, smaller Member States reacted negatively. They considered OCCAR a closed club tailored to accommodate the needs of larger country producers. In particular, they were unwilling to accept the renunciation of the juste retour principle, because such a move was perceived as nothing but an obituary for their small defence industries. This negative reaction on the part of the smaller Member States was based not only on their dissatisfaction with the actual content of OCCAR's rules, but also on the fact that these rules were the outcome of a process from which smaller Member States were bluntly excluded.[55]

The Commission approached the initiative cautiously, with mixed emotions. On the one hand, more European defence equipment was something to be content with. On the other hand, however, the establishment of an armaments structure outside the EU demonstrated the willingness of the big players to commit themselves to an intergovernmental structure, thus reducing the potential influence and role of the Commission. This could explain the coincidence of the publication of Commission's Communication (96) 10 final as an attempt to begin the debate of defence market liberalization within the Union before it was too late.

It is submitted that thus far OCCAR's performance has been quite modest and it certainly has not met the high expectations which accompanied its establishment. It should be understood that OCCAR does not constitute a free defence market among its members—far from it. As already mentioned, it is merely an agency, which manages those collaborative defence programmes that have been assigned to it by its members.[56] This means that OCCAR does not constitute an *exclusive* forum of collaborative projects for OCCAR's members. In addition, although Article 8 of OCCAR's Convention foresees a wide range of activities,[57] this potential has not been exploited yet.

The main reason for the mismatch between potential and actual performance can be found in the lack of political commitment on the part of its members. In addition, it should be underlined that the much celebrated abandonment of juste retour, the main point of friction between larger and smaller Member States, did not

[54] As K Hayward put it: 'If France, Germany and Britain can begin the harmonization process, the others might be persuaded to follow their lead', n 49, above.

[55] J Mawdsley, *The European Union and Defence Industrial Policy*, BICC Paper 31 (Bonn, International Center for Conversion, 2003), 18.

[56] Art 7 Convention on the Establishment of the Organisation for Joint Armaments Co-operation.

[57] Art 8 Convention on the Establishment of the Organisation for Joint Armaments Co-operation stipulates that:

OCCAR shall fulfil the following tasks, and such other functions as the Member States may assign to it: (a) management of current and future cooperative programmes, which may include configuration control and in-service support, as well as research activities; (b) management of those national programmes of Member States that are assigned to it; (c) preparation of common technical specifications for the development and procurement of jointly defined equipment; (d) coordination and planning of joint research activities as well as, in cooperation with appropriate military staffs, studies of technical solutions to meet future operational requirements; (e) coordination of national decisions concerning the common industrial base and common technologies; (f) coordination of both capital investments and the use of test facilities.

lead to the establishment of a competitive environment where value for money is the only criterion for the award of defence contracts. It is suggested that the concept of *juste retour* is often used as a synonym for 'industrial return'. Nevertheless it should be clarified that the concept has a much narrower meaning in the framework of OCCAR. It suffices to cite, in this respect, Article 5 of the OCCAR Convention:

> To enable a strengthening of the competitiveness of the European defence technological and industrial base, the Member States renounce, in their cooperation, the analytical calculation of industrial *juste retour* on a programme-by-programme basis, and *replace it by the pursuit of an overall multi-programme/multi-year balance* . . . [emphasis added]

This necessarily means that the renunciation of juste retour does not signify the absolute prohibition of the concept of 'work-sharing'. It simply introduces a more flexible industrial return mechanism based not on an analytical calculation for individual projects but rather on an overall balance over a series of programmes.

As a result, the 'renunciation of juste retour' should not be read as signifying the abandonment of the concept of industrial return as a whole but rather the concept of industrial return calculated on a programme by programme basis. It also explains why smaller Member States seem to be reluctant to join OCCAR despite the fact that work-sharing is still a rule in the game. It seems that the new industrial return mechanism suits the interests of large country producers best. The latter, due to their wide defence industrial base and their greater spending capability, are able to participate in various projects and as a result secure an overall industrial return. In contrast, smaller Member States with their more limited financial and industrial capabilities are less likely to benefit from this system. .

What is more, the image of OCCAR as the model forum where principles of competition and value for money are best observed is further undermined by the fact that the aforementioned 'global industrial balance' mechanism is not yet fully applicable. In particular, the OCCAR Convention foresees an initial three-year period during which transitional provisions will apply. The latter are stipulated in Annex III of the Convention. According to the latter:

> [H]owever, in accordance to Article 5 of the present Convention, during the three years following entry into force of this Convention:
>
> (a) if the industry of a Member State has received a volume of orders smaller than 66% of its financial contribution, either concerning a *programme*, a *certain phase* or a certain *sub-assembly* of a programme (as far as the complexity of a weapon system justifies that this system is divided beforehand into sub-assemblies),
> (b) if a global imbalance of more than 4% is identified in relation to all programmes, *appropriate actions* will be taken by the Board of Supervisors (BoS) in order to *restore the balance.*
> 2. The efficiency of this procedure, and in particular the percentage rates quoted above shall first be reviewed a year after entry into force and subsequently at regular intervals.
> 3. After the three-year period, there must be an examination of *whether this procedure can be repealed* . . . [emphasis added].

These provisions—especially paragraph 3, which implies that the transitional period may be prolonged—clearly demonstrate that OCCAR is far from being a haven of competition. It remains a forum where political and industrial considerations are strongly present.[58]

3.3. The Letter of Intent (LoI) Framework Agreement

The Letter of Intent is an initiative taken in July 1998 by the defence ministers of six European countries, namely France, Germany, Italy, Spain, Sweden, and the UK. Its purpose is to facilitate the restructuring of the defence industry in Europe.[59] The initiative identified six different areas of interest: security of supply, export procedures, protection of classified information, research and development, exchange of technical information, and standardization of military requirements. Six specialist Working Groups were set up to examine the respective areas.

On the basis of the proposals of the six Working Groups a legally binding international treaty, known as the Framework Agreement, was drafted and subsequently signed by LoI participating countries in July 2000. The ratification cycle was concluded in 2003. The Framework agreement is expected to make a significant contribution to the integration of defence markets of the respective countries, especially in the areas of intellectual property rights, harmonization of military requirements, security of supply, and security of information.

However, it should be emphasized that the Framework Agreement did not go beyond intergovernmental cooperation. It did not even contemplate the establishment of a permanent structure for monitoring and coordination. This is assigned to the Executive Committee, which will convene four times a year. In addition, it did not create a free defence market between signatories. It seems rather that the Agreement is based on the assumption that the respective markets remain distinct and thus aims to facilitate participation in the latter through restructuring of the industry.

4. The Unsuccessful Initiatives of the European Union

The integration of European armaments cooperation into the framework of the EU has always been more a matter of political will than of institutional or legal

---

[58] According to Arts 10 et seq of the OCCAR Convention the highest decision-making authority in the organization is the Board of Supervisors, which consists of the ministers of defence of OCCAR members or their delegates and among other competencies it decides or approves the award of contracts. The members of the Board have the right to vote only in those decisions that relate to a programme in which the country that they represent participates. This arrangement underlines the infiltration of political considerations in OCCAR's decision-making process.

[59] 'Explanatory Memorandum for an Agreement to Facilitate the Restructuring and Operation of the European Defence Industry', British Ministry of Defence.

capability. This becomes evident from Article 17, sentence 4 TEU, which provides that:

[T]he progressive framing of a common defence policy will be supported, *as Member States consider appropriate*, by cooperation in the field of armaments. [emphasis added]

The earlier initiatives undertaken by the Union in the field of defence procurement usually met with reluctance on the part of some of the Member States.

4.1. POLARM

In 1995 the Council of the EU set up an ad hoc Council Working Group, POLARM, as a forum of discussion for armaments policy issues. The work of POLARM has been quite modest,[60] because of lack of agreement among Member States. It was not until 2003 that POLARM agreed on draft recommendations, which were later adopted by the Council.[61] It is submitted that although these documents do not contain any serious commitments they nevertheless show a renewed interest in bringing armaments issues within the auspices of the EU.[62]

4.2. The first initiatives of the European Commission

The European Commission never tried to hide its aspiration to acquire a role in the area of armaments regulation and policy. In 1996 the Commission issued COM (96) 10 final,[63] in which it presented its views with regard to the creation of a European defence equipment market, especially in the areas of competition, state aid, and defence procurement. The Commission proposed the application of already existing instruments of the first pillar such as the public procurement Directives, albeit in a way that takes into account the characteristics of the defence sector. In other words, the Commission suggested to extend its supervisory role in the field of warlike materials, but expressed its willingness to be more moderate in the exercise of this role. Nevertheless, COM (96) 10 final demonstrated that the Commission focused more on the market aspect of the defence market by proposing its integration into the first pillar and underplayed its political side. It has been suggested[64] that this was due to the fact that the Communication, although based

---

[60] Mawdsley, n 51, above. L Ciovachini, Presentation at the conference 'European Armaments Industries, ESDP and Transatlantic Cooperation', Cicero Foundation, Paris, 29–30 March 2001.
[61] Council Resolutions, 'The EU Armaments Sector Restructuring Challenges' and 'Security of Supply', both 16 June 2003.   [62] Schmitt, n 43, above.
[63] COM (96) 10 final, *The Challenges Facing the European Defence Related Industry, a Contribution for Action at European Level*, Brussels, 1996. For an analysis of COM (96) see M Trybus, 'The Challenges Facing the European Defence-Related Industry—Commission Communication COM (96) 08' (1996) 5 *Public Procurement L Rev* CS 98 et seq.
[64] Ulrika Mörth, 'Competing Frames in the European Commission—The Case of the Defence Industry and Equipment Issue', (2000) 7 *J of Eur Public Policy* 182 et seq.

on the proposals of both the Commission's Directorate General (DG) Industry and DG External Relations, was influenced more by the former than the latter.

Subsequently the Commission issued COM (97) 583 final,[65] where it proposed the adoption of a Common Position and an Action Plan for the creation of an integrated defence market. Despite the fact that COM (97) 583 final was more pragmatic in its approach to the defence market, it failed to convince the Council to adopt the draft Common Position. Moreover, the progress of the Action Plan was rather disappointing.[66]

5. Recent Developments within the EU

5.1. The current initiatives of the Commission

The Commission reopened the debate on the organization of the defence market at the European level by issuing COM (2003) 113 final.[67] This document was issued in response to a European Parliament Resolution of 10 April 2002 which invited the Commission to address the issue of armaments in a new Communication. COM (2003) 113 final, without introducing radical substantial changes to the Commission's previous positions, adopts a more moderate style in its discourse, which shows an understanding of the current situation. Whereas the previous Communications present defence market integration as a *precondition* for the establishment of the ESDP[68]—based on the idea that agreement would be easier on the industrial-economic rather than the political front—the present Communication considers defence market integration on the one hand as a logical consequence of the furtherance of the ESDP, witnessed during the last few years, and on the other as a prerequisite, not for the establishment of the latter, but for its credibility.[69] In addition, the language used to refer to the negative consequences of market fragmentation is indicative of the attached political significance. For example, in various instances throughout the communication reference is made to the fact that fragmentation will not only put European companies at risk but will also be detrimental to the EU as a whole.[70]

Moreover, the Commission seems to acknowledge the prerogatives of Member States in the relevant field as well as their political choice to coordinate their defence industrial efforts within the Union, but at least initially outside the first pillar. For this reason the Commission proposes a hybrid approach combining first and second pillar instruments.[71]

---

[65] COM (97) 583 final, *Implementing European Union Strategy on Defence Related Industries*, Brussels, 1997.

[66] E Liinkanen, 'The Role of EU and European Commission Initiatives to Promote a Competitive European Defence Technological and Industrial Base', Forum Europe 5th European Defence Industries Conference, Brussels May 23, 2000.

[67] COM (2003) 113 final, n 2, above.   [68] COM (96) 10 final.

[69] COM (2003) 113 final.   [70] Ibid.   [71] Ibid.

Finally, COM (2003) 113 final identified seven areas where the Commission contemplated further initiatives, namely: standardization, monitoring of defence-related industries, intra-Community transfers, defence procurement, competition policy, export control of dual-use goods, and research and development.

5.1.1. The Green Paper on Defence Procurement

The Green Paper on Defence Procurement[72] is the first of the actions mentioned in COM (2003) 113 final. The latter establishes a consultation process with the stakeholders (national defence ministries, industry, other relevant institutions, and experts) with regard to the clarification of the existing legal framework, namely Article 296 EC, the examination of the suitability of the European public procurement rules for the purposes of defence procurement, and the desirability of the adoption of a specific Community instrument in the area of armaments acquisitions (Defence Procurement Directive). With regard to the clarification of the existing legal framework, the Green Paper announces the adoption of an interpretative Communication which would clarify the scope of Article 296 EC. In this respect the Green Paper repeats the position of the Commission that Article 296 EC does not introduce an automatic exemption of production and trade in arms and munitions from the application of Treaty provision. What is more, this exemption should only be used when derogation is necessary for the protection of the essential interests of the security of the Member States. Moreover, according to the Green Paper the burden of proof lies with the Member States. The interpretative Communication, although not legally binding for the Member States, will oblige the Commission to take action if necessary before the European Court of Justice.

Finally, the Green Paper proposes the adoption of a Defence Procurement Directive which would provide legal certainty and would take into account the idiosyncrasies of the sector. Interestingly, the Green Paper asks whether the Defence Procurement Directive should also cover collaborative projects. As explained below, armament collaborative projects in the EU fall under the supervision of the newly established EDA.

5.2. Recent initiatives of the Council

The European Council in Thessaloniki decided on 19–20 June 2003 to put in place the foundations for the creation of an intergovernmental European Agency in the field of defence capabilities development, research, acquisition, and armaments.[73] As a result the European Defence Agency[74] (EDA) was established by

---

[72] COM (2004) 608 final, *Green Paper on Defence Procurement*, Brussels, 2004. For an analysis see A Georgopoulos, 'The Commission's Green Paper on Defence Procurement' (2005) 14(2) Public Procurement L Rev NA 34 et seq.

[73] Presidency Conclusions, Thessaloniki European Council, Thessaloniki, 19–20 June 2003, para 65.

[74] For an analysis of the European Defence Agency see Aris Georgopoulos, 'The New European Defence Agency: Major Development or Fig Leaf?' (2005) 14(2) Public Procurement L Rev 103

the Council's Joint Action 2004/551/CFSP[75] on 12 July 2004. The mission of the EDA is to support the Council and the Member States in their effort to improve European defence capabilities in the field of crisis management and in the promotion of the ESDP in general.

The EDA has four main tasks: the development of defence capabilities in the field of crisis management, the promotion of European armaments cooperation, the strengthening of the EDTIB, and the enhancement of European Defence Research and Technology.

5.2.1. *The European Defence Agency*

The task of the promotion of European armament cooperation establishes EDA as one of the key actors in the field.

It is submitted that the EDA was not meant to be just a new addition to the already complex institutional structure of European armaments cooperation. Instead, the intention was to streamline the over-congested institutional environment of European armaments cooperation by assimilating structures of cooperation that were outside the EU. This 'streamlining' function has already started with the assimilation of the WEAG by EDA in May 2005.[76] Thus the creation of the EDA brought into effect for the first time European armaments cooperation under the ambit of the EU. It should be borne in mind, however, that the creation of the EDA does not establish an a priori exclusive forum for European armaments cooperation. In theory, participating Member States[77] may engage in collaborative armaments efforts outside the EDA.

From an organizational point of view the EDA has legal personality and is able to conclude contracts with private or public entities and organizations on behalf of the participating Member States—and, in the case of specific ad hoc projects,[78] on behalf of contributing Member States—and be a party to legal proceedings.[79] Nevertheless, the EDA is not be completely independent but operates under the political supervision of the Council, to which it submits regular reports. The Council also issues regular guidelines to the EDA.

The EDA is composed of the Head of the Agency (the Secretary General of the Council of the EU/High Representative of the CFSP), a Steering Board, a Chief Executive, and its own staff.

---

et seq; M Trybus, 'The New European Defence Agency: A Contribution to a Common European Security and Defence Policy and a Challenge to the Community Acquis?' (2006) 43 CML Rev 667–703.

[75] Council Joint Action 2004/551/CFSP of 12 July 2004 on the establishment of the European Defence Agency [2004] OJ L-245/17.

[76] OCCAR remains operational for the time being outside the EU.

[77] EDA comprises all EU Member States apart from Denmark. The latter did not participate in the elaboration and adoption of the Joint Action, in conformity with its 'opt-out' from decisions which have defence implications.

[78] Namely projects in which only *some* of the EDA's Member States participate.

[79] Art 6 of Joint Action 2004/551/CFSP.

The Steering Board is the decision-making body and comprises one representative of each participating Member State and a representative of the Commission—*without voting rights*. It convenes at least twice a year at the level of Ministers of Defence and meetings are chaired by the Head of the Agency. Decisions at the EDA are taken in principle by qualified majority voting (QMV).[80] Nevertheless, if a representative of a participating Member State declares that it intends to oppose a decision taken by QMV for important and stated reasons of national policy, a vote shall not be taken. The representative can refer the matter through the Head of the Agency to the Council or the Steering Board—acting by qualified majority—may do so. The Council will take a decision by unanimity.[81]

The Chief Executive is appointed by the Steering Board for a period of three years extendable for two more years. The Chief Executive is the Head of the Agency's staff and is responsible for the efficient functioning of the Agency. He is also the Agency's legal representative.

With regard to the specific subject matter covered by the EDA it must be emphasized that the latter extends only to European *collaborative* armaments projects. This essentially means that in principle, and pursuant to the EDA's constitution (namely the Joint Action 2004/551/CFSP), the latter would not have jurisdiction in the area of off-the-shelf[82] armaments procurement. In other words there is a prima facie division of labour between the EDA and the Commission: the former would deal with collaborative projects and the latter with off-the-shelf acquisitions.

Nevertheless, it is argued that this picture of harmonious cohabitation has changed significantly with the adoption by the EDA's participating Member States of the so-called 'Code of Conduct' for armaments acquisitions, discussed below.

5.2.2. The Code of Conduct for armaments acquisitions

The Code of Conduct[83] constitutes an intergovernmental, voluntary, non-binding agreement between the EDA's participating Member States with the aim of creating a transparent and open European defence equipment market, where defence contractors from participating Member States will enjoy a level playing field of competition. The Code of Conduct was agreed in November 2005 by the EDA Steering Board[84] and became operational on 1 July 2006. Twenty-two of the twenty-four EDA Member States take part in the new regime.[85]

---

[80] Art 9(2).   [81] Art 9(3).

[82] Namely, equipment already developed and available for purchase.

[83] For a detailed analysis of the Code of Conduct see Aris Georgopoulos, 'The European Defence Agency's Code of Conduct for Armament Acquisitions: A Case of Paramnesia' (2006) 15(2) Public Procurement L Rev 51 et seq.

[84] 'EU Governments Agree on Voluntary Code for Cross-border Competition in Defence Equipment Market', European Defence Agency, Press Release, 21 November 2005, Brussels available at <http://www.eda.europa.eu/news/2005-11-21-1.htm>.

[85] Hungary and Spain initially decided not to join the new regime.

The latter covers hard defence[86] procurement contracts which fulfil the conditions of Article 296 EC[87] and whose value is over €1 million, apart from those explicitly excluded from the latter. These excluded contracts[88] refer to very sensitive areas such as nuclear or cryptographic equipment. At this point it should be underlined that collaborative programmes are not covered by the Code of Conduct. In other words, collaborative projects carried out within the EDA are exempt from the new regime. The significance of this observation is explained in more detail below. The main characteristics of the Code of Conduct are the following:

First, openness and transparency are to be facilitated by a centralized electronic system of dissemination of information on defence contracting opportunities. This is the Electronic Bulletin Board,[89] where the competent authorities of the Member States should publish their defence procurement notices.

Secondly—even though, as already mentioned, the Code of Conduct is applicable to defence contracts which fulfil the requirements of Article 296 EC— Member States agree to invoke Article 296 EC only for compelling and extraordinary reasons of national security. What is more, the invocation must be accompanied by a proper justification. The Code of Conduct is based on the commitment of Member States to avoid the overuse (or abuse) of Article 296 EC in the procurement of hard defence equipment.

Thirdly, there is a system of institutionalized 'peer pressure'. This is linked with the requirement for Member States to justify invoking Article 296 EC and is intended to function as a 'name and shame' exercise. It is argued that this is the only 'stick-like' mechanism in a regime which does not create legally enforceable obligations.

Finally, the EDA acts as the facilitator and monitor of the new regime and will collect data regarding the frequency of the use of Article 296 EC by the Member States in the framework of armaments acquisitions.

It is submitted that the Code of Conduct bears a resemblance to the Coherent Policy Document (CPD), which was intended to create a European defence equipment market within the WEAG. It suffices to note at this point that there

---

[86] Namely, equipment destined for purely military purposes (as opposed to dual-use goods which can be used for both military and non-military purposes and which as a result do not fall within Art 296 EC).

[87] Art 296(1b) EC stipulates that:

Any Member State may take such measures as *it* considers necessary for the protection of the essential interests of its security which are connected with the production of or trade in arms, munitions and war material; such measures shall not adversely affect the conditions of competition in the common market regarding products which are not intended for specifically military purposes. [Emphasis added]

[88] In particular, the following types of defence contract do not fall within the CoC field of application: research and development contracts; collaborative procurements; contracts for chemical, radiological goods and services; nuclear weapons; nuclear propulsion systems; and cryptographic equipment.   [89] Available at <http://www.eda.europa.eu/ebbweb/>.

are three main reasons why the Code of Conduct might prove more successful than its predecessor.[90]

First, the timing of the new initiative is better than that of the Coherent Policy Document. It seems that Member States started to realize the long-term negative effects of fragmentation and introvert defence industrial policies.

Secondly, the system of peer pressure may prove useful in underlining the commitment that Member States undertook when they decided to participate in the new regime.

Finally, from a practical point of view, the centralized[91] system of publication will obviously facilitate the dissemination of information and create a more user-friendly environment. This Code of Conduct is essentially a forum of self-regulation because its voluntary and non-binding character means that it does not create any enforceable obligations.

6. Analysis of the current initiatives

The recent initiatives brought European armaments cooperation under the ambit of the EU. This is an important development in its own right and not only because of its symbolic value. In fact, it signals a significant departure from the recent past which is based on the realization that the ESDP cannot attain its object-ives unless supported by a healthy European defence industrial base. It seems that this realization is shared by all the relevant actors. Moreover, it is evident that the subordination of European armaments cooperation under the EU does not fit the classic first and second pillar structure but appears to be placed—somewhat uncomfortably—in-between them. This has repercussions on the institutional side of European armaments cooperation because it enables both the Commission and the Council to claim a role in the process.

It is also suggested that the parallel initiatives of the Commission and the Council, despite their proclaimed complementarity,[92] are inherently antagonistic. This becomes evident if one observes the various stages of the two initiatives together. It is submitted that this clearly reveals what could be termed as a 'refined institutional game of chess'.

First, remember that the EDA was established only a year after the deliberations at the European Summit in Thessaloniki in 2003. Furthermore, its establishment was disassociated with the adoption of the European Constitutional Treaty discussed by Trybus in Chapter 3 and in particular Article I-41(3) which foresees

---

[90] For a more detailed comparison see Georgopoulos, n 83, above.

[91] Remember that under WEAG's EDEM publication of procurement notices was decentralized.

[92] The complementarity of the initiatives is suggested by both the Commission and the EDA in their various policy documents; see, for example, COM (2005) 626, *Communication from the Commission to the Council and the European Parliament on the results of the consultation launched by the Green Paper on Defence Procurement and on the future Commission initiatives*, December 2005, 10.

the establishment of the Agency, exactly because it had been anticipated that the ratification of the Constitutional Treaty was going to be a demanding process with uncertain outcomes. The hurriedness on the part of the Council to establish the EDA within the course of 2004 could be explained as an immediate response to the re-introduction by the Commission's Communication *Defence—Industrial and Market Issues—Towards an EU Equipment Policy* of the debate over the liberalization of European defence markets which left open the possibility of the introduction of supranational elements in the area. Thus the Council tried to secure the intergovernmental character of European armaments cooperation *even within the EU*.

Secondly, the establishment of the Code of Conduct by the EDA comes immediately after the publication of the Green Paper by the Commission which proposed the adoption of a European Defence Procurement Directive and the publication of the interpretative Communication on Article 296 EC. Both these instruments are intended to increase the *supranational* elements in European armaments integration with the immediate result of securing a more active role for the Commission. Moreover the subtle antagonism between the supranational and intergovernmental actors (namely the Commission and the EDA respectively) is manifested by the fact that despite an initial mutual recognition of an elementary division of labour between the two[93]—the Commission would oversee integration in the field of off-the-shelf armaments procurement while the EDA would be the supervisory authority in the area of armament collaborative projects—both bodies tried to encroach into each others 'subject matters' (jurisdictions). As mentioned above, the Commission's Green Paper raised the issue whether collaborative armaments projects —an area under the supervision of the EDA—should be covered by a Defence Procurement Directive if and when such an instrument was to be adopted. It is clear that the subordination of collaborative projects under the Directive would necessarily entail the expansion of the Commission's jurisdiction, with a simultaneous reduction of the EDA's authority.[94]

On the other hand the Code of Conduct clearly enters into an area which lies beyond the actual subject matter of the EDA (namely the supervision of the use of Article 296 in off-the-shelf acquisitions by Member States). It is self-evident that the Code coincides with the area that the Commission envisages covering in its own initiatives. The suggestions of the Commission that the Code and its own initiatives refer to different segments of the defence market because the former applies to contracts that fulfil the conditions of Article 286 EC whereas the latter applies to armaments acquisitions that do not fulfil these conditions is simplistic and tautological. As argued elsewhere,[95] the issue of when a hard defence contract

---

[93] See, for example, Joint Action 2004/551/CFSP Art 1(1): 'The Agency's mission shall be *without prejudice to the competences of the European Community...*' or Art 5(1): '...the Agency *shall respect the competences of the European Community...*'.

[94] This means that contract awards made by the EDA would be under the scrutiny of the Commission as well as every other defence contracting authority.

[95] Georgopoulos, n 83, above, at 53 and 58.

meets the conditions of Article 296 EC and who decides if this is the case is the main issues of the debate. Nevertheless, it should be underlined that the antagonism between the Commission and the EDA is subtle. This is understandable because a head-on collision would be counter-productive for both. Instead, there is a link for cooperation between the two. It is precisely in this framework that the participation of the Commission in the EDA's Steering Board without voting rights should be understood.

Moreover, it is suggested that that the Code of Conduct makes the possibility for integration through the 'tranquilizer' of a very restrictive interpretation of Article 296 EC by the European Court of Justice even more unlikely. The reason is that with the establishment of the Code of Conduct Member States show that they understand that Article 296 EC has been abused in the past and that they commit themselves—albeit in a non-legally binding way—to correct the situation based on a self-regulatory framework. The Court is much more likely to adopt a deferential approach, at least for the period immediately after the establishment of the Code of Conduct, leaving the Member States to prove their commitment.

7. Conclusions

Until recently the institutional framework of European armaments cooperation was undeniably overloaded. The institutional congestion did little service to the much needed rationalization of European defence industrial efforts. Various bodies with similar mandates and overlapping memberships highlighted an environment of fragmentation and duplication. Moreover, it became clear that initiatives undertaken outside the framework of the EU in the field of armaments cooperation had not produced the desired results.

The current initiatives in the area of European armaments cooperation/integration constitute undeniably positive developments. It seems only natural for an effort, which presents market and security policy elements, to be carried out under the ambit of the only European institutional structure that covers both these areas. In addition, as pointed out in the Final Report of Working Group VIII on Defence, of the European Convention, the EU is the only framework which can attach the 'European label' to this effort.[96] In any case, the subordination of this area under the EU as a necessary condition for the credibility of the ESDP is important per se. What is more, the current initiatives started to contribute to the rationalization of the institutional environment with the assimilation of WEAG/WEAO by the EDA.

Nevertheless, despite some positive first steps, it is argued that the institutional rationalization of European armaments cooperation/integration is anything but complete.

[96] 'Final report', Working Group VIII 'Defence', the European Convention, CONV 461/02, Brussels, 16 December 2002, para 64.

To begin with, OCCAR still operates outside the EU as managerial agency of collaborative projects of the participating countries. More importantly, it seems that the initiatives undertaken within the EU by the Commission, the Council, and subsequently by the EDA reproduced to a certain extent the institutional duplication within the EU. As a result, both the Commission and the EDA claim a role in the European armaments cooperation integration process.

It is submitted that the relation of the EDA with the Commission as stakeholders of the European armaments cooperation/integration is far from resolved. Overlaps of competences amplified by the lack of a clear legal framework inevitably create institutional tensions: a constant reminder of the struggle between the supranational/economic and intergovernmental/security elements of the defence market. In addition, as already discussed, the adoption of the Code of Conduct increases the overlapping of competences between the two bodies since it covers an area which falls under the supervision of the Commission. However, it is argued that the antagonism between the two main actors, namely the European Defence Agency and the European Commission, may in the long run have certain positive effects. Armaments acquisitions is a very sensitive area directly linked with national security concerns. This means that there are not necessarily any easy solutions. If the antagonism between the Commission and the EDA leads to a proper debate for finding the optimum forum and framework for meeting the needs of the creation of a competitive European defence industrial base then this could only be a positive development.

This observation is linked to the fact that even if the initiatives of the Commission and the EDA are to a certain extent antagonistic they are nevertheless interconnected. For example, the Commission's initiatives have nothing to win and everything to lose from a potential failure of the Code of Conduct. This is because the success or failure of the latter is based on the level of commitment of Member States in creating a healthy, integrated European defence industrial base. If this commitment is compromised in the framework of a voluntary, non-binding regime (the Code of Conduct) then the adoption of a more intensive 'first pillar' instrument (the Defence Procurement Directive) becomes logically unfeasible.

Last but not least it should be remembered that armaments acquisitions primarily serve defence purposes. The dialectic of defence procurement with the political environment is a given and the integration effort, in order to be successful, must be able to address it.

As already mentioned, the central role of the Member States in the field of armaments acquisitions remains almost unchallenged. As a result, the success of the current initiatives, especially the EDA and the Code of Conduct, are directly analogous to the level of commitment that Member States will demonstrate. Anything less than a sustained drive to further the development of a healthy European defence industrial base will lead to the loss of another great opportunity, with immediate negative repercussions on the credibility of the ESDP.

PART III

CONSISTENCY OF THE EUROPEAN SECURITY FRAMEWORK

10

Differentiation in EU Foreign, Security, and Defence Policy: Between Coherence and Flexibility

*Ramses A Wessel**

1. Introduction

With the Treaty of Nice (2001) a security and defence policy (ESDP) has finally become part of the competences of the European Union as a subdivision of the Common Foreign and Security Policy (CFSP) that was introduced by the Maastricht Treaty in 1992.[1] While neo-functionalist integration theories might have expected this to happen much sooner, many Member States were (and still remain) hesitant to hand over any powers in this area. Reasons can be found in the close connection between defence policy and the sovereignty of the state as well as in a fear of undermining NATO. This has resulted in a number of compromises which, in turn, raise the question of whether security and defence policy has really been integrated into the legal structure of the EU. No explicit mention is being made in the Union Treaty; yet practice reveals the creation of a number of new organs dealing with the formulation and implementation of military operations (such as the Military Committee and the Political and Security Committee). This half-hearted integration of a new policy area raises a number of legal questions that so far have been left almost untouched in the literature. Since 'security and defence policy' is separated from 'foreign and security policy', one of the key questions concerns the dividing line between the two areas. EU security law is based on

* Professor of the Law of the European Union and other International Organizations, Centre for European Studies and Law Department, University of Twente, the Netherlands. The author wishes to thank the participants in the *Colloquium on European Security Law*, University of Nottingham, 14–15 April 2005 and in particular Martin Trybus and Frederik Naert for their valuable comments. All website addresses cited were active on 17 October 2006, unless otherwise specified.
[1] See in general on the ESDP: R A Wessel, 'The State of Affairs in European Security and Defence Policy: The Breakthrough in the Treaty of Nice' J of Conflict & Security L (2003) 8(2) 265–88 and, more extensively, M Trybus, *European Union Law and Defence Integration* (Oxford: Hart, 2005) ch 3.

both, but at the same time different rules apply for the CFSP and the ESDP. Is it possible for Member States not to participate in the security and defence integration or does the single legal order of the Union prevent this variation? A second question concerns the more general possibilities for closer (or 'enhanced') cooperation. While the Treaty on the one hand allows for groups of Member States to work closer together in the area of the CFSP, the possibilities for an enhanced cooperation in the ESDP are less evident. And, finally, the question is to what extent the proposed new EU Constitutional Treaty further consolidates the somewhat fragmented legal regime on differentiation in the area of foreign, security, and defence policy.

2. Flexibility in the European Union

In order to be able to say something on the special arrangements in the area of foreign, security, and defence policy, a first step is to take a look at the general flexibility regime in the EU. As far as European Community law is concerned, it traditionally builds on the principle of uniformity. This principle implies that all Member States reach a certain objective at the same time and that measures discriminating between Member States are not adopted. Community law is the same for all Member States under all circumstances.[2] However, from the outset exceptions to this rule were accepted, and related to: the participating states, the moment of entry into force of a measure, and/or the attainment of the objective of a measure. Thus, the original EEC Treaty acknowledged closer cooperation between the Benelux countries; transition arrangements were accepted for new Member States and certain Member States were allowed to refrain from participation in the European Monetary System or other areas of cooperation.[3] Secondary legislation also revealed temporary differences between Member States as it sometimes allowed for alternative, optional, or minimum national measures.[4] In addition Article 220 (now 293) of the EC Treaty allowed for separate treaties to be concluded between Member States on subjects connected with the development of the Community.

The past two decades have presented further examples of an erosion of the principle of uniformity. In 1985 the dissolution of border controls became the subject of an extra-Community arrangement between a restricted number of Member States: the Schengen agreement. In 1986 the Single European Act extended and strengthened the harmonization competences of the EEC, while at the same time

---

[2] Cf European Court of Justice, Case C-166/73, *Rheinmühlen* [1974] ECR 19. The principle of uniformity runs through the entire case law of the Court. See R Barents, *Het Verdrag van Amsterdam in werking* (Deventer: Kluwer, 1999) 85.

[3] Examples of the latter include the Protocols to the original EEC Treaty on Luxembourg and German Internal Trade.

[4] See for instance the Groundwater Directive 80/68 ([1980] OJ L-20/43) and the Capital Movements Directive 88/361 ([1988] OJ L-178/5).

allowing Member States to continue to apply national measures on certain grounds and under specified procedures.[5] The 1992 Treaty on European Union (TEU) allows for different speeds to reach the objectives of an Economic and Monetary Union (EMU) as well as for Member States not to participate at all in the EMU. Comparable exceptions were allowed in the fields of, for instance, social policy (UK) and the development of a defence policy (Denmark).

The idea of a possibly fragmented Union played an important role in particular during the negotiations on the Amsterdam Treaty in 1996/97. The different variations of flexibility were frequently presented as harmful to the Union's unity. Thus concepts like *variable geometry, concentric circles*, a *multiple-speed Europe*, or a *Europe à la carte* all seemed to prelude the end of the Union. While these concepts did not make it to the final draft of the Treaty, the development towards a more flexible approach towards cooperation within the EU is reflected in the modifications to the TEU introduced by the 1997 Amsterdam Treaty.

The current TEU, as well as the modified EC Treaty, provides for a number of general and specific arrangements allowing for forms of flexible cooperation between a limited number of Member States. The concept of 'flexible cooperation' or 'differentiation' in the context of the present contribution concerns the situation in which the 27 Member States do not necessarily participate to the same extent in every policy or activity of the Union.[6] The TEU nowhere explicitly refers to the notion of flexibility.[7] However, one can distinguish between at least two broad categories of flexibility within the Unions' legal system. The first category contains the general *enabling clauses* on the basis of which the Council has a competence—through the adoption of secondary legislation—to decide on the establishment of 'enhanced cooperation'. The second category harbours a variety of forms of flexible cooperation linked to specific fields of EU/EC competence, including the so-called *pre-determined* forms of flexibility, ie, forms of differential treatment of certain Member States as laid down in the treaties themselves or in protocols, as well as ad hoc or 'spontaneous' differentiation following an opt-out of Member States with respect to certain decisions.[8]

---

[5] See the old Art 100A(4) EC. The Treaty of Amsterdam extended and to some extent clarified its elements. See the new Art 95 EC.

[6] Cf J A Usher, 'Flexibility: The Amsterdam Provisions', in: T Heukels, N M Blokker, M M T A Brus (eds), *The European Union after Amsterdam, A Legal Analysis* (The Hague: Martinus Nijhoff, 1999) 253.

[7] See G Edwards G and E Philippart, 'Flexibility and the Treaty of Amsterdam: Europe's New Byzantium?', *Centre for European Legal Studies Occasional Paper No 3* (Cambridge: 1997) 12: 'During the legal and linguistic revision of the text agreed in June (1997), the word "flexibility" disappeared. The need for it was no longer important in the domestic politics of the UK'. See also J Shaw, 'The Treaty of Amsterdam: Challenges of Flexibility and Legitimacy' (1998) 63 Eur L J 69.

[8] See more extensively on the theoretical implications of flexibility for the unity of the Union's legal order I F Dekker and R A Wessel, 'The European Union and the Concept of Flexibility. Proliferation of Legal Systems within International Organizations' in N M Blokker and H G Schermers (eds), *Proliferation of International Organizations* (The Hague: Kluwer Law International, 2001) 381–414.

2.1. General EU/EC enhanced cooperation

The first category of flexibility provisions is contained in Title VII EU and introduces a general competence for Member States to use the mechanism to establish 'enhanced cooperation' in, as yet, unidentified areas. Article 43 EU states:

Member States which intend to establish enhanced cooperation between themselves may make use of the institutions, procedures and mechanisms laid down by this Treaty and by the Treaty establishing the European Community [...].

This competence is subject to a number of general and specific conditions—as listed in Article 43 TEU and Articles 27A TEU (on CFSP), 40B TEU (on Police and Judicial Cooperation in Criminal Matters: PJCC) and 11A EC (Community cooperation), Article 11 EC and Article 40 TEU—which to a large extent determine the feasibility of the mechanism of closer cooperation. At first sight these conditions may seem to be obvious, but in fact they raise a number of still unsettled questions of interpretation.[9]

Before the 2004 enlargement of the Union, enhanced cooperation could only be established among a majority of the Member States as Article 43 TEU refers to a minimum of eight participants. However, this provision has not been changed with the increase in the number of Member States, which means that these days less than one third of the Member States would form a sufficient basis for a form of enhanced cooperation.

In making use of the institutions, the states participating in enhanced cooperation are furthermore bound by Article 44 TEU, which provides that the relevant institutional provisions apply. An exception is made with regard to the adoption of decisions by the Council. While all states may take part in the deliberations, only the states participating in enhanced cooperation take part in the adoption of decisions, which implies a de facto derogation from the unanimity rule on issues where it would normally be applied (since it is not required to have *twenty-seven* votes in favour, despite the fact that the legal basis remains the same). In case of qualified majority voting, the rules are adapted according to the number of participating Member States. Except for the administrative costs of the institutions, expenditure is to be borne by the participating Member States, unless the Council unanimously decides otherwise.

2.2. Pre-determined forms of flexibility

The second category of flexibility within the EU/EC legal systems first of all contains the aforementioned *pre-determined* forms of flexible cooperation. While one

---

[9] See also Shaw, n 7, above, 70–6; JA Usher, 'Flexibility: The Amsterdam Provisions' in Heukels, Blokker, Brus (eds), n 6, above, 263–4; and C D Ehlermann, 'Differentiation, Flexibility, Closer Cooperation: The New Provisions of the Amsterdam Treaty', (1998) 246–70 4 Eur L J 253–9.

could say that these forms of differentiation are instances of the concept of enhanced cooperation,[10] it must be taken into account that they are not established through secondary law but find their basis in primary law, and that some of the specific rules differ from the rules attached to the mechanism of enhanced cooperation.

Pre-determined flexibility may either take the form of a permission granted by all Member States to a group of Member States to act together through Union institutions and legislation (eg, the Social Protocol under the Maastricht regime), or it is reflected in the permission given to Member States *not* to participate in an activity in which they should in principle participate as a matter of Union or Community law (eg, the 1991 Protocols on the basis of which Denmark and the UK are not obliged to take part in the third phase of the EMU; and the 1991 Protocol concerning Denmark's non-participation in the elaboration or implementation of measures having defence implications).[11] This last sub-category has gained some popularity under the Treaty of Amsterdam, especially in the context of the new Title in the EC Treaty on the free movement of persons and the integration of the Schengen *acquis* into the legal framework of the Union. Special arrangements were included in Protocols with regard to the UK, Ireland, and Denmark.[12]

Apart from these pre-determined forms of flexibility, the Treaties harbour a variety of general provisions which in one way or another result in a permeation of the principle of uniformity in a specific area of the Union's legal system. These forms of flexibility flow either from possibilities for constructive abstention in voting procedures and partial application of treaties (Article 24 and 34 TEU) or from variations in the system of preliminary rulings (Articles 35 TEU and 68 EC).[13]

3. Enhanced Cooperation in EU Security Law

3.1. The current legal regime and the EU Constitutional Treaty

From the outset, the CFSP was excluded from the formal possibilities for flexible cooperation. While the 'Reflection Group', set up in June 1995 to prepare the Amsterdam Intergovernmental Conference (IGC), left open the possibility of a

---

[10] See, in this context, Art 11(5) EC.

[11] Cf J A Usher, 'Flexibility: The Amsterdam Provisions' in Heukels, Blokker, Brus (eds), n 6, above, 254–6.

[12] Ibid, at 267–71. The position of Norway and Iceland with regard to their participation in the Schengen *acquis* is not mentioned here, because this concerns a form of flexible cooperation outside the Union's legal system. On 17 May 1999 the Council concluded international agreements with these two countries on their involvement in the Schengen *acquis*. See [1999] OJ L-176/35.

[13] Before 'Amsterdam' the EC Treaty already contained such forms of flexibility, for instance those included in Art 95 with regard to the harmonization of national legislation, and in Arts 168 and 169 concerning the area of research and technological development on the basis of which multi-annual framework programmes may be implemented through supplementary programmes involving the participation of certain Member States only.

greater degree of differentiation in CFSP, the Treaty legislator in the end backed down from this idea. The French and the Germans pushed towards improved possibilities for enhanced cooperation, but other states, including Italy, strongly valued a veto-possibility in anything close to defence cooperation. The final draft of the Dutch Presidency still envisaged unanimity for the establishment of CFSP enhanced cooperation, but the IGC in the end decided to limit flexibility in the second pillar to 'constructive abstention' (see below). Missiroli gives the following reason:

[I]t can be argued that, in the end, no European government was really in favour of a specific flexibility clause for the CFSP proper: the smaller countries, in general, for the fear of being outvoted, Italy and Spain for fear of being excluded, Britain for reasons of principle and tradition. Yet even Germany and France did not insist on that point: presumably, the former did not see its urgency after all (and did see, indeed, other ways to bring about enhanced cooperation), while the latter was worried that it might end up infringing a country's right to say 'no' on matters of life and death.[14]

At the time of the negotiations on the Nice Treaty it had become clear that the foreseen enlargement with ten new Member States reinforced the need to re-think the possibilities for differentiation in CFSP as well. This opened up the way to a Union-wide application of Article 43 TEU. Indeed, the current version is no longer restricted to the first and third pillars, and Title VII (on Enhanced Cooperation) explicitly refers to Article 27 in which the specific legal regime on flexibility in CFSP is laid down.[15] Apart from the general conditions under which enhanced cooperation may be established (see above), Articles 27A-E lay down the specific rules on CFSP flexibility. Article 27A provides that:

Enhanced cooperation in any of the areas referred to in this title shall be aimed at safeguarding the values and serving the interests of the Union as a whole by asserting its identity as a coherent force on the international scene. It shall respect:
– the principles, objectives, general guidelines and consistency of the common foreign and security policy and the decisions taken within the framework of that policy,
– the powers of the European Community, and
– consistency between all the Union's policies and its external activities.

Despite these ambitious objectives, the possibilities for developing a flexible CFSP are limited as Article 27B explicitly refers to the implementation of a Joint Action or a Common Position. This means that the contribution of the Nice Treaty in this respect may be less far-reaching than is sometimes proclaimed.[16] In any case,

---

[14] See A Missiroli, *CFSP, Defence and Flexibility*, Chaillot Paper 38 (Paris: Institute for Security Studies, February 2000) 9–10.

[15] See, in general, on flexibility in the CFSP: T Jaeger, 'Enhanced Cooperation in the Treaty of Nice and Flexibility in the Common Foreign and Security Policy', (2002) *Eur Foreign Affairs Rev* 297–316 and M Trybus, 'The Flexibility Phalanx: Differentiation in the Common Security and Defence Policy of the Constitutional Treaty and Beyond', work in progress, 2005 version.

[16] In 2000 in a speech in Warsaw Prime Minister Blair, for instance, claimed that 'there is clearly much greater scope for using enhanced cooperation in the two biggest growth areas of European

it is clear that only the *implementation* of Joint Actions and Common Positions is covered by Article 27B. Hence, the *adoption* of these instruments cannot be subject to enhanced cooperation. The same holds true for the adoption as well as the implementation of any other type of instrument. While one could argue that at least the adoption of Common Strategies (as general policy plans for a specific country or region) should not be subject to differentiation, it is not entirely clear why the implementation of this instrument (through Joint Actions and Common Positions) could not have been part of the regime. After all, Common Strategies have been adopted by the European Council by unanimity, and one can imagine specific parts being implemented by smaller groups of Member States. Along the same lines, one may wonder why enhanced cooperation does not cover the implementation of other 'Decisions' taken by the Council. Indeed, not all CFSP decisions take the form of a Joint Action or a Common Position (as implicitly acknowledged by Article 13, para 3 TEU).[17]

Moreover, for the purposes of this book it is important to note that the introduction of enhanced cooperation in CFSP is not extended to defence policy. According to Article 27B 'it shall not relate to matters having military or defence implications'. This phrase is not unfamiliar in other dimensions of CFSP: it returns in the regime on qualified majority voting (see below, section 4) as well as in the budgetary provisions in Article 28, para 3 (expenditure arising from operations having military or defence implications shall not be charged to the budget of the EC). It is also used on a structural basis in CFSP decisions to remind us of the special position of Denmark in relation to European defence policy (see below). However, the problem remains how to distinguish defence policy from security policy. Within the framework of the TEU, the most obvious interpretation would be that defence policy can only be based on Article 17. This interpretation finds some support in the 1997 Protocol on the position of Denmark (infra), which refers to Article 17 in relation to decisions and actions having defence implications. A similar reference may be found in the new Protocol annexed to the proposed EU Constitutional Treaty, although the scope is widened to Articles III-309–13 (the general Title on security and defence policy) and Article III-295(1), thereby including general guidelines of the European Council. This does not mean that, in turn, all measures related to Article 17 would entail defence implications. The criterion seems to be the 'military' dimension of actions. The reference to 'military and defence policy' in Article 27B TEU as well as the reference to 'civilian and military means' in Article III-309 of the Constitutional Treaty reveal that the Treaty legislator was not unaware of a distinction in this field. For instance, EU police missions would therefore fall under 'security' rather than under 'defence policy'.[18]

---

action: the development of a foreign and security policy and the cross-border fight against crime'. See D Thym, *Ungleichzeitigkeit und europäisches Verfassungsrecht* (Baden-Baden: Nomos, 2004) 163.

[17] Ibid, ch V.   [18] Ibid, 168. In practice ESDP decisions are based on Art 14.

The Constitutional Treaty somewhat modifies the provisions on enhanced cooperation, but more importantly for our topic it extends enhanced cooperation to the CFSP without restricting it to its implementation. Moreover, no general exception was made in relation to the Common Security and Defence Policy, the new name for ESDP. The current legal regime completely excludes any form of enhanced cooperation in security and defence matters and merely allows for 'closer cooperation', that is, cooperation between EU Member States (and possible others) outside the TEU.

In the Constitutional Treaty the general provisions are to be found in Articles I-44 and III-416–23.[19] Article I-44 reveals, inter alia, that enhanced cooperation is to be open to all Member States. This excludes the possibility of excluding certain Member States from CFSP actions. Indeed, the starting point remains the framing of Union-wide policies and enhanced cooperation can only be authorized by the Council as a measure of 'last resort when it has established that the objectives of such cooperation cannot be attained within a reasonable period by the Union as a whole, and provided that at least one third of the Member States participate in it' (para 2). In Article III-419 a difference is made between CFSP and other policy areas in the Constitutional Treaty. Where, on the basis of paragraph 1, the general procedure for the establishment of enhanced cooperation starts with a request to the Commission (followed by a QMV decision of the Council after having consulted the European Parliament), paragraph 2 reflects a more substantive role for the Council in CFSP enhanced cooperation and provides:

The request of the Member States which wish to establish enhanced cooperation between themselves within the framework of the common foreign and security policy shall be addressed to the Council. It shall be forwarded to the Union Minister for Foreign Affairs, who shall give an opinion on whether the enhanced cooperation proposed is consistent with the Union's common foreign and security policy, and to the Commission, which shall give its opinion in particular on whether the enhanced cooperation proposed is consistent with other Union policies. It shall also be forwarded to the European Parliament for information. Authorisation to proceed with enhanced cooperation shall be granted by a European decision of the Council acting unanimously.

Another difference may be found in relation to participation in an enhanced cooperation that is already in progress. On the basis of Article III-420, para 2, in CFSP cooperation not only the Council and the Commission shall be notified, but also the Union Minister for Foreign Affairs. The final (unanimous) decision is taken by the Council, after consulting the Union Minister for Foreign Affairs. The latter may also suggest to the Council that transitional measures may be necessary.

---

[19] See, in general, J Howorth, 'The European Draft Constitutional Treaty and the Future of the European Defence Initiative: A Question of Flexibility', *Eur Foreign Affairs Rev* (2004) 483–508. See, in general, on security and defence in the Constitution: F Naert, 'European Security and Defence Policy in the EU Constitutional Treaty' J of Conflict & Security L (2005) No 2, 187–207. See also M Trybus, Chapter 3 of this volume.

Whenever a form of enhanced cooperation has been established, all Council members may participate in the deliberations, but only the members participating in the enhanced cooperation have a right to vote (Article I-44, para 3). Regarding the voting procedure, Article I-44, para 3 introduces a complex arrangement:

Unanimity shall be constituted by the votes of the representatives of the participating Member States only. A qualified majority shall be defined as at least 55% of the members of the Council representing the participating Member States, comprising at least 65% of the population of these States. A blocking minority must include at least the minimum number of Council members representing more than 35% of the population of the participating Member States, plus one member, failing which the qualified majority shall be deemed attained.

By way of derogation from the third and fourth subparagraphs, where the Council does not act on a proposal from the Commission or from the Union Minister for Foreign Affairs, the required qualified majority shall be defined as at least 72% of the members of the Council representing the participating Member States, comprising at least 65% of the population of these States.

Finally, paragraph 4 confirms that the acts adopted in the framework of enhanced cooperation shall bind only participating Member States and that they shall not be regarded as part of the *acquis* which has to be accepted by candidate states for accession to the Union.

The possibility of using qualified majority voting in enhanced cooperation is extended by Article III-422, allowing the Council to move to QMV (or to use the ordinary legislative procedure) on the basis of a unanimous decision:

1. Where a provision of the Constitution which may be applied in the context of enhanced cooperation stipulates that the Council shall act unanimously, the Council, acting unanimously in accordance with the arrangements laid down in Article I-44(3), may adopt a European decision stipulating that it will act by a qualified majority.
2. Where a provision of the Constitution which may be applied in the context of enhanced cooperation stipulates that the Council shall adopt European laws or framework laws under a special legislative procedure, the Council, acting unanimously in accordance with the arrangements laid down in Article I-44(3), may adopt a European decision stipulating that it will act under the ordinary legislative procedure. The Council shall act after consulting the European Parliament.

To the surprise of many, in the final hour the European Convention adopted the idea of extending the possibility of QMV to defence issues.[20] It seems, however, that the Convention's Presidium pushed its luck; the subsequent IGC decided to included a new paragraph in Article III-422:

3. Paragraphs 1 and 2 shall not apply to decisions having military or defence implications.

This makes the requirement of unanimity (of participating Member States) in common security and defence matters absolute.[21]

---

[20] See Convention Doc 853/03, 2 and the report of the Plenary of 9–10 July 2003.
[21] See also Trybus, n 15, above.

3.2. Ad hoc and permanent structured cooperation

Irrespective of the fact that because of the requirement of unanimity, enhanced cooperation in CSDP may be hard to establish, Article I-41 of the new EU Constitutional Treaty offers interesting alternatives. First of all, paragraph 3 acknowledges the possibility of groups of Member States making their multinational forces available for the purposes of the CSDP. Article III-310 (1) builds on this idea:

Within the framework of the European decisions adopted in accordance with Article III-309 [on the so-called Petersberg tasks], the Council may entrust the implementation of a task to a group of Member States which are willing and have the necessary capability for such a task. Those Member States, in association with the Union Minister for Foreign Affairs, shall agree among themselves on the management of the task.

This is an almost purely intergovernmental way of allowing individual Member States to decide if and how they wish to participate and how they wish to manage the operation. Despite the ad hoc nature of this form of flexibility, one could argue that a de facto enhanced cooperation in the field of defence cooperation is thus foreseen by the Constitution. At the same time, one has to acknowledge that, even in the current pre-Constitutional era, ESDP missions operate in a flexible manner as far as the composition of the troops is concerned: not all Member States participate in all missions, and some missions are even built on the commitment of one state (eg, the role of France in the Congo mission).[22]

In addition to this ad hoc flexibility, paragraph 6 of Article I-41 introduces the notion of 'permanent structured cooperation' for 'those Member States whose military capabilities fulfil higher criteria and which have made more binding commitments to one another in this area with a view to the most demanding missions'. The permanent structured cooperation is further elaborated by Article III-312 and by a special Protocol (No 23).

According to this Protocol the permanent structured cooperation can be seen as an institutionalized form of cooperation in the field of defence policy between able and willing Member States. In that sense it may be regarded as a special form of enhanced cooperation, although the term is not used. It shall be open to any Member State which undertakes to (Article 1):

(a) proceed more intensively to develop its defence capacities through the development of its national contributions and participation, where appropriate, in multinational forces, in the main European equipment programmes, and in the activity of the Agency in the field of defence capabilities development, research, acquisition and armaments (European Defence Agency), and

(b) have the capacity to supply by 2007 at the latest, either at national level or as a component of multinational force groups, targeted combat units for the missions planned, structured at a tactical level as a battle group, with support elements including

---

[22] See also Naert, n 19, above, 202; and Jaeger, n 15, above, 307.

transport and logistics, capable of carrying out the tasks referred to in Article III-309, within a period of 5 to 30 days, in particular in response to requests from the United Nations Organisation, and which can be sustained for an initial period of 30 days and be extended up to at least 120 days.

Obviously, no reference is made to the creation of a 'European army'. Any explicit hints in that direction would have been unacceptable for certain Member States. Nevertheless, the tasks of the participating Member States come close to at least a harmonization of the different national defence policies. According to Article 2 of the Protocol, Member States undertake to:

(a) cooperate with a view to achieving approved objectives concerning the level of investment expenditure on defence equipment;
(b) bring their defence apparatus into line with each other as far as possible;
(c) take concrete measures to enhance the availability, interoperability, flexibility and deployability of their forces, including possibly reviewing their national decision-making procedures;
(d) work together to ensure that they take the necessary measures to make good, including through multinational approaches; and
(e) take part, where appropriate, in the development of major joint or European equipment programmes in the framework of the European Defence Agency.

Moreover, the creation of the so-called European Rapid Reaction Force (ERRF), envisaged by the 1999 Helsinki Headline Goal (60,000 troops),[23] in practice seems to come close to what could be called an 'army', irrespective of the fact that—for political reasons—the Helsinki Document stressed that the ERRF would not amount to 'the creation of a European army'. Interestingly enough, this phrase does not return in the Constitutional Treaty.

Participation will be open to all Member States 'which fulfil the criteria and have made the commitments on military capabilities set out in the Protocol on Permanent Structured Cooperation'. A notification of their intention is to be sent to the Council and to the Union Minister for Foreign Affairs (Article III-312). It is interesting to note that in the decision establishing the cooperation, as well as on the accession of new participants, the Council shall act by a qualified majority vote (in the latter case of participating Member States). This means that the establishment (as well as the further development) of the permanent structured cooperation cannot be blocked by other Member States. In the case of the accession of new participants only members of the Council representing the participating Member States shall take part in the vote. A qualified majority shall be defined as at least 55 per cent of the members of the Council representing the participating Member States, comprising at least 65 per cent of the population of these states. A blocking minority must include at least the minimum number of Council members representing

[23] European Council, Presidency Conclusions, 10–11 December 1999; available at <http://www.consilium.europa.eu/ueDocs/cms_Data/docs/pressData/en/ec/ACFA4C.htm>.

more than 35 per cent of the population of the participating Member States, plus one member, failing which the qualified majority shall be deemed attained.

Participation is not without engagement. If a participating Member State no longer fulfils the criteria or is no longer able to meet the commitments, the Council may adopt (by QMV) a European Decision suspending the participation of the Member State concerned. A special role in this regard is laid down for the European Defence Agency, in assessing the contribution of the participating Member States with regard to capabilities. But voluntary withdrawal is also possible (Article III-312, para 5).

With the introduction of the permanent structured cooperation alongside the general possibility of enhanced cooperation, the new treaty adds to the already existing complexity. As we have seen, any form of enhanced cooperation would be open to all Member States and non-participating states will remain involved in the subsequent decision-making. In contrast, the access of new Member States to an already established form of permanent structured cooperation is in the hands of the participating states only (Article III-312, para 3). There is no automatic right to join in and newcomers will have to 'fulfil higher military capability criteria' (para 1).[24]

3.3. European Defence Agency

Although the European Defence Agency (EDA) is only to be established on the basis of the European Constitution (Article I-41, para 3 and Article III-311), it is already operational on the basis of a Council Joint Action of 12 July 2004.[25] The Agency acts under the Council's authority, in support of the CFSP and the ESDP, but enjoys a separate legal personality (Article 6 of the Joint Action). It has functions in the fields of: defence capabilities development; armaments cooperation; the European defence technological and industrial base and defence equipment market; and research and technology. The mission of the Agency is to support the Council and the Member States in their effort to improve the EU's defence capabilities in the field of crisis management and to sustain the ESDP as it stands now and develops in the future.

The Agency is open to participation by all EU Member States; Member States who wish to participate immediately in the Agency had to notify their intention to do so to the Council and inform the SG/HR at the time of the adoption of the Joint Action. As all Member States, except for Denmark,[26] have done so no major differentiation is to be foreseen in this area. And even at this stage Denmark (or any future EU Member State) may participate in the Agency by notifying its intention to the Council and informing the SG/HR. Nevertheless, the EDA Joint Action differentiates between participants and non-participants and even allows

---

[24] Ibid, 17.

[25] Joint Action 2004/551/CFSP of the Council of [2004] OJ L-245. See also A Georgopoulos, 'The New European Defence Agency: Major Development or a Fig Leaf?' (2005) Public Procurement L Rev 103.

[26] See section 21 of the Preamble of Joint Action 2005/551/CFSP. The participation of Bulgaria and Romania is not yet clear.

for withdrawal. At least in theory, this could amount to further differentiation in the longer run.

However, more differentiation is to be expected with regard to particular projects of the Agency as a difference is made between participating Member States (Member States who participate in the Agency) and contributing Member States (Member States contributing to a particular project or programme). Projects may also be joined by non-Member States (Article 23). Decision-making is in the hands of a 'Steering Board' composed of one representative of each participating Member State, and a representative of the Commission. The Steering Board acts within the framework of the guidelines issued by the Council and meets at the level of the Ministers of Defence of the participating Member States or their representatives. It may, however, also meet in other compositions (such as National Defence Research Directors, National Armaments Directors, and National Defence Planners or Policy Directors). Contributing states may include third parties.

The Agency returns in the EU Constitutional Treaty in Article III-311, which in fact reflects the institutional arrangements of the 2004 Joint Action. Despite its potential to add to further differentiation within the Union, the EDA also aims at consolidating existing arrangements in the area of armaments cooperation. Both the British-French-German-Italian cooperation in OCCAR (later joined by Belgium and Spain as well) and the broader WEAO are eventually meant to be integrated into the EDA.[27]

3.4. Denmark

From the outset, the position of Denmark towards the ESDP has been special. After the 'no' of the first Danish referendum regarding the approval of the Maastricht Treaty and the compromise reached at the Edinburgh Summit directly after, it was clear at the Amsterdam IGC that this position needed to be institutionalized. The Edinburgh compromise that Denmark had no obligation to join the Western European Union (WEU) and would not participate in the adoption and implementation of measures, and actions which have defence implications, was codified in the Protocol on the Position of Denmark to the Amsterdam Treaty in 1997 and maintained in Nice four years later.

In the Constitutional Treaty the position of Denmark in this regard returns in Protocol 20, Article 5:

With regard to measures adopted by the Council pursuant to Article I-41, Article III-295(1) and Articles III-309 to III-313 of the Constitution, Denmark does not

---

[27] OCCAR is based on the Convention on the Establishment of the Organisation for Joint Armaments Co-operation and is based in Bonn. The Western European Armaments Organization (WEAO) was established in the framework of the Western European Union (WEU) and has as its members Austria, Belgium, Czech Republic, Denmark, Finland, France, Germany, Greece, Hungary, Italy, Luxembourg, the Netherlands, Norway, Poland, Portugal, Spain, Sweden, Turkey, and the UK. See Burkard Schmitt, *European Armaments Cooperation: Core Documents*, Chaillot Paper No 59 (Paris: Institute for Security Studies, 2003). See also A Georgopoulos, Chapter 9 of this volume.

participate in the elaboration and the implementation of decisions and actions of the Union which have defence implications. Therefore Denmark shall not participate in their adoption. Denmark will not prevent the other Member States from further developing their cooperation in this area. Denmark shall not be obliged to contribute to the financing of operational expenditure arising from such measures, nor to make military capabilities available to the Union.

The unanimity of the members of the Council, with the exception of the representative of the government of Denmark, shall be necessary for the acts of the Council which must be adopted unanimously.

The rules on qualified majority voting are the same as for the establishment of the permanent structured cooperation (supra). All provisions referred to in Article 5 of the Protocol are related to the CSDP. It is striking that no reference is made to Article III-295, para 2. Paragraph 1 establishes the competence of the European Council to define the general guidelines for the CFSP, including for matters with defence implications. Irrespective of the absence of a reference to defence implications in paragraph 2, this provision deals with the implementation of the guidelines, by the Council, in the form of European Decisions. This opens the way for Denmark to participate in the adoption of European Decisions once these do not entail defence implications, but are nevertheless part of ESDP. In practice Denmark indeed already participates in, for instance, the EU Police Mission in Bosnia and Herzegovina, but not in the military Operation ALTHEA in the same country or in any other military operation.[28]

3.5. Common defence

The Nice Intergovernmental Conference did reach an agreement on 'the progressive framing of a common defence policy', but Article 17 continues to refer to a 'common defence' as a future possibility. At the same time all references to the WEU as the 'defence arm' of the EU were deleted. Is this the end of the WEU and hence of a European collective defence arrangement? No: since no consensus could be reached on the transfer of the original core function of the WEU to the EU, the collective assistance agreement laid down in Article V of the Modified Brussels Treaty is untouched. This provision reads:

If one of the High Contracting Parties should be the object of an armed attack in Europe, the other High Contracting Parties will, in accordance with the provisions of Article 51 of the Charter of the United Nations, afford the Party so attacked all the military and other aid and assistance in their power.

The WEU decided to have its residual functions and structures in place by 1 July 2001 so as to enable the Member States to fulfil the commitments arising from Articles V and IX (on the WEU Assembly). This means that by now the WEU is

---

[28] See more extensively on the composition of the missions F Naert, Chapter 4 of this volume.

essentially returned to the organization that was originally set up to deal with collective defence matters between the Benelux countries and the UK and France in 1948: the Brussels Treaty Organization. Although the 1948 Brussels Treaty was also intended to intensify the economic, social, and cultural collaboration between the Member States,[29] the collective self-defence paragraph (at that time Article IV) soon proved to be the key provision.

As only ten EU members are (full) members of the WEU, this results in a form of differentiation with regard to common defence.[30] In the current EU Treaty a future transfer of the collective—or 'common' in perhaps somewhat more supra-national EU terms—defence provision from the WEU to the EU is made dependent on a decision by the European Council only (which may nevertheless need to be adopted by the individual Member States in accordance with their respective constitutional requirements—Article 17). An inclusion of the defence clause in the Union treaty would not only be in line with the established defence policy, but also with the goals the EU has set for itself: 'to organise, in a manner demonstrating consistency and *solidarity*, relations between the Member States and between their peoples' (Article 1); 'to safeguard the common values, fundamental interests, independence and integrity of the Union . . .'; and 'to strengthen the security of the Union in all ways' (Article 11).

This seems to be acknowledged by the Treaty legislator, as the proposed EU Constitutional Treaty finally seems to include a common defence clause, albeit somewhat hidden in Article I-41, para 7:

If a Member State is the victim of armed aggression on its territory, the other Member States shall have towards it an obligation of aid and assistance by all the means in their power, in accordance with Article 51 of the United Nations Charter. This shall not prejudice the specific character of the security and defence policy of certain Member States.

This comes close to the current obligation in Article V of the WEU Treaty. Therefore it is striking that the same provision, in paragraph 2, still refers to 'common defence' as an aim to be achieved:[31]

The common security and defence policy shall include the progressive framing of a common Union defence policy. This will lead to a common defence, when the European Council, acting unanimously, so decides. It shall in that case recommend to the Member States the adoption of such a decision in accordance with their respective constitutional requirements.

Taking into account that according to the Helsinki (1999) and Laeken (2001) Declarations 'the development of military capabilities does not imply the creation

---

[29] The official name of the WEU Treaty is still the 'Treaty of Economic, Social and Cultural Collaboration and Collective Defence'.

[30] Full members of WEU are: Belgium, France, Germany, Greece, Italy, Luxembourg, the Netherlands, Portugal, Spain, and the UK.

[31] Nevertheless, Art I-16(1) still uses the term 'might lead', thereby suggesting a possibility rather than an objective. See also Naert, n 19, above, 192.

of a European army', it is puzzling what it is the European Council will have to decide on. Nevertheless, it is a fact that the original draft presented by the Convention included the possibility of closer cooperation as regards mutual defence. Draft Article I-40(7) stated that '[u]nder this cooperation, if one of the Member States participating in such cooperation is the victim of armed aggression on its territory, the other participating States shall give it aid and assistance by all means in their power, military or other, in accordance with Article 51 of the United Nations Charter.' Despite the fact that this would allow the 'neutral' states (Austria, Finland, Ireland, and Sweden) not to participate, they opposed this clause because, as they said, 'Formal binding security guarantees would be inconsistent with our security policy or constitutional requirements'.[32] If one compares the draft provision with the final text in the Constitutional Treaty, one may wonder whether there is much difference in practice. Even now there seems to be quite a strict mutual defence obligation and in both cases account has been taken of the special position of the neutral states.[33]

This is even more the case when the so-called 'Solidarity clause' in Article I-43, is taken into account. This clause does not restrict common defence to 'armed aggression', but in fact extends the obligation to terrorist attacks:

The Union and its Member States shall act jointly in a spirit of solidarity if a Member State is the object of a terrorist attack or the victim of a natural or man-made disaster. The Union shall mobilise all the instruments at its disposal, including the military resources made available by the Member States, to:

(a) – prevent the terrorist threat in the territory of the Member States;
   – protect democratic institutions and the civilian population from any terrorist attack;
   – assist a Member State in its territory, at the request of its political authorities, in the event of a terrorist attack;
(b) assist a Member State in its territory, at the request of its political authorities, in the event of a natural or man-made disaster.

Paragraph 2 refers to Article III-329 for more detailed arrangements. There we can find a coordinating role of the Council as well as the procedure: the arrangements for the implementation of the Solidarity clause shall be defined by a European Decision adopted by the Council acting on a joint proposal by the Commission and the Union Minister for Foreign Affairs.

However, after the Madrid terrorist attacks in March 2004, the European Council issued a 'Declaration on Solidarity Against Terrorism',[34] in which Article III-329 of the Constitutional Treaty is already incorporated, although the Declaration does not refer to a role for the Union as such, but refers to the 'Member States acting jointly'. In addition, the Declaration leaves it to the Member States to

---

[32] See their letter of 4 December 2003; A Missiroli, *From Copenhagen to Brussels: European Defence: Core Documents*, Chaillot Paper No 67 (Paris: Institute for Security Studies, 2003) 432. See also Trybus, n 15, above, 19.   [33] See more extensively H Krieger, Chapter 8 of this volume.
[34] Brussels European Council, 25–26 March 2004, Presidency Conclusions.

'choose the most appropriate means to comply with this solidarity commitment'. Irrespective of the legal nature of this Declaration,[35] one may see this as a further possibility for differentiation. At least until the entry into force of the Constitution, the Union as such will not have a role to play in this regard and it is up to (groups of) Member States to organize their responses in a rather ad hoc manner.

4. Other Forms of Differentiation in EU Security Law

4.1. Constructive abstention

A special form of differentiation can be established on the basis of the so-called 'constructive abstention' clause, introduced by the Amsterdam Treaty in 1997. The clause is generally regarded as a compromise between the states that aimed for QMV and enhanced cooperation in CFSP matters and those that wished to hold on to the status quo of the Maastricht regime. Compared to enhanced cooperation—allowing Member States to give a positive boost to integration in the area of the CFSP—constructive abstention is more negative as it is basically a decision not to oppose a further step.[36] In the current EU Treaty constructive abstention found its place in Article 23, paragraph 1:

Decisions under this title shall be taken by the Council acting unanimously. Abstentions by members present in person or represented shall not prevent the adoption of such decisions.

When abstaining in a vote, any member of the Council may qualify its abstention by making a formal declaration under the present subparagraph. In that case, it shall not be obliged to apply the decision, but shall accept that the decision commits the Union. In a spirit of mutual solidarity, the Member State concerned shall refrain from any action likely to conflict with or impede Union action based on that decision and the other Member States shall respect its position. If the members of the Council qualifying their abstention in this way represent more than one third of the votes weighted in accordance with Article 205(2) of the Treaty establishing the European Community, the decision shall not be adopted.

This provision makes clear that differentiation may only occur in case the abstaining Member States qualifies its abstention in a formal declaration. This way the special position of the non-participating Member States is not only institutionalized, but it is also clear what its position is. Unity and coherence is being achieved both by the rule that the non-participants shall refrain from any action that could be in conflict with the adopted decision and by the fact that this form of differentiation is not possible when the group of non-participating states represents more than one third of the votes. While the 'loyalty obligation' should certainly be seen

---

[35] See on this question: M Reichard, 'The Madrid Terrorist Attacks: A Midwife for EU Mutual Defence?' (2004) *Zeitschrift für Europarechtliche Studien* 313–34.

[36] Cf Jaeger, n 15, above, 320 and D Galloway, *The Treaty of Nice and Beyond* (Sheffield: Sheffield Academic Press, 2001) 134–6.

as a legal obligation, both its nature and the absence of jurisdiction of the Court of Justice place its enforcement in the hands of the Council.

As the Treaty only refers to 'a formal declaration' Member States remain free to give any reason they want for non-participation. Abstaining for purely financial reasons is therefore not excluded, resulting in systematic 'free-riding'. Indeed, using the system this way would turn out to be 'destructive', rather than 'constructive'.[37] In terms of the size of the potential group there is a striking difference with enhanced cooperation: on the basis of constructive abstention a group would have to represent at least two thirds of the weighted votes in the Council, whereas under enhanced cooperation groups may consist of eight Member States only.

Article 23 explicitly refers to decisions taken by the Council. This implies that decisions (including Common Strategies) adopted by the European Council are excluded from the constructive abstention rules. While it has been argued that constructive abstention could also be used for decisions that can be taken by QMV, the general view—based on both the Treaty text and the ratio of the very notion of constructive abstention—is that it is meant for unanimous voting procedures only.[38] On the other hand, irrespective of an explicit reference in the Treaty, implementation decisions seem to be covered by the constructive abstention regime, even when they would be adopted by QMV. After all, if a Member State is not 'obliged to apply the decision', it will also not be asked to apply any implementing measure based on the decision.

The possibility of joining Common Positions and Joint Actions at a later stage is also not regulated by the Treaty, but nothing seems to stand in the way of Member States joining in. In the case of Common Positions this would simply mean an adherence to the policy laid down therein; in the case of Joint Actions, there may be practical as well as financial implications. However, blocking the participation of former 'outs' does appear to be in conflict with the notion that forms of differentiation should only occur in the last resort.

Can constructive abstention also be used in the case of the adoption of decisions in the area of the security and defence policy? As paragraph 1 of Article 23 is not restricted to general CFSP decisions, the answer should be in the affirmative. 'Decisions having military or defence implications' are excluded in paragraph 2 only, which deals with the possibility of QMV. This means that even in the area of the ESDP one can imagine decisions being taken which are supported by a restricted group of 'able and willing' Member States. Based on its general exception, there does not seem to be a need for Denmark to use the constructive abstention clause in these cases.

In the EU Constitutional Treaty, the possibility of constructive abstention returns in Article III-300 in similar wordings. Decisions having military or defence implications remain to be excluded from QMV decision-making (see also Article IV-444 on the simplified revision procedure).

---

[37] Missiroli, n 32, above, 15.   [38] See more extensively Thym, n 16, above, 155.

4.2. The implementation of a Joint Action and the Security Council

From the outset the TEU has accepted the possibility of differentiation where the implementation of Joint Actions is concerned. Article 14, paragraph 6 allows for Member States to deviate from Joint Actions ('take the necessary measures as a matter of urgency') in cases of imperative need arising from changes in the situation and failing a Council decision. Moreover, paragraph 7 acknowledges the possibility of 'grave difficulties' for Member States to implement a Joint Action. Although this should be discussed in the Council, to seek an appropriate solution, this provision implicitly takes the possibility into account that one or more Member States does not participate in the implementation of certain Joint Actions.[39] Both possibilities return in the Constitutional Treaty in Article III-297, paragraphs 4 and 5.

Another possibility for differentiation may be found in the provision that the permanent members of the UN Security Council (France and Britain) seem to enjoy a certain freedom to pursue their national interests in the position they take in the Security Council. After all, on the basis of Article 19 TEU they have to defend the positions of the Union only when they do not have to compromise 'their responsibilities under the provisions of the United Nations Charter'. While this possibility for differentiation can hardly be expected to be acceptable in the case of binding CFSP acts, it reflects a potential threat to the coherence of other Union positions. Nevertheless, it is difficult to come up with examples of cases where the responsibilities of the permanent members of the Security Council under the UN Charter would lead to a legal conflict with their EU obligations. As one observer holds, a political conflict can, however, be imagined:

It appears that by including a reminder of their UN responsibility, France and Britain intended to stress the awareness of their partners in the Union that they will continue to pursue their particular geopolitical interests in the Security Council where they remain free to do so, and perhaps even that they consider the sensible security interest dealt with in the Security Council to override all other possible interests, including the aims of the EU.[40]

Article III-305, paragraph 2 of the Constitutional Treaty repeats the current provision. A minor difference is that the new provision is not restricted to the permanent members of the Security Council, but refers in general to 'Member States which are members of the Security Council'. This opens the possibility of a larger group of EU Member States deviating from earlier positions of the Union once related issues are on the agenda of the Security Council during their two-year term as non-permanent member.

---

[39] See also Jaeger, n 15, above, 300 and C D Ehlermann, 'Differentiation, Flexibility, Closer Cooperation: The New Provisions of the Amsterdam Treaty', EUI Working Paper, 1997, VI.5.
[40] Jaeger, ibid, 301.

5. Differentiation in ESDP Practice and Operations?

Since the end of 1998 the EU has been actively developing its security and defence policy.[41] The 1992 TEU had already been an important first phase in the on-going quest to consolidate Western European defence cooperation. A closer defence cooperation was planned in the original version of this treaty, albeit that its Article J.4 clearly reflected the compromise, as it referred extremely carefully to 'the eventual framing of a common defence policy, which might in time lead to a common defence'. Another international organization, the WEU, would be asked to 'elaborate and implement decisions and actions of the Union which have defence implications'. On the basis of this provision one could easily be led to believe that we would never witness the creation of an ESDP. Nevertheless, even this carefully phrased compromise obviously helped recalcitrant Member States (the UK in particular) to get used to the idea of a future role for the EU in this area. The Amsterdam Treaty (1997, entry into force in 1999) turned Article J.4 into Article 17, and took another subtle step forward by formulating a common defence policy as an *objective* of the European Union, rather than a mere *possibility*.

On 15 November 1999, for the first time in its history, the Council of the European Union met informally in the composition of Ministers for Foreign Affairs and Ministers of Defence.[42] While this may seem a logical step in the light of current developments, it highlights the revolution that has taken place within the EU during the past few years. Previously, meetings of defence ministers were unthinkable within the EU framework. During this meeting France and the UK launched their plan for a rapid reaction force, an idea that was adopted by the European Council in Helsinki in December 1999 when it decided to develop an autonomous military capacity. Probably to reassure (the parliaments of) certain Member States, the somewhat ambiguous sentence was added that this does not imply the creation of a European army. Nevertheless, all developments pointed in the direction of a sincere attempt on the part of the EU to create a military force. The European Council formulated a 'headline goal' and decided that by the year 2003 Member States must be able to develop rapidly and then sustain forces 'capable of the full range of Petersberg tasks, including the most demanding, in operations up to corps level; up to 15 brigades, or 50,000–60,000 persons'. These forces should be self-sustaining with the necessary command and control and intelligence capabilities, logistics, and other combat support services and, additionally, appropriate naval and air elements. The readiness requirement is 60 days, with some units at very high readiness, capable of deployment within days or

---

[41] See more extensively R A Wessel, 'The State of Affairs in European Security and Defence Policy: The Breakthrough in the Treaty of Nice' J of Conflict & Security L (2003) 8(2).

[42] Conclusions of the General Affairs Council of 15 November 1999, Council Press Release No 12642/99 (*Presse* 344). The first formal meeting of the Defence Ministers took place in May 2002; see Conclusions of the General Affairs Council, 13–14 May 2002.

weeks.[43] Indeed, in May 2003 the Council confirmed that the EU now has operational capability across the full range of Petersberg tasks. Nevertheless, the goals set in Helsinki in 1999 were not attained and in May 2004 the Council approved a new 'Headline Goal 2010'.[44] This new capabilities commitment includes the establishment of so-called 'battlegroups': 'force packages at high readiness as a response to a crisis either as a stand-alone force or as part of a larger operation enabling follow-on phases'. On decision-making, the ambition of the EU is to be able to take the decision to launch an operation within five days of the approval of the so-called Crisis Management Concept by the Council. On the deployment of forces, the ambition is that the forces start implementing their mission on the ground no later than ten days after the EU Decision to launch the operation. While the composition of the foreseen battlegroups is not yet clear (they will have to be ready by 2007), one may expect smaller groups of Member States cooperating in them.

The results of these developments found their way into the Treaty of Nice, which was adopted in December 2000. On the basis of that treaty, Article 17 TEU was modified as follows: the second subparagraph of paragraph 1 on the relationship with the WEU was deleted; the same holds true for the first three subparagraphs of paragraph 3 on the role of the WEU in the implementation of EU Decisions with defence implications. This means that the Union has been given the competence to operate within the full range of the Petersberg tasks: 'humanitarian and rescue tasks, peacekeeping tasks and tasks of combat forces in crisis management, including peacemaking' (Article 17, para 2). In that respect it is odd that Article 17 still refers to the 'progressive framing of a common defence policy' after that same policy has entered into force on the basis of the same article. Provisions like these reveal the fact that, although a final consensus was reached on an ESDP, some Member States are more eager to lay everything down in treaty arrangements than others. Nevertheless one cannot overlook the gradual development from the first provision in the Maastricht Treaty ('the *eventual* framing of a common defence policy, which *might in time* lead to a common defence'), to the Amsterdam Treaty ('the *progressive* framing of a common defence policy, which *might* lead to a common defence'), and finally to Nice where all references to the WEU were deleted, thereby making the EU itself responsible for the elaboration and implementation of decisions and actions which have defence implications. In the EU Constitutional Treaty this arrangement returns in Article I-16.

---

[43] See on the feasibility of this headline objective, for instance R de Wijk, 'Convergence Criteria: Measuring Input or Output' (2000) *Eur Foreign Affairs Rev* 397–417; as well as the NATO Parliamentary Assembly Interim Report 'Building European Defence: NATO's ESDI and the European Union's ESDP', Rapporteur Van Eekelen, 5 October 2000.

[44] Conclusions of the External Relations Council, 17 May 2004. On financing, see also for the Athena mechanism: Council Decision 2004/197/CFSP of 23 February 2004, [2004] OJ L-63/68, as

By now the ESDP provisions have been put into practice and the Union is, and has already been, engaged in a number of operations. The first was Operation 'Concordia'. On 31 March 2003 the EU formally took over NATO's Operation Allied Harmony in the Former Yugoslav Republic of Macedonia, an operation contributing to a stable, secure environment. This decision has been made possible following the agreements reached by the EU and NATO concerning EU-led operations.[45] Regarding the financing of military operations, the Council had already agreed on a solution in June 2002: costs lie where they fall. In other words: contributing Member States pay their own expenses, although certain expenses (for instance arising from communication, medical arrangements, and the appointment of local personnel) will be charged in accordance with the GNP scale.[46]

In general the operations reveal a large degree of support on the part of the Member States. Nevertheless, it is clear that in many operations not all Member States participate and that, if they do, contributions differ greatly. At the same time, only Denmark formally withheld its participation on a structural basis, which raised the question of the legal basis for the non-participation of the other Member States. After all, the current treaty excludes enhanced cooperation for matters having military and defence implications. Practice thus reveals a form of differentiation that is not foreseen (or perhaps even explicitly excluded) by the treaty. The fact that almost all operations are at the same time characterized by an extensive participation of non-Member States, substantively adds to the variation.[47]

Irrespective of this complex picture, the fact remains that the operations are all 'Union' operations and were based on unanimously adopted Council decisions. In that respect, the final composition of the troops may be less relevant. The same seems to hold true for multinational forces of some Member States. The possibility of making these forces available to the Union is foreseen by the EU Constitutional Treaty (Article I-41, para 3). And, as we have seen, the establishment of the so-called permanent structured cooperation will be embedded within the Union's institutional framework (compare also Article I-41, para 6).

---

amended by Council Decision 2004/925/EC of 22 December 2004, [2004] OJ L-395/31 68 and by Council Decision 2005/68/CFSP of 24 January 2005, [2005] OJ L-27/29 59.

[45] See M Reichard, 'Some Legal Issues Concerning the EU-NATO Berlin Plus Agreement' Nordic J of Intl L (2004) 37–68.

[46] Conclusions of the General Affairs Council of 17 June 2002. With regard to the EU Police Missions, however, it was also agreed that certain costs will be financed out of the community budget; see Council Joint Action 2003/141/CFSP of 27 January 2003, OJ L-53, 28 February 2003. See also Article III-313 of the Constitutional Treaty: '[...] 2. Operating expenditure to which the implementation of this Chapter gives rise shall also be charged to the Union budget, except for such expenditure arising from operations having military or defence implications and cases where the Council decides otherwise'.   [47] See F Naert, Chapter 4 of this volume.

6. Conclusion

A true common foreign, security, and defence policy depends on the positioning of the Union as a cohesive force in international relations. In fact, the whole purpose of establishing a CFSP in the first place was to make an end to the often diverging foreign policies of the Member States. A subsequent fragmentation of the Union's external policy due to à la carte constructions would run counter to the very notion of a common policy.[48] The 'constitutionalization process' which resulted in the EU Constitutional Treaty in 2004 further strengthened this idea. The further consolidation of foreign, security, and defence policy and in particular the explicit treaty base of the latter explains why the starting points have been maintained.

On the other hand, the current treaty as well as the Constitutional Treaty explicitly allow for differentiation in the areas of CFSP and CSDP. While both enhanced cooperation and ad hoc regimes are foreseen, CSDP flexibility depends on actual participation of Member States (and third States) in specific operations. The question most frequently asked is whether this variation in foreign, security, and defence policy has consequences for the unity of the Union's legal order.[49] Political analyses will certainly point to the negative effects of too much fragmentation on the positioning of the Union as a united global force. While there will certainly be much truth in this presumption, legal analyses could be used to take the discussion one step further. Two points could be made in this respect. First, there is no doubt that the way in which flexibility is regulated in the current treaties (including the Constitutional Treaty) adds to the complexity. The different forms that have been described above all have their own creation, accession, and decision-making rules and differences have been created between the CFSP and the ESDP/CSDP. At the same time, however, it is through the complex restrictions on flexibility that the Treaty legislator attempts to maintain a grip on the cooperation between smaller groups of Member States and to prevent too much variation from occurring. Indeed, despite the introduction of enhanced cooperation in the CFSP as a means to make it less dependent on the whims of individual states, it has not been used in practice.

The second point is that regulation of flexibility in the CFSP/ESDP may prevent extra-EU initiatives by Member States, which could be even more harmful for the unity of the Union. Irrespective of its complexity, the current (and planned) legal regime on differentiation in the CFSP/ESDP provides a framework in which the institutions play a leading role and through which initiatives by

---

[48] See more extensively on this point R A Wessel, 'Fragmentation in the Governance of EU External Relations: Legal Institutional Dilemmas and the New Constitution for Europe' in J W de Zwaan et al (eds), *The European Union—An Ongoing Process of Integration* (The Hague: TMC Asser Press, 2004) 123–40.   [49] See ibid more extensively and for references.

groups of able and willing Member States are embedded in the Union legal order. As long as operations are fully embedded in the Union's institutional framework and non-participating states refrain from actions that would harm their character as Union operations, they do not seem to be a threat to consistent external action. On the contrary, history has shown that the further development of the ESDP needs some room for smaller-scale initiatives. The new Constitutional Treaty continues to offer possibilities in this respect.

11

Security and Defence Policy within the Context of EU External Relations: Issues of Coherence, Consistency, and Effectiveness

Panos Koutrakos *

1. Introduction

The European Security Strategy, presented by the EU High Representative Javier Solana and approved by the European Council in December 2003, states that 'Europe should be ready to share in the responsibility for global security and in building a better world'.[1] To that effect, it asserts the need, amongst others, of being more active in pursuing the strategic objectives of the Union in ways that would cover 'the full spectrum of instruments for crisis management and conflict prevention at our disposal, including political, diplomatic, military and civilian, trade and development activities'.[2]

The intention of the Union to rely upon the full panoply of its instruments and policies in order to 'assert its identity on the international scene'[3] renders the European Security and Defence Policy (ESDP) within the system of EU international relations. This raises questions about the linkages between the ESDP and the policies carried out in the context of the Community legal order. In any multilevel system of governance, coherence is a challenge. In the case of the EU it is even more so as its international role is defined by a variety of actors, both supranational and intergovernmental, developing a variety of interacting policies pursuant to distinct, albeit, interrelated, sets of rules.

This multiplicity of institutions, rules, and processes has been viewed as a source of considerable confusion. In his latest book, Timothy Garton Ash argues that:

Europe has a hundred left hands and none of them knows what the right hand is doing. Trade, development aid, immigration policy, education, cultural exchanges, classic

* Professor of European Law, University of Bristol, United Kingdom. All website addresses cited were active on 10 February 2006, unless otherwise specified.
[1] *A Secure Europe in a Better World—European Security Strategy* (Brussels: 12 December 2003) at 1.
[2] Ibid, at 11.   [3] Art 2 TEU.

diplomacy, arms sales and anti-proliferation measures, counter-terrorism, the fight against drug and organized crime: each European policy has an impact, but the effects are fragmented and often self-contradictory.[4]

In other words, the issue of consistency has a clear practical content. In terms of the efficiency of EU actions, it rationalizes the allocation of resources and prevents duplication; it also seeks to maximize the effects of the desired outcomes by managing the synergies between different actions. Furthermore, the extent to which the EU ensures the consistency of its policies is directly relevant to its credibility as an international actor and affects, directly or indirectly, its ability to intervene on the international scene and relate to other international actors.

The need for consistency is acknowledged in the Treaty on European Union (TEU) expressly. Article 1 third subparagraph states that the task of the Union 'shall be to organise, in a manner demonstrating consistency and solidarity, relations between the Member States and between their people'. In terms of the ways in which this may be achieved, Article 3 reads as follows:

The Union shall be served by a single institutional framework which shall ensure the consistency and continuity of the activities carried out in order to attain its objectives while respecting and building upon the *acquis communautaire*.

In its second subparagraph, Article 3 TEU confers upon the Council and the Commission the duty to ensure the consistency of the Union's external activities as a whole in the context of its external relations, security, economic, and development policies. In order to achieve this objective of consistency, the Council and the Commission are to cooperate and, in accordance with their respective powers, ensure the implementation of the above policies. As if the point had not already been brought home, Article 13(3) third subparagraph TEU states that the Council 'shall ensure the unity, consistency and effectiveness of action by the Union'.

This proliferation of references to the need for consistency illustrates awareness of the challenges raised by the coexistence of the formally distinct but materially and institutionally interacting pillars and policies. These challenges have also been analysed in the light of the need for coherence of the Union's external action. The European Security Strategy, for instance, refers to the coherence of the Union's actions as one of the central policy implications for the Union's role in the world.[5] In a Report on Conflict Prevention, the Common Foreign and Security Policy (CFSP) High Representative pointed out that:

. . . the central issue for the Union is one of coherence in deploying the right combination and sequence of instruments in a timely and integrated manner. This demands greater

---

[4] Timothy Garton Ash, *Free World* (London: Penguin, 2005) 218.

[5] For an early analysis of the requirement of consistency, see N Neuwahl, 'Foreign and Security Policy and the Implementation of the Requirement of "Consistency" under the Treaty on European Union' in D O'Keefe and P Twomey (eds), *Legal Issues of the Maastricht Treaty* (London: Chancery Law, 1994) 227.

coherence and complementarity at several levels: between the instruments and capabilities available within each pillar, between the pillars themselves, between Member State and Community activities, and between the Union and its international partners in conflict prevention.[6]

In examining the ESDP within the context of EU external relations, this analysis will focus on the various linkages between the development of the former and the regulation of the latter. In particular, it will seek to identify mechanisms which, irrespective of their source, aim at ensuring the absence of contradictions and the development of interconnections between the relevant policies. The increasing emphasis on the interaction between the various external policies of the Union and their relevance to the development of the ESDP renders such issues central to the effectiveness of the Union's international actions.

This chapter does not purport to provide an exhaustive analysis of the ways in which the organization and conduct of ESDP interact with the law and policy of EU external relations. Instead, it aims at shedding some light on a number of dimensions of the requirement of consistency and coherence which characterize the position of the ESDP within the EU external relations system. The analysis will be structured as follows. First, it will examine the normative dimension of consistency by outlining the effects that the substantive interaction between security policy and external relations law may have on the legal autonomy of the respective sets of rules. Secondly, it will highlight the political dimension of the need for coherence by focusing on the interactions between development cooperation and conflict prevention. Thirdly, it will identify certain areas where EU institutions and the Member States have developed practical mechanisms aiming at managing the conduct of ESDP and its interactions with EU external relations in an efficient manner.

2. The Normative Dimension of the Requirement for Consistency

At the core of the development of ESDP as part of the system of policies which enables the EU to assert its identity on the international scene is its relationship with the Community legal order and the legal repercussions of their interactions. As a matter of principle, these are addressed in primary law. On the one hand, Article 46 TEU excludes the CFSP provisions from the jurisdiction of the Court of Justice. On the other hand, Article 47 TEU stipulates that 'nothing in this Treaty shall affect the Treaties establishing the European Communities or the

---

[6] Report to the Council, 14088/00, Brussels, 30 November 2000 at 5. In terms of the links between development and other Community policies, Art 178 EC states that the Community 'shall take account of the objectives [of its development policy] in the policies that it implements which are likely to affect developing countries'.

subsequent Treaties and Acts modifying or supplementing them'. And, of course, there is the reference to the requirement that the Union activities be carried out 'while respecting and building upon the *acquis communautaire*' in Article 3 TEU.

Therefore, the normative dimension of the requirement of consistency is central to the functioning of the EU's constitutional order. The Court of Justice has made it clear that this requirement is by no means a statement of merely rhetorical significance by assuming the role of adjudicating where the dividing line between the pillars lies. This became apparent in the *Airport Transit Visa* case, an annulment action brought by the Commission challenging the adoption of a Joint Action under the third pillar.[7] The measure in question aimed at introducing common rules on issuing visas for transit through the international areas of the airports of the Member States. The Court was asked whether that measure ought to have been adopted under the pre-Amsterdam provision of Article 100c EC. The Council and the British Government objected to the admissibility of the action by challenging the jurisdiction of the Court. They argued that the annulment of acts adopted beyond the Community legal order was excluded from it pursuant to Article 46 TEU.

In its judgment, the Court asserted its jurisdiction in no uncertain terms. By relying upon Article 47 TEU, it pointed out that Article 46 TEU makes it clear that the EC Treaty provisions on the powers of the Court of Justice and the exercise of those powers applied to Article 47 TEU. It then concluded as follows:[8]

It is therefore the task of the Court to ensure that acts which, according to the Council, fall within the scope of [then] Article K.3(2) of the Treaty of the European Union do not encroach upon the powers conferred by the EC Treaty on the Community.

It follows that the Court has jurisdiction to review the content of the [Joint Action] in the light of Article 100c of the EC Treaty in order to ascertain whether the Act affects the powers of the Community under that provision and to annul the [Joint Action] if it appears that it should have been based on Article 100c of the EC Treaty.

Whilst the Commission's action was dismissed and the third pillar was affirmed as the correct legal framework for the contested Joint Action, the significance of this judgment is considerable. By asserting its jurisdiction in order to preserve the boundaries of the Community legal order, the Court highlights the normative dimension of the element of consistency in the conduct of EU external relations as a whole. In other words, the political assessment of how best to ensure the effectiveness of the Union's external policies may not be dissociated from the requirement that the *acquis communautaire* be respected.

The implications of the Court's approach became apparent in the recent judgment of the Grand Chamber in Case C-176/03 *Commission v Council*.[9] The subject matter of this annulment action was Framework Decision 2003/80/JHA which lays down a number of environmental offences in relation to which the

---

[7] Case C-170/96 *Commission* v *Council* [1998] ECR I-2763. The measure challenged by the Commission was Joint Action 96/197 [1996] OJ L-63/8.   [8] Ibid, paras 16–17.
    [9] [2005] ECR I-7879.   [10] [2003] OJ L-29/55.

Member States are required to introduce criminal penalties.[10] The Commission argued that that measure should have been adopted under the environmental provisions of the EC Treaty which provided for majority voting. The Council, and ten Member States which intervened in its support, counter-argued that the Community lacked the competence to require Member States to impose criminal penalties in respect of the environmental offences falling within the scope of the Framework Decision.

The very first point made by the Court in its judgment is to reiterate the ratio of Article 47 TEU and to reaffirm the jurisdiction of the Court in cases of encroachment upon Community powers. It then went on to annul the Framework Decision on the basis of the following two considerations. On the one hand, the substantive provisions of the contested measure introduced partial harmonization of national criminal laws in order to protect the environment whilst, in principle, neither criminal law nor criminal procedures fall within the Community's competence. On the other hand, this principle 'does not prevent the Community legislature, when the application of effective, proportionate and dissuasive criminal penalties by the competent national authorities is an essential measure for combating serious environmental offences, from taking measures which relate to the criminal law of the Member States which it considers necessary in order to ensure that the rules which it lays down on environmental protection are fully effective'.[11]

The combined effect of the judgments in *Airport Transit Visas* and *Environmental Crimes* illustrates that the effectiveness and consistency of ESDP may not be dissociated from the integrity and effectiveness of the Community legal order. Therefore, the competence of the Community to act in accordance with the rules and processes laid down in primary law may not be undermined pursuant to a political decision that a non-Community law instrument should be adopted. Moreover, the above judgments put the role of the Court of Justice at the very centre of the system of rules which underpin the effort of the Union to assert its identity on the international scene. The corollary of this approach is the compliance by the Community judiciary with the limits of its jurisdiction as laid down in TEU. Therefore, the Court of First Instance has not examined the substance of actions against the CFSP and third pillar measures in the context of actions seeking to establish liability[12] or of annulment proceedings.[13]

---

[11] N 9, above, para 48.

[12] See Case T-338/02 *Segi, Araitz Zubimendi Izaga and Aritza Galarraga* v *Council*, Order of 7 June 2004, [2004] ECR II-1647, at paras 41 et seq. AG Mengozzi delivered his Opinion on appeal (Case C-354/04P) on 26 October 2006 where, whilst agreeing with the CFI on the point of jurisdiction, he argued that national courts were under a Union law duty to acknowledge their jurisdiction to hear actions of this kind, in the name of respect for fundamental rights and the judicial protection this should entail.

[13] See Case T-349/99 *Miskovic against Council* [2000] OJ C-79/35 challenging Council Dec 1999/612/CFSP and Case T-350/99 *Karic against Council* [2000] OJ C-79/36 challenging Council Dec 1999/62/CFSP, both removed ([2001] OJ C-161/50 and 51 respectively). There is an annulment action brought by the Commission under Article 230 EC against a Council Decision implementing a Joint Action in relation to the Moratorium on Small Arms and Light Weapons: Case C-91/05 *Commission* v *Council* [2005] OJ C-115/10.

The normative dimension of the requirement of consistency has been further developed by the Court in cases where the substantive choices made by the legislature and the executive may impinge upon Community policies. A case in point is the adoption of trade measures with security policy implications in general, and export restrictions in particular. Export measures fall within the scope of the Common Commercial Policy (CCP). Set out in Article 133 EC, as amended first at Amsterdam[14] and then, in a disconcertingly convoluted manner, at Nice,[15] the CCP is shaped pursuant to unilateral measures and international agreements adopted by the Council by qualified majority vote. In the areas covered by the CCP, the Member States are excluded from acting, except under a specific Community law authorization.[16] The principle of exclusivity, coupled with the requirement for majority voting, has led to the CCP being viewed as 'represent[ing] the EC at the height of its legal powers, control, and supremacy over the Member States'.[17]

The interaction between the Community's trade policy and the Union's security and defence policy raises serious legal questions. Are the Member States free to rely upon non-Community legal mechanisms in order to impose trade restrictions on third countries? If so, to what extent and in which circumstances? In a limited number of judgments, delivered in the 1990s, the Court was called upon to answer these questions. A number of these cases were about restrictions on the export of dual-use goods imposed unilaterally by Member States. Products which may be of both civil and military application, dual-use goods become increasingly significant in the light of the rapid technological progress in the defence-related industries. Whilst exports of products are regulated under the CCP, in the context of which the Council has adopted secondary legislation,[18] the special nature of dual-use goods appeared to question the appropriateness of that framework. In *Richardt*, the Luxembourg authorities restricted the export of such products which were in transit from Paris to Moscow and initiated criminal proceedings against the exporter on the ground of the absence of an export licence required under national law.[19] The Court held that the Community rules applicable on

---

[14] On the Amsterdam amendment, see O Blin, 'L'Art 113 CE après Amsterdam' (1998) 420 *Revue du Marche commun et de l'Union européenne* 447

[15] On the Nice amendments, see M Cremona, 'A Policy of Bits and Pieces? The Common Commercial Policy after Nice' (2001) 4 Cambridge Ybk of Eur Legal Studies 61 at 73 and C Herrmann, 'Common Commercial Policy after Nice: Sisyphus Would Have Done a Better Job' (2002) 39 CML Rev 7 at 17.

[16] *Opinion 1/75 (re: OECD Local Cost Standard)* [1975] ECR 1355 at 1364, *Opinion 1/78* [1979] ECR 2871, Case 41/76 *Suzanne Criel, née Donckerwolcke and Henri Schou v Procureur de la Republique au Tribunal de Grande Instance, Lille and Director General of Customs* [1976] ECR 1921, Case 174/84 *Bulk Oil (Zug) AG v Sun International Limited and Sun Oil Trading Company* [1986] ECR 559 and Case 5/84 *Tezi Textiel BV v Commission* [1986] ECR 887.

[17] D McGoldrick, *International Relations Law of the European Union* (London: Longman, 1997) 70.

[18] Council Regulation 3918/92 on common rules on exports (Export Regulation) [1991] OJ L-372/31 amending Council Reg 2603/69 [1969] (II) OJ, English ed, 590.

[19] Case C-367/89 *Criminal Proceedings against Aimé Richardt and Les Accessoires Scientifiques SNC* [1991] ECR I-4621.

transit did allow Member States to impose restrictions and pointed out that, in doing so, the exceptional clause the EC laid down in Article 30 EC should be complied with. That provision covered public security, a concept which the Court interpreted broadly so as to apply to both domestic and international security. However, it was made clear that, as a deviation from the principle of free movement, the relevant right of the Member State should be interpreted strictly so as to ensure that the national measures under review are such as to serve the interests laid down therein and 'they do not restrict intra-Community more than is absolutely necessary'.[20] The determination of compliance with the principles of necessity and proportionality was left to the national court.

The judgment in *Richardt* indicated that, whilst broadly interpreted, public security would not be seen as providing the Member States with a *carte blanche* to deviate from Community law and the ensuing supervision of the Court of Justice.[21] This became more apparent in the subsequent judgments in *Werner*[22] and *Leifer*.[23] These cases were about a requirement for an export licence imposed under German law on exports of dual-use goods in order to protect the peaceful coexistence of nations and the conduct of the external relations of Germany. What rendered that requirement problematic was the existence of secondary legislation setting out the principle of free exportation. To the argument that trade measures with foreign and security policy implications fell beyond the scope of Community law, the Court responded as follows:[24]

The specific subject-matter of commercial policy, which concerns trade with non-member countries and, according to Article [133] is based on the concept of a common policy, requires that a Member State should not be able to restrict its scope by freely deciding, in the light of its own foreign policy or security requirements, whether a measure is covered by Article [133].

The requirement that Community policies should not be impinged upon by non-Community measures on the basis of security policy considerations was further clarified in *Centro-Com*, where the Court ruled that 'while it is for Member States to adopt measures of foreign and security policy in the exercise of their national competence, those measures must nevertheless respect the provisions adopted by the Community in the field of the common commercial policy provided for by Article 133 of the Treaty'.[25]

In asserting that the ESDP development should not undermine the Community legal order, the relevant case law defines the requirement for respect

---

[20] Para 20. See also Case 72/83 *Campus Oil Ltd v Minister for Industry and Energy* [1984] ECR 2727, paras 32–7.

[21] For an analysis of the judgment, see I Govare and P Eeckhout, 'On Dual Use Goods and Dualist Case Law: The *Aime Richardt* Judgment and on Export Controls' (1992) 29 CML Rev 941.

[22] Case C-70/94 *Fritz Werner Industrie-Ausruestungen GmbH v Germany* [1995] ECR I-3189.

[23] Case C-83/94 *Criminal Proceedings against Peter Leifer and Others* [1995] ECR I-3231.

[24] Case C-70/94 *Werner*, n 22 above, para 11.

[25] Case C-124/95 *The Queen, ex parte Centro-Com Srl v HM Treasury and Bank of England* [1997] ECR I-81 at para 27.

of the *acquis communautaire* and Article 47 TEU in a very specific fashion: rather than general statements of merely rhetorical significance, they are viewed as legal imperatives compliance with which is central to the constitutional development of the Union's legal order. By assuming the role of ensuring respect for these requirements, the Court of Justice assumes, yet again, a constitutional function which renders it at the very centre of the multi-level Union legal order. In terms of the position of the Member States, rather than putting forward an absolute uncompromising construction of the Community legal order, the Court has recognized the wide discretion that Member States enjoy in protecting their security in ways they deem necessary. The outer limit of that discretion is compliance with the requirements of necessity and proportionality which is to be assessed by national courts. Indeed, the case law on export restrictions on dual-use goods is underpinned by an interpretation of Community law as a legal system whose outer limits are carefully defined and rigorously protected whilst its substantive content is sufficiently flexible to accommodate national concerns over security policy considerations.[26]

Another noteworthy feature of the Court's approach is that the Member States and the Community legislature have responded to it in a positive fashion. The case of exports of dual-use goods is a case in point. Prior to the above case law, exports of dual-use goods were regulated on the basis of rules laid down in two measures, namely Regulation 3381/94 adopted under Article 133 EC[27] and Council Decision 94/942/CFSP.[28] The former measure set out the common rules governing such exports, essentially based on a system of export licences granted by national authorities, whereas the latter measure laid down the criteria pursuant to which such licences were to be granted and the scope of products which would fall within that system. The main tenet of this set of rules, that is to render the modus operandi of trade measures with foreign policy implications beyond the CCP, soon proved to be flawed in legal terms and unnecessary in practical terms.[29] Following the case law of the Court, the relevant rules were duly amended and incorporated in a single instrument adopted under Article 133 EC which expressly refers to the relevant rulings.[30]

This section has outlined the role of the Court of Justice in ensuring that the quest for a consistent and coherent international presence for the Union, with an

---

[26] For this interpretation, see P Koutrakos, *Trade, Foreign Policy and Defence in EU Constitutional Law* (Oxford: Hart Publishing, 2002) ch 6.   [27] [1994] OJ L-367/1.

[28] [1994] OJ L-367/8. This was amended a number of times by the following Council measures: Dec 95/127/CFSP [1995] OJ L-90/2; Dec 95/128/CFSP [1995] OJ L-90/3; Dec 96/423/CFSP [1996] OJ L-176/1; Dec 96/613/CFSP [1996] OJ L-278/1; Dec 97/100/CFSP [1997] OJ L-34/1; Dec 97/173/CFSP [1997] OJ L-52/1; Dec 97/419/CFSP [1997] OJ L-178/1; Dec 97/633/CFSP [1997] OJ L-266/1; Dec 98/106/CFSP [1998] OJ L-32/1; Dec 98/232/CFSP [1998] OJ L-92/1; Dec 99/54/CFSP [1999] OJ L-18/1; and Dec 2000/243/CFSP [2000] OJ L-82/1.

[29] See P Koutrakos, 'Exports of Dual-Use Goods under the Law of the European Union' (1998) 23 Eur L Rev 235.

[30] Council Reg 1334/2000 [2000] OJ L-159/1 amended by Council Reg 149/2003 [2003] OJ L-30/1 and Council Reg 1504/2004 [2004] OJ L-281/1.

effective ESDP as a vital component, would not encroach upon the legal integrity of the Community legal order. This function has another aspect worth considering, namely, the extent to which, in carrying out its function as the ultimate adjudicator of the Union legal order in an assertive manner, the Community judiciary has an impact on the effectiveness of Union action. It is noteworthy that the assertion of its jurisdiction is accompanied by deference to the substantive choice made by the Union institutions as to the effectiveness of their action. In *Bosphorus*, for instance, the Court of Justice interpreted a Council Regulation providing for the impounding of any aircraft owned by a person or undertaking based in or operating from Yugoslavia, broadly: it was irrelevant whether the owner exercised any control over the day-to-day operation of the aircraft, as a conclusion to the contrary 'would jeopardize the effectiveness of the strengthening of the sanctions, which consist in impounding all means of transport of [Serbia and Montenegro] and its nationals . . . in order further to increase the pressure on that republic'.[31] Similarly, the function of the sanctions regime was deemed of such 'especial importance'[32] pursuing 'an objective of general interest so fundamental for the international community'[33] that it could, and indeed did, justify 'negative consequences, even of a substantial nature'[34] for non-absolute fundamental rights.[35] A similar approach was adopted in *Ebony Maritime* in relation to a Regulation prohibiting the entry of commercial traffic into Yugoslav territorial waters.[36] It was also adopted more recently, albeit not uncontroversially, by the Court of First Instance in *Kadi*[37] and *Yussuf*.[38] In these cases, Article 308 EC, along with Articles 301 and 60 EC, was used so as to enable the Community to implement a CFSP measure which provided for smart sanctions, that is, sanctions targeting specific individuals, with no link to the exercise of authority in a given state.[39]

---

[31] Case C-84/95 *Bosphorus Hava Yollari Turizm ve Ticaret AS v Minister for Transport, Energy and Communications and others* [1996] ECR I-3953 at para 18.   [32] Ibid, para 25.

[33] Ibid, para 26.   [34] Ibid, para 23.

[35] For criticism of this position, see I Canor, ' "Can Two Walk Together, Except They be Agreed?" The Relationship Between International Law and European Law: The Incorporation of United Nations Sanctions against Yugoslavia into European Community Law through the Perspective of the European Court of Justice' (1998) 35 CML Rev 137. However, see the unanimous judgment by the Grand Chamber of the European Court of Human Rights according to which there was no manifest deficiency in the protection of the applicant's ECHR rights by the Court of Justice in Case C-84/95 *Bosphorus*: see *Bosphorus Hava Yollari v Ireland*, App No 45036/98, judgment of 30 June 2005.

[36] Case C-177/95 *Ebony Maritime SA and Loten Navigation Co Ltd v Prefetto della Provincia di Brindisi and others* [1997] ECR I-1111 at paras 23 et seq.

[37] Case T-315/01 *Kadi v Council and Commission*, [2005] ECR II-3649 (now on appeal in Case C-402/04P)

[38] Case T-306/01 *Yusuf v Council and Commission*, [2005] ECR II-3533 (now on appeal in Case C-415/05P). See also Case T-253/02 *Ayadi* and Case T-94/04 *Hassan*, delivered on 12 July 2006, not yet reported, where the CFI elaborated on the role of national courts.

[39] For early criticism on the Court's approach, see M-G Garbagnati Ketvel, 'The jurisdiction of the European Court of Justice in respect of the Common Foreign and Security Policy' (2006) 66 ICLQ 77 at 111 et seq. But see the annotation by C Tomuschat in (2006) 43 CMLRev 537 and N Lavranos, 'Judicial Review of UN Sanctions by the Court of First Instance' (2006) 11 EFA Rev 471.

3. Coherence as a Political Imperative

Development cooperation is another area of EU external relations whose links to ESDP become increasingly prominent. It is, in particular, regarding conflict prevention that this interaction appears more acute. The European Security Strategy states that 'security is a precondition for development since conflicts not only destroy productive and social infrastructure but also encourage criminality, deter investment and make normal economic activity impossible'.[40]

In June 1997 the Council adopted a Resolution on Coherence between the Community development cooperation and its other policies.[41] The Resolution sets out a number of procedural arrangements which would ensure that policy incoherence would be addressed effectively. First, in its proposals to the Council, the Commission is invited to highlight any coherence questions which may arise in relation to development cooperation. To that effect, the idea of coherence impact assessments is raised. Secondly, any policy incoherence ought to be discussed in the Council pursuant, in principle, to a report by the Commission. Thirdly, the Commission is invited to present regular reports to the Council on questions of coherence which could also include specific proposals. Fourthly, the Commission is invited to investigate the use of joint monitoring procedures with developing countries for the prompt identification of possible incoherencies. Fifthly, in cases where there is a special need for policy coherence, joint Council meetings and consultation between experts are recognized as potentially useful.

Then the Council identifies four themes which underlie development policy and in relation to which the question of coherence is significant, namely, peace-building, conflict prevention and resolution, food security, fishery and development, migration and development. In relation to the first theme, the Council points out that development assistance may be relevant if it is designed and implemented to address the root causes and precipitating factors of violent conflicts in ways that are relevant to local circumstances. To that effect, it is pointed out that primary responsibility for conflict prevention lies with the people concerned and, therefore, development policy should take into account the important role of civil society and its institutions, including women and women's organizations. As a first step, the Council recommends that further consideration is given to elaborating further the role of development instruments in conflict prevention, to the formulation of development programmes to address the root causes of violent conflicts, to the identification of specific measures aimed at ensuring the coherence and complementarity of development and other policies, and to support as appropriate for the building of capacity at regional, sub-regional, national, and local levels to prevent, manage, and resolve conflicts.

---

[40] *A Secure Europe in a Better World—European Security Strategy* (Brussels: 12 December 2003) at 2–3.
[41] The Resolution was adopted by the Development Council on 5 June 1997.

In dealing with the interactions between development and conflict prevention, the above Resolution is underpinned by an understanding of coherence as a distinctly indeterminate concept. Not only does it spell this out expressly[42] but it also permeates the tenor of the document and the actions it suggests. Linked to this element is the paramount role of the political choice which underpins the quest of coherence. Issues such as the overall direction of the various interacting policies, the prioritization of objectives, and the methods pursuant to which effectiveness is ascertained, are the subject of a policy choice which, in itself, is bound to be subject to other internal and external factors of an economic and political nature. The Resolution expressly acknowledges that 'coherence is...dependent upon political choices'[43] and is underpinned by a distinct reluctance to suggest concrete measures. This is apparent not only in relation to migration and development, where development aid is seen as 'hardly hav[ing] a decisive impact...in view of the complexity of the phenomenon' and the focus is suggested to be on the need for more information, but also in relation to the other themes which underpin development policy. In relation to food security, for instance, the issue of coherence between development cooperation, trade, and agricultural policies· is addressed as a topic for discussion with the governments of the Member States.[44]

In other words, the need for coherence between development and ESDP, whilst acknowledged, appears to be viewed as the subject matter of a multi-level process of reflection. The language of the Resolution in its concluding part is indicative of the overall underlying approach: the Council 'will continue its reflection on coherence in policy areas which are likely to affect developing countries'. The combination of the emphasis on the political dimension of coherence and the proceduralization of its monitoring is noteworthy: it is recalled that it has been this combination which underpinned the development of the EU foreign policy system, not only in its early days within the framework of the European Political Cooperation, but also following its insertion into the EC Treaty by the Single European Act.

The link between development and security policy is becoming increasingly important. It was also acknowledged more recently by the Council, the Representatives of the Governments of the Member States meeting within the Council, the European Parliament, and the Commission. In a Joint Statement adopted in November 2003, *The European Consensus on Development*, a common vision was set out in order to provide the Union with values, objectives, principles, and means for development.[45] Under the EU vision on development, reference is made to policy coherence. It is in that context that reference is made to insecurity and violent conflict as two of the biggest obstacles to achieving the Union's

---

[42] 'The Council...recognises that coherence is difficult to measure...': ibid in I-Introduction.

[43] Ibid.

[44] Similarly, in relation to fishery and development, it is stated that special attention should be paid to projects aiming at improving the research on, and scientific knowledge of, fishery resources, as well as those enabling improved monitoring. [45] 14820/05.

Millennium Development Goals.[46] The European Council welcomed the adoption of the Joint Statement in December 2005. In this context, the political dimension of the requirement of coherence is also clear. One of the factors which would shape it would be the implementation of the European Security Strategy. This sets out three strategic objectives for the EU, namely, to address the threats to its security as early as possible and with recourse to a variety of instruments, to build security in its neighbourhood, and to contribute to the establishment of an international order based on effective multilateralism. To that effect, reference is made to the need 'to develop a strategic culture that fosters early, rapid, and when necessary, robust intervention'.[47] The European Security Strategy is a document whose precise implications in concrete terms are yet to be determined.[48] However, it is indicative of an increasingly self-confident Union whose intention is to raise its visibility on the international scene.

It should be pointed out that the interaction between the development and security policies is shaped in an incremental manner whereby the relevant linkages emerge not only in direct and obvious but also in indirect and subtle ways—and no less effective for that.[49] The above overview merely highlighted the political element which is inherent in the definition, monitoring, and assessment of the requirement of coherence. Its prominent role increases the significance of other mechanisms aimed at ensuring the effective conduct of ESDP within the context of EU external relations in a manner characterized by coherence and consistency.

4. Managing Consistency

The normative dimension of consistency, safeguarded by the Court of Justice, and the political dimension of coherence, highlighted by the Union institutions, set out the outer limits within which the Union may carry out its security and defence policy in order to assert its identity on the international scene. This section will focus on three issues which are central to the management of ESDP and will seek to identify the thread that brings them together.

---

[46] These include the eradication of extreme poverty and hunger, the achievement of universal primary education, the promotion of gender equality and empowerment of women, the reduction of the mortality rate of children, improved maternal health, fight against HIV/AIDS, malaria and other diseases, environmental sustainability and the development of a global partnership for development.

[47] *A Secure Europe in a Better World—European Security Strategy* (Brussels: 12 December 2003) at 11.

[48] See S Duke, 'The European Security Strategy in a Comparative Framework: Does it Make for Secure Alliances in a Better World?' (2004) 9 *Eur Foreign Affairs Rev* 459 and A Toje, 'The 2003 European Union Security Strategy: A Critical Appraisal' (2005) 10 *Eur Foreign Affairs Rev* 117.

[49] See B Martenczuk, 'Community Cooperation Policy and Conflict Prevention' in V Kronenberger and J Wouters (eds), *The European Union and Conflict Prevention—Policy and Legal Aspects* (The Hague: TMC Asser Press, 2004) 189.

4.1. Agreements with third countries on participation in conflict prevention operations

In carrying out its relations with the outside world, the EU is endowed with express treaty-making power. This has been the case with the European Community since its inception: on the one hand, primary law has provided for an increasing number of areas in which the Community, either on its own or with the Member States, could negotiate, conclude, and implement international agreements;[50] on the other hand, the Court developed the principle of implied competence which enabled the Community to act externally in areas where internal competence has been provided.[51] The development of the Community's external policies originates in its legal personality, which is expressly laid down in Article 281 EC.[52] It is the absence of express legal personality of the Union which renders the negotiation and conclusion of international agreements in the area of ESDP an issue of acute significance and sensitivity. Article 24 TEU enables the Council to conclude agreements with one or more states or international organizations in implementation of the CFSP provisions. Such agreements are negotiated by the Presidency, assisted by the Commission as appropriate.[53] The debate centred around this procedure, as to whether the Union is endowed with implied legal personality, is beyond the scope of this chapter.[54] It should just be noted that Article I-7 Constitutional Treaty would endow the Union with express legal personality.

This section focuses on agreements establishing a framework for the participation of third countries in EU crisis management operations. Such agreements have been concluded so far with Bulgaria,[55] Iceland,[56] Norway,[57] Romania,[58] and Ukraine.[59] To that effect, the structure of the above agreements and the

[50] One of the first such areas has been the Common Commercial Policy (Art 133 EC).

[51] Case 22/70 *Commission* v *Council (re European Road Transport Agreement)* [1971] ECR 263.

[52] On the development of the Community's external competences, see P Eeckhout, *External Relations of the European Union* (Oxford: OUP, 2004) chs 2–4 and P Koutrakos, *EU International Relations Law* (Oxford: Hart Publishing, 2006) chs 1–3.

[53] In accordance with Art 24(2) and (3) TEU, such agreements are concluded unanimously when they cover an issue for which unanimity is required for the adoption of internal decisions and by qualified majority when adopted in order to implement a Joint Action or common position. According to Art 24(5), '[n]o agreement shall be binding on a Member State whose representative in the Council states that it has to comply with the requirements of its own constitutional procedure; the other members of the Council may agree that the agreement shall nevertheless apply provisionally'. Finally, Art 24(6) TEU provides that such agreements shall be binding on the EU institutions.

[54] See, for instance: E Denza, *The Intergovernmental Pillars of the European Union* (Oxford: OUP, 2002) at 174–7; R A Wessels, *The European Union's Foreign and Security Policy—A Legal Institutional Perspective* (The Hague: Kluwer Law International, 1999) ch 7; S Marquardt, 'The Conclusion of International Agreements under Art 24 of the Treaty on European Union' in V Kronenberger (ed), *The European Union and the International Legal Order: Discord or Harmony?* (The Hague: TMC Asser Press, 2001) 333. [55] [2004] OJ L-46/50.

[56] [2005] OJ L-67/2.   [57] [2005] OJ L-67/8.   [58] [2005] OJ L-67/14.

[59] [2005] OJ L-182/29.

mechanisms established therein are identical. In terms of their scope, they apply to both civilian and military crisis operations and emphasize the decision-making autonomy of the Union, both in their preamble and in a standard clause repeated in all Agreements.

The agreements address a number of issues which are bound to arise in any such operation. First, the agreement sets out the general provisions which would govern such operations. The third State undertakes to associate itself with the Joint Action by which the Union decides to conduct a crisis management and with any subsequent Joint Action in accordance with the specific provisions of the agreement and any other subsequent arrangement. The status of personnel and forces of the third country is defined with reference to the specific agreement concluded between the Union and the state in which the operation is conducted. As for jurisdiction, the third country is to exercise it over its personnel without prejudice to the above agreement and is also responsible for answering any claims from or concerning any of its personnel. Both the Union and the third party to each agreement undertake to make a declaration including a waiver of claims against each other.

The agreements, then, set out the general conditions for participation in civilian crisis management operations. In terms of the chain of command, personnel seconded by the third State should conduct themselves solely with the interests of the EU operation in mind, whilst remaining under the full command of their national authorities. The Head of Mission exercises operational control and is responsible for the day-to-day management of the operation whereas a National Contingent Point of Contact, appointed by the third State, represents that state's contingent in the operation and is responsible for its day-to-day discipline.

Similarly, the agreements set out the general conditions for participation in military crisis management operations, under which all forces and personnel remain under the full command of their national authorities which transfer the operational and tactical command to the EU Operation Commander. The third States have the same rights and obligations in terms of the day-to-day management of the operation as any participating EU Member State and their national contingent is represented by a Senior Military Representative who is to consult with the EU Force Commander.

Finally, there is provision for further technical and administrative arrangements should they prove necessary for the implementation of the agreements. These are to be concluded, on behalf of the EU, by the CFSP High Representative. In case of non-compliance, the agreements provide for the right of termination by serving notice of one month whereas there is a general provision for the right of denunciation effective six months after receipt of notification. Finally, the agreements with Norway, Iceland, and Ukraine provide for their review at least every three years, whereas those with Bulgaria and Romania provide for their amendment by mutual written agreement between the parties.

The alignment of third countries with the Union's approach to international affairs in specific cases has not been uncommon. On various occasions, third countries have been associated with Common Positions adopted by the Council under Title V TEU.[60] Indeed, following the insertion of Article 24 TEU, a number of agreements were concluded on the participation of third countries in the military crisis management operation in Bosnia and Herzegovina (Operation ALTHEA), namely with Switzerland,[61] Morocco,[62] Argentina,[63] New Zealand,[64] and Chile.[65] However, the conclusion of agreements setting out the general framework for participation in crisis management operations is indicative of a gradual shift from a case-by-case approach to a more clearly thought out and managed approach.[66] In policy terms, this signifies the commitment of the Union to act along with third States in areas covered by its ESDP. Furthermore, their content as well as their raison-d'être also illustrate a more structured approach to the practical aspects of the Union's crisis management operations. In the light of the emphasis on the political choices underpinning coherence and the latter's indeterminate content, which is bound to be ascertained on a case-by-case basis, as outlined above in this chapter, this approach provides a noteworthy alternative to the quest for efficiency in the conduct of ESDP operations. Viewed from this angle, it is consistent with the approach adopted by EU institutions in other areas where foreign and security policy interacts with EU external policies.

4.2. Economic sanctions against third countries

Sanctions against third countries are imposed under Articles 301 and 60 EC by a Council Regulation adopted by QMV following the adoption of a Common Position under Title V TEU.[67] In December 2003 the Council approved a set of guidelines on implementation and evaluation of sanctions in the framework of the CFSP.[68] These guidelines were drawn up by the Working Party of Foreign Relations Counsellors and then discussed by the Political Committee which submitted them to COREPER. They constitute the first effort by the EU to enhance the effectiveness of its sanctions regimes in a comprehensive manner. In the context of this analysis, the guidelines are interesting both for their content and for what they omit. Their scope covers 'the entire process from imposition of restrictive measures, through effective monitoring of their application, to developing a more consistent approach for reporting and assessing the effectiveness of the restrictive measures'.[69]

---

[60] See V Kronenberger, 'Common Foreign and Security Policy: International Law Aspects of the Association of Third States with the Common Positions of the Council of the European Union' in Kronenberger (ed), n 54, above, 351.   [61] [2005] OJ L-20/42.

[62] [2005] OJ L-34/47.   [63] [2005] OJ L-156/22.   [64] [2005] OJ L-127/28.

[65] [2005] OJ L-202/40.

[66] To that effect, see the first preambular paragraph to all Council Decisions concluding the Agreements, eg, Council Dec 2005/495/CFSP on the Agreement with Ukraine [2005] OJ L-182/28.

[67] See Koutrakos, n 26, above, ch 4.

[68] Council conclusions 15535/03 (PESC 356) of 8 December 2003.

[69] PESC 757, FIN 568 at para 2.

The guidelines lay down the main principles underpinning issues such as targeted measures, exemptions, expiration or review of sanctions, implementation of UN Security Council Resolutions, and jurisdiction. In various cases, they put forward standard wording to be applied to various matters and they raise the issue of the time difference between the adoption of the Common Position and that of the Council Regulation. In addition, the establishment of a 'Sanctions Formation' of the Foreign Relations Counsellors Working Group was approved with the express aim of sharing experience and developing best practice in the implementation and application of sanctions. Consistently with the overall tenor of the guidelines, the mandate of this new Council body is defined in terms of specific, practical aspects of sanctions management, therefore including, amongst others, collecting all information available on alleged circumventions of EU sanctions and other international sanctions regimes, assisting in evaluating the results and difficulties in the implementation of sanctions, and examining all relevant technical issues relating to the implementation of EU sanctions.

The guidelines on sanctions have a clear focus on the practical and specific issues that the management of sanction regimes raises. Not only is this document short on statements of merely rhetorical significance, but it also states quite early on that it does not address the political process leading to the decision to impose or repeal restrictive measures.[70] Viewed as an effort to disentangle the effectiveness of the implementation of sanctions from the web of political difficulties and legal complexities that surround the adoption of such measures, the guidelines illustrate a useful and interesting approach.

4.3. Military capabilities

Another area whose regulation and management test the effectiveness of ESDP operations is the development of the Union's military capabilities. The serious problems facing the European industries in that area, both structural and economic, are well-known.[71] However, the fragmentation of defence industries has proved very difficult for the Member States to address. This has been partly due to the self-evident political sensitivity of the issue and partly due to the somewhat ambiguous legal position of defence industries which is widely perceived, albeit unjustifiably, to be entirely beyond the Community legal framework.[72] However, a highly fragmented European defence industry riddled with economic problems would always prove to be an inherent limit to the effectiveness and efficiency of ESDP. It leads to duplication of certain resources and scarcity of others, it slows

[70] Ibid, at para 2.

[71] See K Hartley, 'Defence Industries' in P Johnson (ed), *Industries in Europe: Competition, Trends and Policy Issues*, 2nd edn (Cheltenham: Edward Elgar, 2003).

[72] See Koutrakos, n 26, above, at 182–97. See also M Trybus, 'The EC Treaty as an Instrument of Defence Integration: Judicial Scrutiny of Defence and Security Exceptions' (2002) 39 CML Rev 1347.

down the ability of multinational forces to engage in rapid deployment, it makes the practical arrangements for the effective deployment of such forces very difficult to manage, and it undermines the ability of the EU to invest in defence research and development.

In an initiative undertaken in the late 1990s, the European Commission put forward a comprehensive approach to the restructuring and consolidation of the defence industries of the Member States. Based on an assessment of the economic problems and challenges facing their fragmented state in an increasingly globalized market,[73] it adopted a document entitled, *Implementing European Union Strategy on Defence Related Industries.*[74] This suggests a detailed set of legal measures which was comprehensive in scope and covered areas such as public procurement, defence and technological development, standardization and technical harmonization, competition policy, structural funds, export policies, and import duties on military equipment. This document articulated the need for a wide synergy of Community, EU, national, and international measures whilst affirming the link between their subject matter and the core of national sovereignty.

However, this initiative was not taken up by the Member States. In response to a request by the European Parliament, the Commission returned to the issues raised by the need for the consolidation of the defence industries in 2003. In a document adopted that year, it reiterated the need for a coherent cross-pillar approach to the legal regulation of defence industries with special emphasis on standardization, intra-Community transfers, competition, procurement, exports of dual-use goods, and research.[75]

The process of the drafting and signing of the Constitutional Treaty has led to a renewed focus on the problems and challenges facing the defence industries. It is recalled that the Constitutional Treaty provides for the establishment of an agency, the European Defence Agency, which is specialized in the area of defence capabilities development, research, acquisition, and armaments (Article I-41(3) subpara 2). According to that provision, the function of the Agency will be:

... to identify operational requirements, to promote measures to satisfy those requirements, to contribute to identifying and, where appropriate, implementing any measure needed to strengthen the industrial and technological base of the defence sector, to participate in defining a European capabilities and armaments policy, and to assist the Council in evaluating the improvement of military capabilities.

At the time of writing, to state that the Constitutional Treaty is moribund is to display an optimistic disposition. And yet, the process of its drafting and its

---

[73] COM(96) 10 final, *The Challenges Facing the European Defence-Related Industry. A Contribution for Action at European Level*, adopted on 24 January 1996.

[74] COM(97) 583 final, adopted on 12 November 1997.

[75] COM(2003) 113 final, *European Defence—Industrial and Market Issues. Towards an EU Defence Equipment Policy* (adopted on 11 March 2003).

signing gave rise to a certain momentum in relation to the management of the
economic aspects of security. This has been apparent at various levels. Following a
decision by the Thessaloniki European Council in June 2003, the Council set up
an intergovernmental agency in the field of defence capabilities. Having responded
to the European Council, the Council adopted a Joint Action on the establishment
of the European Defence Agency in July 2004.[76] The objective of the Agency is 'to
support the Council and the Member States in their effort to improve the EU's
defence capabilities in the field of crisis management and to sustain the ESDP as it
stands now and develops in the future' without prejudice to either the competences
of the EC or those of the Member States in defence matters.[77]

On another front, the Commission responded to the European Security
Strategy[78] by focusing on 'the combined and relatively untapped strengths of the
"security" industry and the research community in order to effectively and innova-
tively address existing and future security challenges'.[79] To that effect, it has now
produced a document about the need to focus on research and development in the
area of security.[80] The main tenet of this proposal is the development of a coherent
security research programme at EU level which would be 'capability-driven, targeted at the development of interoperable systems, products and services useful
for the protection of European citizens, territory and critical infrastructures as
well as for peacekeeping activities' whilst also directly linked to 'the good functioning of such key European services as transport and energy supply'.[81] Four different areas are targeted: consultation and cooperation with users, industry, and
research organizations under the umbrella of a European Security Research
Advisory Board; the establishment of a European Security Research Programme
implemented as a specific programme with its own set of procedures, rules for participation, contracts, and funding arrangements; cooperation with other institutional actors established under the CFSP and ESDP framework and especially the
European Defence Agency; and the establishment of a structure which would
ensure the flexible and effective management of the European Security Research
Programme. In addition to the above, the Commission also adopted a Green
Paper on Defence Procurement.[82] In this document it asks for the clarification of
the legal status of defence industries under Community law and suggests the
adoption of a Directive which would coordinate the award of contracts on defence
goods, services, and work.

Some of the above developments are examined elsewhere in this volume.[83]
In terms of this analysis, suffice it to point out that there is a thread which brings

---

[76] 2004/551/CFSP [2004] OJ L-245/17. See also Council Dec 2003/834/EC creating a team to
prepare for the establishment of the agency in the field of defence capabilities development, research,
acquisition, and armaments [2003] OJ L-318/19.   [77] Ibid, Arts 2(1), 1(2), and 2(2).
[78] See n 1, above.
[79] COM(2004) 72 final, *Towards a Programme to Advance European Security through Research and
Technology.*   [80] COM(2004) 590 final, *Security Research: The Next Step.*
[81] Ibid, at 4.   [82] COM(2004) 608 final.
[83] See A Georgopoulos, Chapter 9 of this volume.

the above developments together: they illustrate a clearer focus on the elaboration of practical mechanisms which would enable the implementation of a more efficiently managed ESDP. This emphasis on the management of ESDP is quite clear in relation to the objectives outlined and the work carried out by the European Defence Agency. Its Chief Executive, Mr Nick Witney, stated that:

one element of our work programme for [2005] is to come back to our Steering Board by the end of the year with some sensible performance measures . . . Performance measures I have in mind include a financial target for spending an increasing proportion of European defence R&T funds on a collaborative basis and possibly something based on criteria for 'usability' of forces, which NATO has pioneered.[84]

This emphasis on the management of military capabilities is also illustrated by some of the short-term projects on the development of which the Agency has focused, namely a command control and communication study, armoured fighting vehicles, and unmanned aerial vehicles.

The clearer focus on the management of defence industries has produced some interesting results. In November 2005 the Defence Ministers of all the Member States, except Denmark, agreed a voluntary code on defence procurement which would take effect on 1 July 2006.[85] This is a voluntary, non-binding intergovernmental regime aiming at encouraging Member States to apply competition rules on a reciprocal basis on contracts worth more than €1m and without prejudice to their rights as laid down in primary law. Member States undertake to ensure 'maximising fair and equal opportunities' for all suppliers based in other Member States by publicizing procurement opportunities through a single online portal provided by the EDA. They also undertake to introduce transparent and objective criteria for selecting bidders and awarding contracts.

Furthermore, in December 2005, the Commission reiterated its intention to work towards the possibility of the adoption of a Directive on public procurement which would apply in cases not covered by the exceptional proviso of Article 296 EC or in cases where the Member States chose not to rely upon it. The Commissioner responsible for Internal Market and Services pointed out that:

. . . action to clarify and improve EU law on defence procurement is imperative. We must now put our foot on the gas. The future of Europe's defence industry is at stake. To deliver real benefits we are almost certainly going to have to go beyond a code of conduct and an interpretative communication.[86]

It is early to ascertain the precise practical implications that the developments outlined in this section may produce in terms of the effectiveness of ESDP. Their intergovernmental features are all too clear, be it in terms of the organization and

---

[84] Interview in (2005) *NATO Rev* Issue 1, available at <http://www.nato.int/docu/review/2005/issue1/english/interview_b.html>.
[85] <http://ue.eu.int/ueDocs/cms_Data/docs/pressData/en/misc/87058.pdf>.
[86] IP/05/2534 of 6 December 2005.

tasks of the EDA or the nature of the undertakings laid down in the Code of Conduct. However, to dismiss them for this reason as irrelevant would be to ignore the legal and political context within which these developments arise. A gradual and steady shift of emphasis on a clearer definition of the international role of the Union has followed the drafting and signing of the Constitutional Treaty. In terms of its content and objectives, that Treaty gave prominent position to the international role of the EU. This was also clearly illustrated by the Rome Declaration, adopted at the European Council summit in October 2003, which launched the 2004 Intergovernmental Conference. In the area of ESDP, and its ultimate fate notwithstanding, the Constitutional Treaty created a momentum which is illustrated by the above developments. This momentum appears to be characterized by a proceduralization of the relevant policies and a shift of emphasis on the elaboration of structured and practical tools aiming at addressing specific aspects of ESDP.

That this momentum and the initiatives to which it has given rise are clearly focused on the management of security and defence is not only welcome but also consistent with the development of the law of EC external relations. The case law on the competence of the Community to negotiate and conclude international agreements and the extent to which it coexists with the Member States is interesting in this respect. For instance, the Court of Justice has consistently sanctioned the formula of mixity, whereby the Community and the Member States conclude an international agreement together, by rendering exclusivity for the Community competence the exception rather than the rule.[87] Instead, it has developed a variety of mechanisms aiming at ensuring the effective management of mixity which vary in nature, including: a wide, albeit rather ill-defined, construction of the Court's jurisdiction to interpret mixed agreements;[88] an increasingly prominent focus on the principle of close cooperation which binds both the Member States and the Community institutions in the process of negotiation, conclusion, and application of international agreements;[89] and an increasingly prominent role for national courts in the process of the application of mixed agreements.[90] The mechanisms aiming at the effective management of EC external relations summarized above are intrinsically interlinked—it is their cumulative effects which determine an ever-developing system of external relations.[91]

---

[87] See *Opinion 1/94 (WTO Agreements)* [1994] ECR I-5267 and the *Open Skies* rulings such as Case C-467/98 *Commission* v *Denmark* [2002] ECR I-9519. For an analysis of this line of case law, see Eeckhout, n 52, above at chs 2–3 and Koutrakos, n 52, above at chs 1 and 3.

[88] See P Koutrakos, 'The Interpretation of Mixed Agreements under the Preliminary Reference Procedure' (2002) 7 *Eur Foreign Affairs Rev* 25.

[89] See *Ruling 1/78* [1978] ECR 2151 at paras 34–36, *Opinion 2/91 (re: ILO)* [1993] ECR I-1061 at para 36, *Opinion 1/94, (WTO Agreements)* [1994] ECR I-5267 at paras 108–9, and *Opinion 2/00 (re: Carthagena Protocol)* [2001] ECR I-9713 at para 18,

[90] See, for instance, Case C-89/99 *Schieving-Nijstad vof and Others and Robert Groeneveld* [2001] ECR I-5851.

[91] This theme, and its links to the regulation and management of the internal market, is developed in P Koutrakos, 'The Elusive Quest for Uniformity in EC External Relations' (2002) 4 Cambridge Ybk of Eur Legal Studies 243. Case C-459/03 Commission v Ireland (re: MOX Plant) [2006] ECR I-4635, paras 175–82.

The increasing activity on the economic aspects of security, and the momentum in the development of ESDP, with their emphasis on the incremental management of clearly-targeted areas, may prove to be a significant component of the overall system of policies shaping the Union's international role as defined in the *European Security Strategy*.

5. Conclusion

This chapter outlined a number of issues raised by the efforts of the Union institutions and the Member States to structure and carry out the ESDP in an effective manner which would also ensure its consistency and coherence with other EU external policies. By examining the normative dimension of the requirement of consistency and the central constitutional role assumed by the Court of Justice and, on the other hand, the inherently political choices which underpin the definition and assessment of coherence, it highlighted the two ever-present factors which the quest for effective action would have to take into account. The momentum characterizing recent developments on the organization and practical underpinnings of ESDP appears to complement these parameters in an interesting and useful manner. By focusing on the management of areas central to the effective conduct of ESDP, the Union institutions and the Member States develop an additional mechanism to link the Union's security policy to the general system of EU external relations law. In practical terms, neither the approach of the Court of Justice, nor individual political initiatives, nor the specific tools for managing the practical underpinnings of ESDP would ensure, in themselves, the effectiveness of ESDP and its coherence and consistency with other external policies. Instead, it is the interaction of these approaches and their cumulative effects which would determine the extent to which the Union succeeds in 'asserting its identity on the international scene'.

12

EU-NATO Relations: Consistency as a Strategic Consideration and a Legal Requirement

*Fabien Terpan**

1. Introduction

During the Cold War, Europeans and Americans were not always of the same opinion regarding the future of the Atlantic Alliance. The USA wanted the Europeans to increase their defence spending in order to better contribute towards a collective defence and they placed the emphasis on interoperability with European soldiers working alongside US forces. The Europeans wanted to prevent the de-coupling which could have resulted from a US proposal being detrimental for the Alliance (such as the US Strategic Defence Initiative). These disagreements, however, had limited practical impact, because the allies had no choice but to share the same strategic goal: facing the USSR.

At the end of the Cold War, it was questionable whether NATO still retained a purpose.[1] Thanks to a shift in its strategy, the Alliance found a new raison d'être, both in Europe[2] and 'out of area'. At a Rome summit, in November 1991, NATO heads of state and government adopted a strategic concept[3] which took into account the new international context. They decided that NATO should not rely so much on nuclear weapons and that the size of NATO's integrated military

* Maître de conférences in public law, Institute of Political Studies, Grenoble, France. All website addresses cited were active on 17 October 2006, unless otherwise specified.

[1] A Forster and W Wallace, 'What is NATO for?', (2001–2) *Survival*, 43(4) 107–22; R D Asmus, R D Blackwill, and F S Larrabee, 'Can NATO Survive?', *Washington Quarterly*, Spring 1996, 79.

[2] Ensuring that the US would remain engaged strategically on the European continent, preserve the relationship between the USA and European countries, reach out to the newly sovereign states of Central Europe, and help shape Russia's future.

[3] The Alliance's Strategic Concept, Approved by the Heads of State and Government Participating in the Meeting of the North Atlantic Council in Washington DC on 23 and 24 April 1999, in M Rutten (ed), *From St Malo to Nice, European Defence: Core Documents*, Chaillot Paper 47, May 2001, 24.

forces should be reduced in order to improve their mobility, flexibility, and adapt-
ability. Rapid reaction capability, as well as key resources like communications,
command, control and intelligence (C3I), or strategic airlift, were acknowledged
as the main instruments required, facing the biggest security risks of the post-Cold
War era, ie, ethnic and regional crises. Whereas a collective defence capability was
maintained, a broader role was assigned to NATO, including security dialogue
and cooperation—especially with new partners in Central and Eastern Europe—
as well as crisis management and peacekeeping. NATO's military command structure and defence planning were also adapted in the light of future requirements
for crisis management and peacekeeping.

Despite these positive steps towards adapting the role of NATO, transatlantic
relations have faced new challenges[4] and the necessity to retain NATO does not
seem to be so obvious for all concerned. Whereas the USA is willing to go it alone
instead of cooperating with its European partners—especially since 11 September
2001—the Europeans want to play a more active role in international politics by
developing a Common Foreign and Security Policy (CFSP),[5] strengthened by a
European Security and Defence Policy (ESDP).[6] At a Maastricht summit, in
February 1992, the EU began to craft its own post-Cold War destiny. As a result,
the parallel processes in NATO and the EU have a profound impact on one
another, and the question of whether the CFSP/ESDP is compatible or not with
NATO inevitably arises.

By common agreement, NATO has retained control of collective defence, as
written in Article 5 of the Washington Treaty. However there is no formal
separation—or division of labour—between the operations that the EU could
undertake under Article 17 para 2 of the Treaty on European Union (the
so-called 'Petersberg tasks')[7] and those that NATO would lead. If EU-NATO
relations are to be fruitful, there must be consistency between what is decided
in both organizations with regard to security and defence matters. In both
NATO and the EU there is a legal basis for the development of a European
role in security and defence. When one looks at overall objectives and main
principles, there is consistency between the EU and NATO. This does not
guarantee that both organizations will evolve in the same direction: arrangements must be made in order to put this theory into practice. NATO-EU
relations are facing big challenges which require clarification from both the
Europeans and the Americans.

---

[4] J B Steinberg, 'An Elective Partnership: Salvaging Transatlantic Relations', [2003] *Survival*,
45(2) 113–46.

[5] F Terpan, *La politique européenne de sécurité commune de l'Union européenne* (Brussels: Bruylant,
2003).

[6] F Terpan (ed), *La politique européenne de sécurité et de défense, L'Union européenne peut-elle gérer
les crises?* (Toulouse: Presses de l'Institut d'études politiques de Toulouse, 2004).

[7] Humanitarian and rescue tasks, peacekeeping tasks, and tasks of combat forces in crisis management, including peacemaking.

2. Legal Basis for the Development of ESDI and ESDP

Both NATO and the EU have created legal means by which Europe is involved in security and defence matters, through the creation of a 'European Security and Defence Identity' (ESDI) within NATO and of a 'European Security and Defence Policy' (ESDP) within the EU.

During the 1990s, the term ESDI was used within both organizations. In a declaration of the Atlantic Council, at the end of the London summit (July 1990), the allies spoke of the 'creation of a European identity in security and defence'.[8] The same term was included in the first NATO strategic concept[9], adopted in Rome (November 1991), and a similar expression was used by the Europeans in a 'declaration on WEU (Western European Union)' added to the Maastricht Treaty (February 1992): 'WEU Member States agree on the need to develop a genuine European security and defence identity and a greater European responsibility on defence matters'.

In 1999, whereas ESDI was recognized as an essential part of the Alliance (Washington summit, April 1999),[10] the EU started to use the term ESDP (Cologne and Helsinki summits, June and December 1999).[11] This decision to build a European Union 'policy' within the framework of the CFSP—much more than a simple 'identity'—indicated a political will to exist outside NATO, but it also raised the question of the consistency between this new policy and NATO's ESDI. This question has not yet been clearly answered, if one looks at the political dimensions of transatlantic relations. However, there are, both in NATO and in the EU, legal requirements for consistency between ESDI and ESDP.

---

[8] London Declaration on a Transformed North Atlantic Alliance, Issued by the Heads of States and Government Participating in the Meeting of the North Atlantic Council, 5–6 July 1990, available at <http://www.nato.int/docu/comm/49-95/c900706a.htm>.

[9] The Alliance's New Strategic Concept, Adopted by the Heads of States and Government Participating in the Meeting of the North Atlantic Council in Rome on 7–8 November 1991, available at <http://www.nato.int/docu/comm/49-95/c911107a.htm>.

[10] We welcome the new impetus given to the strengthening of a common European policy in security and defence by the Amsterdam Treaty and the reflections launched since then in the WEU and—following the St Malo Declaration—in the EU, including the Vienna European Council Conclusions. This is a process which has implications for all Allies. We confirm that a stronger European role will help contribute to the vitality of our Alliance for the 21st century, which is the foundation of the collective defence of its members.

Washington Summit Communiqué, Issued by the Heads of State and Government Participating in the Meeting of the North Atlantic Council, in Washington, DC on 24 April 1999, Press Release NAC-S(99)64, available at <http://www.nato.int/docu/pr/1999/p99-064e.htm>.

[11] Declaration on Strengthening the European Common Policy on Security and Defence, European Council, Cologne, 3–4 June 1999, in Rutten (ed), n 3, above, 54. Presidency Conclusions, II. European Common Policy on Security and Defence, European Council, Helsinki, 10–11 December 1999, in Rutten (ed), n 3, above, 82.

2.1. The European Security and Defence Policy and its relations with NATO

2.1.1. *The Maastricht and Amsterdam treaties: compliance with NATO*

The treaties of Maastricht and Amsterdam, which paved the way for the creation of an ESDP, contain no provisions that really threaten the Atlantic Alliance.

In February 1992 the Treaty on European Union (TEU), adopted in Maastricht, created a 'common foreign and security policy', which 'shall include all questions related to the security of the Union, including the eventual framing of a common defence policy, which might in time lead to a common defence' (Article J4). The same article of the Treaty made it clear that the CFSP should comply with NATO:

The policy of the Union in accordance with this article shall not prejudice the specific character of the security and defence policy of certain Member States and shall respect the obligations of certain Member States under the North Atlantic Treaty and be compatible with the common security and defence policy established within that framework.

While the EU asked the WEU—as 'an integral part of the development of the Union'—'to elaborate and implement decisions and actions of the Union which have defence implications' (Article J.4–2), a declaration (No 30) issued by the then nine members of the WEU and included as an annex to the TEU confirmed that the WEU should 'act in conformity with the positions adopted in the Atlantic Alliance'.[12] As written in declaration No 30: 'WEU will be developed as the defence component of the European Union and as a means to strengthen the European pillar of the Atlantic Alliance'.[13]

In 1992–3 this idea of a 'European pillar', which derived from the aforementioned provisions of the TEU, could have two opposite meanings: the recognition of NATO's primacy or the creation of a European caucus within NATO. Some would argue that the use of the WEU as a means to implement a European defence policy was a sign that NATO was considered as the first priority. Others would say that the link between the WEU and the EU already showed a European will to be more autonomous and to possibly define common positions before Atlantic summits.[14]

---

[12] This requirement is limited to those Member States which are also members of the Atlantic Alliance.

[13] In the same declaration, it is also stated that: 'WEU will form an integral part of the process of the development of the European Union and will enhance its contribution to solidarity within the Atlantic Alliance'.

[14] In Maastricht, the EU has agreed that its representatives 'in international organizations' (NATO included) 'shall cooperate in ensuring that the common positions and common measures adopted by the Council are complied with and implemented' (Art J.6 of the Maastricht Treaty). This article was modified by the Treaty of Amsterdam: 'Member States shall coordinate their action in international organisations and at international conferences' (Article 19 of the consolidated version of the TEU).

Whilst the Treaty of Amsterdam brought a few modifications to the TEU, none changed the nature of the existing relationship between the EU and NATO. The article on security and defence (Article 17 of the consolidated version of the TEU) is now written as follows:

the common foreign and security policy shall include all questions relating to the security of the Union, including the progressive framing of a common defence policy...which might lead to a common defence, should the European Council so decide.

NATO's primacy seems to be reinforced by a direct reference to the defence requirements of the North Atlantic Treaty:

The policy of the Union in accordance with this Article shall not prejudice the specific character of the security and defence policy of certain Member States and shall respect the obligations of certain Member States, *which see their common defence realised in the North Atlantic Treaty Organisation (NATO), under the North Atlantic Treaty* and be compatible with the common security and defence policy established within that framework.

The only provision which could lead to divergences between the EU and NATO is the one related to the possibility of an integration of the WEU into the Union.[15] In this respect, the Treaty of Amsterdam can be seen as the starting point of a process leading to the integration of the main functions of the WEU within the EU.

2.1.2. *The institutionalization of the ESDP: between European autonomy and preservation of the Atlantic alliance*

Following the entry into force of the Treaty of Amsterdam on 1 May 1999, the Cologne European Council (June 1999)[16] decided that the role fulfilled by the WEU would be progressively undertaken by the EU. This decision meant that the EU itself would be in charge of the newly-created ESDP, which developed without a proper revision of the Treaty on European Union. The Cologne document did not place any emphasis on NATO, except in one phrase which stated that the European capability should not cause 'prejudice to NATO actions'.

This evolution was due to a profound change in the policy of the UK with regard to security and defence issues. At the Franco-British summit in Saint Malo in December 1998, Prime Minister Blair and President Chirac issued a brief statement which stated that the EU 'must have the capacity for autonomous action, backed up by credible military forces, the means to decide to use them, and a readiness to do so, in order to respond to international crises'.[17] This statement made the creation of an EU-based security and defence policy possible and at

---

[15] Article 17: 'The Union shall accordingly foster closer institutional relations with the WEU with a view to the possibility of the integration of the WEU into the Union, should the European Council so decide'.

[16] Declaration on Strengthening the European Common Policy on Security and Defence, European Council, Cologne, 3–4 June 1999, in Rutten (ed), n 3, above, 54.

[17] Joint Declaration, British-French Summit, Saint-Malo, 3–4 December 1998, in Rutten (ed), n 3, above, 8.

the same time made competition with NATO likely. Indeed, the declaration acknowledged that the EU would need appropriate structures and capabilities in situation analysis, sources of intelligence, strategic planning, ie, in areas where NATO and the USA had pre-eminence. Of course, this goal was to be conciliated with the necessity to avoid 'unnecessary duplication' with NATO's assets and structures, but it was symbolic of a new ambition.

The Saint-Malo declaration, by finding a compromise between Atlanticism and Europeanism, opened the way for the institutionalization of ESDP by the European Council in Cologne (June 1999), Helsinki (December 1999), and Feira (June 2000). ESDP was not given a proper legal basis but was set up through political declarations. Nevertheless, the decisions taken in 1999 by the European Council were in line with the dispositions of the Maastricht and Amsterdam treaties, especially regarding the issue of EU-NATO relations. The EU Member States stated that EU-led operations would only be undertaken in circumstances where NATO was not engaged, and they pointed out that unnecessary duplications with NATO structures and forces should be avoided. However, the decision taken by the Helsinki European Council to establish a 'Headline Goal' for EU Member States in terms of their military capabilities[18] was a challenge for NATO. Would the EU—with an effective capacity to undertake military operations—become a competitor to NATO?

The EU Constitutional Treaty[19] would have provided a clear legal basis for the ESDP, if the French and the Dutch had not rejected it. However, as far as NATO was concerned, Article I-41 para 2 of the Constitutional Treaty was equivalent to Article 17 para 1 TEU, with the same direct reference to NATO, including the notions of compatibility with NATO's security and defence policy and the emphasis on 'the obligations of certain Member States, which see their common defence realised . . . under the North Atlantic Treaty'. In the field of crisis management, the new treaty did not bring major improvements.

As far as territorial protection was concerned, the Constitutional Treaty would have had some impact on EU-NATO relations. In Article I-40 para 7, the possibility for Member States to help each other in case of an armed attack was anticipated:

If a Member State is the victim of armed aggression on its territory, the other Member States shall have towards it an obligation of aid and assistance by all means in their power, in accordance with Article 51 of the United Nations Charter.

This clause on mutual defence was written in a way that could be compatible with the neutrality of certain Member States, as it was not specified that each country

---

[18] The objective of the Headline Goal—popularly called the 'European rapid reaction force'—is to enable the EU, by the year 2003, to deploy and sustain for at least one year military forces of up to 60,000 troops to undertake the full range of the so-called Petersberg tasks.

[19] [2004] OJ C-310, 16 December 2004. See also M Trybus, Chapter 3 of this volume.

would have to use military means. However, aid and assistance were considered as legal obligations and as a commitment for automatic action. In this respect, Article I-40 para 7 was very close to Article 5 of the WEU Brussels Treaty, but it suffered from the same important limitation: mutual assistance was not a realistic option as the Europeans did not possess the means of territorial common defence. In the short term, there was no risk of real competition between NATO and the EU in collective defence as the development of a European defence capability was only hypothetical. Indeed, the building of integrated military structures still depended on a unanimous decision from the European Council. In the long term, the inclusion of a mutual assistance clause in the TEU could have been considered as another step towards the militarization of the EU. And a risk of competition— at least a potential one—could have resulted from the entry into force of the Constitution.

The solidarity clause of Article I-43 raised the same kind of questions. The wording of this article made it clear that the EU could use military means to protect a Member State, in other situations than an 'armed attack', that is to say outside the scope of Article I-40 para 7:

The Union and its Member States shall act jointly in a spirit of solidarity if a Member State is a victim of terrorist attacks or natural or man-made disasters. The Union shall mobilise all the instruments at its disposal, including the military resources made available by the Member States to prevent the terrorist threat on the territory of a Member State.

The solidarity clause has been somehow anticipated on a political level by a declaration on Combatting Terrorism made in March 2004. So the principle of solidarity against terrorism might have some kind of role, even if the Constitutional Treaty is not ratified. What consequences would EU solidarity have on EU-NATO relations? The answer is difficult to give as the concrete implications of solidarity have not been specified. It could be argued, however, that solidarity against terrorism is less demanding in terms of military resources and would not lead to unfruitful competition between the EU and NATO.

2.2. The building of an ESDI within NATO

It is doubtful whether the ESDP could have been created without the previous acceptance of the ESDI within the Alliance. In the early 1990s, the USA gave strong support to the idea of a European 'pillar' within NATO. This was also the position defended by some key EU Member States, especially the UK, which did not welcome —until 1999—any defence policy directly implemented within the EU framework, because it would destabilize NATO. At the end of the 1990s, the USA accepted that the EU should develop a more autonomous capacity by creating an ESDP related to NATO, but within the framework of the EU.

2.2.1. *A 'European identity in security and defence'*

When, in 1989, James Baker, as US Secretary of State, pronounced the term 'new atlanticism', he paved the way for the creation of a European pillar within NATO. As previously indicated, in 1990–1, NATO members agreed on the idea of a 'European identity in security and defence'.[20] Actually, it was not the purpose of the North Atlantic Treaty to increase the European contribution to crisis management, but the Treaty did not forbid such an evolution. There was no legal argument to restrain the Allies from building the ESDI through a political declaration.

In November 1990[21] a joint US-EC declaration acknowledged the process of European identity-building in the field of economy, foreign policy, and security. One month later, in the Brussels declaration of the North Atlantic Council, a reference was made to the efforts that the Europeans were making 'to strengthen the security dimension in the process of European political integration'. The ministers also stated that 'a European security identity and defence role, reflected in the construction of a European pillar within the Alliance, will not only serve the interests of the European states but also help to strengthen Atlantic solidarity'.[22]

However, the US attitude was somewhat ambiguous. For the Americans, the idea of a European pillar within NATO was a way to hinder the creation of a European defence policy outside NATO. In 1990–1 the reluctance of the US administration to accept the concept defended by the Franco-German tandem within the intergovernmental conference on political union was revealed. Mr J Dobbins, a Department of State official, met with European officials to convince them of the necessity of staying within the NATO framework.[23] The 'Bartholomew Telegram' sent to the WEU identified US pre-conditions for the creation of a CFSP.[24]

Despite these hesitations, the ESDI was officially recognized during the Rome summit in November 1991, whereas the CFSP, as defined by the Maastricht European Council, was welcomed by the Atlantic Council held in Brussels in December 1991. Later on, the assertion that ESDI is an integral part of NATO development was made on important occasions, especially during the meetings of the Atlantic Council in Brussels (January 1994) and Berlin (June 1996).

2.2.2. *A European 'capacity for autonomous action'*

The Washington summit of the Atlantic Council, in April 1999, was a major step in the development of the European defence policy. At this meeting, the creation

[20] London Declaration on a Transformed North Atlantic Alliance, Issued by the Heads of States and Government Participating in the Meeting of the North Atlantic Council, 5–6 July 1990, available at <http://www.nato.int/docu/comm/49-95/c900706a.htm>.

[21] *Bulletin of the European Union*, 11–1990.

[22] Final Communiqué, North Atlantic Council, Brussels, 17–18 December 1990, available at <http://www.nato.int/docu/comm/49-95/c901218a.htm>.

[23] K H Cerny, 'The US Gropes for a Policy toward Post-Cold War Europe' in Mario Telo (ed), *Vers une nouvelle Europe? Towards a New Europe?* (Brussels: Etudes Européennes, 1992) 160.

[24] M Anand, F Anthony, and W William, 'A Common European Defence?' (1992) 34(2) *Survival*, 105.

of the ESDP—officially announced two months later during the Cologne summit of the European Council—was accepted. The Heads of State and Government acknowledged 'the resolve of the European Union to have the capacity for autonomous action so that it can take decisions and approve military action where the Alliance as a whole is not engaged'.[25] By doing so, they admitted a certain degree of autonomy for the EU, but without making it clear what the term autonomy really meant. They not only accepted the building of an ESDI within NATO but also the development of an ESDP to be implemented outside the scope of the Alliance. Of course, this progress towards the acceptance of ESDP is still limited by the reaffirmation of the political primacy of NATO, ESDP operations being initiated 'where the Alliance as a whole is not engaged'.

Undoubtedly, the EU and NATO have created a legal basis for European actions in the field of security and defence. This is 'soft law'—declarations of the Atlantic Council, provisions of the TEU outside the scope of the European Court of Justice[26]—but soft law is enough to exert influence: the strengthening of the cooperation between the EU and NATO since 1992–3 has shown that declarations on ESDI-ESDP gave enough incentives to bring these two organizations closer together within a context that could have resulted in the complete opposite. That does not mean binding rules are useless. A permanent treaty could help to make EU-NATO relations clearer and would certainly encourage the member countries to discipline themselves, instead of making ESDI-ESDP a controversial subject. But, as we will argue later, some political clarifications are needed prior to the adoption of an EU-NATO treaty.

In any case, the process of building a European defence capability reached a peak with the adoption of a joint EU-NATO declaration on ESDP in December 2002,[27] which established a strategic partnership in crisis management. This partnership is based on the following principles: effective mutual consultation; autonomy of the EU and NATO in decision-making; respect for the UN Charter; and mutually reinforcing the development of the military capabilities within the two organizations.

The Allies have made clear the continued crucial role of NATO in crisis management and conflict prevention, and have reaffirmed that NATO remains the foundation of the collective defence of its members.[28] But at the same time, they have stated that a stronger European role will help contribute to the vitality of the Alliance, specifically in the field of crisis management. And they also welcomed

[25] Washington Summit Communiqué, available at <http://www.nato.int/docu/pr/1999/p99-064e.htm>.
[26] The provisions of the treaties concerning the powers of the Court of Justice do not apply to the provisions of Title V TEU (Common Foreign and Security Policy): see Art 46 TEU.
[27] EU-NATO Declaration on ESDP, 16 December 2002, Press Release (2002/142), available at <http://www.nato.int/docu/pr/2002/p02-142e.htm>.
[28] The Brussels and Washington treaties both contain a commitment for the allies to help each other in the event of external aggression.

the ESDP, and defined its purpose: adding 'to the range of instruments already at the European Union's disposal for crisis management and conflict prevention in support of the CFSP' and strengthening 'the capacity to conduct EU-led crisis management operations, including military operations', 'where NATO as a whole is not engaged'.[29]

Is the set of principles included in the declaration of December 2002 really coherent? Obviously, some crucial problems remain unsolved. Consultation must be effective, but should the allies consult each other under any circumstances? Should it be the case in a situation of urgency? Is respect of the UN Charter still considered as an important principle when the USA has decided to send military forces to Iraq without any resolution of the UN Security Council, just a few weeks after the adoption of the EU-NATO strategic partnership? The allies should make it clear what kind of 'capacity for autonomous action' they want for the EU. As the Europeans depend heavily upon US assets within NATO, it cannot be more than a cautious and limited form of autonomy.

The arrangements negotiated by the EU and NATO to strengthen their cooperation may help to understand how the aforementioned principles materialize.

3. Arrangements for Cooperation between the EU and NATO

Since the beginning of the 1990s, the allies have searched for practical ways in which to fully cooperate in the fields of security and defence. As early as 1991, while creating the CFSP, the Europeans took into account the necessity of strengthening cooperation between the WEU and NATO. The declaration on the WEU annexed to the Treaty of Maastricht stated that the:

WEU is prepared to develop further the close working links between WEU and the Alliance and to strengthen the role, responsibilities and contributions of WEU Member States in the Alliance. This will be undertaken on the basis of the necessary transparency and complementarity between the emerging European security and defence identity and the Alliance.[30]

Transparency and complementarity, which were primarily NATO concepts set out in 1990,[31] served to formalize arrangements between the WEU and NATO during the 1990s, and between the EU and NATO since 1999.

---

[29] EU-NATO Declaration on ESDP, n 27, above.

[30] Declaration on WEU, annex to the Treaty on European Union, 7 February 1992.

[31] As it was written by the Members' Heads of States and Governments in the declaration issued at the end of their meeting, 'we emphasise ... the importance of safeguarding complementarity and transparency between the two processes of the adaptation of the Alliance and of the development of European security co-operation': Final Communiqué, North Atlantic Council, Brussels, 17–18 December 1990, available at <http://www.nato.int/docu/comm/49-95/c901218a.htm>.

3.1. The arrangements between the (WEU) EU and NATO

3.1.1. *WEU-NATO arrangements*

The principles of transparency and complementarity, reflecting the concept of interlocking institutions, strongly influenced the negotiations between the WEU and NATO after the adoption of the Maastricht Treaty. Consultation on a permanent basis has been considered a privileged means for creating transparency between the WEU and NATO. In November 1992 a first document was adopted which established rules for contacts and meetings at different levels and rules for information-sharing.[32] Complementarity was the goal of operational agreements between NATO and the WEU (November 1992), NATO and Eurocorps (January 1993), and NATO and Eurofor-Euromarfor (May 1995). It was decided that forces made available to the WEU could be used in NATO operations, if WEU Member States decided thus. Additionally, the possibility of the WEU using NATO's Combined Joint Task Forces (especially the CJTF's headquarters) was agreed by Heads of State and Government at a NATO Brussels summit (January 1994).[33]

In June 1996, at NATO's Berlin and Brussels foreign and defence ministerial meetings,[34] NATO and the WEU negotiated larger framework agreements which served as the basis for creating a European pillar within NATO. The WEU would be permitted to make use of certain NATO assets—including staff officers, military equipment not available to the WEU Member States, the Deputy SACEUR (Supreme Allied Commander Europe), and NATO's new Combined Joint Task Forces—in circumstances when NATO as a whole chose not to be involved. NATO would identify types of 'separable but not separate' capabilities, assets and support assets—especially Headquarters (HQ), HQ elements, and command structures—which could be made available if the North Atlantic Council so decided.

To be more precise, the Berlin-Brussels agreements included the following points: taking WEU requirements into account in NATO's defence planning procedures for developing forces and capabilities;[35] introducing procedures for identifying NATO assets and capabilities on which the WEU might wish to draw with the agreement of the North Atlantic Council; establishing multinational European command arrangements within NATO, which could be used to prepare, support, command, and conduct an operation under the political control

---

[32] Agence Europe, 5–7 November 1992.

[33] The notion of Combined Joint Task Forces (CJTF) emerged during a meeting of the Defence Ministers in Travemünde, October 1993.

[34] Final Communiqué, North Atlantic Council, Berlin, 3 June 1996, Press Communiqué M-NAC-1(96)63, available at <http://www.nato.int/docu/pr/1996/p96-063e.htm>.

[35] The WEU began contributing to the Alliance defence planning process in 1997 by providing an input to the 1997 Ministerial Guidance.

and strategic direction of the WEU;[36] introducing consultation and information-sharing arrangements to provide the coordination needed throughout a WEU-led operation undertaken with NATO support; and developing military planning and exercises for illustrative WEU missions. These different elements are of crucial importance given that the WEU—and now the EU—does not have the capacity to act alone for most crisis management operations. A European mission should not be launched without using NATO assets, and more precisely US assets within NATO.

The concept of separable but not separate capabilities should allow the WEU to conduct an operation under its own political control and strategic direction. But the assets requested could be made available to the WEU by a decision of the North Atlantic Council taken on a case-by-case basis. Conditions for their transfer to the WEU, as well as for monitoring their use and for their eventual return or recall, would be registered in a specific agreement between the two organizations. During the operation, NATO would monitor the use of its assets, thanks to a political liaison with the WEU.[37]

The decisions taken in Berlin and Brussels helped the WEU to become operational but at the same time recognized—at least implicitly—NATO's primacy. The ministerial communiqué presented the Alliance as 'the essential forum for consultation among its members' (3 June 1996). Even if it was not said, it implied that NATO comes first and the WEU second. And the concept of NATO first means America's primacy, as a lot of capabilities in some critical areas—including large transport aircraft, intelligence, and satellite-based communications—belong not to NATO itself but to the USA.[38]

Following the Berlin-Brussels decisions, France and the USA had a major disagreement over command arrangements within NATO. France wanted the subordinate commands in Southern Europe[39] to be headed up by Europeans, which was refused by the USA. France also wanted the WEU to have an automatic right to use NATO assets whereas the USA preferred to keep a right of refusal, arguing that a lot of these assets were American. The French did not succeed in their efforts to convince the Americans, which was not surprising. At that time, the main shortcoming of the ESDI was clearly revealed. An evolution towards autonomy would imply a qualitative and quantitative leap in European

---

[36] Under these arrangements the Deputy Supreme Allied Europe Commander Europe (Deputy SACEUR) was given a distinct role, both in normal times and in the context of WEU-led operations, in relation to the forces to be made available to the WEU. Regarding WEU-led operations, it was decided that D-SACEUR could be used by the WEU as its own strategic commander. The practical arrangements were drawn up by the Atlantic Council in July 1997 and finally adopted in April 1999, during the Washington summit.

[37] A WEU-NATO Working Group held on 10 September 1998 reviewed procedures for consultations in the event of a WEU-led operation using NATO capabilities.

[38] NATO owns a very little in terms of capabilities: headquarters; command, control and communications; some logistics, and 17 airborne warning and control surveillance aircraft.

[39] Allied Forces Southern Europe (AFSOUTH).

military assets. Otherwise, autonomy would remain just a word and dependence a reality.

In April 1999, during the Washington Atlantic summit, the Berlin-Brussels arrangements were reaffirmed. In the Washington communiqué, the NATO allies stated their readiness to 'adopt the necessary arrangements for *ready access* by the European Union to the collective assets and capabilities of the Alliance'.[40] They also made this access more certain by saying that there would be '*assured* access to NATO planning capabilities able to contribute to military planning for EU-led operations' and a '*presumption of availability* to the EU of the pre-identified NATO capabilities and common assets for use in EU-led operations'. Of course, this is not a legally binding document. The commitment, which is only political, tries to compensate for the lack of European military means, but it certainly does not eliminate European reliance on US assets. Access to NATO capabilities may be 'assured', but nothing could force the USA to put its military forces under the control of the EU, if it does not want to do so.

In June 1999 the Cologne European Council decided that the European defence policy would be implemented by the EU directly and would integrate the WEU structures and functions necessary to accomplish the Petersberg missions. The WEU was maintained for two main reasons: the clause on mutual defence (Article V of the Brussels Treaty)[41] and the role of the Assembly as a useful parliamentary forum on security and defence issues. But as far as crisis management was concerned, the EU would not rely on the WEU any more, so it became necessary to negotiate new arrangements between the EU and NATO. In the meantime, NATO and the WEU continued to work together in order to complete and implement arrangements,[42] but only to make the necessary transition with the EU. At their meeting in Marseilles in November 2000, the WEU Ministers decided to suspend routine NATO-WEU consultation mechanisms.

3.1.2. *ESDP-NATO arrangements*

The ESDP-NATO relations are based on the mechanisms that were established between NATO and the WEU, especially the decisions taken in Berlin and Brussels in June 1996, including the concept of using separable but not separate NATO assets and capabilities for EU-led operations. However, with the transfer of responsibilities from the WEU to the EU, the relationship between NATO and the EU has taken on a new dimension, reflected in developments within

---

[40] Washington Summit Communiqué, available at <http://www.nato.int/docu/pr/1999/p99-064e.htm>.

[41] 'If any of the High Contracting Parties should be the object of an armed attack in Europe, the other High Contracting Parties will, in accordance with the provisions of Article 51 of the Charter of the United Nations, afford the Party so attacked all the military and other aid and assistance in their power.'

[42] Joint testing and evaluation of procedures were undertaken. A joint NATO-WEU crisis management exercise was held in February 2000.

both organizations, and leading to the creation of a 'strategic partnership' (December 2002).

If this strategic partnership is to be effective, two kinds of arrangements must be found between the EU and NATO, as stated in the Washington declaration in April 1999: a means of ensuring the development of effective mutual consultation, cooperation, and transparency between the EU and the Alliance; and practical arrangements for EU access to NATO planning capabilities and NATO's assets and capabilities. The full set of arrangements is referred to as 'Berlin Plus'. From 1999 to 2002 the EU and NATO were blocked from formalizing the arrangements because of manoeuvres by Greece and Turkey. 'Berlin Plus' was finalized in March 2003.

As far as mutual consultation, cooperation, and transparency are concerned, the dialogue between the Alliance and the EU has steadily intensified in accordance with the decisions taken in Washington. During the European Council summit in Cologne in June 1999, the EU decided to develop arrangements for full consultation, cooperation, and transparency with NATO. At Santa Maria de Feira (June 2000), the EU added that 'consultations and cooperation' should be developed regarding 'full respect for the autonomy of EU decision-making', and proposed to NATO. This would involve the creation of four joint NATO-EU Ad Hoc Working Groups to discuss security issues such as: procedures for the exchange of classified information and intelligence; modalities for EU access to Alliance assets and capabilities; capability goals (including issues relating to the Alliance's defence planning system); and the definition of permanent arrangements for EU-NATO consultation. These procedures have been working since mid-2000, allowing the Europeans to defend common positions and to make clear what the EU expects from NATO.

Meetings of the European Council in Nice and of the North Atlantic Council in Brussels in December 2000 registered further progress. Both organizations agreed that consultation and cooperation would be developed between them on questions of common interest relating to security and effective defence and crisis management, so that crises could be met with the most appropriate military response. An exchange of letters took place in January 2001 between the Secretary General of NATO and the Swedish Presidency of the EU, defining the scope of cooperation and the modalities of consultation between the two organizations: consultation between the EU Political and Security Committee (COPS) and the Atlantic Council (every two months); consultations between ministers (every six months), military committees (four times a year), Secretary General and military staff (on a routine basis). According to the arrangements, both organizations are committed to stepping up consultations in times of crisis. In March 2003 a NATO-EU Agreement on the security of information,[43] part of the larger 'Berlin

---

[43] Agreement between the EU and NATO on the security of information, [2003] OJ L-80/36, 27 March 2003.

plus' arrangements, was signed, covering the exchange of classified information under reciprocal security protection rules. This document was meant to facilitate consultations in the context of a crisis management operation (especially an EU-led operation making use of NATO assets and capabilities). And specific arrangements were set out to ensure that the EU and NATO would consult each other in the context of an EU-led crisis management operation using NATO assets.

Finally, on the basis of a document approved by the European Council in December 2003 and called 'European Defence: NATO/EU Consultations, Planning and Operations', in 2005 the EU set up a permanent cell at SHAPE and NATO established permanent liaison arrangements with the EU Military Staff (EUMS).

As far as EU access to NATO assets is concerned, the decisions made in Washington (April 1999) were reflected in the declarations issued by the European Council in Cologne (June 1999) and Feira (June 2000). In Nice (December 2000), the European Council adopted a document on EU access to NATO which implemented the Washington 1999 declaration. The 'Berlin Plus' arrangements, finalized on March 2003, provided the basis for NATO-EU cooperation in crisis management by allowing EU access to NATO's collective assets and capabilities for EU-led operations. On this subject, the arrangements cover four main elements.

The first is assured EU access to NATO planning. At the early stages, before a decision has been taken to launch an operation, the EU Military Staff works in close cooperation with SHAPE in Mons to define the military strategic options. After the decision is taken on the basis of 'Berlin Plus', NATO provides the operational planning required. The second element is that NATO should make available a European command option for EU-led operations. The Operation Commander should be NATO's Deputy SACEUR, who should play a pivotal role between the EU and NATO. So it is crucial in terms of European autonomy that the D-SACEUR is a European. The other command elements such as the EU Force Commander and the EU Force Headquarters deployed in the theatre should be provided either by the EU or by NATO. The third element gives details on the way the EU should use NATO assets and capabilities. These assets and capabilities are identified in a list and procedures for their release; monitoring, return, and recall are set out in a specific agreement (known as the 'Model Contract'). The last element is about arrangements for coherent and mutually-reinforcing capability requirements.

'Berlin Plus' is a series of useful arrangements tied together with the so-called 'Framework Agreement' which consists of an exchange of letters between the EU's High Representative and the NATO Secretary General dated 17 March 2003. Some uncertainties remain as to the extent to which the EU is able to act autonomously in crisis management, but this 'Berlin Plus' package of agreements forms the basis for practical work between the EU and NATO and has been implemented through several EU-led operations.

3.2. The EU-NATO arrangements in practice

A few days after the 'Berlin Plus' arrangements were finally adopted, the EU-led Operation Concordia succeeded the NATO-led mission 'Allied Harmony' in the Former Yugoslav Republic of Macedonia (31 March 2003). It was the first time that NATO assets had been made available to the EU. In line with the Berlin Plus arrangements, NATO's D-SACEUR was appointed as Operation Commander. NATO gave support to the EU on strategic, operational, and tactical planning. An EU-Operation Headquarters (OHQ) was set up at NATO's Supreme Headquarters Allied Powers Europe (SHAPE) in Mons, Belgium to assist the Operation Commander. And an 'EU Command Element' (EUCE) was established at AFSOUTH (Allied Forces Southern Europe) in Naples, Italy. The Chief of Staff of AFSOUTH also became Chief of Staff of the new EUCE, assisted by an EU Director for Operations. This structural organization guaranteed the link between the EU and NATO's operational chain of command.

Operation EUFOR-ALTHEA is another good example of the EU working within the framework of the Berlin Plus arrangements. Once again, NATO's D-SACEUR was the EU Operation Commander and the EU had access to NATO's assets and planning.

In addition to the ESDP operations under Berlin Plus, the EU-NATO arrangements have been implemented through close cooperation on issues such as terrorism and non-proliferation (in the wake of the terrorist attacks of 11 September 2001), or capability development.

As early as 12 September 2001, the Secretary General of NATO was participating in the deliberations of the EU General Affairs Council held on 12 September in order to analyse the international situation following the attacks the previous day. Since then, the EU and NATO institutions have exchanged information on their activities in the field of the protection of civilian populations against chemical, biological, radiological, and nuclear attacks. At the Prague Summit of NATO (2002) they agreed a new military concept for defence against terrorism, which states that NATO forces must be able to 'deter, disrupt and defend' against terrorists, wherever the interests of the allies demand it.

As far as capabilities are concerned, concerted planning of capabilities development and mutual reinforcement between NATO's Capability Commitment (Prague, 2002) and the EU's European Capabilities Action Plan (ECAP) have become an integral part of the NATO-EU agenda. NATO's experts provide military and technical advice, starting from the preparation to the implementation of the ECAP. A NATO-EU Capability Group was established in May 2003. The European capability shortfall is certainly the major problem in the building of a European defence identity. This is a problem that endangers the Atlantic Alliance as well as the ESDI. Solutions must be found in both organizations if ESDP is to be coherent with the development of a European pillar within NATO. In line with the Washington declaration and the Berlin Plus arrangements, the improvement of defence capabilities needs to be more than a common goal for the EU and NATO but the subject of close cooperation.

A lot has been done to develop the relationship between the EU and NATO, through EU treaties, the declarations of the Atlantic Council and the European Council, joint EU-NATO or EU-US declarations, EU-NATO agreements... A European security and defence identity has been built within NATO and a European security and defence policy has been accepted outside NATO. ESDI and ESDP have been developed in a consistent way and in a spirit of mutual reinforcement. However, a lot of ambiguities still remain in the definition of principles and rules which apply to EU-NATO relations.

4. The Challenges of EU-NATO Relations

EU-NATO relations currently face three major challenges. First, it has been often said that the EU would only take the lead of a crisis management operation in those situations where 'NATO as a whole is not engaged'. The idea was for this to lead to a kind of subsidiarity between the EU and NATO, but if this is the case a definition of this complex notion needs to be found. Secondly, and on a more practical level, EU-NATO rules and mechanisms should not be implemented if they do not allow European and NATO forces to be interoperable. Thirdly, the allies—especially EU Member States and the USA—need to make clear what kind of partnership they want.

4.1. Subsidiarity

According to the EU and NATO's official positions, the ESDP is not supposed to take the lead in crisis management operations when the USA intends to partici-pate. This principle of subsidiarity implies that common action is the rule, whereas separate actions should remain the exception. Whenever the Americans do not wish to be involved, the Europeans should decide to undertake an ESDP operation and might use NATO assets, if the NATO Council agrees. This situa-tion could pose three kinds of problems.

First, the principle that the EU will act only 'where NATO as a whole is not engaged' most probably implies that NATO comes first, the EU being a second-hand solution. It should be interpreted in a different way by countries, like France, which would deny this right of first refusal and give priority to a European military intervention even in those situations where NATO would be prepared to take the lead. However, there is no reason to oppose NATO to the EU since most of the EU's Member States are also members of the Atlantic Alliance, and provided that a NATO refusal does not prevent the EU from launching its own operation.

Consequently, the second problem is the capacity for the EU to act alone as a genuine military player. What would be done if NATO is not engaged because of an earlier US refusal and if the EU wants to launch an operation? There would be no problem if the EU possesses enough capabilities. As many European military forces are double-hatted, ie, available in both the EU and NATO, it could even be 'NATO-EU' assets and capabilities. But in these cases, when the EU would not have the capabilities needed, American assets within NATO would be required and, of course, the USA could not be forced to supply assets. Because of the European capabilities shortfall, the EU's process of 'autonomization' (cf 4.3. below) would certainly be hindered.

Thirdly, the principle of subsidiarity may lead to work-sharing between the EU and NATO. However, it may be difficult to find the right criteria for a clear distinction between the EU and NATO's sphere of action.

NATO could be involved in areas of European-American common interest, whereas Europeans and Americans would act alone in areas where no common interest can be identified. But giving a precise view of what the interests of each partner are could prove to be difficult. The EU cannot limit its scope of action to the European continent (plus Africa), whereas NATO would be more and more engaged outside Europe, especially in the Middle East, in accordance with current US priorities. Whilst the USA cannot decide that it is no longer interested in the affairs of the 'old continent', the EU cannot refuse to take on international responsibilities.

If a geographical criterion is not appropriate, the division of labour could be 'functional' and/or related to the kind of tasks implemented by each organization. For example, it could be: civilian tasks for the EU, military tasks for the USA and NATO; military-humanitarian tasks for the EU, peacekeeping and peace enforcement for the USA and NATO; peacekeeping for both the EU and the USA/NATO (depending on the situation), and peace enforcement for the USA and NATO. This kind of functional work-sharing is more likely to develop, because of the divergence of capabilities between Europe and the USA. The ESDP would be limited to low-intensity operations whereas the USA—within or with-out NATO—in providing the logistics, strategic air and sea-lift, intelligence, and air-power, would be in charge of the high-intensity operations. Such a division of labour would benefit those countries which do not advocate the idea of an autonomous Europe. But it is doubtful whether this solution could be politically sustainable. It would create different perceptions of risks and costs, and would not be a good incentive for political cooperation between Europeans and Americans. Moreover, some EU Member States would not accept such a limitation in the building of this policy, because they have higher ambitions for the ESDP: even if it is a long-term ambition, they advocate an enlargement of the Persterberg missions and an evolution towards a more powerful Europe.

Finally, there seems to be no division of labour when one looks at the declarations made by both organizations. What do the decisions taken in Washington

(April 1999) and in the subsequent meetings imply? The Washington communiqué acknowledged the possibility of the EU having a 'capacity for autonomous action', 'when the alliance as a whole is not engaged', without any detail or distinction between the situations where NATO should or should not be engaged. Moreover, the decision to make NATO's assets and capabilities available to the EU for EU-led operations will be taken 'on a case-by-case basis', according to NATO's new Strategic Concept adopted during the same Washington summit. Therefore, subsidiarity should be interpreted in a more pragmatic way. NATO should be engaged, anywhere and for any kind of operation, as agreed by all the allies. An ESDP operation should be decided, anywhere and for any kind of mission, if the EU Member States agree (and in those cases where no consensus exists in favour of a NATO operation). The ESDP operations should use NATO assets (including US assets) if all the allies (the USA included) agree, and should rely on its own capabilities whenever the USA refuses to allow NATO assets to be made available (if this were to be the case, the EU would be limited to very low-intensity ARTEMIS-type operations). At the moment, the European 'capacity for autonomous action' is rather limited, due to the EU's poor military capabilities. The more the military shortcomings are rectified, the more the capacity for autonomous action will increase. Thus, subsidiarity is a flexible concept which may lead to a different kind of work-sharing between the EU and NATO, depending on the political will of the member countries and most of all depending on the military capacity of the European countries.

4.2. Interoperability

NATO forces already work together in complex and difficult missions, some of them undertaken under the political control of the EU. Will it still be possible to do this in the near future? Or will the growing divergence between the USA and Europe's capabilities make cooperation on the operational level more and more difficult? Indeed, working together seems to be ever-increasingly hard for the allies because of the USA's lead in military technology. The USA's increasing preeminence in some areas such as communications or data processing—areas of major importance as they enable communication between forces and the coordination of the actions of those forces—is a problem. If cooperation is becoming a challenge because of the military gap between the allies, the Americans should decide to go it alone more and more often, instead of using NATO. This was certainly one reason for the US decision to undertake its own operation in Afghanistan, deliberately avoiding NATO. Interoperability has always been an issue within NATO. It may become a more serious problem in the post-Cold War era, because the trends in military modernization show a major discrepancy between the USA and EU Member States.

However, interoperability is considered a legal requirement within both NATO and the EU. In Washington (April 1999) NATO launched a Defence

Capabilities Initiative aimed at improving the Alliance's capabilities in five main areas: mobility; sustainability; effective engagement; survivability; and interoperability (focused on command, control and information systems). From the EU side, the ESDP provides a political incentive for modernizing Europe's military forces (the Headline Goal and the Capabilities development mechanism) and ensures that they remain interoperable with the US ones. The EU-NATO declaration on ESDP, in December 2002, recognized the need for arrangements to be put in place to ensure that the development of the capability requirements common to the two organizations continues to be mutually reinforcing. Consistency between NATO's Defence Capabilities Initiative (DCI) and the EU's capabilities development mechanism is of major relevance.[44]

4.3. A more balanced partnership between the EU and the USA?

The USA has long been concerned that European military weakness is harmful to NATO and to US interests. Europe's inability to contribute to high-end operations, in a more equal way, provides the arguments to those in the USA who see Europe as unwilling ever to take on its fair share of the burden.

The ESDP, whilst enhancing the European capacity for crisis management, addresses the constant refrain from the USA about 'burden sharing' within the Alliance. The USA should welcome ESDP because the Headline Goal focuses on the development of military capacities that can also contribute to NATO and its DCI. Moreover, both the EU and NATO's legal framework seem to guarantee that ESDP will not be detrimental to NATO. Nevertheless, ESDP continues to raise some issues of serious concern for the USA which need to be resolved to ensure that NATO and EU actions through ESDP will be compatible with one another. What if the ESDP develops outside NATO and is in competition with NATO's structure and processes? The (Helsinki) goal of creating a force of up to 60,000 people could not be seen as producing a real competitor for NATO (or the USA), but it seems to be enough to create US concern. As Ms Madeleine Albright said as long ago as 8 December 1998, a few days after the Franco-British summit at Saint-Malo, European autonomy could lead to three major threats, called the 'three-D's': decoupling, duplication, and discrimination.[45]

If defence planning takes place both within the EU and within NATO, there could be inconsistencies, incompatibilities, and inefficiencies. The ESDP may stimulate greater European defence spending, but that spending might go primarily on purchasing capabilities that NATO already has in abundance.

---

[44] Consistency between ESDP and NATO also implies that methods of defence planning be compatible, and implies that one methodology be implemented for important capabilities like command, control, communications, and intelligence (C3I).

[45] M K Albright, US Secretary of State, 'The Right Balance will Secure NATO's Future' *Financial Times*, 7 December 1998.

The ESDP could also lead some allies to believe that they can meet the military requirements of the Headline Goal without facing the more expensive demands of the NATO Defence Capabilities Initiative. The Headline Goal included the decision to create capabilities in those areas where the WEU was supposed to use NATO (US) assets under the Brussels-Berlin agreement (C3I, and strategic transport).[46]

The ESDP could also lead to a 'European caucus' within NATO. Despite its limited military capabilities, the EU has a potential that the Alliance does not, ie, a foreign policy which is still in the making but which covers the whole spectrum of policy actions, including crisis management. This is why the USA fears that the EU could become a new international power and a competitor for NATO and the USA. The major challenge is to find a clear definition of what has been called, in Washington, a European 'capacity for autonomous action'. On this specific and central issue, the Americans are opposed to the position defended by France—the most ambitious for ESDP among EU member—alone or within the Franco-German tandem.

4.3.1. The French position on ESDP and NATO

From a French viewpoint, the EU must be an autonomous actor in terms of both decision-making and operational capabilities. Autonomy implies a capacity to defend those positions which can differ from American ones and a capacity to act alone whenever a military intervention proves necessary.

However, the purpose of the French foreign policy is not to build the European defence policy in opposition to that of the USA, but to be able to make its own choices. NATO must be preserved but it must evolve in a way that 'allows the European security and defence identity to emerge', which implies 'an increased political cooperation among the Europeans inside NATO, and more and more responsibilities for the Europeans within the organization'.[47] For France, being part of the alliance is important provided that the EU plays a major role in it, and can talk on an equal basis with the USA.

However, France has been trying to convince the Americans and its EU partners that the preservation of the alliance is considered a priority goal. On several occasions during the 1990s France took a position in favour of the transformation of NATO and its adaptation to the post-Cold War era (eg, the adoption of a new NATO concept, and the decision to create Combined Joint Task Forces). France even announced, on 5 December 1995, its decision to participate in the meetings of the military Committee and of the Atlantic Council. This was an historical moment, as France had retired from the NATO military bodies in 1966, following a decision taken by President de Gaulle. Of course, the decision to become closer

---

[46] From the US point of view, the building of a European large air transport, for example, is not a priority because such capacities are already available within NATO (ie, US aircraft such as C-17 and C-130J).   [47] *Livre blanc sur la défense 1994* (Paris: Éditions 10/18, 1994) 66.

to the alliance was pragmatic: as French soldiers were involved in NATO crisis management operations (UNPROFOR), it was necessary for France to be present in those bodies whose decisions could have a direct impact on the situation of French military forces. But the decision was also political: it was meant to ensure that the ESDI was accepted inside NATO. As Charles Zorgbibe said, 'the end of the French exception could be considered, surprisingly, as a condition of a renewed position for France in international politics'.[48]

In the 1990s France did become closer to NATO as a new equilibrium between Europe and the USA had been reached within the Atlantic organization (whether thanks to new agreements between the EU and NATO or to the SHAPE reforms). However France's integration into NATO stopped when the USA refused to give the Southern-Europe Command to a European officer. The NATO Rapid Reaction Force is welcome, provided that 'it develops in a way compatible with the agreements reached by some Member States within the European Union'. 'The basic elements of this force should be used by one organization or the other without right of first use'.[49] And France would fully participate in the alliance if only 'the European defence identity is permanent and visible'[50] and provided that NATO continues to be adapted in a way which allows the EU to be autonomous in the management of crises.

This adaptation depends upon both the USA as a partner and the EU Member States. The Europeans need to have the military resources to be credible as far as crisis management is concerned. If they rely too much upon the US military assets available in NATO, they will not be able to make their own decisions. Of course, EU-US arrangements in NATO can help to clarify the situation. France is very aware of the need to ensure that Europeans have military control over operations that are led by Europeans. But whatever institutional and operational arrangements there can be, it will not make the EU autonomous if the success of the crisis management operation depends heavily on the military support given by the USA. Officially, Paris says that the EU should avoid unnecessary duplication of NATO assets. But no doubt this is mostly rhetoric. For France, the Europeans should make an effort in key domains (intelligence, command and communication systems, and transport) in order to enhance ESDP and make it more effective and credible. This could imply some duplication. Defence planning and headquarters are another good example: if the EU is to lead an operation, it cannot rely on CJTF headquarters.

---

[48] C Zorgbibe, '*Des guerres de sécession yougoslaves au rapprochement de la France de l'OTAN*' in Pierre Pascallon (ed), *Les interventions militaires extérieures de l'armée française* (Brussels: Bruylant, 1997) 273.

[49] *Sommet de l'OTAN, Conférence de presse de M Jacques Chirac, président de la république, après la réunion des chefs d'Etat et de gouvernement*, 21 novembre 2002, *Documents d'actualité internationale, No 2*, 15 January 2003, 60–3.

[50] *Discours du président Chirac à la réunion annuelle des ambassadeurs à L'Elysée*, 29 August 1996, *Documents d'actualité internationale, No 20*, 15 October 1996.

The French position was presented in this chapter because it is certainly the most ambitious in terms of European autonomy, but France is not the only country to provide ideas in the field of security and defence. Germany, Belgium, and other countries, including the UK, have made proposals that could increase the European capacity for autonomous action. The new equilibrium between Europe and America depends on the consensus that will be found among Europeans.

4.3.2. The USA and the evolution of European autonomy

The evolution towards a more balanced transatlantic relationship also depends upon the position of the US administration.[51] The EU countries, especially those which are very close to the USA, such as the UK, Italy, or the Netherlands, must try to convince the US administration that the development of a credible ESDP is the best option for the future of transatlantic relations. And France has a role to play in making it clear that its main goal is not to build a European power in opposition to the USA.

The international environment, after 11 September 2001[52] and above all after the crisis over Iraq,[53] does not seem favourable to the establishment of a balanced transatlantic relationship. Is the idea of an equal partnership still realistic in such a context?

The EU countries and the USA share the same democratic aspirations for their societies. To oppose a unilateralist and militaristic America to a pacifist Europe is a caricature. Americans and Europeans identify very similar issues as their primary concerns: foreign policy, particularly international terrorism, and weapons of mass destruction. Of course, the method used by the Europeans and the Americans to solve these problems differ, the latter being more inclined to military action. But some years ago, in the Balkans, the USA was not so eager to deploy forces on the ground. In the future, an EU backed up by a strong ESDP should be more and more involved in peacekeeping and crisis management, both militarily and diplomatically.

From 1998 to 2001 the international context seemed to be in favour of a rise of European power (thanks to the creation of a credible ESDP) and a more balanced transatlantic relationship. Since 2001, it seems to show a gap between the EU and the USA. But now that the crisis over Iraq has lessened, the context should make another change in a way that could be favourable to the alliance. The problems that the Bush administration is facing in dealing with post-war Iraq may lead the USA to a more multilateral approach to foreign relations. Even a country as

---

[51] J Thomson, 'US Interests and the Fate of the Alliance', (2003–4) 45(4) *Survival*, 207–220. Robert E Hunter, *The European Security and Defense Policy, NATO's Companion—or Competitor?* (Cambridge and Leiden: RAND Europe, 2003).

[52] P H Gordon, 'NATO After 11 September', (2001–2) 43(4) *Survival*, 89–106.

[53] I H Daalder, 'The End of Atlanticism', (2003) 45(2) *Survival*, 147–66.

powerful as the USA cannot continue to take decisions without having a minimum level of legitimacy and consent.

There needs to be solid political and military dialogue between the EU and NATO. Preferably, it should be a dialogue based on an equal partnership. Transparency should not mean that the Europeans cannot defend common positions within NATO. The declaration of the WEU members, included in the Maastricht Treaty's final act, already evokes the necessity to introduce common positions in all consultations between allies (point 4).

However the arrangements between the ESDP and NATO do not guarantee a balanced partnership between Europeans and Americans. The EU still relies a lot upon NATO assets. If a portion of NATO's assets and structures can be made available for use by the EU, the decision to transfer these means to the EU can be vetoed by the USA. For most crisis management operations, the Europeans cannot go it alone, because the ESDI and even the ESDP are not completely independent entities. If the USA wants ESDP to avoid 'unnecessary duplication', it must reassure the Europeans that NATO would release its assets. This might convince most of the EU Member States but not those Members insisting on European independence. For the latter, the creation of a new set of military forces—for example, the development of the A400M transport aircraft—that would duplicate NATO's resources could turn the EU into an autonomous player. There are political and financial reasons to avoid 'unnecessary duplication'. But the qualifier 'unnecessary' can be interpreted in many different ways. Duplication should be defined 'unnecessary' as soon as a specific capability exists within the NATO framework. But some duplication could nevertheless be agreed upon in order to give the EU an autonomous capacity for crisis management. Without a significant strengthening of their capacities, the Europeans will be forced to act in limited cases, ie, when the USA agrees to transfer NATO assets to the ESDP and under a kind of political control from the US side.

If the Europeans decide to make the necessary efforts to build a more equal partnership, they need more capabilities (necessary 'duplications'). But they should avoid any aggressive rhetoric that could be interpreted by the US administration and the US Congress as a will to break the link between the EU and NATO ('de-linking' and 'de-coupling').

5. Conclusion

The EU-NATO link is a practical necessity: for the Europeans who rely too much on the support of the USA and for the Americans who claim burden-sharing. It is also a political necessity: for the Europeans who need American involvement in international and—most of all—European security and for the Americans who may benefit from the help of partners, even if unilateralism is promoted by the

Bush administration. These necessities are reflected in legal rules and political declarations adopted by the allies.

But a lot of uncertainties remain, due to political divergences between the EU
Member States, and between the Europeans and the Americans. If a permanent
treaty is to be signed within the framework of the Atlantic Alliance, clarifications
have to be made, as regards subsidiarity, interoperability, and equal partnership.
But, in the short term, it is doubtful whether EU-NATO relations can be
strengthened by treaty provisions. Since the end of the Cold War difficult compromises have been found among member countries which do not exactly share
the same vision of EU-NATO relations. Only a strong consensus could lead to a
revision of the North Atlantic Treaty or to the negotiation of a new treaty whose
purpose could be the EU/NATO link in crisis management. Such a consensus
explained the signature of the Washington Treaty in 1949. The Allies were tied
together by the existence of a global threat coming from the USSR; this situation
came to an end in 1989–91. But common interests still remain, which, through
soft law and political declarations, are enough to create a European security
defence element, both in the EU and in NATO. We entered a period of experi-
mentation which could be punctuated by a new transatlantic partnership. One
day, the 'strategic partnership' of the 2002 EU-NATO declaration could be
enclosed within a real international agreement. If the Europeans want this partnership to be more equal, if they want to take their part in international security,
they need to give themselves the necessary means of a credible defence policy. The
weakness of Europe, in terms of armament and military resources, is a source of
ambiguity and difficulties. It is only through the development of ESDP means
that the EU can negotiate a permanent treaty with the USA based on an equal
partnership.

13

The Organization for Security and Co-operation in Europe and European Security Law

Marco Odello *

1. Introduction

The analysis of developments, problems and issues concerning the concept of European security law cannot be properly outlined without dealing with the Organization for Security and Co-operation in Europe (OSCE).[1] As with its predecessor, the Conference for the Security and Co-operation in Europe (CSCE),[2] the term 'security' is included in the name of the organization. Security is a wide concept with not always well defined limits. Compared to the idea of defence, as a military related concept, the area of security can expand and include both military and non-military components. With its initial 35 founding states, and present 55 participating states, the OSCE has been the largest organization in the widened European region since well before the end of the Cold War, ranging from the USA and Canada to Russia and Central Asia, including relationships with Japan. For this reason, it is not possible to speculate on the concept of European security law without dealing with the pan-European organization par excellence. The content of the concept of security used in official OSCE documents will be related to other organizations to provide the general framework of the developments concerning the definition(s) of this concept. It is not the purpose of this chapter either to

* Lecturer in Law, University of Wales, Aberystwyth, United Kingdom. All website addresses cited were active on 17 October 2006, unless otherwise specified.

[1] On the OSCE there is a wide literature. See M Bothe, N Ronzitti, and Allan Rosas (eds), *The OSCE in the Maintenance of Peace and Security* (The Hague/London/Boston: Kluwer Law International, 1997); R E Rupp and M M McKenzie, 'The Organization for Security and Cooperation in Europe: Institutional Reform and Political Reality', in M M McKenzie and P H Loedel, *The Promise and Reality of European Security Cooperation: States, Interests, and Institutions* (Westport and London: Praeger, 1998).

[2] The CSCE officially changed its name to OSCE in January 1995. In this chapter we shall use the acronym OSCE, unless reference is made to specific CSCE documents.

evaluate or discuss political and strategic issues, which should not be underestimated in the analysis and assessment of any international institution.[3] The analysis of the present chapter is limited to some aspects of OSCE's action in the area of international security. The main purpose is to evaluate whether the legal and institutional structures of the organization either undermine its future role as the leading European organization, or may represent an advantage compared to other, mainly European, organizations.

The OSCE as an international entity—with not clearly defined legal personality—raises some relevant questions that will be mentioned in the present work. Due to the fact that the organization is non-treaty based, the nature of the organization itself, of its organs, of its powers (mainly 'legislative' ones), and their relevance in international law may raise some problems in relationship to their legal value, future legal developments, and activities. Issues which are under present discussion have been addressed by the OSCE in the report entitled *Common Purpose: Towards a More Effective OSCE* presented in June 2005.[4] The areas of intervention of the organization, expression of the wide concept of security, also need an evaluation with respect to general international law. They need an assessment in relationship to the UN Charter, as the primary responsible organization in the field of international security. Possible problems of institutional coordination and treaty-making capacity of the existing institutions will be discussed. This analysis will focus on the potential role of the OSCE in developing a specific legal framework—a European security law—both in partnership with other European organizations and in relationship with the UN. In conducting a broad analysis of the aims, purposes, and work of the OSCE, an assessment of the organization's adequacy to deal with the development of a pan-European security law should be provided.

2. Concepts of Security

The concept of security does not have clear borders and has expanded its margins and purposes over the recent decade.[5] It should be neither confused nor misused with the term 'defence'. Even though in many cases both terms are used as synonymous, it should be stressed that the term defence has a clear military component. Ministers of Defence are national organs in charge of the armed forces in

---

[3] See generally S V Scott, *International Law in World Politics: An Introduction* (Boulder, CO: L Rienner Publishers, 2004); M Byers (ed), *The Role of Law in International Politics: Essays in International Relations and International Law* (Oxford: Oxford University Press, 2001).

[4] *Common Purpose: Towards a More Effective OSCE*, Final Report and Recommendations of the Panel of Eminent Persons on Strengthening the Effectiveness of the OSCE, 27 June 2005, available at <http://www.osce.org/documents/cio/2005/06/15432_en.pdf>. See M Odello, 'Thirty Years after Helsinki: Proposals for OSCE's Reform' (2005) 10(3) JCSL 435–49.

[5] On the concept of security see B Buzan, O Wæver, and J de Wilde, *Security: A New Framework for Analysis* (Boulder, CO: Lynne Rienner Publishers, 1998).

a given state. NATO[6] represents a typical 'collective defence', or alliance organization,[7] with a primarily military component to ensure military action of Member States in case of external military threats.[8]

A further term of art is 'collective security',[9] based on collective self-regulation when 'a group of states attempts to reduce security threats by agreeing to collectively punish any member state that violates the system's norms'.[10] Therefore, collective security is mainly centred on issues within the area of interest and within the geographical borders, of security organizations, and its regulations at universal level are defined in Chapter VII of the UN Charter. Nevertheless, some regional organizations have their own systems of collective security, as in the case of the Organization of American States (OAS) and the Inter-American Treaty of Reciprocal Assistance.[11]

The term security has been used in different contexts with different meanings.[12] It can, and generally does, include defence elements, as part of a general 'security' policy or activity. But it has recently expanded to include the concept of 'human security' that 'complements state security, enhances human rights and strengthens human development'.[13]

The OSCE has been one of the first international institutions to employ the term in a wide perspective, matching security to the term cooperation. Still under the threat of the Cold War, the Helsinki Final Act of 1975,[14] the founding document of the organization, expressed a wide list of elements to be taken into consideration to ensure that European states 'can live in true and lasting peace free from any threat to or attempt against their security'. States recognized the 'indivisibility of security' and 'the close link between peace and security' in Europe.

In other contexts, the concept and areas of security have expanded, particularly since the end of the Cold War. The Agenda for Peace presented by UN Secretary General Boutros-Ghali in 1992,[15] despite focusing on issues of preventive diplomacy, peacemaking and peacekeeping, also recognized that several 'sources of

---

[6] North Atlantic Treaty, Washington DC, 4 April 1949, available at <http://www.nato.int/docu/basictxt/treaty.htm>.

[7] See M Brenner (ed), *NATO and Collective Security* (Basingstoke: Macmillan, 1998).

[8] North Atlantic Treaty, Arts 5 and 6.

[9] For a discussion on collective security see G W Dowson (ed), *Collective Security beyond the Cold War* (Ann Arbour: The University of Michigan Press, 1994); N D White (ed), *Collective Security Law* (Aldershot: Ashgate, 2003); N D White, 'On the Brink of Lawlessness: The State of Collective Security Law' (2002) 13(1) Indiana Intl & Comparative L Rev 237–251.

[10] C A Kupchan, 'The Case for Collective Security' in Dowson (ed), ibid, 42.

[11] Inter-American Treaty of Reciprocal Assistance, Rio de Janeiro, 2 September 1947, OAS, Treaty Series Nos 8 and 61.

[12] See generally, E Krahmann (ed), *New Threats and New Actors in International Security* (New York, Basingstoke: Palgrave Macmillan, 2005); P Hough, *Understanding Global Security* (New York, London: Routledge, 2004).

[13] Commission on Human Security, *Human Security Now*, New York, 2003, 2, available at <http://www.humansecurity-chs.org/finalreport/English/FinalReport.pdf>.

[14] CSCE, *Final Act*, Helsinki, 1 August 1975, 14 ILM (1975) 1292.

[15] UN, SG, *An Agenda for Peace*, UN Doc A/47/277–S/24111, 17 June 1992.

conflict and war are pervasive and deep',[16] such as 'brutal ethnic, religious, social, cultural or linguistic strife',[17] and 'economic despair, social injustice and political oppression'.[18] This led the UN Secretary General to say that 'the efforts of the Organization to build peace, stability and security must encompass matters beyond military threats'.[19] Other European organizations and the OAS have included wider concepts of security in recent official documents.

As far as NATO is concerned, mention should be made of the 1991 Alliance Strategic Concept,[20] the 1997 Madrid Declaration,[21] the 1999 Strategic Concept,[22] and the 2002 Prague Summit Declaration.[23] Within the EU, we should refer to the European Security Strategy presented by Mr Javier Solana in 2003.[24] Solana's document identifies new key threats 'which are more diverse, less visible and less predictable' than the traditional attacks on state sovereignty. They include terrorism, proliferation of weapons of mass destruction, regional conflicts, state failure, and organized crime.[25] Outside the European context, the 2003 Declaration on Security in the Americas,[26] adopted by the Special Conference on Security, is worth mentioning. The American Declaration on Security affirms that the 'new concept of security in the Hemisphere is multidimensional in scope' and includes old and new threats. Some of them match with the 2003 European Security Strategy, but others further expand the limits of security, including:

... terrorism, transnational organized crime, the global drug problem, corruption, asset laundering, illicit trafficking in weapons, and the connections among them ... extreme poverty and social exclusion ... natural and man-made disasters, HIV/AIDS and other diseases, other health risks, and environmental degradation ... trafficking in persons ... attacks to cyber security ... the potential for damage to arise in the event of an accident or incident during the maritime transport of potentially hazardous materials, including

[16] Ibid, para 5.   [17] Ibid, para 11.
[18] Ibid, para 15.   [19] Ibid, para 13.
[20] NATO, *The Alliance's Strategic Concept*, agreed by the Heads of State and Government participating in the meeting of the North Atlantic Council Rome, 8 November 1991, available at <http://www.nato.int/docu/basictxt/b911108a.htm>.
[21] Madrid Declaration on Euro-Atlantic Security and Cooperation, Issued by the Heads of State and Government, Madrid, 8 July 1997, available at <http://www.nato.int/docu/pr/1997/p97-081e.htm>.
[22] Approved by the Heads of State and Government participating in the meeting of the North Atlantic Council in Washington DC on 23 and 24 April 1999.
[23] Issued by the Heads of State and Government participating in the meeting of the North Atlantic Council in Prague on 21 November 2002.
[24] *A Secure Europe in a Better World. European Security Strategy*, document proposed by Javier Solana and adopted by the Heads of State and Government at the European Council in Brussels on 12 December 2003, published by the European Institute for Security Studies, Paris, available at <http://www.iss-eu.org/solana/solanae.pdf>.   [25] Ibid, 6–9.
[26] OAS, *Declaration on Security in the Americas*, adopted in Mexico City at the third plenary session of 28 October 2003, OEA/SerK/XXXVIII CES/DEC1/03 rev 1 (28 October 2003), available at <http://www.oas.org/documents/eng/DeclaracionSecurity_102803.asp>. See M Odello, 'International Security in the Western Hemisphere: Legal and Institutional Developments' (2005) XXI *Anuario de Derecho Internacional* 379–411.

petroleum and radioactive materials and toxic waste ... [and] the possibility of access, possession, and use of weapons of mass destruction and their means of delivery by terrorists.[27]

These threats also receive a different spatial delimitation in the two documents. While the American Declaration focuses its attention and corresponding action within the Western Hemisphere, Solana considers that some of the threats such as regional conflicts and state failure, which could happen outside Europe, and might have an impact on European security, need some form of intervention from the EU to ensure Member States' security.[28] This development may lead to EU action beyond the territorial limits of its Member States,[29] and raises a series of legal issues concerning the limitations on the use of force under international law,[30] and the relationship with the UN,[31] as in the case of the 1998 NATO bombing of Yugoslavia. NATO provides a more limited area of activity, mainly due to its Charter limitations and military alliance purposes. But since the 1991 NATO Rome Summit[32] it was recognized that '[i]n contrast with the predominant threat of the past, the risks to Allied security that remain are multi-faceted in nature and multi-directional, which makes them hard to predict and assess',[33] and has stressed the importance of building confidence and security through dialogue, arms control, disarmament, and non-proliferation measures,[34] and forms of fighting against terrorism.[35]

Trends mentioned at regional level have been followed by the UN. In December 2004, the document *A More Secure World: Our Shared Responsibility*,[36] presented by the UN Secretary General on international threats and security, defined a wide concept of security, and tried to identify new forms and areas of intervention related to suggestions for reforms of the UN system to deal with them.

If the wider concept of security, as briefly outlined here, is taken to its logical conclusion, collective security could be defined not only as a 'system of all against one', that means providing collective measures against the state violator of the

---

[27] OAS, ibid, para 4(m).

[28] This task has been assumed by the EU with the incorporation of the so-called WEU Petersberg tasks that included the possibility of peacekeeping missions and humanitarian activities outside the limits of the organization's geographical borders: see *Nato Handbook*, 2001, ch 15, available at <http://www.nato.int/docu/handbook/2001/hb150401.htm>. See also Eugenia López-Jacoiste Díaz (ed), *La política de seguridad y defensa en Europa* (Pamplona: EUNSA, 2006).

[29] See F Naert, Chapter 4 of this volume.

[30] See N Tsagourias, Chapter 5 of this volume.

[31] See N D White, Chapter 14 of this volume.

[32] NATO, n 20, above; see also M Wörner, 'NATO Transformed: The Significance of the Rome Summit' (1991) 39(6) *NATO Rev* 3–8.　　　　　　　　　　　　　　　　[33] Ibid, para 8.

[34] Ibid, paras 23–33.　　　　[35] NATO, 2002 Prague Summit Declaration, paras 3, 4, 7, 8, 10.

[36] UN, High-level Panel on Threats, Challenges and Change, *A More Secure World: Our Shared Responsibility*, UN doc A/59/565, 2 December 2004; see S Bouwhuis, 'Report of the High-level Panel on United Nations Reform' (2005) 79 Australian L J 278–81; M Odello, 'Commentary on the United Nations' High-level Panel on Threats, Challenges and Change' (2005) 10(2) JCSL 231–62. On different issues related to the report see (2005) XXI *Anuario de Derecho Internacional* 3–131.

system, but it might also include collective actions to prevent threats, such as the traditional threat of the use of force, and to deal with situations that can endanger the 'security', broadly interpreted, of one or more members of an international organization. These threats represent imminent possible security threats for the 'collectivity of states', when states can be structured either as universal or regional organizations. This seems to be the recent tendency adopted by several organizations, not only dealing with 'security' in military terms, but also for organizations traditionally dealing with other issues, such as the EU. It should be stressed here that the wide approach to security, as it will be shortly presented, was at the very origin of the OSCE and of its action.

3. Security Issues within the OSCE

When dealing with the definition of security within the OSCE, several documents that have addressed the issue since the origin of the organization must be taken into consideration. They range from the 1975 Helsinki Summit Final Act, the constitutive document of the CSCE, to the Charter for European Security, adopted at the Istanbul Summit in 1999.[37] The comprehensive debate on security within the OSCE led to the identification of a series of issues that would define the broad concept of security in the wide European context. The Helsinki Final Act identified three main security related areas, commonly referred to as 'baskets'. The first set (Basket I) deals with the politico-military aspects of security, and includes principles considered of fundamental importance for the relations among participating states, the so-called 'Decalogue',[38] and confidence-building measures in military matters. The second set (Basket II) includes cooperation in a wide selection of issues, including economics, science and technology, and the environment. The third set (Basket III) deals with 'cooperation in humanitarian and other fields'.[39] It is the basis for the so-called 'Human Dimension',[40] to use the OSCE

[37] Other relevant documents including security issues are: the 1990 Paris Summit, the 1992 Helsinki Summit, the 1994 Budapest Summit, and the 1996 Lisbon Summit. Also relevant for the discussion of the concept of security in the area of OSCE are: Follow-up Meeting 1980–3, *Concluding Document*, Madrid, 11 November 1980 to 9 September 1983, The Security Model Discussion 1995–6, *Report of the Chairman-in Office to the Lisbon Summit Review Meeting*, Lisbon 1996. The Istanbul Summit, 18–19 November 1999, adopted a *Final Declaration* and a *Charter for European Security* divided into four parts: I Our Common Challenges; II Our Common Foundations; III Our Common Response; IV Our Common Instruments; V Our Partners for Co-operation; and VI Conclusion, OSCE Istanbul Summit, *Istanbul Documents 1999*, Cm 4560, January 2000.

[38] The ten fundamental principles are contained in the *Declaration on Principles Guiding Relations between Participating States* of the Helsinki Final Act.

[39] This formula refers to different human rights issues under the headings of 'human contacts', 'information', 'co-operation in the field of culture', and 'co-operation in the field of education'.

[40] The expression 'Human Rights Dimension' was introduced by the 1989 Vienna Concluding Document and defined as 'the undertakings entered into in the Final Act and in other CSCE documents concerning respect for all human rights and fundamental freedoms, human contacts and other

jargon, referring to human rights. The Act also mentioned various issues related to the Mediterranean area[41] in a series of final recommendations. It should be mentioned here that the OSCE has concentrated its activities within Central and Eastern Europe, including parts of Asia,[42] because of the destabilization produced in transition countries after the end of the Communist regimes. In 2003 the Mediterranean partnership[43] received renewed attention,[44] but still with very limited concrete actions in this region of the world.

The 1999 Charter for European Security[45] widened the concept of security defined in the Helsinki Act and in subsequent documents. It recognized that 'threats to security can stem from conflict within States as well as from conflicts between States' and for that reason both types of conflict 'represent a threat to the security of all OSCE participating States'.[46] International terrorism, organized crime, and drug trafficking 'represent growing challenges to security', and are linked to the 'destabilising accumulation and uncontrolled spread of small arms and light weapons'.[47] Acute economic problems and environmental degradation are related to the already existing areas of cooperation in the fields of economy, science, and technology.[48] These issues are not supposed to derogate the existing ones. They add further elements to the areas of cooperation among states within the OSCE in the effort of providing security. The broad sense of security within the OSCE is expressed in the following terms in paragraph 9 of the Charter:

> We will build our relations in conformity with the concept of common and comprehensive security, guided by equal partnership, solidarity and transparency. The security of each participating State is inseparably linked to that of all others. We will address the human, economic, political and military dimensions of security as an integral whole.

To ensure stability and security the Charter for European Security has also widened its possible forms of action. These include the development of OSCE's role in peacekeeping and the ability to carry out police-related activities to assist states in maintaining the primacy of law.[49] The option mentioned in paragraph 16 of the Charter is very relevant, which foresees the urgent procedure for consultation and actions that may be required in the case of a participating state 'seeking

---

issues of a related humanitarian character'; see generally A Bloed and P van Dijk (eds), *The Human Dimension of the Helsinki Process* (Dordrecht: Martinus Nijhoff, 1991).

[41] Mention of the Mediterranean was also made in the second part of the 1992 Helsinki Document, 'The CSCE and the management of change'. On some occasions the idea of a parallel conference on Security and Co-operation in the Mediterranean (CSCM) has been mentioned, but without consistent developments.

[42] The Asian Partners for Co-operation (APCs) are: Japan, Republic of Korea, Thailand, Afghanistan, and Mongolia.

[43] The six Mediterranean Partners for Co-operation (MPCs) are: Algeria, Egypt, Israel, Jordan, Morocco, and Tunisia.

[44] OSCE, Eleventh Meeting of the Ministerial Council, *OSCE Strategy to Address Threats to Security and Stability in the Twenty-First Century*, Maastricht, 1–2 December 2003, MC DOC/1/03, 2 December 2003.   [45] *Charter for European Security*, n 37, above.

[46] Ibid, para 2.   [47] Ibid, para 4.   [48] Ibid, para 5.   [49] Ibid, para 1.

assistance in realizing its right to individual or collective self-defence in the event that its sovereignty, territorial integrity and political independence are threatened'. The same paragraph clearly establishes the commitment by states that actions will be taken 'in conformity with our OSCE responsibilities'. But there is no clear reference to which forms the reaction might take, and under which rules it would be carried out. The only reference, in the initial part of the paragraph, is to the Code of Conduct on Politico-Military Aspects of Security.[50]

The Code of Conduct, adopted during the OSCE Budapest Summit in December 1994, is one of the relevant rule-setting documents in the area of security. It deals with different areas of security, even if its title seems to concentrate on the political and military aspects of security.[51] It provides a link between military matters and democratic and human rights issues. The Code is an original and unique instrument adopted in the field of military and security issues. It links security to mutual confidence, respect for human rights, humanitarian law, and state control over its armed forces.

The most recent document concerning the definition of security has been adopted in the form of Follow-up Decisions taken at the Maastricht Ministerial Council in December 2003.[52] It makes reference to the areas mentioned before, and also stresses its attention to the economic and environmental dimensions of security.[53] Issues related to the definition of security provide the wide context in which the OSCE is supposed to work to ensure 'security' to states participating in the organization. But the mandate of the organization should be matched also with the nature and powers of the organization. In fact, organizations should deal with their mandate under the general rules of international law and in compliance with the rules established by their constitutive documents. The peculiar status and structure of the OSCE need briefly to be addressed, and this will be the content of the next part of this chapter.

4. The Organization

Before analysing the areas of activity and the possible role of the OSCE in shaping a European security law, some legal matters related to the international status of the OSCE should be mentioned.[54] The legal status of the OSCE is relevant in

---

[50] OSCE, *Code of Conduct on Politico-Military Aspects of Security*, DOC FSC/1/95, 3 December 1994, available at <http://www.osce.org/documents/fsc/1994/12/4270_en.pdf>.

[51] On the Code of Conduct of Politico-Military Aspects of Security see V-Y Ghebali and Alexander Lambert, *The OSCE Code of Conduct on Politico-Military Aspects of Security: Anatomy and Implementation* (Leiden/Boston: Martinus Nijhoff, 2005); G de Nooy (ed), *Cooperative Security, the OSCE, and its Code of Conduct* (The Hague/London/Boston: Kluwer Law International, 1996).

[52] OSCE, *OSCE Strategy to Address Threats to Security and Stability in the Twenty-First Century*, n 44, above.   [53] Ibid, Pt I, paras 5 and 14.

[54] See C Berger, 'OSCE and International Law' (1996) 24 International J of Legal Information 36–47; Nigel D White, *The Law of International Organisations*, 2nd edn (Manchester: Manchester University Press, 2005) 52–4.

relationship to other issues that in part depend on this primary issue. The OSCE could play a more active role in the construction and management of a pan-European security system,[55] but the organization needs appropriate legal tools to deal with the task. The report *Common Purpose: Towards a More Effective OSCE*,[56] suggests the adoption of a treaty to provide the OSCE with legal personality and therefore full capacity to act under international law.

Compared to other European organizations, such as the EU, NATO, and the Council of Europe, the OSCE has intrinsic legal weaknesses that have not been solved yet, and might undermine the organization's role in developing and managing a proper system of European security law. It is not the purpose here to develop a full analysis of the legal personality and powers of the OSCE, but rather to raise some issues, and foresee some possible solutions.

The participating states at the Conference on Security and Cooperation in Europe signed the Final Act in Helsinki on 1 August 1975,[57] still under the threat of the Cold War, and facing the policy of détente. States decided to keep the organizational structure in the form of periodical meetings,[58] called Summit, Follow-Up, and Intersessional Meetings.[59] This procedure developed a sort of *forum*, or 'concert', called the 'Helsinki Process', with a small secretariat dealing with the organization of meetings. For this reason, there were not Member States, but 'participating States', as they are still called in official OSCE documents. Later on, the CSCE moved from being a 'process' to an 'institution',[60] and finally to an 'organization', the OSCE, due to a smooth reform process which took the form of successive Summit Declarations, but that never led to the adoption of a formal treaty under international law.[61]

The new name was supposed to change nothing of the legal structure or personality of the organization.[62] Paragraph 29 of the 1994 Budapest Summit affirmed that 'The change in name from CSCE to OSCE alters neither the

[55] See OSCE, *Charter for European Security*, Istanbul, November 1999, para 51; D Stuart, 'NATO's Future as a Pan-European Security Institution' (1993) 41(4) *NATO Review* 15–19.

[56] See OSCE Parliamentary Assembly and Swiss Institute for World Affairs, *Colloquium on 'The Future of the OSCE'*, Report, Washington, 5–6 June 2005, available at <http://www.osce.org/documents/pa/2005/06/15378_en.pdf >.

[57] *Common Purpose: Towards a More Effective OSCE*, n 4, above, 19–20.

[58] CSCE, *Final Act*, Helsinki, 1 August 1975 (1975) 14 ILM 1293.

[59] On the negotiation and an early analysis of the legal nature of the Helsinki Final Act see H S Russell, 'The Helsinki Declaration: Brobdingnag or Lilliput?' (70) 2 AJIL (1976) 244–9.

[60] Summits were the most important meetings where new relevant commitments could be defined and adopted. A series of 'follow-up meetings' took place in Belgrade (4 October 1977–8 March 1978), Madrid (11 November 1980–9 September 1983) and Vienna (4 November 1986–19 January 1989). Intersessional meetings were also held with the aim of maintaining momentum between follow-up meetings.

[61] D McGoldrick, 'The Conference on Security and Cooperation in Europe—From Process to Institution', in B S Jackson and D McGoldrick (eds), *Legal Visions of the New Europe*, (London: Graham & Trotman, 1993) 159.

[62] It could be envisaged that the Charter of Paris, adopted at the 1990 Paris Summit of Heads of State and of Government, which stated the 'institutionalization' process of the CSCE into the OSCE, could be used as a 'codification document', reaffirming the documents and principles adopted by previous Summits and Conferences, see McGoldrick, ibid, 152.

character of our CSCE commitments nor the status of the CSCE and its institutions'. It should be noted that the same paragraph included reference to the Rome Decision on Legal Capacity and Privileges and Immunities, and affirmed that participating states 'will, furthermore, examine possible ways of incorporating their commitments into national legislation and, where appropriate, of concluding treaties'. This statement shows a willingness to treat the organization as an international subject with its own privileges and immunities, including legal capacity, and in particular to ensure adequate protection to its personnel when on missions abroad.

The question to consider, if the OSCE is an international organization, is whether it is properly equipped to act in an international scenario, and to deal with the variety of activities linked to the broad concept of international security. We shall briefly address some issues that might help in the definition of the issue under discussion.

Definitions of characteristics of international organizations are not uniform.[63] Commentators on international organizations identify several criteria.[64] They include membership (two or more states), common aims defined by members, and 'a formal structure of a continuous nature established by an agreement such as a treaty or constituent document'. Once these criteria are met, an international organization comes into existence. It is quite clear that the OSCE fulfils most of the criteria. Membership seems to be met by the original 35 and present 55 participating States. A formal structure has been achieved, mainly in 1994, when the Budapest Summit reshaped the existing institutions and reinforced their capability to govern and manage the 'organization'.[65] In particular, the Secretary General and the Chairman in Office (CiO) are two entities who cover the role of a permanent secretariat, the first mainly dealing with 'internal' administrative issues, the second with 'external' representation activities. Other organs, such as the Ministerial Council, the Senior Council, and the Permanent Council meet regularly and take decisions and deal with the regular activity of the organization, and are the expression of participating states' will in collegiate organs. There are permanent institutions with a general mandate, such as the OSCE Secretariat, and others with a specific mandate, such as the Office for Democratic Institutions and Human Rights (ODIHR), and the High Commissioner on National Minorities (HCNM). Among the institutions non-permanent structures should also be

---

[63] On the debate on the OSCE's legal status see I F Dekker and R A Wessel, *'Van CVSE naar OVSE'* (2002) 31(4) *Vrede en Veiligheid* 425–38; C Bertrand, *'La nature juridique de l'Organisation pour la Sécurité et la Coopération en Europe (OSCE)'* (1998) 102(2) *Revue Générale de Droit International Public* 365–406; M Sapiro, 'Changing the CSCE into the OSCE: Legal Aspects of a Political Transformation' (1995) 89(3) AJIL 631–7; J F Prevost, *'Observations sur la nature juridique de l'Acte Final de la Conférence sur la Securité et la Coopération en Europe'* (1975) *Annuaire Français de Droit International* 129–53.

[64] See Clive Archer, *International Organizations*, 3rd edn (London and New York: Routledge, 2001) 30–3.

[65] See Chittharanjan F Amerasinghe, *Principles of the Institutional Law of International Organizations*, 2nd edn (Cambridge: Cambridge University Press, 2005) 9.

included, such as country Missions and Field Activities, working in different areas of conflict prevention, negotiation, and assistance to national authorities in the accomplishment of the human dimension commitments, and in the field of conflict resolution. These are organs with permanent international staff, amounting to about one thousand people recruited internationally.[66] Most of these structures and institutions act on the basis of a mandate, and develop their activities separately from the states that endorsed them.

A more difficult task concerns the definition of a constituent document that should govern the activities of the organization under international law. The 1975 Helsinki Act is not, properly defined, an international treaty. Some commentators consider that the Helsinki Final Act has the characteristics of a Memorandum of Understanding, without legal character, which merely defines political and moral commitments.[67] This position was actually included in several official Summit documents adopted by OSCE states. Without entering into the dispute on the nature of memoranda and treaties, some other justifications might help in defining the legal nature of the OSCE commitments.

If the main documents adopted by State Summits, despite their names (Final Act, Declaration, etc), are not treaties in the sense defined by the 1969 Vienna Convention the question arises as to whether they might nonetheless have some legal effect. Here the concepts of 'soft' law and 'customary' law may provide the necessary legal background. Soft law 'usually refers to any international instrument other than a treaty containing principles, norms, standards, or other statements of expected behaviour'.[68] The use of declarations, principles, etc, defined generally as soft law can be considered the starting point for setting rules and principles, that may evolve into hard law, be it either treaty or customary law. The OSCE has been defined by Klabbers as a 'soft organization'.[69] Keeping this in mind, the analysis of the main documents adopted within the OSCE shows a repetition of principles and rules that can be considered the foundation of the cooperation and action among the participating states. If custom is created by the repetition of acts for a certain period of time, and states consider it mandatory from the legal point of view, then the custom becomes a rule crystallized in the form of customary law. The OSCE itself defines the outcome of its law-making process in the following terms: 'the fact that OSCE commitments are not legally binding does not detract from their efficacy. Having been signed at the highest

[66] For Schermers and Blokker it seems that the gradual 'institutionalization' of the CSCE and the change of the name make it an organization, at least since the 1994 Budapest Declaration: see Henry G Schermers and Niels M Blokker, *International Institutional Law*, 4th edn (Boston: Martinus Nijhoff Publishers, 2003) 23.

[67] See OSCE, *Annual Report on OSCE Activities 2003*, 182 available at <http://www.osce.org/documents/sg/2004/05/2677_en.pdf>.

[68] See A Aust, *Modern Treaty Law and Practice* (Cambridge: Cambridge University Press, 2000) 28.

[69] D Shelton, 'International Law and "Relative Normativity"', in M D Evans (ed), *International Law* (Oxford: Oxford University Press, 2003) 166.

political level, they have an authority that is arguably as strong as any legal statute under international law'.[70]

This means that the OSCE produces commitments that have an authority comparable to other legal rules. Furthermore, the organization may contribute to the definition of further rules by way of subsequent practice.[71] In the following section the rules that establish the legal commitments of the participating states in relation to the OSCE will be addressed.

5. Basic Principles of the OSCE

OSCE's official documents provide quite a number of rules that are relevant for the purpose of providing international security. They include the so-called Decalogue, which expresses rules of general customary law and general principles of international law.[72] The Decalogue was adopted in 1975 as a set of fundamental principles governing the reciprocal relations among the participating states and for ensuring the equal standing of all states within the organization.[73] The ten principles include sovereign equality of states, inviolability of frontiers, and non-intervention in internal affairs of states.[74] Because the CSCE was established during the Cold War, the principles represent the minimum common denominator at a time of confrontation between blocs, and include the Declaration of Principles of International Law, adopted in 1970 by the UN General Assembly.[75] But the Decalogue did not provide any major novelty in the area of legal tools for strong cooperation and integration.

In any case, since the adoption of the 1975 Helsinki Final Act, participating states have always made reference in final Summit declarations to 'their common adherence to the principles [. . .] in conformity with the Charter of the United Nations, as well as their common will to act, in the application of these principles, in conformity with the purposes and principles of the Charter of the United Nations'.[76]

---

[70] J Klabbers, 'Institutional Ambivalence by Design: Soft Organizations in International Law'(2001) 70 Nordic J of Intl L 403–21.

[71] OSCE, *Handbook*, 3rd edn (Vienna: July 2002) 3, available at <*http://www.osce.org/publications/osce/2005/04/13858_222_en.pdf*>.

[72] See D Akande, 'International Organisations' in Evans (ed), n 69, above, 281–2.

[73] See generally M N Shaw, *International Law*, 5th edn (Cambridge: Cambridge University Press, 2003) 68–88, 92–9.

[74] For a legal analysis of the Principles, see Russell, n 59, above, 263–71.

[75] The ten principles are: I Sovereign equality, respect for the rights inherent in sovereignty; II Refraining from the threat or use of force; III Inviolability of frontiers; IV Territorial integrity of States; V Peaceful settlement of disputes; VI Non-intervention in internal affairs; VII Respect for human rights and fundamental freedoms, including the freedom of thought, conscience, religion or belief; VIII Equal rights and self-determination of peoples; IX Co-operation among States; X Fulfilment in good faith of obligations under international law.

[76] UN General Assembly, *Declaration of Principles of International Law Concerning Friendly Relations and Cooperation among States in Accordance with the Charter of the United Nations*, GA Res 2625, 25 UN GAOR Supp (No 28) 121, UN Doc A/8082 (1970).

Furthermore, the 1975 Helsinki Final Act includes some specific measures that were envisaged to make those principles more effective. The participating states reaffirmed that 'they will respect and give effect to refraining from the threat or use of force'. To reinforce that commitment they also reaffirmed a series of principles including the purposes and principles of the UN Charter, the non-use of force, disarmament measures, and the peaceful solution of disputes. These principles were then reiterated in later Summits, generally in a shorter form, such as in the 1990 Paris Charter for a New Europe[77] and in the 1999 Istanbul Charter for European Security.[78] Participating states referred to the basic rules and principles in the following terms:

> We reaffirm our full adherence to the Charter of the United Nations, and to the Helsinki Final Act, the Charter of Paris and all other OSCE documents to which we have agreed. These documents represent our common commitments and are the foundation for our work.[79]

Apart from the aforementioned general principles there are other specific rules that could be considered as part of the legal development of the OSCE. At least three basic principles have been regularly included in the main documents which deserve some consideration here in view of the legal commitments in the area of security. One is the qualification of the OSCE 'as a regional arrangement under Chapter VIII of the Charter of the United Nations'.[80] This 'upgrade' of the organization was included in the 1992 Helsinki Summit after the end of the Cold War, and was aimed at strengthening the role of the OSCE, particularly in the area of peacekeeping, under the pressure of the emerging conflict in Yugoslavia. The second principle is to be found in two other statements, parallel to this declaration. The first is the recognition of the OSCE 'as a primary organization for the peaceful settlement of disputes within its region and as a key instrument for early warning, conflict prevention, crisis management and post-conflict rehabilitation'. The second statement is the affirmation that the OSCE 'is the inclusive and comprehensive organization for consultation, decision-making and cooperation in its region'.[81] Nevertheless, OSCE states 'recognize the primary responsibility of the United Nations Security Council for the maintenance of international peace and security and its crucial role in contributing to security and stability' of the region.

The third principle covers a very wide are, to be discussed later in this chapter, and has always been a feature of the OSCE. It is the so-called 'Human Dimension', meaning the international rules related to human rights, a central issue within the organization's activities that has expanded over the years. The Human Dimension has developed a series of principles, in particular in the area of

---

[77] CSCE, 1975 Helsinki Summit, *Declaration on Principles Guiding Relations between Participating States.*
[78] They were included in the section called 'Friendly Relations among Participating States, CSCE, Paris Charter for a New Europe' (1991) 30 ILM 190 et seq.
[79] They were included in the section called 'Our Common Foundations'.
[80] OSCE, 1999 Istanbul Summit, *Charter for European Security*, n 37, above, Pt II, para 7.
[81] CSCE, 1992 Helsinki Decisions, ch III, para 3.

minority rights, freedom of expression, election, and military submission to democratic institutions, which provide a set of rules and guidelines for the regular activities of the OSCE and its organs and institutions.

6. A Possible Legal Status for the OSCE

The set of rules that govern the aims and activities of the OSCE represent quite detailed mechanisms that allow the organization to work. The rules might therefore be defined as an 'evolving constitution' based on a series of agreements of participating states. With the repetition of their mandatory nature as the foundation of the work of the organization, the rules mentioned above have at least the status of soft law and in several cases they may represent customary law. This consequence was already envisaged by Schachter, under the application of the principle of 'good faith' to the commitments defined in the declarations adopted in the framework of the OSCE.[82] Some of the principles, such as the peaceful solution of disputes and the respect of sovereignty, have already acquired the status of general principles of international law. Furthermore, paragraph 12 of the 1999 Charter for European Security affirms that the 'Principles [...] apply to any organization or institution whose members individually and collectively decide to adhere to them'. This might be interpreted as a surrogate formula to bind new participating members, both individual states and organizations, to the established principles of the organization, which could not otherwise be mandatory, due to the lack of a foundational treaty to which other international subjects might adhere.

If the criteria match the main requirements for the existence of an international organization, then the OSCE would be a proper international organization,[83] with international personality, subject of and to international law.[84] This implies that the organization and its organs are bound by general international law, can act under international law, and may be responsible internationally.[85] This is a relevant issue in defining the limits and fields of action of the OSCE in developing and applying a legal security framework, an issue which will be the basis of the further analysis in this chapter.

If the OSCE has no legal personality, as generally stated, then the organization would not have any international rights or duties. The participating states would be held responsible for the actions developed by the OSCE.

---

[82] OSCE, *Charter for European Security*, n 37, above, Pt II, para 7.

[83] O Schachter, *International Law in Theory and Practice* (Dordrecht/Boston/London: Martinus Nijhoff, 1991), ch VI, particularly 100–1.

[84] On the same position see P Sands and P Klein, *Bowett's Law of International Institutions*, 5th edn (London: Sweet & Maxwell, 2001) 201.

[85] P Koojimans rejects this conclusion, considering that the OSCE 'is not treaty-based and therefore has no international personality': P Koojimans, 'The Code and International Law', in Nooy, n 51, above, 33.

Despite the unsettled issue of the legal status of the OSCE, the organization has developed several tools, institutions, and mechanisms in the field of security. They can be seen as part of a European security framework, contributing to a European security law.

7. OSCE's Tools in the Area of Security

The 1975 Helsinki Final Act provided a diplomatic framework for a European security policy based on cooperation among states through a regular process of consultation. This led to a soft institutional structure, with quite limited powers and means. The structure did not foresee any use of force among states as a way to deal with the traditional meaning of collective security. Nevertheless, the CSCE is supposed to have played a relevant role in the demise of totalitarian regimes in Central and Eastern Europe, in particular through the development of human rights standards.[86]

An important step towards the creation and reinforcement of security mechanisms was taken at the 1992 Helsinki Summit (also called Helsinki-II).[87] The second part of the Declaration, entitled 'The CSCE and the management of change', tried to make the CSCE more 'operational and effective'. The measures included new tools for conflict prevention and crisis management, the creation of a High Commissioner on National Minorities (HCNM), and the possibility of peacekeeping missions. During the Third Ministerial Council, held in Stockholm in 1992, there was a reference to the fact that 'in association with efforts to bring about political solutions, stability can be enhanced by armed contingents for peacekeeping purposes. The deployment and conduct of such operations must be in accordance with the norms of international law and CSCE principles'.[88] But the OSCE has not been able, or willing, to use peacekeeping with a military dimension. It has fared better with so-called field missions that are characterized by a strong civilian component.

In general terms the OSCE has developed a security framework by strengthening the link between domestic and international orders.[89] This is shown by the importance accorded to the development of democratic institutions and the protection of minorities as fundamental elements of regional stability and security. Different tools are envisaged for the attainment of security. They include arms

[86] Schachter considered that this last consequence was not applicable to the OSCE political commitments: n 83, above, 101.

[87] See D C Thomas, *The Helsinki Effect: International Norms, Human Rights, and the Demise of Communism* (Princeton: Princeton University Press, 2001).

[88] CSCE, 1992 Helsinki Summit (1992) 31 ILM 1385 et seq. For a thorough analysis of this meeting, see A Heraclides, *Helsinki-II and its Aftermath* (London and New York: Pinter Publishers, 1993).

[89] CSCE Third Ministerial Council meeting held in Stockholm (14–15 December 1992), Decision n 6.

control, disarmament, and confidence and security-building measures (CSBMs) which represent the politico-military Dimension of the OSCE.[90] The so-called Human Dimension, which entails mechanisms to deal with the internal issues of states, provides a greater involvement of the OSCE. The mechanisms comprise the Office for Democratic Institutions and Human Rights, the HCNM, and the so-called Long-term Missions.[91] Other institutions involved in this broad area are the Representative on Freedom of the Media, and the Coordinator of OSCE Economic and Environmental Activities, who works mainly with the Chairman-in-Office, the Permanent Council, and other OSCE institutions to address economic, social, and environmental aspects of security.[92] Finally, another set of tools is mainly represented by the traditional mechanisms of Peaceful Settlement of Disputes, now institutionalized by the Convention on Conciliation and Arbitration[93] and the Geneva-based Court.[94] Nevertheless, the last institution has never been used. It seems that diplomatic solutions of disputes are handled more within the political arena and other institutions, such as the HCNM,[95] provided by the OSCE than through more institutionalized forms of dispute resolution mechanism. In this section the main areas of activity developed by the OSCE in the field of security will be addressed to provide a picture of its role in the development of security law within the European context.

8. Confidence and Security-Building Measures and Arms Control

To contribute to peace and security in Europe, the 35 initial states (today 55 states) which adopted the Helsinki Final Act in 1975 decided to eliminate 'the causes of tension' using new ways to 'strengthen confidence among them' and thus to contribute to increasing stability and security in Europe. The original mechanisms, inherited from the Cold War, of both the CSCE and OSCE, were based

[90] G Flynn and H Farrell, 'Piecing Together the Democratic Peace: The OSCE, Norms, and the "Construction" of Security in Post-Cold War Europe' (1999) 53(3) *International Organization* 516.

[91] On the issue, see V-Y Ghebali and D Warner, *The Politico-Military Dimension of the OSCE: Arms Control and Conflict Management Issues*, PSIO Occasional Paper No 2 (Geneva: HEI/PSIO, 2005).

[92] See V-Y Ghebali, 'The OSCE Long-Term Missions Experience, 1992–2004: A Global Assessment' in Ghebali and Warner, n 51, above.

[93] The ENVSEC Initiative was launched in 2002. It represents a joint programme among UNDP, UNEP, OSCE, and NATO: see <http://www.envsec.org/>.

[94] CSCE, Convention on Conciliation and Arbitration, Third Meeting of the Council of Ministers, Summary of Conclusions Decision on Peaceful Settlement of Disputes, Annex 2, Stockholm, 15 December 1992, available at <http://www.osce.org/documents/mcs/1992/12/4156_en.pdf>.   [95] See <http://www.osce.org/cca/>.

on the 'confidence and security-building measures' (CSBMs) that would lead to increased 'transparency', confidence, and cooperation among states, and on decision-making procedures governed by consensus.[96]

CSBMs were negotiated in several meetings in Vienna, after the 1989 Summit. They consist of a package of information exchange mechanisms and verification regimes used as a fundamental tool to reduce the threat of large-scale conventional conflict in Europe.[97] The activities related to the CSBMs are mainly developed within the Forum for Security Cooperation. There are different mechanisms adopted to facilitate the exchange of information among participating states regarding their military forces and activities. The mechanisms may be divided into two main areas. The first type of information is related to the armed forces in general, the second to specific aspects of armaments controls. They will be quickly presented hereafter. The general information on defence exchange among participating states includes the following mechanisms:

- Annual Exchange of Military Information,[98] where participating states exchange information on the organization and manpower of their military forces, and also on major weapons and equipment systems, and their planned deployments for the coming year.
- Each year states have to provide information on their defence planning and military budgets.[99] These include the size, structure, training, and equipment of their armed forces, as well as defence policy, doctrines, and budgets.
- Military contacts, annual calendars, and constraining provisions[100] consist of a series of contacts and cooperation between participating states in the military areas. They include visits to air bases and other military facilities, observation visits and demonstrations of new types of major weapons systems, and information on any forthcoming military activities which are also subject to prior notification.
- Global exchange of military information, like the annual exchange, foresees the reciprocal exchange of information on major weapons and equipment systems and personnel, but includes all forces worldwide, not just those in the territory of the participating state.

[96] For an analysis of the HCNM mandate, see O A J Brenninkmeijer, *The OSCE High Commissioner on National Minorities: Negotiating the 1992 Conflict Prevention Mandate* PSIO Occasional Paper No 5 (Geneva: HEI/PSIO, 2005).

[97] See E Schlager, 'The Procedural Framework of the CSCE: From the Helsinki Consultations to the Paris Charter' (1991) 12 Human Rights L J 221–7. The *Charter for European Security* established that 'We will continue to uphold consensus as the basis for OSCE decision-making' (para 10), n 37, above.

[98] On the issue see Graeme P Auton, 'Multilateral Security Regimes: The Politics of CFE and CSBMs' in McKenzie and Loedel (eds), n 1, above, ch 8.

[99] The annual exchange is part of the Vienna Document 1999, and takes place no later than 15 December each year.

[100] The information should be provided no more than three months after national approval of the military budget, and is part of the Vienna Document 1999.

A further set of more specific forms of information-sharing regards weapons, including the compilation of an annual questionnaire. They consist of:

- The Small Arms and Light Weapons[101] mechanism, which deals with: national marking systems; manufacture control procedures; export policy, procedures and documentation, and control over brokering; and destruction techniques and procedures.
- Conventional Arms Transfers through which participating states share information each year on their exports and imports of conventional weapons, including battle tanks, ACVs (Armoured Combat Vehicles), artillery systems, combat aircraft, attack helicopters, warships and missiles, and missile launchers.[102] Participating states also complete a questionnaire on their policy, practices, and procedures concerning the export of conventional arms and related technology.
- Code of Conduct Questionnaire based on the Code of Conduct on Politico-Military Aspects of Security, which established certain commitments on participating states regarding the conduct and control of their armed forces. States share information on the implementation of these obligations through a questionnaire.
- Chemical Weapons Convention Questionnaire provides information by states on their ratification process for the Chemical Weapons Convention. Through the Anti-Personnel Landmines Questionnaire the participating states share information on their policies and practices regarding anti-personnel landmines.

These mechanisms are probably among the most remarkable developments in the creation of a series of commitments among OSCE states to provide a valuable source of confidence and détente among former potential enemy states. Despite their non-legally binding nature, they have helped states in developing strong commitments in the sensitive area of disarmament and arms control.

These mechanisms are integrated and completed by some documents that fall within the traditional disarmament and armed control multilateral treaties. They include the Treaty on Conventional Armed Forces in Europe (CFE),[103] which binds only 23 states, and the Treaty on Open Skies (entered into force on 1 January 2002, with 26 signatories),[104] which 'establishes the regime, to be known as the Open Skies regime, for the conduct of observation flights by States Parties over the territories of other States Parties' (Article 1.1). The Forum for Security

---

[101] The Vienna Document 1999 established that participating states must provide information on their annual plans for such contacts no later than 15 November each year.

[102] The Document on Small Arms and Light Weapons contains seven information exchanges, the first set of which took place by 30 June 2001.

[103] These categories are identical to those of the UN Register of Conventional Arms.

[104] OSCE, *Treaty on Conventional Armed Forces in Europe*, signed in Paris on 19 November 1990. See K Homan, 'The Adapted CFE Treaty: A Building Block for Cooperative Security in Europe' (2000) 2 *Helsinki Monitor* 52–7.

Cooperation has also adopted the OSCE Document on Small Arms and Light Weapons,[105] which deals with many aspects related to the trafficking, exporting, law enforcement, stockpiling and destruction of small arms, and the OSCE Document on Stockpiles of Conventional Ammunition.[106]

The CSBMs also include an emergency mechanism, which allows a state to ask another state for urgent clarification of military manoeuvres within 48 hours. In the case of a non-satisfactory reply, the state can ask for an emergency meeting of the Conflict Prevention Centre. A parallel mechanism was introduced during the crisis in Yugoslavia. This is an emergency mechanism approved during the 1991 CSCE Council of Minister in Berlin. It could be triggered in the case of a 'serious emergency situation which may arise from the violation of one of the Principles of the Final Act or as the result of major disruptions endangering peace, security, or stability'.[107] Under this mechanism, any state can ask for information to be provided within 48 hours, and in the event of an unsatisfactory reply twelve states can request an emergency session of the Committee of Senior Officers (CSO). The CSO may adopt recommendations for the solution of the dispute, but the problem with this mechanism is that it requires the consensus of all participating states. Therefore, when it was used during the crisis in Yugoslavia, it was blocked by the negative vote of the concerned state. To overcome the veto power involved in the consensus rule, the Prague Council of Ministers approved the consensus minus one rule in 1992.[108] This new rule was used to suspend Yugoslavia from its participation in all OSCE meetings and therefore to avoid its negative vote concerning measures against it. Nevertheless, the measure adopted against the state could be enforced only outside its territory, such as the embargo, to respect the principle of state sovereignty as established in Principle I of the Helsinki Final Act.

9. The Human Dimension

The Human Dimension is probably the best developed tool dealing with security in the OSCE context.[109] The Human Dimension brings broad issues of international human rights law into the area of security, establishing a fundamental relation between peace and conflict prevention. In developing this area of activity, the OSCE respected the use of the universal terminology in the field of human

---

[105] OSCE, Treaty on Open Skies, Helsinki, 24 March 1992, available at <http://www.osce.org/documents/doclib/1992/03/13764_en.pdf>.

[106] OSCE, Forum for Security Co-operation, *Document on Small Arms and Light Weapons*, 24 November 2000, FSC DOC/1/00.

[107] OSCE, Forum for Security Co-operation, Document on Stockpiles of Conventional Ammunition, 19 November 2003, FSC DOC/1/03.

[108] See A Bloed, *The Conference on Security and Co-operation in Europe: Analysis and Basic Documents, 1972–1993*, 2nd edn (Dordrecht: Kluwer Academic, 1993).

[109] OSCE, Second Meeting of the Council, Prague, 30–31 January 1992, available at <http://www.osce.org/documents/mcs/1992/01/4142_en.pdf>.

rights,[110] ensuring a uniform standard and compatibility with other human rights treaties developed at global and regional level. Provisions concerning the freedom of religion, freedom of movement, security of persons, national minorities, rule of law, human contacts and information were included in the 1989 Vienna Document.[111] The Charter of Paris further expanded this area to cover economic cooperation, culture, the environment, migrant workers, and the Mediterranean area. States are committed to comply with the relevant provisions of the Summit Declarations, but commitments are not limited to mere political declarations. The OSCE has developed several interstate monitoring procedures for the control of the application of standards that fall within the Human Dimension. They include the Vienna Mechanism[112] and the Moscow Mechanism,[113] which can be activated either by OSCE states towards another participating state, or by a state seeking advice in specific areas of the Human Dimension. In the field of minority rights the Moscow Mechanism was envisaged to deal with crises within states. The mechanism provides for the possibility of sending a mission of independent experts or a rapporteur to a participating state to investigate the human rights situation. This decision can be taken without the consent of the concerned state, applying the rule of consensus minus one. Nevertheless, decisions on the measures to be taken should be discussed and approved by the CSO on the basis of consensus, therefore limiting again any possible enforcement measure. The Moscow Mechanism has so far been used five times, by the 12 European Community states to investigate atrocities against the civilian population in Croatia and Bosnia Herzegovina (1992); by Estonia to improve its legislation in the areas of universally accepted human rights norms (1992); by Moldova to advance its legislation and implementation of minorities' rights and interethnic relations (1993); in June 1993, by the CSCE Committee of Senior Officials vis-à-vis Serbia-Montenegro to investigate human rights violations, although because of the Federal Republic of Yugoslavia's lack of cooperation, the mission could not be operated; and finally by ten OSCE participating states[114] to examine all matters relating to the conduct of the investigation resulting from the reported attack on 25 November 2002 on President Niyazov, in Turkmenistan (December 2002–March 2003).

The leading institutional organ in the area of Human Dimension is the ODIHR, created in 1991, although the recognition of the importance of minority rights for

[110] See Bloed and van Dijk (eds), n 40, above.

[111] In particular, terminology was drawn from the UN International Covenant on Civil and Political Rights (1966). On the issue, see Ludmilla Alexeyeva, 'Human Rights: The Helsinki Process' (1990) Proceedings of the American Society of Intl L 113–30.

[112] The 1989 Vienna Conference started a series of Conferences on the Human Dimension: Paris (1989), Copenhagen (1990), and Moscow (1991).

[113] Established in the Vienna Concluding Document of 1989, 'Human Dimension of the CSCE', paras 1–4.

[114] Established at the last meeting of the Conference on the Human Dimension in Moscow in 1991 (paras 1–16) and amended by the Fourth Meeting of the Council, Rome 30 November–1 December 1993 (Decisions of the Fourth Council Meeting, ch IV, para 5).

the purposes of security[115] also led to the creation of the HCNM in 1992.[116] The ODIHR deals with four main areas: assistance of democratic processes, monitoring the implementation of the OSCE Human Dimension in participating states, cooperation with intergovernmental and non-governmental organizations, and integration of the Human Dimension into the security activities of the OSCE.[117] The ODIHR has been particularly active in the electoral process in Bosnia under Annex 3 of the Dayton Peace Accords,[118] with quite pervasive powers[119] compared to the traditional OSCE missions that will be mentioned later. The ODIHR is also actively involved in a number of missions in countries participating in the OSCE.

In the field of national minorities, the main role of the HCNM is to provide 'an instrument of conflict prevention at the earliest possible stage'. Nevertheless, it does not deal with individual or collective complaints by minorities. The express consent by a state to the HCNM's involvement in minorities' issues concerning that state is not required, but the HCNM is not completely autonomous in carrying out its tasks. Once the political organs of the OSCE are officially involved in a specific case concerning minorities, the HCNM's activities depend on decisions taken by those organs.[120]

Other mechanisms and programmes have been developed recently to deal with specific aspects of the Human Dimension. Some of them are particularly relevant in relation to security issues. They include: anti-terrorism; freedom of expression, freedom of religion and belief; tolerance and non-discrimination; monitoring places of detention; trial monitoring; use of the death penalty; and states of emergency. All these programmes work under specific mandates and in cooperation with other OSCE bodies, in particular in monitoring and supporting activities within participating states and in Long-term Missions.

10. Peacekeeping and Long-term Missions

Peacekeeping is still not a clearly defined tool, and even the main organization involved in this field, the UN, has been confronted by both practical organizational issues and the clear definition of its legal regulation and limits.[121] In 1992

---

[115] Germany, the USA, Austria, Canada, the UK, Greece, Ireland, Italy, Norway, and Sweden.

[116] Reference to minority rights was included in the 1999 Vienna Document. On the importance of minority issues for security see Li-Ann Thio, 'Developing a "Peace and Security" Approach towards Minorities' Problems' (2003) 52(1) ICLQ 115–50.

[117] CSCE, 1992 Helsinki Summit, Decisions, ch II, para 1.

[118] The mandate of the ODIHR is included in several documents, in particular the 1990 Charter of Paris for a New Europe, the 1992 Helsinki Follow-up Documents, the 1993 Rome Council Meeting, and the 1994 Budapest Review Conference.

[119] Dayton Peace Accords, signed in Paris on 14 December 1995, available at <http://www1.umn.edu/humanrts/icty/dayton/daytonaccord.html>.

[120] See M Sica, 'The Role of the OSCE in the Former Yugoslavia after the Dayton Peace Agreement', in Bothe, Ronzitti, and Rosas (eds), n 1, above.

[121] CSCE, 1992 Helsinki Summit, Decisions, ch II, para 16.

the Helsinki Summit, under the euphoria generated by the end of the Cold War and facing international pressure to deal with the conflict in Yugoslavia, included the peacekeeping[122] option in the mechanisms for dealing with crisis management, providing also quite detailed rules, compared to the UN Charter which is actually silent on this issue. The rules concerning the establishment of peacekeeping operations are included in Chapter III of the 1992 Helsinki Document,[123] subsequently confirmed by paragraph 46 of the Istanbul Charter.[124] The document establishes that 'CSCE peacekeeping activities may be undertaken in cases of conflict within or among participating states to help maintain peace and stability in support of an ongoing effort at a political solution'.[125] It is foreseen that OSCE's peacekeeping operations 'will involve civilian and/or military personnel' and its activities may assume a variety of forms, including observer and monitor missions and larger deployments of forces. Peacekeeping activities could be used, inter alia, to supervise and help maintain cease-fires, to monitor troop withdrawals, to support the maintenance of law and order, to provide humanitarian and medical aid, and to assist refugees. The mandate seems to include a wide range of actions. Nevertheless, there are quite clear limitations provided in the same document. They include the fact that OSCE peacekeeping operations 'will not entail enforcement action';[126] they will 'require the consent of the parties directly concerned';[127] they 'will be conducted impartially';[128] and they 'cannot be considered a substitute for a negotiated settlement and therefore must be understood to be limited in time'.[129]

Because of these limitations, the OSCE has not established peacekeeping missions. As a parallel or alternative tool, the OSCE has developed instead a huge number of so-called Long-term Missions. Some of these missions could fit in the peacekeeping structure, and fulfil the requirements. Others include negotiation powers, institution-building activity, and human rights monitoring. The term 'mission' makes these actions more acceptable to the states involved in them, probably due to the fact that in some way it does not make reference to a situation of conflict, traditionally linked to the term peacekeeping as a result of UN practice. Different names are used to indicate this type of activity, such as 'field missions', and they have been addressed as 'other field activities' if they do not correspond to the Long-term Mission patterns. For instance, in the case of Chechnya the term mission was avoided, and it was replaced by the more neutral expression 'OSCE Assistance Group'. The main OSCE activities in this field since 1992 have been in connection with the crisis in Yugoslavia. OSCE Long-term Missions have

---

[122] J T O'Neill and N Rees, *United Nations Peacekeeping in the Post-Cold War Era* (Abingdon: Routledge, 2005); N D White, *Keeping the Peace: The United Nations and the Maintenance of International Peace and Security* (Manchester: Manchester University Press, 1993).

[123] N Ronzitti, 'OSCE Peace-keeping', in Bothe, Ronzitti, and Rosas (eds), n 1, above, ch 8.

[124] CSCE, 1992 Helsinki Summit Decisions, ch III, *Early warning, conflict prevention and crisis management (including fact-finding and rapporteur missions and CSCE peacekeeping)*, paras 17–56.

[125] See n 37, above.   [126] CSCE, 1992 Helsinki Summit Decisions, n 124, above, para 17.

[127] Ibid, para 22.   [128] Ibid, para 23.   [129] Ibid, para 24.

been also classified under different headings: conflict prevention; crisis management; post-conflict rehabilitation; and liaison office.[130] At present there are fifteen missions in most European and Central Asian countries.[131] The problem with the missions is that they are neither defined nor regulated in any OSCE official document. They do not fit in with the provisions of the 1992 Helsinki Decisions on fact-finding and rapporteur missions.[132] Missions can develop activities of good-offices and mediation, such as the definition of the status of the Transdniestrian region by the OSCE Mission in Moldova. Human rights monitoring is particularly evident in Bosnia Herzegovina, where the Mission monitors the human rights situation and the development and implementation of legislation through a network of field officers. The OSCE Mission in Kosovo (OMIK) supervises elections and police education; and there is a Border Monitoring Operation in Georgia (December 2001). Missions to the Baltic States have dealt with political and economic reforms and minority rights, with particular attention to the issue of the Russian minorities in the Baltic, a matter of friction between the Baltic and the Russian governments. In this context the OSCE has worked in the field of assessing the legislation of the new Republics in the light of non-discrimination rules. In some cases, missions were sent to countries or areas in distress. This was the case in Georgia, Moldova, Tajikistan, and Chechnya. In the case of Chechnya, the OSCE sent an 'OSCE Assistance Group' (1994–7) trying to facilitate the cease-fire between the parties. During the crisis in Yugoslavia, the OSCE managed to send missions to Kosovo, Sandjak, and Vojvodina. But with the suspension of Serbia from any OSCE meeting in 1992, members of the mission were expelled in July 1993. During the worst period of the conflict, between 1991 and 1995, the OSCE did not actually take action in the Balkans. It came to the fore again with the Dayton Peace Accords in December 1995 when it was involved in a wide mission concerning elections, refugees, human rights, and a mandate in the area of confidence-building and arms control actions within the sub-region among the former parties to the conflict.[133]

This brief description of missions shows that there are no established formulae as missions are built within a legal and institutional vacuum, and they are defined mainly by the practice of OSCE decision bodies. They include cooperation between the OSCE and states usually employing existing mechanisms, such as the ODIHR, the HCNM, and other programmes, such as election monitoring,

---

[130] Ibid, para 25.

[131] V Abadjian, 'OSCE Long-Term Missions: Exit Strategy and Related Problems' (2000) 1 *Helsinki Monitor* 24. For a list of present and past missions, including their mandates and tasks, see OSCE, *Survey of OSCE Long-Term Missions and other OSCE Field Activities*, 12 September 2006, at <http://www.osce.org/documents/cpc/2005/08/3242_en.pdf>.

[132] Fact-finding and rapporteur missions are foreseen in 1992 Helsinki Decisions, ch III, paras 12–16.

[133] See R E Rupp and M M McKenzie, 'The Organization for Security and Cooperation in Europe: Institutional Reform and Political Reality', in McKenzie and Loedel (eds), n 1, above, 132–4.

mainly within the area of the Human Dimension. Missions have therefore been defined 'as "soft institutions" in a broader "soft-law" framework'.[134] They are based on the acceptance and conditions of the state involved, and usually they have to perform their activities with a limited number of personnel.

11. OSCE's Relationship with Other International Organizations

By 1992, because of the crisis in the Balkans, there was a strong interest in developing the role of the OSCE in conducting peacekeeping operations with its own forces.[135] This idea was based on the possible development of cooperation with the UN (under Chapter VIII of the UN Charter), and with other European organizations, in particular NATO, the Western European Union (WEU), and the Commonwealth of Independent States (CIS). At the same time, NATO identified the OSCE, and the UN, as potential organizations that could mandate peacekeeping operations where NATO could take part.[136] The legal justification for OSCE's role was the identification of the OSCE as a regional arrangement under Chapter VIII of the UN Charter. The 2005 OSCE Permanent Council decision 670[137] shows the trend in establishing a more formal basis for cooperation with other organizations. The document identifies the basis 'for enhanced cooperation on the existing legal *acquis* of the Council of Europe and the OSCE's political commitments'. Along the same lines, in 2004 the EU Council approved a document, within the European Security and Defence Policy,[138] on cooperation with the OSCE in dealing with crisis management.[139]

The OSCE introduced the issue of cooperation with other institutions and organizations in some of its declarations. The Platform for Cooperative Security, included in the December 1996 OSCE Lisbon Document,[140] developed this idea, but in quite vague terms.[141] Possible cooperation with other institutions is

---

[134] A Rosas and T Lahelma, 'OSCE Long-Term Missions', in Bothe, Ronzitti, and Rosas (eds), n 1, above, 189.

[135] M M McKenzie and P H Loedel, 'Introduction: States and Institutions in European Security', in McKenzie and Loedel (eds), n 1, above, 12.

[136] NATO, Ministerial Meeting of the North Atlantic Council, *Final Communiqué*, Oslo, 4 June 1992, paras 10–11, available at <http://www.nato.int/docu/comm/49-95/c920604a.htm>.

[137] OSCE, Permanent Council, Decision No 670, *Cooperation between the Organization for Security and Co-operation in Europe and the Council of Europe*, PCDEC/670, 28 April 2005.

[138] See F Naert, Chapter 4 of this volume.

[139] EU, 2630th Council Meeting, General Affairs and External Relations, Brussels, 13 December 2004, under the issue 'Cooperation with the OSCE—Crisis Management' approved document 15387/1/04 REV1.

[140] OSCE, Lisbon Summit, *Lisbon Document*, Lisbon, 3 December 1996, DOCS/1/96, available at <http://www.osce.org/documents/mcs/1996/12/4049_en.pdf>.

[141] G P Auton, 'Multilateral Security Regimes: The Politics of CFE and CSBMs', in McKenzie and Loedel (eds), n 1, above, 153.

mentioned in Paragraph 2 of the Platform for Cooperative Security, and in Part III of the 1999 Istanbul Declaration. It is stated that the Principles of the OSCE 'apply to any organization or institution whose members individually or collectively decide to adhere to them' and that the OSCE, playing a 'key integrating role', could offer 'a flexible coordinating framework to foster cooperation, through which various organizations can reinforce each other drawing on their particular strength'. At the same time it affirmed that the OSCE does not 'intend to create a hierarchy of organization or a permanent division of labour among them'. These two documents left a too ambiguous framework for possible cooperation mechanisms.

The first example of institutional cooperation between the OSCE and the UN was the Mission in Georgia.[142] The mission was established in 1992[143] to address the conflict in Georgia and 'to promote negotiations between the conflicting parties in Georgia which are aimed at reaching a peaceful political settlement'.[144] In 1997, on the basis of UN Security Council resolution 1077,[145] a Memorandum of Understanding (MoU) was signed between the OSCE and the UN Human Rights Office in Abkhazia, Georgia.[146] The MoU provides the OSCE Mission to Georgia with powers to implement the relevant parts of its mandate in monitoring the human rights situation in Abkhazia, and supporting the activities of the UN Human Rights Office. The mandate was further expanded to include anti-terrorist implementation of UN resolution 1373[147] and election technical assistance.[148]

Another example of OSCE's cooperation with the UN is the OSCE Mission in Kosovo. Following UN Security Council Resolution 1244[149] the OSCE Permanent Council adopted a decision[150] to work with the UN in the implementation of that resolution. It is affirmed that the OSCE Mission in Kosovo 'will constitute a distinct component within the overall framework of the United Nations Interim Administration Mission in Kosovo (UNMIK), with a specific mandate'. In general terms, the OSCE would 'take the lead role in matters relating to institution- and democracy-building and human rights'. The mandate then specifies the various areas of activity of the mission. The work of the OSCE in the field has developed quite pervasive powers. In fact, the OSCE has been involved in: the organization of elections; the organization of political parties; the establishment of an Ombudsman institution in cooperation with the United Nations

---

[142] On the mission see OSCE, *Survey of OSCE Long-Term Missions and Other OSCE Field Activities*, SECINF/33/05, 26 August 2005, 11–15.

[143] CSCE, CSO Meeting, 6 November 1992, Journal No 2, Annex 2.

[144] CSCE, CSO, *Modalities and Financial Implications*, 13 December 1992.

[145] UN Security Council Resolution 1077, 22 October 1996.

[146] The Human Rights Office in Abkhazia, Georgia (HROAG) was established on 10 December 1996.   [147] UN, SC resolution 1373, 28 September 2001.

[148] Through the OSCE's Georgia Elections Assistance Programme (GEAP).

[149] UN SC resolution 1244, 10 June 1999.

[150] OSCE, Permanent Council, Decision No 305, 1 July 1999.

High Commissioner on Human Rights; the strengthening of the rule of law, including helping to re-establish a judicial system based on democratic principles and human rights; and the area of mass-media, including independent media support, regulations, laws and standards, media monitoring, and Radio-TV Kosovo. Nevertheless, neither in UN Resolution 1244 nor in OSCE Decision 305 is there any reference to the 'regional agreements' defined in Chapter VIII of the UN Charter, and therefore the Mission seems to fall outside this general framework.

The widened concept of security, outlined at the beginning of this chapter, may also undermine the possibility of cooperation between different European organizations. NATO is shifting from a strictly 'defensive alliance' to a 'security organization' so that it is becoming 'difficult to distinguish NATO's enlarged mandate from the overall approach of the Conference on Security and Cooperation in Europe'.[151] The same can be held true with regard to other European organizations, in particular the EU.[152] The latter, having assumed a broad concept of security, including military operations, includes the possibility of using force in its actions, which could take place both within and outside the European region.

Cooperation with NATO has been established in some cases. Since 1992, NATO has identified the possibility of acting under the mandate of the OSCE in the field of peacekeeping operations.[153] Since that time, forms of coordination have been established, including the participation of high officials in meetings of each organization. They included the conclusion, in November 1990, of the Treaty on Conventional Armed Forces in Europe by the then 22 Member States of NATO and the former Warsaw Pact members.

On the operative side, in 1996 and 1997 NATO protection was provided to support the OSCE's administration of general and municipal elections in Bosnia and Herzegovina. The same occurred in 1997 in Albania when the OSCE monitored the resulting elections and NATO provided security. The NATO-led Kosovo force (KFOR) supported the OSCE Kosovo Verification Mission in 1999. In Bosnia and Herzegovina the NATO-led Implementation Force (IFOR) and its successor SFOR have cooperated with the OSCE in the implementation of the Dayton Peace Agreement. IFOR supported the OSCE in its preparations for elections, providing security and logistical support. IFOR and SFOR also supported the OSCE in implementing Article II (CSBMs) and Article IV (Sub-Regional Arms Control Agreements) of the Dayton Agreement, by providing relevant data on weapons cantonments. NATO has also cooperated closely with the OSCE in the Former Yugoslav Republic of Macedonia (FYROM). Although the safety and security of international monitors remains primarily the responsibility of FYROM, a NATO task force was created in September 2001 in order to provide additional security. Cooperation includes the provision of military protection for

---

[151] W Bowens et al, 'The OSCE and the Changing Role of NATO and the European Union' *NATO Rev* 41, n 3 (June 1994), 21–5.   [152] See H Krieger, Chapter 8 of this volume.
[153] NATO, Oslo Ministerial Conference, n 136, above.

OSCE civilian personnel in the field. Furthermore, it seems that the missions in conflict situations are not coordinated by the OSCE, but by other organizations, such as the UN or NATO. Therefore, there is no clear move towards a leading coordination role of the OSCE in the area of security in Europe.

The relationship between the OSCE and the EU has not been very intense. In some missions, such as the EUPM in Bosnia,[154] special agreements for the participation of OSCE states were foreseen. In some cases the EU participates with OSCE, NATO, and the Stability Pact for South Eastern Europe[155] in the 'Ohrid Process on Border Management and Security in South-East Europe'. For the time being cooperation between the EU and the OSCE has not produced formal legal instruments. There is a general tendency at political level to improve forms of cooperation and coordination, but they have not yet been transformed into proper legal agreements.

12. The OSCE and European Security Law

Some of the issues mentioned above are relevant to the definition of a possible role of the OSCE as a comprehensive organization dealing with security in Europe. The classification of the OSCE as an international organization implies that it is acting within the international system, despite its doubtful status under international law. The problem comes when dealing with the legal consequences of OSCE's acts. As mentioned above, international institutions can perform quite different tasks. In the field of legislative or normative powers they can play a relevant role.[156] They may produce new norms on the basis of their legal constitutions. In this case, they may develop new norms as foreseen by the powers attributed to their organs, or may develop new rules that are usually justified on the basis of the inherent powers[157] of the organization. International organizations may also develop new rules in their role of convenors or promoters of new treaties among states participating in the organization.

In all the main documents adopted by the OSCE there is a clear reference to respect of the purposes and principles of the UN Charter, the full support of the UN, and the 'common will to act, in the application of these principles, in conformity with the purposes and principles of the Charter of the United Nations'.[158] The OSCE is also defined as a 'regional agreement under Chapter VIII of the United

---

154 See F Naert, Chapter 4 of this volume.

155 Stability Pact for South Eastern Europe, SCSP Constituent Document, Cologne, 10 June 1999, available at <http://www.stabilitypact.org/constituent/990610-cologne.asp>.

156 On these powers see Sands and Klein, n 84, above, ch 11.

157 On inherent powers see White, n 54, above, 87–9.

158 CSCE, *Declaration on Principles Guiding Relations between Participating States*, Helsinki Final Act; OSCE, Eleventh Meeting of the Ministerial Council, *OSCE Strategy to Address Threats to Security and Stability in the Twenty-First Century*, n 44, above, Maastricht, 1 and 2 December 2003, MC DOC/1/03, 2 December 2003, Section I, para 2.

Nations and a primary organisation for the peaceful settlement of disputes within its region and a key instrument for early warning, conflict prevention, crisis management and post-conflict rehabilitation'.[159] The Charter for European Security added the recognition of the 'primary responsibility of the United Nations Security Council for the maintenance of international peace and security and its crucial role in contributing to security and stability' in the region.[160] It also recognized the rights and obligations under the UN Charter, including non-use of force or threat of force, and the peaceful solution of disputes 'as set out in the United Nations Charter'.[161]

The reference to the UN Charter's principles and purposes is relevant in the analysis of the role of the OSCE within a general framework for the definition of European security law. In fact, if the OSCE might play a major role in the field of security, expanding its tasks and forms of intervention, and work in coordination with other European organizations, in particular with the EU and NATO, it is quite relevant that the envisaged mechanisms should respect the general provisions defined by the UN Charter.

Nonetheless, some legal problems can be envisaged. First and foremost they derive from the nature of the OSCE. It is a non-treaty-based organization, whose commitments adopted as final acts of summits are considered to create mere political and moral compromise, but not legally binding norms. As there is no founding treaty, a constitutional text, to which states are legally bound, on which legal norms would the actions taken by the OSCE be based? The problem consists in assessing how the rules concerning collective security should be considered binding for the OSCE. Two solutions might be envisaged. The first is the one mentioned above, based on the UN membership of all OSCE participating states, and therefore based on the individual obligations of states *uti singuli*. It might be argued that the OSCE participating states, being members of the UN, would be automatically bound by the UN Charter obligations. But it is clear from the past that UN membership does not ensure full respect of international law and the principles enshrined in the UN Charter, as the 1999 NATO bombing of Yugoslavia clearly showed. The second option is based on the fact that by creating an organization states establish a new entity. If that entity has international legal personality it is distinct from the individual subjects that are part of it. Therefore, another basis for binding the OSCE as a subject of international law must be found. One could be the reference to the respect of general international law as applicable to any subject of the international community, and therefore to international organizations as well. As we have assumed in this chapter that the OSCE is an international legal subject, it follows that the organization is bound by international rules concerning the use of force, in particular those provided in the UN Charter.

---

[159] OSCE, *Charter for European Security*, n 37, above, para 7.   [160] Ibid, para 10.
[161] Ibid, para 11.

Of course, this solution cannot resolve a further problem, the indeterminacy of the applicable rules by the OSCE. In fact, in case of need, it would be quite a complex task to exactly define which rules would be applicable in a given case. If it is still quite complex to properly apply the UN Charter, which is framed in legal terms, with established rules of procedure, and has been interpreted for almost sixty years, what could happen when we try to apply a mixture of documents, some very wide and framed in general, or political terms, without legal basis and legal language, which should be interconnected and interrelated among them? The task seems hard, indeed. Nevertheless, it is quite clear that from the analysis of the OSCE documents, and on the basis of its Decalogue, that the use of force, even in the case of collective security actions, must be excluded.

It is not appropriate to consider the OSCE as an organization dealing with collective security in the narrow sense. As we mentioned at the beginning of this chapter, the concept of collective security implies the possibility of mechanisms for enforcement action, when one or more states violates the rules of the system. This procedure is defined in the UN Charter, in particular within Chapter VII. But when dealing with the OSCE, the rules on which the organization is based show that the consent of the state(s) involved is considered an essential element. Even the exceptions to the rule, the consensus minus one and minus two, provide for possible measures taken outside the territory of a state, and not against the sovereign integrity of that state.

In case of either international or internal conflict, the application of some principles of the Decalogue, such as inviolability of frontiers, self-determination, non-intervention, sovereign equality, and the human dimension elements seem at odds.[162] The problems emerged during the Yugoslavian crisis and the subsequent recognition and admission of the new independent states to the OSCE show the difficulty of dealing with the punctual application of the established principles. Nevertheless, as all these principles are not absolute in character, it is considered that the two contrasting principles of self-determination and the inviolability of frontiers can find a solution in favour of the former principle, when the self-determination is not effective in a non-democratic state.[163]

Concerning the rule of consensus, again it was during the Yugoslav crisis that the first exception to the principle of equality of states arose. In 1992 the CSCE Prague Council of Ministers introduced the new rule within the Human Dimension section 'in order to further develop the CSCE's capability to safeguard human rights, democracy and the rule of law through peaceful means'. This included the possibility 'that appropriate action may be taken by the Council or the Committee of Senior Officials (CSO), if necessary in the absence of the consent of the state concerned in cases of clear, gross and uncorrected violations of

---

162 A Rosas, 'Internal Conflicts and the CSCE Process' (1992) 3(2) *Helsinki Monitor* 5–9.
163 F Ermacora, 'Rights of Minorities and Self-Determination', in Bloed and van Dijk (eds), n 40, above, 205.

relevant CSCE commitments'.[164] The actions taken were limited to 'political declarations and other political steps to apply outside the territory of the state concerned' and were limited to the Human Dimension, and not to all CSCE commitments.[165] As a consequence, Yugoslavia representatives were suspended first from participating in decisions concerning the crisis,[166] and later from partici- pation in all CSCE meetings.[167] Suspension did not imply expulsion, as it would be difficult to expel a state from a non-organization such as the CSCE was supposed to be at that time. But even in this case, the decision would meet some criticism. First, there is no reference to any kind of suspension of voting rights in any CSCE official document. The possibility of adopting decisions thanks to the 'suspension' of the state concerned is, of course, an advantage, compared for instance to the veto power in the UN Security Council, but the legality, or at least the conformity of the measure in relationship to the Decalogue, is quite questionable. Secondly, the decision is debatable in particular with reference to Principle I concerning sov- ereign equality, and the respect for the rights inherent to sovereignty, and possibly Principle IX relating to cooperation among states. Thirdly, the 'consensus minus one' rule, as it is now called, directly violates the principle that consensus is the common rule for the adoption of decisions within the OSCE. Therefore this deci- sion should have been adopted by consensus, to justify it under the rules of procedure of the OSCE. Are these new voting rules legally justified? If these rules were adopted and other states did not reject them, they are actually creating customary rules in the field of procedural powers of the organs of the OSCE. We consider that these cases can be also taken as a further example of the 'evolving constitution' of the OSCE as an international organization.

The rule of consensus was again modified with the rule of consensus minus two that would require abstention in decisions concerning two states involved in a dis- pute. It seems that this rule could expand to consensus minus-N, in the case of N number of states involved in a dispute. In this case the OSCE could take actions short of military force. As the Yugoslav experience shows, the OSCE could adopt measures falling within the area of sanctions foreseen by Article 41 of the UN Charter. Nevertheless, those actions should be taken by regional organizations following the authorization of the UN Security Council, as stated in Article 53(1) of the UN Charter. But actions under Article 42 of the UN Charter, implying the use of force against a state, seem not to be authorized by the Decalogue and the principles developed within the OSCE. Therefore they should exclude any trad- itional collective security measure by the OSCE.

---

[164] CSCE, *Prague Document on Further Development of CSCE Institutions and Structures*, Section on 'Safeguarding Human Rights, Democracy and the Rule of Law', (1992) 31 ILM 976 at 987.

[165] See McGoldrick, n 61, above, 161.

[166] Committee of Senior Officers, Decision of 10 June 1992.

[167] Committee of Senior Officers, Decision of 8 July 1992. For an analysis of the suspension see V Perry, 'The OSCE Suspension of the Federal Republic of Yugoslavia' (1998) 4 *Helsinki Monitor* 44–54.

A further problem can be foreseen by paragraph 16 of the Charter for European Security when it establishes that urgent consultation and actions may be required in the case of a participating state 'seeking assistance in realizing its right to individual or collective self-defence in the event that its sovereignty, territorial integrity and political independence are threatened'.[168] The relevant OSCE documents do not provide clear rules and procedures to deal with these cases. Several legal issues can be pointed out. First, the concept of threat is not clear. In the cited passage it seems to get a wide meaning, as it is not limited to external aggression, so it might be invoked also in cases of internal strife that endanger the survival of the state. Secondly, in cases of threat from another state, it is not specified whether the threat should come from a participating state of the OSCE, from a non-participating state, or from both. In any case, the OSCE should apply and follow the principles established by the UN Charter, in particular those foreseen in Article 51 of the Charter, which include the obligation of states to 'immediately report' to the Security Council the measures taken, and establish the priority of the Security Council 'to take at any time such action as it deems necessary in order to maintain or restore international peace and security'. Some clarification of this issue can be taken from paragraph 19 of the Code of Conduct which states that:

In the event of armed conflict, they [the participating states] will seek to facilitate the effective cessation of hostilities and to seek to create conditions favourable to the political solution of the conflict. They will cooperate in support of humanitarian assistance to alleviate suffering among the civilian population, including facilitating the movement of personnel and resources dedicated to such tasks.

This rule puts a limitation on the type of activities that can be taken by states in cases of armed conflict: humanitarian assistance, more than collective security military measures. This conclusion should be considered in conformity with the general provisions contained in the OSCE documents.

Due to the characteristics of the OSCE, a possible role in the field of traditional collective security, involving the use of force against a state, should be excluded, at least on the grounds of the existing principles and rules governing the work of the organization. The provision included in paragraph 16 of the Charter for European Security seems to deal with the general right to individual and collective self-defence, generally admitted in international law, and not with the development of a collective security system within the OSCE region, even if in some cases the border between the two concepts might be blurred, in particular in cases when

---

[168] This principle is also reaffirmed in the Code of Conduct, para 5, where it is stated that:

Participating States are determined to act in solidarity if CSCE norms and commitments are violated and to facilitate concerted responses to security challenges that they may face as a result. They will consult promptly, in conformity with their CSCE responsibilities, with a participating State seeking assistance in realizing its individual or collective self-defence. They will consider jointly the nature of the threat and actions that may be required in defence of their common values.

the aggression would be conducted by a participating state against another participating state. In this case, the collective reaction could fit both in collective self-defence and in collective security action.

13. Conclusions

From the previous analysis some conclusions can be drawn regarding the possible role of the OSCE as a main actor in the development of a European security law. The limitations affecting the rule-making capacity and procedural aspects, due to the unclear legal position of the organization, have been underlined during the analysis in this chapter. To be a fully-fledged security organization, dealing with all areas of security, including collective security measures, the OSCE should change its original status. It might adopt a treaty, as suggested by the recent report,[169] with rules concerning the conduct of such types of operation. This change might meet a negative reaction from some states, and would also put at risk the survival of the organization, as some states would not be interested in providing stronger mechanisms.[170]

The OSCE should not necessarily include an armed branch in its activities to be a security organization. This mission is already taking forms within the new institutional developments of both NATO and the EU. The OSCE should learn from its experience and further develop the 'soft diplomacy' that is the main tool for dialogue and security, based on preventive action. Due to the fact that most of the present conflicts, even within the OSCE region, are intra-state conflicts, the best approach to security, defined in the wide terms that have been presented at the beginning of this chapter, should focus on issues concerning human rights, minorities, migration, democratic institutions, disarmament, etc. This complex of tasks that are usually included in so-called preventive diplomacy and early warning action should provide better tools for preventing conflicts, both internal and international, in Europe. The military option, of course, may be the last resort, as expressed by the UN Charter, but it does not always provide the best results, and it can cause more damage than the problem it tries to tackle. Now that the confrontation of the Cold War is over, new forms and areas of cooperation should be envisaged. Security issues, as mentioned in this chapter, are not only related to military confrontation. This vision is still a Cold War inheritance. In the

---

[169] *Common Purpose: Towards a More Effective OSCE*, n 4, above.

[170] The problem of future developments has been mentioned by the CiO in its statement addressed to the NATO North Atlantic Council held in Brussels, on 26 January 2005, with reference to the Triple 'R' Agenda, which includes Revitalize, Reform, and Rebalance, and has led to the appointment of the Panel of Eminent Persons, on 15 February 2005, to review the OSCE's effectiveness and make recommendations on its future.

wide context of security threats, the OSCE still remains an essential instrument for the development of peaceful relations and of peaceful tools for dealing with actual threats to security in the wide pan-European region.

The OSCE, despite its institutional weakness, has been the most successful organization in the development of confidence-building measures among former potential enemy states in the area of security in Europe. This role might be reinforced, through the negotiation of new treaties concerning cooperation in wide security matters, including terrorism, armaments, environment, migration, etc, which may be relevant for the security of European states and where the OSCE could provide the best negotiating environment. The wider geographical coverage of the new instruments would be a positive outcome if compared to EU and NATO membership.

There should be better coordination with other organizations, in particular with the Council of Europe,[171] in the areas of common interest, including not only the general protection of human rights and fundamental freedoms, but also the development of democratic institutions, the rule of law, and legal reforms in the area of human rights. New legal procedures should be foreseen as part of the development of effective mechanisms to ensure democratic governance in all European countries, including minority rights, as a proper tool to work in the prevention of conflicts. Cooperation with NATO has already been established in the area of disarmament and arms control, and should be enhanced in the future.

The OSCE could participate with other European organizations, in particular with NATO and the EU, in some enforcement measures in the framework of collective security actions. Nevertheless, it should abstain from actions including the use of force, due to its statutory limitations. Other organizations seem more willing to use force, such as NATO, and possibly the future EU. The OSCE could cooperate in applying sanctions and in political and diplomatic measures to solve the dispute peacefully. In some cases, it might participate with other organizations in peacekeeping missions, clearly defined in its mandate, and in cooperation with the host state, within the regional area of its concern, providing the civilian support operation. But it would be highly risky for the OSCE to get involved in military-style operations, as its legitimacy would be strongly undermined, with possible danger for its future activities.

Finally, it seems that the OSCE would better contribute to the development of early-warning, negotiation and peaceful solution of disputes. It could be an example for other regional organizations in the field of cooperative security,

---

[171] Council of Europe, Third Summit of Heads of State and Government, *Warsaw Declaration*, Warsaw 16–17 May 2005, available at <http://www.coe.int/t/dcr/summit/20050517_decl _varsovie_en.asp>.

instead of pushing itself into the enforcement of collective security measures with military actions. In a growing regionalization of international relations, the OSCE could contribute with its experience and membership to a wider concept of security, also within the UN system, as provided by Chapter VIII of the UN Charter.[172] But still the legal and institutional framework would need clearer rules and procedures, as the action of the organization should be better defined and the obligations of participating states better identified.

---

[172] On regionalism and security see L Van Langenhove, 'Towards a Regional World Order' (2004) 41 *UN Chronicle* n 3, 12–13.

14

The EU as a Regional Security Actor within the International Legal Order

Nigel D White *

1. Introduction

In 1945 when the UN was established its 'primary' purpose was to maintain and, where necessary, restore international peace and security.[1] The UN Charter envisaged the universal organization it constituted working on security matters alongside regional security actors. More widely, the UN Charter also formed part of the post-1945 international legal order, contributing in varying degrees to the principles and rules governing the use of military force, the imposition of non-forcible measures, and the protection of human rights and self-determination. In the period 1956–92 the impact of these international rules and institutions on the predecessors of the EU was limited, though there were isolated instances of the European actor taking non-forcible measures through the instrument of European Political Cooperation (EPC).[2] With the EU's entry as a serious security actor on the international stage in 1992 with the adoption of the Maastricht Treaty, it became more pressing to evaluate the position, powers, and limitations of the EU in the international legal order.

The UN has since its inception acted in the sphere of peace and security in accordance with its purposes, while the EU has been a more recent entrant into this field. The UN has also been active in the areas of human rights promotion and more recently democracy promotion as it develops a wider concept of security. The EU's foreign policy has also been driven by these concerns. Increasingly, the activities of the EU and the UN overlap. Sometimes the overlap results in cooperation, sometimes lack of coordination and sometimes confrontation.

---

* Professor of International Law, University of Sheffield, UK and Director of the Centre for Law in its International Context. All website addresses cited were active on 17 October 2006, unless otherwise specified.

[1] *Certain Expenses of the United Nations (Art 17, Paragraph 2, of the Charter)*, Advisory Opinion, [1962] ICJ Rep 151, 167.

[2] M E Smith, *Europe's Foreign and Security Policy* (Cambridge: Cambridge University Press, 2004), 90–116.

The questions to be considered within this chapter concern the rights and duties of the EU and the UN in international law in the related areas of peace and security, human rights, and democracy, as well as the legal relationship between the two bodies. This will then provide a clearer framework within which better cooperation can be achieved. Furthermore, the process of situating the organizations within the international legal order should result in enhancing the legitimacy and arguably the effectiveness of the two organizations, whether they act singly or together. It is important to identify the underlying principles governing the organizations and their activities. It will be argued that there are fundamental (legal) principles underlying the function of collective security in the international community that have to be recognized and reinforced if we are to have organizational activity that is not just simply discretionary or arbitrary.

2. A Subject of International Law?

The EU and the UN are significant players on the international scene to the extent that the post-Westphalian vision of the international political order being dominated by states and the international legal order being dependent on the consent of states is no longer accurate.[3] States are still extremely important but so are international organizations—why else do powerful states keep coming back to the UN to seek approval for their military actions? The collective non-forcible measures taken by the EU against Zimbabwe from 2002[4] appear to be more acceptable to the international community than such measures taken under customary international law by states acting alone or in unison. The basis for these actions is that both organizations have powers separate to, and, in some instances, different from or even greater than, those belonging to Member States.

In anodyne legal terms the label international legal personality is used to signify that organizations meeting certain criteria are separate corporate legal entities capable of acting independently in law from states.[5] That the UN has such a legal nature has not been in doubt since 1949, when the International Court recognized it.[6] Its significance is sometimes lost though. What it means is that, for instance, the UN Security Council representing the UN in security matters is capable of making wide-ranging decisions that potentially extend beyond any that could have been made by the Member States either individually or collectively. The creation of international criminal tribunals, of post-conflict administrations, and the raft of anti-terrorist measures are the main recent examples. Some of these may be controversial, but the controversy is about the extent of the corporate power of the Council, rather than its existence.

---

[3] For a classical statement of international law see *Lotus* Case, 1927, PCIJ, Ser A, No 10 at 18.

[4] See below.

[5] N D White, 'Discerning Separate Will', in W P Heere (ed), *From Government to Governance* (The Hague: TMC Asser Press, 2004) 31.

[6] *Reparation for Injuries Suffered in the Service of the United Nations*, [1949] ICJ Rep, 174 at 178–9.

The continuing debate about the legal personality of the EU since the Maastricht Treaty of 1992 has arguably weakened the EU as an actor on the international stage.[7] Though there now seems to be more consensus on the EU having such independence,[8] the lack of any express recognition is a reflection of a core of doubt at a political, rather than legal, level. The failure of the 2004 Treaty Establishing a Constitution for Europe, with its explicit recognition of legal personality, has continued this uncertainty.[9] It can be contended that for the EU to be a credible security actor it is better viewed as an international legal person. Otherwise it will just be an unincorporated association of states, with no separate rights and duties from Member States. It would for all intents and purposes be no stronger legally than the Commonwealth or the OSCE, which merely act as cyphers for the Member States. The relative weakness of these organizations as security actors is well known.

Of course the Union is more than an unincorporated association of states, more than a modern day Concert of Europe. It has separate powers and separate responsibilities from the Member States. However, to date some of the EU's security policies appear to have been characterized by a confusion as to whether it is the Member States (or some of them) acting collectively or whether it is the organization taking action. This has happened both internally, for instance in the case of Austria in 2000,[10] and externally, for instance in the case of Iran and nuclear technology from 2003.[11]

While personality allows an organization to take separate decisions, in some cases to make law, it also brings with it duties. As international legal persons, organizations are bound by principles of international law.[12] There appears to be no doubt that organizations possessing international legal personality and being active in international relations are subject, at the very least, to *jus cogens* or peremptory norms of international law, such as those prohibiting aggression and genocide, and other basic principles, for example, of human rights, such as nondiscrimination, or those governing the environment, such as the no harm and precautionary principles.[13] Furthermore, it is not acceptable for states to establish organizations that are not bound by the basic principles of international law that

---

[7] K P E Lasok, *Law and Institutions of the EU*, 7th edn (London: Butterworths, 2001) 31.

[8] J Klabbers, 'Presumptive Personality: The European Union in International Law', in M Koskenniemi (ed), *International Legal Aspects of the EU* (The Hague: Kluwer, 1998) 243; R Wessel, 'Revisiting the International Legal Status of the EU' (2000) 5 *Eur Foreign Affairs Rev* 507; D Curtin and I Dekker, 'The European Union as "Layered" International Organisation: International Unity in Disguise', Paul Craig and Gráinne De Búrca (eds), *The Evolution of EU Law* (Oxford: Oxford University Press, 1990) 83–136.   [9] OJ -310/47, 24 December 2004, Art I-7.

[10] M Happold, 'Fourteen Against One: The EU Member States' Response to Freedom Party Participation in the Austrian Government' (2000) 49 ICLQ 953.

[11] W Q Bowen and J Kidd, 'The Iranian Nuclear Challenge' (2004) 80 *Intl Affairs* 257.

[12] N D White, *The Law of International Organisations*, 2nd edn (Manchester: Manchester University Press, 2005) 40–1.

[13] See also P Sands and P Klein, *Bowett's Law of International Institutions*, 5th edn (London: Sweet and Maxwell, 2001) 458–9.

bind states.[14] This makes it clear that states cannot establish international bodies that can carry out acts prohibited in international law for their members.

The purpose of this chapter will be to consider the rights and duties under international law of the EU as an international legal person acting in the field of peace and security. Before doing that, though, it is necessary to consider whether the EU is also subject to the limitations on regional organizations found in the provisions of the UN Charter.

3. A Regional Arrangement within the Terms of the UN Charter?

The issue to be considered in this section is whether the EU is a 'regional' collective security organization in the sense of Chapter VIII of the UN Charter. Chapter VIII purports to govern the relationship between the UN and regional arrangements or agencies in issues of peace and security. Schermers and Blokker include regional organizations within a somewhat wider category of 'closed' organizations which 'seek only membership from a closed group of states and no members from outside the group will be admitted'.[15] Of course there may be some debate about whether an applicant country is within the group or not, as with the case of Turkey and Russia and the EU, but the contrast with universal organizations which are normally open to all states,[16] is clear. It would seem that attempts at further refinement of the concept of regional organization are fraught with difficulty. To define regionalism in terms of geographical proximity is immediately appealing but in practice very difficult to judge as the endless debates about where Europe ends in a geographical sense illustrate only too well. Furthermore, 'the criterion of common cultural, linguistic, or historical relations'[17] is also imprecise and likely to cause as many disputes as it solves.[18]

In reality, regional organizations are non-universal groupings of states that are essentially self-defining in terms of membership and objects and purposes,[19]

---

[14] *Matthews* v *The United Kingdom* (1999) 28 EHRR 316 at para 22 (ECHR).

[15] H G Schermers and N M Blokker, *International Institutional Law*, 4th edn (Leiden: Martinus Nijhoff, 2003) 42.   [16] See for example Art 4 UN Charter.

[17] W Hummer and M Schweitzer, 'Art 52', in B Simma (ed), *The Charter of the United Nations*, 2nd edn (Oxford: Oxford University Press, 2002) 821.

[18] For further discussion see P Taylor, *International Organisations in the Modern World* (London: Pinter, 1993) 7; A Abass, *Regional Organisations in the Development of Collective Security* (Oxford: Hart, 2004) 1–26; E D Mansfield and H V Milner, 'The New Wave of Regionalism', in P F Diehl (ed), *The Politics of Global Governance* (Boulder, CO: Lynne Rienner, 2001) 314–16; M P Karns and K A Mingst, *International Organisations: The Politics and Processes of Global Governance* (Boulder, CO: Lynne Rienner, 2004) 145–53.

[19] See for instance Art 1 of the OAS Charter that provides that the organization is a regional one within the meaning of the UN Charter.

but generally have as their aim the protection or achievement of certain values, such as peace and security or economic prosperity among their membership. The principal ones often share similar goals and values to the UN, ranging across peace and security, human rights and justice, to economic and social well-being, but on a regional level. Thus the potential for overlap between the functions and activities of the UN and regional organizations is considerable.

It is clear that the African Union, the Organization of American States, the League of Arab States, the European Union, and the Association of South East Nations are leading examples of regional organizations. It is also clear that organizations such as the Economic Community of West African States and the *Mercado Commun Del Sur* (MERCOSUR) in South America are also within the broad concept of regionalism as sub-regional bodies. There are other organizations that should be included within the concept of regionalism such as the Organization for Security and Co-operation in Europe (OSCE), though its membership is not confined to European states.[20] However, the North Atlantic Treaty Organisation (NATO) has 'claimed for long not to be a regional organisation but a collective self-defence organisation based upon article 51 of the UN Charter, in order to avoid the application of Chapter VIII'.[21] It is contended, however, that when NATO steps beyond the confines of self-defence, it cannot be but a regional organization for 'functional purposes'.[22]

The EU is certainly a regional body in the economic sense, having a well-developed level of integration between members of the European Community. It is also developing competence with regard to foreign and security policy.[23] Unlike the established regional organizations of the Americas and Africa, which are often concerned with controlling their membership, the EU's security policy is principally external to its membership, relating to threats to or breaches of the peace within or by states that are not members of the EU. This, though, does not disqualify it as a regional organization. The relatively harmonious state of European affairs means that its main concern in security matters is external, though one should not underestimate the propensity of the continent towards violence, as history shows. The election of an extreme right-wing government in Austria in 2000 and the reaction of the EU to it,[24] as well as the threat from terrorism as illustrated by the Madrid bombings of 11 March 2004 and the London bombings of 7 July 2005, show that European security is as much an internal issue as an external one.

---

[20] See the Budapest Document of the OSCE (1994) 15 Human Rights L J 259–72, when the Conference on Security and Cooperation in Europe (CSCE), established since the Helsinki Final Act of 1975, was declared to be the OSCE. The CSCE had already declared in 1992 that it was a regional arrangement in the sense of Chapter VIII of the UN Charter.

[21] C Dominicé, 'Co-ordination Between Universal and Regional Organizations', in N M Blokker and H G Schermers (eds), *Proliferation of International Organizations: Legal Issues* (The Hague: Kluwer, 2001) 69.   [22] Ibid, 70.

[23] See R A Wessel, 'The State of Affairs in EU Security and Defence Policy: The Breakthrough in the Treaty of Nice' (2003) 8 J of Conflict and Security, L 265.

[24] M Happold, 'Fourteen Against One', n 10, above, 953–63.

In general terms, although the EU has not expressly stated that it comes within Chapter VIII (unlike, for instance, the OAS and the OSCE), it has not tried to opt out of the UN Charter system for collective security. Nevertheless, the proposition that the EU comes within Chapter VIII of the UN Charter is not necessarily that clear-cut. In the text of the Treaty on European Union there is a clear statement that the Union in defining and implementing a foreign and security policy shall safeguard its values and preserve peace and security 'in conformity with' and 'in accordance with' the principles of the UN Charter.[25] The principles of the UN Charter are contained in Article 2 of that treaty. Although there is no specific reference to Chapter VIII of the Charter (Articles 52 to 54) in the TEU, it is argued later in this chapter that conformity with the principles of the Charter requires compliance with the rules governing the use of force (contained in Article 2(4)), an integral element of which is the UN Security Council's power to authorize states to use force under Chapter VII (Article 42), or regional arrangements under Chapter VIII (Article 53).

Interestingly though, in the two Security Council authorizations to EU forces to date—ALTHEA in Bosnia (2004) and ARTEMIS in the D R Congo (2003)— the Security Council authorized the forces under Chapter VII (ie, Article 42) rather than Chapter VIII (ie, Article 53) of the UN Charter.[26] Such practice is not incompatible with the presupposition that the EU is a regional arrangement within the meaning of Chapter VIII, for as past Security Council resolutions of the mid-1990s authorizing NATO in Bosnia show,[27] the important issue is gaining Security Council authority to use force, and Chapter VII is the normal method of granting this. This may also be explicable given that both the Bosnian and Congolese forces contained troops from outside the EU and it was therefore more sensible to direct the authorization at the Member States of the UN (including EU states) undertaking the military action. The normal method for the Security Council to authorize Member States to use force is to act under Chapter VII.

Although its future is now in serious doubt, it is still important to consider the Treaty Establishing a Constitution for Europe of 2004, to see whether it would have constituted a clearer signal on the issue of whether the EU is a regional organization within the meaning of Chapter VIII of the UN Charter. The Treaty has a more elaborate set of security provisions and also has an increased number of references to the EU acting in conformity with the principles of the UN Charter and international law.[28] Again, though, there are no specific references

---

[25] Art 11 TEU, OJ C-3255, 24 December 2002.

[26] SC Res 1575, 22 November 2004 (Bosnia); SC Res 1484, 30 May 2003 (DRC).

[27] SC Res 770, 13 August 1992.

[28] Art I-3(4), in relation to upholding and promoting its values; Art I-41(1) in relation to peace-keeping and conflict prevention; Art III-292(1) in relation to the principles that should guide EU action on the international scene; Art III-292 (2) in relation to common policies and actions of the EU.

to Chapter VIII of the UN Charter: the only specific Charter provision mentioned is Article 51 (Chapter VII), which preserves the right of individual or collective self-defence in response to an armed attack and reference to which is found in the Constitutional Treaty's mutual defence clause.[29] The Constitutional Treaty does state that the Union 'shall promote multilateral solutions to common problems, in particular within the framework of the UN',[30] and that the Union 'shall establish all appropriate forms of cooperation with the organs of the UN and its specialised agencies',[31] but these are not specific enough obligations to expressly incorporate Chapter VIII.

On balance though, as the following analysis will show, it is difficult for the EU to deny that it is subject to Chapter VIII. Although it is clearly within the founding states' competence to establish a closed organization by delimiting membership in certain ways, once such an organization is created having as one of its objects and purposes the maintenance or restoration of peace and security, then it is subject to the rules of international law on the use of force, which include the provisions of Chapter VIII of the UN Charter.

4. The UN, the EU, and International Law

Debates about the legal relationship between the UN and regional organizations have tended to focus on Article 53 of Chapter VIII of the UN Charter, which provides that 'enforcement' action by regional bodies has to be authorized by the UN Security Council.[32] A great deal of debate has surrounded issues of interpretation of Article 53, concerning for instance issues of implicit authorization, acquiescence amounting to authorization, and retrospective authorization.[33] Further debate focuses on Article 103 of the UN Charter, which provides that obligations

---

[29] Art I-41(7).   [30] Art III-292(1), 2nd para.

[31] Art III-327(1). See further Art III-305 of the Constitution which deals with EU Member States' obligations when acting within other international organizations, including the obligation on states that are members of the Security Council to 'defend the positions and interests of the Union, without prejudice to their responsibilities under the UN Charter'. This is similar to Art 19 of the existing TEU.

[32] Art 53 of the Charter provides in part that 'the Security Council shall . . . utilize such regional arrangements or agencies for enforcement action under its authority. But no enforcement action shall be taken under regional arrangements without the authorization of the Security Council'. In contrast to enforcement action, when regional organizations take action to defend one of their members from external armed attack, Art 51 of the UN Charter permits the right of collective self-defence 'until the Security Council has taken measures necessary to maintain international peace and security'.

[33] See most recently U Villani, 'The Security Council's Authorization of Enforcement Action by Regional Organisations' (2002) 6 Max Planck Ybk of United Nations L 535; E de Wet, 'The Relationship between the Security Council and Regional Organisations during Enforcement Action under Chapter VII of the United Nations Charter' (2002) 71 Nordic J of Intl L 1; C Walter, 'Security Council Control over Regional Action' (1997) 1 Max Planck Ybk of United Nations L 129.

of Member States under the UN Charter prevail over obligations arising under any other treaties, thereby implicitly including treaties establishing regional organizations.[34] Both of these provisions indicate that there are elements of a hierarchical relationship between the UN and regional organizations such as the EU. While not dismissing the importance of such issues, this chapter tries to look more deeply at the relationship between the UN and the EU in order to more fully understand its underpinnings. It may be that the formalities of the UN Charter represent no real threat to the autonomy of the EU as a security actor, or it may be that they do represent something more fundamental than a formal treaty commitment made by members of the UN either in 1945 or when they subsequently joined.

In traditional international legal terms, the presumption must be against hierarchies. They smack too much of a constitutional system, rather than the traditional contractual system of inter-state relations. In an international system which is still state-dominated and horizontally constructed there must be legitimate reasons for a hierarchy within bodies set up by states. Hierarchies are antithetical to the Westphalian paradigm of sovereign equal nation states recognizing no superior. Even in the post-1945 era of the growth of international organizations there must be a presumption against hierarchies.

Nevertheless, in those two key constitutional provisions mentioned above, Articles 53 and 103, the founders of the UN Charter, the representatives of the international community at the time, not only created an international organization, they provided legal structuring to the relationship both between the UN and regional bodies such as the EU, and between the UN and its Member States (including Member States of the EU). As Bernhardt states, Article 103 means that 'the Charter has a higher rank and that obligations derived from the Charter shall prevail', being part of the Charter's aspiration to 'be the "constitution" of the international community accepted by the great majority of States'.[35] Ress and Brohmer states that under Article 53 a 'regional organisation functions as a subsidiary organ of the UN'.[36]

The distinctive features of the hierarchy provisions in the UN Charter must be borne in mind. While Article 53 is referring to enforcement action by other international organizations within a collective security context, and places authority in the hands of the Security Council, Article 103 refers to obligations on states under international agreements. Bernhardt thinks that the character of the Charter as 'the basic document or "constitution" of the international community' signifies that this superiority extends beyond treaty obligations, but this appears doubtful in practice.[37] There is no clear institutional arbiter of Article 103, though the

---

[34] Art 103 provides that 'In the event of a conflict between the obligations of the Members of the United Nations under the present Charter and their obligations under any other international agreement, their obligations under the present Charter shall prevail'. See Rudolph Bernhardt, 'Art 103', in Simma (ed), n 17, above, 1292–1302.   [35] Bernhardt, 'Art 103', ibid, 1295.
[36] Ress and Brohmer, 'Art 53', ibid, 860.   [37] Bernhardt, 'Art 103', ibid, 1299.

Security Council is relying increasingly on its effect to drive through its anti-terrorist legislation, first against Libya in 1992,[38] and then more widely after the terrorist attacks of 11 September 2001.[39]

The *primary* obligations on states (including EU Member States) under the UN Charter, and thus those that prevail over other treaty obligations by virtue of Article 103 are, in reality, quite limited. The primary obligations are contained in Article 2: the duties of good faith, the peaceful settlement of disputes, not to threaten or use force, and to assist the UN. Other significant ones include the pledge in Article 56 of the Charter to promote higher standards of living, conditions of economic, social progress and development; solutions to international economic and social health problems; cooperation on cultural and educations matters; and respect for and observance of human rights and fundamental freedoms. The normative content of these obligations in the field of economic, social, and human rights matters has been developed by significant constitutional laws since the Universal Declaration of Human Rights in 1948.[40] In addition, there are also important *secondary* obligations arising out of Security Council resolutions binding under the UN Charter by virtue of Article 25.[41]

Thus in practice the hierarchy provisions of the UN Charter are being moulded by the Security Council. This is explicitly provided for in Article 53 regarding regional bodies and enforcement action, while the combination of Articles 25 and 103 has in practice given the Security Council crude supranational powers over Member States. There is some debate to be had about whether these supranational powers relate only to enforcement action as befits an executive body, or whether the Council has legitimately extended them to acquire more of a legislative competence.[42]

Still there remain vast areas of regional organizational activity that are free from UN duties that might prevent regional Member State compliance with regional laws. In these areas, in their operational activities, it is largely a question of practical cooperation between different organizations rather than issues of legal competences. In these activities the primary legal framework for regional organizations, indeed any organization that has international legal personality, is international law. Thus in economic matters—issues of social policy—regional organizations have considerable autonomy. Of course, their decisions may be subject to rules of international law governing human rights for instance (as international legal persons they are bound by such laws), but they cannot be blocked by the Security Council, or directed by the General Assembly or the specialized agencies, except

---

[38] SC Res 748, 31 March 1992.   [39] SC Res 1373, 28 September 2003.

[40] GA Res 217A, 1948.

[41] Art 25 of the UN Charter states that '[t]he Members of the United Nations agree to accept and carry out the decisions of the Security Council in accordance with the present Charter'.

[42] For discussion see M Happold, 'Security Council Resolution 1373 and the Constitution of the United Nations' (2003) 16 Leiden J of Int'l L 593; S Talmon, 'The Security Council as World Legislature' (2005) 99 AJIL 175.

perhaps in a soft law sense. Indeed in most areas, regional organizations are subject to the same international norms as the UN, and both types of organizations contribute to the creation of international law. In some areas of international law, regional organizations can be more developed, as is still the case with the European system of human rights law, and is clearly the case with European economic law as developed by the EC.

In fact in most areas outside collective security matters, and subject to the still relatively rare application of Article 103, the relationship between the UN system and regional systems is not one of institutional hierarchy. In fact, both UN and regional institutions are subject to international law, as international legal persons. There are increasing issues of conflict of norms emerging from regional entities such as the EU, and universal organizations such as the UN Security Council and the World Trade Organisation, with those of international law.[43] Such legal regimes (EU law, UN Law, WTO law) cannot evade fundamental obligations under human rights law for instance, so that sanctions regimes applied by the Security Council, or trade regimes upheld by the WTO's Dispute Settlement Body, or anti-terrorist measures produced by the European Council must all be compatible with basic human rights provisions found in the international and regional human rights treaties.

Indeed, in most collective security matters, Chapter VIII of the UN Charter makes it clear that regional organizations such as the EU have autonomy in diplomacy, in peaceful settlement, and implicitly in the case of consensual peacekeeping, subject to a reporting requirement.[44] It is not proposed in this chapter to look in detail at the whole range of security activities undertaken by the EU, but to consider the issues where there are disputes about hierarchy under the formal provisions of the UN Charter, regarding both non-forcible and forcible measures taken in a security context. These disputes show that there is a complex interplay between the formal provisions of the UN Charter and rules of international law to which all organizations with international legal personality are bound.

5. Non-forcible Measures

As has been stated, regional organizations have a great deal of autonomy in economic matters internal to their regions and membership. International laws are sometimes kept at bay for policy reasons,[45] but there is an acceptance that they are applicable. However, when regional organizations start to flex their economic

---

[43] See for example J Pauwelyn, *Conflict of Norms in Public International Law: How WTO Law Relates to other Rules of International Law* (Cambridge: Cambridge University Press, 2003).

[44] See Arts 52 and 54, UN Charter.

[45] S Peers, 'Fundamental Rights or Political Whim? WTO Law and the European Court of Justice', in Grainne de Burca and Joanne Scott (eds), *The EU and the WTO: Legal and Constitutional Questions* (Oxford: Hart Publishing, 2001) 111 at 130.

muscles problems arise, particularly when they may be trying to coerce non-Member States into changing their behaviour.

It may be argued that in some of these instances of external action regional organizations such as the EU are simply pooling the existing international legal rights of Member States to take collective non-forcible countermeasures to combat breaches of obligations owed *erga omnes*.[46] Normally under international law non-forcible countermeasures are taken bilaterally by a state that has been the victim of a violation of international law against the state in breach. They are temporary measures aimed at seeking to restore normal relations between the parties. Essentially what would otherwise be a temporary breach of international law by the victim state is permitted as a proportionate response to the initial breach by the responsible state.[47] However, if the violation constitutes a breach of a fundamental norm, for example aggression or genocide, then it has been argued that all states have a right to take countermeasures against the state in breach.[48] If those countermeasures do not go beyond the accepted limitations upon that doctrine, then although they are enforcing *international* community obligations, international law arguably recognizes the right of *regional* organizations like the EU to do so. It is a controversial right though.[49] While the International Law Commission (ILC) recognized the existence of *erga omnes* obligations in its 2001 Articles on State Responsibility, it was silent on how to enforce them.[50] In addition, a great deal of regional practice is not so clear. In a number of instances it goes beyond the limited doctrine of countermeasure and in reality constitutes sanctions. While countermeasures are aimed at encouraging the restoration of a legal relationship, sanctions have more punitive and coercive aims.[51]

If regional organizations are exercising sanctioning powers beyond the application of collective countermeasures then they appear to be claiming to have greater rights than the combined rights of the Member States.[52] It could be

---

[46] The concept of *erga omnes* refers to the extent of the interest that other states have in seeing fundamental rules complied with. All states—not only the state which is the victim of a violation of a fundamental rule—have an interest in invoking the responsibility of the state in breach. See further M N Shaw, *International Law* 5th edn (Cambridge: Cambridge University Press, 2003) 116–18.

[47] D Alland, 'Countermeasures of General Interest' (2002) 13 Eur J of Intl L 1221 at 1221.

[48] J Crawford, *The International Law Commission's Arts on State Responsibility* (Cambridge: Cambridge University Press, 2002) 283.

[49] See D Alland, n 47, above, 1221; P Klein, 'Responsibility for Serious Breaches of Obligations Deriving From Peremptory Norms of International Law and United Nations Law' (2002) 13 Eur J Intl L 1241; E Zoller, *Peacetime Unilateral Remedies: An Analysis of Countermeasures* (Dobbs Ferry, NY: Transnational, 1984) 104–5; A Cassese, *International Law*, 2nd edn (Oxford: Oxford University Press, 2005) 275.

[50] Arts 41 and 54 of the ILC's Arts on Responsibility of States for Internationally Wrongful Acts (2001). See Crawford, n 48, above, 302.

[51] N D White and A Abass, 'Countermeasures and Sanctions', in Malcom D Evans (ed), *International Law*, 2nd edn (Oxford, Oxford University Press, 2006), 512; Zoller, n 49, above, 106; G Abi-Saab, 'The Concept of Sanction in International Law', in V Gowlland-Debbas (ed), *United Nations Sanctions and International Law* (The Hague: Kluwer, 2001) 32.

[52] But see F L Morrison, 'The Role of Regional Organisations in the Enforcement of International Law', in J Delbrück (ed), *The Allocation of Law Enforcement Authority in the International System*

argued that when they are exercising the power to impose economic sanctions inter partes, within the regional membership, then the members of the regional organizations have consented to this. But upon what basis can such organizations exercise these sanctioning powers externally, for instance in the case of the EU sanctions against Burma in 2000 and Zimbabwe in 2002, both taken without any Security Council authority?[53] From where does a regional organization claim to get its power of global governance when imposing sanctions against third States outside its region?

In general terms the enforcement of international law is not by any means wholly centralized in international institutions, but at the same time self-help by states has been severely restricted since 1945. The lacuna in the enforcement of fundamental rules that this process has left has arguably been filled by states taking collective countermeasures, and by regional organizations, along with the UN, when it is able to act, enforcing international law. Following this line of argument, in principle when fundamental rules of international law are being breached, regional communities of states should be able to take global action. On this basis non-forcible sanctioning power, not clearly belonging to individual states, can be claimed by a regional actor such as the EU for the enforcement of fundamental rules.

Again, the argument is controversial since the enforcement of international law by the taking of non-forcible coercive measures has been much reduced for the state, as shown by the narrow doctrine of countermeasures codified by the ILC in 2001. If this is the case why should it be less restrictive for the regional actor? The answer must be because of the greater legitimacy action by a regional grouping of states brings. This must then depend upon the level of constitutional development in the relevant regional organization, for the more checks and balances and the greater the democratic development, the more legitimate the decision, and the less likely that a regional hegemon will dominate the decision.[54] Although there is clearly a democracy deficit within the EU,[55] it has greater legitimacy in this regard, evidenced by the fact that it has direct elections to the European Parliament.

There is certainly practice by regional organizations that suggests economic sanctions do not require the authorization of the Security Council under

---

(Berlin: Duncker and Humblot, 1995), 39 at 46–7, where he states that organizations cannot have more powers than Member States.

[53] For Burma see Regulation No 1081/2000, 22 May 2000 [2002] OJ L-122, 24 May 2000—covering equipment for suppression, freezing of funds of persons related to important government functions—due to human rights violations. For Zimbabwe see Regulation 310/02, 18 February 2002—relating to the freezing of funds and assets of members of government and ban on export of suppression equipment—due to human rights violations [2002] OJ L-050, 21 February 2002—see also Council Regulation 313/2003, [2003] OJ L-046, 20 February 2003).

[54] For criticisms of regional organizations in this regard see S N MacFarlane and T G Weiss, 'Regional Organisations and Regional Security' (1992) 2 *Security Studies* 16 at 29–34.

[55] R Burchill, 'The Future or Failure of Democracy in the EU' (2001) 7 Eur Public L 307.

Article 53,[56] but it is only the EU's practice in this matter that has been consistently external, starting in the 1980s with its measures taken against Argentina for its invasion and occupation of the Falklands.[57] The EU's ability to undertake external non-forcible enforcement action is not argued to be a unique competence, but is a product of its more advanced constitutional development, and its concern with developing an external foreign policy (which is also an issue of advanced regional development).

Regional organizations such as the EU are claiming external competence over international matters, competence that states do not have. Or to put it more subtly, when the EU engages in economic coercion, it is not subject to so much criticism as when individual states engage in such activity. The UN's position on economic measures undertaken by regional bodies is equivocal—from San Francisco to the debates in the 1960s about sanctions imposed by the OAS, it has never been clear that Article 53 covers non-forcible measures, requiring the authorization of the Security Council. It is of course possible that the UN (Council or Assembly) could censure sanctions that it felt went beyond the Charter or the principle of non-intervention,[58] just as it has done for individual states, for example in relation to the US embargo of Cuba.[59] Many of the internal (Haiti-OAS) and external (Iraq-EU, Federal Republic of Yugoslavia-EU) regional sanctions regimes imposed in the 1990s[60] have actually complemented to a large degree the UN's own measures, even though they may have technically preceded them. This signifies that the precise nature of the relationship between the UN and regional organizations on non-forcible measures has not been fully developed.

The situation seems to be that there is a presumption in favour of regional organizations like the EU possessing a power to impose economic sanctions against members, and in certain circumstances (where fundamental rules are being breached), against third States. While it might have been the intention of the drafters of the UN Charter to put any coercive enforcement measures (whether forcible or not) under the authority of the Security Council, this has not been the case in practice.[61] The main reason for this is because the basic freedom to trade or to shape economic relations between states has not been prohibited, though it has been curtailed, in the post-1945 era. Against this background of international law

---

[56] Comments by R Wolfrum in Delbrück (ed), n 52, above, 91.
[57] EC Regulation 877/82, [1982] OJ L-102/1.
[58] Shaw, n 46, above, 1039:

The principle of non-intervention is part of customary international law and founded upon the concept of respect for the territorial sovereignty of states. Intervention is prohibited where it bears upon matters which each state is permitted to decide freely by virtue of the principle of state sovereignty ... Intervention becomes wrongful when it uses methods of coercion in regard to such choices, which must be free ones.

[59] See for example GA Res 56/9, 4 December 2001.
[60] See White and Abass, n 51, above, 520–1. See EC Regulation 2340/90, [1990] OJ L-213/1 re Iraq; EC Regulation 3300/91, [1991] OJ L-315/1 and EC Regulation 1432/92 [1992] OJ L-151/4 re the Federal Republic of Yugoslavia. [61] C Dominicé, n 21, above, 82.

where there is no clear prohibition on economic coercion[62] (somewhat perversely given the very narrow doctrine of countermeasures), other international legal persons can utilize such freedoms. Or to put it another way, the clouds of obscurity that surround economic coercion when undertaken by a state are largely lifted when undertaken by an organization. Of course, the universal organization is endowed with such powers without any doubt,[63] but because the universal rules of the Charter do not prohibit economic coercion, it is also the case that in certain circumstances, regional organizations have a similar power.[64] Attempts to argue that the prohibition on the use of force in Article 2(4) of the Charter also covered economic force or coercion, as well as armed force, failed.[65] Thus against the background of a lack of a clear prohibition, regional organizations such as the EU have asserted a right of economic coercion.

6. Military Measures

Just as a state's right to take non-forcible measures has been restricted (but not prohibited) in the post-1945 era, a state's right to take military action has also been (more severely) restricted in the new world order of 1945. In their unilateral military actions, once states have gone beyond the right of self-defence, they are acting beyond what is clearly lawful.[66] There may be attempts to develop the law of self-defence to allow for defence of individuals in other countries,[67] or to deal with imminent or indeed latent threats,[68] but the presumption of illegality of such unilateral operations must be contrasted with the presumption of legality if the Security Council authorizes such operations.[69] The question then becomes whether regional organizations like the EU have a similar competence.

Here the debate is no longer about the interpretation of Article 53, which, as will be recalled, requires enforcement action by regional bodies to be authorized by the UN Security Council. If 'enforcement action' has any meaning at all it must cover aggressive military action, action that would otherwise be unlawful if it were

---

[62] O Y Elagab, *The Legality of Non-Forcible Counter-Measures in International Law* (Oxford: Clarendon Press, 1988) 212–13; White and Abass, 'Countermeasures and Sanctions', in M Evans (ed), n 51, above, 521–4.

[63] Art 41, UN Charter.

[64] Though they might be restricted by the principle of non-intervention—see White and Abass, 'Countermeasures and Sanctions', in M Evans (ed), n 62, above, 521.

[65] J Paust and A P Blaustein, 'The Arab Oil Weapon—A Threat to International Peace', (1974) 68 AJIL 410 at 417.   [66] Arts 2(4) and 51, UN Charter.

[67] For discussion of the arguments for humanitarian intervention as providing for a further lawful means of using force see S Chesterman, *Just War or Just Peace? Humanitarian Intervention and International Law* (Oxford: Oxford University Press, 2002); J L Holzgrefe and R O Keohane (eds), *Humanitarian Intervention: Ethical, Legal and Political Dilemmas* (Cambridge: Cambridge University Press, 2003); B D Lepard, *Rethinking Humanitarian Intervention: A Fresh Legal Approach Based on Fundamental Ethical Principles* (Pennsylvania: Penn State University Press, 2003).

[68] C Henderson, 'The Bush Doctrine from Theory to Practice' (2004) 9 J of Conflict and Security L 3.   [69] Arts 42 and 53, UN Charter.

not permitted. The very idea of authorization in Article 53 assumes that otherwise the action would be illegal, a situation which applies to military enforcement action which is prohibited by Article 2(4) of the UN Charter,[70] but not economic enforcement (or at least not all of it).[71] While 'enforcement' action may have been interpreted more restrictively than the 1945 consensus to exclude (at least presumptively) economic sanctions, if it still retains its core meaning it must cover military enforcement action, thus requiring Security Council authorization.

The continued application of Article 53 to military enforcement action by regional organizations is not just a result of the terms of the provision itself, but is underpinned by the other hierarchy provisions of the Charter. More fundamentally it is underpinned by the peremptory nature of the prohibition on the threat or use of force.[72] Some regional military enforcement (including robust peacekeeping) practice appears contrary to Article 53, for example the action of the OAS in the Dominican Republic in 1965, the Arab League in Lebanon in 1976, and of ECOWAS in Liberia and Sierra Leone in the 1990s and beyond.[73] This might be argued to have undermined this provision if it were not part of the more fundamental hierarchies of the UN Charter: first, Article 103 regarding the Charter obligation to refrain from the use of force, and secondly of international law, namely the *jus cogens* obligation to refrain from the use of force. The Security Council, by virtue of Article 42 of the UN Charter, is specifically allowed to take military action in response to threats to the peace, breaches of the peace, and acts of aggression.[74] The Council's power is part of the Charter rules governing the use of force, as is the right of self-defence belonging to individual states, and both are part of the peremptory norm as well.[75] Thus it is the case that, backed by the hierarchy provisions of the Charter (Articles 53, 103), and by the hierarchy provisions of international law, the Security Council has powers of military enforcement not possessed by states or by regional organizations.[76]

---

[70] Art 2(4), UN Charter provides:

All Members shall refrain in their international relations from the threat or use of force against the territorial integrity or political independence of any state, or in any other manner inconsistent with the purposes of the United Nations.

[71] Villani, n 33, above, 539.

[72] I Brownlie, *International Law and the Use of Force by States* (Oxford: Oxford University Press, 1963), 488–9; Shaw, n 46, above, 117–18.   [73] White, n 12, above, ch 8.

[74] Art 42 provides in part that:

Should the Security Council consider that measures provided for in Art 41 would be inadequate or have proved inadequate, it may take such action by air, sea, or land forces as may be necessary to maintain or restore international peace and security . . .

[75] *Jus cogens* are not confined to customary rules according to Bernhardt, 'Art 103', in Simma (ed), n 17, above, 1294.

[76] See J Delbrück, 'The Impact of the Allocation of International Law Enforcement Authority on the International Legal Order', in Delbrück (ed), n 52, above, 135 at 158:

International law is increasingly developing elements of a hierarchical order as is evidenced by the way international law enforcement authority is allocated, and even more so by [the way] its exercise is conceptualised ie by police-like enforcement of norms of 'public interest'.

In other words, there are two basic hierarchies in international law. First of all those provisions in the UN Charter that provide for Council authority over non-defensive uses of force, and that provide that Charter obligations including the obligation to refrain from the threat or use of force, prevail over other treaty obligations. Secondly, there are the recognized fundamental norms of the international community or *jus cogens*,[77] which include the prohibition of the threat or use of force. These two combine to effectively protect the rules governing the use of force from any real erosion by contrary regional practice, unlike the rules governing economic sanctions where the ambiguous term 'enforcement action' in Article 53 is not backed up by clear customary rules, and certainly not by any peremptory rules, to prohibit non-forcible measures by regional organizations.

There may be greater leeway in the case of economic measures (where a state has some freedom on trading matters), allowing a collection of states in a region powers of coercion. However, there is no real freedom in use of force matters where there is a clear prohibition on the use of force—a fundamental restriction in international law, allowing only limited exceptions. This is bolstered by Articles 103 and 53 of the Charter. In other words, it is a combination of universal international law,[78] and the powers of the universal organization (the UN) that gives universalism a certain supremacy over regionalism in use of force matters. In military matters regional organizations thus only have autonomy in collective self-defence (a right clearly belonging to states),[79] and peacekeeping (if consensual),[80] but not in enforcement action.

7. The Legitimacy of the Security Council

The argument that in matters of use of force the UN has a certain supremacy over the EU and other regional actors is countered by criticism of the legitimacy of the decision-making process in the Security Council.[81] Can the authority of the UN

---

[77] Jus cogens are fundamental (peremptory) rules from which no derogation is allowed. They contain obligations upon states (and other actors) not to commit certain acts. See Art 53, Vienna Convention on the Law of Treaties 1969.

[78] J Charney, 'Universal International Law' (1993) 87 AJIL 529.

[79] Art 51 was drafted to accommodate the rights of regional organizations to undertake actions in collective self-defence: Brownlie, n 72, above, 270.

[80] On the importance of consent for peacekeeping, distinguishing it from military enforcement, see the International Court's advisory opinion in *Certain Expenses of the United Nations* [1962] ICJ Rep 151. For a discussion of regional peacekeeping and enforcement see C Gray, *International Law on the Use of Force*, 2nd edn (Oxford: Oxford University Press, 2004) 282–327.

[81] See N Tsagourias, 'The Shifting Laws on the Use of Force and the Trivialization of the UN Collective Security System: The Need to Reconstitute It' (2003) XXXIV Netherlands Ybk of Intl L 55. But see comments by C Schreuer in J Delbrück (ed), n 52, above, at 86, where he argues that the Council is more representative than the Assembly where small states that contribute very little to the budget can win a vote.

be undermined by the undoubted selectivity and lack of representation in Security Council decision-making?[82] Furthermore, does this signify that the failure to take military enforcement measures by the Council allows states or regional bodies to take action in its stead—as occurred in the case of NATO military enforcement action to bring an end to the repression in Kosovo in 1999?[83] There seem to be some implications of this type of approach in the EU's Security Strategy of 2003,[84] the 1999 Security Protocol of ECOWAS,[85] and the 2000 Constituent Treaty of the AU.[86] Claims to take military action in these documents can be interpreted very widely indeed, and yet they are subject to much more muted criticism when compared to the US claims to use force in a wide range of situations in the National Security Strategy or Bush Doctrine of 2002.[87] It seems that they have greater legitimacy because they were adopted by regional organizations representing the collective view of groups of states.

It may be argued that the European Council of 25 states, or the NATO Council of 26 states, acting by and large by consensus, are more representative than the UN Security Council of 15 states with an in-built hierarchy. However, it must be pointed out that the European Council represents European states only, while the Security Council, for all its defects, represents the international community.[88] At the UN's founding constitutional moment in 1945,[89] it was the international

---

[82] See N D White, 'The Will and Authority of the UN Security Council After Iraq' (2004) 17 Leiden J of Intl L 645.

[83] See the debate between Simma and Cassese. B Simma, 'NATO, the UN and the Use of Force: Legal Aspects' (1999) 10 Eur J of Intl L 1; A Cassese, '*Ex Injuria ius Oritur:* Are We Moving Towards International Legitimation of Forcible Humanitarian Countermeasures in the World Community?' (1999) 10 Eur J of Intl L 23.

[84] 12 December 2003. At 7 the Strategy states that 'we should be ready to act before a crisis occurs', tackling such threats not 'by purely military means'.

[85] See Arts 3(a), 22(c), and 25(c), Art 22(c) provides for 'humanitarian intervention in support of humanitarian disaster'.

[86] Art 4(h) provides for 'the right of the Union to intervene in a Member State pursuant to a decision of the Assembly in respect of grave circumstances, namely: war crimes, genocide and crimes against humanity'. However, it is worth noting that in the 2002 Protocol Relating to the Establishment of the Peace and Security Council of the African Union, there are provisions that show greater deference to the UN Charter rules. Art 17(1) provides that 'in the fulfilment of its mandate in the promotion and maintenance of peace, security and stability in Africa, the Peace and Security Council shall cooperate closely with the United Nations Security Council, which has primary responsibility for the maintenance of international peace and security...'. Art 17(2) further states that 'where necessary, recourse will be made to the United Nations to provide the necessary financial, logistical and military support for the African Union's activities in the promotion and maintenance of peace, security and stability in Africa, in keeping with the provisions of Chapter VIII of the UN Charter on the role of Regional Organisations in the maintenance of international peace and security'.   [87] Henderson, 'The Bush Doctrine', n 68, above.

[88] Art 24(1), UN Charter states that:

... in order to ensure prompt and effective action by the United Nations, its Members confer on the Security Council primary responsibility for the maintenance of international peace and security, and agree that in carrying out its duties under this responsibility the Security Council acts on their behalf.

[89] See D Sarooshi, *The United Nations and the Development of Collective Security* (Oxford: Oxford University Press, 1999) 26–32.

community as a whole creating something unique,[90] that only the international community (ie, all states acting together in another constitutional moment) could subsequently take away. The founders also established fundamental universal rules such as the non-use of force, which can only remain valid if they are ultimately regulated by universal organizations. This signifies that only the UN can authorize any derogations from the prohibition of the use of force beyond a state's inherent right of individual or collective self-defence. Regional self-authorization would be subject to too much abuse—the genie of a regional world police force would be let out of the lamp, and it would be very difficult to put back.[91] Indeed, the likelihood of competing regional police forces would be great. Consequently, instead of having universal rules governing the use of force, potentially conflicting regional rules would emerge.

Nevertheless, the universal organization is in need of significant improvement. The problems of legitimacy in the Security Council signify the need for either a more representative/accountable Council exercising its primary responsibility for peace and security[92] in a proactive consistent manner, or a re-invigoration of the subsidiary powers of the General Assembly recognized in 1950 in the Uniting for Peace Resolution.[93] However, weaknesses in the universal organization do not signify that regional organizations can step in to fill the gaps, at least in matters of military enforcement. The international community created a universal organization to police universal rules, something not possessed by individual states, or even non-universal organizations. As has been stated, only the international community as a whole could take this away. Until that happens, we are stuck with the Security Council, currently with its in-built selectivity, and a very limited Assembly with subsidiary powers to recommend enforcement measures that can be exercised in exceptional circumstances.

Unfortunately, the inaction of the Security Council to deal with the crimes against humanity being committed in the Darfur region of Sudan[94] from 2003 onwards is evidence of the continued failure of the Council to take action in all cases of serious violations of international law. The smokescreen sent up by its reference of the matter to the International Criminal Court in March 2005[95] should not distract from the fact that all the Council could achieve, in the sense of taking

[90] See comments by C Schreuer in J Delbrück (ed), n 52, above, 82, who states that 'the evolving regime of the United Nations now goes beyond the sum total of the powers of individual states'. It is argued here that, at least on paper, this was the case in 1945.

[91] Simma, 'NATO'. But see Abass, n 18, above, 204 and T Farer, 'The Role of Regional Collective Security Arrangements', in T G Weiss (ed), *Collective Security in a Changing World* (Boulder, CO: Lynne Rienner, 1993).   [92] Art 24(1), UN Charter.

[93] GA Res 377, 3 November 1950. See further N D White, 'The Legality of Bombing in the Name of Humanity' (2000) 4 J of Conflict and Security L 27; S D Bailey and S Daws, *The Procedure of the UN Security Council*, 3rd edn (Oxford: Clarendon, 1998) 296.

[94] That this level of abuse has occurred is determined by a commission set up by the Council itself. See report of the International Commission of Inquiry on Violations of International Humanitarian Law and Human Rights Law in Darfur (UN doc S/2005/60).

[95] SC Res 1593, 31 March 2005.

meaningful action to prevent crimes being committed, was a mere threat of non-forcible measures.[96] By locking up the rules on the use of force on the matter of enforcing fundamental rules of international law in the Security Council, the drafters created an inherently selective and weak system. To unlock those rules in favour of regional organizations, however, may prove to be more disastrous. The better course is for a reformed and legitimate Council to emerge out of the current pressure for change.[97] Though the recent World Summit (14–16 September 2005) does not move the issue of structural reform of the Security Council forward, the EU and its Member States (including the two permanent members of the Council) should actively promote and support such reform.

The World Summit did, however, endorse the idea that the Security Council had a responsibility to protect in instances of crimes against humanity and similar offences. The actual commitment was less forthright than that recommended by the High Level Panel in 2004[98] but welcome nonetheless.

We are prepared to take collective action, in a timely and decisive manner, through the Security Council, in accordance with the UN Charter, including Chapter VII, on a case by case basis in cooperation with relevant regional organizations as appropriate, should peaceful means be inadequate and national authorities manifestly fail to protect their populations from genocide, war crimes, ethnic cleansing, and crimes against humanity.[99]

In the future, in certain situations of grave human rights abuses, the Security Council should be less able to hide behind its hitherto discretionary façade. If it does then its failure to comply with the standard set by the UN itself will erode its legitimacy to the point of no return. It is also interesting to note the reference to cooperation with regional organizations in ensuring that vulnerable populations are protected. Potentially this may become important if the Council is blocked or is otherwise unwilling to grant authority to a regional organization that is prepared to take measures in genuine cases of crimes against humanity.

Neither the EU, nor its members, should support the maintenance of the status quo, nor should they support illegitimate or unlawful Security Council measures. For instance, in its relationship to the International Criminal Court, the Security Council must use its power of referral of situations to the Court under Article 13 of the Rome Statute to support a wider security policy, not as an excuse for a lack of such. Further, it should not use its power of deferral of situations under Article 16 of the Rome Statute to protect permanent members' troops from being subject to the jurisdiction of the ICC.[100] The fact that the

---

[96] SC Res 1556, 30 July 2004; SC Res 1564, September 2004.

[97] See Report of the Secretary General, 'In Larger Freedom: Towards Security, Development and Freedom for All' (UN, 2005) paras 167–70.

[98] Report of the High Level Panel on Threats, Challenges and Change (UN, 2004), recommendation 55.   [99] GA Res 60/1, 24 October 2005.

[100] SC Res 1422, 12 July 2002. See R Cryer and N D White, 'The Security Council and the International Criminal Court: Who's Being Threatened?' (2002) 8 *Intl Peacekeeping Ybk* 143.

Council has done both of these things in the short period of time that the ICC has come into being reflects badly on the Security Council, increasing pressure for meaningful reform.

8. Conclusion

It could well be argued that there are too many contradictions in the above analysis, in particular the argument that the EU is a regional organization subject to the authority of a body—the Security Council—that has been heavily criticized. Doesn't this decrease the effectiveness of the EU as a regional actor? It is difficult enough to get agreement within the EU to take action without submitting to international requirements. The answer to these questions is that in instances where fundamental principles govern then the EU or any other actor has no choice, if it wishes its actions to be accepted by the international community, but to comply with these rules. It can argue to change the rules and the mechanisms. It should lobby strongly for a reformed Security Council.

It is not suggested that the EU is actively considering circumventing the Security Council, but circumstances will arise in which it is faced with the issue. It is important that regional organizations respect the rules of international law. Although we speak of a democracy deficit in the EU it is not hard to imagine regional organizations with little or no democracy, dominated by a hegemon, willing to intervene by force in states with little justification or provocation. Furthermore, if one accepts that regional organizations can act autonomously in military matters, there is no validity in arguing that universal laws are somehow still applicable to ad hoc groupings of states, or indeed an individual state that declares it is acting on behalf of the international community. The invasion of Iraq in 2003 might seem to have been just such a case with the UK and USA acting without UN authority, but the importance of the reaction of most of the rest of the world in not recognizing the legality of such actions should not be underestimated.

With its recent activities in the security field, what could be labelled 'hard' security action of a military nature, to add to its pattern of practice in sanctions over the years, the EU has entered onto the regional and international security stage. But as an international legal person it, like any other subject of international law, is subject to the obligations of international law, as well as the rights conferred upon it. Furthermore, the autonomy that legal personality brings enables a security organization to take action over and above that possessed by individual Member States. This helps to explain the EU's sanctioning competence in its external relations. However, the duties of international law mean that the EU must comply with the rules governing the use of force. These prevail over any inconsistent EU obligation (whether created by the TEU or by secondary legislation), by virtue of Article 103 of the UN Charter and by virtue of the peremptory nature of the rules governing the use of force. This means that to take military enforcement action (as opposed to defensive or consensual action), the authority of the Security Council must be secured. States can gain Security Council authority under Chapter VII, while regional organizations can do so under Chapter VIII. It follows then that the EU, as a regional security actor with separate will, is bound by the provisions of Chapter VIII.

Thus in the matter of military enforcement action, the UN Security Council still has constitutional authority on its side, by dint of the Charter and by reason of the peremptory rules of international law, but as with other constitutional systems it is dependent upon issues of legitimacy, authority, and loyalty. If the UN Security Council cannot uphold the fundamental principles of the Charter and of international law,[101] then authority may pass elsewhere, not only to regional organizations that we may have confidence in but also ultimately to individual powerful states. This would lead to a degradation of the most basic rules in any system, namely those governing the use of force. Thus the EU must resist the temptation to seek short-term gains by taking military action outside the framework of international law, for the longer-term consequences for the fragile international legal order may be profound and destabilizing. It is better for the EU to use its considerable influence to improve the universal organization and to deepen its cooperation with it.

---

[101] The Security Council is not restricted in its actions under Chapter VII to dealing with breaches of international law: see H Kelsen, *The Law of the United Nations* (London: Stevens, 1950) 294. However, as Vera Gowlland-Debbas argues 'the development of the concept of fundamental community norms logically calls for centralised and institutionalised mechanisms to ensure their respect and compliance' (V Gowlland-Debbas, 'Introduction' in V Gowlland-Debbas (ed), n 51, above, 8). See further V Gowlland-Debbas, 'Security Council Enforcement Action and Issues of State Responsibility' (1994) 43 ICLQ 55.

CONCLUSION

15

Conclusions on the Current State of European Security Law

Nigel D White and Martin Trybus

The EU is a significant actor on the international scene to the extent that the post-Wesphalian vision of the international political order being dominated by states and the international legal order being dependent on the consent of states is no longer truly accurate. States are still extremely important but so are international organizations—why else do Member States take joint actions and seek, and act under, the authority of the EU when taking military measures? Sometimes such measures amount to Member States exercising their sovereign rights under the auspices of the EU, on other occasions they are being taken as an exercise of the rights and powers of the EU per se.

There is no doubt that since 1992, and to a lesser extent before that, the EU has become an important regional security organization though it still has a significant way to go before it can match the economic power of the first pillar of the Maastricht temple—the EC. While it can use its economic might to help it pursue its security aims, and related human rights and democracy protection aims, through trade and development agreements with other states, the EU will not become a central security actor until it can develop an effective military option. As was pointed out by Martin Trybus in Chapter 2, this was realized in the 1950s but the political will was not present until the end of the Cold War and the tumultuous events that have happened on the edges of Europe that forced European leaders to reconsider that shelved idea.

This book has focused to some degree on the development of the EU's military capacity, in relatively small-scale operations in Macedonia, the Democratic Republic of the Congo and others as fully reviewed by Frederik Naert in Chapter 4, to the larger operation in Bosnia from December 2004. Considerable progress has been made on operational (legal) aspects of deploying such forces. Furthermore, as discussed by Nicholas Tsagourias in Chapter 5, there is some conceptual room for the development of EU peacekeeping operations until they run up against firm rules of international law. There is also debate to be had as to whether the military option should be truly military in the NATO sense or whether it should reflect more the civilian roots of the development of the European enterprise. There is a clear tension between a civilian approach to security and the, admittedly problematic, development of a European armaments policy, as discussed in Chapter 9 by Aris Georgopoulos.

A significant start has been made down the road to developing military capacity, but the EU is still an infant military actor, not yet strong enough or predictable enough to challenge the established security actors—NATO, the UN, and of course, sovereign states. The advent of the EU as a security actor will not prevent recourse to unilateralism, as the invasion of Iraq in 2003 shows, though it might help reduce it. The EU represents another possible collective way of tackling security problems, especially ones that have an impact on the European continent. However, as Ademola Abass' discussion of the Congo operation in Chapter 6 shows, the EU is prepared to go outside its geographical area, thus distinguishing it from other regional organizations such as the OAS or the AU that are more inward-looking. In so doing though it must develop frameworks of cooperation with both the relevant regional organizations and the UN.

The EU's expansive approach to security is explicable by the fact that the EU, through its first limb, has combined economic and foreign policy matters, through the promotion of human rights and democracy as well as using sanctions to send messages to aggressors. A long-term approach to security requires attention not just to the absence of war (the so-called negative peace) but also to the positive aspects of developing peace and security through promoting human rights and democracy around the globe. The EU, though not yet out of infancy as a security actor, has an institutionalized foreign, security, and defence policy that is far more developed than its regional counterparts elsewhere, as shown by Panos Koutrakos in Chapter 11.

Growing security competence brings problems of integration into the wider collective security system, and the consequent issue of inter-institutional relationships. Further, while imputed international legal personality allows the EU to take separate decisions, in some cases to make law, it also brings with it duties. As international legal persons, organizations are bound by principles of international law. This means that organizations are bound, for instance, by basic principles of human rights law, so that the EU cannot simply promote human rights: it is itself bound by them, in its peacekeeping operations or in its sanctions regimes for instance.

The continuing background debate about the legal personality of the EU since the Maastricht Treaty of 1992 created this new entity has in the past weakened the EU as an actor on the international stage. Though there now seems to be near consensus on the EU having personality, the lack of any express recognition is a reflection of a core of doubt at a political, rather than legal, level about the Union's status as an outward-looking, autonomous international organization. This would be clarified if the 2004 Constitutional Treaty were to come into force, though this looks extremely doubtful.

Of course the Union is more than an unincorporated association of states, a modern day Concert of Europe. It has separate powers and separate responsibilities from the Member States. Indeed, in many ways the EU is far more than a standard inter-governmental organization, and has facets of a proto-state. In sovereign states, though, there is almost always a clear centralization of foreign policy power in the government. In the case of the EU to date, however, some of its security and human rights policies appear to have been characterized by a confusion as to whether it is the Member States (or a few of them) acting together or whether it is the organization taking action. This has happened both internally, for instance in the case of Austria in 2000, and externally, for instance in the case of Iran and nuclear technology from 2003. Ramses Wessel's analysis, in Chapter 10, shows that there is a long way to go before full coherence is achieved in foreign, security, and defence policy. Indeed, with expansion in membership, and with many different approaches to defence and security within the membership, it may well be that clear principles on differentiation will be the best outcome that can be achieved.

For a number of years the EU has applied human rights policies externally within first pillar measures through human rights clauses in trade and cooperation agreements with third countries. Violation has led to the suspension of agreements with a number of countries. Second pillar measures in the form of non-forcible measures have also been taken in support of human rights—for example against Haiti (1994), Yugoslavia (1994), Nigeria (1995), Burma (2000), and Zimbabwe in 2002. Panos Koutrakos' analysis, in Chapter 11, of such issues from the angle of external relations shows both the strengths and weaknesses of the Union in this regard. It does show, however, development.

Of relevance to the promotion of democracy by the EU is that the democratic entitlement can be seen as firmly tied to the right of self-determination, in its internal aspect. As an international actor the EU is bound to respect this fundamental principle of international law and to ensure that the wishes of the people are respected when promoting democracy, and furthermore that minorities are protected.

The historical necessity of minorities protection is recognized in the Council of Europe's European Framework Convention on the Protection of National Minorities of 1995, where there is a clear link made between the issue of the protection of minority rights and the issue of security. The preamble declares that 'upheavals of European history have shown that the protection of national minorities is essential to stability, democratic security and peace in this continent'. A clear link between security and minority rights is to be found in the office and work of the OSCE's High Commissioner on National Minorities established at the 1992 Helsinki Conference with the specific task of reducing national minority tensions that might endanger the peace between the OSCE states. The High Commissioner's interventions in Albania, Estonia, Hungary, Kazakhstan, Macedonia, and Ukraine for example have often proved to be crucial in preventing an internal as well as international breakdown.

There is a specific link in the High Commissioner's mandate between security and minority rights, as one would expect from an organization that has been based on a more integrated concept of security as shown by Marco Odello in Chapter 13.

In many of the situations mentioned in the book the EU and the UN have acted in cooperation. For example, in the imposition of non-forcible measures or sanctions the two organizations acted in relative harmony in the cases of Haiti, Yugoslavia, and Sudan. In other instances the EU has acted alone—for example, in the case of Zimbabwe. As Nigel White shows in Chapter 14, while it is desirable that the two organizations do not act in a contradictory way when taking non-forcible measures, in reality international law does not provide any clear limitations upon regional organizations acting independently in taking such measures, though of course they must meet other requirements of international law. In particular they should not violate the human rights of the population of the target state. The advanced state of EU integration does not exempt it from the rules of international law.

Additionally, when taking military action of an enforcement kind, the EU is also subject to the additional requirement of UN Security Council authority (Article 53, UN Charter). These are military measures that are not consensual or peacekeeping operations as the EU undertook in Macedonia in 2003, or actions undertaken in individual or collective self-defence. In other military operations to date, those that potentially have enforcement elements—in Bosnia from December 2004 and in the Congo in 2003—the EU has acted under a mandate of the Security Council.

The UN Charter expressly states in Article 53 that regional arrangements must act with Security Council authorization when taking enforcement action. Though there has been ambiguity over whether this covered economic enforcement action, there is little doubt that it covers military enforcement action. It can be argued that this certainly does not improve the effectiveness of regional organizations as security actors, since it subjects them to the vagaries of the veto in the UN Security Council whenever authority is sought.

The problem for those that would argue for regional military autonomy in these urgent instances is that the Charter provisions requiring Security Council authority under Chapters VII and VIII of the Charter are specific exceptions to the most fundamental rule in the international legal system—that prohibiting the threat or use of force in Article 2. The rule prohibiting the threat or use of force is not only one of the obligations in the UN Charter that by virtue of Article 103 of that Charter prevail over obligations in any other treaty (including one establishing a regional organization), it is also recognized as a peremptory norm of international law from which there is no derogation. In these circumstances a clear hierarchy of rules is established by reason of the Charter (Articles 53 and 103) and by reason of general principles of international law (*jus cogens*).

Of course, there may be an argument to the effect that the EU is not a regional security actor in the sense of Chapter VIII of the UN Charter and so there is no need for the EU to seek the Council's blessing. It is true that the EU's security actions seem to be in the main external to it, against Zimbabwe or elements in the Congo for instance, while the classical regional organization—the OAS—in the main acts internally against Member States. However, it would seem even more important for the EU to be governed by the universal principles of the Charter as well as international law when it is not acting within its membership. Furthermore, internal security issues will become ever more important to the EU following the bomb blasts in Madrid in 2004 and London in 2005. It is interesting to note that in the Outcome Document of the UN World Summit at the UN the provisions of Chapter VIII of the UN Charter are reiterated and the EU is specifically mentioned along with the AU.[1]

Terrorism is a security matter of utmost importance to both the UN and the EU. Their actions against suspected terrorists do seem to be based on a shared vision of how to deal with the threat, though again both organizations must ensure that the anti-terrorist measures they take must be compatible with basic human rights, especially those concerning due process, fair trial, and detention.

It must not be forgotten that Chapter VIII gives regional organizations considerable autonomy in security matters. It still remains true, however, that crucial to the strengthening of the international legal system based on universal rules is a more legitimate and accountable UN Security Council. The problem of legitimacy in the Security Council signifies the urgent need for a more representative/accountable Council exercising its primary responsibility for peace and security in a proactive, consistent manner. The EU, and in particular France and the UK as permanent members of the Security Council, should actively work towards this end.

It is not being suggested that the EU is actively considering circumventing the Security Council, but circumstances will arise in which it is faced with the issue. It is important that regional organizations respect the rules of international law. Although we speak of a democracy deficit in the EU it is not hard to imagine regional organizations with little or no democracy, dominated by a hegemon, willing to intervene by force in states with little justification or provocation. Furthermore, if one accepts that regional organizations can act autonomously in military matters, why can't an ad hoc grouping of states, or indeed an individual state that declares it is acting on behalf of the international community in so doing?

Collective security is not divisible into regions, though it is desirable to have strong regional security bodies. Threats to the peace do not often respect territorial boundaries, as is shown by the recent upsurge in international terrorism. The consequences of this for the EU have been shown by Mirko Sossai in Chapter 7.

---

[1] GA Res 60/1, World Summit Outcome, 24 October 2005, para 93.

It is not possible therefore to build a collective security system from jigsaw pieces made up of regional security organizations. There is a need for a universal organization to police universal rules and to coordinate military actions that may involve regional actors and states. Without this institutional and normative glue, a multi-bloc system of security would disintegrate into competing, and potentially warring, power blocs.

Indeed, within regions, there can be a number of actors dealing with aspects of security or security related matters. In Europe, there has been mention in this conclusion of the work of the Council of Europe and the OSCE, which both take a human security approach, concentrating on human rights including minorities issues and democracy concerns. NATO on the other hand has traditionally been based on 'hard' security issues—the defence of states that are parties to the 1949 treaty. However, since the end of the Cold War, and provoked by the crisis in Kosovo in 1999, NATO now shares a similar vision on humanitarian or the so-called 'Petersberg' tasks to the EU. The growing convergence, at least in claimed competence, between NATO and the EU will be taken further if the Constitutional Treaty, or at least the mutual defence clause, comes into force. In Chapter 8 Heike Krieger makes a very good argument to the effect that confrontation with NATO on the key security issues can and should be avoided. As Fabien Terpan has shown in Chapter 12, although efforts have been made to coordinate the actions and policies of these two organizations, and there has been a sharing of assets, there is still much serious work to be done in developing a coherent approach to security issues, one that is compatible with international law.

As Martin Trybus has shown in Chapter 3, the failure of the Constitutional Treaty of 2004 is certainly not the end of the development of European security. The EU has, in the past, shown resilience and innovation in the face of what appeared to be insurmountable problems that hamstrung the organization. This book has shown a number of ways that the organization can overcome its current difficulties to develop a coherent security policy based on the rule of law.

Bibliography

Abass, A, *Regional Organisations and the Development of Collective Security: Beyond Chapter VIII of the UN Charter* (Oxford: Hart Publishing, 2004)

Abi-Saab, G, *The United Nations Operation in Congo, 1960–1964* (Oxford: Oxford University Press, 1978)

Amerasinghe, C F, *Principles of the Institutional Law of International Organisations* (Cambridge: Cambridge University Press, 1996)

——, *Principles of the Institutional Law of International Organizations*, 2nd edn (Cambridge: Cambridge University Press, 2005)

Archer, C, *International Organizations*, 3rd edn (London and New York: Routledge, 2001)

Ash, T G, *Free World* (London: Penguin, 2005)

Aust, Anthony, *Modern Treaty Law and Practice* (Cambridge: Cambridge University Press, 2000)

Bailey, S D and Daws, S, *The Procedure of the UN Security Council*, 3rd edn (Oxford: Clarendon, 1998)

Beaumont, P, Lyons, C, and Walker N (eds), *Convergence & Divergence in European Public Law* (Oxford: Hart Publishing, 2002)

Beckett, E, *The North Atlantic Treaty, the Brussels Treaty and the Charter of the United Nations* (London: Stevens & Sons, 1950)

Bernardt, R (ed), *Encyclopedia of International Law* (Amsterdam/New York/Oxford: North Holland, 1982)

Bianchi, A (ed), *Enforcing International Law Norms against Terrorism* (Oxford: Hart, 2004)

Bloed, A, *The Conference on Security and Co-operation in Europe: Analysis and Basic Documents, 1972–1993*, 2nd edn (Dordrecht: Kluwer Academic, 1993)

—— and van Dijk, P (eds), *The Human Dimension of the Helsinki Process* (Dordrecht: Martinus Nijhoff, 1991)

Blokker, N M and Schermers, H G (eds), *Proliferation of International Organizations: Legal Issues* (The Hague: Kluwer Law International, 2001)

Bloom, W, *Personal Identity, National Identity and International Relations* (Cambridge: Cambridge University Press, 1990)

Bothe, M, Ronzitti, N, and Rosas, A (eds), *The OSCE in the Maintenance of Peace and Security* (The Hague/London/Boston: Kluwer Law International, 1997)

Bourantosnis, D and Evriviades, M (eds), *A United Nations for the Twenty-First Century: Peace, Security and Development* (The Hague/London/Boston: Kluwer Law International, 1996)

Bowett, D W, *United Nations Forces* (London: Stevens & Sons, 1964)

Brenner, M (ed), *NATO and Collective Security* (Basingstoke: Macmillan, 1998)

Brownlie, I, *Principles of Public International Law*, 6th edn (Oxford: Oxford University Press, 2003)

Burke, J, *Al Qaeda, Casting a Shadow of Terror* (London: Penguin, 2004)

Buzan, B, Wæver, O, and de Wilde, J, *Security: A New Framework for Analysis* (Boulder, Colorado: Lynne Rienner, 1998)

Byers, M (ed), *The Role of Law in International Politics: Essays in International Relations and International Law* (Oxford: Oxford University Press, 2001)

Calliess, C and Ruffert, M (eds), *Kommentar des Vertrages über die Europäische Union und des Vertrages zur Gründung der Europäischen Gemeinschaft*, 2nd edn (Neuwied: Hermann Luchterhand Verlag, 2002)

Cannizzaro, E (ed), *The European Union as an Actor in International Relations* (The Hague/London/Boston: Kluwer Law International, 2001)

Cassese, A, *International Law*, 2nd edn (Oxford: Oxford University Press, 2005)

Chesterman, S, *Just War or Just Peace? Humanitarian Intervention and International Law* (Oxford: Oxford University Press, 2002)

Coicaud, J-M and Heiskanen, V, *The Legitimacy of International Organisations* (Tokyo: United Nations University Press, 2001)

Coomans, F and Kamminga, T (eds), *Extraterritorial Application of Human Rights Treaties* (Antwerp: Intersentia, 2004)

Craig, P and Harlow, C, *Lawmaking in the European Union* (Kluwer Law International: London/The Hague/Boston, 1998)

—— and de Búrca, G, *EU Law*, 3rd edn (Oxford: Oxford University Press, 2002)

—— and—— (eds), *The Evolution of EU Law* (Oxford: Oxford University Press, 1999)

de Burca, G and Scott, J (eds), *The EU and the WTO: Legal and Constitutional Questions* (Oxford: Hart Publishing, 2001)

de Nooy, Gert (ed), *Cooperative Security, the OSCE, and its Code of Conduct* (The Hague/London/Boston: Kluwer Law International, 1996)

de Zwaan, J W, Jans, J H, Nelissen FA, and Blockmans, S (eds), *The European Union—An Ongoing Process of Integration* (The Hague: TMC Asser Press, 2004)

Delbrück, J (ed), *The Allocation of Law Enforcement Authority in the International System* (Berlin: Duncker and Humblot, 1995)

Denza, E, *The Intergovernmental Pillars of the European Union* (Oxford: Oxford University Press, 2002)

Diehl, P F (ed), *The Politics of Global Governance* (Boulder, Colorado: Lynne Rienner, 2001)

Dinstein, Y, *War, Aggression and Self-Defence*, 3rd edn (Cambridge: Cambridge University Press, 2001)

Dowson, G W (ed), *Collective Security beyond the Cold War* (Ann Arbour: University of Michigan Press, 1994)

Doyle, M (ed), *Peacemaking and Peacekeeping for the New Century* (Oxford: Rowman and Littlefield Publishers, 1996)

Duke, S, *The EU and Crisis Management Development and Prospects* (Maastricht: EIPA, 2002)

——, *The Elusive Quest for European Security: From EDC to CFSP* (Houndsmills: Macmillan Press, 2000)

Dumoulin, A, Mathieu, R and Sarlet, G, *La Politique Européenne de Sécurité et de Défense De l'opératoire à l'identitaire* (Brussels: Bruylant, 2003)

Dupuy, R-J, (ed) *A Handbook on International Organizations*, 2nd edn (Leiden/Boston: Martinus Nijhoff, 1998)

Durch, W J (ed), *The Evolution of Peacekeeping: Case Studies and Comparative Analysis* (New York: St Martin's Press, 1993)

Eeckhout, P, *External Relations of the European Union: Legal and Constitutional Foundations* (Oxford: Oxford University Press, 2004)

Elagab, O Y, *The Legality of Non-Forcible Counter-Measures in International Law* (Oxford: Clarendon Press, 1988)

Eliassen, K E (ed), *Foreign and Security Policy in the European Union* (Sage: London, 1998)

Evans, M D (ed), *International Law*, 2nd edn (Oxford: Oxford University Press, 2006)

Fijnaut, C, Wouters, J, and Naert, F (eds), *Legal Instruments in the Fight against International Terrorism: A Transatlantic Dialogue* (Leiden/Boston: Martinus Nijhoff, 2004)

Franck, T, *Recourse to Force* (Cambridge: Cambridge University Press, 2002)

Freedman, L (ed), *Military Intervention in European Conflicts* (Oxford: Blackwell, 1994)

Fursdon, E, *The European Defence Community: A History* (London: Macmillan, 1980)

Galloway, D, *The Treaty of Nice and Beyond* (Sheffield: Sheffield Academic Press, 2001)

Geiger, R, *EUV, EGV: Vertrag über die Europäische Union und Vertrag zur Gründung der Europäischen Gemeinschaft*, 3rd edn (Munich: CH Beck, 2000)

Ghebali, V-Y and Lambert, A, *OSCE Code of Conduct on Politico-Military Aspects of Security: Anatomy and Implementation* (Leiden/Boston: Martinus Nijhoff, 2005)

Gnesotto, N (ed), *EU Security and Defence Policy: The First Five Years (1999–2004)* (Paris: EU ISS, 2004)

Gordenker, L and Weiss, T (eds), *Soldiers, Peacekeepers and Disasters* (Basingstoke: Macmillan, 1991)

Gowlland-Debbas, V (ed), *United Nations Sanctions and International Law* (The Hague: Kluwer Law International 2001)

Gray, C, *International Law on the Use of Force*, 2nd edn (Oxford: Oxford University Press, 2004)

Harris, D J, O'Boyle, M, and Warbrick, C, *Law of the European Convention on Human Rights* (London: Butterworths, 1995)

Hayward, J (ed), *The Crisis of Representation in Europe* (London: Frank Cass, 1995)

Heere, W P (ed), *From Government to Governance* (The Hague: TMC Asser Press, 2004)

Heisbourg, F, *Hyperterrorisme: la nouvelle guerre* (Paris: Odile Jacob, 2001)

Henckaerts, J-M and Doswald-Beck, L, *Customary International Humanitarian Law*, Vol 1 (Cambridge: Cambridge University Press, 2004)

Henderson, K (ed), *Back to Europe: Central and Eastern Europe and the European Union* (London: UCL Press, 1999)

Henkin, L, *Foreign Affairs and the United States Constitution* (Oxford: Clarendon Press, 1996)

Heraclides, A, *Helsinki-II and its Aftermath* (London and New York: Pinter Publishers, 1993)

Heukels, T and McDonnell, A, *Action for Damages in Community Law* (The Hague/London/Boston: Kluwer, 1997)

——, Blokker, N M, and Brus, M M (eds), *The European Union after Amsterdam, a Legal Analysis* (The Hague: Martinus Nijhoff, 1999)

Higgins, R, *United Nations Peacekeeping, 1946–1967: Documents and Commentary Vol 3: Africa* (Oxford: Oxford University Press, 1980)

Hirsch, M, *The Responsibility of International Organisations Towards Third Parties: Some Basic Principles* (The Hague/London/Boston: Martinus Nijhoff, 1995)

Holland, M (ed), *The Failure of European Political Cooperation Essays on Theory and Practice* (London: Macmillan, 1991)

Holzgrefe, J L and Keohane, R O (eds), *Humanitarian Intervention: Ethical, Legal and Political Dilemmas* (Cambridge: Cambridge University Press, 2003)

Hough, P, *Understanding Global Security* (New York, London: Routledge, 2004)

Hoyer, W and Kaldrack, G (eds), *Europäische Sicherheits- und Verteidigungspolitik* (Baden-Baden: Nomos, 2002)

Hunter, R E, *The European Security and Defense Policy, NATO's Companion—or Competitor?* (Cambridge/Leiden: RAND Europe, 2003)

Ifestos, P, *European Political Cooperation* (Aldershot: Avebury, 1987)

Ipsen, K, *Rechtsgrundlagen und Institutionalisierung der Atlantisch-Westeuropäischen Verteidigung* (Hamburg: Heitman, 1967)

Jackson, B S and McGoldrick, D (eds), *Legal Visions of the New Europe* (London: Graham & Trotman, 1993)

Johnson, P (ed), *Industries in Europe: Competition, Trends and Policy Issues*, 2nd edn (Cheltenham: Edward Elgar, 2003)

Jorgensen, K E (ed), *European Approaches to Crisis Management* (The Hague/London/Boston: Kluwer, 1997)

Kalin, W (ed), *Human Rights in Times of Occupation: The Case of Kuwait* (Berne: Law Books in Europe, 1994)

Karns, M P and Mingst, K A, *International Organisations: The Politics and Processes of Global Governance* (Boulder, Colorado: Lynne Rienner, 2004)

Kelsen, H, *The Law of the United Nations* (London: Stevens, 1950)

Klabbers, J, *An Introduction to International Institutional Law* (Cambridge: Cambridge University Press, 2002)

Kleine, M, *Die militärische Komponente der Europäischen Sicherheits- und Verteidigungspolitik* (Baden-Baden: Nomos Verlag, 2005)

Koskenniemi, M, *International Law Aspects of the European Union* (The Hague/Boston/London: Martinus Nijhoff, 1998)

Koutrakos, P, *Trade, Foreign Policy and Defence in EU Constitutional Law: The Legal Regulation of Sanctions, Exports of Dual Use Goods and Armaments* (Oxford: Hart Publishing, 2001)

——, *EU International Relations Law* (Oxford: Hart Publishing, 2006)

Krahmann, E (ed), *New Threats and New Actors in International Security* (New York/Basingstoke: Palgrave Macmillan, 2005)

Kronenberger, V (ed), *The European Union and the International Legal Order* (The Hague: TMC Asser Press, 2001)

—— and Wouters, J (eds), *The European Union and Conflict Prevention: Legal and Policy Aspects* (The Hague: TMC Asser Press, 2004)

Langton, C (ed), *The Military Balance 2001–2002* (Oxford: Oxford University Press, 2001)

Laqueur, W, *The New Terrorism Fanaticism and Arms of Mass Destruction* (Oxford: Oxford University Press, 1999)

Lasok, K P E, *Law and Institutions of the EU*, 7th edn (London: Butterworths, 2001)

Laursen, F S and Vanhoonacker, S (eds) *The Intergovernmental Conference on Political Union: Institutional Reforms, New Policies and International Identity of the European Community* (Maastricht: European Institute of Public Administration, 1992)

Lepard, B D, *Rethinking Humanitarian Intervention: A Fresh Legal Approach Based on Fundamental Ethical Principles* (Pennsylvania: Penn State University Press, 2003)

Lerner, D and Aron, R , *France Defeats EDC* (New York: Frederick A Praeger, 1957)

Lie, T, *In the Cause of Peace* (New York: Macmillan, 1954)

Magone, G J, *A Short History of International Organization* (New York: McGraw-Hill, 1954)

Marauhn, T, *Building a European Security and Defence Identity: The Evolving Relationship between the Western European Union and the European Union* (Bochum: Universitätsverlag N Brockmeyer, 1996)

Maresceau, M (ed), *Enlarging the European Union: Relations between the EU and Central and Eastern Europe* (London: Longman, 1997)

McGoldrick, D, *International Relations Law of the European Union* (London: Longman, 1997)

McKenzie, M M and Loedel, P H, *The Promise and Reality of European Security Cooperation: States, Interests, and Institutions Cooperation* (Westport/London: Praeger, 1998)

Ministry of Defence, UK, *The Manual of the Law of Armed Conflict* (Oxford: Oxford University Press, 2004)

Muller, A S, *International Organisations and their Host States* (The Hague/London/Boston: Kluwer, 1995)

Nuttall, S, *European Political Co-operation* (Oxford: Clarendon Press, 1992)

Nutting, A, *Europe Will Not Wait: A Warning and a Way Out* (London: Hollis & Carter, 1960)

O'Keefe, D and Twomey, P (eds), *Legal Issues of the Maastricht Treaty* (London: Wiley Chancery Law, 1994)

O'Neill, J T and Rees, N, *United Nations Peacekeeping in the Post-Cold War Era* (Abingdon: Routledge, 2005)

Osterdahl, I, *Threat to the Peace: The Interpretation by the Security Council of Article 39 of the UN Charter* (Stockholm: Almquiest & Wiksell International, 1998)

Pascallon, P (ed), *Les interventions militaires extérieures de l'armée française* (Brussels: Bruylant, 1997)

Pauwelyn, J, *Conflict of Norms in Public International Law: How WTO Law Relates to Other Rules of International Law* (Cambridge: Cambridge University Press, 2003)

Provost, R, Crawford, J, and Bell, J, *Human Rights and Humanitarian Law* (Cambridge: Cambridge University Press, 2002)

Quinlan, M, *European Defense Cooperation: Asset or Threat to NATO?* (Washington DC: Woodrow Wilson Center Press, 2001)

Ronzitti, N, *Rescuing National Abroad through Military Coercion and Intervention on Grounds of Humanity* (Dordrecht/Boston/Lancaster: Martinus Nijhoff, 1985)

Royal Defence College and Royal Institute for International Relations (eds), *Able and Willing* (Brussels: Belgian Ministry of Defence, 2004)

Rummel, R (ed), *Toward Political Union: Planning a Common Foreign and Security Policy in the European Community* (Baden-Baden: Nomos Verlagsgesellschaft, 1992)

Russell, R, *A History of the United Nations Charter: The Role of the United States 1940–1945* (Washington DC: The Brookings Institution, 1958)

Salomon, A, *L'ONU et la Pais: Le Conseil de Sécurite et le réglement pacifique des différends* (Paris: Editions Internationales, 1948)

Sands, P and Klein, P, *Bowett's Law of International Institutions*, 5th edn (London: Sweet & Maxwell, 2001)

Sarooshi, D, *The United Nations and the Development of Collective Security: The Delegation by the UN of its Chapter VII Powers* (Oxford: Oxford University Press, 1999)

——, *International Organizations and the Exercise of their Sovereign Powers* (Oxford: Oxford University Press, 2005)

Schachter, O, *International Law in Theory and Practice* (Dordrecht/Boston/London: Martinus Nijhoff, 1991)

Schermers, H G and Blokker, N M, *International Institutional Law: Unity within Diversity*, 3rd edn (The Hague/London/Boston: Martinus Nijhoff Publishers, 1995)

—— and ——, *International Institutional Law*, 4th edn (Boston: Martinus Nijhoff, 2003)

Scholz, R (ed), *Europa der Bürger?* (Cologne: Hanns-Martin-Schleyer-Stiftung, 2002)

Scott, S V, *International Law in World Politics: An Introduction* (Boulder, Colorado: Lynne Rienner, 2004)

Shaw, M N, *International Law*, 5th edn (Cambridge: Cambridge University Press, 2003)

Simma, B (ed), *The Charter of the United Nations*, 2nd edn (Oxford: Oxford University Press, 2002)

Smith, M E, *Europe's Foreign and Security Policy* (Cambridge: Cambridge University Press, 2004)

Sutterlin, James, *The United Nations and the Maintenance of International Peace and Security: A Challenge to be Met* (Connecticut: Praeger, 1995)

Taylor, P, *International Organisations in the Modern World* (London: Pinter, 1993)

Telo, M (ed), *Vers une nouvelle Europe?, Towards a New Europe?* (Brussels: Etudes Européennes, 1992)

Terpan, F, *La politique européenne de sécurité commune de l'Union* (Brussels: Bruylant, 2003)

—— (ed), *La politique européenne de sécurité et de défense, L'Union européenne peut-elle gérer les crises?* (Toulouse: Presses de l'Institut d'études politiques de Toulouse, 2004)

Thomas, D C, *The Helsinki Effect: International Norms, Human Rights, and the Demise of Communism* (Princeton: Princeton University Press, 2001)

Thym, D, *Ungleichzeitigkeit und europäisches Verfassungsrecht* (Baden-Baden: Nomos, 2004)

Tomuschat, C (ed), *Rechtsprobleme einer europäischen Sicherheits- und Verteidigungspolitik* (Heidelberg: Muller, 1997)

Trybus, M, *European Defence Procurement Law: International and National Procurement Systems as Models for a Liberalised Defence Procurement Market in Europe* (The Hague/London/Boston: Kluwer Law International, 1999)

——, *European Union Law and Defence Integration* (Hart Publishing: Oxford, 2005)

United Nations Department of Public Relations, *The Blue Helmets: A Review of United Nations Peacekeeping*, 2nd edn (New York: UN Department of Public Information, 1990)

Varwick, J (ed), *Die Beziehungen zwischen NATO und EU: Partnerschaft, Konkurrenz, Rivalität?* (Opladen: Barbara Budrich Verlag, 2005)

von Kielmansegg, S, Graf, *Die Verteidigungspolitik der Europäischen Union* (Stuttgart: Boorberg, 2005)

von Plate, B (ed), *Europa auf dem Weg zur kollektiven Sicherheit?* (Baden-Baden: Nomos Verlag, 1994)

Walter, C, Vöneky, S, Röben, V, and Schorkopf, F (eds), *Terrorism as a Challenge for National and International Law: Security versus Liberty?* (Berlin: Springer, 2004)

Warnken, M, *Der Handlungsrahmen der Europäischen Union im Bereich der Sicherheits- und Verteidigungspolitik* (Baden-Baden: Nomos, 2002)

Weiss, T G (ed), *Collective Security in a Changing World* (Boulder Colorado: Lynne Rienner, 1993)

—— (ed), *Beyond Subcontracting: Task-Sharing with Regional Arrangements and Service-Providing NGOs* (Basingstoke: Macmillan, 1998)

Wellens, K and Suy, E (eds), *International Law: Theory and Practice Essays in Honour of Eric Suy* (The Hague: Martinus Nijhoff, 1998)

Wessel, R A, *The European Union's Foreign and Security Policy: A Legal and Institutional Perspective* (The Hague/London/Boston: Kluwer Law International, 1999)

White, N D, *The Law of International Organisations* (Manchester: Manchester University Press, 1996)

——, *The Law of International Organisations*, 2nd edn (Manchester: Manchester University Press, 2005)

——, *Keeping the Peace: The United Nations and the Maintenance of International Peace and Security* (Manchester: Manchester University Press, 1993)

——, *Keeping the Peace*, 2nd edn (Manchester: Manchester University Press, 1997)

—— (ed), *Collective Security Law* (Aldershot: Ashgate, 2003)

Zoller, E, *Peacetime Unilateral Remedies: An Analysis of Countermeasures* (Dobbs Ferry, NY: Transnational, 1984)

Index

Complete titles of organizations are used as main headings but subheadings use abbreviations e.g. North Atlantic Treaty Organization (NATO) as a main heading, but NATO as a subheading. A complete list of abbreviations is given on pages ix–xii